Advertising
Principles & Practice

Advertising
Principles & Practice
7TH edition

WILLIAM WELLS
University of Minnesota

SANDRA MORIARTY
University of Colorado

JOHN BURNETT
University of Denver

PEARSON
Prentice Hall

Upper Saddle River, New Jersey 07458

Library of Congress Cataloging-in-Publication Data

Wells, William, 1926-

    Advertising : principles & practice / William Wells, John Burnett, Sandra Moriarty.-- 7th ed.

       p. cm.

    Includes bibliographical references and index.

    ISBN 0-13-146560-0

    1. Advertising. I. Title: Advertising principles & practice. II. Title: Advertising principles and practice. III. Burnett, John, 1944- IV. Moriarty, Sandra E. (Sandra Ernst) V. Title.

    HF5823.W455 2006

    659.1--dc22

2005047639

Acquisitions Editor: Katie Stevens
Vice President/Editor-in-Chief: Jeff Shelstad
Marketing Manager: Ashaki Charles
Assistant Editor: Melissa Pellerano
Editorial Assistant: Rebecca Lembo
Developmental Editor: Elisa Adams
Media Project Manager: Peter Snell
Associate Director Production Editorial: Judy Leale
Production Editor: Theresa Festa
Permissions Coordinator: Charles Morris
Manufacturing Buyer: Diane Peirano
Design Director: Maria Lange
Designer: Steve Frim
Interior Design: dePinho Graphic Design
Cover Design: Steve Frim
Director, Image Resource Center: Melinda Reo
Manager, Rights and Permissions: Zina Arabia
Manager, Visual Research: Beth Brenzel
Manager, Cover Visual Research & Permissions: Karen Sanatar
Image Permission Coordinator: Carolyn Gauntt
Photo Researcher: Melinda Alexander
Manager, Print Production: Christy Mahon
Composition: Pre-Press Company, Inc.
Full-Service Project Management: Pre-Press Company, Inc.
Printer/Binder: Courier-Kendallville/Phoenix

Credits and acknowledgments borrowed from other sources and reproduced, with permission, in this textbook appear on appropriate page within text and on pages 571–573.

Pearson Education LTD.
Pearson Education Singapore, Pte. Ltd
Pearson Education, Canada, Ltd
Pearson Education–Japan

Pearson Education Australia PTY, Limited
Pearson Education North Asia Ltd
Pearson Educación de Mexico, S.A. de C.V.
Pearson Education Malaysia, Pte. Ltd

10 9 8 7 6 5 4 3 2 1

We wish to dedicate this book to all our students present, past, and future who have taught us about how people respond to advertising, as well as inspired us to better understand these responses.

Brief Contents

PART 1   FOUNDATIONS

  1 Introduction to Advertising   3

  2 Advertising's Role in Marketing   29

  3 Advertising and Society   59

PART 2   PLANNING AND STRATEGY

  4 How Advertising Works   97

  5 The Consumer Audience   125

  6 Strategic Research   155

  7 Strategic Planning   179

PART 3   EFFECTIVE ADVERTISING MEDIA

  8 Print and Out-of-Home Media   209

  9 Broadcast Media   241

  10 Interactive and Alternative Media   269

  11 Media Planning and Buying   291

PART 4   EFFECTIVE ADVERTISING MESSAGES

  12 The Creative Side and Message Strategy   325

  13 Copywriting   355

  14 Design and Production   385

PART 5   INTEGRATION AND EVALUATION

  15 Direct Response   421

  16 Sales Promotion, Events, and Sponsorships   451

  17 Public Relations   475

  18 Special Advertising Situations   503

  19 Evaluation of Effectiveness   531

  Glossary   557

  Credits   571

  Notes   575

  Index   581

Contents

Preface xxi

PART I   FOUNDATIONS

1 Introduction to Advertising 3

 Volkswagen Sings a New Song With iPOD® 3

WHAT IS ADVERTISING? 5
Defining Modern Advertising, 5 • The Key Concepts of Advertising, 5

THE ROLES AND FUNCTIONS OF ADVERTISING 6
The Marketing Role, 8 • The Communication Role, 8 • The Economic Role, 8 • The Social Role, 10 • The Functions of Advertising, 10

THE KEY PLAYERS 10
The Advertiser, 10 • The Advertising Agency, 13 • The Media, 15 • The Suppliers (Vendors), 16 • The Target Audience, 16

TYPES OF ADVERTISING 17

WHAT MAKES AN AD EFFECTIVE? 19
The Important Role of Objectives, 19 • Effectiveness and Award Shows, 20

THE EVOLUTION OF ADVERTISING 21

THE CURRENT ADVERTISING SCENE 21
An Expanded View of Advertising, 21 • Integrated Marketing Communication, 22 • Globalization, 23

A MATTER OF PRACTICE: Driving on the Road of Life 9
A MATTER OF PRINCIPLE: The Greatest Commercial Ever Made 12
THE INSIDE STORY: Why Do I Love Advertising? 14
IT'S A WRAP: Effective Advertising Drives Volkswagen's Success 24

Summary 25
Key Terms 26
Review Questions 26
Discussion Questions 26
Class Project 26
Hands-On: Introduction to Advertising 27

2 Advertising's Role in Marketing 30

 Puma Is One Cool Cat 30

WHAT IS MARKETING? 31
Key Concepts in Marketing, 31 • The Marketing Concept: Focus on Customers, 31 • The Concept of Exchange, 32 • The Concept of Branding, 33 • The Concept of Added Value, 35

THE KEY PLAYERS AND MARKETS 37
The Marketer, 37 • Suppliers and Vendors, 38 • Distributors and Retailers, 39 • Types of Markets, 39

THE MARKETING PROCESS 41
Marketing Research, 42 • Key Strategic Decisions, 42 • Marketing Mix Strategies, 42

HOW AGENCIES WORK 45
Types of Agencies, 47 • How Agency Work is Organized, 49 • How Agencies Make Money, 51

INTERNATIONAL MARKETING 52
Organizing for International Marketing, 52 • International Marketing Management, 52

THE DYNAMICS OF MODERN MARKETING 52

A MATTER OF PRINCIPLE: It's Pure and It Floats 34

A MATTER OF PRACTICE: Marketing a Passion for Doughnuts 46

THE INSIDE STORY: The Day-to-Day Job of an Account Executive 50

IT'S A WRAP: Puma Leaps Forward 53

Summary 54
Key Terms 54
Review Questions 55
Discussion Questions 55
Class Project 55
Hands-On: WWP's Owner—a British Knight with
Every (Marketing) Weapon at His Disposal 56

3 Advertising and Society 59

Advertising's Social Role 61
Advertising's Role in Shaping or Mirroring Society, 61 • Social and Cultural Considerations in
International Advertising, 62

REVIEW AND REGULATION OF ADVERTISING 62
Advertising's Legal Environment, 62

ADVERTISING'S REGULATORY ENVIRONMENT 66
The FTC, 66 • Food and Drug Administration, 70 • Federal Communications Commission, 70 • Other
Regulatory Bodies, 70 • International Laws and Regulations, 70

MEDIA REVIEW OF ADVERTISING 72
Self-Regulation, 72 • Self-Discipline, 73 • Industry Self-Regulation, 73 • Public and Community
Review, 74

ADVERTISING ETHICS 75
Poor Taste and Offensive Advertising, 75 • Reinforcing Stereotypes, 76 • Body Image and Self-
Image, 79 • Targeting Children, 79 • Misleading Claims and Other Message Strategies, 80 •
Advertising Controversial Products, 84

DETERMINING WHAT IS ETHICAL 86
The Social Ethic, 86 • Professional Ethics, 87 • International Standards and Codes, 88 • Personal
Ethics, 88

A MATTER OF PRINCIPLE: Cheesecake or Good Targeting? 77

THE INSIDE STORY: Breaking Into Madison Avenue 89

IT'S A WRAP: Lessons from the Losers 90

Summary 90
Key Terms 91
Review Questions 91
Discussion Questions 91
Class Project 92
Hands-On: Boycott This! 92

PART-ENDING CASE Chick-fil-A: Foundations 94

PART II   PLANNING AND STRATEGY

4 How Advertising Works   97

SignBoy Is a Hole in One for FootJoy   97

HOW ADVERTISING WORKS AS COMMUNICATION   99
The Communication Model, 99 • Advertising as Communication,
100 • Adding Interaction to Advertising, 102

THE EFFECTS BEHIND ADVERTISING EFFECTIVENESS   102
The Simple Answers, 102 • The Facets Model of Effective Advertising, 103

PERCEPTION   104
The Components of Perception, 104 • The Subliminal Issue, 106

COGNITION   106
The Components of Cognition, 106

THE AFFECTIVE OR EMOTIONAL RESPONSE   109
The Components of Affective Response, 109

ASSOCIATION   110
The Components of Association, 110 • Brand Transformation, 111 • Association Networks, 113

PERSUASION   113
The Components of Persuasion, 113 • Involvement's Role in Persuasion, 116

BEHAVIOR   116
The Components of Behavior, 116

A MATTER OF PRINCIPLE: Does Subliminal Advertising Work?   107
A MATTER OF PRACTICE: It's Green, It's Squishy, It's Guacamole!   112
THE INSIDE STORY: The Curiosity-arousing Function of Antidrug Ads   118
IT'S A WRAP: SignBoy is a Sign of Success for FootJoy   119
Summary   120
Key Terms   120
Review Questions   121
Discussion Questions   121
Class Projects   121
Hands-On: How Advertising Works: If It Walks Like the Aflac Duck   122

5 The Consumer Audience   125

So What Do You Crave?   125

HOW DOES CONSUMER BEHAVIOR WORK?   126
The Consumer Audience, 127

CULTURAL AND SOCIAL INFLUENCES ON CONSUMER DECISIONS   127
Culture, 128 • Subcultures, 129 • Social Class, 129 • Reference Groups, 129 • Family,
130 • Demographics, 131

PSYCHOLOGICAL INFLUENCES THAT MOTIVATE CONSUMERS   135
Perception and State of Mind, 135 • Motivations, 139 • Attitudes and Values, 139 • Personality,
139 • Psychographic Influences, 140

BEHAVIORAL INFLUENCES ON CONSUMER DECISIONS   144
Usage Behavior, 144 • Innovation and Adoption, 144

THE CONSUMER DECISION PROCESS   145
Influences on B2B Decision Making, 146

SEGMENTING AND TARGETING   147
To Segment or Not to Segment? 147 • Targeting the Right Audience, 150

A MATTER OF PRACTICE: Choice Hotels Says "Thanks for Traveling" 136

THE INSIDE STORY: The Grand Myth of Early Adoption 143

IT'S A WRAP: Making Cravers One of Ours 151

Summary   151
Key Terms   152
Review Questions   152
Discussion Questions   152
Class Projects   152
Hands-On: Toyota Goes After Tuners   153

6 Strategic Research   157

 Leaping Over Learning   157

RESEARCH: THE QUEST FOR INTELLIGENCE AND INSIGHT   157
Types of Research, 157

THE USES OF RESEARCH   162
Market Information, 162 • Consumer Insight Research, 162 • Media Research, 163 • Message Development and Evaluation Research, 163

RESEARCH METHODS USED IN ADVERTISING PLANNING   165
Background Research, 165 Consumer Research, 166 • Choosing a Research Method, 171

RESEARCH CHALLENGES   172
Globalization, 172 • New Media Technology, 172 • Internet and Virtual Research, 173 • Embedded Research, 173 • Insightful Analysis, 174

A MATTER OF PRACTICE: The Army Marches to a Different Drummer   164

THE INSIDE STORY: The Power of Design Personas   167

IT'S A WRAP: Leap Into a Total Learning System   174

Summary   175
Key Terms   175
Review Questions   175
Discussion Questions   175
Class Projects   176
Hands-On: What Lies Beneath? Making a Choice   176

7 Strategic Planning   179

 The Legendary Service of Citizens Bank   179

STRATEGIC PLANNING   181
The Business Plan, 182 • The Marketing Plan, 183 • The Advertising or IMC Plan, 184

BASIC STRATEGIC PLANNING DECISIONS   185
Typical Advertising or IMC Plan Outline, 185 • Situation Analysis, 186 • Advertising Objectives and Strategies, 188 • Segmenting and Targeting, 189 • Positioning Strategy, 190 • Budgeting, 193 • Evaluation: Determining Effectiveness, 194

ACCOUNT PLANNING: WHAT IS IT?   194
The Research Foundation, 195 • Consumer Insight, 195 • The Communication Brief, 198 • Personal Characteristics of a Planner, 199

THE INSIDE STORY: Exploiting the Dot—Repositioning a Luxury Coffee Brand   192

A MATTER OF PRACTICE: Everybody's Favorite Soul Food   196

IT'S A WRAP: Proving That a Bank Is Not Typical 201

Summary 202

Key Terms 202

Review Questions 202

Discussion Questions 202

Class Projects 203

Hands-On: Unscrambling the NASCAR Fan 203

PART-ENDING CASE Chick-fil-A: Planning and Strategy 204

PART III EFFECTIVE ADVERTISING MEDIA

8 Print and Out-of-Home Media 209

 Apple Tops the Charts with Digital Music 209

THE MEDIA INDUSTRY 211

BASIC MEDIA CONCEPTS 212
Planning and Buying, 212 • Reach and Frequency, 212 • Impressions, 212 • Media Key Players, 213

PRINT MEDIA 213

NEWSPAPERS 214
The Structure of the Newspaper Industry, 214 • Types of Newspaper Advertising, 217 • Newspaper Readership, 218 • The Advantages and Disadvantages of Advertising in Newspapers, 219 • The Future of the Newspaper Industry, 220

MAGAZINES 220
Types of Magazines, 221 • Distribution and Circulation, 223 • Magazine Advertising, 223 • Magazine Readership Measurement, 224 • Advantages and Disadvantages of Advertising in Magazines, 225 • The Future of Magazine Advertising, 226

PACKAGING 226

OUT-OF-HOME ADVERTISING 227
Outdoor Advertising, 227 • On-Premise Signs, 230 • Posters, 230 • Transit Advertising, 231

DIRECTORY ADVERTISING 233

USING PRINT ADVERTISING 235

A MATTER OF PRACTICE: International Truck Delivers the Goods 222

THE INSIDE STORY: Kellogg's Special K 2-Week Challenge 232

IT'S A WRAP: iPod® Dances to Tunes 235

Summary 236

Key Terms 236

Review Questions 237

Discussion Questions 237

Class Projects 237

Hands-On: Next Month's Issue: Credibility 238

9 Broadcast Media 241

  A Drugstore Goes Online 241

BROADCAST MEDIA 243

RADIO 243
The Structure of the Radio Industry, 243 • Radio Advertising, 244 • The Radio Audience, 246 • Advantages and Disadvantages of Advertising on Radio, 248 • Using Radio Effectively, 249 • Trends in Radio/Audio Advertising, 249

TELEVISION 249
Structure of the Television Industry, 250 • Television Advertising, 255 • The Television Audience, 257 • Advantages of Advertising on Television, 259 • Disadvantages of Television Advertising, 259 • Changes and Trends in Broadcast Television, 261

FILM AND VIDEO 262
Advantages and Disadvantages of Movie Advertising, 262

PRODUCT PLACEMENT 263
Advantages and Disadvantages of Product Placements, 263

USING BROADCAST ADVERTISING EFFECTIVELY 263

A MATTER OF PRACTICE: Starbucks Makes TV Less Intrusive 256

THE INSIDE STORY: Selling a Political Party with Humor 260

IT'S A WRAP: Using TV to Demonstrate Convenience 264

Summary 265
Key Terms 265
Review Questions 265
Discussion Questions 266
Class Projects 266
Hands-On: Will Radio Listeners Finally Get Sirius with Howard Stern? 266

10 Interactive and Alternative Media 269

  eBay Reinvents the Marketplace 269

INTERACTIVE MEDIA 271

THE INTERNET 271
E-Business and Marketing Communication, 271 • The Internet and Marketing Communication, 274

INTERNET ADVERTISING 276
Purpose of Internet Advertising, 277 • Types of Internet Advertising, 277 • Off-line Advertising for Web Sites, 278 • The Internet Audience, 278 • Advantages and Disadvantages of Internet Advertising, 279 • The Web in International Advertising, 280 • Changes and Trends in Internet Advertising, 280

E-MAIL ADVERTISING 281
Spam, 281 • Viral Marketing, 282

ALTERNATIVE AND NEW MEDIA 282
Advertainment, 282 • New Internet Practices, 283 • Video Games, 284 • Wireless Communication, 284 • Nonelectronic New Media, 285 • Guerilla Marketing, 285

THE INSIDE STORY: Entertaining the User Through Web Site Redesign 272

A MATTER OF PRINCIPLE: Cookies and G-Mail 273

IT'S A WRAP: eBay Rewrites the Rules for e-Marketers 286

Summary 287
Key Terms 287

Review Questions 287
Discussion Questions 287
Class Projects 288
Hands-On: BMW Knows the ABC's of C to B 288

11 Media Planning and Buying 291

 Archipelago Rings the Bell 291

MEDIA PLANNING AND BUYING 293
The Aperture Concept, 293

THE MEDIA PLAN 293
Media Research: Information Sources, 293

MEDIA OBJECTIVES 297
Exposure and GRPs, 297 • The Reach Objective, 298 • The Frequency Objective, 299 • Effective Frequency, 300

MEDIA STRATEGIES 300
Delivering on the Objectives, 300 • Target Audience Strategies, 301 • Media Mix Selection, 303 • Cost Efficiency: CPM and CPP, 305 • Scheduling Strategies, 306 • The Media Budget, 308 • Global Media Planning, 308

A SAMPLE MEDIA PLAN FOR PIZZA HUT 310
Situation and Consumer Analysis, 310 • Media Objectives and Aperture Strategies, 310 • The Media Mix, 310 • The Flowchart: Scheduling and Budgeting Allocation, 312

MEDIA BUYING 313
Media Buying Specifics, 313 • Global Media Buying, 316

MEDIA PLANNING CHANGES AND CHALLENGES 316
Unbundling Media Buying and Planning, 316 • Online Media Buying, 317 • New Forms of Media Research Needed, 317

A MATTER OF PRACTICE: Polaroid Zones In 302

THE INSIDE STORY: The Reality of Budget Cuts 309

IT'S A WRAP: The Open Show Opens the Door for Archipelago 317

Summary 318
Key Terms 318
Review Questions 318
Discussion Questions 319
Class Projects 319
Hands-On: P&G Puts the Medium Before the Message 319

PART-ENDING CASE Chick-fil-A: Effective Advertising Media 321

PART IV EFFECTIVE ADVERTISING MESSAGES

12 The Creative Side and Message Strategy 325

 MSN Takes Wing 325

THE ART AND SCIENCE OF CREATIVE ADVERTISING 327
The ROI of Effective Advertising, 327 • Creative Thinking, 330 • The Creative Process: How to Get an Idea, 332

CREATIVE STRATEGY 334
Message Objectives, 334 • Head and Heart Strategies, 334

FACETS OF CREATIVE STRATEGY 336
Messages That Drive Perception, 336 • Messages That Drive Cognition, 338 • Messages That Touch Emotions, 340 • Messages That Persuade, 340 • Messages That Transform a Product into a Brand, 342 • Messages That Drive Action, 344 • Message Approaches, 344 • Delivering on the Objectives and Strategies, 345

PLANNING AND MANAGING CREATIVE STRATEGY 345
The Creative Brief, 345 • Message Execution, 347 • Managing the Global Creative Strategy, 348 • the Go/No-Go Decision, 349

THE INSIDE STORY: How Does a Quintessentially American Brand Introduce Itself en Español? 343

A MATTER OF PRINCIPLE: Finding a Universal Truth About Cats 349

IT'S A WRAP: MSN's Butterfly Emerges as a Winning Big Idea 350

Summary 351
Key Terms 351
Review Questions 351
Discussion Questions 352
Class Projects 352
Hands-On: How Do You Put a Price on Great Creative?
Ask McCann-Erickson 353

13 Copywriting 355

 Frontier's Tales About Tails 355

COPYWRITING: THE LANGUAGE OF ADVERTISING 357
The Copywriter, 357 • Advertising Writing Style, 358

COPYWRITING FOR PRINT 360
How to Write Headlines, 360 • How to Write Other Display Copy, 363 • How to Write Body Copy, 364 • Print Media Requirements, 365

HOW TO WRITE RADIO COPY 367
The Tools of Radio Copywriting, 368 • The Practice of Radio Copywriting, 369 • Planning the Radio Commercial: Scripts, 369

HOW TO WRITE TELEVISION COPY 369
Tools of Television Copywriting, 374 • Planning the TV Commercial, 376

WRITING FOR THE WEB 378
Banners, 378 • Web Ads, 380 • Other Web Formats, 380

COPYWRITING IN A GLOBAL ENVIRONMENT 380

THE INSIDE STORY: Selling Newspaper Classifieds on the Radio 370

A MATTER OF PRACTICE: "Hello. London Calling with a Jaguar Just for You." 375

A MATTER OF PRINCIPLE: The Ocean Speaks 379

IT'S A WRAP: Talking Animals on the Tarmac 381

Summary 381
Key Terms 382
Review Questions 382
Discussion Questions 382
Class Projects 383
Hands-On: Beautiful Just the Way You Are, Finds Ogilvy 383

14 Design and Production   385

 The Work of a Lifetime   385

VISUAL COMMUNICATION   386
Visual Impact, 387 • The Art Director, 387

PRINT ART DIRECTION   389
Illustrations and Photos, 389 • Color in Print, 390 • Typography, 391 • Layout and Design, 394

PRINT PRODUCTION   399
Print Media Requirements, 399 • Art Reproduction, 400

TELEVISION ART DIRECTION   404
Video Graphics, 405 • TV and Film Requirements, 406

BROADCAST PRODUCTION   407
Producing TV Commercials, 407 • The TV Production Process, 408

EFFECTIVE WEB DESIGN   412
Action and Interaction, 413

A MATTER OF PRACTICE: Kitty Slickers and Cat Herders   404

A MATTER OF PRINCIPLE: Honda "Cog" Gets It Right, But Not the First Time   411

THE INSIDE STORY: The Best and Worst of Site Design   413

IT'S A WRAP: Imagine a Legendary Lifestyle   414

Summary   414
Key Terms   415
Review Questions   415
Discussion Questions   416
Class Projects   416
Hands-On: The Future Definition of Advertising   417

PART-ENDING CASE Chick-fil-A: Effective Advertising Messages   418

PART V   INTEGRATION AND EVALUATION

15 Direct Response   421

 What's Holding You Back from a Harley?   421

THE PRACTICE OF DIRECT MARKETING   423
Advantages and Disadvantages of Direct Marketing, 424 • Direct Marketing and Direct-response Advertising, 424

DATABASE MARKETING   428
Lists, 429 • Data-driven Communication, 430 • Customer Relationship Management (CRM), 432

THE KEY PLAYERS   432
The Advertisers, 432 • The Agencies, 433 • The Media Companies, 433 • The Customers, 433

THE TOOLS OF DIRECT MARKETING   435
Direct Mail, 435 • Catalogs, 437 • Telemarketing, 438 • Direct-response Advertising, 440 • The Internet and Direct Response, 442

INTEGRATED DIRECT MARKETING   443
Linking the Channels, 444 • Creating Loyalty, 444

GLOBAL CONSIDERATIONS IN DIRECT MARKETING   445

A MATTER OF PRINCIPLE: The Principles of Data-driven Relationships   431

THE INSIDE STORY: Shaping the World of Miss Hall's School   434

A MATTER OF PRACTICE: GEICO Delivers a "Good News" Story 441

IT'S A WRAP: Living the Harley Dream 445

Summary 446

Key Terms 446

Review Questions 447

Discussion Questions 447

Class Projects 447

Hands-On: I Won't Be Calling, But Let's Talk: Telemarketers Respond to the Do-Not-Call Registry 448

16 Sales Promotion, Events, and Sponsorships 451

History's Lost and Found Auction Block 451

THE PRACTICE OF SALES PROMOTION 453
Changes in the Promotion Industry, 453 • Reasons for the Growth of Sales Promotion, 454 • Categories of Sales Promotion, 455

CONSUMER PROMOTIONS 455
Types of Consumer Promotions, 455 • How to Use Consumer Promotions, 458

TRADE PROMOTIONS 461
Types of Trade Promotion, 461 • How to Use Trade Promotion, 462

PROMOTIONS THAT CROSS THE LINES 464
Sponsorships and Event Marketing, 464 • Other Promotional Support, 465 • Interactive and Internet Promotions, 465 • Loyalty Programs, 466 • Partnership Programs, 466

PROMOTION STRATEGY 467
Promotion Objectives, 468 • The Issue of Brand Building, 468 • Promotion Integration, 469 • Promotion Effectiveness, 470

A MATTER OF PRACTICE: Brown Sugar and Honey: I Love Those Links! 457

THE INSIDE STORY: The Phaeton Test Drive Program at W Hotels™ 459

IT'S A WRAP: History Channel Finds a Winning Promotion Idea 471

Summary 471

Key Terms 472

Review Questions 472

Discussion Questions 472

Class Projects 472

Hands-On: Upromise Uses Values Marketing to Pay for College 473

17 Public Relations 475

Kids Are Hungry. Believe It! 475

THE PRACTICE OF PUBLIC RELATIONS 477
Public Opinion, 478 • Reputation: Goodwill, Trust, and Integrity, 478 • Comparing Public Relations and Advertising, 478 • Types of Public Relations Programs, 480

PUBLIC RELATIONS PLANNING 483
Research and SWOT Analysis, 483 • Targeting, 484 • Objectives and Strategies, 484 • The Big Idea, 486 • PR's Role in IMC, 486

PUBLIC RELATIONS TOOLS 487
Advertising, 487 • Publicity, 489 • Publications, 492 • Videos/DVDs, CDs, and Books, 493 • Speakers and Photos, 493 • Displays and Exhibits, 493 • Special Events and Tours, 493 • Online Communication, 496

EFFECTIVENESS AND PR EXCELLENCE 497
Excellence in Public Relations, 498

A MATTER OF PRACTICE: "I Love Smoke-Free NYC" 479

THE INSIDE STORY: The Spokane Stampede: A Sales Mission to Calgary 495

IT'S A WRAP: P&G Works Globally 499

Summary 499
Key Terms 500
Review Questions 500
Discussion Questions 500
Class Projects 500
Hands-On: Oprah Helps People Live Their Wildest Dreams, with Some Help from Pontiac
501

18 Special Advertising Situations 503

 Novell Speaks Your Language 503

RETAIL ADVERTISING 504
Retail Advertising Strategies, 505 • Creating the Retail Ad, 507 • The Media of Retail Advertising, 509

BUSINESS-TO-BUSINESS ADVERTISING 510
Types of Business-to-Business Advertising, 510 • B2B Buying Behavior, 513 • Creating B2B Advertising, 513 • B2B Advertising Media, 514

NONPROFIT OR SOCIAL MARKETING 515
Cause and Mission Marketing, 516 • Nonprofit Marketing, 516

INTERNATIONAL ADVERTISING AND MARKETING COMMUNICATION 518
Stages of Market Development, 518 • The Global Versus Local Debate, 519 • Planning Global Marketing Communication Programs, 521 • Planning a Global Advertising Strategy, 523 • The IMC Factor in Global Advertising, 525

A MATTER OF PRACTICE: Fred Makes the IT Manager a Hero 511

A MATTER OF PRINCIPLE: The Great American Bake Sale Cooks Up Donations 517

THE INSIDE STORY: The "Mr. CONTAC" Campaign in Japan: A Case Study 524

IT'S A WRAP: Giving Voice to the Bottom Line 527

Summary 527
Key Terms 528
Review Questions 528
Discussion Questions 528
Class Projects 529
Hands-On: A New Alliance Turns Google Yellow 529

19 Evaluation of Effectiveness 531

 Changing Perceptions from the Mailroom to the Board Room 531

EVALUATING EFFECTIVENESS 533
Types and Stages of Evaluation, 533 • Factors to Be Evaluated, 534 • Copy-testing Services, 534

STAGES OF COPY TESTING 535
Message Development Research, 536 • During Execution: Concurrent Testing, 537 • Posttesting: After Execution Research, 540

MEDIA EVALUATION 542
Evaluating Audience Exposure, 542 • Advertising ROI and Media Efficiency, 543

CAMPAIGN AND IMC EVALUATION *544*
Marketing Communication Evaluation, 544 • IMC Consistency, 548 • Special Advertising Situations, 548

THE INSIDE STORY: Volvo Road Tests the "Starting a Family" Campaign   *536*

A MATTER OF PRACTICE: Research Finds Moments of Truth for IBM   *538*

IT'S A WRAP: What Can Brown Do for You?   *550*

Summary   *551*
Key Terms   *551*
Review Questions   *551*
Discussion Questions   *551*
Class Projects   *552*
Hands-On: Lovin' It at McDonald's Again   *552*

PART-ENDING CASE Chick-fil-A: Integration and Evaluation   *554*

Glossary   *557*
Credits   *571*
Notes   *575*
Index   *581*

Preface

WHAT MAKES ADVERTISING EFFECTIVE?

During the 2005 Super Bowl an ad for Anheuser-Busch called "Applause" showed people in an airport spontaneously applauding a group of American troops returning home. Even the audience watching from their living rooms was inclined to join in with applause as part of this graceful display of respect and appreciation. It was touching. Memorable. Beautifully photographed. And the people seemed real. But was it an effective ad? What was it trying to accomplish?

Advertising can cause you to stop and watch, or even stop and think. It can make you laugh, or squirm in your seat, or bring tears to your eyes. It can inspire you to read about a new product or remember a favorite brand when you're walking down the aisle in a supermarket. Advertising can also leave you free to change the channel or turn a page without being aware of having seen the ad at all.

So what is effective advertising? Is it advertising that gets talked about? Is it advertising like the Anheuser-Busch commercial that inspires you to applaud? In other words, is it advertising that affects people or is it advertising that gets results and can be measured? What, exactly, does it mean to say that an advertisement "works?" Ultimately advertising is evaluated on its ability to generate a desired consumer response based on meeting a set of carefully crafted objectives.

In most cases, you have little idea what the objectives of an ad were because that information generally isn't made public. However, we contacted the winners of various effectiveness award programs and wrote the stories in this book based on the "briefs," the documents advertisers write to explain the decisions behind their advertising. That means the strategy becomes more transparent and you can actually read the objectives, as well as the results. These aren't hypothetical campaigns or stories clipped from magazines. We work with the real planning documents and we talk to the people who developed the advertising.

Advertising is part inspiration and part hard work. In this 7th Edition of *Advertising: Principles and Practice* we take you behind the scenes of many award-winning campaigns to uncover the hard work and explain the objectives, as well as the inspiration behind some great advertising campaigns. You will see how the ideas come together; you will live through the decision-making; and you will understand the risks that the creators of the advertising faced.

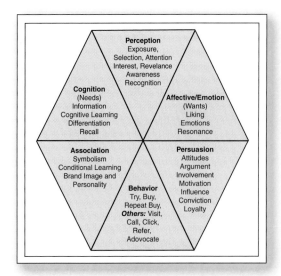

THE FACETS MODEL: PICTURING ADVERTISING EFFECTIVENESS

Advertising is complex and there are many different ways advertising can "affect" people. At the most basic level, advertising works if people pay attention to it, become aware of the brand, and remember both the brand and the advertising. That's impact at the perceptual level. But an advertisement may also be designed to create five other general types of responses: It may provide useful information, touch emotions, give a brand a personality, change consumer attitudes, and cause people to act.

The 7th Edition of *Advertising: Principles and Practice* has organized this discussion of advertising effects for you in the form of a Facets Model. This illustration and the ideas it represents are used throughout the book to help you remember what we mean by effectiveness when we explain such things as how advertising works, how objectives are decided upon, and how an advertisement is evaluated based on its objectives.

ORGANIZATIONAL CHANGES AND THEMES

Table of Contents

The book is the same length in terms of the number of chapters, however, there are two new chapters dealing with interactive media and evaluation of effectiveness. The international and campaigns chapters have been eliminated as separate chapters; however, their content has been integrated throughout remaining chapters.

Part 1: Foundations

In the 7th edition, former chapters 2 and 3 exchange places. The new organization provides the platform to discuss practicing advertising and marketing communication in socially responsible ways.

Chapter 1: Introduction to Advertising
Chapter 2: Advertising's Role in Marketing
Chapter 3: Advertising and Society

Part 2: Planning and Strategy

We begin with Chapter 4, "How Advertising Works," which was Chapter 6 in the previous edition. We also introduce a new model of how advertising works—The Facets Model—that will be used in other chapters, such as planning and message strategy.

Chapter 4: How Advertising Works
Chapter 5: The Consumer Audience
Chapter 6: Strategic Research
Chapter 7: Strategic Planning

Part 3: Effective Advertising Media

This part now consists of four chapters with a free-standing interactive chapter. In addition, the more complex discussion of planning and buying has been moved to the end of this section.

Chapter 8: Print and Out-of-Home Media
Chapter 9: Broadcast Media
Chapter 10: Interactive and Alternative Media
Chapter 11: Media Planning and Buying

Part 4: Effective Advertising Messages

The three creative chapters continue here as before, with the direct-response chapter moving to Part V.

Chapter 12: The Creative Side and Message Strategy
Chapter 13: Copywriting
Chapter 14: Design and Production

Part 5: Integration and Evaluation

The three other functional areas of marketing communication—direct response, sales promotion, public relations—continue in this book but are now grouped together in Part V. Retail, business-to-business and international are now combined into one chapter focusing on special advertising situations. The former campaign chapter, which dissected a campaign in-depth, has been eliminated on the advice of our reviewers, and the content that framed the discussion of the campaign is now in the Strategic Planning chapter. We added a summary chapter on evaluating effectiveness.

Chapter 15: Direct Response
Chapter 16: Sales Promotion, Events, and Sponsorships
Chapter 17: Public Relations
Chapter 18: Special Advertising Situations
Chapter 19: Evaluation of Effectiveness

Strong Brand Focus

The launch of the iPod is one example of how the 7th edition addresses strong brands with advertising and IMC. In Chapter 8 you will learn about how the iPod was launched with great print and broadcast ads. The introduction also included partnership programs with companies like Volkswagon and the launch of iTunes, its sister music system. You'll learn about the importance of iPod's buzz marketing programs and the variety of marketing communication tools utilized to get people talking about the new product. Advertising has reached the stage where it sometimes isn't enough to have a great commercial, slogan or jingle. The industry has moved to integrated marketing communication (IMC), which coordinates all the ways an organization communicates about its products, services, or ideas.

Advertising: Principles and Practice was the first advertising or promotion text to feature the topic of IMC. We give it even greater emphasis in this edition by threading the IMC perspective throughout the book. That's why *Advertising: Principles and Practice* has always contained chapters on direct marketing, sales promotion, and public relations. It is important that advertising be planned and evaluated as one element, albeit an important one, within this constellation of messages. Here are some related concepts and techniques used in support of an integrated campaign:

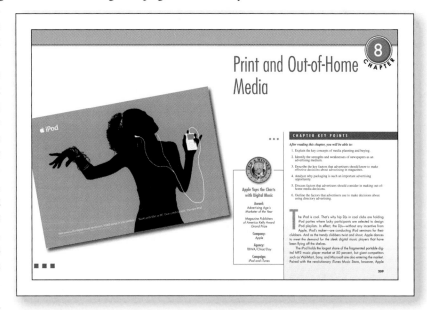

Account Planning: Effective advertising, as well as effective marketing communication in all its forms, is based on an understanding of consumers—what they want from a product, how they relate to a brand, and how they respond to various types of brand messages. Consequently, effective advertising and IMC programs rely on practices, such as account planning, which is a research and planning technique designed to uncover insight into consumer beliefs and behavior. This

edition of *Advertising: Principles and Practices* has increased the coverage of account planning in an attempt to better explain how planners derive insight from research. The KFC story in Chapter 7 about how the meaning of the quintessentially American brand was adapted to appeal to British consumers provides insight into the thinking of account planners.

International Context: Chapter 13 explains how Jaguar uses a "London Calling" theme to sell its distinctive British cars in the U.S. As electronic communication has exploded around the globe, advertising has been embedded in a web of international marketing strategies. Even if an advertiser isn't operating internationally, there's a good chance the competition is, which adds to the complexity of the planning, particularly for brands that are being marketed internationally and creates a challenge for a consistent brand strategy—what to change and what to keep the same?

Because of the importance of the international context, we have included an international discussion in most of the chapters. In addition, the basic discussion from the old international chapter is now included within Chapter 18, Special Advertising Situations. The goal is to make the international perspective a seamless part of all the discussions. To that end, various chapters have chapter opening stories, A Matter of Practice boxes, and Inside Stories from outside the U.S.

EFFECTIVENESS

It's clear from the headlines in industry publications that advertisers want to know if their ads and other marketing communication efforts work. But of equal concern is the return advertisers get on their investment in advertising. Accountability is the word. Advertising costs money—a lot of money in many cases—and advertisers want proof that their advertising and marketing communication is efficient, as well as effective. That's why we make the claim—and, yes, this is an advertisement—that:

> *ADVERTISING: PRINCIPLES AND PRACTICE* **Is the book to read to learn about effective advertising**

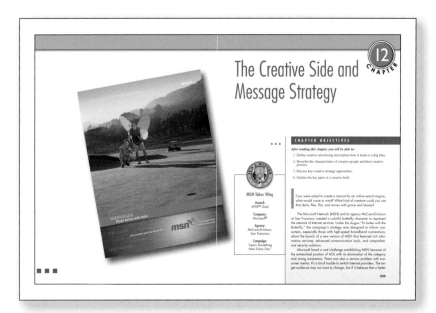

You will learn in this book that all advertising claims need to be supported. We are making a bold claim, but here is how we back it up:

The Effectiveness Award Winners

Every chapter opens with a story about work that has been recognized as effective, such as the development of the butterfly mascot for the Microsoft network (MSN), which is featured in Chapter 12. Most of these stories are EFFIE award-winning campaigns recognized by The New York American Marketing Association as outstanding examples of effectiveness, the Direct Marketing Association's Echo Awards, the Public Relations Society of America's Silver Anvil, and the Sales Promotion Association's Reggie Awards.

It's a Wrap

At the end of each chapter we loop back to the opening campaign story and show you why it was successful. We match the results to the objectives and provide the data used by professionals to determine whether the advertising worked. In the MSN "butterfly" story, for example, we document the success MSN had with this campaign in acquiring new customers for its Internet service.

A Matter of Practice

We continue to feature the "A Matter of Practice" box, which discusses effective professional practice. These boxes examine effectiveness tactics, such as the Starbucks' foray into television advertising using a technique that is less intrusive than the usual TV commercial.

IT'S A WRAP

MSN'S BUTTERFLY EMERGES AS A WINNING BIG IDEA

No matter how much the creative people or the client or the account executive may like an idea, if it doesn't communicate the right message or the right product personality to the right audience at the right time, it is not effective. That's the science of advertising messages; the art side comes from creative Big Ideas that have stopping power and break through the competitive clutter.

MSN's "Butterfly" campaign is a good example of both the art and science of advertising. It was designed to motivate consumers to consider MSN as an alternative to AOL and to sign up for the new service. By tapping into what consumers truly want from their Internet service provider—a more useful experience—the McCann team developed an impactful advertising campaign. It has been recognized as effective because it delivered on its objectives:
- Generate switching momentum from AOL to MSN: The campaign resulted in 715,000 AOL users switching to MSN.
- Increase Internet subscriptions: The total MSN subscriptions grew 31 percent with a significant increase during the six-week online campaign.

A Matter of Principle

Staying true to the book's title—*Advertising: Principles and Practice*—every chapter also features principles that guide the industry of advertising, as well as the issues that complicate it. These boxes may feature a discussion on subliminal advertising in Chapter 4 and the use of cookies in email in Chapter 10. Other times, a principle is a simple statement of a fundamental truth that draws together the discussion of a key point and summarizes it as an important rule that guides professional practice.

Inside Story

Catch the spirit of Sonia Montes, an account executive at Young and Rubicam and graduate of the Michigan State University advertising program, who tells you in her own words why she loves advertising. One of the reviewers' favorite features of *Advertising: Principles & Practice* is The Inside Story, which are boxes that spotlight the thoughts and experiences of young advertising professionals. You'll enjoy the insights of these professionals from agencies big and small, as well as other companies from all parts of the United States and abroad.

Showcase Work

We collected examples of outstanding work contributed by young professionals who have been nominated by their faculty. We included ads like these in past editions, but this time we are showcasing the work in order to give more credit to these people and the schools and professors who trained them.

Practical Tips

These are ideas that you can apply on the job, in an internship, or in your coursework. Building on past editions, the Tips in this edition include when to use print and broadcast media, tips for creating original ideas, and how to create effective direct mail pieces.

Hands-On Cases

This popular feature continues in the 7th Edition. At the end of the chapter, you have the chance to become advertising decision makers yourself by analyzing a real-world

SHOWCASE

Gander Mountain carries a wide selection of supplies and gear at great prices. The employees at the stores are all outdoor experts who don't just sell gear; they also use it as they participate in outdoor activities themselves. The agency determined that communication for Gander Mountain should focus on these "outdoor experts" as well as on customers and their outdoor experiences. This ad was contributed by Trent Walters, a graduate of the University of North Texas advertising program, where he was selected by the American Advertising Federation as one of its "Most Promising Students." He is now an account supervisor at the Richards Group in Dallas, Texas.

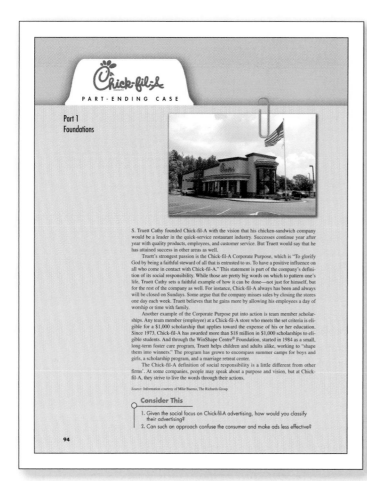

advertising case. You will be challenged to think critically about the many pieces of the puzzle that must work together to create successful ads. New companies examined include Wal-Mart and its corporate image advertising in Chapter 1, AFLAC's duck in Chapter 4, and the BMW "Films" campaign which is revolutionizing Internet advertising in chapter 10.

Part-Ending Cases

Every part ends with an updated Chik-fil-A case. These cases illustrate how the key topics of every chapter must work together to create an advertising campaign with a consistent message.

Suggested Class Projects

To really understand what effective advertising is and how it is done, you have to do it yourself. We help by providing Suggested Class Projects at the end of each chapter that allow you to work together in teams as advertisers do. They also invite you to learn how to use the Internet as a research and creative tool. For example in Chapter 7 you are asked to create a positioning statement for car models, in Chapter 12 you are asked to brainstorm about creative concepts to encourage people to use alternative transportation, and in chapter 13 you are asked to transform print ads into broadcast commercials.

SUPPLEMENTS FOR INSTRUCTORS AND STUDENTS

Instructor's Manual

Contains chapter overviews and key points, plus detailed chapter outlines, incorporating key terms from the text. Also includes support for end-of-chapter material, along with additional class projects and assignments.

- *New feature:* "Outside Examples" offer instructors additional lecture material for each chapter. The examples may include extensions of concepts or company examples briefly mentioned in the chapter, or new material that further develops a key concept in the text.
- *New feature:* "Professors on the Go!" was created with the busy professor in mind. This helpful feature brings key material upfront in the manual, where instructors who are short on time can take a quick look and find key points and assignments to incorporate into a lecture without having to page through all the material provided for each chapter.

Test Item File

Contains over 2,800 questions. Each chapter consists of multiple-choice, true/false, essay, and short-answer questions, with page references and difficulty levels provided for each question.

- *New feature:* An entire section dedicated to application questions. This resource provides real-life situations that take students beyond basic chapter concepts and vocabulary and asks them to apply their advertising knowledge.

PC/MAC TESTGEN

Prentice Hall's test generating software is available from the *Instructor's Resource Center (IRC) Online* (www.prenhall.com/wellsburnett) or from the *IRC on CD-ROM*.

- PC/Mac compatible; preloaded with all of the Test Item File questions.
- Manually or randomly view test bank questions and drag-and-drop to create a test.
- Add or modify test bank questions using the built-in Question Editor.
- Print up to 25 variations of a single test and deliver the test on a local area network using the built-in QuizMaster feature.

Free customer support is available at media.support@pearsoned.com or 1-800-6-PRO-FESSOR between 8:00 A.M. and 5:00 P.M. CST.

NEW! Instructor's Resource Center

All instructor resources are password protected and available for download via **www.prenhall.com/wellsburnett**. For your convenience, these resources are also available on the Instructor's Resource CD-ROM.

- *Instructor's Manual:* View this resource chapter-by-chapter or download the entire manual as a .zip file.
- *Test Item File:* View chapter-by-chapter or download the entire test item file as a .zip file.
- *TestGen for PC/Mac:* Download this easy-to-use software; it's preloaded with the Seventh Edition test questions and a user's manual.
- *Image bank (On CD only):* Access many of the images, ads, and illustrations featured in the text. Ideal for PowerPoint customization.
- *PowerPoints:* When it comes to PowerPoints, Prentice Hall knows one size does not fit all. That's why we offer instructors more than one option.
- *PowerPoint BASIC:* This simple presentation includes only basic outlines and key points from each chapter. It integrates no animation or forms of rich media, which makes the total file size manageable and easier to share online or via email. BASIC was also designed for instructors who prefer to customize PowerPoints and who want to be spared from having to strip out animation, embedded files, or other media rich features.
- *PowerPoint MEDIA RICH (On CD only):* This media rich alternative includes basic outlines and key points from each chapter, plus advertisements and art from the text, images from outside the text, discussion questions, Web links, and embedded video snippets from the accompanying video library. It's the best option if you want a complete presentation solution. Instructors can further customize this presentation using the image library featured on the IRC on CD-ROM.

Color Overheads

Features 15-20 color acetates per chapter selected from the Media Rich set of PowerPoints; includes images from text.

Video

In order to enrich your advertising course, the accompanying video library offers a variety of video segments. Some segments take students on location, profiling well-known companies and their marketing and advertising strategies. Others offer a behind-the-scenes look at a typical day in the life of various advertising employees at different levels in the agency, providing insight into what skills are really needed to succeed in the field. Additionally, a collection of commercial advertisements are included in the video library. These serve as a great tool to demonstrate to your students what works—and what doesn't—in the field of advertising. You may download the Video Guide from the Instructor's Resource Center.

New! Media Guide

Are your students still struggling with the media aspect of advertising? Are you looking for an innovative new way to introduce the various forms of media to your students? Brand new to this edition, the Media Guide, complete with rate cards, gives an in-depth explanation of each form of media. In addition, you will have many short- and long-term project options to choose from, geared around each of the media channels discussed. After reviewing the various forms of media, your students will then be asked to rate which is best, given the information in the guide, ensuring that they understand the form that can best suit their future business's needs. For electronic manipulation, the rate cards can be downloaded from the Companion Website at **www.prenhall.com/wellsburnett**. At the request of the professor, the Media Guide can be packaged for FREE with new copies of this textbook. Contact your Prentice Hall representative for the package ISBN.

Companion Website

This FREE site serves as a valuable resource for students in preparing for exams. Two student quizzes per chapter are offered. The Concept Check Quiz is administered prior to reviewing the chapter, in order to assess the students' initial understanding. The Concept Challenge Quiz is administered after reviewing the chapter to assess the students' comprehension. Also featured on the site is the text glossary. You can reach the Companion Website by visiting **www.prenhall.com/wellsburnett**.

Contributors

The "Practice" idea in the book's title—*Advertising: Principles and Practice*—is supported in this edition by involving many professionals from a variety of areas. Professionals were used in the initial planning to review chapters in their own areas of expertise and provide information to update the book. Young professionals are also writing the Inside Story boxes and their creative work is shown in the Showcase feature. We appreciate the work and contributions of these people and would like to thank them in this section.

PROFESSIONAL ADVISORS

Constance Cannon Frazier

Senior Vice President, AAF Mosaic Center and Education Services

Constance Cannon Frazier joined the American Advertising Federation (AAF) AS senior vice president, AAF Mosaic Center and education services. As leader of these vitally important programs, Frazier oversees continuing efforts to promote multiculturalism in the industry, as well as steer the AAF's educational programs, which include the Most Promising Minority Students and the AAF Mosaic Awards. As head of the AAF's education services, Frazier promotes the organization's 210 college chapters and oversees programs such as the National Student Advertising Competition. She also heads the AAF's internship and scholarship programs, encouraging students to pursue advertising as a career. In addition to extensive professional experience in the advertising industry, Frazier achieved an outstanding record in advertising education at Howard University, where she was the coordinator of the advertising and public relations sequence. The American Advertising Federation (AAF), which is headquartered in Washington, D.C., is the trade association that represents 50,000 professionals in the advertising industry.

Marty Horn

Senior Vice President, Group Director—Strategic Planning & Research DDB, Chicago

Marty Horn is a Senior Vice President, Director of Brand Planning at DDB, one of the country's—and one of the world's—largest advertising agencies. He directs all consumer research and development of creative strategies for State Farm and ALL-TEL. In addition to his client duties, Marty oversees the *DDB Life Style Study,* the largest and longest-running survey of its kind on American attitudes, interests and desires. Marty has published articles in the *Journal of Advertising, Journal of Advertising Research* and the *International Journal of Sports and Event Marketing.* He is currently on the Board of Directors of the Association for Consumer Research. Marty has Bachelors and Masters Degrees in Communications from the University of Connecticut.

Adam S. Kruse

Senior Research Analyst, MPG (Media Planning Group), Boston

Adam S. Kruse is a Senior Research Analyst in the Research and Modeling group at MPG (Media Planning Group) in Boston, MA. Before MPG, he was a Research Analyst in Media Research at Starcom in Chicago. He is a Phi Beta Kappa graduate of the William Allen White School of Journalism at the University of Kansas. He also received his M.S. in Integrated Marketing Communications at the University of Colorado, Boulder.

Susan Mendelsohn, Ph.D.

President, Susan Mendelsohn Consultants, Chicago

Susan is President of Susan Mendelsohn Consultants, a Chicago-based company that specializes in brand building and developing creative and integrated communication strategies. She possesses exceptional account planning experience including planning in the profit and not-for-profit sectors with clients and brands in over 60 industries. Client experience includes Chock full o'Nuts, Quaker (Gatorade, snacks, all cereals), The Field Museum, Jim Beam brands, Sesame Workshop, Hasbro, The Goodman Theatre and P&G. Susan is also an adjunct professor of marketing for The School of the Art Institute of Chicago. Prior to that, she was Executive Vice President, Director of Planning for Young & Rubicam and Senior Vice President, Group Planning Director for FCB Worldwide both in Chicago. Before that, Susan worked in New York City for Saatchi & Saatchi, Griffin Bacal Inc., DMB&B. Her doctorate and MS degrees are in Human Development from Syracuse University. She earned her BA cum laude in Psychology from the University of Denver (Phi Beta Kappa). Susan currently serves as Chairman for the Midwest APG

(Account Planning Group) and is a frequent speaker and writer in her field.

Ivan L. Preston

Journal Communications Professor Emeritus, University of Wisconsin

Ivan L. Preston is Journal Communications Professor Emeritus at the University of Wisconsin-Madison after being on the faculty for 31 years. His Ph.D. is from Michigan State. He previously worked in advertising and has written two books on deceptive advertising (*The Great American Blow-Up* and *The Tangled Web They Weave*), along with a number of law review articles. He has participated in law cases on behalf of advertisers and government regulators, and also spent time in Washington as inhouse consultant to the Federal Trade Commission.

William H. Weintraub

Chief Marketing Officer (retired), Coors Inc., Boulder CO

Bill received his B.S. in Communications from the University of Illinois and his M.B.A. in from Northwestern. He began his career at Procter & Gamble, managing a range of brands for 15 years. Over the next 20 years, Bill was Chief Marketing Officer at Kellogg, then Tropicana, and then Coors. Through his career, Bill received a number of awards, including *BrandWeek's* Marketer of the Year. He now teaches at the University of Colorado, while serving on various boards.

Karl Weiss

President/CEO, Market Perceptions, Inc.

Karl Weiss, founder and president of Denver-based Market Perceptions, Inc. has 15 years experience in marketing research, with special expertise in research design and statistical analysis. Karl holds an MBA with an emphasis in marketing research and B.S. degrees in marketing and statistics. His background in statistical methods, coupled with experience in marketing research, provides clients with expertise ranging from defining study objectives to design and analysis. Karl's goal in founding Market Perceptions was to build a research firm that allowed clients to become closer to their research, "experience their data" rather than be subjected to it. By turning traditional printed research reports into multimedia presentations with integrated voice and data, Market Perceptions brings clients to a much closer understanding of how their companies and brands are perceived by the outside world.

Christine Wright-Isak

Ph.D. Founder and President, Northlight Marketing, Inc.

Dr. Wright-Isak was educated at the University of Chicago, where she received her Ph.D.. In New York she applied her training to marketing research for a variety of client companies while at Omnicom (BBDO Advertising) and then at Young & Rubicam Advertising. Her client work includes GE "We Bring Good Things to Life," and the launch of two new brands: Lever 2000 soap and Colgate Total Toothpaste. At Y&R Dr. Wright-Isak was the corporate reputation specialist for clients such as DuPont, Kodak, and Johnson & Johnson. In 1998, at the request of several clients, Dr. Wright-Isak launched the strategic market research firm Northlight Marketing, Inc. In 1999, the Advertising Research Foundation awarded her a Gold Ogilvy, the industry's highest award for outstanding research, for her contribution to the launch of Colgate Total. Throughout her business career, she has continued to be an active participant in the academic community by conducting independent research and publishing in academic journals. Most recently she has joined the faculty of Florida Gulf Coast University to teach Marketing and Advertising courses.

SHOWCASE CONTRIBUTORS

We would like to thank the following professionals who contributed their work to illustrate the book with Showcase features.

Mike Dattolico is a freelance art director and a graduate of the University of Florida. Since earning degrees in Advertising & English Literature, Michael ventured to England and is finishing up a postgraduate degree in Creative Advertising. On finishing, he will further pursue a career as an Art Director in London. In addition, he is in the process of publishing his first book, "Broken Roses: a poetic tale." Dattolico's work was nominated to be featured in this book by Professor Elaine Wagner, University of Florida.

Chris Hutchinson is an art director at Wieden + Kennedy in Portland, Oregon. He started at Bulldog-Drummond in San Diego after graduating from the University of Oregon with a degree in advertising. In his spare time he makes films. Hutchinson was nominated by Professor Charles Frazer, University of Oregon.

Ingvi Logason is a principal in his own firm, HÉR&NÚ Marketing Communications in Reykjavik, Iceland. A graduate of Western Florida University, he was nominated by Professor Tom Groth.

Lara Mann is a copywriter at FHB Advertising in Orlando, Florida. A 2001 advertising graduate from the University of Florida, she was nominated by Professor Elaine Wagner, University of Florida.

Amy Niswonger is a 2001 graduate of Miami University, Oxford, Ohio, where she was named Most Promising Minority Student by the American Advertising Federation (AAF). She is a graphic designer at the Cleveland, Ohio-based Nova Creative Group. Using both her marketing and graphic design degrees, she is creating unique pieces for the agency's regional clients. She was nominated by Connie Frazier, Senior Vice President, AAF Mosaic Center and Education Services.

Trent Walters, a 1997 graduate of the University of North Texas, is an account supervisor at The Richards Group in Dallas. He has worked on a number of the agency's major accounts including Nokia, the STARZ! Movie channel, AT&T Broadband, and Motel 6, in addition to his current assignment with the Gander Mountain account. Walters was also named a Most Promising Minority Student by the American Advertising Federation (AAF). He and his work were nominated by Professor Sherri Broyles, University of North Texas.

INSIDE STORY CONTRIBUTORS

Other contributors include the professionals who wrote stories about their work, which are featured in the Inside Story boxes. Their biographies are included at the end of their Inside Story, but we would like also to thank them here on the contributors page.

Ryan Ali, Account Executive, Ziccardi Partners Frierson Mee, New York

Cheri Anderson, Principal Consultant, SRI Consulting, Menlo Park, California

Masura Ariga, Strategic Planning Director, Dentsu, Tokyo, Japan

Heather Beck, Media Coordinator, Stern Advertising, Cleveland, Ohio

John Butler, Senior Marketing and Communication Strategist, Witeck-Combs Communications, Washington D.C.

Tammie DeGrasse, Account Supervisor, McCann-Erickson, New York

Amy Hume, Associate Media Director, Starcom Worldwide, Chicago

Ingvi Logason, Principal, HÉR&NÚ Marketing Communications, Reykjavik, Iceland

Harley Manning, Research Director, Site Design and Development, Forrester Research Jennifer Montague, National Accounts Director, Swivel Media San Francisco

Sonia Montes, Account Executive, Young & Rubicam, Chicago

Karl Schroeder, Copywriter, Nonbox, Portland, Oregon

Peter Stasiowski, Art Director, Gargan Communication, Dalton, Massachusetts

Eric Telchin, Designer, Washingtonpost.com Entertainment Guide, Washington D.C

Carson Wagner, Assistant Professor, University of Texas

ACADEMIC REVIEWERS

We would like to thank the following professors for their time in reviewing the sixth edition and for their valuable comments in shaping the seventh edition. We would especially like to thank Mike Weigold for his creative work and tireless energy in writing the Hands On Cases for this edition.

Susan Alessandri, Syracuse University

Andrew Aylesworth, Bentley College

Frederick DeCasperis, Siena College

Olan Farnall, California State University at Fullerton

Jooyoung Kim, Iowa State University

John Murphy, University of Texas at Austin

Ronald Stanton, Emerson University

Michael Weigold, University of Florida

The Mandate for Effectiveness

At a big meeting of advertising executives, Peter Sealey, former senior executive at Coca-Cola and Apple Computer and now a consultant, observed that "We are on the threshold of making advertising accountable." *Advertising Age* editor Rance Crain responded, "That's easier said than done."

Today, advertising finds itself in a serious bind. With a continuing weak economy, the tragedy of 9/11, and new technology that may threaten the way advertising operates, there is a need to justify the huge amounts of money spent of advertising.

Advertising will only survive and grow if it focuses on being accountable. Advertisers expect results. They want to know that their advertising works; is effective. That means the objectives they state for their advertising are being met. Clients expect proof, and, for the most part, that proof must lead to or actually produce sales.

The basic premise of this book is that advertising must be effective. To that end, we teach you about the complexities and intricacies of advertising strategies that produce effective results—ads that work, ads that touch people's emotions, stick in their minds, and move them to action. Because we are so concerned about effectiveness, we will introduce most chapters with an ad that has won an award that recognizes the effectiveness of the message.

Advertising is part art and part science and there are no easy answers to the questions of accountability and effectiveness. The industry has some things figured out but it is still searching for answers. As we journey through this story of advertising principles and practices you will join in the search.

In Chapters 1 and 2, the first part of the book, we will introduce the two professional areas of advertising and marketing. We will define them, identify their principles, and describe their practices. Chapter 3, the last chapter in Part I, will look at these two professional areas in terms of their place in society—the contributions they make as well as the criticisms they elicit.

Part I provides the "big picture" of advertising. The rest of the book will provide the depth and detail you need to be an informed user, or maybe even creator, of the advertising you see all around you. It's a fascinating business and we hope you will love the stories we have to tell about how great ads come to life.

Source: Rance Crain, "Change in Air at ANA, MPA; Problem is How to get There," *Advertising Age*, November 3, 2003, p. 23.

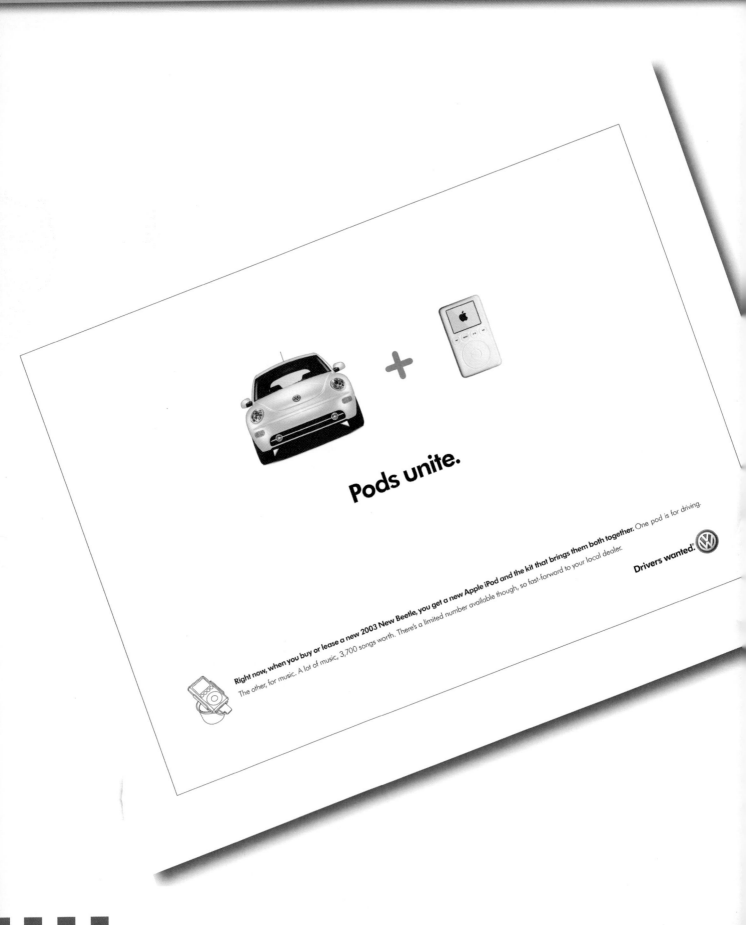

Pods unite.

Right now, when you buy or lease a new 2003 New Beetle, you get a new Apple iPod and the kit that brings them both together. One pod is for driving. The other, for music. A lot of music, 3,700 songs worth. There's a limited number available though, so fast-forward to your local dealer.

Drivers wanted.

Introduction to Advertising

CHAPTER

1

Volkswagen Sings a New Song with iPod®

Client:
Volkswagen of America

Agency:
Arnold Worldwide, Boston

Campaign:
"Pods Unite"

Award:
Gold Effie®, Silver Reggie*

---

*The EFFIE® award is given for advertising effectiveness. It is awarded by the New York American Marketing Association. The REGGIE award is given by the Promotion Marketing Association.

CHAPTER KEY POINTS

After reading this chapter, you will be able to:

1. Define advertising and explain its key components.

2. Discuss the roles and functions of advertising within society and business.

3. Identify the key players and their roles in creating advertising.

4. Explain the different types of advertising.

5. Summarize the characteristics of effective advertising and explain why it is always goal directed.

6. Analyze the changes affecting the advertising industry.

The good times roll for Volkswagen when its advertising, under the guidance of the Boston-based agency Arnold Worldwide, is winning awards. And Volkswagen's advertising has been on a hot streak since the mid-1990s, winning bookcases full of prizes for advertising effectiveness, as well as for creativity.

Most recently, an award-winning promotion offered an Apple iPod with the purchase of the New Beetle hardtop. The headline capitalized on the design, functional, and technological similarities between the iPod and the New Beetle, as a way of reminding people about what makes the New Beetle special.

Here's how the campaign evolved.

By 2003 Volkswagen and its agency Arnold Worldwide realized that the New Beetle was becoming old news since it was now

3

five years old. New products like the Mini Cooper were stealing its position as the "gotta have it" car. The successful launch of the new Beetle convertible earlier in the year had also cannibalized sales of the hardtop New Beetle.

To make things even more difficult, auto sales in general were down, and the marketplace was dominated by what Volkswagen saw as extravagant financial incentives like 0% down and thousands of dollars in rebates. Many manufacturers were sacrificing profits in order to gain, or simply maintain, market share.

Volkswagen opted not to join the incentive-and-discount fray, which would risk turning the most unique car on the road into a commodity. The marketing challenge and the advertising agency's objective, then, was to find a way to make the New Beetle hardtop seem fresh and more of a value than the competition.

So Arnold took a different path and found inspiration not in traditional automotive marketing, but in the practices of other unique brands. When looking at the Apple brand, for example, Arnold planners felt as though they were looking in a mirror. Both Apple and Volkswagen were "underdog" brands with a focus on leading design and technology. The consumers in VW's market, which it calls "Drivers," are active, confident, and independent people who love to drive. Further research confirmed that Volkswagen's "Drivers" love music and are early adopters of emerging technology. Comparing them to Apple's iPod users, Arnold found that they were a perfect match in terms of their interests and lifestyles.

By joining forces with Apple, VW capitalized on the obvious synergies between the two brands. Arnold found a way to add more tangible value to the New Beetle by including an iPod and a custom car-connectivity kit with the purchase of every New Beetle hardtop sold during the campaign. The headline of the campaign read, "Pods Unite."

The measurable objectives were to reach a sales goal of 5,200 units in two months and document that each sale came through the New Beetle/iPod promotion. Other measurable objectives included generating test drives at the dealerships by qualified customers who received a targeted direct-mail piece, and attracting apple.com users to the promotion's mini-Web site.

Source: Adapted from 2004 EFFIE Awards Brief for Volkswagen New Beetle + iPod: "Pods Unite" campaign. The brief was provided by Volkswagen of America and Arnold Worldwide; Alison Overolt, "The 'Pods Unite' Ad," *Fast Company* (October 2003): 36.

VW is an example of advertising that has been highly effective over the years. To see why, and to appreciate why the "Pods Unite" campaign was so successful, in this chapter we will examine what advertising is, how it is defined, and how it works.

The chapter starts with a definition of advertising and an explanation of some of advertising's most basic concepts. Then it provides some basic information about the roles and functions of advertising, the key players in advertising, and the various types of advertising. Here at the beginning of the twenty-first century we find an emphasis in the industry on advertising's effectiveness, and that concept is also introduced in this chapter. Finally, the chapter concludes with a review of advertising as a dynamic profession, identifying changes today and tomorrow that may affect the way advertising is defined in the future.

WHAT IS ADVERTISING?

You have been reading, watching, listening, and looking at advertising since you were a child. So it may seem a little silly to ask, "What is advertising?" An educated observer, however, looks at advertising as something more than a sales message that occupies the space in and around news stories, magazine features, and TV programs. In fact, it's a complex form of communication that operates with objectives and strategies leading to various types of impact on consumer thoughts, feelings, and actions. In this book, we're interested in great advertising and what principles and practices make it successful and effective. Effectiveness is a theme in this book and that means we will focus our attention on ads that create the consumer responses desired by the advertiser.

In a way, advertising is simple. It's about creating a message and sending it to someone, hoping they will react in a certain way. You've seen it all your life in the many thousands of commercials you've watched on television and the ads you've read in magazines, on billboards and the Internet, and in other places.

Advertising becomes controversial when questions arise about how it influences people and whether that is a good thing. Some say they hate it and that it makes us do things we don't really want to do. Others see it as a fashion guide or as entertainment with good jokes, great music, and fascinating images. We'll examine some of these issues later in the book, beginning with Chapter 3. But there is no doubt that advertising can be effective at influencing people. Advertising has evolved as society has changed: It has had an effect on society and at the same time society has had an effect on advertising.

Defining Modern Advertising

A standard definition of advertising has five basic components:

- Advertising is a paid form of communication, although some forms of advertising, such as public service announcements (PSAs), use donated space and time.
- Not only is the message paid for, but the sponsor is identified.
- Most advertising tries to persuade or influence the consumer to do something, although in some cases the point of the message is simply to inform consumers and make them aware of the product or company. In other words, it is strategic communication driven by objectives, and these objectives can be measured to determine whether the advertising was effective.
- Advertising reaches a large audience of potential consumers.
- The message is conveyed through many different kinds of mass media, which are largely nonpersonal. What that means is that advertising isn't directed to a specific person, although this is changing with the introduction of the Internet and more interactive media.

A modern definition, then, would be: **Advertising** is paid persuasive communication that uses nonpersonal mass media—as well as other forms of interactive communication—to reach broad audiences to connect an identified sponsor with a target audience.

The Key Concepts of Advertising

In describing advertising we refer to four broad factors: strategy, creative idea, creative execution, and creative media use. (Figure 1.1) All demand creative thinking from the advertising professionals who are responsible for their development and implementation. We'll refer to these dimensions often, and you will soon understand them as rich concepts that serve as a foundation for the practice of advertising.

These are also the fundamental elements professionals use to analyze the effectiveness of their advertising efforts. In other words, professionals critique the strategy, the creative idea, the execution of their advertising ideas, and the way the message is delivered through appropriate media.

Let's see more specifically what these four elements are.

- *Advertising strategy.* Strategy is the logic and planning behind the advertisement that gives it direction and focus. Every effective ad implements a sound strategy. The

Four Fundamental Elements of Advertising

Strategy, the creative idea, the advertising executions, and the media must work together for an ad to be truly effective.

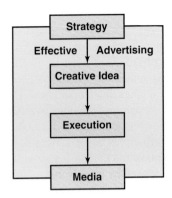

advertiser develops the ad to meet specific objectives, carefully directs it to a certain audience, creates its message to speak to that audience's most important concerns, and runs it in media (print, broadcast, or the Internet, for instance) that will reach its audience most effectively.

- *Creative idea.* The creative concept is the ad's central idea that grabs your attention and sticks in your memory. The "Pods Unite" campaign for VW, for example, connects two innovative products in a way that relates to the emotional connection Volkswagen owners have with their cars. The word *creative* describes a critical aspect of advertising that drives the entire field of advertising. Planning the strategy calls for imaginative problem solving: The research efforts need to be creative, and the buying and placing of ads in the media require creative thinking.
- *Creative execution.* Effective ads are well executed. That means that the details, the photography, the writing, the acting, the setting, the printing, and the way the product is depicted all reflect the highest production values available to the industry. Advertising often sets the standard or establishes the cutting edge for printing, broadcasting, and Internet design because clients demand the best production their budget allows.
- *Creative media use.* Every message has to be delivered somehow. Most advertisers use media—communication channels that reach a broad audience, such as television, magazines, or the Internet. Deciding how to deliver the message sometimes can be just as creative as coming up with the big idea for the message, a point we'll discuss more in Part 3.

Good advertisers know that how you say something and where you say it is just as important as what you say. What you say and where you say it comes from strategy, whereas how you say it is a product of creativity and execution. Strategy, the creative idea, its execution, and the media used all determine the effectiveness of an advertisement.

ROLES AND FUNCTIONS OF ADVERTISING

Over time, as the practice of advertising has evolved, it has played many different roles. It started out as a way to identify the maker of goods and that continues to be an important role today. As technology, such as the printing press, made it possible to reach a wider audience, advertising became more focused on providing commercial information along with identification of the product's maker.

Because of the advances of industrialization, which made it possible to produce more goods than the local market could absorb, advertising took on the role of creating demand for a product, which was done through two techniques: hard-sell approaches that use reasons to *persuade* consumers, and soft-sell approaches that build an *image* for a brand and touch consumers' emotions. An ad trumpeting a special reduced price on a tire is an example of a **hard-sell** approach; the long-running Michelin ad campaign that shows a baby sitting inside a tire is **soft sell**. (It's selling the tires' durability and reliability without saying that specifically; rather it symbolizes reliability with an image that touches your emotions.) In effect, these two approaches represent the art and science of advertising.

SHOWCASE

These ads use unexpected visuals—a parody on a common package for a soap detergent and a can of soup—to call attention to a special promotion on CDs by Virgin Megastores. These ads were contributed by Chris Hutchinson, a graduate of the advertising program at the University of Oregon and an art director at Weiden + Kennedy in Portland, Oregon.

But as the proliferation of media made it more difficult for any one message to get people's attention, a need developed for more creative techniques that would make an impact, such as the ads for Virgin Megastore. Creativity remains a key factor in evaluating the impact of an advertising idea and is an important characteristic of successful advertising.

In the early 2000s, as the economy slowed down, marketers have become concerned about accountability and the return they are getting on the money they invest in advertising. As a result, advertising professionals find themselves needing to prove that their work is effective—that it delivers the results the marketer has specified for the advertising. This intense emphasis on accountability is the reason that effectiveness is a key theme in this book. Every chapter opens with a case that details an example of effective work and ends, in It's a Wrap, with a discussion of the results of the work—in other words, how the advertising professionals determined or proved that the work was, in fact, effective. In order to better understand how advertising works, let's consider the four roles advertising plays in business and in society:

1. Marketing
2. Communication
3. Economic
4. Societal

The Marketing Role

The process a business uses to satisfy consumer needs and wants by providing goods and services is called **marketing**. The marketing department or manager is responsible for selling a company's product, which can be goods (computers, refrigerators, soft drinks), a service (restaurant, insurance, real estate), or an idea (support an organization, believe in a candidate). Products are also identified in terms of their **product category**. By category, we mean the classification to which the product is assigned—that is, Levi's is in the jeans category, Harley-Davidson is in the motorcycle category. The particular group of consumers thought to be potential customers for the goods and services constitute the **target market**.

Principle
A product can be services and ideas, as well as goods.

    The tools available to marketing include the *product* (the way it is designed, packaged, and how it performs), its *price,* and the means used to distribute or deliver the product to a *place* where the customer can buy it. Marketing also includes a method for communicating this information to the consumer called *marketing communication,* or *promotion.* These four tools—product, price, place (distribution), and promotion—are collectively referred to as the **marketing mix** or the four Ps, and we will discuss them in more detail in the next chapter. Advertising, of course, is one of the most important marketing communication tools.

    Marketing professionals are also involved with the development of a **brand**, which is the distinctive identity of a particular product that distinguishes it from its competitors. Colgate, for example, is one brand of toothpaste and Crest is another. They are produced by different companies and compete directly against one another. The Matter of Practice box explains how VW used brand-building advertising in support of its marketing program for the New Beetle hardtop.

The Communication Role

Advertising is a form of mass communication. It transmits different types of market information to connect buyers and sellers in the marketplace. It both informs and transforms the product by creating an image that goes beyond straightforward facts. The broad term **marketing communication** includes advertising, but it also includes a number of related communication techniques used in marketing—such as sales promotion, public relations, direct response, events and sponsorships, packaging, and personal selling. Table 1.1 summarizes the strengths of advertising.

The Economic Role

Advertising tends to flourish in societies that enjoy some level of economic abundance, in which supply exceeds demand. In these societies, advertising moves from being primarily informational to creating a demand for a particular brand.

TABLE

1.1 Strengths of Advertising as a Marketing Technique

Strengths	Examples
Can reach a mass audience	A commercial on the Super Bowl reaches 150 million consumers.
Introduces products	Windows 98 was simultaneously introduced in multiple world markets.
Explains important changes	MTN Cellular's ads explain changes in its technology.
Reminds and reinforces	Pepsi-Cola has been advertised continuously over the last 50 years.
Persuades	Nike campaigns have helped increase sales by 300% during the last decade.

A MATTER OF PRACTICE

Driving on the Road of Life

Given that Volkswagen is one of the greatest brands in the history of marketing, it is hard to believe that it almost went out of business in North America.

When Arnold Worldwide took over the Volkswagen account in 1994, its research discovered that consumers perceived the brand as unreliable and of poor quality. Volkswagen's heritage as an affordable, well-engineered car for people with a unique attitude toward life had gotten lost. Deep down, Arnold planners knew that if they could tap into this heritage and deliver on Volkswagen's key strengths, the brand could be brought back to life.

The agency's research uncovered the affection that Volkswagen loyalists continued to hold for the brand. It also discovered there was a position in the marketplace between overpriced European cars and the everyday driving experience offered by Asian and domestic competitors.

The agency's breakthrough "Drivers Wanted" campaign was launched in 1995–1996 and continues as the umbrella theme for all Volkswagen advertising. This award-winning theme captured the spirit of Volkswagen's tribe of loyal drivers and effectively rebuilt demand for the brand.

Arnold's creative team brought the theme to life by telling stories that were half about driving and half about living—about energetic, young people actively driving and experiencing their cars, feeling the road and everything around them. It placed the reader or viewer inside the car. And it placed the car in drivers' lives. The campaign all came together with the line "On the road of life, there are passengers and there are drivers. Drivers wanted."

"Drivers wanted" is much more than a catchy phrase. It carved out a place in the market that Volkswagen could own; it defined a distinctive target audience. Demographically, its "Drivers" were younger, more educated, and more affluent than average consumers. But most importantly, they loved to drive. They were different and proud of it. They were active participants in life. They were *Drivers.*

After all, the "Drivers Wanted" theme reflects a spirit rooted in Volkswagen's DNA: fun-to-drive cars for active people. And from the start, it resonated with the target audience.

The campaign's measurable objectives focused on increasing sales, brand awareness, intention to purchase, and the recall of its new advertising campaign. In effect, it sought to establish a unique and memorable relationship with a distinctive target audience.

The results? Sales turned around immediately and the most important measures of the brand's health—based on the objectives of awareness, purchase consideration, and ad recall—skyrocketed. Every measure of advertising effectiveness continued to rise year after year. Today, "Drivers wanted" is the most recognizable brand slogan in the auto industry.

Source: Adapted from The 2003 EFFIE Awards Brief; provided by Volkswagen of America and Arnold Worldwide.

If you sold your soul in the 80s, here's your chance to buy it back.

Drivers wanted.

© 1998 Volkswagen 1-800-DRIVE VW or www.vw.com

There are two points of view about the way advertising creates economic impact. In the first, advertising is seen as a vehicle for helping consumers assess value, through price as well as other information—such as quality, location, and reputation. Rather than diminishing the importance of price as a basis for comparison, advocates of this school view the role of advertising as a means to objectively provide price–value information, thereby creating a more rational economy.

In the second perspective, advertising is seen as so persuasive that it decreases the likelihood that a consumer will switch to an alternative product, regardless of the price charged. In other words, by focusing on other positive attributes, the consumer makes a decision on nonprice benefits—such as a psychological appeal. This is presumed to be the way images and emotions can be used to influence consumer decisions.[1] Neither of these perspectives on the role of advertising has been verified. It's likely that advertising plays both roles.

The Societal Role

Advertising also has a number of societal roles. It informs us about new and improved products, helps us compare products and features, and generally keeps us informed about innovations and issues. It mirrors fashion and design trends and adds to our aesthetic sense. It has an educational role in that it teaches about new products and how to use them. It helps us shape an image of ourselves by setting up role models that we can identify with, and it gives us a way to express ourselves in terms of our personalities and sense of style through the things we wear and use. There are both negative and positive dimensions to these social roles, which we will discuss in more detail in Chapter 3.

The Functions of Advertising

Looking at advertising's roles in society has given us the big picture, but now we need to focus more closely on what an advertiser might expect to get from advertising—why, in other words, it chooses to use advertising. From the advertiser's perspective, advertising, in general, performs seven basic functions:

- Builds awareness of products and brands
- Creates a brand image
- Provides product and brand information
- Persuades people
- Provides incentives to take action
- Provides brand reminders
- Reinforces past purchases and brand experiences

Consider This

1. Do the four roles—marketing, communication, economic, and societal—describe advertising as you see it?
2. Can you think of other roles advertising plays?

THE KEY PLAYERS

The advertising industry is complex because it has a number of different organizations involved in making decisions and executing advertising plans. The accompanying Matter of Principle box about the greatest television commercial ever shown introduces a number of these key players and illustrates how they all make different contributions to the final advertising. The players include the advertiser or client, the agency, the media, the supplier, and the audience. They all have different perspectives and objectives and a great advertisement is produced only when they come together as a team with a common vision. Let's look at each of these in turn.

The Advertiser

Advertising begins with the **advertiser**, the person or organization that uses advertising to send out a message about its products. In the "*1984*" story in the matter of principle box, the Apple company was the advertiser and Steve Jobs, the company's CEO, made the final decision to run the controversial commercial. The list in Table 1.2 shows the biggest U.S. advertisers in terms of their categories.[2]

The advertiser initiates the advertising effort by identifying a marketing problem that advertising can solve. The VW story is an example of how an advertiser struggles to maintain its position in a changing market, and also how its agency helps as a partner in developing a communication strategy to address the problem.

To better understand how that works, consider how VW's advertising evolved. Ask anyone who grew up in the 1960s and they can provide a litany of the legendary ads created by the Doyle Dane Bernbach advertising agency for the original VW Beetle affectionately known as "the Bug." They fondly remember such lines as "Think Small," "Lemon," "The Egg Car," "Ugly is Only Skin Deep," "Mass Transit" (a group of nuns in the bus), and, on television, "How does the snow plow driver get to his snow plow?" With such a tradition as an advertising leader, how does VW and its current agency continue this legacy of success? In fact, VW went through some hard times and was almost ready to drop out of the U.S. market. That's why the "Drivers Wanted" campaign was so important.

The creative genius behind the early VW Beetle ads made the car an advertising icon. Ads like this one are frequently cited in lists of the greatest advertising because they turned automotive marketing upside down by advertising smallness when everyone else was advertising largeness.

TABLE 1.2 Biggest U.S. Advertisers in Terms of Categories

1. Automotive
2. Retail
3. Movies, media, and advertising
4. Food, beverages, and confectionery
5. Medicines and proprietary remedies
6. Financial services
7. Telecommunications
8. Toiletries, cosmetics, and personal care
9. Airline travel, hotels, and resorts
10. Restaurants
11. Direct-response companies
12. Home furnishings, appliances, supplies
13. Insurance and real estate
14. Computers, software, Internet
15. Government, politics, and organizations
16. Apparel
17. Beer, wine, and liquor
18. Audio and video equipment and supplies
19. Sporting goods, toys, and games
20. Entertainment and events

A MATTER OF PRINCIPLE
The Greatest Commercial Ever Made

The advertiser was Apple, the product was its new Macintosh, and the client—the person handling the advertising responsibility and making decisions—was Steve Jobs, Apple's CEO and co-founder, who wanted "a thunderclap" ad. The agency was California-based Chiat/Day. The medium was television's Super Bowl. The supplier was legendary British film director Ridley Scott of *Alien* and *Blade Runner* fame. The audience was the 96 million people watching Super Bowl XVIII that day in January 1984, and the target audience was all those in the audience who were trying to decide whether they should buy a personal computer.

It's a basic principle in advertising: The combination of the right product at the right time in the right place with all the right people involved can create something magical—Jobs's thunderclap. In this case it also required a cast of 200 and a budget of $900,000 for production and $800,000 for the 60-second time slot. So it wasn't a small effort.

The storyline was a takeoff on George Orwell's science-fiction novel about the sterile mind-controlled world of *1984*. An audience of mindless gray-skinned drones (actually skinheads from the streets) watch a massive screen image of "Big Brother" spouting an ideological diatribe. And then an athletic young woman in bright red shorts runs in, chased by helmeted storm troopers, and throws a large sledgehammer at the screen. The destruction of the image is followed by a burst of fresh air blowing over the open-mouthed drones as they "see the light." In the last shot the announcer reads the only words in the commercial as they appear on screen: "On January 24th, Apple Computer will introduce Macintosh. And you'll see why 1984 won't be like *1984*."

Was it an easy idea to sell to the client?

First of all, some of the Apple executives who first saw the commercial were terrified that it wouldn't work because it didn't look like any commercial they had ever seen. After viewing it, several board members put their heads down in their hands. Another said, "Who would like to move on firing Chiat/Day immediately?" Supposedly Apple's other founder, Steve Wozniak, took out his checkbook and told Jobs, "I'll pay for half if you pay for the other half." The decision to air the commercial finally came down to Jobs, whose confidence in the Chiat/Day creative team gave him the courage to run the ad.

Was it effective?

On January 24 long lines formed outside computer stores carrying Apples, and the entire inventory sold out in one day. The initial sales goal of 50,000 units was easily surpassed by the 72,000 units sold in the first 100 days and more would have been sold if Apple had been able to keep up with the demand.

The *1984* commercial is one of the most talked about and most remembered commercials ever made—the best of the decade, the best 50 commercials ever made, etc. Every time there is a list of the best commercials, it sits at the top, and it continues to receive accolades into the twenty-first century. If you haven't seen it, then check it out on apple-history.com or www.uriah.com/apple-qt/1984.html and decide for yourself.

And remember, the commercial ran only once—admittedly it was a very expensive spot on the television program that has the highest viewership of the year, but it was seen only once by its target audience.

But it did turn the Super Bowl from just another football game into the advertising event of the year. What added to its impact was the hype before and after it ran. People knew about the spot because of press coverage prior to the game and they were watching for it. And post-coverage of the game was as likely to talk about "*1984*" as the football score. Advertising became news and watching the commercial became an event. That's why *Advertising Age*'s critic Bob Garfield calls it "the greatest TV commercial ever made."

The debate continues about whether the "Big Brother" character was designed to represent IBM. What do you think?

Consider This

1. Why is "*1984*" considered to be a great commercial?
2. Does this commercial fit the classic definition of advertising? Identify and explain the elements in the commercial that lead you to your conclusion.

Sources: Kevin Maney, "Apple's '1984' Super Bowl Commercial Still Stands as Watershed Event," *USA Today* (January 28, 2004 3B; Liane Hansen, host, "Steve Hayden Discusses a 1984 Apple Ad Which Aired During the Super Bowl," National Public Radio Weekend Edition, February 1, 2004; Cleveland Horton, "Apple's bold '1984' Scores on All Fronts," *Advertising Age*, (January 1, 1990) 12, 38; Bradley Johnson, "10 Years after '1981': The Commercial and the Product That Changed Advertising," *Advertising Age*, (June 1994) 1, 12–14; Curt's Media, "The 1984 Apple Commercial: The Making of a Legend," http://www.isd.net/cmcalone/cine/1984.html.

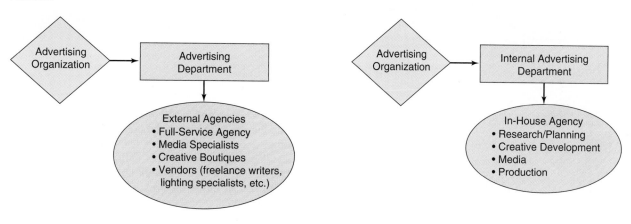

WHEN THE ADVERTISER DOESN'T HAVE AN IN-HOUSE AGENCY

Advertising Organization → Advertising Department → External Agencies
- Full-Service Agency
- Media Specialists
- Creative Boutiques
- Vendors (freelance writers, lighting specialists, etc.)

WHEN THE ADVERTISER HAS AN IN-HOUSE AGENCY

Advertising Organization → Internal Advertising Department → In-House Agency
- Research/Planning
- Creative Development
- Media
- Production

FIGURE 1.2 Sample Structures of the Advertising Process

The advertiser also makes the final decisions about the target audience and the size of the advertising budget. This person or organization also approves the advertising plan, which contains details outlining the message and media strategies.

Finally, the advertiser hires the advertising agency; in other words, the advertiser becomes the agency's client. As the client, the advertiser is responsible for monitoring the work and paying the bills for the agency's work on its account. That use of the word *account* is the reason agency people refer to the advertiser as "the account" and the agency person in charge of that advertiser's business as "the account manager."

The Advertising Agency

The second player in the advertising world is the advertising agency or department that creates the advertising. Advertisers hire independent agencies to plan and implement part or all of their advertising efforts as Chiat/Day did for Apple and the Arnold company did for Volkswagen in the opening story. This working arrangement is known as the agency–client partnership. The "*1984*" story demonstrates how important it is to cultivate a strong sense of trust between these two partners.

In 2002–2003 ad agency gross income was $10.6 billion worldwide, according to *Advertising Age*'s annual agency report. The top three U.S. ad agencies were J. Walter Thompson, Leo Burnett, and McCann-Erickson Worldwide. Japanese-based Dentsu, Inc. is the largest agency in the world. Arnold Worldwide of Boston is the agency that produced the most recent EFFIE-winning campaign work for VW; it is ranked fourteenth among U.S. agencies and had billings of $1.2 billion in 2003.

An advertiser uses an outside agency because it believes the agency will be more efficient in creating an advertisement or a complete campaign than the advertiser would be on its own. Successful agencies such as Arnold Worldwide typically have strategic and creative expertise, media knowledge, workforce talent, and the ability to negotiate good deals for clients. The advertising people working for the agency are experts in their areas of specialization and passionate about advertising, as the Inside Story illustrates.

There are several ways advertisers organize to manage their advertising. Large advertisers—either companies or organizations—participate in the advertising process either through their in-house agencies or through their advertising departments, as we see in Figure 1.2.

The Advertising Department Most large businesses have **advertising departments**. Their primary responsibility is to act as a liaison between the marketing department and the advertising agency (or agencies) and other vendors. Depending on the business, the

THE INSIDE STORY

Why Do I Love Advertising?

Sonia Montes, Senior Account Executive, Leo Burnett/Lapiz

I always knew I wanted to be in the ad business. As a child I filmed "commercials" with my parents' video camera. Throughout high school I admired Angela Bower (*Who's the Boss*) and thought Amanda Woodward (*Melrose Place*) had the best life. In college, I did well in my advertising classes and became heavily involved with the American Advertising Federation (AAF) student chapter. Although by graduation I should have had an inclination of what to expect, I still had a very glamorized image of the ad business. No textbook or TV show could have prepared me for what I was about to learn.

"Where's the Beef?"

There are no 3-hour-long lunches in the ad business. At least not since I've been in the industry. Most days, I'm lucky if I have a quick lunch at my desk . . . *while* I'm working. Long hours and late nights are practically an industry standard. I try to remind myself that most of my friends experience similar workdays in their business fields.

"Think Different."

One of the hardest things about being in the advertising business is actually describing to others what I do on a daily basis. Advertising is a dynamic, fast-paced environment, so every day my job is different. There are always new ideas, new creative strategies, and new problems to solve. Having analytical, writing, and presentation skills and the ability to reason through problems and think from other people's point of view is a necessity. While this is exciting, I always remember that someone else can do it better, which makes me work harder to stay competitive. You need to thrive on stress and challenges to survive advertising.

"It's the Real Thing."

So why do I stay in advertising? Well, I'm lucky. I work in a creative environment with young, passionate, forward-thinking people. It's a challenging field that keeps me on my toes daily. Above all, advertising is fun. I've learned that it's not surprising to be asked to wear a hot-pink wig or to see an art director stand on top of a table during client meetings. While my co-workers' hairstyles range from Mohawks to shaved heads, many of us have one thing in common. We are die-hard advertising addicts, constantly blazing our way to a brighter tomorrow with style and good company.

Sonia graduated from Michigan State University in 2000 with a BA in advertising. While at MSU, she was president of her student AAF chapter, the largest chapter in the country at that time, and she was named one of the 25 Most Promising Minority Students in Communications 2000 by the AAF. She began her career at FCB Chicago and has worked on such brands as S. C. Johnson and Kraft. She is currently a Senior Account Executive at Leo Burnett/Lapiz.

Nominated by Professor Carrie La Ferle, Michigan State University

involvement of the marketing department can vary tremendously from company to company. The individual in charge of the advertising department may carry a title such as Director of Advertising or Advertising Manager. Typically, that person has extensive experience in all the facets of advertising. In fact, many have had jobs on the agency side, so they may have worked with advertisers in various capacities and are familiar with their operations.

As indicated, the task of the advertising manager and the staff is to facilitate the interaction between the company's marketing department and the agencies. Many companies may have hundreds of agencies working for them, although they normally have an **agency-of-record**, which does most of their business and may even manage the other agencies. Tasks performed by the advertising department include the following: It selects the agencies; coordinates activities with vendors, such as media, production, photography, fulfillment; makes sure the work gets done as scheduled; and determines whether the work has achieved prescribed objectives.

The In-House Agency Companies that need closer control over their advertising have their own in-house agencies. Large retailers, for example, find that doing their own advertising provides cost savings as well as the ability to meet deadlines. Some fashion companies, such as the Ralph Lauren company, also create their own advertising in house in order to maintain complete control over the brand image and the fashion statement it

TABLE 1.3 Big Media

Company	Revenue and Employees	Businesses
Time Warner New York	$39.57 billion 80,000	America Online, HBO, Time Inc., Turner Broadcasting, Time Warner Cable, Time Warner Books, Warner Bros. Entertainment, Warner Music Group, New Line Cinema
Disney Burbank, CA	$27.06 billion 112,000	ABC, ESPN, Disney Channel, ABC Radio, Radio Disney, ABC News On-Demand (video), WDIG (wireless news), theme parks (Walt Disney World and EPCOT, Disneyland, Disneyland in Paris, Tokyo Disney), Walt Disney Studios including Touchstone Pictures, Miramax, and Buena Vista
Viacom New York	$26.59 billion 122,770	CBS, MTV, Paramount Pictures, Paramount Television, Blockbuster, Simon & Schuster, Nickelodeon, Showtime, Infinity Radio and Outdoor, Spelling Television, UPN, BET cable and BET Jazz, Paramount Parks, and 19 TV stations
Comcast Philadelphia	$18.35 billion 59,000	Cable, broadband Internet, SportsNet, E! Entertainment Television, The Golf Channel, Style, Outdoor Life Network, G4, CN8—The Comcast Network, Comcast SportsNet (Philadelphia and Mid-Atlantic), Philadelphia 76ers (NBA), Philadelphia Flyers (NHL), two Philadelphia indoor sports arenas
News Corp. Sydney, Australia	$17.47 billion 36,900	DirectTV, Fox, 20th Century Fox, HarperCollins, Fox News Channel, Fox Sports, XFX, Sky Television, Fox Television, *The Australian, New York Post, Times* of London, Smartsource, donna hay

Source: Adapted from "Big Entertainers," *Wall Street Journal* (February 12, 2004): A8; Emily Nelson & Joe Flint, "Comcast's Big Play for Mickey," *Wall Street Journal* (February 12, 2004): B1; http://www.timewarner.com; http://www.viacom.com; http://www.newscorp.com.

makes. An **in-house agency** performs most, and sometimes all, of the functions of an outside advertising agency.

The Media

The third player in the advertising world is the media. The **media player** is composed of the channels of communication that carry the message from the advertiser to the audience, and in the case of the Internet, it carries the response from the audience back to the advertiser. (Note that *media* is plural when it refers to various channels, but singular—*medium*—when it refers to only one form, such as newspaper.)

The development of mass media has been a central factor in the development of advertising because mass media offers a way to reach a widespread audience.

We refer to these media as *channels* of communication or *media vehicles* but they are also companies, such as your local newspaper or radio station. Some of these media conglomerates are huge, such as Time Warner and Viacom (see Table 1.3).

Each media vehicle (newspaper, radio or TV station, billboard company, etc.) has a department in place that is responsible for selling ad space or time. Each medium tries to assist advertisers in comparing the effectiveness of various media as they try to make the best choice of media to use. Many of the media organizations will assist advertisers in the design and production of advertisements. That's particularly true for local advertisers using local media, such as a retailer preparing an advertisement for the local newspaper.

The primary advantage of advertising's use of mass media is that the costs for time in broadcast media, for space in print media, and for time and space in interactive and support media are spread over the tremendous number of people that these media reach. For example, $2 million may sound like a lot of money for one Super Bowl ad, but when you consider that the advertisers are reaching more than 500 million people, the cost is not so extreme. So one of the big advantages of mass-media advertising is that it can reach a lot of people with a single message in a very cost-efficient form.

A media sales representative typically meets the advertiser or the advertiser's representative (probably an advertising agency) and tries to convince this person that the medium is a good delivery vehicle for the advertiser's message. For example, a marketing representative

Principle
Mass media advertising can be cost effective because the costs are spread over the large number of people reached by the ad.

for media provider *Qwest Dex* (Yellow Pages directory) calls on hundreds of prospective users of the Dex directory. The purpose of the visit is to describe the research supporting the use of this medium as an advertising vehicle, discuss the various advertising designs, offer assistance in designing an ad, and outline the conditions of buying space in the directory.

The Suppliers (Vendors)

The fourth player in the world of advertising is the group of service organizations that assist advertisers, advertising agencies, and the media in creating and placing the ads: the **suppliers**, or **vendors**, who provide specialized services. Members of this group include artists, writers, photographers, directors, producers, printers, as well as self-employed free-lancers and consultants, among others. In the "*1984*" story, the movie director Ridley Scott was a supplier in that Chiat/Day contracted with him to produce the commercial.

The array of suppliers mirrors the variety of tasks that it takes to put together an ad. Other examples include freelance copywriters and graphic artists, photographers, song-writers, printers, market researchers, direct-mail production houses, telemarketers, and public relations consultants.

Why hire a vendor? For many reasons. The advertisers may not have expertise in that area; they may be overloaded, or they may want a fresh perspective. Another reason to rely on vendors is cost: Vendors' services are often cheaper than the services of someone in-house.

The Target Audience

All advertising strategy starts with the identification of the customer or prospective customer—the desired audience for the advertising message.

The character of the **target audience** has a direct bearing on the overall advertising strategy, especially the creative strategy and the media strategy. The task of learning about the target audience is laborious and may take thousands of hours and millions of dollars to accomplish. Fortunately, we now have data-gathering technology that not only reduces the time and cost of doing the research but also improves the accuracy of information about customers. This information is collected every time you buy products using a scanner, complete a warranty **target audience**/guarantee card, join a book or CD club, or sign up for America Online.

Purchasers are not always the product users. In the case of cold cereal, for example, parents may purchase the cereal but kids consume it and definitely influence the purchase. Kellogg might actually have two target audiences for a children's cereal and would, therefore, design one ad for the kids target audience and another for the parents target audience. It's critical, then, that advertisers recognize the various target audiences they are talking to and know as much about them as possible.

Interactive technology has created a new world of targeting and ads can now be customized to individual consumers to some extent. This customization is growing and will make it even more important to know the target audience and create ads that speak to individual needs. When you go to the Web site Amazon.com, for example, it can greet you with a suggestion on a book or album that might be of interest based on what you have purchased in the past.

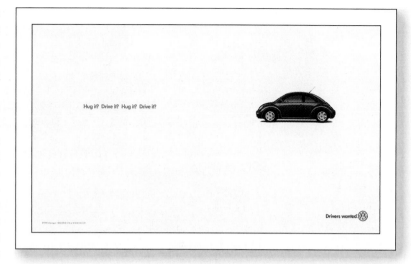

The Loyal Volkswagen Tribe Understanding the unique relationship Volkswagen has with its owners was a key to the success of the "Drivers Wanted" campaign. In taking over the struggling account in 1994, Arnold's planners went to work and uncovered an interesting insight: There was a loyal tribe of Volkswagen owners who loved their vehicles, even through the difficult years. These people were younger, more educated, and more affluent than average automotive consumers. But most importantly, they loved to drive—their cars were more than utilitarian objects designed to get from point A to point B. They were active participants in the driving experience—they were Drivers!

In the "Pods Unite" campaign, this audience was tightened. Because of the need to make an immediate impact on sales, the iPod "Drivers" market was further defined as those intending to purchase within the next three months. The creative and media strategies were then designed to connect with these "in-the-market buyers" who were actively considering a purchase and specifically targeted to those among the in-the-market buyers who were interested in music and new technologies.

TYPES OF ADVERTISING

Advertising is complex because so many different advertisers try to reach so many different types of audiences. Considering all these different advertising situations, we can identify seven major types of advertising.

- *Brand.* The most visible type of advertising is national consumer, or brand advertising. **Brand advertising**, such as that for Volkswagen's New Beetle, the Apple Macintosh, or Polo focuses on the development of a long-term brand identity and image.
- *Retail or Local Advertising.* A great deal of advertising focuses on retailers or manufacturers that sell their merchandise in a certain geographical area. In the case of retail advertising, the message announces facts about products that are available in nearby stores. The objectives tend to focus on stimulating store traffic, and creating a distinctive image for the retailer. Local advertising can refer to a retailer, such as T.J. Maxx, or a manufacturer or distributor who offers products in a fairly restricted geographic area.
- *Direct-Response Advertising.* Direct-response advertising can use any advertising medium, including direct mail, but the message is different from that of national and retail advertising in that it tries to stimulate a sale directly. The consumer can respond by telephone or mail, and the product is delivered directly to the consumer by mail or some other carrier. Of particular importance in direct-response advertising has been the evolution of the Internet as an advertising medium.
- *Business-to-Business Advertising.* Business-to-business advertising (B2B) is sent from one business to another. For example, it includes messages directed at companies distributing products, as well as industrial purchasers and professionals such as lawyers and physicians. B2B is not directed at general consumers. Advertisers place most business

advertising in professional publications or journals. The ad for Interland is an example of a typical business-to-business ad.

• *Institutional Advertising.* Institutional advertising is also called *corporate advertising.* These messages focus on establishing a corporate identity or winning the public over to the organization's point of view. Many of the tobacco companies are running ads that focus on the positive things they are now doing, and the leukemia ads for America's Pharmaceutical Companies are also adopting that focus.

• *Nonprofit Advertising.* Not-for-profit organizations, such as charities, foundations, associations, hospitals, orchestras, museums, and religious institutions, advertise for customers (hospitals, for example), members (the Sierra Club), and volunteers (the Red Cross), as well as for donations and other forms of program participation.

• *Public Service Advertising.* Public service announcements (PSAs) communicate a message on behalf of some good cause, such as stopping drunk driving (for example, messages from Mothers Against Drunk Driving) or preventing child abuse. These advertisements are usually created by advertising professionals free of charge and the media often donate the necessary space and time.

We see, then, that there isn't just one kind of advertising. In fact, advertising is a large and varied industry. Table 1.4 summarizes the types, roles, and functions of advertising that we have just examined. All types of advertising demand creative, original messages that are strategically sound and well executed. But most of all, they must be effective, so let's close our introduction to advertising with a more in-depth discussion of what we mean by effectiveness.

TABLE 1.4   Advertising Types, Roles, and Functions: A Summary

Types	*Roles*	*Functions*
Brand	Marketing	Brand/product awareness
Retail/local	Communication	Brand image
Direct-response	Economic	Product/brand information
Business-to-business	Societal	Persuasion
Institutional		Incentives to take action
Nonprofit		Reminder/reinforcement
Public service		

WHAT MAKES AN AD EFFECTIVE?

Great ads are effective ads and effective ads are ads that work—they deliver the message the advertiser intended and consumers respond as the advertiser hoped they would. Ultimately, advertisers such as Volkswagen and Apple want consumers to buy and keep buying their goods and services. To get to that point, ads must first communicate a message that motivates consumers to respond in some way.

What are the characteristics of effective ads that impact on consumer response? To move consumers to action, they must gain their attention, which was the purpose of the riveting story in the "*1984*" commercial. The ad must then hold their interest long enough to convince consumers to change their purchasing behavior and try the product, which sometimes means switching brands, and then stick with the product and buy it again. For a restaurant or car dealer, the real measure of the advertisement's effectiveness is whether the customers come back again. That depends upon their satisfaction with the product, but it also is a function of the power of the advertising to remind customers of the brand and their positive feelings about it.

In general, an ad or campaign works if it creates an impression for a product or brand, influences people to respond in some way, and separates the product or brand from the competition in the mind of the customer. Chapter 4 explains these effectiveness characteristics in more detail.

Initially, consumers may be interested in watching an ad for its entertainment value, as happened with the "*1984*" commercial. If the ad is sufficiently entertaining, they may remember it. However, they may also learn that the ad relates to a personal need and provides them with relevant information about how to satisfy that need. The ad may also offer enough incentive for consumers to risk change because it shows how to satisfy their needs without worrying about unexpected consequences, such as dissatisfaction with the product. Further, ads may reinforce product decisions and remind customers of how their needs have been satisfied. These are all different types of effects that an advertising message can achieve and therefore they can be seen as characteristics of effective advertising.

This institutional ad for a trade association uses a heart-tugging visual and copy to show consumers the value of the organization's activities: producing pharmaceutical drugs that help save lives.

The Important Role of Objectives

The one characteristic that is most important in terms of effectiveness is the idea that advertising is purposeful; it is created to have some effect, some impact on the people who read or see the message. Determining effectiveness, in other words, depends on setting a goal in terms of the impact advertisers hope to create in the minds of the people who read, view, or listen to the ads. We refer to this as advertising's **effects**, the idea being that effective advertising messages will achieve the advertiser's desired impact on the target audience. The desired impact is formally stated as an **objective**, which is the measurable goal or result that the advertising is intended to achieve. The advertising works if it achieves that objective.

Ads and their goals work on two levels. First, they satisfy consumers' objectives by engaging them with a relevant message that catches their attention, speaks to their interests, and remains in their memories. And second, from the company's perspective, the ads achieve the company's marketing objectives, which are usually related to growth and sales and contribute to the success of the business. Also, the advertising achieves its own objectives, which are creating the communication effects in terms of the consumer responses that support the marketing objectives.

Principle
When an ad "works," that means it delivers specific results that meet its stated objectives.

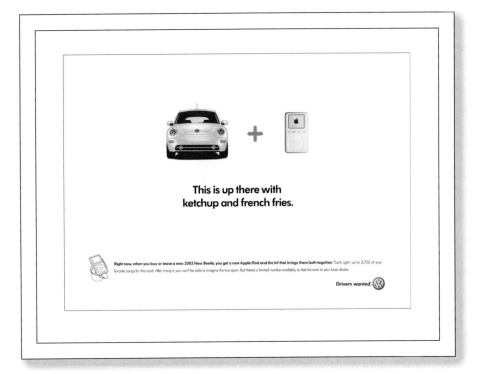

This is up there with
ketchup and french fries.

Right now, when you buy or lease a new 2003 New Beetle, you get a new Apple iPod and the kit that brings them both together. That's right, up to 3,700 of your favorite songs for the road. After trying it, you won't be able to imagine the two apart. But there's a limited number available, so fast-forward to your local dealer.

Drivers wanted: VW

■ ■ ■

To dramatize the connection between the Volkswagen New Beetle and the iPod, the campaign used the idea of logical pairs, such as ketchup and french fries, to dramatize the connection between the two.

To analyze the relationship between objectives and results, consider the VW "Drivers Wanted" campaign. Over the years, the campaign has been driven by three types of objectives: brand awareness, ad recall, and consideration (intend to buy). It first won an EFFIE award in 1998 for its effectiveness in accomplishing these three objectives.

"Drivers Wanted" was recognized again in 2002 with an EFFIE award for its long-term impact on the brand. This award recognizes a special category of advertising effectiveness called "Sustained Success" and it is given to only a few of the most successful advertising campaigns that are truly outstanding year after year.

So what were the results that garnered this Sustained Success award for Volkswagen and its agency partner, Arnold Worldwide? Over the seven-year period since the "Drivers Wanted" campaign launched in 1995, Volkswagen sales increased 213 percent. Brand awareness, a measure that is difficult to move, rose dramatically, increasing 218 percent. Purchase consideration, a measure of the target audience's intention to buy the brand, climbed 200 percent. Finally, advertising recall more than doubled, moving up 250 percent since the beginning of the campaign. In the end, however, the campaign has been successful for a decade because it established a more meaningful and intimate dialogue with its customers and it serves as an effective platform for continuing promotional ideas, such as the "Pods Unite" campaign.

Effectiveness and Award Shows

This chapter opened with the VW "Pods Unite" campaign, which was identified as award-winning advertising. The EFFIE award, which is a shortened form of the word *effective,* is given by the New York Chapter of the American Marketing Association (AMA) to advertising that has been proven to be effective. That means the campaigns were guided by measurable objectives, and evaluation after the campaign ran determined that the effort did, in fact, meet or exceed the objectives. Other award shows that focus on effectiveness are the Advertising and Marketing Effectiveness (AME) awards by the New York Festivals company and the Institute of Practitioners Award (IPA) by a London-based advertising association.

But are all award-winning ads effective ads? Not necessarily. There are a number of other award shows that judge other factors such as creative ideas (the CLIOS by a private award show company, the One Show by a New York–based advertising association, and the Cannes Awards by a French award show company), media plans (*Adweek*'s Media Plan of the Year), and art direction (the New York Art Director's Award Show).

Other professional areas also have award shows that reward such things as clever promotional ideas (the REGGIES given by the Promotion Marketing Association) and outstanding public relations efforts (the Silver Anvil by the Public Relations Society of America [PRSA]). There are many other award shows that may be mentioned in this book, but this quick introduction should give you some idea of the effort marketing communication professionals make to recognize outstanding work. We'll be referring to these awards throughout this book because we like to use these award winners as cases, and hopefully you will be able to learn about various types of best practices from these award winners. Another way to learn about great advertising is to look at how these best practices have evolved.

Award shows have been around for a long time, as has the search for new ways to do great advertising. The next section gives you a brief review of how the practice of advertising has evolved.

Consider This

1. In your own words, explain what makes effective advertising.
2. Analyze the opening VW story based on your explanation of effectiveness.

THE EVOLUTION OF ADVERTISING

Now that we have discussed the types, functions, and players of advertising, let's investigate how the principles and practices of advertising developed.[3] The practice of advertising as it has evolved has been dynamic, as noted in Figure 1.3. The figure divides the evolution of advertising into six stages. The first stage is the "Age of Print." Ads were primarily like classified advertising in format and print media carried them. Their objective was to deliver information. The primary medium of this age was the newspaper.

The second stage we label "Industrial Revolution and Emergence of Consumer Society," a period when advertising grew in importance and size because of numerous social and technological developments. The purpose of advertising was to devise an effective, efficient communication system that could sell products to a widely dispersed marketplace. National media developed as the country's transportation system grew.

The "Modern Advertising Era" is the third stage in the evolution of advertising. The Agency Era is the period when the advertising industry grew and organizations specializing in modern professional advertising developed. To compete in a crowded marketplace and build demand for brands the Creative Era showcased an emphasis on new creative practices.

In the early 1970s the "Accountability Era," which is the beginning of the industry-wide focus on effectiveness, emerged. Clients wanted ads that produced sales so the emphasis was on research and measurement. In the early 1990s, the advertising industry recognized that advertising had to pay its own way and prove its own value.

Finally, the tragedy of September 11, 2001, is still very much on the minds of citizens around the world. Advertising has changed in some obvious ways. Immediately following the attacks, the advertising industry rushed to change ads that were seen by the public as insensitive. Also, advertisers ran fewer ads, as the economy faltered in the wake of the tragedy and the boom, then bust, of the Internet economy. Accountability became even more important in a tight economy and advertisers demanded proof that their advertising was truly effective.

THE CURRENT ADVERTISING SCENE

Advertising continues to be a dynamic profession that is constantly changing. What are the current issues and trends, and what's ahead for the advertising industry? Above all, what is "the new advertising"?

An Expanded View of Advertising?

Electronic media, such as the Internet and wireless communication, are changing the media landscape and making more intimate, interactive, and personalized forms of communication much more important to advertisers.

A big debate at the Cannes Festival several years ago, for example, centered on whether the innovative BMW "Hire" campaign, which was primarily based on the use of short action films on the Internet, counted as advertising. It was creative; it got attention; it sold cars—but it didn't look like advertising. So is it advertising? Of course it is. It's just the next step in the evolution of advertising. And advertisers are pushing their agencies to keep up with these changes.

1441 Johannes Gutenberg creates moveable type

Mid-1400s Printed handbills

1472 First ad in English "Pyes of Salisbury"

1600s Newspapers emerge

1622 First ad in London's Weekly *Relations News*

1655 First use of the term "advertising"

1704 First U. S. newspaper to carry ads

1841 Volney Palmer becomes first ad sales agent (Boston)

1850 George P. Rowell becomes first ad space wholesaler (Boston)

1850s First branded items such as Baker's Chocolate appear in stores

1864 J. Walter Thompson forms JWT agency, first account executive

1872 First Ward's illustrated mail-order catalog

1879 Procter & Gamble introduces Ivory soap

1880s John Powers pioneers copywriting: focuses on news

1888 George Eastman creates first Kodak camera

Age of Print

Industrial Revolution and Emergence of Consumer Society

This early English ad, written by William Caxton in 1477, is an example of printed ads in the 15th century.

In this 1869 ad, George P. Rowell's Ad-Wholesaling agency used testimonial from a satisfied customer to promote the agency.

FIGURE 1.3 **Advertising Timeline**

This is where real creativity lies—not just in the development of a big idea for a magazine ad or a television commercial, but in the use of new ways of reaching and communicating with people. The BMW "Hire" campaign also used events, such as a gathering of faithful viewers on a corner in New York City in a live-action scene related to one of the online mini-movies. Such novel ideas create **buzz**, which means people talk about the event, the idea, and the brand.

Likewise, Jeep has had great success with its summer camps; it invites its owners to come and learn how to drive off-the-road and test themselves in such driving conditions. Is the objective to sell Jeeps? Yes, in a way. These satisfied owners might buy another Jeep the next time they buy a car, but the camp idea is more about building a strong customer relationship. Jeep knows that these people become advocates for the brand and they are the best salespeople Jeep can have. They spread the word, and word of mouth is one of the strongest forms of persuasion that exists. Is Jeep's camp advertising? It's creative; it's marketing communication; and it sells cars—so it must fit somewhere into the new world of "advertising." Of course, it's not traditional advertising in nonpersonal mass media, but it expands the activities that engage the creative ideas of advertising professionals who seek new ways to connect with consumers.

"New advertising," then, is more personal and interactive and more likely to employ creative new uses of communication opportunities beyond the traditional mass media.

Integrated Marketing Communication

One of the biggest trends affecting advertising is the development of the integrated marketing communication (IMC) approach, which also is expanding the scope of what we have referred to as the "new advertising." We mentioned earlier that advertising is only one type of marketing communication. As you might imagine, keeping all these various communication tools coordinated is a major task. In some cases advertising uses these other forms of marketing communication such as sales promotion to build consumer interest, and in other cases it merely interacts with them—advertising, for example, is used to announce the Jeep camp, which stands on its own as a major promotional event.

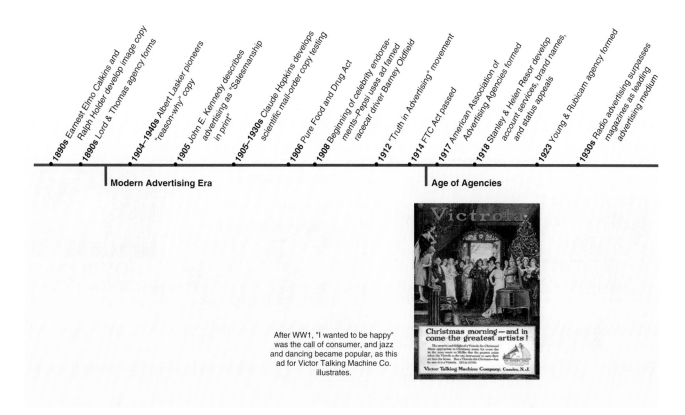

1890s Earnest Elmo Calkins and Ralph Holder develop image copy

1890s Lord & Thomas agency forms

1904–1940s Albert Lasker pioneers "reason-why" copy

1905 John E. Kennedy describes advertising as "Salesmanship in print"

1905–1930s Claude Hopkins develops scientific mail-order copy testing

1906 Pure Food and Drug Act

1908 Beginning of celebrity endorsements—Pepsi uses ad famed racecar driver Barney Oldfield

1912 "Truth in Advertising" movement

1914 FTC Act passed

1917 American Association of Advertising Agencies formed

1918 Stanley & Helen Resor develop account services, brand names, and status appeals

1923 Young & Rubicam agency formed

1930s Radio advertising surpasses magazines as leading advertising medium

Modern Advertising Era

Age of Agencies

After WW1, "I wanted to be happy" was the call of consumer, and jazz and dancing became popular, as this ad for Victor Talking Machine Co. illustrates.

The important thing to remember is that all these other areas deliver messages, just as advertising does, and it is important to have them all work together if there is to be a coherent brand message. **Integrated marketing communication (IMC)** is the practice of unifying all marketing communication tools so they send a consistent, persuasive message promoting company goals.

In addition to the profusion of marketing communication tools, the brand's **stakeholders**—all those groups of people who have an interest in the brand—includes employees, vendors and suppliers, distributors, investors, government and regulators, the community, watchdog groups, the media, and so forth. So the audience is as complex as the tools used to reach them.

In companies that use IMC, marketers coordinate all these marketing communication messages to create synergy, which means each individual message has more impact working jointly to promote a product than it would working on its own. The goal is to create strategic consistency across all messages a customer receives.[4]

But IMC also considers all messages that consumers receive about a brand, whatever the source. And it includes messages to—and from—all stakeholders who are involved with the brand. So the communication world for a brand becomes dramatically more complex than just doing a single advertisement. Advertising is part of this new world and, in the eyes of many advertising professionals, it should be the lead function.

The practice of advertising will continue to evolve as the dynamic industry adjusts to changes in its environment with less emphasis on the nonpersonal and mass-media elements and more on interactive communication, as well as more sense of advertising's place within a coordinated program of communication efforts. There are other trends related to the widening of the definition of advertising and the growth of IMC.

Globalization

The IMC trend and technological improvements in communication have made it possible for companies to have more of a dialogue with their customers, moving marketing communication—and advertising—further away from the one-way model of communication

1932 John Caples applies scientific methods to mail-order copy and headlines

1940 Clyde Bedell develops "selling stratagems"

1950s TV becomes important advertising medium

1950s Rosser Reeves develops "Unique Selling Proposition"

1960s Leo Burnett creates brand icons and "inherent drama"

1960s David Ogilvy develops research-based image advertising and storytelling

1960s Bill Bernbach focuses on the art of persuasion

1980s–1990s Mergers, globalization

1990s–2000s IMC, niche marketing, growth of interactive technology, relationship marketing, mass customization

2001 Advertising takes on new responsibilities

Creative Era | Accountability Era

In the 1950s – TV becomes an important advertising medium.

This ad created by Bill Bernbach reflects his appeal to emotions.

Who can forget Pepsi's use of celebrity endorsements in the 1980s?

GOD BLESS AMERICA

Due to the 9/11 attacks, advertising takes on a new responsiblilty.

FIGURE 1.3 continued

that has dominated its evolution. This trend is complicated by the increasing globalization of marketing programs. In the early 1990s the trade barriers throughout much of Europe came down, making it the largest contiguous market in the world. Eastern Europe, India, Russia, and China have at least partially opened their markets to international marketing. As advertisers move into these markets, ad agencies are forming huge multinational operations with international research and media-buying capabilities.

The advertising question is whether to practice global or local advertising: Should advertisers standardize ads or advertising strategies across all cultures or should they adapt their strategies to local markets? How much consistency does a brand and its advertising need to maintain as it moves across borders? Because of the importance of understanding the underlying cultural issues that affect advertising, we devote Chapter 19 to the topic of international advertising.

IT'S A WRAP

EFFECTIVE ADVERTISING DRIVES VOLKSWAGEN'S SUCCESS

■ ■ ■ Effective advertising is recognized in a number of ways: through sales results, through communication impact, and in awards won. Throughout this book we will feature brand stories that represent award-winning marketing communication. In the case of Volkswagen's "Pods

Unite" promotion with the Apple iPod, the campaign was recognized by industry awards, winning both the EFFIE and the Promotion Marketing Association's REGGIE awards.

In addition to the awards, the "Pods Unite" campaign was effective in surpassing the sales goal of 5,200 by 14 percent, which also reversed the negative sales trend that had been noted before the campaign began. The response to the direct-mail piece was at a 3 percent level, which was 200 percent above the objective. Approximately 750,000 unique apple.com users clicked on the "Pods Unite" minisite.

Not only did the promotion meet its objectives, it also resulted in great publicity with mentions on *The Today Show,* as well as articles in *Fast Company, USA Today* and *The Chicago Tribune.* Such free publicity not only caught attention and added to the buzz about the "Pods Unite" campaign, it helped keep the Volkswagen New Beetle top of mind without costing the company its precious marketing dollars.

The story about Volkswagen told throughout this chapter makes the point that advertising has played an important role in the ups and downs of the company. The Beetle ads of the 1960s by the Doyle Dane Bernbach agency are classic examples of some of the best advertising that has ever been created. And the more recent award-winning work in the 1990s by the Arnold agency has helped rebuild the VW brand in the United States and put it back on the road to profitability. The important lesson from that experience is that if the cars aren't attractive to their market, then the advertising will probably not be effective no matter how creative it is. But when the product connects with the consumer, the advertising can have tremendous impact on the target audience.

It's not an accident that the great VW ads of the 1960s and the 1990s have coincided with periods of great sales for the car company. Effective advertising delivers the right message in the right way through the right medium at exactly the right time to touch the hearts and move the minds of the target audience.

■■■ Summary

1. **Define advertising and identify its key components.** Advertising is (1) paid (2) persuasive communication that uses (3) nonpersonal mass media and other forms of interactive communication to reach (4) broad audiences to connect (5) an identified sponsor with (6) a target audience.

2. **Discuss the roles and functions of advertising within society and business.** Advertising fulfills a (1) marketing role, (2) communication role, (3) economic role, and (4) a societal role.

3. **Identify the key players and their roles in creating advertising.** The five key players in the advertising industry are advertisers, advertising agencies, media, vendors, and the target audience. A firm's advertising can be handled either internally by an in-house agency or externally by an advertising agency. Companies often have advertising departments to either handle the firm's advertising or oversee the work of an agency.

4. **Explain the different types of advertising.** There are seven types of advertising and they are appropriate for certain distinct marketing communication situations. They are: (1) brand, (2) retail or local, (3) direct-response, (4) business-to-business (B2B), (5) institutional, (6) nonprofit, and (7) public service,

5. **Summarize the characteristics of effective advertising and why it is goal directed.** Effective ads work on two levels: They engage the mind of the consumer and at the same time deliver a selling message. Effective advertising is purposeful, which means it accomplishes its objectives.

6. **Analyze the changes affecting the advertising industry.** Advertising is a dynamic industry that changes as the consumers, technology, and the marketplace change. This chapter discusses three types of changes: (1) The definition of advertising is expanding as technology makes it possible for "new advertising" to be more personal and interactive. (2) Integrated marketing communication (IMC) is also expanding the scope of advertising by involving it more closely in a mix that uses various marketing communication tools to deliver a consistent message and brand image. (3) Globalization demands that international advertisers consider whether their messages should be standardized across all cultures and localized and adapted to local markets. Localization is more personalized but complicates the consistency problem.

■■■ Key Terms

advertiser, p. 11
advertising, p. 5
advertising department,
    p. 13
agency-of-record, p. 14
brand, p. 8
brand advertising, p. 17
business-to-business (B2B)
    advertising, p. 17
buzz, p. 22

direct-response advertising,
    p. 17
effects, p. 19
hard-sell, p. 6
in-house agency, p. 15
institutional advertising, p. 18
integrated marketing
    communication (IMC),
    p. 23

local advertising, p. 17
marketing, p. 8
marketing communication,
    p. 8
marketing mix, p. 8
media, p. 15
nonprofit advertising, p. 18
objective, p. 19
product category, p. 8

public service advertising,
    p. 18
retail advertising, p. 17
soft sell, p. 6
stakeholders, p. 23
suppliers, p. 16
target audience, p. 16
target market, p. 8
vendors, p. 16

■■■ Review Questions

1. Explain the five key components of the advertising definition.
2. Define marketing and explain advertising's role in marketing.
3. Who are the five key players in the world of advertising and what are the responsibilities of each?

4. List and describe the seven types of advertising introduced in this chapter.
5. Why is effectiveness important to advertisers?
6. What is IMC and why is it important for advertisers?

■■■ Discussion Questions

1. "I'll tell you what great advertising means," Bill Slater, a finance major, said during a heated discussion. "Great advertising is the ability to capture the imagination of the public—the stuff that sticks in the memory, like the Budweiser Frogs, or that Aflac duck—that's what great is," he says. "Bill, you missed the point," says Phil Graham, a marketing major. "Advertising is a promotional weapon. Greatness in advertising means commanding attention and persuading people to buy something. No frills, no cuteness—great advertising has to sell the public and keep them sold," he adds. How would you enter this argument? How do you define great advertising?

2. You belong to an organization that wants to advertise a special event it is sponsoring. You are really concerned that the group not waste its limited budget on advertising that doesn't work. Outline a presentation you would make to the

group's board of directors that explains the concept of advertising effectiveness. In this situation, what would be effective and what wouldn't be? What are the kinds of effects you would want the advertising to achieve? How would you know if it works?

3. Chris Jameson has just joined the advertising department faculty in a university after a long professional career. In an informal talk with the campus advertising club, she is put on the spot about career choices. The students want to know which is the best place to start: with an advertiser (a company) or with an advertising agency. How should she respond? Should she base her answer on the current situation or on how she reads the future? What factors in the changing dynamics of advertising would affect her recommendation?

■■■ Class Project

1. Form groups of five or six students. Have a spokesperson contact one or two advertising agencies. Question one or more key people about the changes that have taken place in their agencies and the industry during the last five years. (Prepare a list of questions ahead of time.) What kinds of changes do they expect in the next five years? Meet to write a three- to five-page report.
2. Consult the Web site of any advertising agency. Does the agency in any way make a claim about accountability or effectiveness for the work it produces for its clients?

HANDS-ON

CASE

Introduction to Advertising

The Day That Wal-Mart Dropped the Smiley Face

Retail giant Wal-Mart annually spends close to a half billion dollars on advertising, so the company's decision in the first month of 2005 to run full-page ads in more than 100 newspapers was not really surprising. What was surprising was the copy in those ads, which said nothing about low-priced toasters or new music CDs. Instead, the ads featured a photo of workers in their blue Wal-Mart smocks and a letter from Wal-Mart CEO Lee Scott. Scott's letter was blunt and to the point: "When special-interest groups and critics spread misinformation about Wal-Mart, the public deserves to hear the truth. Everyone is entitled to their own opinions about our company, but they are not entitled to make up their own facts."

Not the sort of message many would expect from a company whose television ads often feature a yellow "smiley-face" flying around a Wal-Mart store lowering prices. But it is a clear sign that Wal-Mart believes it can no longer afford to ignore several societal trends that threaten the company's success and profitability.

Wal-Mart is the largest and most successful retailer in the world. It employs more people than any other private company in the United States (almost 1.2 million) and has world-wide sales of over a quarter *trillion* dollars, more than four times that of its nearest competitor. The foundation of this impressive record is the company's ability to keep its promise of customer-friendly service and low prices.

But with success comes attention and not all of it good. Several lawsuits claim Wal-Mart shorts overtime pay and one lawsuit claimed female employees face discrimination in pay and promotions. Wal-Mart's expansion plans have also run into trouble, as some cities and states, citing concerns ranging from low wages, inadequate benefits, environmental damage, and harm to local economies, have passed laws to make it difficult or impossible for Wal-Mart to build its giant superstores.

In response to past criticisms of its diversity policies, Wal-Mart created company-wide postings of promotional opportunities, created a new position for a director of diversity, and slashed the bonuses of managers who fail to achieve diversity hiring targets. Scott himself stands to lose $600,000 from his annual bonus if Wal-Mart does not meet diversity goals. Recent years have also seen the CEO spend more time meeting with investors, community groups, and the media.

But in recent years Wal-Mart has begun to use advertising as a way of addressing criticisms that the company is not a good employer. At first, much of this advertising was "soft-sell," emphasizing happy Wal-Mart employees. The new campaign is clearly more direct: The copy seeks to address misperceptions about employee wages and benefits, noting that full-time company employees are paid an average of $9.68—substantially higher than what is required by federal law ($5.15). The copy also notes that a majority of Wal-Mart employees said benefits were important to them when they chose to take a job at the retailer. Complementing the ads is a public relations campaign in select cities using employees and press conferences. In Tampa, Florida, for example, employee Michael Martin told reporters, "I'm making more after working four years at Wal-Mart than I did after nine years at Winn-Dixie." Martin, a department manager, noted, "I left Winn-Dixie because I couldn't get a promotion. Here I got one after six months."

Why is the company using a new approach? "For too long, others have had free rein to say things about our company that just are not true," said Lee Scott, president and chief executive officer. "Our associates [Wal-Mart speak for employees] are tired of it and we've decided to draw our own line in the sand." It is too soon to know if the campaign will succeed, although some are already skeptical. According to retail marketing consultant Jordan Zimmerman, aggressive image campaigns like Wal-Mart's are rare and costly. And ads that directly address the company's critics will not likely replace the company's regular brand advertising (including the smiley face), which is not scheduled to change any time soon. But the new ads do constitute a small change in the nature of the dialogue Wal-Mart has with consumers and society. Only time will tell if they help Wal-Mart to stay on top.

Consider This

1. What is Wal-Mart doing with its latest campaign? What are the difficulties involved in such an effort?
2. A recent *Advertising Age* article noted that Wal-Mart customers are less likely to read newspapers and more likely to watch television than the population as a whole. Why, then, did Wal-Mart choose newspapers for its new campaign?
3. Analyze this Wal-Mart campaign and explain its purpose referring to the discussion in this chapter of the roles and functions of advertising. What is its primary purpose? Do you think it will be effective at accomplishing that purpose?

Sources: Claire Atkison, "Prices and People Stressed in Retail Titan's Advertising," *Advertising Age* (October 6, 2003): 3; Jack Neff, "Store Ads Still Treated as Promotion," *Advertising Age* (February 9, 2004): 44; Kourtney Stringer, "In Ad Blitz, Wal-Mart Counters Public Image as Harsh Employer," *Wall Street Journal* (January 14, 2005): B3; "Our Commitment to Communities," http://walmartstores.com/wmstore/wmstores/Mainnews.jsp; Mark Albright, "Wal-Mart Fires Back." *St. Petersburg Times* (January 13, 2005); Ann Zimmerman, "Wal-Mart to Hit Latest Sales Goal After Late Surge," *Wall Street Journal* (January 4, 2005): B2.

Advertising's Role in Marketing

Puma Is One Cool Cat

Award:
*Prophet's 2003
Branding Hit*

*Cool Brand leader by the
UK's Brand Council*

Company:
Puma

Agency:
Gyro Worldwide

Campaign:
*The Puma and Mini
Marketing Partnership*

CHAPTER KEY POINTS

After reading this chapter, you will be able to:

1. Define the role of advertising within marketing.

2. Explain how the four key concepts in marketing relate to advertising.

3. Identify the key players in marketing and how the organization of the industry affects advertising.

4. List and explain the six critical steps in the marketing process.

5. Summarize the structure of the advertising agency industry and how agencies work with their clients on the marketing side.

6. Analyze the changes in the marketing world and what they portend for advertising.

Puma and its leaping cat logo are cool. The German athletic shoe company's innovative retro designs are intended to appeal to trendy individualists who like to make a style statement with its stylish low-top sneakers. Puma's success in a crowded market is what led Prophet—a leading management consulting firm that specializes in the integration of brand, business, and marketing strategy—to name it one of its top three brands.

The German-born CEO, Jochen Zeitz, explains why individualism is so important to the shoe company: "Like the puma as an animal is not a herd animal, we also want people and our brand to stand for individuality and as such, we position the brand so it [blends] sport, lifestyle, and fashion in a unique way."

The brand stays hip through design innovation and also by linking up with other hot icons, such as outfitting the tennis great Serena Williams, which created a distinctive brand attitude. Puma's brand consulting company, Gyro Worldwide, is a Philadelphia-based agency that works under the consumer's radar to attract cutting-edge trend influencers.

Similarly Puma's Nuala yoga collection is a successful partnership with model Christy Turlington. Puma's sponsorship of the Jamaican Olympic team through 2008 is promoted in print ads featuring the colorful H. Street shoe in magazines such as *Spin* and *Vibe.*

In the partnership with the BMW Mini praised by the Prophet folks, Puma sells a black, two-piece driving shoe called the "Mini Motion" shoe, which is marketed as an accessory to the car. The shoe is similar in design to a Formula 1 racing shoe with a flexible inner slipper and a sturdier outer shoe that provides ankle support and traction. The slipper provides comfort on long trips, or even around the house, and the outer shoe can be worn outdoors, as well as in city traffic where it combats the strain from frequent shifting of gears.

As part of the collaborative effort, the Mini car used functional footwear elements, like air mesh, for the seats. Puma's logo and its signature "formstripe" is used on the car's exterior.

Another new line features boots inspired by 1950s boxing shoes, as well as black shoes stitched to look like old-time hockey skates. Apparel is equally fashionable, with a line of unisex garments patterned after martial arts robes.

Even though its ideal target is a style-conscious person who values individualism, Puma knows it has to also reach a wider audience—a more mainstream consumer—in order to stay in business. To do that it uses a television campaign linked to the Athens Olympics. The company expects to earn growth from this market by reminding audiences of Puma's traditions in soccer, track, and baseball.

Although its worldwide sales are approaching $1.7 billion, Puma is still a small player in the U.S. athletic footwear market. SportScan, an independent market research firm, says Puma has a 0.25 percent market share and is dwarfed by giants Nike and Reebok. Its growth trends have erased the 1980s image of the company as a commodity product with no distinctive image—a strategy, or rather lack of one, that almost destroyed the brand.

Puma is also growing because of its unusual approach to distribution and its market segmentation. Its marketing strategy delivers both exclusivity and a mass market audience, selling its edgy designs to trendy retailers and then placing its more mainstream products in stores like Foot Locker. Foot Locker might sell the GV special, a style based on a retro Puma tennis shoe from its glory days 30 years ago; at the same time an independent fashion store might carry a basketball shoe in fabrics like snakeskin or lizard.

The same innovative spirit drives Puma's marketing communication that often uses nontraditional ways to connect with customers. Retailers praise Puma for its creativity in designing eye-catching in-store merchandising displays. Recognizing the importance of word of mouth, guerilla marketing programs promote the brand on the street and on the feet of its devotees. Puma also uses viral marketing, a technique that spreads the word about new products through an online network of users.

Clever ideas include promotions at sushi restaurants during the 2003 World Cup, which was held in Japan and South Korea. Puma got a well-known sushi chef to create a special Puma sushi roll that was served in select Japanese restaurants in cities around the world. These restaurants also discreetly announced the sponsorship in its Puma-branded chopsticks, sake cups, and napkins. At the same time, Puma partnered with the Terence Conran design shop to sell an exclusive version of its World Cup soccer boot, holding weekend sushi-making events at the home furnishings store.

An advertiser like Puma needs an effective campaign to help its products succeed in the marketplace. However, to succeed a product must also offer customers value, and much of the value is created by marketing decisions that determine the product's design and ease of use, as well as its distribution, pricing, and marketing communication. Because advertising is just one part of the total marketing effort, it's unlikely that an advertising person could create effective advertising without a thorough understanding of the client's marketing program.

This chapter explains the basic principles of marketing but it does so from the perspective of advertising's role in marketing. It also takes a look at the advertising agency, its variations, and its structures, and it examines the key role the client–agency relationship plays in executing an integrated marketing communication strategy.

WHAT IS MARKETING?

Marketing is the way a product is designed, tested, produced, branded, packaged, priced, distributed, and promoted. The American Marketing Association (AMA) defines it as "an organizational function and a set of processes for creating, communicating, and delivering value to customers and for managing customer relationships in ways that benefit the organization and its stake holders."[1]

Traditionally, the objective of most marketing programs—such as Puma's—has been to sell a product (athletic shoes) or a service or an idea, in the sense that the United Way and the Army are trying to convince people to donate, volunteer, or sign up. The goal has been to match a product's availability—and the company's production capabilities—to the consumer's need, desire, or demand for the product.

Key Concepts in Marketing

The practice of marketing is still evolving. However, some concepts are critical to our understanding of it as it is today: the marketing concept and the concepts of exchange, branding, and added value. All of these have important implications for advertising and for advertising's role in marketing. Let's look briefly at each.

The Marketing Concept: Focus on Customers

Historically marketers developed a product and then tried to find a market for it. More recently successful marketers try to include the customer in the product design and development process. The **marketing concept** is an approach that suggests marketing should focus first on identifying the needs and wants of the customer, rather than on finding ways to sell products that may or may not meet customers' needs. The product- or corporate-focused approach is still used, particularly in areas where product innovation is important, such as high technology.

Today, marketers know that to compete effectively they must focus on their customers' problems and try to develop products to solve them. Some of the businesses that have adopted this perspective include Harley Davidson, Intel, and United Parcel Services

Principle
A company that operates with a *marketing concept* philosophy focuses on satisfying its customers' needs and wants.

We'll help you relieve stress even before your vacation.

UnitedEscapes packages can take care of your travel needs with the lowest price guaranteed.

Hawaii – 5 day/4 night air+car+hotel packages found from as low as **$614***
Caribbean – 5 day/4 night air+hotel packages found from as low as **$579***
Las Vegas – 3 day/2 night air+hotel packages found from as low as **$218***

For more information, or to book your UnitedEscapes® package today, visit **united.com/escape**

UNITED Escapes

After eight years of being voted best frequent flyer program, where else is there to go? Up, of course.

Mileage Plus is proud to have been voted the best frequent flyer program for the past eight years by the readers of *Business Traveler* magazine. And we know the best way to thank you is to make the program even better. To join or to find out more, visit united.com/joinmp today.

UNITED Mileage Plus®

These two ads, both by United Airlines, demonstrate a consumer focus in the United Escapes vacation-planning ad versus a corporate orientation in the Mileage Plus frequent flyer ad.

(UPS), all now recognized as leaders in customer-focused marketing. Consider how you buy a computer from Dell. Online you check the various options and then you specify what you want. You pay for it, and Dell builds it for you and delivers it 10 days later. Why aren't more companies like Dell selling products that are designed to really meet their customers' needs?[2]

The marketing concept suggests two marketing steps. First, determine what the customer needs and wants. Second, develop, manufacture, market, and service goods that fill those particular needs and wants—that is, create solutions for customers' problems. Both these steps are addressed in advertising planning through consumer research and the methods used by planners to develop insight into consumer decision making. This information feeds back into marketing plans where it can stimulate new product developments that are better designed to meet customer needs.

In advertising, the difference lies in the focus of the ad: Is it on the consumer, or on the company? Although a customer focus is thought to be the strongest approach, there are still times when a product- or company-focused approach is appropriate. United Airlines uses a customer-focused approach for its Escapes vacation-planning service and a product focus for its Mileage Plus frequent flyer program.

The Concept of Exchange

Marketing helps to create **exchange**, that is, the act of trading a desired product or service to receive something of value in return. The company makes a product and offers it for sale at a certain price; the customer gives money to the company to buy that product. Money is exchanged for goods.

What do we exchange? Marketers use the word *product* to refer to goods like cars, refrigerators, and computers; to services provided by restaurants and sellers of insurance and real estate; and to ideas generated in politics, universities, and nonprofit associations.

SOMEWHERE ON AN AIRPLANE A MAN IS TRYING TO RIP OPEN A SMALL BAG OF PEANUTS.

There are a number of meanings associated with the Harley-Davidson brand. We know that Harley is a biker's bike and it appeals to people who live on the edge and aren't concerned with convention and traditional values.

So in using the word *product* we are referring to this larger world of things that are sold in exchange for something from the customer. The company, for example, could be an orchestra and the experience of attending a concert is given in exchange for the price of a ticket. In political advertising, a donation may be given in return for a sense of affiliation with and support for a particular political philosophy.

In addition to economic exchange, marketing also facilitates communication exchange. Advertising provides information, as well as the opportunity for customer–company interaction. So *exchange* has two meanings in marketing, with the communication aspect being particularly important to advertising. In other words, people have to know about it before they can buy it or sign up for it or donate to it. Thus marketing is only as effective as the communication practices that make people aware of its products.

The Concept of Branding

Branding is the process of creating a special meaning for a product, one that makes it distinctive in the marketplace and in its product category, just as your name makes you unique in your community. That special meaning, or **brand image**, is the result of communication, as well as your own personal experiences with the product.

Harley-Davidson, for example, carried an "outlaw" image from its early association as the bike of choice for the Hell's Angels. More recently that meaning has been shaded so that it still has an edgy, slightly dangerous image but it's now acceptable for everyone from accountants to lawyers and even college professors to be seen riding one.

Branding transforms a product into a **brand**, which is a distinctive identity for a product. Think about the importance of a brand when you give a gift to a loved one. There's a big difference between giving a watch in a Tiffany box and giving one in a Wal-Mart box. The Tiffany box and logo signals a high-quality, status product.

Tiffany's brand image also sends messages. A brand can signal status, quality, or good value; sometimes it's a "cool factor." Why is a Coach handbag worth $150 dollars when a nearly identical one without that brand name sells for $15? The reason is the value we place on the Coach brand as well as the brand's meaning as a quality, high-status product.

A brand, and the advertising behind it, creates familiarity: We're more comfortable buying brands we know. For that reason, a familiar brand is important when we make

Principle
Effective branding transforms a product by creating a special meaning for it.

A MATTER OF PRINCIPLE
It's Pure and It Floats

A basic principle of branding is that a brand takes on meaning when it makes a product distinctive within its product category. The Procter & Gamble company accomplished that by creating identity elements for its brand, Ivory, before anyone had thought of making a bar of soap a distinctive product. The Ivory brand identity system also called attention to innovative features of the product. Here's the background story about how Ivory came to be one of the first and most successful brands of all time.

Before the Civil War, homemakers made their own soap from lye, fats (cooking grease), and fireplace ashes. It was a soft, jellylike yellowish soap that would clean things adequately, but if it fell to the bottom of a pail, it dissolved into mush. In Victorian times, the benchmark for quality soap was the highly expensive castile bar—a pure white soap imported from the Mediterranean and made from the finest olive oil.

William Procter and James Gamble, who were partners in a candle-making operation, discovered a formula that produced a uniform, predictable bar soap, which they provided in wooden boxes to both armies during the Civil War. This introduced the concept of mass production and opened up a huge market when the soldiers returned to their homes with a demand for the bars of soap. But the bars were still yellow and sank to the bottom.

Procter & Gamble (P&G) hired a chemist to create a white bar equivalent to the legendary castile bar, which was the first use of science-based research and development (R&D) to design a product. In 1878 P&G's white soap was invented. It was a modest success until the company began getting requests for the "soap that floats." It turns out that an accident in whipping the ingredients together had added enough air to some of the bars to make them lighter than water. This production accident led to one of the world's greatest statements of a product benefit: "It floats."

Other decisions also helped make it a branding breakthrough. In 1879 one of the P&G family was in church listening to a scripture about ivory palaces and proposed that the white bar be renamed Ivory Soap. So a great product now had a great name as well as a great product benefit. Rather than asking for soap—soap was soap—and taking a bar from the barrel, customers could now ask for a specific product that they liked by name.

But that wasn't the end of P&G's branding innovativeness. A grandson, determined to match the quality of the legendary castile soap, again turned to a chemist to determine the purity of both castile and Ivory. The research found that the total impurities in Ivory added only to 0.56 percent, which was actually lower than the castile bars. By turning that to a positive, P&G could make the claim that its Ivory is "99 and 44/100 percent pure" and thus was born one of the most famous slogans in brand history.

Consider This

1. What made Procter & Gamble's Ivory Soap special? What separated it from its competitors in the bar soap category? Is there an actual point of difference?
2. Marketers believe that people will pay a higher price for a successfully branded product. Do you agree or disagree? Explain, based on your experiences as a consumer.

Sources: Charles Goodrum and Helen Dalrymple, *Advertising in America* (New York: Harry N. Abrams, 1990); Laurie Freeman, "The House That Ivory Built: 150 Years of Procter & Gamble," *Advertising Age* (August 20, 1987): 4–18, 164–220; "P&G History: History of Ivory," www.pg.com, June 2004.

TABLE
2.1   **Top 25 Corporate Brands**

Corp Brand	Corp Brand Value ($ billion)	Sales ($ billion)
1. Procter & Gamble	107.4	47.0
2. Microsoft	103.1	34.3
3. Merck	91.3	22.5
4. Intel	80.2	30.1
5. Eli Lilly	76.4	12.6
6. IBM	71.0	89.1
7. Cisco Systems	69.6	19.8
8. Medtronic	61.4	8.6
9. UPS	58.2	33.5
10. PepsiCo	56.1	27.0
11. General Electric	54.2	132.9
12. Goldman Sachs	46.6	23.6
13. Coca-Cola	45.6	21.0
14. Anheuser-Busch	43.0	14.1
15. Pfizer	41.8	45.2
16. Johnson & Johnson	37.9	41.9
17. Viacom	37.0	26.6
18. Citigroup	35.5	94.7
19. Kimberly-Clark	31.3	14.3
20. Colgate-Palmolive	29.4	9.9
21. Aflac	20.3	11.4
22. Nike	19.7	11.2
23. General Mills	17.5	10.8
24. Kellogg	16.2	8.8
25. Harley-Davidson	15.7	4.6

Source: "Top U.S. Corporate Brands," *Forbes* (April 2, 2004), www.Forbes.com.

major purchases such as cars and home appliances, because we have a sense that there is less risk in buying them than in choosing products whose makers we don't know.

Branding is particularly useful to consumers buying clothing and fashion items, such as Polo (Ralph Lauren), Rolex, Gucci, Diesel, Oakley, and Doc Martens, where self-identity may also be linked to the brands we buy and wear. These brands are fairly complex psychological messages whose meanings are built up over time through advertising.

The basic principles of branding evolved initially through the marketing innovations of Procter & Gamble, particularly the development of its Ivory Soap brand. As the Macintosh "*1984*" commercial in Chapter 1 represents one of the all-time great ads, Ivory represents one of the all-time great marketing stories.

When a **brand name** or **brand mark** is legally protected through registration with the Patent and Trademark Office of the Department of Commerce, it becomes a **trademark**. The trademark Intel Inside has become an important part of Intel's marketing strategy. **Brand equity** is the reputation, meaning, and value that the brand name or symbol has acquired over time. It measures the financial value the brand contributes to the company.

The Concept of Added Value

The reason marketing and advertising activities are useful, both to consumers and to marketers, is that they add value to a product. Added value means a marketing

or advertising activity makes the product more valuable, useful, or appealing. A motorcycle is a motorcycle but a Harley-Davidson Fat Boy or Road King is a highly coveted bike because of its brand image. Here are examples of other factors, in addition to advertising, that provide **added value**: The more convenient the product is to buy, the more valuable it is to the customer. Likewise, the lower the price, the more useful features a product has, or the higher its quality, the more a customer may value it. Ensuring the product's utility and convenience is one of the tasks of customer-oriented marketing, as we discussed above.

Advertising not only can showcase the product's value but it also may add value by making the product appear more desirable or more of a status symbol. Providing news and useful information of interest to consumers is another way that advertising adds value, as shown in the YMCA "New Equipment" ad.

Basic business practices also add value. Local retailers that compete with big chains such as Wal-Mart, Office Depot, or Home Depot can survive only if they find some way to offer value other than price. For example, a small Oklahoma chain of office supply stores called SPC Office Products holds its own against Staples and Office Depot by having more knowledgeable employees on the floor to answer customer questions than its giant competitors do.[3] The additional service adds value for its customers.

Branding is a special case of added value because the value it adds is purely psychological. Nike's image, which focuses on the performance of outstanding athletes, has been constructed primarily through advertising. The "swoosh" logo is recognized worldwide by customers who like Nike's products and associate themselves with outstanding athletic performance.

SHOWCASE

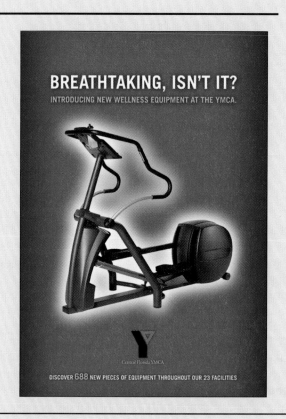

■ ■ ■

A shipment of fitness equipment delivered to YMCA centers wasn't just new; it was state of the art. A series of print ads, direct mail, and in-center banners put a spotlight on the flashy new equipment. This ad was contributed by Lara Mann, a graduate of the University of Florida advertising program, who is now a copywriter at FHB Advertising in Orlando, Florida.

Consider This

1. Experts believe that a successfully branded product can ask a premium price. What is the logic behind that notion. Where do you see it working or not working?
2. Do you buy branded products? If so, in what product categories and why?

THE KEY PLAYERS AND MARKETS

The marketing industry is a complex network of professionals, all of whom are involved in creating, producing, delivering, and selling something to customers. There are four important categories of key players including the marketer, suppliers or vendors, distributors and retailers, and agencies. We'll discuss the first three here and agencies will be discussed in more depth in the last section of this chapter.

The Marketer

The **marketer**, also referred to as the advertiser or the client (from the agency's point of view), is any company or organization behind the product—the organization, company, or manufacturer producing the product and offering it for sale. The 10 top global marketers, in respect to media spending, are displayed in Table 2.2.

In most companies of any size, the marketing function is handled by a marketing department and represented in the corporate hierarchy by a vice president or director of marketing. The marketing function is usually set up as a department with a number of people managing brands, products and product lines, and marketing services, which includes suppliers such as marketing researchers and marketing communication agencies. Marketing is also a function in nonprofit and governmental organizations, such as hospitals, museums, zoos, orchestras, Junior Achievement, and the United Way.

Some companies may have a **product** or **brand management** organizational structure with managers who handle the marketing responsibility. A product or brand manager is the person responsible for all the strategic decisions relating to the brand's product design and manufacture as well as the brand's pricing, distribution, and marketing communication. Procter & Gamble was a pioneer in establishing the brand management concept.

TABLE 2.2   Top 10 Global Marketers by Media Spending

Rank Spending 2002	2001	Advertiser	Headquarters	Total Ad (in millions)
1	1	Procter & Gamble Co.	Cincinnati	$4,479
2	3	Unilever	London/Rotterdam	3,315
3	2	General Motors Corp.	Detroit	3,218
4	6	Toyota	Toyota City, Japan	2,405
5	5	Ford Motor Co.	Dearborn, Mich.	2,387
6	4	Time Warner	New York	2,349
7	7	DaimlerChrysler	Auburn Hills, Mich./ Stuttgart, Germany	1,800
8	10	L'Oréal	Paris	1,683
9	9	Nestlé	Vevey, Switzerland	1,547
10	16	Sony	Tokyo	1,513

Source: "Top 100 Global Marketers," Advertising Age (November 10, 2003): 28.

Suppliers and Vendors

The materials and ingredients used in producing the product are obtained from other companies, referred to as suppliers and vendors. Their work also determines the quality of the final product, and the ingredients they provide, as well as the cost of their materials, and is a big factor in determining the product's price. This can be very complex. Think about the automotive industry and all the pieces and parts that go into a car. The phrase **supply chain** is used to refer to this complex network of suppliers who produce components and ingredients that are then sold to the manufacturer. Sometimes other companies acting as brokers are involved in selling the supplies to the manufacturer and other companies may be employed to deliver the goods.

In marketing theory, every contribution from the supply chain adds value to the product. In marketing practice these suppliers and vendors are partners in the creation of a successful product. They are also partners in the communication process and their marketing

SHOWCASE

■ ■ ■

Gander Mountain carries a wide selection of supplies and gear at great prices. The employees at the stores are all outdoor experts who don't just sell gear; they also use it as they participate in outdoor activities themselves. The agency determined that communication for Gander Mountain should focus on these "outdoor experts" as well as on customers and their outdoor experiences. This ad was contributed by Trent Walters, a graduate of the University of North Texas advertising program, where he was selected by the American Advertising Federation as one of its "Most Promising Students." He is now an account supervisor at the Richards Group in Dallas, Texas.

communication may relate to the brand, particularly in the practice called **ingredient branding**, which means acknowledging a supplier's brand as an important product feature. Think about how important the reputations of Gore-tex and Intel are to manufacturers who use these ingredients.

Distributors and Retailers

The **distribution chain** or **distribution channel** refers to the various companies that are involved in moving a product from its manufacturer into the hands of its buyer. These **resellers**, or intermediaries, may actually take ownership of the product and participate in the marketing, including the advertising. Similar to the supply chain, everyone involved in the distribution chain—distributors, wholesalers, brokers, dealers, and retailers—adds value to the product. They also are involved in a chain of advertising.

Wholesalers and retailers, for example, are important parts of the channel and each is capable of influencing, supporting, and delivering advertising messages. The primary strength of the wholesaler is personal selling. Wholesalers do not advertise often; however, in some instances they may use direct mail, trade papers, or catalogs to reach retailers. The advertising copy tends to be simple and straightforward, and the focus is on product, features, and price. Conversely, retailers are quite good at advertising, especially local advertising. Retailers' main concern is that the advertising be directed at *their* customers as opposed to the customers of the manufacturers.

The Gander Mountain story showcases the importance of advertising by retailers and the manufacturers whose products they sell. Gander Mountain is a hunting, fishing, and camping retailer located in the upper Midwest. The print ad shown here focuses on actual employees of the company who give voice to the advertising's tagline, "We live outdoors."

Types of Markets

In addition to reviewing the key players, let's also consider the types of markets in which these advertising professionals and their companies work. The word **market** originally meant the place where the exchange between seller and buyer took place. Today we speak of a market not only as a place (the Rocky Mountain market), but also as a particular type of buyer—for example, the youth market or the motorcycle market. The phrase **share of market** (or market share) refers to the percentage of the total market in a product category that buys a particular brand.

When marketing strategists speak of markets, they generally refer to groups of people or organizations. As Figure 2.1 shows, the four main types of markets are (1) consumer, (2) business-to-business (industrial), (3) institutional, and (4) reseller. We can

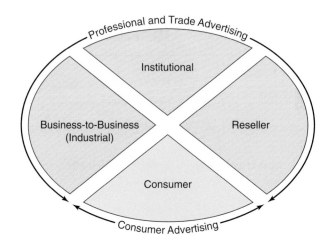

The Four Main Types of Markets
The consumer market is only one of four markets.

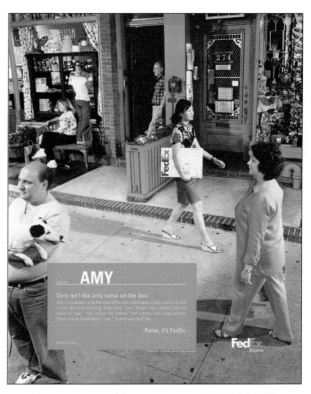

This group of ads demonstrates advertising directed at the four types of markets: consumer (Keds), business-to-business (FedEx), institutional (GE aircraft engines), and channel (Sunkist Growers, Inc.)

further divide each of these markets by size or geography, such as local, regional, national, or international.

- *Consumer markets.* Consumer markets consist of people who buy products and services for personal or household use. As a student, you are considered a member of the consumer market for companies that sell jeans, athletic shoes, sweatshirts, pizza, music, textbooks, backpacks, computers, education, checking accounts, bicycles, travel and vacations, along with a multitude of other products that you buy at drug and grocery stores, which the marketing industry refers to as **package goods**.
- *Business-to-business (industrial) markets.* Business-to-business markets consist of companies that buy products or services to use in their own businesses or in making other products. General Electric, for example, buys computers to use in billing and inventory control, steel and wiring to use in the manufacture of its products, and cleaning supplies to use in maintaining its buildings. Ads in this category usually are heavier on factual content than on emotional appeals.
- *Institutional markets.* Institutional markets include a wide variety of profit and non-profit organizations—such as hospitals, government agencies, and schools—that provide goods and services for the benefit of society. Universities, for example, are in the market for furniture, cleaning supplies, computers, office supplies, groceries, audiovisual material, and paper towels and toilet paper, to name a few. Such ads are very similar to business-to-business ads in that they are heavy on copy and light on visuals and emotional appeals.
- *Channel markets.* The channel market is made up of members of the distribution chain, which is what we call resellers, or intermediaries. Resellers are wholesalers, retailers, and distributors who buy finished or semifinished products and resell them for a profit. Microsoft and its retailers are part of the reseller market. Prestone is a wholesaler that distributes its de-icing fluid and other products to retailers. Companies that sell products and services such as trucks, cartons, and transportation services (airlines, cruise ships, and rental car agencies) consider resellers their market. *Channel marketing* is more important now that manufacturers consider their distributors to be important partners in their marketing programs. Giant retailers, particularly Wal-Mart, are becoming more powerful and can even dictate to manufacturers what products their customers want to buy and how much they are willing to pay for them.

Businesses spend most of their advertising dollars on consumer markets, although business-to-business advertising is becoming almost as important. Firms usually advertise to consumers through mass media such as radio, television, newspapers, general consumer magazines, and direct-response advertising media (that is, direct mail and online). They typically reach the other three markets—industrial, international, and reseller—through trade and professional advertising in specialized media, such as trade journals, professional magazines, and direct mail.

THE MARKETING PROCESS

Marketing is a process for doing business. The process begins with marketing research, which leads marketers to make a set of key strategic and tactical decisions that guide the deployment of the marketing mix. These steps are listed below followed by brief explanations of each. In later chapters on research and planning we'll explore these topics in more detail.

Step 1: Research the consumer market and the competitive marketplace and develop a situation analysis.

Step 2: Set objectives for the marketing effort.

Step 3: Assess consumer needs and wants relative to the product, segment the market into groups that are likely to respond, and target specific markets.

Step 4: Differentiate and position the product relative to the competition.

Step 5: Develop the marketing mix strategy: Select product design and performance criteria, pricing, distribution, and marketing communication.

Step 6: Evaluate the effectiveness of the strategy.

Marketing Research

The marketing process begins with research into markets, consumers, and the competitive situation. The objective for planners is to know as much as they can about the marketplace so they can make informed and insightful strategic decisions. Part of marketing research is focused on gathering information from already existing and published **secondary research** and from **primary research**, which is original research undertaken to answer specific questions.

But the second part of research is **situation analysis**, which identifies the brand's strengths and weaknesses, as well as corporate and market opportunities and threats. Interpreting marketing information in terms of strengths, weaknesses, opportunities, and threats (**SWOTs**) helps managers turn data into insights. The goal of marketing research is both information and insight.

Key Strategic Decisions

Marketing planners use research to develop strategies for approaching their markets. These strategies in turn give direction to the planning of advertising. There are three key strategic decisions:

Objectives   The marketer's first step after the research is done is to set objectives for the marketing effort. Usually these objectives are business measures, such as increased sales levels or share of market,

Segmenting and Targeting   The next step is to assess whether there are identifiable groups within the market whose needs and wants intersect with the product and its features—this is called *segmentation.* In customer-focused marketing the product may actually have been designed with the involvement of a particular segment. Then planners assess the needs of these groups, as well as their propensity to respond and decide which groups to *target*, which means they become the focus of the marketing communication efforts.

Differentiation and Positioning   Planners also assess the competition and decide where their product's point of **differentiation** lies and then make some decisions about how to present or *position* the product within this competitive environment relative to consumer needs. **Positioning** refers to how consumers view and compare competitive brands or types of products—how they see a brand relative to the other brands in the category.

Setting objectives, targeting, segmentation, differentiation, and positioning are basic marketing strategy decisions but they are also critical factors that affect advertising strategies. So although we briefly introduce these key marketing strategic decisions here, we'll discuss them in much more detail in later chapters where we introduce advertising planning and message strategies. These key strategic decisions are also important because they give direction to the marketing mix decisions.

Marketing Mix Strategies

As Figure 2.2 shows, marketers use the four main elements of the marketing mix to achieve their objectives. We referred to these in Chapter 1 as the four Ps and we'll describe their relationship to advertising following the list below. The **marketing communication mix** or *promotion,* which includes advertising, is one of these marketing elements; to a marketing manager communication is just one part of marketing, no more important than *product, price,* or distribution (*place*).

1. *Product.* Includes product design and development, product operation and performance, branding, and the physical dimensions of packaging.
2. *Place (Distribution).* Includes the channels used in moving the product from the manufacturer to the buyer.

Product	Distribution
• Design and Development • Branding • Packaging • Maintenance	• Distribution Channels • Market Coverage • Storage

Price	Communication
• Price Copy • Psychological Pricing • Price Lining • Value Determination	• Personal Selling • Advertising • Sales Promotion • Direct Marketing • Marketing/Public Relations • Point-of-Sale/Packaging

FIGURE 2.2

The Four Elements of the Marketing Mix
These four elements, and their related tools, serve as the basics of marketing.

3. *Price.* Includes the price at which the product or service is offered for sale and the level of profitability the price establishes.
4. *Promotion (Marketing Communication).* Includes personal selling, advertising, public relations, sales promotion, direct marketing, events and sponsorships, point-of-sale, and the communication aspects of packaging.

We introduced advertising and markting communication in Chapter 1, but let's review the other three marketing mix elements.

The Product   The product is both the object of the advertising and the reason for marketing. A product exists within a **product category**, which is a class of similar products—for example, Puma is in the athletic shoe category, as are Nike and Reebok. Marketing begins by asking a set of questions about the product offering. In line with the marketing concept, these questions should always be asked from the consumer's perspective: What product attributes and benefits are important? How is the product perceived relative to competitive offerings? How important is service? How long should the product last? Customers view products as "bundles of satisfaction" rather than just physical things, so what are the meanings they attach to the product and its competitors?

Distribution   It does little good to manufacture a fantastic product that will meet customers' needs unless you have a mechanism for delivering and servicing the product and receiving payment. The two channel factors that affect advertising reflect the distance

Celestial Seasonings uses its distinctive packages to send messages to consumers about its marketing position. How do you think the package reinforces the brand image?

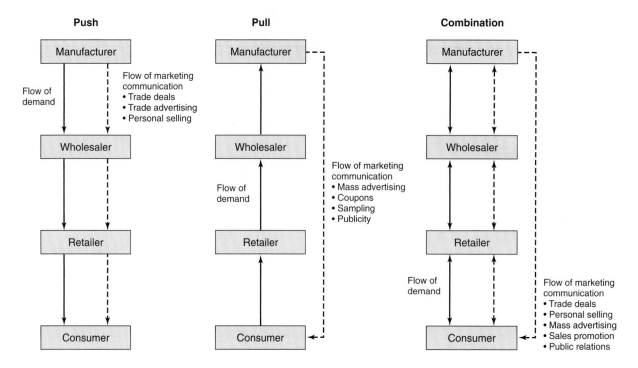

FIGURE 2.3 Push, Pull, and Combination Strategies

Advertising and other communication strategies are a major part of both a pull and push strategy.

between the manufacturer and the customer. **Direct-marketing** companies, such as Lands' End and Burpee Seeds, distribute their products directly without the use of a reseller. What you are more familiar with is more properly described as **indirect marketing**, where the product is distributed through a channel structure that includes one or more resellers. The products you see in a supermarket or discount store are all marketed indirectly through a complex channel marketing system.

Manufacturers often expect retailers in these indirect channels to participate in advertising programs. Through **cooperative** (or **co-op) advertising** allowances, the producers share with the reseller the cost of placing the advertisement.

A number of strategic distribution decisions develop from the overall marketing strategy, and these in turn affect advertising strategy.

- *Market Coverage Strategy.* Market coverage means the geographic distribution of the product, which is particularly important for the media strategy.
- *Push and Pull Strategies.* A **pull strategy** directs marketing efforts at the consumer and attempts to pull the product through the channel by intensifying consumer demand. Marketers using this strategy emphasize consumer advertising, along with incentives such as coupons, rebates, free samples, and sweepstakes. Little is expected from resellers other than to stock the product. In contrast, a **push strategy** directs marketing efforts at resellers, and success depends on the ability of these intermediaries to market the product, which they often do with advertising. Advertising may be targeted first at resellers to gain their acceptance, then at consumers through joint manufacturer–reseller advertising. Most marketers use a combination strategy of push and pull. Figure 2.3 summarizes these strategies.

Pricing The **price** a seller sets for a product is based not only on the cost of making and marketing the product but also on the seller's expected profit level. Certain psychological factors also affect the price. Ultimately, the price of a product is based on what the market will bear, the competition, the economic well-being of the consumer, the relative value of the product, and the consumer's ability to gauge the value.

With the exception of price information delivered at the point-of-sale, advertising is the primary vehicle for telling the consumer about price. The term **price copy**, which is the focus of much retail advertising, designates advertising copy devoted primarily to this type of information. A number of pricing strategies influence advertising strategy.

- **Customary** or expected pricing uses a single, well-known price for a long period of time. Movie theaters and manufacturers of candy use this pricing strategy. Advertisers communicate a dramatic or temporary price reduction through terms such as *sale, special,* and *today only.*
- **Psychological pricing** strategies use advertising to manipulate the customer's judgment of value. For example, ads showing prestige pricing—in which a high price is set to make the product seem worthy or valuable—are accompanied by photographs of the "exceptional product" or by copy consisting of logical reasons for this high price. Psychological pricing is often used when a marketer is targeting affluent consumers.

Marketing Communication and Personal Sales   We talked about marketing communication in the previous chapter but one type of communication is particularly important to marketing programs. **Personal sales** uses face-to-face contact between the marketer and a prospective customer. In contrast to most advertising, whose effects are often delayed, marketers often use personal selling to create immediate sales to people who are shopping for some product. Personal sales is also used in business-to-business marketing to reach key decision makers within a company who can authorize a purchase.

The different types of personal selling include sales calls at the place of business by a field representative (field sales), assistance at an outlet by a sales clerk (retail selling), and calls by a representative who goes to consumers' homes (door-to-door selling).

Marketing Strategy Evaluation

Most of the steps outlined in this discussion of the marketing process are contained in a document called a **marketing plan**, prepared usually for a year's activity. Once the planning period has been completed, marketers generally make an effort to evaluate the plan based on how well it met its stated objectives. This is the last step in the marketing process, and it measures the effectiveness not only of the marketing strategy, but also of the advertising effort.

Consider This

1. What are the steps in the marketing process and how do they relate to advertising?
2. Why do marketers consider the competition when making their key marketing strategy decisions?

In this section we examined the marketing process and how advertising supports the marketing function. Let's stop for a moment to consider the story of Krispy Kreme® and its marketing program. After this, we conclude the chapter with the role and structure of advertising agencies and how they work with a client and its markting department.

HOW AGENCIES WORK

We've talked about the marketing process and identified points in the marketing effort where advertising is particularly important. So who does the work of advertising, and how do these professionals work with the marketing department or the company behind the marketing?

A marketer may have a contractual relationship with one agency, called the **agency-of-record (AoR)**, or with many. Usually marketers have different agencies for different types of marketing communication tasks, but sometimes they hire several agencies in the same area because they believe the competition will result in better work. Regardless of the arrangement, the agency–client relationship and contract is one that takes a lot of nurturing in order to work effectively. Ideally, the relationship is a partnership working together on behalf of the brand.

A MATTER OF PRACTICE
Marketing a Passion for Doughnuts

When Krispy Kreme opened its first store in the Fort Worth, Texas, market 40 people were waiting in a line at 5 A.M. to ensure they'd be among the first to sample the legendary hot, freshly made doughnuts. What makes Krispy Kreme such a hit with its customers?

As with all good marketing plans, it starts with the product: The proprietary recipe for the yeast dough and glazing, along with the company-designed equipment that produces a perfect doughnut shape and cooks it to the perfect point of softness is at the heart of the success of Krispy Kreme.

The result is a perfect doughnut with a taste that some of its passionate fans say is addictive.

Krispy Kreme's stores are another element that attracts Krispy Kreme fanatics. Its trademark glass and chrome architecture is actually a doughnut bakery with a retail unit added in front. The stores even have a viewing window so you can see your favorite indulgence being made as you watch.

Since its customers are so loyal to the brand and other prospective customers have been presold on Krispy Kremes by their friends, price doesn't seem to be a factor. In other words, like most big brands, Krispy Kremes can charge a premium price because people value the product so highly.

Distribution procedures continue to evolve. The company started off in the 1930s as a bakery that distributed its doughnuts to other stores to sell. Soon after, people began stopping by to ask whether they could buy hot doughnuts fresh from the plant. The demand was so great that company founder, Vernon Carver Rudolph, cut a hole in the wall of the factory in order to sell the hot doughnuts direct to his delighted customers.

Marketing communication has also been innovative. What made customers really seek out Krispy Kreme was the opportunity to get a hot doughnut fresh out of the fryer. In order to get the word out that fresh goods were available, a franchise owner in the 1970s bought a window shade and had a sign company print "Hot Doughnuts Now" on it. When his store finished a batch of doughnuts, he'd pull down the window shade. Now all stores have neon signs that are turned on to proclaim the same mouthwatering message.

Today Krispy Kreme produces more than 7.5 million doughnuts a day and more than 2.7 billion a year. It has more than 310 stores in 41 states, as well as in international locations in Canada, Mexico, Asia, Europe and Eastern Europe, and Australia. It saw solid growth until the anti-carbohydrate craze affected some of its customer base. But that downturn in the U.S. market has been compensated for by growth in international markets.

But Krispy Kreme isn't sitting on its glazed laurels; it continues to innovate, particularly in the area of distribution. You've probably noticed packages of the company's

doughnuts in grocery and convenience stores, even department stores, such as the legendary Harrod's store in London. The off-premise boxes of Krispy Kremes also offer an opportunity for people who have never visited a Krispy Kreme store to sample the product.

More recently the company has been outfitting specially designed trucks as mobile stores complete with viewing windows to bring the hot, fresh doughnuts to fairs and other major events. The management is also experimenting with centralized bakeries in order to bring the hot-fresh, doughnut concepts to small stores in locations where a full-size store might not be feasible.

For many years the success of Krispy Kreme was due to word of mouth by customers who were passionate about its doughnuts. Its primary marketing communication was with nonprofit organizations who sold Krispy Kreme doughnuts in their fund-raising efforts.

In its early years, therefore, Krispy Kreme used very little advertising to build the business. However, after signing up with GSD&M, a high-profile agency in Austin, Texas, known for its creative product, Krispy Kreme is determining how to advertise in ways customers will respect and that don't diminish the image and personality of the brand.

Consider This

1. How has Krispy Kreme used the elements of its marketing mix to build its business?
2. Do you think Krispy Kreme's marketing strategies are faithful to the marketing concept? Why or why not?

Sources: Scott Livengood, "Krispy Kreme Looks to Its Global Roll-Out," *Financial Times* (March 15, 2004): 6; Krispy Kreme online press kit, www.krispykreme.com, February 2004; Aetna Smith and Barry Shlachter, "Krispy Kreme Phenomenon Continues to Be a Sweet Deal," *Denver Post* (March 3, 2003): 1C, 8C; Scott Hume, "Model Behavior," *Restaurants and Institutions* (July 1, 2001): 28–38; Tim O'Brien, "Krispy Kreme Deliver at the Ohio State Fair," *Amusement Business* (September 2, 2002): 12.

Why should a company sign a contract with an advertising agency? Hiring an agency has four main benefits: It provides specialized services, objective advice, experienced staffing, and tailored management of all advertising activities and personnel.

Ultimately, the primary benefit of hiring an ad agency is that it can implement the creative vision of the client, and help it to reach its advertising goals. Each agency tends to have its own style—one for which it is known. Note the ads of three different agencies for the three branches of the U.S. military. Do you perceive a difference in style? Which do you think would be most effective?

Types of Agencies

We are primarily concerned with advertising agencies in this book, but other areas such as public relations, direct marketing, sales promotion, and the Internet also have agencies that provide specialized services (and since they are all part of an integrated marketing communication approach, we have separate chapters on these functions later in this book).

The top or biggest agencies are what we call full-service agencies, but there are other ways that agencies organize their services for their clients, including specialized agencies and media-buying services. As discussed in Chapter 1, advertising also can be handled internally by the advertiser either in an in-house agency or an advertising department.

Full-Service Agencies   In advertising, a **full-service agency** is one that includes the four major staff functions: account management, creative services, media planning and buying, and account planning, which is also joined with research. A full-service advertising agency will also have its own accounting department, a traffic department to handle internal tracking on completion of projects, a department for broadcast and print production (usually organized within the creative department), and a human resources department.

The top agency brands worldwide are shown in Table 2.3. They are all full-service agencies.

Specialized Agencies   Many agencies do not follow the traditional full-service agency approach. They either specialize in certain functions (writing copy, producing art, or media buying), audiences (minority, youth), industries (health care, computers, agriculture, business-to-business communication), or markets (minority groups such as Asian, African American, or Hispanic). In addition, there are specialized agencies in all marketing communications areas, such as direct marketing, sales promotion, public relations, events

TABLE 2.3 World's Top 10 Agency Brands

Rank 2003	Rank 2002	Agency	Headquarters	Worldwide Gross Income 2003	Worldwide Gross Income 2002
1	1	Denstu	Tokyo	$1,864.1	$1,442.6
2	3	BBDO Worldwide	New York	1,237.5	1,062.7
3	2	McCann-Erickson Worldwide	New York	1,220.1	1,176.5
4	4	J. Walter Thompson Co.	New York	1,178.5	996.9
5	5	Publicis Worldwide	Paris	1,066.0	1,040.9
6	6	DDB Worldwide Communications	New York	1,214.6	1,176.9
7	7	Leo Burnett Worldwide	Chicago	1,072.3	1,029.3
8	9	TBWA Worldwide	New York	771.0	665.9
9	8	Euro RSCG Worldwide	New York	756.1	733.3
10	10	Ogilvy & Mather Worldwide	New York	1,135.4	1,109.4

Notes: Figures are in millions of U.S. dollars. Worldwide agency brands are defined as international networks associated with the agency and the agency's U.S. brand. Specialty units (direct marketing, sales promotion, research, etc.) and independent subsidiaries are excluded at both the U.S. and international levels.

Sources: "World's Top 10 Core Agency Brands," Advertising Age (April 19, 2004): S13.

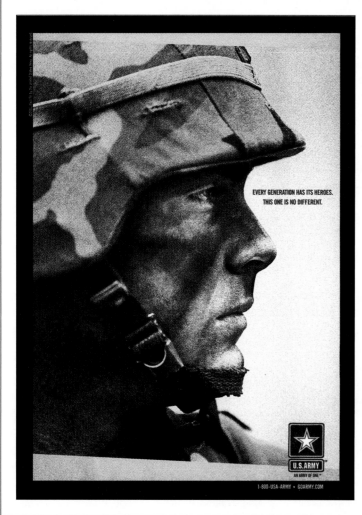

and sports marketing, and packaging and point-of-sale. There are also one-client agencies such as the Focus agency in Dallas that serves only GTE.

Recall from Chapter 1 that there are also in-house agencies and freelancers. Here we will discuss creative boutique and media buying-services.

- *Creative boutiques.* Creative boutiques are ad agencies, usually small (two or three people to a dozen or more), that concentrate entirely on preparing the creative execution of client marketing communications. The focus of the organization is entirely on the idea, the creative product. A creative boutique will have one or more writers or artists on staff. There is no staff for media, research, or strategic planning. Typically, these agencies can prepare advertising to run in print media, outdoors, and on radio and television. Creative boutiques usually serve companies but are sometimes retained by advertising agencies when they are overloaded with work.
- *Media-buying services.* Agencies that specialize in the purchase of media for clients are called *media-buying services.* They are in high demand for many reasons but three reasons stand out. First, media has become more complex as the number of choices grows—think of the proliferation of new cable channels, magazines, and radio stations. Second, the cost of maintaining a competent media department has escalated. Third, media-buying services often buy media at a low cost because they can group several clients' purchases together to develop substantial buying power.

How Agency Work Is Organized

If the agency is large enough, it usually has a chief executive officer, perhaps one or two vice presidents, and several different functional areas. We concentrate here on five of those areas: account management, creative development and production, media planning and buying, account planning and research, and internal services.

Account Management

The **account management** department acts a liaison between the client and the agency. It ensures that the agency will focus its resources on the client's needs. It develops its own point of view regarding the research and strategy, which the account manager presents to the client. The account manager is also responsible for interpreting the client's marketing strategy for the rest of the agency. Linda Wolf, the president of the Leo Burnett advertising agency, described an account management executive as needing "financial acumen, a passion for the creative product, and the ability to build client relationships."[4] The Inside Story focuses on the work of an account executive.

Once the client (or the client and the agency together) establishes the general guidelines for a campaign or advertisement, the account management department supervises the day-to-day development within these guidelines. Account management in a major agency typically has three levels: *management supervisor,* who provides leadership on strategic issues and looks for new business opportunities; *account supervisor,* who is the key executive working on a client's business and the primary liaison between the client and the agency; and the *account executive* (as well as assistant account executives), who is responsible for day-to-day activities and operates like a project manager.[5] Sometimes a fourth level may exist: the *account director,* who is above the account supervisor. A smaller agency will combine some of these levels.

Creative Development and Production

The creative members of the agency are the creative directors, creative department managers, copywriters, art directors, and producers. In addition to these positions, the broadcast production department and the art studio are two other areas where creative personnel can apply their skills. Generally, the creative department has people who create and people who inspire (*creative directors*). A *creative group* includes people who write (*copywriters*), people who design ideas for print ads or television commercials (*art directors*), and people who convert these ideas into television or radio commercials (*producers*). Many agencies will employ an art director and a copywriter who work well together, and build a support group around them.

Media Planning and Buying

Agencies that don't rely on outside media specialists will have a media department that recommends to the client—or another department—

INSIDE STORY

The Day-to-Day Job of an Account Executive

Tammie DeGrasse, Account Supervisor, McCann-Erickson, New York

So what exactly do you do in advertising?" That is by far the most common question I am asked once someone finds out I'm in Account Management. "Do you create the ads?" "Do you choose the actors?" "Do you decide which magazines to run in?" To be honest, I don't think my own mother has it figured out, yet. I've since realized that the best way to define what we, as account people, do in advertising is . . . make it all happen. To use a simple analogy, an account manager is like the supervisor in a car factory's assembly line. We don't physically connect part A to part B; but we do make sure every department fully understands what the car is supposed to look like and how it should run to ensure that it will be created effectively and efficiently, so it can sell.

That's just the big picture; my day-to-day duties aren't so lofty. Now, I could break it down and give you an idea of my typical 9-to-5 day; but to be honest, in advertising there's no such thing as "typical" or "9-to-5." My day entails anything and everything to make sure the job gets done. Whether it's literally running tapes to NBC, viewing casting reels for the next commercial, researching our clients' top competitors, watching focus groups describe what they think makes a good ad (that's always fun), or attending television shoots . . . my days are anything but typical. Some highlights during my career at McCann

include watching a handful of celebrities read our scripts in a recording session and even having myself featured in a national newspaper ad (Hey, anything to get the job done, right?).

Nonetheless, it's been amazing so far and a valuable learning experience every step of the way.

For those of you considering entering the advertising industry, deciding which area to concentrate in can be difficult. Every department is so equally appetizing; anyone would have trouble figuring out what the best fit for him or her might be. Being that I possess leadership qualities, enjoy strategizing, and like to get my hands in just about everything, Account Management seemed like my perfect fit. For others it may not be so easy, so I strongly suggest learning more about the specifics of every group. Keep in mind that there are pros and cons to each and only you can decipher which end of the factory assembly line you would be best to work on. That's all for now—have to run . . . client dinner in ten minutes. Best of luck to all of you!

Tammie DeGrasse graduated magna cum laude from Florida State University, in the spring of 2000. She then began her career at McCann-Erickson as an Assistant Account Executive, working on two multimillion-dollar accounts (Gateway and Burger King); she was promoted to Account Executive after a little more than a year on the job and is now an Account Supervisor.

Nominated by Professor Kartik Pashupati, Florida State University

the most efficient means of delivering the message to the target audience. That department has three functions: planning, buying, and research. These media experts may represent one-half of the physical space occupied by an ad agency. Because media is so complex, it is not unusual for some individuals to become experts in planning, others in buying, and still others in doing research about trends and examining characteristics of consumers using different media.

Account Planning and Research   A full-service agency usually has a separate department specifically devoted to planning and sometimes to research. Today the emphasis in agency research is on developing an advertising message that focuses on the consumer's perspective and relationship with the brand. An **account planner** is a type of planner who gathers all available intelligence on the market and consumers and acts as the voice of the consumer. Account planners are strategic specialists who prepare comprehensive recommendations about the consumer's wants, needs, and relationship to the client's brand, and how the advertising should work to satisfy those elements based on insights they derive from consumer research. Most major agencies conduct consumer research to make the advertising more focused and appropriate to the target audience. They also purchase research from companies that specialize in this area.

Internal Agency Services   The departments that serve the operations within the agency include the traffic department and print production, as well as the more general financial services and human resources or personnel.

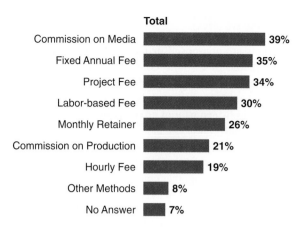

Agency Compensation
Agencies derive their revenues from two main sources: commission and fees.

Source: Jack Feuer, "What Clients Think about Media," *Adweek* (June 4, 2001): 42.

The **traffic department** is responsible for internal control and tracking of projects to meet deadlines. The account executive works closely with the assigned traffic coordinator or traffic manager to review deadlines and monitor progress. The traffic department is the lifeblood of the agency, and its personnel keep track of everything that is happening there. Taking a layout, a visual, and a page of copy and turning them into a four-color magazine page or a full-page newspaper advertisement is the work of the **print production department**. Thanks to versatile graphics software, much of this work is now done on the computer.

How Agencies Make Money

Agencies derive their revenues and profits from three main sources: commissions, fees, and retainers. A **commission** is the amount an ad agency charges the client as a percentage of the media cost. For example, if the $85,000 cost of media to the agency has a 15 percent commission allowance, the agency adds $12,750 to the $85,000 when billing the client. The standard 15 percent commission has been criticized by clients as being too high and a practice that pushes agencies to use more expensive media. For those accounts still using a commission approach, this rate is rarely 15 percent; it is more likely subject to negotiation between agency and client.

Most advertisers now use a fee system either as the primary compensation tool or in combination with a commission system. The **fee** system is comparable to the means by which advertisers pay their lawyers and accountants. The client and agency agree on an hourly fee or rate. This fee can vary by department or it could be a flat hourly fee for all work regardless of the salary level of the person doing the work. Charges are also included for out-of-pocket expenses, travel, and other standard items. All charges are billed to the client, and no commission is added to the media cost. Figure 2.4 shows the use of commission and fees as compensation for U.S. ad agencies.

There are also instances where an agency is put on a monthly or yearly **retainer**. The amount billed per month is based on the projected amount of work and the hourly rate charged. This system is most commonly used by public relations agencies.

The most recent trends in agency compensation are for advertisers to pay agencies on the basis of their performance. One consultant recommends that this arrangement be based on paying the agency either a percentage of the client's sales or a percentage of the client's marketing budget. Procter & Gamble is the pioneer in trying to apply this new system.[6]

Consider This

1. What are the major areas in an agency? Explain their work responsibilities.

2. If you were to apply for a summer job in an agency, in which department would you want to work? Why? Which of your own skills are relevant to that area?

INTERNATIONAL MARKETING

In most countries markets are composed of local, regional, and international brands. A **local brand** is one marketed in a single country. A **regional brand** is one marketed throughout a region (for example, North America or Europe). An **international brand** is available virtually everywhere in the world. Advertising that promotes the same product in several countries is known as **international advertising**. It did not appear in any organized manner until the late nineteenth century.

Saturation of the home country market isn't the sole reason companies venture outside the home market. International marketing and advertising is also prompted by research that shows market potential for products in other countries, by mergers and acquisitions with foreign businesses, and by moves into other markets to preempt development by competitors.

Export marketing and advertising are not the exclusive province of large companies. Bu Jin, an innovative company in Boulder, Colorado, creates and markets martial arts products. With only eight full-time employees, its products fill a high-end international market worldwide. Most of Bu Jin's business is driven by its catalog. Many service providers also market internationally. Airlines and transportation companies that serve foreign markets, such as UPS, are in effect exporting a service.

Organizing for International Marketing

Once the exporter becomes nationalized in several countries in a regional bloc, the company often establishes a regional management center and transfers day-to-day management responsibilities from the home country to that office. For instance, Coca-Cola has several regional offices around the world to support its international markets.

A company that has domestic operations and established regional operations in Europe, Latin America, North America, the Pacific, or elsewhere, faces the question of whether to establish a world corporate headquarters. Part of the reason for making such a decision is to give the company a truly global perspective: a corporate philosophy that directs products and advertising toward a worldwide market. Unilever and Shell (both of which have twin world headquarters in the United Kingdom and the Netherlands), IBM, Nestlé, and the advertising holding company Interpublic have changed to a global management structure.

International Marketing Management

Regardless of the company's form or style of management, the shift from national to international management requires new tools for advertisers, including one language (usually English), one control mechanism (the budget), and one strategic plan (the marketing strategy).

The choice of an advertising agency for international advertising is influenced not only by many of the same considerations as the choice of a domestic agency, but also by the decision on whether to standardize its messages across all markets or localize them to accommodate local cultural differences. If the company wants to take a highly standardized approach in international markets, it is likely to favor an international agency that can handle advertising for the product in both the domestic and the international market. A localized advertising effort, by contrast, favors use of advertising agencies in many countries for both planning and implementation of the advertising.

THE DYNAMICS OF MODERN MARKETING

Marketing continues to be challenged to prove its effectiveness. The only defense against such challenges is a concerted effort to demonstrate the accountability of marketing and its positive impact on the organization's return on investment. There are also several changes in the way marketing is conducted that are making marketing more accountable, efficient, and effective. They include integrated marketing, relationship marketing, and permission marketing.

- *Integrated marketing.* Similar to IMC, integrated marketing is focused on better coordinating marketing efforts.[7] Integrated marketing means all areas of the marketing mix, including marketing communication, work closely together to present the brand in a coherent and consistent way. The basic premise is that everything communicates something about the brand—the price delivers a message, the place where you buy the product delivers a message, the way it handles or performs delivers a message. And, of course, the marketing communication delivers messages. The objective of integrated marketing, then, is to manage all these messages so they are consistent.[8]

- *Relationship marketing.* Another trend in modern marketing is relationship marketing, which means marketing that considers all the firm's stakeholders, whether employees, distributors, channel members, customers, agencies, investors, government agencies, the media, or community members. Relationship marketing is driven by communication and therefore is best accomplished through an IMC program. **Customer relationship management (CRM)** is a recent trend that uses databases to drive communication with customers and keep track of their interactions with a company.

- *Permission marketing.* The practice of inviting prospective customers to sign up or self-select themselves into a brand's target market in order to receive marketing communication is referred to as permission marketing. This practice has become more feasible with the development of interactive communication technologies, such as the Internet, that allow firms to customize their marketing messages. Advertising can contribute to this change, such as when it announces a new product and invites interested consumers to contact the company for additional information.

Consider This

1. How do trends in the marketing industry, such as integrated marketing, affect advertising?

2. Can advertising be a factor in relationship-marketing or permission-marketing programs? In what way?

IT'S A WRAP

PUMA LEAPS FORWARD

The opening story about Harley touched on a number of key concepts in marketing planning, such as the customer-focused marketing concept, the concepts of exchange, added value and, most importantly, the concept of branding. The story also referred to many of the key players in marketing such as customers, dealers, and its advertising agency.

Puma, a small player in the athletic shoe market, does not attempt to outspend its competitors. Instead it uses a highly strategic marketing effort to set the brand apart and give it a distinctive personality. Its market communication creates an attitude for the brand, as well as sales.

Puma's internal marketing philosophy is a factor in the brand's resurrection. The CEO calls it the "blue mountain strategy." He explains, "We may not be the biggest or tallest mountain, but if we want to differentiate ourselves, we want to be the blue mountain that stands out not for its size but for how we do things."

That philosophy has guided everything from advertising budgets, to product distribution and promotional partners. Puma, for example, spends around $4 million on advertising in the United States, compared to around $130 million for Nike and $45 million for Reebok. In spite of the relatively tiny ad budget, Puma reported a 48 percent sales increase in 2002. Puma's sales jumped to $121 million, up from $82 million in 2001 and $58 million in 2000.

▪▪▪ Summary

1. **Define the role of advertising within marketing.** Understanding how marketing works and the role advertising plays within the marketing strategy is essential for successful advertising. The success of marketing depends on whether a business can create a competitive advantage that results in an exchange and advertising showcases those advantages. Advertising helps a company to match a product's availability—and the company's production capabilities—to the consumer's need, desire, or demand for the product.

2. **Explain how the four key concepts in marketing relate to advertising.** The four key marketing concepts are the marketing concept, and the concepts of exchange, branding, and added value. The (1) *marketing concept* focuses first on the needs of the consumer in designing product offerings rather than the goals and needs of the company. (2) *Exchange* refers to the way a company makes and offers something and what a consumer gives in return to obtain that product (good, service, or idea). Advertising offers an information exchange in support of the marketing exchange. (3) *Branding* uses advertising to create a special meaning for a product that makes it distinctive in the marketplace. (4) *Added value* means a marketing or advertising effort makes the product more valuable, useful, or appealing to a consumer.

3. **Identify the key players in marketing and how the organization of the industry affects advertising.** The four important categories of key players in marketing are the marketer, suppliers or vendors, distributors and retailers, and agencies. The *marketer* is the advertiser—the company or organization that produces the product and offers it for sale. *Suppliers and vendors* are companies that provide the materials and ingredients used in running a business and producing a product. The *distribution* chain or channel refers to the various companies—distributors, wholesalers, brokers, dealers, and retailers—involved in moving a product from its manufacturer to the buyer. *Agencies* are the marketing communication companies that help marketers promote their products.

4. **List and explain the six critical steps in the marketing process.** The six steps in the marketing process include: (1) researching the consumer market and the competition to develop a situation analysis; (2) setting the marketing objectives, which are usually expressed in terms of sales and market share; (3) assessing consumer needs and wants and using that information to segment the market into groups of likely prospects for the product, and then targeting specific markets that are most likely to be profitable; (4) differentiating and positioning the product relative to the competition; (5) developing the marketing mix strategy in terms of product design and performance, pricing, distribution, and promotion; and (6) evaluating the effectiveness of the marketing strategy.

5. **Summarize the structure of the advertising agency industry and how agencies work with their clients on the marketing side.** The advertising industry is organized into full-service agencies, specialized agencies such as creative boutiques and media-buying services, as well as in-house agencies and advertising departments within the marketer's company. In advertising agencies, work is handled by account managers who are the liaison with the client; creative departments who write and design the advertising; media planners and buyers who place the advertisements in the media; account planners and researchers who develop research to obtain insights about consumer behavior and preference; as well as other internal agency services that help the company operate its business.

6. **Analyze the changes in the marketing world and what they portend for advertising.** In addition to an increase in international marketing, some of the other marketplace changes that affect the way advertising operates within a marketing program include integrated marketing—which is a focus on integrating all the marketing mix decisions and communication—relationship and permission marketing.

▪▪▪ Key Terms

account management, 49
account planner, 50
added value, 36
agency of record (AoR), 45
brand, 33
brand equity, 35
brand image, 33
brand management, 37
brand mark, 35
brand name, 35
branding, 33

business-to-business market, 41
channel market, 41
commission, 51
consumer market, 41
cooperative (co-op) advertising, 44
customer relationship management (CRM), 53
differentiation, 42
direct marketing, 44
distribution chain, 39

distribution channel, 39
exchange, 32
fee, 51
full-service agency, 47
indirect marketing, 44
ingredient branding, 39
institutional market, 41
integrated marketing, 52
international advertising, 52
international brand, 52
local brand, 52
market, 39

marketer, 37
marketing communication mix, 42
marketing concept, 31
marketing plan, 45
media-buying services, 49
package goods, 41
permission marketing, 53
personal sales, 45
positioning, 42
price, 44
price copy, 45

primary research, 42
print production department, 51
product category, 43
product management, 37

pull strategy, 44
push strategy, 44
regional brand, 52
relationship marketing, 53
reseller, 39

retainer, 51
secondary research, 42
share of market, 39
situation analysis, 42
supply chain, 38

SWOTs, 42
trademark, 35
traffic department, 51

Review Questions

1. Where does advertising fit within a marketing program?
2. What are the four key marketing concepts that give direction to advertising?
3. In general, outline the structure of the marketing industry and explain where advertising fits and how it relates to the various key players.
4. Outline the key steps in the marketing process.
5. Explain how agency work is organized. In other words, what are the primary functions or professional areas found in an agency?
6. Explain relationship marketing and permission marketing.

Discussion Questions

1. Find an example of an advertisement that you think demonstrates the marketing concept and another ad that you think does not represent an effective application of the marketing concept. Compare the two and explain why you evaluated them as you did.
2. Professor Baker tells her advertising class that advertising's relationship to marketing is like the tip of an iceberg. As the class looks puzzled, she explains that most (80 percent) of the iceberg cannot be seen. "It's the same with the consumer's perception of how much of marketing is advertising-related," Baker explains. What is Baker trying to illustrate with the iceberg analogy?
3. This chapter stressed integration of advertising with other components of the marketing mix. If you were in marketing management for Kellogg cereals, how would you see advertising supporting product, price, and place? Could advertising improve each of these functions for Kellogg? Explain your answer.
4. As this chapter states, Coca-Cola is the most recognizable brand in the world. How did the company achieve this? What has the company done in its marketing mix in terms of product, price, distribution, and marketing communications that has created such tremendous brand equity and loyalty? How has advertising aided in building the brand? You might want to visit Coca-Cola's Web site for help: www.coca-cola.com
5. Imagine you are starting a company to manufacture fudge. Consider the following decisions:
   a. Describe the marketing mix you think would be most effective for this company.
   b. Describe the marketing communication mix you would recommend for this company.
   c. How would you determine the advertising budget for your new fudge company?
   d. What brand image would you recommend for your fudge?

Class Project

1. Interview the manager of a large retail outlet store in your area, such as Target, Kmart, or Wal-Mart. Assess how the retailer uses various elements of the marketing communication mix. Study a few diverse products, such as food items, blue jeans, and small appliances. You might even talk to the automotive service department. Write a report, making conclusions about how advertising comes into play.
2. Assess the Web sites of three ad agencies. What differences in offerings do you observe? (See Table 2.3 for some agency names. Do a search for their home pages on a search engine such as Yahoo! or Google.)

HANDS-ON

WPP's Owner—a British Knight with Every (Marketing) Weapon at His Disposal

To the uninformed, nothing about Martin Sorrell or his company, the WPP group, may be quite what it seems. Although he was awarded a knighthood, Sir Martin is anything but a reserved aristocrat. And while WPP is one of the four largest agency holding companies in the world, the initials actually stand for Wire & Plastic Products, the British company Sorrell used to gobble up some of the world's most famous advertising agencies. The roster of agencies now under the WPP's wing includes industry leaders Ogivly and Mather, Burson-Marsteller, Hill & Knowlton, Young & Rubicam, and J. Walter Thompson, to name just a few.

Large conglomerates like WPP made frequent head-lines in the 1990s, a period of great consolidation in the advertising industry. Faced with harsh economic and business realities, individual advertising agencies chose to give up independent existence in order to become parts of large communication companies that offered clients all the tools for an integrated campaign, including advertising, direct marketing, public relations, and sales promotion. In the new millennium, dealing with one (or several) of the four large holding companies, WPP Group (England), Interpublic (U.S.), Publicis Groupe (France), and Omnicom (U.S.), is the way the world's biggest advertisers do business.

While each of the conglomerates is led by a charismatic and dynamic individual, none appears to have an edge on Sorrell, who was described in a recent *Fortune* article as ". . . confident, witty, and a tad arrogant, talking rapidly about the future of advertising and the challenges of keeping fractious clients and ad agencies happy." *Fortune* also noted that "In an industry populated by shameless schmoozers, the 59-year-old Sorrell is in a league of his own."

These characteristics have served Sorrell well. In 2004 he squared off against rival Publicis Groupe and its CEO, Maurice Levy, in pursuit of one of the last great independent agencies, Grey Advertising, New York. During the battle *Advertising Age* opined that Publicis had a big advantage because Levy and Grey chair Edward Meyer were friends and had spoken about merging in the past. In addition, both Grey and Publicis created ads for consumer giant Procter & Gamble, while WPP agency Ogilvy & Mather counted P&G's competitor Unilever among its most important clients. (It is customary for agencies not to work for competing accounts.) A Unilever spokesperson, asked for his thoughts about the possibility of working with an agency that created ads for his most important rival, suggested that "In the past, we've not seen it to be such a

good idea." But nobody familiar with Martin Sorrell was surprised when at the end of the day he convinced Grey to sign with WPP and persuaded Procter & Gamble to stay as well.

Unlike many of his peers, Sorrell has never written a word of copy, nor has he ever penciled a print design or directed a broadcast commercial. Sorrell's talents are organizational and strategic; although he is an expert in the world of finance, Sir Martin cautions, "I may be a bean counter, but I'm not an accountant." To drive home the point he posed for WPP's annual report surrounded by lima and pinto beans.

So how does Martin Sorrell continue to win in the high-stakes agency world? His vision, developed years before most of his rivals caught on, that twenty-first-century clients would want a complete menu of marketing communication services, all of which work synergistically, is one important reason for his success. Tenacity, energy, focus, and a willingness to do whatever is needed to win are also traits that come to mind. All these are illustrated in the story of Sorrell's drive to land Korean giant Samsung when the company put its advertising up for review in the spring of 2004. Samsung spends almost $400 million each year supporting its brands, which is reason enough for agencies to salivate for the account. Sorrell believes that the company holds even greater appeal because of his forecast that advertising growth in the twenty-first century will come disproportionately from Asia.

So Sorrell did whatever he could to attract Samsung's attention. Like any savvy agency head, he assigned his best people to generate creative ideas to pitch to Samsung executives. But unlike most agency heads, he didn't stop there. After discovering that a Samsung-financed museum was having a grand opening in Seoul, Sorrell jumped on a plane and ended up being the only agency person there. Samsung executives found themselves receiving e-mails from Sorrell at all times of the day and night. Peter Stringham, marketing director of HSBC, a company that Sorrell landed after several years of trying, commented, "Martin can be quite persistent. He was there from the first meeting to the last. He'd pitched to us a couple of times before and not gotten the account, but he'd had his eye on it for years."

Needless to say, in the fall of 2004, Samsung announced it was awarding its account to WPP. In the new millennium, British knights may not wear armor, carry a crest, or rescue damsels in distress. But Sir Martin Sorrell knows how to triumph in the competitive world of advertising agencies.

Consider This

1. Why do large clients like Samsung wish to work with giant holding companies like WPP instead of with smaller agencies?
2. What qualities help Sorrell to be successful? Why are these qualities so important for his company's success?
3. Explain how Martin Sorrell wins clients and builds positive agency–client relationships. How does he see the agency's role in marketing?

Sources: "Sorrell Cashes In on $30M Incentive Bonus," *Advertising Age* (September 27, 2004); Brian Steinberg and Erin White, "Grey Global Could Go Many Ways; Advisers Explore Options; Publicis Link Is Possible, as Both Firms Serve P&G," *Wall Street Journal* (Eastern edition) (June 29, 2004): B3; Nelson D. Schwartz, "Bigger and Bigger: Martin Sorrell Wants WPP to Be the World's Largest Marketing Machine. With His Most Recent Acquisition, He's Almost There," *Fortune* (November 29, 2004): 146; Erin White, "WPP Group's Tough-Love Artist; Neil French's Role Includes Making Candid Appraisals of Agencies' Global Talent," *Wall Street Journal* (October 20, 2003): B9; Erin White, "WPP Deal Puts Pressure on Havas; Pact to Buy Grey Solidifies Power of Four Big Firms, Leaving French Rival in Cold," *Wall Street Journal* (Eastern edition) (September 14, 2004): B14.

Advertising and Society

The most offensive and dumbest ads of the decade

CHAPTER KEY POINTS

After reading this chapter, you will be able to:

1. Discuss the shape-versus-mirror debate.

2. Analyze the legal topics that guide advertising practice.

3. List the key regulatory agencies and their responsibilities.

4. Explain the way the advertising industry regulates itself.

5. Critique the key ethical issues that challenge the practice of advertising.

6. Outline three ways to determine if an advertising decision is ethical.

n 2003 *Adweek* ran a feature on what it described as "the lowest moments in advertising" during the previous decade. Many of these advertisements are on the list because, in their search for creative ideas and attention-getting images, they challenge the ethical standards of the industry. Whatever the reason, they have been dubbed winners, or rather losers, in an award show that most advertisers would rather not enter.

Most of the advertisements are on the list because they are tasteless, insensitive, or offensive. For example, at the top of the list was Calvin Klein's notorious 1995 campaign that used a style of lighting and staging reminiscent of a porn movie to show prepubescent teens in their underwear. The ads for CK jeans were pulled under threat of criminal charges from the FBI and the Justice Department.

There has been a remarkable range of insensitive ideas. In the emotional days after 9/11, a number of advertisers tried to find ways to tie in with sensitivity to the traumatic event; one that grated was a billboard for Kenneth Cole that proclaimed, "God Dress America!" Viewer complaints forced Fox Sports Net to pull an ad for its Best Damn Sports Show Period that featured heavyweight boxer Mike Tyson as a baby-sitter; the fact that Tyson is a convicted rapist, is known for biting off part of the ear of Evander Holyfield, and has threatened to "eat the children" of another rival didn't seem to occur to Fox Sports Net.

Benetton has used ads that shock as a way to position itself as a fashion house that cares about social issues, but *Adweek* described its ad supplement featuring death-row prisoners as over the top. The features used celebrity-style photos and a sympathetic interview style that seemed to glamorize its subjects, even as it exploited them. Part of the outrage was because the victims didn't even rate a mention although the killers were memorialized.

Other ads on the list were offensive because they played with stereotypes. For example, a Super Bowl spot for Just for Feet shows a barefoot black man running through the wilderness tracked by a patrol in a Humvee. *Adweek* wondered why no one realized that there's something wrong with the Great White Hunter tracking a black African as a wild beast. The client became the first to sue its agency for malpractice. Similarly a postcard campaign for the Toyota RAV4 showed a male African American mouth, exaggerated lips, white pearly teeth, and a gold Toyota Rav4 SUV emblazoned on one of the teeth. The Reverend Jesse Jackson observed that "All that's missing is a watermelon."

An ad for the Nike ACG Air Goat made fun of the handicapped. It promised the shoe would help the runner avoid running into trees and becoming a "drooling, misshapen nonextreme trail-running husk of my former self." Consumers, the disabled, and their advocacy groups were outraged. Nike and the agency apologized and said, "We have stepped over the line with this advertisement, and there is no excuse for it."

When you read stories like this, you can't help but ask yourself why these advertisements were ever made. It's unlikely the advertiser or agency was trying to deliberately engage in offensive and insensitive practices, so what is behind the decision to use such questionable strategies? The answer lies in the driving need to produce something that is creative and attention getting. These ads may get attention, but it's the wrong kind of attention. Some of these ads have even generated action by governmental regulators, as well as outcries from the public.

This chapter, which is focused on advertising's role in society, will look at two topics: advertising regulation and advertising ethics. First we'll review the various types of regulation and regulatory bodies involved in overseeing the practice of advertising. Then, because ultimately the problem lies not with regulation but with a sense of professional ethics, we will review the key ethical issues that concern advertising practitioners.

ADVERTISING'S SOCIAL ROLE

Advertising takes place in a public forum in which business interests, creativity, consumer needs, and government regulations meet. Sometimes ads are controversial. And sometimes they are just bad, as the *Adweek* list illustrates. But some criticisms of advertising go deeper and take us to the core of advertising's visible social role.

The excessive, misleading, and false claims made by patent medicine makers in the early twentieth century generated the first regulation of advertising through the Pure Food and Drug Act of 1906. Advertising's economic role also has been criticized in the way it creates *demand,* which means people want or feel a need to buy and use a product. **Demand creation**, which means using an external message to drive people to feel a need or want, is an economic force that drives progress and the search for better products. Advertising plays an important role in creating and sustaining that force. Viagra™ is a good example of a product that exists only because advertising created demand for it. Demand creation becomes a question of ethics when social critics charge that the demand is artificial and the products really aren't needed—that people's wants are being manipulated unnecessarily.

Advertising is also a factor in the increased cost of branded products. Some argue that the costs are offset by the efficiencies that come from mass production and marketing, but economic as well as social and cultural concerns remain.

We know, however, that advertising also supports brands we like, as well as teaches us how to use new products that make our lives easier and our health better. Advertising is used in social marketing to support good causes. In and of itself, advertising is not evil. So why are there so many questions and dilemmas in looking at the social role of advertising? Although we believe advertising is a force for good in society, we will discuss the social concerns and ethical questions in order to provide a larger framework for a discussion of the role it plays in modern society.

Advertising's Role in Shaping or Mirroring Society

The second half of the twentieth century is notable for the rise of a materialistic consumer culture in the Western world. Did advertising create this culture, or did it simply reflect it? At what point does advertising cross the line between *reflecting* social values and *creating* them? Critics argue that advertising has repeatedly crossed this line, influencing vulnerable groups, such as children and young teenagers, too strongly.

This shape-versus-mirror debate is the most central issue we need to address in considering advertising's role in society. What drives consumers to behave or believe as they do? Is it advertising, or is it other forces? Why do women buy cosmetics, for example? Are they satisfying a deep cultural need for beauty or were they manipulated by advertising to believe in the hope that cosmetics offer? Or have their family and friends socialized them to believe they look better with cosmetics than without?

Can advertising manipulate people? In general, critics of advertising tend to believe that advertising has the power to shape social trends and the way people think and act. Some critics argue that advertising has the power to dictate how people behave. They believe that even if an individual ad cannot control our behavior, the cumulative effects of nonstop television, radio, print, Internet, and outdoor ads can be overwhelming.

On the other hand, advertising professionals tend to believe that the best they can do is spot trends and then develop advertising messages that connect with them. If people are interested in saving money, then you will see ads that use frugality as an advertising strategy. Advertisers believe advertising mirrors values rather than sets them.

In fact, advertising and society's values are probably interactive, so the answer to the debate may simply be that advertising *both* mirrors and shapes values. Advertising planners spend huge amounts of money and time trying to identify people's motivations before they develop message strategies. They must, then, be searching for something deeper than the impact of a previous ad.

We also know that advertising planners search for insights into consumer behavior. Do people save money for their retirement, or spend on more luxurious bathrooms—and why? What leads people to be concerned for their future financial health or encourages them to look upon their homes as "cocoons," a nest or place where they can retreat from the world? How interested are they in environmental issues? These tendencies are social trends that marketers and advertisers have found from their research and then used to develop advertising strategies.

Social and Cultural Considerations in International Advertising

Many oppose the move to a global perspective because of concerns about the homogenization of cultural differences. **Marketing imperialism** or **cultural imperialism** is a term used to describe what happens when Western culture is imposed on others, particularly cultures such as the Middle East, Asian, and African cultures. Some Asian and Middle Eastern countries are critical of what they see as America's materialism and disrespectful behavior toward women and elders. They worry that international advertising, as well as international media, will encourage their young people to adopt these viewpoints.

Cultural differences are very real and we will talk more about them in Chapter 5; consider, however, that respect for culture and local customs is so important that insensitivity to local customs can make an ad completely ineffective. Customs can be even stronger than laws. When advertising to children age 12 or over was approved in Germany, for example, local customs were so strong that companies risked customer revolt by advertising. In many countries, naming a competitor in comparative advertising, as we do, is considered bad form.

Customs are often more subtle and, as a result, are easier to violate than laws. Quoting an obscure writer or poet would be risky in the United States, where people would not respond to the unknown author. In Japan the audience would respect the advertiser for using the name or become embarrassed at not knowing a name they were expected to recognize. A campaign that made such a reference might irritate U.S. audiences and engage Japanese consumers.

Companies starting to do business in the Middle East have to learn new selling methods because the region is so devoutly religious. There are major restrictions on how women are presented in advertising. Many Asian cultures emphasize relationships and social, group, or community context. In some Asian cultures it is not considered proper for a young person to have direct eye contact with an older person; likewise, touching can be inappropriate. To be effective, the advertising message must recognize these cultural differences, and that can only be done by having as a partner a local agency or consultant who knows the culture well enough to identify potential cultural gaffes.

Consider This

1. If you were to develop your own definition or statement of advertising's social role, how would you word it based on what you have read?
2. What is cultural imperialism and how might that be a problem in international advertising?

REVIEW AND REGULATION OF ADVERTISING

Advertising is regulated or monitored by a number of bodies and groups. Figure 3.1 identifies the organizations with oversight responsibility for advertising and groups them in terms of five categories: government, media, industry, public or community groups, and the competition.

Advertising's Legal Environment

Let's look first at governmental oversight, which includes two topics: law and regulation. Congress legislates laws, while courts interpret those laws in specific situations to create case law. In this section, we examine two pivotal areas of case law—trademarks and copyright protection, and the First Amendment—as they pertain to advertising.

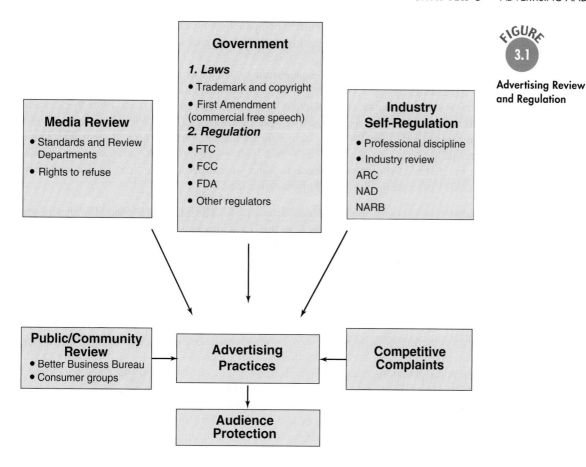

FIGURE
3.1

**Advertising Review
and Regulation**

Trademark and Copyright Protection   A **trademark** is a brand, corporate, or store name or a distinctive symbol that identifies the seller's brand and thus differentiates it from the brands of other sellers. A trademark must be registered through the Patent and Trademark Office of the Department of Commerce, which gives the organization exclusive use of the mark, as long as the trademark is maintained as an identification for a specific product. Under the Lanham Trademark Act of 1947, the Patent Office protects unique trademarks from infringement by competitors. Because trademarks are critical communication devices for products and services, they are important in advertising.

Even an audio trademark is protected, as a case in the European Union illustrates. A distinctive audio sound based on the noise of a cock crowing and the way it was represented in Dutch had been registered with the EU's trademark office. When this sound "trademark" was used by a different company, the first company sued for trademark infringement.[1]

A recent trademark issue is protection for uniform resource locators (URLs), which are Internet domain names. Advertisers must remember that URLs have to be registered and protected just like any other trademark. They are issued on a first-come, first-served basis for any domain name not identical to an existing brand name.[2]

A **copyright** gives an organization the exclusive right to use or reproduce original work such as an advertisement or package design for a period of time. Common designs or symbols, however, cannot be copyrighted. Controls for copyright protection are provided by the Library of Congress. Advertising is a competitive business in which me-too ads abound. Copyrighting of coined words, phrases, illustrations, characters, and photographs can offer some protection from other advertisers who borrow too heavily from their competitors.

Copyright infringement can occur when a product is used in an ad without proper permission. For example, the retailer Gap was sued by On Davis, a maker of high-priced metal eyewear, when the eyeglasses were used in a Gap ad without permission. The designer behind the glasses explained that he wanted Gap to not include his eyewear because his high-status glasses "aren't compatible in my mind with jeans and sweatshirts." He also claimed the image of his high-end fashion product was hurt by being associated with a mass retailer, such as Gap.[3]

Copycat ads that use the message strategy of another advertiser may also be subject to copyright infringement charges. For example, a commercial for a Sega NBA videogame was a scene-by-scene copy of Nike's "Frozen Moment" ad from 1996 that featured Michael Jordan. The spot shows fast-paced basketball action and then shifts to slow motion to show riveted fans neglecting things that are going on around them. The ad then returns to normal speed and closes with a Jordan slam dunk. Nike ads have been parodied in the past but the company choose to file a lawsuit because the Sega ad was not a commentary but rather a direct steal of a creative idea.[4]

Advertising and the First Amendment The most basic federal law that governs advertising is the First Amendment to the U.S. Constitution. The First Amendment states that Congress shall make no law "abridging the freedom of speech, or of the press." How have courts applied the First Amendment to advertising? First Amendment protection extends to **commercial speech**, which is speech that promotes commercial activity. However, that protection is not absolute; it is often restricted and the Supreme Court generally applies a different standard to commercial speech.

Protection of advertising as commercial speech has varied over the years. In 1980, in conjunction with its ruling on *Central Hudson Gas and Electric v. Public Service Commission of New York,* the Supreme Court established a test that determines to what extent the government can restrict advertising. This decision also stipulated the degree to which advertising is considered commercial speech.

A number of cases have attempted to change the common view of advertising as commercial speech. Most notably, the Supreme Court struck down a Massachusetts law that restricted tobacco advertising. Free speech advocates applauded the decision while critics of tobacco companies lamented. Although no one expects advertising to have the same constitutional protection of free speech that is given to individuals, courts throughout the country are narrowing the gap.

Although there is freedom in the United States for commercial free speech, it is not as widely valued as other forms of free speech such as that enjoyed by the press and filmmakers. The Supreme Court believes that there is a "commonsense difference" between commercial speech and other types, such as news; however, the "commonsense difference" is not defined and hard for advertisers to identify.[5]

In other words, the Supreme Court does permit some restrictions on commercial speech. For example, the Court has held that false or misleading commercial speech can be banned. Even truthful commercial speech can be restricted if the government can prove the public good demands such restrictions.[6] The courts have also ruled that such acts as the federal ban on junk faxes are valid and that businesses' right to commercial speech does not include printing their advertisements on other people's fax machines.[7]

Essentially, the Supreme Court has ruled that only truthful commercial speech is protected, not misleading or deceptive statements. Because the Supreme Court continues to reinterpret how the First Amendment applies in different cases, advertisers need to keep close track of legal developments. Table 3.1 lists some key First Amendment Court decisions that affect advertising.

Two recent cases show how varied First Amendment case law can be. The Supreme Court's 1996 decision in *44 Liquormart, Inc. v. Rhode Island* signaled strong protection for companies under the First Amendment. The Court struck down two Rhode Island statutes created to support the state's interest in temperance. Both statutes banned the advertisement of alcohol prices. The first statute prohibited advertising alcohol prices in the state except on signs. The second statute prohibited the publication or broadcast of alcohol price ads. The Supreme Court held that Rhode Island's statutes were unlawful because the ban abridged the First Amendment's guarantee of freedom of speech.

In contrast, a sharply divided (5–4) Supreme Court rejected a First Amendment challenge by California fruit growers who objected to part of a federal agricultural marketing

3.1	**First Amendment Rulings on Commercial Speech**

Valentine v. Christensen (1942)

First Amendment does not protect purely commercial advertising because that type of advertising does not contribute to decision making in a democracy.

Virginia State Board of Pharmacy v. Virginia Citizens Consumer Council (1976)

States cannot prohibit pharmacists from advertising prices of prescription drugs because the free flow of information is indispensable.

Central Hudson Gas & Electric Corporation v. Public Service Commission of New York (1980)

Public Service Commission's prohibition of promotional advertising by utilities is found to be unconstitutional, placing limitations on government regulation of unlawful, nondeceptive advertising.

Posadas de Puerto Rico Associates v. Tourism Company of Puerto Rico (1986)

Puerto Rican law banned advertising of gambling casinos to residents of Puerto Rico.

Cincinnati v. Discovery Network (1993)

Court ruled that the Cincinnati City Council violated the First Amendment's protection of commercial speech when it banned news racks of advertising brochures from city streets for aesthetic and safety reasons, while permitting newspaper vending machines.

Edenfield v. Fane (1993)

Court ruled that Florida's prohibition of telephone solicitation by accountants was unconstitutional.

44 Liquormart, Inc. v. Rhode Island (1996)

Court ruled that two Rhode Island statutes that banned advertising for alcohol prices were unconstitutional.

Glickman v. Wiliman Bros. (1997)

Court ruled that a mandatory generic advertising program, issued in accord with marketing orders of the Agricultural Marketing Act, did not infringe upon the free speech rights of fruit growers.

agreement that mandated they spend a certain amount of their federal money on generic product advertising and promotion (*Glickman v. Wiliman Bros. & Elliott, Inc.*). Does this decision diminish the protection of advertising under the First Amendment? Some legal experts contend that the focus on coerced speech rather than commercial speech suggests otherwise.

Nike has been involved in an important corporate speech case that involves a company's right to defend itself in the court of public opinion.[8] The issue revolves around a California Supreme Court ruling that Nike's public statements about its overseas labor practices were subject to claims of false and deceptive advertising. The press releases and ads in question said the company was doing a good job with its overseas labor practices but could do better. Nike's supporters said the California court's action amounted to applying a gag order—making it impossible for companies to respond to charges and defend themselves. The judge said that Nike's defense was no more than another form of advertising and deserved only limited First Amendment protection. Supporters of the Court's decision believe that advocacy press releases and ads should be subject to the same standards that govern other types of ads, and that includes review for possibly misleading and deceptive statements. As this chapter was written, this litigation is still working its way through the courts.

Changes in who sits on the Supreme Court as well as the makeup of the regulatory commissions can also influence the interpretation of First Amendment protection for advertisers.

Consider This

1. What are trademarks and copyrights and why is there legal protection for them?
2. Does your university or college have a legally protected trademark? How is it monitored?

ADVERTISING'S REGULATORY ENVIRONMENT

In addition to the Federal Trade Commission, the Food and Drug Administration and the Federal Communications Commission are dynamic components of the advertising regulatory environment. Let's look in more depth at their missions, and the type of advertising practices that they regulate.

The FTC

Established by Congress in 1914 to oversee business, the Federal Trade Commission (FTC) is the primary agency governing the advertising industry. Its main focus with respect to advertising is to identify and eliminate ads that deceive or mislead the consumer. Some FTC responsibilities are to

- initiate investigations against companies that engage in unfair competition or deceptive practices.
- regulate acts and practices that deceive businesses or consumers and issue cease-and-desist orders where such practices exist. Cease-and-desist orders require that the practice be stopped within 30 days (a cease-and-desist order given to one firm is applicable to all firms in the industry).
- fine people or companies that violate either (1) a trade regulation rule or (2) a cease-and-desist order given to any other firm in the industry.
- fund the participation of consumer groups and other interest groups in rule-making proceedings.[9]

Specifically, the FTC oversees false advertising of such items as foods, drugs, cosmetics, and therapeutic devices. That oversight includes such things as health and weight-loss business practices, 900 numbers, telemarketing, and advertising that targets children and the elderly. The FTC monitors the ratings system and the advertising practices of the film, music, and electronic games industries. Periodically it issues progress reports to Congress on youth-oriented entertainment advertising to make sure that ads for products with potentially objectionable content—primarily violent or sexual content—are not seen on media targeted to youth. The FTC's reports to Congress cover advertising on television and Web sites as well as print media.

The existence of a regulatory agency such as the FTC influences advertisers' behavior. Although most cases never reach the FTC, advertisers prefer not to risk long legal battles with the agency. Advertisers are also aware that competitors may complain to the FTC about a questionable advertisement. Such a move can cost the offending organization millions of dollars.

Table 3.2 lists important advertising legislation, most of which shows the growing authority of the FTC to regulate advertising.

Regulating Deception   Ultimately, advertisers want their customers to trust their products and advertising, so many take precautions to ensure that their messages are not deceptive, misleading, or unreasonable. **Deceptive advertising** is advertising intended to mislead consumers by making claims that are false or by failure to make full disclosure of important facts, or both. The current FTC policy on deception contains three basic elements:

1. *Misleading.* Where there is representation, omission, or practice, there must be a high probability that it will mislead the consumer.

TABLE

3.2 **Advertising Legislation**

Pure Food and Drug Act (1906)

Forbids the manufacture, sale, or transport of adulterated or fraudulently labeled foods and drugs in interstate commerce. Supplanted by the Food, Drug and Cosmetic Act of 1938; amended by Food Additives Amendment in 1958 and Kefauver-Harris Amendment in 1962.

Federal Trade Commission Act (1914)

Establishes the commission, a body of specialists with broad powers to investigate and to issue cease-and-desist orders to enforce Section 5, which declares that "unfair methods of competition in commerce are unlawful."

Wheeler-Lea Amendment (1938)

Prohibits unfair and deceptive acts and practices regardless of whether competition is injured; places advertising of foods and drugs under FTC jurisdiction.

Lanham Act (1947)

Provides protection for trademarks (slogans and brand names) from competitors and also encompasses false advertising.

Magnuson-Moss Warranty/FTC Improvement Act (1975)

Authorizes the FTC to determine rules concerning consumer warranties and provides for consumer access to means of redress, such as the "class action" suit. Also expands FTC regulatory powers over unfair or deceptive acts or practices and allows it to require restitution for deceptively written warranties costing the consumer more than $5.

FTC Improvement Act (1980)

Provides the House of Representatives and Senate jointly with veto power over FTC regulation rules. Enacted to limit the FTC's powers to regulate "unfairness" issues in designing trade regulation rules on advertising.

The Telemarketing and Consumer Fraud Act and Abuse Protection Act (1994)

Specifies that telemarketers may not call anyone who requests not to be contacted. Resulted in the Telemarketing Sales Rules.

2. ***Reasonableness.*** The perspective of the "reasonable consumer" is used to judge deception. The FTC tests reasonableness by looking at whether the consumer's interpretation or reaction to an advertisement is reasonable.
3. ***Injurious.*** The deception must lead to material injury. In other words, the deception must influence consumers' decision making about products and services.[10]

This policy makes deception difficult to prove because the criteria are rather vague and hard to measure. It also creates uncertainty for advertisers who must wait for congressional hearings and court cases to discover what the FTC will permit.

Regulating Substantiation   Claim substantiation is an area of particular concern to the FTC in determining whether or not an advertisement is misleading. The advertiser should have a reasonable basis for making a claim about product performance or run the risk of an FTC investigation. Food claims, such as those focused on calories or carbohydrates, have to be supported by research about nutrition. Consequently, an advertiser should always have data on file to substantiate any claims it makes in its advertisements. Also, it is best if this research is conducted by an independent research firm.

The FTC determines the reasonableness of claims on a case-by-case basis. In general, the FTC considers these factors:

• ***Type and specificity of claim made.*** For example, Computer Tutor claims you can learn the basics of using a computer by simply going through its three-CD set.
• ***Type of product.*** FedEx promises a certain delivery time, regardless of weather, mechanical breakdown, and so forth. This product has a great many uncontrollable variables compared to Heinz ketchup, which the company promises will be thick.

guess who's been counting carbs for over 85 years?

With 3 grams of net carbs per delicious serving," you can watch your carbs and still enjoy the consistently fresh taste of Planters.

*5g total carbs less 2g fiber (calorie free) = 3g net carbs. Remember to count calories. 170 calories/serving of peanuts.

PUT OUT THE
GOOD
STUFF.
planters.com

■ ■ ■
This ad for Planters Peanuts makes a claim of "3 grams of net carbs" that the company must be able to substantiate. Food marketers do extensive research in order to determine what health claims they can prove for their products.

• *Possible consequences of the false claims.* A Web site that claims it is secure can cause serious damage to its customers if, in fact, it is not secure.
• *Degree of reliance on the claims by consumers.* Business-to-business customers depend on the many claims made by their vendors. Therefore, if XPEDX (yes, that's how it's spelled), a manufacturer of boxes and other packages, claims in its ad that it can securely deliver any size product, it had better deliver.
• *The type and accessibility of evidence available for making the claim.* The type of evidence could range from testimonials from satisfied customers to complex product testing in multiple laboratories. It could be made available through an 800 number request or online.

Remedies for Deception and Unfair Advertising   The common sources of complaints concerning deceptive or unfair advertising practices are competitors, the public, and the FTC's own monitors. If a complaint seems justified, the commission can follow several courses of action: consent decrees, cease-and-desist orders, fines, corrective advertising, substantiation of advertising claims, and consumer redress.

• *Consent Decrees* A **consent decree** is the first step in the regulation process after the FTC determines that an ad is deceptive. The FTC simply notifies the advertiser of its finding and asks the advertiser to sign a consent decree agreeing to stop the deceptive practice. Most advertisers do sign the decree to avoid the bad publicity and the possible $10,000-per-day fine for refusing to do so.

Duracell® was forced to modify one of its ads after Energizer® complained that the ad inferred that Duracell CopperTop batteries would last three times longer than other heavy-duty and super-heavy-duty batteries. The ad didn't mention Energizer by name, but Energizer charged the ad was "false and misleading" because consumers would think the comparison was with other alkaline batteries, such as Energizer. In fact, the CopperTop does not last longer than other alkaline batteries. The ad was modified with a disclaimer.[11]

Sometimes the remedy can be more costly than simply modifying an ad. Federal marshals banned two health products—Crave Away and Aide Crème—after the company was accused of false advertising. According to the U.S. attorney's office, the products' claims weren't approved by the Food and Drug Administration (FDA) and hence they were "making false and unsubstantiated claims."[12]

• *Cease-and-Desist Orders* When the advertiser refuses to sign the consent decree and the FTC determines that the deception is substantial, it issues a **cease-and-desist order**. The process leading to the issuance of a cease-and-desist order is similar to a court trial. An administrative law judge presides. FTC staff attorneys represent the commission, and the accused parties are entitled to representation by their lawyers. If the administrative judge decides in favor of the FTC, the judge issues an order requiring the respondents to cease their unlawful practices. The advertiser can appeal the order to the full five-member commission.

• *Corrective Advertising* The FTC may require **corrective advertising** when consumer research determines that an advertising campaign has perpetuated lasting false beliefs. Under this remedy, the FTC orders the offending person or organization to produce messages for consumers that correct the false impressions the ad made. The purpose of corrective advertising is not to punish an advertiser but to prevent it from continuing to deceive consumers. The FTC may require a firm to run corrective advertising even if the campaign in question has been discontinued.

A landmark corrective advertising case is *Warner-Lambert v. FTC*. According to the FTC, Warner-Lambert's campaign for Listerine mouthwash, which ran for 50 years, had been deceiving customers, leading them to think that Listerine could prevent or reduce the severity of sore throats and colds. The company was ordered to run a corrective advertising campaign, mostly on television, for 16 months at a cost of $10 million. The case is significant for two reasons. First, the Supreme Court gave the FTC the power to apply remedies to both past and ongoing campaigns to curtail future deceptions. Second, the Court rejected the argument that corrective advertising violates the advertiser's First Amendment rights.

Interestingly, after the Warner-Lambert corrective campaign ran its course, 42 percent of Listerine users continued to believe that the mouthwash was being advertised as a remedy for sore throats and colds, and 57 percent of users rated cold and sore throat effectiveness as a key reason for purchasing the brand.[13] These results raised doubts about the effectiveness of corrective advertising and have affected recent court decisions.

The 1998 decision also prompted the commission (specifically Commissioner Orson Swindle) to publish a statement on the logic of the practice of corrective advertising. In addition to concurring that there is no evidence that corrective advertising works, Commissioner Swindle also noted that the assumption that corrective advertising should run the same length of time as the deceptive ad had run is erroneous.

• *Consumer Redress* The Magnuson-Moss Warranty-FTC Improvement Act of 1975 empowers the FTC to obtain consumer redress when a person or a firm engages in deceptive practices. The commission can order any of the following: cancellation or reformation of contracts, refund of money or return of property, payment of damages, and public notification.

• *Advertising Agency Legal Responsibility* With the resurgence of the FTC has come a new solution for deception within the FTC and in the federal courts: Make the ad agency liable instead of the advertiser. To quote former FTC chairperson Janet Steiger, "An agency that is involved in advertising and promoting a product is not free from responsibility for the content of the claims, whether they are expressed or implied. You will find the commission staff looking more closely at the extent of advertising involvement."[14] Essentially, an agency is liable for deceptive advertising along with the advertiser when the agency is an active participant in the preparation of the ad and knows or has reason to know that it is false or deceptive.

Agencies should heed the FTC's warnings. Several FTC actions and court cases in the early 1990s show that agencies must be prepared to defend their advertising practices. For example, a federal court found that Wilkinson, the maker of the Ultra Glide® shaving system, intended to make misleading claims about Gillette and halted the campaign. The court awarded Gillette damages of nearly $1 million, to be paid by Wilkinson, and another $1 million to be paid by Wilkinson's agency, Friedman Benjamin.

Consider This

1. What are the primary responsibilities of the FTC?
2. Do you think the remedies for deceptive and unfair advertising are adequate? Why or why not?

Food and Drug Administration

The Food and Drug Administration (FDA) is the regulatory division of the Department of Health and Human Services that oversees package labeling, ingredient listings, and advertising for food and drugs. It also determines the safety and purity of foods and cosmetics. In particular, the FDA is a watchdog for drug advertising, specifically in the controversial area of direct-to-consumer ads for prescription drugs. Its job is first to determine whether drugs are safe and then to see that these drugs are marketed in a responsible way. Marketing includes promotional materials aimed at doctors, as well as consumers.

For pharmaceutical companies, advertising is a commercial free speech issue and the industry has brought pressure on the FDA to make direct-to-consumer advertising rules for prescription drugs more understandable, simpler, and clearer.[15]

Federal Communications Commission

The Federal Communications Commission (FCC), formed in 1934 to protect the public interest in radio and television broadcast communications, can issue and revoke licenses to broadcasting stations. The FCC also has the power to ban messages, including ads, that are deceptive or in poor taste. The agency monitors only advertisements that have been the subject of complaints and works closely with the FTC to eliminate false and deceptive advertising. The FCC takes actions against the media, whereas the FTC is concerned with advertisers and agencies.

Other Regulatory Bodies

In addition to the FTC, the FDA, and the FCC, several other federal agencies regulate advertising. Most other federal agencies that regulate advertising are limited to a certain type of advertising, product, or medium, as we see in Table 3.3. We have already discussed the Patent Office and the Library of Congress and their roles in protecting copyrights and trademarks. Let's now look at other key regulatory agencies.

Bureau of Alcohol, Tobacco, and Firearms   The Bureau of Alcohol, Tobacco, and Firearms (BATF) within the Treasury Department regulates deception in advertising and establishes labeling requirements for the liquor industry. This agency's power comes from its authority to issue and revoke annual operating permits for distillers, wine merchants, and brewers. Because there is a danger that public pressure could result in the banning of all advertisements for alcoholic beverages, the liquor industry strives to maintain tight controls on its advertising.

The U.S. Postal Service   The Postal Service regulates direct-mail and magazine advertising and has control over the areas of obscenity, lotteries, and fraud. Consumers who receive advertisements in the mail that they consider sexually offensive can request that no more mail be delivered from that sender. The postmaster general also has the power to withhold mail that promotes lotteries. Fraud can include a number of activities that are questionable, such as implausible, get-rich-quick schemes.

The States' Attorneys General   The National Association of Attorneys General tries to regulate advertising at the state level. Members of this organization have successfully brought suits in their respective states against such advertising giants as Coca-Cola, Kraft, and Campbell Soup. More recently, numerous attorneys general have led the way against the tobacco industry and have supported the advertising restrictions discussed earlier.

International Laws and Regulations

As advertisers, agencies, and media become more and more global, it will be imperative that the players understand the local ethical standards and laws in the countries in which they operate.

Marketing practices, such as pricing and price advertising, vary in their legal and regulatory restrictions. Distribution is particularly troublesome in some local markets, partic-

TABLE

3.3   Specialized Government Agencies That Affect Advertising

Agency	Effect on Advertising
Federal Trade Commission www.ftc.gov	Regulates credit, labeling, packaging, warranties, and advertising.
Food and Drug Administration www.fda.gov	Regulates packaging, labeling, and manufacturing of food and drug products.
Federal Communications Commission www.fcc.gov	Regulates radio and television stations and networks.
U.S. Postal Service www.usps.gov	Controls advertising by monitoring materials sent through the mail.
Bureau of Alcohol, Tobacco, and Firearms www.atf.treas.gov	Division of the U.S. Treasury Department that regulates advertising for alcoholic beverages.
U.S. Patent Office www.uspto.gov	Oversees trademark registration to protect against patent infringement.
Library of Congress www.loc.gov	Provides controls for copyright protection.

ularly those that operate with many small retailers. In Japan, distribution arrangements are handled through long and complicated negotiations that often involve the participation of a local business partner. Such problems with pricing and distribution can affect the way a brand is presented and the brand image itself can be affected.

Some product categories, such as over-the-counter (OTC) drugs, are particularly difficult because regulations about their marketing and advertising are different in every country. There are also bans on advertising for certain types of products. Thailand has laws banning tobacco ads, as does Hungary. In Hong Kong, outdoor display advertising of tobacco products was banned. Malaysia has banned most forms of tobacco advertising, including print, TV, radio, and billboards. However, these bans are fairly ineffective as a result of **indirect advertising**—advertising that features a product other than the primary (controversial) product. Examples of these techniques in Malaysia are quite plentiful. Billboards with the Salem, Benson & Hedges, and Winston names dot the landscape, but they're not advertising cigarettes. They're advertising their travel, clothing, and restaurant businesses.

International advertisers do not fear actual laws; they fear not knowing those laws. For example, a marketer cannot advertise on television to children under 12 in Sweden or Germany, cannot advertise a restaurant chain in France, and cannot advertise at all on Sunday in Austria. In Malaysia, jeans are considered to be Western and decadent, and advertising for them is prohibited. A commercial can be aired in Australia only if it is shot with an Australian crew; likewise in Malaysia all the production has to be done in the country and the talent have to be Malaysians.

There also are differences in the legal use of various marketing communication tools. A contest or promotion might be successful in one country and illegal in another. Direct marketing is also considered an invasion of privacy in some European countries and is forbidden.

Because of the difficulty of understanding the legal situation in each country, international advertisers try to work with either local agencies or with international agencies that have local affiliates. The important thing is to have someone in the country who knows the local laws and can identify potential legal problems.

MEDIA REVIEW OF ADVERTISING

The media attempts to regulate advertising by screening and rejecting ads that violate their standards of truth and good taste. Most networks have a Standards and Practices Department that screens every ad and gives approval before the ad can run. Each individual medium has the discretion to accept or reject a particular ad. For example, *The Reader's Digest* does not accept tobacco and liquor ads, and many magazines and television stations do not show condom ads. In the case of the major television networks, the standards and guidelines designed by the Advertising Review Council (ARC), an industry group, serve as the primary standard.

The First Amendment gives any publisher the right to refuse to publish anything the company does not want to publish and this sometimes creates battles between media companies and advertisers. For example, some billboard companies in Utah are refusing to run billboards for a Wasatch Beer company brand named Polygamy Porter. The brand's slogan "Why have just one!" and headlines like "Take Some Home for the Wives" are deemed offensive to the state's Mormon population. A similar brouhaha arose when the state's Brighton Ski Resort promoted its four-person lifts with a billboard during the Salt Lake City Olympics that said, "Wife. Wife. Wife. Husband." The billboard company that banned the beer ads received letters both for and against its stand, which indicates the difficulty of such decisions.[16]

The FTC is pressuring magazines and newspapers, in particular, to stop running ads for weight-loss products that it says are misleading. Publishers, however, jealously guard their decision-making rights and resist being pressured by either government agencies or advertisers. But there are some debatable areas where the media have restricted advertising. For example, in 2003 a case was brought before the Superior Court of New Jersey demanding that an injunction be issued to keep CNN from refusing to run ads for the IDT telecommunication company. The IDT commercials claimed that its giant competitors—AT&T, Sprint, Verizon, and WorldCom—charge more because of bad business decisions and that's why IDT can charge less. IDT says the ban was discriminatory and contrary to the government's policy of encouraging competition.

More recently a political advocacy group, MoveOn, sponsored a contest to find the best commercial opposed to the George Bush presidency and hoped to run it during the Super Bowl. The winning ad, "Child's Play," was a polished, subtle, sobering spot questioning the Bush administration's rampant deficit spending. After the winner was named, CBS refused to air the ad claiming it was too controversial, even though it had accepted an ad from the White House.[17] A newspaper editorial that protested what it called the "myopic" CBS decision said it was sad that "outlandish propaganda spots by the White House were accepted but not a respectful, if hard-hitting, political ad."[18]

SELF-REGULATION

Rather than wait for laws and regulatory actions, responsible advertisers take the initiative and establish individual ethical standards that anticipate and even go beyond possible complaints. Such a proactive stance helps the creative process and avoids the kinds of disasters that result from violating the law or offending members of society.

Advertisers regulate themselves more stringently than do government agencies. There are three types of self regulation:

- *Self-discipline.* An organization, such as an advertising agency, develops, uses, and enforces norms within its own practices.
- *Industry self-regulation.* The industry develops, uses, and enforces norms.
- *Self-regulation with outside help.* The advertising industry voluntarily involves nonindustry people, such as the Better Business Bureau or the media, in the development, application, and enforcement of norms.

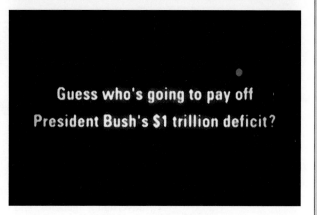

Guess who's going to pay off
President Bush's $1 trillion deficit?

Self-Discipline

Virtually all major advertisers and advertising agencies have in-house ad review procedures including reviews by agency and client attorneys. Typically the attorneys are concerned with the claims—how they are phrased and substantiated. Are the claims verifiable? Is there research and data to prove the truth of the claims? Is there anything in the wording that could be misinterpreted or is misleading? Is there anything deceptive in the visual images?

Several U.S. companies (Colgate-Palmolive, General Foods, AT&T) have their own codes of behavior and criteria that determine whether advertisements are acceptable. Companies without such codes tend to have informal criteria that they apply on an ad-by-ad basis. At a minimum, advertisers and agencies should have every element of a proposed ad evaluated by an in-house committee, lawyers, or both.

CBS refused to allow the MoveOn organization to buy space on the Super Bowl for an ad that won its anti-Bush advertising contest. What do you think: Should the media have the right to refuse political statements like these?

Industry Self-Regulation

In the case of both advertisers and advertising agencies, the most effective attempts at pure self-regulation have come through industry groups, such as the Advertising Review Council (ARC) and the Better Business Bureau (BBB). In 1971 several professional advertising associations in conjunction with the Council of Better Business Bureaus established the National Advertising Review Council, which negotiates voluntary withdrawal of national advertising that professionals consider deceptive. The National Advertising Division (NAD) of the Council of Better Business Bureaus and the National Advertising Review Board (NARB) are the two operating arms of the National Advertising Review Council. None of these are government agencies.

The NAD is a full-time agency made up of people from the field of advertising. It evaluates complaints submitted by consumers, consumer groups, industrial organizations,

The NARB Appeal Process
Consumers or groups submitting a complaint to NAD and NARB go through this process. The ultimate power of NAD and NARB is the threat of passing the claim to the FTC. Usually, cases are settled before that point.

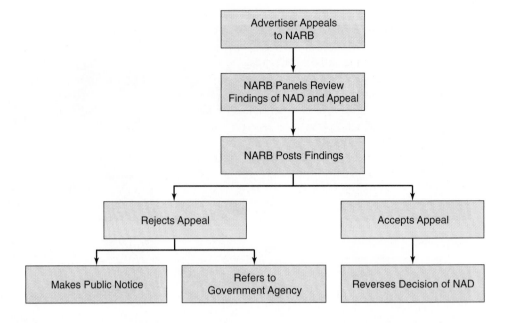

and advertising firms. NAD also does its own industry monitoring. After NAD receives a complaint, it may ask the advertiser in question to substantiate claims made in the advertisement. If such substantiation is deemed inadequate, NAD representatives ask the advertiser to change or withdraw the offending ad. When a satisfactory resolution cannot be found, NAD refers the case to NARB.

The NARB is a 50-member regulatory group that represents national advertisers, advertising agencies, and other professional fields. When the advertiser appeals a case to NARB, it faces a review panel of five people: three advertisers, one agency person, and one public representative. This NARB panel reviews the complaint and the NAD staff findings and holds hearings to let the advertiser present its case. If the case remains unresolved after the process, NARB can (1) publicly identify the advertiser and the facts about the case and (2) refer the complaint to the appropriate government agency (usually the FTC). Although neither NAD nor NARB has any real power other than threatening to invite government intervention, these groups have been effective in controlling cases of deception and misleading advertising. Figure 3.2 summarizes the NARB appeal process.

Competitive Complaints   Not only do the media and agencies screen ads; the competition is also on the lookout for deceptive claims and advertising strategies that reflect poorly on the brands. *Comparative advertising,* which we'll discuss later in this chapter, is a big red flag and advertisers that engage in this practice know that their research in support of their competitive claims has to be impeccable.

But there are other ways an advertisement can harm a brand. For example, Absolut Vodka pulled an ad after Vail Resorts threatened to sue. The ad showed the distinctive vodka bottle, which has been used for a decade, to put a twist on a visual pun in the shape of a cast for a broken leg. The words "Absolut Vail" were scrawled across it.[19]

Public and Community Review

The public is also involved in the advertising review process through actions by community, local business, and consumer activist groups.

- *Local Groups* At the local level, self-regulation has been supported by the Better Business Bureau (BBB). The BBB (www.bbb.org) functions much like the national regulatory agencies, and also provides local businesses with advice concerning the legal aspects of advertising. Approximately 250 local and national bureaus, made up of advertisers, agencies, and media, have screened hundreds of thousands of advertisements for possible violations of truth and accuracy. Although the BBB has no legal

power, it does receive and investigate complaints and maintain files on violators. It also assists local law enforcement officials in prosecuting violators. The ease with which the BBB can be accessed on the Internet has prompted businesses to be more careful about complying with its standards.
- **Consumer Activist Groups** Activist groups of all kinds monitor advertising practices. The Action for Children's Advertising group follows the practices of advertisers who market to children and will file complaints with industry boards or regulatory agencies if they see advertisements that they consider questionable. The consumer group Public Citizen inspired the FDA to require warnings on print ads for certain types of nicotine products. Groups that are focused on media literacy also review the performance of advertisers. For example, the Cultural Environment Movement is a nonprofit coalition of independent organizations and individuals that focuses on fairness, diversity, and justice in media communication.[20]

Consider This

1. In what ways does advertising regulate its own practices?
2. Do you think the advertising industry is sincere in trying to regulate its own practices? How could the industry prove to you that this is a serious industry-wide concern?

ADVERTISING ETHICS

Advertising law and regulations can only go so far in ensuring ethical practices by advertising. Ultimately professionals in the industry have to be guided by their own ethical principles. **Ethics** is a set of moral principles that guide actions and create a sense of responsible behavior. It's about being able to analyze ethical questions and dilemmas in professional decision making in terms of the concepts of right and wrong to determine one's obligation and responsibility to do the right thing.[21]

Is it ethical to include in an ad an offensive double meaning or illustrations that portray people in negative stereotypical situations? Is it all right to stretch the truth when making a claim about a product? Can you criticize a competitor's product even though you know it is basically the same as your own?

It's fairly easy to see the right answers in these situations. However, in most marketing and advertising decisions, the right path is not as easy to discern. Business ethics automatically refocus business decisions on a higher plane than the expediencies of the bottom line. McDonald's decision, for example, to eliminate its super-sized products is an example of doing the right thing even if it means losing some business opportunities.

To help you better understand how ethics applies to advertising decisions, we will discuss a variety of ethical issues that challenge the standards of advertising professionals. Then we'll conclude with a discussion of how an advertising professional makes ethical advertising decisions. We'll discuss six key issues: taste and offensive advertising, stereotyping, body and self-image problems, targeting strategies, problems with advertising claims and other message strategies, and the issues surrounding the marketing of controversial products.

Poor Taste and Offensive Advertising

Although certain ads might be in bad taste in any circumstance, viewer reactions are affected by such factors as sensitivity to the product category, the time the message is received (for example, in the middle of dinner), and whether the person is alone or with others when viewing the message. Some things on television, for example, that might not bother an adult when alone would make that person uncomfortable if children were watching. Also, questionable ads become offensive in the wrong context. Advertisers and media outlets must try to be sensitive to such objections.

We all have our own ideas about what constitutes good taste. Unfortunately, these ideas vary so much that creating general guidelines for good taste in advertising is difficult. Different things offend different people. In addition, taste changes over time. What was offensive yesterday may not be considered offensive today. A 1919 *Ladies' Home Journal* deodorant advertisement that asked the question, "Are you one of the many women who are troubled with excess perspiration?" was so controversial that 200 readers immediately canceled their subscriptions. By today's standards that advertisement seems pretty tame. Today's questions of taste center on the use of sexual innuendo, nudity, vulgarity, and violence.

The Breckenridge Ski Resort pulled an ad campaign that was designed to appeal to young men with lines like "The hill may dominate you. But the town will still be your bitch." Some young skiers in the resort's target market saw no problem with the language, although the campaign was criticized as distasteful by women's groups, community leaders, residents, and business leaders.[22]

One beer company was sued for violating public taste by using the slogan, "Good beer. No Shit." The argument against it charged that such language is offensive to many people and particularly inappropriate for children who cannot be protected from seeing and hearing the slogan.

Sex in Advertising   Although the use of sex in advertising is not new, the blatancy of its use is. Advertising that portrays women (or men) as sex objects is considered demeaning and sexist, particularly if sex is not relevant to the product. Ads for cosmetics and lingerie fall into a gray area because sex appeals for these products are usually relevant; the ethical question, then, is: How sexy is too sexy? Advertising Women of New York (AWNY) sponsors an annual award to showcase advertising that features women in sexist or offensive ways. The practice of using cheesy images is discussed in the Matter of Principle box.

Reinforcing Stereotypes

A **stereotype** is a representation of a cultural group that emphasizes a trait or group of traits that may or may not communicate an accurate representation of the group (blondes are dumb, Italians are sexy). Sometimes the stereotype is useful (athletes are fit) and aids communication by using easily understood symbolic meanings, but sometimes the stereotype relies on a characteristic that is negative or exaggerated and, in so doing, reduces the group to a caricature. That's what Nike accomplished with its ad lampooning the disabled.

Principle
Stereotyping is negative when it reduces a group of people to a caricature.

The issue of stereotyping also raises the shape-versus-mirror question. For example, stereotyping women as sex objects is a practice that is deeply embedded in our culture. When a woman is portrayed as a sex object in an advertisement it is reflecting or linking to a cultural value, however negatively some might see that value. On the other hand, using such a strategy also makes advertising a participant in shaping and reinforcing that cultural value.

Diversity Issues   If we believe that advertising has the ability to shape our values and our view of the world, then it is essential that advertisers become aware of how they portray different groups. Conversely, if we believe that advertising mirrors society, advertisers have a responsibility to ensure that what is portrayed is accurate and representative. Diversity has become an issue as advertisers struggle to target, as well as portray, people outside the white, straight mainstream market.

A few adventurous companies have even begun to show images suggesting homosexuality in advertising to general audiences through mass media. Such images have appeared fairly extensively in mainstream fashion advertising for brands such as Calvin Klein, Benetton, and Banana Republic. The coming-out episode of ABC's *Ellen* was groundbreaking in more ways than just programming: It was the first time advertisers used prime-time network TV to reach gay and lesbian viewers.

Commercial Closet is a nonprofit journalistic and educational organization that seeks to raise awareness about how the gay community is portrayed in advertising. Its Web site primarily analyzes mainstream commercials that represent the gay community as a minor-

A MATTER OF PRINCIPLE
Cheesecake or Good Targeting?

Women have appeared partially undressed on calendars and other advertising for decades. However, the use of what's sometimes called a "cheesecake" strategy has come under fire from women for just as long a time. This is one practice that continues to challenge the industry because the technique tends to succeed at getting the attention of men who are the target for these ads.

So what if it offends women? They aren't the target, right? Like most ethical questions, this one gets caught up in business decisions.

The issue got a new life recently when several beer advertisers began running ads with scantily clad women. The one that got the most criticism was a Miller Light commercial aimed at male sports fans and called "catfight," which was the winner of the "Grand Ugly" award by the Advertising Women of New York (AWNY) for portraying women in the most offensive manner (see it at aef.com museum under the "Good, Bad, and Ugly" awards).

The spot, which was presented as a fantasy dreamed up by two guys in a bar, was described by *Adweek* critic Barbara Lippert as showing "two buxom bimbos" in swimsuits mud-wrestling, a match that degenerated into something she described as having lesbian overtones. To try to keep it on the side of political correctness, the girlfriends of the two guys at the bar looked on with scorn as their guys enjoyed the fantasy play.

It isn't just in the United States where concern about sexism has to be considered by advertisers. In France, where nudity in advertising has been much more acceptable, the advertising industry has agreed to a tough new code of conduct to ensure "respect for the dignity of women" and has set up a hot line for the public to use to complain if they are offended by vulgarity or sexism.

The issue is whether the sex appeal is gratuitous; in other words, is it relevant to the product? Even if it is relevant—and some will argue that sexy "babes" appeal to beer-drinking males—does it degrade women (or men, in those cases where a "hunk" is used to appeal to women)? What's degrading to one person may not be offensive to another, so this decision needs to be made based on research that determines whether most people believe it to be degrading or offensive. Finally, is the brand meaning sullied when the advertising uses cheesecake?

Consider This

1. What are the ethical issues underlying debates about sexism in advertising?
2. Do you think marketers whose products are targeted at young men should also consider the reactions of women when reviewing an advertising idea that might be considered sexist? Why or why not?

Sources: John Lichfield, "French Advertisers Promised a Cover-up in Battle over Nudity," *The Independent* (November 29, 2003): 17; Hillary Chura, "Miller Set to Roll Catfight Sequels," *Advertising Age* (February 17, 2003): 1, 35; Hillary Chura, "Miller: Another Round of Raunch," *Advertising Age* (March 17, 2003): 1, 30; Lisa Sanders, "'Catfight' Wins AWNY 'Grand Ugly' Ad Award," *Advertising Age* (April 1, 2003); Christopher Lawton, "Miller, Coors Still Bet Sex Sells Beer," *Wall Street Journal* (June 10, 2003): B3; Barbara Lippert, "'Taste'-less," *Adweek* (January 20, 2003): 16.

ity. The Commercial Closet Web site is devoted to "raising awareness of something no one has thought of before: How the gay community is portrayed as a minority group in advertising."

Gender Roles   Television is a powerful socializing agent and is particularly influential in the area of gender identity. One of the most important lessons it teaches is how people fit into culturally shared gender and racial roles. The way women are cast as characters in commercials, as well as programs, can create or reinforce cultural stereotypes.[23]

Historically, advertising has portrayed gender in distinct and predictable stereotypes. Men are usually shown as strong, independent, and achievement oriented; women are shown as nurturing and empathetic, but softer and more dependent, and they are told that the products being advertised will make their lives less stressful and more manageable. Men are often negatively stereotyped as well. For example, in a Wyeth Flu-mist® ad, a bumbling dad sends his kids to school in summer clothes during a snowstorm, and in a Honda Pilot ad, the father acts like a drooling wolf. The Society for the Prevention of Misandry in the Media has been formed to protest such silly portrayals.[24]

Harmful female stereotypes take a number of forms. Women are portrayed as indecisive, childlike, frivolous, and only interested in shopping; obsessed with men or their own physical appearance; submissive to men; or simple housewives, superwomen, and sexual objects. Such stereotypes aren't just the province of beer and tire ads. An example of an upscale advertisement that plays with women's stereotypes is a newspaper ad for IWC Schaffhausen, a high-end Swiss watch. The headline says, "Almost as complicated as a woman. Except it's on time." The ad ran in the *London Times,* among other prestigious publications.

A study of gender representation in 1,300 prime-time commercials in the late 1990s found that although women make most purchases of goods and services, they are still underrepresented as primary characters during most prime-time commercials, except for health and beauty products. Women are still cast as younger, supportive counterparts to men. Older women are still the most underrepresented group. Television commercials, in other words, still perpetuate traditional stereotypes of women and men.[25]

However, some advertisers are recognizing the diversity of women's roles. But with the effort to portray women as more than housewives came a different problem. Beginning in the 1980s, advertisements focused on briefcase-toting professional women. Consider the commercial in which a NASA engineer, who is also a working mother, tells us the benefits of serving her children a powdered breakfast drink. The image of Supermom has been displaced by the image of Superwoman.

A Chicago conference hosted in 2003 by the Advertising Educational Foundation asked, "How Is Advertising Shaping the Image of Women?"[26] The answer, in spite of the number of women moving into leadership positions in the advertising industry, is that advertising doesn't seem to be any freer of sexual stereotypes. University of Illinois professor Linda Scott said that although things had been improving, ground has been lost in the last 10 years.

Racial and Ethnic Stereotypes   Critics charge that racial and ethnic groups are stereotyped in advertising. Even though most in the industry would deny it, that charge was evident in the "Just for Feet" ad that showed a black man being hunted down like a wild animal. In one study of the prototypical images of African Americans, the researchers found that blacks are portrayed in commercials as staying in the background and having little to say (except in ads designed exclusively for black publications). Men are athletic, tall, dark, handsome, fashionable, outgoing, and not family connected. Women like to shop and are seen as fair-skinned with wavy hair, quiet, petite, and supportive. The most frequently used black images are of black children or teenagers.[27]

A study of Asians in television commercials found that they were treated similarly to females in general. In other words, they were underrepresented and given lesser roles. Even the more frequent use of younger Asian characters isn't culturally sensitive.

One myth is that members of minority groups are all the same. The Hispanic market is a case in point. In 2000 the Hispanic population in the United States was over 30 million, 15 percent of the total. Still, there is a misconception that all Hispanic consumers are alike, when nothing could be further from the truth: There are major differences in groups whose ancestry is Spanish, Mexican, Cuban, Puerto Rican, or from a South American country, such as Colombia or Argentina.

Senior Citizens   Another group that critics say is often subject to stereotyping is senior citizens, a growing segment of the population with increasing amounts of disposable income. Critics often object to the use of older people in roles that portray them negatively.

Barbara Champion, president of Champion & Associates, a research firm specializing in the maturing market, made the following observation: "The needs of maturing consumers, depending on mental and physical acuity as well as life-stage factors, are often different from one another. Whether a consumer is an empty-nester whose children have grown up and left home, a grandparent, a retiree, a widow, or one in need of assisted living, for example, will greatly affect how, when, and why goods and services are purchased."[28] Many of the ads for Viagra speak to a specific segment of the population, and do so in a tasteful, tactful way.

In a focus group of women in their 50s, participants had trouble keeping their comments polite when viewing a series of health care ads that showed older women in primarily sedentary activities. One explained that even though she has arthritis, she still wants to see ads show arthritis sufferers working out in a gym, rather than "silver-haired couples walking along the beach with a golden retriever."[29]

Consider This

1. What ethical values does the use of stereotyping violate?
2. Do you think stereotyping is a real problem or are some people overly concerned about political correctness? Defend your viewpoint.

Body Image and Self-Image

Advertising has been criticized for glorifying glamorous looks in both men and women. In an interview on NPR, author Jean Kilbourne, who is the author of *Can't Buy My Love: How Advertising Changes the Way We Think and Feel,* said that "ads are aimed at the very heart of girls' insecurities" because of the ideal image of beauty that they portray—"an absolutely perfect-looking young woman who's incredibly thin."[30]

Playing on consumers' insecurities about their appearance presents advertisers with a classic ethical dilemma because self-image advertising can also be seen as contributing to self-improvement. Sometimes, however, such strategies are questionable because they lead to dangerous practices. Some critics charge that women place their health at risk in order to cultivate an unrealistic or even unhealthy physical appearance.

To discover how flagrant or subtle this message is, a group of researchers tested the "thin ideal" on college-age women, the group most vulnerable to this message and to high incidences of eating disorders. They found that students did not perceive any danger in advertisements using excessively thin fashion models as a stereotypical portrayal of beauty. The respondents in the study reacted strongly to other female stereotypes but were far less concerned about images promoting the "thin ideal." The authors concluded that although there are many female stereotypes used in advertising that are irritating, offensive, and demeaning, none is potentially more dangerous to health than the "thin ideal."[31]

The same problem of stereotyping based on physical appearance exists for men, particularly young men, although the muscular body ideal—V-shaped body with a well-developed chest and arm muscles and wide shoulders tapering down to a narrow waist—may not lead to the same health-threatening reactions that young women face, unless men resort to steroids. Other stereotyped male images are the rugged western Marlboro man and the clueless Dagwood type.

The standard of attractiveness is a sociocultural phenomenon that advertising mirrors, as well as shapes. Responsible advertisers have, therefore, begun using models of more normal size and weight as a way to reduce the pressure on young people, who seem to be the most open to messages about cultural standards of beauty and physical attractiveness.

Targeting Children

As the earlier story about the Breckenridge Ski Resort illustrated, an ad can be offensive to the general public even if it's accepted by the target audience. Advertisers would be wise to conduct the necessary research to gauge the standards of taste for the general population as well as the specific target audience.

Because mass media are seen or read by people outside the target audience, such testing can be tricky. The problem is that if you aim to satisfy everyone, you may not connect with the primary target audience. This is a serious dilemma in creating advertising, and one not easily resolved. An even more serious problem is targeting vulnerable groups, such as children.

Advertising to children continues to be one of the most controversial topics in the industry. After a 1988 study found that the average child saw more than 20,000 TV commercials per year, a heated debate ensued. One side favored regulation because of children's inability to evaluate advertising messages and make purchase decisions. The other side opposed regulation because members of that group believed many self-regulatory mechanisms already existed and the proper place for restricting advertising to children was in the home.

In response, the FTC initiated proceedings to study possible regulations of children's television. Despite the FTC's recommendations, the proceedings did not result in new federal regulations until 1990. In the interim, self-regulation in the advertising industry tried to fill this void.

The National Advertising Division (NAD) of the Council of Better Business Bureaus set up a group charged with helping advertisers deal with children's advertising in a manner sensitive to children's special needs. The Children's Advertising Review Unit (CARU), established in 1974, evaluates advertising directed at children under the age of 12.

In 1990 Congress passed the Children's Television Advertising Practice Act, which placed 10.5-minute-per-hour ceilings for commercials in children's weekend television programming and 12-minute-per-hour limits for weekday programs. The act also set rules requiring that commercial breaks be clearly distinguished from programming, barring the use of program characters to promote products.

Advocates for children's television continue to argue that many stations made little effort to comply with the 1990 act and petitioned the FCC to increase the required number of educational programs to be shown daily. In 1996, broadcasters, children's advocates, and the federal government reached an agreement requiring all TV stations to air three hours of children's educational shows a week.

Marketing alcohol to black teens is an issue because of the use of rappers like Ice-T to promote malt liquors and the dozens of pages of alcohol ads that appear in black youth-culture magazines such as *Vibe*. A Georgetown University study says the alcohol beverage industry is marketing far more heavily to African American young people than to others in that age group.

Misleading Claims and Other Message Strategies

Advertising claims are considered to be unethical if they are false, misleading, or deceptive. We talked about misleading and deceptive ads in the discussion of FTC regulation. In the drive to find something to say about a product that will catch attention and motivate the audience to respond, advertisers sometimes stretch the truth. *False advertising*, which is a type of misleading advertising, is simply untrue.

For an example of false and deceptive advertising, consider how Sony Pictures made the *Adweek* losers list after it invented a movie reviewer named David Manning. The mythical reviewer, of course, gave Sony's pictures great reviews. *Newsweek* investigated and Sony Pictures admitted its marketing department had invented Manning. As *Adweek* observed, overnight he went from "poster personality to a poster boy for deceptive advertising." The state of Connecticut launched an investigation into a potential violation of its Unfair Trade Practices Act.

The target of the heaviest criticism for being misleading is weight-loss advertising, as well as other back-of-the-magazine self-improvement advertisements for health and fitness products. In a study of 300 weight-loss ads, the FTC found that ads for weight-loss products sometimes make "grossly exaggerated" claims and that dieters need to beware of ads for dietary supplements, meal replacements, patches, creams, wraps, and other products. The study found that 40 percent of the ads made at least one representation that was almost certainly false and 55 percent made a claim that was very likely false or at least lacked adequate substantiation.[32]

Misleading claims are not just a problem in the United States. The London-based Barclays credit card company was forced (by the U.K. Office of Fair Trading, which is equivalent to the FTC in the U.S.) to withdraw an advertising campaign that promised "0 percent forever." The ad was deemed deceptive because borrowers would enjoy the 0 percent interest rate for only as long as it took for the balance to be cleared. In other words, all new spending on the card would be charged the standard interest rate.[33]

Manipulative Advertising   Most advertising is designed to create demand and touch the emotions. So in a sense, a manipulative message is a natural outcome of persuasion. However, there are times and situations where ethical issues arise. For example, there can be manipulative ads that play on the emotions in order to create inappropriate or overly intense feelings. A radio commercial that recorded the last moments of a child and his father before they died in a car accident was criticized as emotionally manipulative, even though the ad was part of a buckle-up campaign.

Another area that gets attention in the media is subliminal advertising. Generally, we assume that messages are seen and heard consciously. However, it is also possible to communicate symbols that convey meaning but are below the threshold of normal perception. These kinds of messages are called subliminal. A **subliminal message** is transmitted in such a way that the receiver is not consciously aware of receiving it. This usually means that the symbols are too faint or too brief for the consumer to clearly recognize them. We'll discuss subliminal advertising in terms of how it works, or doesn't work, in the next chapter.

Puffery   Not all exaggerated claims are seen as misleading. **Puffery** is defined as "advertising or other sales representations, which praise the item to be sold with subjective opinions, superlatives, or exaggerations, vaguely and generally, stating no specific facts."[34] Campbell Soup, for example, has used the slogan "America's Favorite Food," which is vague and exaggerated and can't really be proven or disproved. It's a classic example of puffery, generally deemed to be of little concern to regulators looking for false or misleading claims because it is so innocuous.

Because obviously exaggerated "puffing" claims are legal, the question of puffery is mainly an ethical one. According to the courts, consumers expect exaggerations and inflated claims in advertising, so reasonable people wouldn't believe that these statements ("puffs") are literal facts. Virtually everyone is familiar with puffery claims for certain products: Sugar Frosted Flakes are "g-r-r-eat," send Hallmark cards if you "want to send the very best," and "nothing outlasts an Eveready battery."

However, empirical evidence on the effectiveness of puffery is mixed. Some research suggests that the public might expect advertisers to be able to prove the truth of superlative claims, and other research indicates that reasonable people do not believe such claims. Advertisers must decide what claims are and are not socially responsible and when the puffery is unbelievable or over the top.[35]

Principle
Puffery may be legal, but if it turns off the target audience then nothing is gained by using such a message strategy.

The Uniform Commercial Code (UCC), a set of laws that govern sales and other commercial matters, distinguishes between mere "puffing" and statements about a product's performance or qualities that create an "express warranty." Under the UCC, a general statement praising the value of a product (such as "the Best Seafood Restaurant") does not create an express warranty. More concrete representations, however, might (for instance, "our fish are never frozen").

The UCC recognizes that advertisers cannot be expected to prove or live up to every general, glorifying statement made about a product. After all, it's only a company's opinion that its product is the best on the market. No one would want to, or could, prove the reasonableness or rationality of such opinions. However, a proposed draft of UCC sections relating to express warranties would make all statements about a product part of the sale agreement. This could mean that all product statements create an express warranty, which could transform advertising as we know it.

Comparative Advertising   Although it is perfectly legitimate to use **comparative advertising** that compares the advertiser's product favorably against a competitor, there are regulations for those uses that are challenged as misleading. Advertisers face the common threat that competitors will misrepresent their products, prices, or some other attributes.

■ ■ ■

This TV commercial demonstrates the acceleration speed of the Volvo 850 Turbo Sportswagon compared to the BMW 328i. What legal issues do you think the company and its agency had to consider with this type of ad?

While no one expects a competitor to be totally objective, there are certain guidelines for protecting advertisers from unfair comparisons. The Lanham Act seeks damages from an advertiser who "misrepresents the nature, characteristics, qualities, or geographic origin in comparative advertising."

Comparative advertising is permitted in the United States, but the ads must compare similar products. Also, companies can't claim that their prices are lower than the competition unless they can prove that the same products are sold at other places for higher prices. Under the Lanham Act, companies or plaintiffs are required to prove five elements to win a false advertising lawsuit about an ad containing a comparative claim. They must prove that:

1. False statements have been made about either product.
2. The ads actually deceived or had the tendency to deceive a substantial segment of the audience.
3. The deception was "material" or meaningful. In other words, the plaintiff must show that the false ad claim is likely to influence purchasing decisions.
4. Falsely advertised goods are sold in interstate commerce.
5. The suing company has been or likely will be injured as a result of the false statements, by either loss of sales or loss of goodwill.

In addition to the Lanham Act, consumers also may rely on state laws governing unfair competition and false ad claims if the consumer is the victim of a false comparative claim. In California, for example, the Business and Professional Code prohibits "unlawful, unfair, or fraudulent business practices" and "unfair, deceptive, untrue, or misleading" advertising.

| TABLE 3.4 | American Association of Advertising Agencies' Ten Guidelines for Comparative Advertising |

1. The intent and connotation of the ad should be to inform and never to discredit or unfairly attack competitors, competing products or services.

2. When a competitive product is named, it should be one that exists in the marketplace as significant competition.

3. The competition should be fairly and properly identified but never in a manner or tone of voice that degrades the competitive product or service.

4. The advertising should compare related or similar properties or ingredients of the product, dimension to dimension, feature to feature.

5. The identification should be for honest comparison purposes and not simply to upgrade by association.

6. If a competitive test is conducted, it should be done by an objective testing service.

7. In all cases the test should be supportive of all claims made in the advertising that are based on the test.

8. The advertising should never use partial results or stress insignificant differences to cause the consumer to draw an improper conclusion.

9. The property being compared should be significant in terms of value or usefulness of the product to the consumer.

10. Comparisons delivered through the use of testimonials should not imply that the testimonial is more than one individual's, unless that individual represents a sample of the majority viewpoint.

Source: James B. Astrachan, "When to Name a Competitor," Adweek (May 23, 1988): 37. Copyright American Association of Advertising Agencies. Reprinted by permission.

The American Association of Advertising Agencies has 10 guidelines that advertisers should follow to ensure truthful comparative advertising. These are shown in Table 3.4.

Endorsements A popular advertising strategy is the use of a spokesperson who endorses a brand; that's a perfectly legal strategy, unless the endorser doesn't actually use the product. An **endorsement** or **testimonial** is any advertising message that consumers believe reflects the opinions, beliefs, or experiences of an individual, group, or institution. However, if consumers can reasonably ascertain that a message does not reflect the announcer's opinion, the message isn't an endorsement and may even be misleading.

Because many consumers rely on endorsements to make buying decisions, the FTC investigates endorsement advertising. Endorsers must be qualified by experience or training to make judgments and they must actually use the product. If endorsers are comparing competing brands, they must have tried those brands as well. Those who endorse a product improperly may be liable if the FTC determines there is a deception.

Demonstrations Product demonstrations in television advertising must not mislead consumers. This mandate is especially difficult for advertisements of food products because such factors as hot studio lights and the length of time needed to shoot the commercial can make the product look unappetizing. Think about the problems of shooting ice cream under hot lights. Because milk looks gray on television, advertisers often substitute a mixture of glue and water. The question is whether the demonstration falsely upgrades the consumers' perception of the advertised brand. The FTC evaluates this kind of deception on a case-by-case basis.

One technique some advertisers use to sidestep restrictions on demonstrations is to insert disclaimers or "supers"—verbal or written words in the ad that indicate exceptions to the advertising claim made. One example is a 30-second spot for Chrysler's Jeep Cherokee that begins with bold shots of the vehicle and music swelling in the background. Suddenly, the message is less clear; for several seconds five different, often lengthy disclaimers flash on the screen in tiny, eye-straining type, including "See dealers for details and guaranteed claim form" and "Deductibles and restrictions apply."

Consider This

1. What is the biggest ethical problem that advertising claims may face?
2. Evaluate the potential of comparative advertising, endorsements, and demonstrations to cause ethical problems. In each case, what would you look for as a "red flag"?

Advertising Controversial Products

Principle
The ethical responsibility for selling a controversial or unsafe product lies with the marketing department; however, advertising is often in the spotlight because it is the visible face of marketing.

Advertising reflects the marketing and business ethics of its clients and, because of its visibility, sometimes gets the blame for selling controversial, unsafe, or dangerous products. For example, products that were once considered not suitable to advertise—such as firearms, gambling, hemorrhoid preparations, feminine-hygiene products, pantyhose and bras, laxatives, condoms, and remedies for male erectile dysfunctions—have become acceptable, although advertising for them may still be offensive to some people.

Unhealthy or Dangerous Products   Before an agency can create an ad for a client, it must consider the nature of the client company and its mission, marketing objectives, reputation, available resources, competition, and, most importantly, product line. Can the agency and its staff honestly promote the products being advertised? Several agencies have resigned from profitable tobacco-advertising accounts, for example, because of the medical evidence about the harm cigarettes cause. But obviously not every agency has made the same decision. In cases where the agency works on a controversial account, there are still ethical ways to approach the business. One way to make ethical decisions is to choose the route that does no one harm.

Because there has been so much negative publicity about the health effects of eating a steady diet of heavily processed food, food companies—particularly fast-food producers such as McDonald's and KFC—have reacted to charges of culpability in the nation's obesity problem. Kraft, for example, pulled a TV commercial for its Oreo cookies because it portrayed a too-sedentary lifestyle that is not in line with the company's new set of advertising guidelines. The company also has allocated millions of dollars to fund public-education projects about nutrition and obesity and launched a variety of what the company claims are healthier versions of existing products.[36]

The point is that marketers are now being forced to consider the social, as well as nutritional, impact of their products. It used to be that consumers were considered responsible for the products they chose to buy, but in a new era of social responsibility, principled marketers are now more responsible for the negative effects of the products they choose to sell. Responsibility has become a new business principle in some industries that never thought they were the focus of ethical questions.

Tobacco   One of the most heated advertising issues in recent years has been proposed new restrictions on the advertising of tobacco. Cigarette advertising on television and radio has been banned since 1971. Proponents of the ban on cigarette advertising argue that since cigarettes have been shown to cause cancer as well as other illnesses, encouraging tobacco use promotes sickness, injury, or death for the smoker and those inhaling second-hand smoke. The restriction of advertising on those products would result in fewer sales and fewer health problems for America as a whole.

In recognition of the growing public concerns about cigarette marketing, tobacco companies have voluntarily curbed their advertising and pulled ads from magazines with high levels of youth readership and from most outdoor billboards. Most major tobacco companies also run antismoking ads aimed at teenagers. Critics charge that these efforts aren't enough.

Opponents of advertising bans counter with the argument that prohibiting truthful, nondeceptive advertising for a legal product is unconstitutional. They feel that censorship is more of a problem than advertising a legal, although unhealthful, product. Opponents of the ban also cite statistics demonstrating that similar bans in other countries have proved unsuccessful in reducing tobacco sales.

In 1996 the FDA established a set of restrictions applicable to tobacco advertisers. Among these were a ban on outdoor ads within 1,000 feet of a school or playground and a rule that limited ads to black-and-white, text only, in magazines with 55 percent readership under the age of 18. The restrictions also stipulated that $150 million be provided to fund antismoking ads targeting children. Following the 1996 action, 46 states have received initial payments from the $206 billion Master Settlement Agreement to be supplied by tobacco companies over a 25-year period. Approximately half the money goes to fund TV and print ads warning children about the dangers of smoking; the other half pays for promotions such as loyalty cards, all-expenses-paid teen summits, and various events.[37]

Banning tobacco advertising is not unique to the United States. In fact such restrictions are even greater in Europe and Asia. More than 20 countries in Europe have adopted prohibitions or outlawed tobacco advertising.[38] A near-total advertising ban in the United Kingdom took effect in early 2003 and in 2005 a similar European Union ban will take effect.

Alcohol Television advertising for liquor hasn't been banned; however, there has been a voluntary restriction on such advertising by the companies themselves and most networks have also refused to accept alcohol advertising. However, in 2002 Smirnoff broke the taboo and began running "responsible drinking" ads on *Saturday Night Live* and *Comedy Central.*

The biggest issue for the spirits industry, however, is charges of advertising to underage drinkers. In 2003 the FTC became so concerned that it asked a number of the major companies to detail their marketing practices and target audiences, as well as explain how they had implemented the promises made in the FTC's 1999 report to Congress.[39] About the same time a lawsuit filed in the District of Columbia charged that alcohol marketers are actively engaged in trying to establish brand loyalty among underage consumers.[40]

Liquor executives contend that they will follow voluntary advertising guidelines to avoid images and time slots that appeal to kids. That promise has been hard to keep because every major brand is trying to win over young consumers.

The beer industry has been the target of strong criticism for several years. Anheuser-Busch pulled its beer advertising from MTV to avoid drawing fire for marketing to underage drinkers, and moved its spots to VH-1, a similar network that targets 25- to 49-year-olds. This decision was partly the result of a study by *Advertising Age* that tracked MTV commercial viewership and found that 50 percent of the viewers were underage.[41] Although it is unlikely that beer advertising will be banned, some companies sensitive to public opinion have initiated proactive programs that educate and discourage underage drinkers.

Prescription Drugs In 1997 the FDA loosened its controls on pharmaceutical companies, and as a result, the amount of prescription drug advertising has skyrocketed. While these print and TV ads have proven very successful in terms of increased sales, various consumer groups, government agencies, and insurance companies have been quite critical of them. In one study, for example, the National Institute of Health Care Management found that direct-to-consumer prescription advertising has led to an increase in requests for costlier drugs, when the less expensive generic drug would be just as effective.[42]

Also, some doctors claim that they are being pressured to write inappropriate prescriptions because their patients are influenced by the drug ad claims; other doctors appreciate that the advertising has caused consumers to become more active in managing their own health and more informed about their drug options.

Consider This

1. In your opinion, what is the most critical ethical issue faced by advertising professionals?

2. What is advertising's role in the advertising of controversial, unsafe, and dangerous products? Explain how you arrived at your answer.

SHOWCASE

To solve a local image crisis, Shell used a campaign based on the slogan "Shell—with you all the way." The campaign demonstrated how Shell was involved and "traveled" with you from youth to adulthood, from your work to your home, from the present to the future and to the end of your destination—shaping society that you wanted to build, with you. This ad was contributed by Ingvi Logason, principal in HER&NU, Reykjavik, Iceland, who got his degree in advertising from Western Florida University.

DETERMINING WHAT IS ETHICAL

How do we evaluate advertising's ethical performance? There are laws and regulations governing the practice of advertising, but there are also codes of conduct, as well as personal and professional decision-making guidelines. One set of guidelines spells out these three types of criteria that need to be considered when making an advertising decision.[43]

1. **The social ethic**. The Golden Rule (Do unto others as you would have them do unto you.)
2. **The professional ethic**. What would be viewed as proper by an objective panel of my professional colleagues?
3. **The personal ethic**. Would I feel comfortable explaining this action to the general public on TV? (A variation is: Would I be comfortable explaining this decision to my mother?)

The Social Ethic

Our concept of right and wrong is based on moral rules, personal and professional standards, and cultural values. In Western cultures the values most often association with ethics are morality, honesty, virtue, fairness, respect, and integrity. The Golden Rule—do unto others as you would have them do unto you—is a cardinal principle of ethics. On another level responsibility based on the Golden Rule could be rephrased as "do no harm."

Looking at ethics from the opposite side of the coin, unethical practice usually involves illegal or questionable practices, such as lying, misleading, deceiving, or harming other people through insensitivity, confusion, irritation, or a conflict of values.

Applying ethical values and principles to marketing and advertising is necessary if these fields are to be socially responsible. **Social responsibility**—a corporate philosophy based on ethical values—motivates a business to perform a useful function within society and to make its impact on society positive rather than negative—and that includes its advertising, as well as other business practices. Oil companies often find themselves charged with practices that contribute to ecological problems. After a series of bad publicity articles in Iceland about Shell Oil, the company realized it needed to emphasize the company's positive environmental programs. Overall the campaign was a success story; the company reported a 20 percent increase in "very positive to the company" responses and a 40 percent positive increase in answers to the question "I experience the company positively/negatively."

Social responsibility includes treating employees and other stakeholders with sensitivity, as well as avoiding practices that hurt the environment, the community, or society.[44] Social responsibility also motivates businesses to support good causes. Johnson & Johnson, for instance, supports the Susan G. Komen Foundation and its breast cancer research and awareness-building campaigns. (We will further discuss social responsibility in the section on social marketing in chapter 17.)

Professional Ethics

Professionals in advertising by and large see themselves as ethical people. However, the public tends to see them differently, as the polls show. In an Honesty and Ethics Poll by the Gallup organization, advertising practitioners ranked forty-third out of 45 occupational categories.[45] That suggests the public is not persuaded that advertising professionals are guided by ethical standards. Industry standards can provide help with a decision about what is or is not ethically correct.

Professional ethics are often expressed in a **code of standards** that identifies how professionals in the industry should respond when faced with ethical questions. The American Association of Advertising Agencies (4As) begins its "Standards of Practice" with the line: "We hold that a responsibility of advertising agencies is to be a constructive force in business." The core of the statement is called The Creative Code and it is reproduced here in Figure 3.3.

In the wake of highly public business scandals such as the collapse of Enron, many firms are responding with their own codes of ethics. If this subject interests you, you can

We, the members of the American Association of Advertising Agencies, in addition to supporting and obeying the laws and legal regulations pertaining to advertising, undertake to extend and broaden the application of high ethical standards. Specifically, we will not knowingly create advertising that contains:

- False or misleading statements or exaggerations, visual or verbal
- Testimonials that do not reflect the real opinion of the individual(s) involved
- Price claims that are misleading
- Claims insufficiently supported or that distort the true meaning or practicable application of statements made by professional or scientific authority
- Statements, suggestions, or pictures offensive to public decency or minority segments of the population.

We recognize that there are areas that are subject to honestly different interpretations and judgment. Nevertheless, we agree not to recommend to an advertiser, and to discourage the use of, advertising that is in poor or questionable taste or that is deliberately irritating through aural or visual content or presentation.

Comparative advertising shall be governed by the same standards of truthfulness, claim substantiation, tastefulness, etc. as apply to other types of advertising.

FIGURE
3.3

The 4As Creative Code

look up these codes in a collection compiled by the Center for the Study of Ethics in the Professions at the Illinois Institute of Technology: http://ethics.iit.edu/codes/.

International Standards and Codes Standards of professional behavior are not found only in the United States or other Western countries. Singapore, for example, has an ad code specifically designed to prevent Western-influenced advertising from impairing Asian family values. Malaysia's requirement that all ads be produced in the country not only keeps that country's advertising aligned with its own standards and cultural values, it also cuts back dramatically on the number of foreign ads seen by its public. Advertisers who violate the ethical code of conduct in Brazil can be fined up to $500,000 or given up to a five-year prison sentence. This punishment would certainly prompt an advertiser to be careful.

In the Netherlands, industry members have encouraged the formation of an "ethical office" to oversee all agencies, advertisers, and media. That office is responsible for reviewing advertisements to ensure that they comply with the Dutch Advertising Code and general ethical principles. In Swedish advertising agencies, an executive known as the "responsible editor" is trained and experienced in marketing law; that editor reviews all the advertisements and promotional materials to ensure that they are legally and ethically acceptable.

Personal Ethics

In advertising, a code of ethics is just a starting point. Ethical decisions are usually complex and involve navigating a moral maze of conflicting forces—strategy versus ethics, costs versus ethics, effectiveness versus ethics, etc. They demand the ability to do what ethicists call "moral reasoning."[46] In the end, if you are an advertising professional making a decision about a strategy or an executional tactic to be used in an advertisement, you must be aware of industry standards, as well as the ethical questions that underlie the core issues we have discussed in this chapter.

Principle
Decisions about ethics are made based on laws and regulations, on professional codes, but more importantly, on an internal moral compass that senses when something is right or wrong.

But more importantly, personal judgment and moral reasoning rests on an intuitive sense of right and wrong, a moral compass that tells you when an idea is misleading, insensitive, too over-the-top, or too manipulative. And then you need the courage to speak up and tell your colleagues. An understanding of advertising's ethical issues will help you develop that sense. If you feel you fit this challenge, consider the recommendations in the Inside Story box on how to find a job in advertising.

The Practical Tips box suggests some ethical questions professionals in advertising can ask themselves as they confront an ethical dilemma. Note that the list is organized into three categories: The first covers the big picture of social impact, followed by the two areas of most concern in the actual practice of advertising—decisions about advertising strategies and their execution tactics.

Practical Tips

An Ethics Checklist for Advertisers

In terms of its social impact, does advertising . . .

- violate pubic standards of good taste?
- reinforce negative stereotypes?
- damage people's self-image and create insecurities?
- promote materialism?
- create false wants and false hope?
- contribute to cultural pollution?
- market dangerous products?

In terms of its strategic decisions, does an advertisement . . .

- target vulnerable groups?
- harm children?

THE INSIDE STORY
Breaking Into Madison Avenue

By Ryan Ali, Account Senior Executive Ziccardi Partners Frierson Mee, New York

The word *graduation* often brings fear and anxiety to many seniors who speak the phrase, or for that matter, begin to think about life after college. But for many of you, who journey to the top ad agencies in New York, that will start much earlier than the day that you hear your name called. You have to break through the clutter of thousands of students, all of them headed to New York, because they think they are the best of the best.

Here is some advice to help make the transition from classroom to boardroom a smooth one:

1. Even before you say goodbye to college, start doing your research as early as six months prior to graduation. What type of agency do you want? You can target smaller boutique agencies or aim for a larger, more corporate environment. Keep in mind that you will be working twelve-hour days your first year at any agency, and the culture is very important.
2. Did I mention research? Trade publications are a great way for you to immerse yourself into the world of advertising. Pick up *AdAge and Adweek*, and register at sites that post creative materials such as www.agency-compile.com. Mentioning a recent article or a new creative review could bring new insight into your interview.
3. Establish contacts. Whether it's alumni, people at a bar, or even people on the subway, you never know who could point you in the right direction. Once you have a contact, which doesn't have to be in HR, ask to meet over coffee or something casual. This is an excellent way for you to gain some insider perspective, not to mention help you get your resumé to HR. There is a

good chance that your professor still has some connections with some former students who will agree to meet with you.
4. Find a recruiter. Human Resource departments are inundated with resumés. If you're a catch, a top industry recruiter can help your resumé reach the desk of an HR Manager.
5. Consider freelancing. It's all about timing. Whether or not an agency wins an account can determine their need to hire. Wet your feet early on. Many agencies and marketing departments would consider hiring freelancers for short-term work. This is an excellent way to make connections, and if a position opens up, HR might call you first.
6. Follow up. Even if you run into someone, ask for a card. The thank-you note is a very important aspect of the interview/meeting process. From my experience, it's the personalized written notes that have received the most attention.

This is probably one of the most cut-throat, aggressive, and demanding industries to work in. Luckily, you have already started to prepare for the journey by making contacts, and this will ultimately land a job at a top advertising agency.

Ryan Ali graduated in 2000 from Florida State University with degrees in Communications and Graphic Design. His first job was also in New York with TBWA/Chiat Day.

Nominated by Professor Kartik Pashupati, Florida State University

- appeal to base motivations such as envy and greed?
- drive demand for unnecessary purchases?
- prey on people's fears unnecessarily?
- undercut people's self-image and self-concept?
- make unsubstantiated claims?

In terms of its tactics, does an advertisement . . .

- use ideas, words, or images that are offensive or insensitive?
- use inappropriate stereotypes?
- manipulate people's emotions unnecessarily?
- make false, deceptive, or misleading claims?
- use unfair comparisons?
- create endorsements or demonstrations that exaggerate or lie?
- use scare or shock tactics?
- use puffery?

Consider This

1. The 4As Creative Code lists unethical behaviors. What positive, ethical behaviors does the code implicitly recommend?
2. Create a personal code of ethics for a group to which you belong. Identify the key values, as well as actions you think would be a violation of the code. Do you believe such a code can have any impact on the organization and its members? Why or why not?

IT'S A WRAP

LESSONS FROM THE LOSERS

Most of the top winners on the *Adweek* list of losers were there because they were offensive—the Calvin Klein kiddie porn ads, the Kenneth Cole "God Dress America" billboard, the Benetton death-row supplement, and the Mike Tyson commercial for Fox Sports Net. Stereotyping was also a problem in the "Just for Feet" commercial, the Nike spot, and the Toyota postcard. The Sony Pictures Entertainment movie posters that featured great reviews by a nonexistent movie reviewer was a lie—false, as well as deceptive.

Some of the ads on the *Adweek* list, however, were there because they simply were dumb. For example, muffler giant Midas used an ad with an elderly woman standing with her back to the camera in front of two Midas employees. As they explained the company's lifetime guarantee, the senior pulled down her top and asked the surprised guys, "What can you do with these?"

Finally, a commercial for Nuveen Investments that starred Christopher Reeve, the late actor who became a paraplegic due to a spinal cord injury, showed the Superman star rising out of his wheelchair and walking. The point of the ad was that "in the future, so many things will happen in the world." It was described by *Adweek* as creepy, emotionally exploitive, as well as confusing and a source of false hope for other paralyzed people.

What all the *Adweek* losers have in common is a lapse in judgment by the people who created the ads. Somewhere there was a breakdown in that internal moral compass that tells advertising professionals when they have gone over the line.

The increasing power of advertising, both in terms of money (we spend more annually educating consumers than we spend educating our children) and in terms of communication dominance (the mass media can no longer survive without advertising support), has made these concerns more prominent than ever. The evidence demonstrating the manipulative power of advertising may be shaky because so many other factors contribute to the choices we make. Still, some advertisers are not objective and often slant or omit information to their benefit, as well as use their advertisements to deceive the public. That's why the industry has a complex set of regulations, self-regulations, and oversight bodies that keep watch for these unethical practices.

Summary

1. **Discuss the shape-and-mirror debate.** The shape-versus-mirror debate is a central issue in considering advertising's role in society. Critics of advertising tend to believe that advertising has the power to shape social trends and the way people think and act; advertising professionals tend to believe that advertising mirrors values rather than sets them.

In fact, advertising and society's values are probably interactive, so the answer may simply be that advertising *both* mirrors and shapes values.

2. **Analyze the legal topics that guide advertising practice.** The are two pivotal areas of case law—trademarks and

copyright protection, and the First Amendment—that pertain to advertising. The Patent Office protects unique trademarks from infringement by competitors; the Library of Congress protects copyrights, the distinctive symbols that identify brands. The First Amendment generally protects commercial speech, which is speech that promotes commercial activity, but the protection is qualified and subject to some limitations.

3. **List the key regulatory agencies and their responsibilities.**
   - The FTC is the agency primarily concerned with identifying and eliminating deceptive advertising.
   - The FDA oversees advertising related to food and drugs.
   - The FCC monitors advertising broadcast by radio and television stations.
   - Other regulatory bodies with some advertising oversight include the Bureau of Alcohol, Tobacco, and Firearms, the U.S. Postal Service, the Patent office, the Library of Congress, and the states' Attorneys General offices.

4. **Explain the way the advertising industry regulates itself.** Advertising agencies have in-house ad review procedures and legal staff that monitor the creation of advertising. The industry has a number of bodies that review advertising, such as the Advertising Review Council (ARC), the National Advertising Division (NAD) of the Better Business Bureau, and the National Advertising Review Board (NARB). Other bodies include the various media review boards, competitors who are concerned about unfair advertising that might harm their brands, and public and community groups that represent either local or special-interest groups.

5. **Critique the key ethical issues that challenge the practice of advertising.** A number of advertising practices generate ethical questions in such areas as offensive advertising, stereotypes, body image, advertising to children, false and misleading advertising, and questionable practices surrounding such message strategies as puffery, comparative advertising, endorsements, demonstrations, and the advertising of controversial or dangerous products.

6. **Outline the ways professionals determine if an advertising practice is ethical.** Ultimately ethical decision making comes down to a personal sense of what's right and what's wrong. To help with these decisions professionals consider social responsibility, professional codes and standards, and personal moral reasoning.

Key Terms

cease-and-desist order, 68
code of standards, 87
commercial speech, 64
comparative advertising, 81
consent decree, 68

copyright, 63
corrective advertising, 69
cultural imperialism, 62
deceptive advertising, 66
demand creation, 61

endorsement, 83
ethics, 75
indirect advertising, 71
marketing imperialism, 62
puffery, 81

social responsibility, 87
stereotype, 76
subliminal message, 81
testimonial, 83
trademark, 63

Review Questions

1. Explain the debate over whether advertising shapes or mirrors society. If you were to take a side in this debate, which side would you be on?
2. Explain how trademarks and copyrights are legally protected, and why the First Amendment is important to advertisers.
3. In addition to the FTC, what other governmental bodies are involved in regulating advertising practices?
4. Explain the three ways in which self-regulation operates in the advertising industry.
5. Define ethics and explain how it relates to advertising.
6. How do you determine what is ethical? If you are called upon to make a decision about the promotion of an event for one of your groups, where does the ultimate consideration lie?

Discussion Questions

1. Zack Wilson is the advertising manager for the campus newspaper. He is looking over a layout for a promotion for a spring break vacation package. The headline says, "Absolutely the Finest Deal Available This Spring—You'll Have the Best Time Ever If You Join Us in Boca." The newspaper has a solid reputation for not running advertising with questionable claims and promises. Should Zack accept or reject this ad? Why?
2. The Dimento Game Company has a new basketball video game. To promote it, "Slammer" Aston, an NBA star, is

signed to do the commercial. In it, Aston is shown with the game controls as he speaks these lines: "This is the most challenging court game you've ever tried. It's all here—zones, man-to-man, pick and roll, even the alley-oop. For me, this is the best game off the court." Is Aston's presentation an endorsement? Should the FTC consider a complaint if Dimento uses this strategy? What would you need to know to determine if you are safe from a challenge of misleading advertising?

3. Find an ad that you think is deceptive or offensive. What bothered you about the ad? Should the medium have carried it? Who would act more effectively in judging a case like this: the government or the advertising industry? Explain.

4. A pharmaceutical company has repackaged a previously developed drug that addresses the symptoms of a scientifically questionable disorder affecting approximately 5 percent of women. While few women are affected by the "disorder," the company's advertising strategy is comprehensive, including dozens of television, radio, and magazine ads. As a result, millions of women with symptoms similar to those of the disorder have sought prescriptions for the company's drug. In turn, the company has made billions of dollars. What, if any, are the ethical implications of advertising a remedy to a mass audience when the affected group is small? Is the company misrepresenting its drug by conducting a "media blitz"? Why or why not?

■■■ Suggested Class Project

1. Select three print ads that you feel contain one or more of the ethical issues discussed in this chapter. Ask five people (making sure they vary by gender, age, or background) how they feel about the ads. Conduct a short interview with each of your subjects; it would be helpful to have a list of questions prepared. Write a report on their opinions and response to your questionnaire. Don't be afraid to include your own conclusions about the ads. What differences or similarities do you see across the responses?

2. Check the Web sites of three big-name companies such as:

   • Mc Donald's (www.mcdonalds.com)
   • Avon (www.avon.com)
   • Ben & Jerry's (www.benjerry.com)

   Write a two- to four-page report on their efforts to be socially responsible. How is the company's social responsibility position reflected in its advertising?

HANDS-ON

CASE 3

Boycott This!

A recent ad for a Nike hiking shoe used copy that was probably intended to be humorous. The copy suggested that Nike's shoe could help the user avoid turning into ". . . a drooling, misshapen non-extreme-trail-running husk of my former self, forced to roam the earth in a motorized wheelchair with my name embossed on one of those cute little license plates you get at carnivals. . . . " Marcie Roth, an advocacy director for the National Council on Independent Living, didn't find it funny. "Nike is trying to be sensationalist, and they're doing it on the backs of the disabled," thundered Roth, adding, "We won't tolerate it." Nike apologized and immediately pulled the ad. But Roth announced that her group was interested in more than just an apology, because the disabled, in Roth's words, had been "dissed." Nike was asked to include disabled actors in its ads and hire a greater number of disabled workers. Otherwise, suggested Roth, Nike could expect a boycott.

Boycotts are certainly one way for consumers to let advertisers know when they've gone too far. While some advertisers, notably Benetton, delight in creating controversy, the vast majority try to avoid the unwanted attention and possible loss of sales that a boycott might bring. Armed with this knowledge, consumers and interest groups regularly threaten boycotts and there are several Web sites that track the dozens of product boycotts that are occurring at any given time. Recently the Web site "Ethical Consumer" listed boycotts of Adidas (for allegedly using kangaroo skin in the manufacture of some boots), Air France (for allegedly transporting primates), Bayer (for allegedly supporting policies favoring the use of genetically modified crops), and even entire nations (Israel, China, Morocco, and Turkey).

Although Ethical Consumer's rationales for supporting boycotts appear motivated by left-leaning or progressive concerns, conservative groups use them too. The American Family Association, based in Tupelo, Mississippi, has sent tens of thousands of e-mails threatening boycotts to advertisers Geico, Best Buy, Foot Locker, and Finish Line. The AFA is not upset with the ads placed by these companies, but rather with the program in which the ads appear: *South Park.* The AFA claims its e-mail campaigns caused Lowe's, Tyson, ConAgra, and Kellogg's to stop placing ads in ABC's surprise hit *Desperate Housewives.*

Some companies resist boycott pressures. Proctor & Gamble ignored AFA pressure to stop its support for gay-friendly legislation in Cincinnati. Subway Vice President Chris Carroll said his company ignored threatened boycotts caused by the company's decision to run ads in a documentary that was unflattering to Democratic presidential nominee John Kerry.

And then there's Pepsi. In 2003 the brand signed hip-hop artist Ludacris to appear in a "fun-oriented" campaign, but outspoken cable show host Bill O'Reilly immediately ripped Pepsi and urged "...all responsible Americans to fight back and punish Pepsi for using a man who degrades women, who encourages substance abuse, and does all the things that hurt . . . the poor in our society. I'm calling for all Americans to say, 'Hey, Pepsi, I'm not drinking your stuff. You want to hang around with Ludacris, you do that, I'm not hanging around with you.'"

A Pepsi representative appearing on O'Reilly's show denied that the artist's provocative lyrics (one album featured a song called "Move Bitch") were relevant to the Pepsi campaign. But the following day Pepsi canceled the campaign. For viewers of a certain age, the entire affair was reminiscent of the controversy that erupted several years earlier when Pepsi canceled ads featuring Madonna after she appeared in a controversial music video. But

Pepsi's decision did not mark the end of the controversy. After the announcement, Ludacris and the Hip-Hop Summit Action Network, an organization run by his producer, Russell Simmons, threatened their own boycott. Following several days of negotiations, the second boycott was called off. Ludacris would not be a spokesperson for Pepsi, but the soft-drink giant agreed to a deal to make a multimillion-dollar donation over several years to the rapper's foundation.

Consider This

1. What do you think about consumer boycotts? Are they unhealthy attempts to infringe on the speech rights of others? Or are they a healthy sign that consumers can take action against the ethical lapses of advertisers?
2. How should a company respond to the threat of a boycott? Consider the different responses of Nike, Subway, Lowe's, Proctor & Gamble, and Pepsi. How well do you think each of these companies reacted to boycott pressure? Did any of the companies hurt their brand because of the way they reacted to boycotts?
3. How would you review advertising ideas that you suspect are controversial and might generate a backlash? Is it ever justified to "push the envelope" in the areas of good taste and social responsibility? How would you decide if such approaches are effective?

Source: Associated Press, "Hip-hop Group Calls Off Pepsi Boycott," February 13, 2003; Candice Choi, "Nike Ad Spurs Disabled to Boycott," DiversityInc.com, October 24, 2000; Jack Neff, "Christian Group Spooks Advertisers," *Advertising Age* (October 25, 2004); Ethical Consumer, http://www.ethicalconsumer.org/boycotts/boycotts_list.htm.

PART-ENDING CASE

Part 1
Foundations

S. Truett Cathy founded Chick-fil-A with the vision that his chicken-sandwich company would be a leader in the quick-service restaurant industry. Successes continue year after year with quality products, employees, and customer service. But Truett would say that he has attained success in other areas as well.

Truett's strongest passion is the Chick-fil-A Corporate Purpose, which is "To glorify God by being a faithful steward of all that is entrusted to us. To have a positive influence on all who come in contact with Chick-fil-A." This statement is part of the company's definition of its social responsibility. While those are pretty big words on which to pattern one's life, Truett Cathy sets a faithful example of how it can be done—not just for himself, but for the rest of the company as well. For instance, Chick-fil-A always has been and always will be closed on Sundays. Some argue that the company misses sales by closing the stores one day each week. Truett believes that he gains more by allowing his employees a day of worship or time with family.

Another example of the Corporate Purpose put into action is team member scholarships. Any team member (employee) at a Chick-fil-A store who meets the set criteria is eligible for a $1,000 scholarship that applies toward the expense of his or her education. Since 1973, Chick-fil-A has awarded more than $18 million in $1,000 scholarships to eligible students. And through the WinShape Centre® Foundation, started in 1984 as a small, long-term foster care program, Truett helps children and adults alike, working to "shape them into winners." The program has grown to encompass summer camps for boys and girls, a scholarship program, and a marriage retreat center.

The Chick-fil-A definition of social responsibility is a little different from other firms'. At some companies, people may speak about a purpose and vision, but at Chick-fil-A, they strive to live the words through their actions.

Source: Information courtesy of Mike Buerno, The Richards Group.

Consider This

1. Given the social focus on Chick-fil-A advertising, how would you classify their advertising?
2. Can such an approach confuse the consumer and make ads less effective?

Peeling an Onion

Developing an advertising plan depends upon how well you understand how consumers think and act. This general area is called consumer behavior, a topic we will consider in the first two of these four chapters in this section on planning.

The first chapter considers how consumers respond to advertising messages; the second chapter focuses on defining and targeting the consumer audience considering the various factors that influence their behavior. The third chapter presents the important role of research in providing information about customers, as well as their responses to advertisements. The last chapter in the section pulls everything together in a discussion of how the information about how consumers think, act, and respond to advertising messages drives the development of an advertising plan.

It should be clear that all four of these chapters reflect this book's customer focus perspective. They overlap in so many ways. Consumer insight, for example, is critical to planning, and yet it is derived from an understanding of consumer behavior that is only acquired through research. We'll discuss consumer insight in the planning chapter, however, as you will see, it is a central concept for all these chapters.

The central topic, in other words, is the consumer and these chapters, like peeling an onion, will uncover various aspects and details of consumer behavior. The customer focus, however, always remains at the core of the discussion.

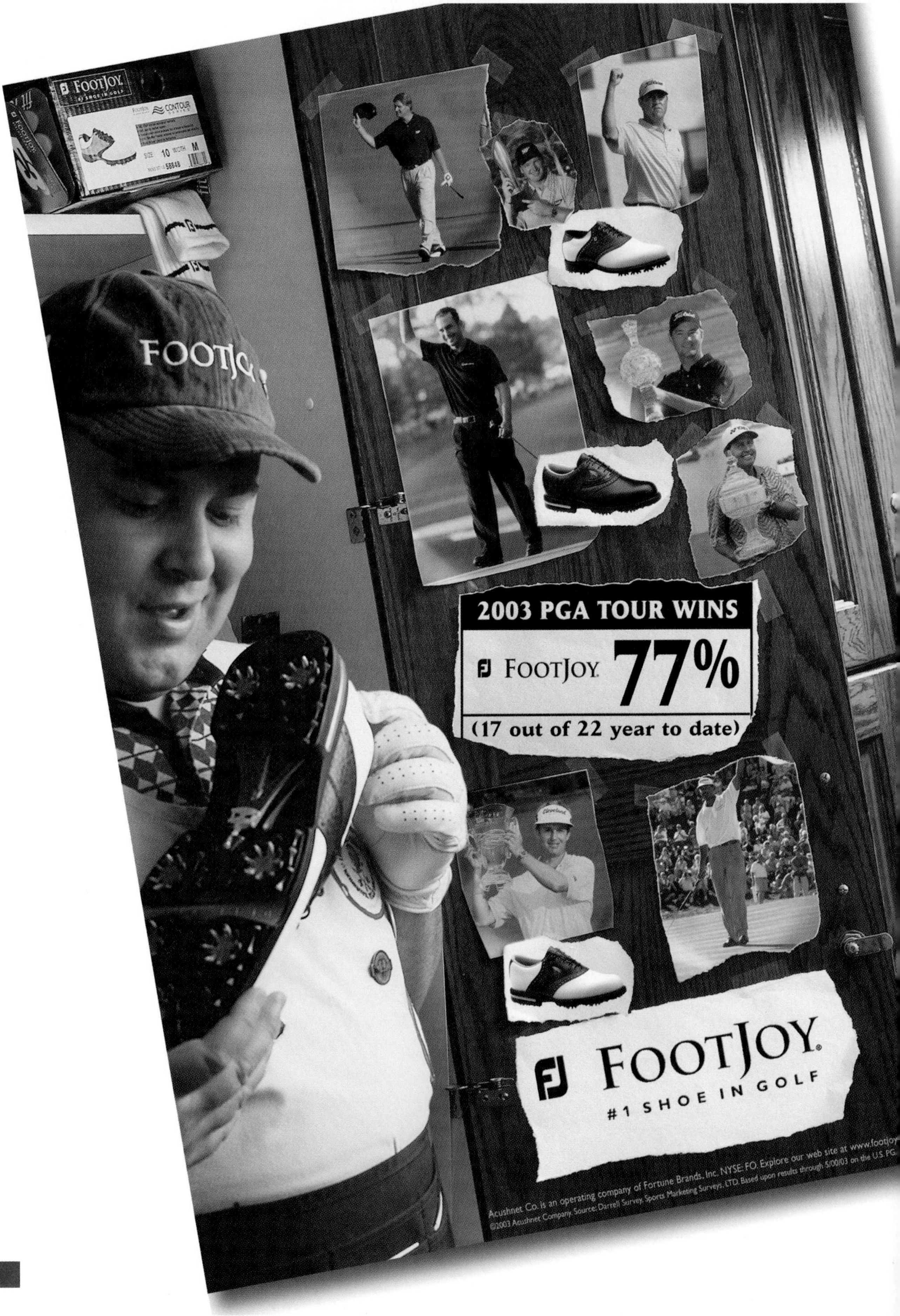

FOOTJOY
#1 SHOE IN GOLF
SIZE 10 WIDTH M
FOOTJOY
2003 PGA TOUR WINS
FOOTJOY 77%
(17 out of 22 year to date)
FOOTJOY
#1 SHOE IN GOLF
Acushnet Co. is an operating company of Fortune Brands, Inc. NYSE: FO. Explore our web site at www.footjoy
©2003 Acushnet Company. Source: Darrell Survey, Sports Marketing Surveys, LTD. Based upon results through 5/00/03 on the U.S. PG

How Advertising Works

4

C H A P T E R

SignBoy Is a Hole in One for FootJoy

Award:
EFFIE® Gold

Company:
FootJoy® golf shoes

Agency:
Arnold Worldwide

Campaign:
FootJoy "SignBoy"

CHAPTER KEY POINTS

After reading this chapter, you will be able to:

1. Demonstrate why communication is a key factor in advertising effectiveness.

2. Explain the Facets Model of Advertising Effects to show how brand advertising works.

3. List the six key effects that govern consumer response to advertising messages.

f you're like most Americans, your closet probably contains more recreation shoes than dress shoes. We have become a society of shoe specialization, especially as far as our recreation is concerned: shoes for walking, others for running, and still others for other sports.

FootJoy (FJ) has been making top-of-the-line golf shoes since 1857, and has been the number-one shoe on the PGA Tour since they started keeping tabs on shoe counts in 1945. FootJoy has also been the market leader since that time, leading the market with shares of greater than 50 percent on average. In the late 1990s, however, the company saw a decline in market share. This 2 percent drop was primarily because new competitors were entering the market and were introducing golf shoes with contemporary designs and technology.

Nike was one of these strong new competitors, with its huge marketing budget and the endorsement of Tiger Woods. Nike's brand of golf shoes was positioned as cool and stylish, while the FootJoy brand was perceived as a golf shoe your father or mother might wear. Nike was a fearful rival with deep pockets in sporting goods, but FootJoy was still the giant in golf.

The challenge was clear. FootJoy had to retain its position as the shoe of choice for the world's best golfers, while creating a new image of being young, cool, and with-it. If it could match the Nike image and continue to offer a superior product, it could increase sales and build on its market share.

In partnership with the advertising agency Arnold Worldwide, FootJoy created the SignBoy character in 1998 to present the FootJoy message in an entertaining and fun manner. In a golf tournament the sign boy is the standard bearer who carries the sign with the scores behind the group of pros playing together on a fairway.

FootJoy's SignBoy character is not only that, but represents an overly enthusiastic fan who aspires to be a sign boy on Tour someday. He's enamored with golf, knows all the professional golfers and details of each tournament, and knows everything about FootJoy's golf shoes, as well as other golf products, such as FootJoy's outerwear and StaSof gloves.

A superfan who is funny, loveable, silly, and a little naive, the FJ SignBoy character drives a beat-up old Impala, lives at home in a room decorated with golf posters, photos of professional players, and memorabilia (for example, a little plastic bag with a divot from the eighteenth fairway in Augusta and a giant cardboard check given to one of the FootJoy pros, which he tried to cash at an ATM).

SignBoy knows all the FootJoy products and the pros who wear them. SignBoy has made up nicknames for them or uses their nicknames, such as "DL3" for Davis Love III or "Lumpy" for Tim Herron. In return, the SignBoy character is loved by FootJoy pros and other golf enthusiasts.

He has become the spokesperson across all FootJoy's media and creative messages. His dialogue with the pros, both real and imagined, provides the opportunity to talk about the product features and benefits in an entertaining, even funny, manner. He can deliver technical discussions about the shoe and do it in a way that is interesting and memorable. Of course, he says FootJoy over and over in the commercials so the repetition creates high memorability. The SignBoy campaign has been a huge success for FootJoy and helped the brand continue in its leadership position with 58 percent of the market, an increase of 12 percent since SignBoy's inception. We explain more about the effectiveness of this campaign in the It's a Wrap section at the end of this chapter.

Great advertising is advertising that has an impact. It is effective because it creates the desired effect on the audience and generates the intended response. Advertisers, however, can't evaluate the effectiveness of their advertising unless they have some idea what effects these messages are designed to achieve.

In this chapter we'll look at the effects behind the concept of effectiveness. First we'll look at advertising as communication, focusing on some key communication concepts that are used to analyze the effectiveness of advertising. Then we'll look at various types of consumer responses to advertising and other marketing communication messages in order to identify the key message effects, which we present as a model of advertising effects.

A Basic Communication Model

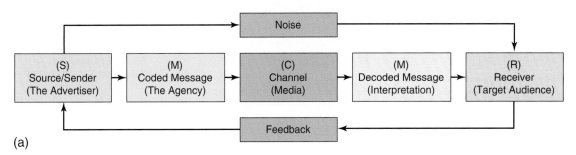

(a)

An Interactive Communication Model

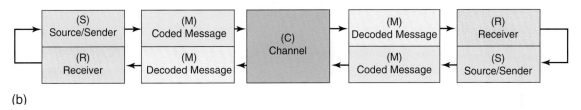

(b)

FIGURE 4.1 **A Basic Communication Model and an Interactive Communication Model**

Mass communication (a) is a one-way process: The message moves from the source to the receiver. Interaction communication (b) is a conversation or dialogue and the source and receiver change positions as the message bounces back and forth between them.

HOW ADVERTISING WORKS AS COMMUNICATION

Advertising is, first of all, a form of communication. In a sense, it is a message to a consumer about a product. It gets attention, provides information and sometimes a little bit of entertainment, and tries to create some kind of response, such as a sale. The legendary David Ogilvy, founder of the advertising agency that bears his name, explained his view of advertising as conversation:

> I always pretend that I'm sitting beside a woman at a dinner party, and she asks me for advice about which product she should buy. So then I write down what I would say to her. I give her the facts, facts, facts. I try to make it interesting, fascinating, if possible, and personal—I don't write to the crowd. I try to write from one human being to another. . . . And I try not to bore the poor woman to death, and I try to make it as real and personal as possible.[1]

In reality, however, advertising is not a conversation. Most advertising is not as personal or as interactive as a conversation because it relies on mass communication, which is indirect and complex. Although other forms of marketing communication—such as personal selling and telemarketing—can deliver the personal contact of a conversation, Ogilvy's comparison ignores the challenge that advertising faces in getting the attention of a largely disinterested audience.

The Communication Model

Mass communication is usually thought of as a process, sometimes referred to as the SMCR model of communication. In Figure 4.1a it is depicted in a communication model that outlines the important players and steps. It begins with a **source (S)**, a sender who *encodes* a **message (M)**—puts it in words and pictures. The model explains how communication works: The message is presented through **channels** of communication **(C)**, such as a newspaper,

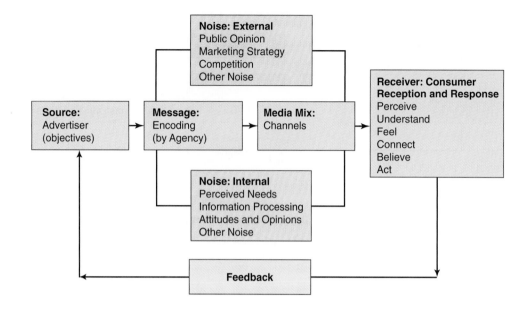

FIGURE
4.2 **Advertising Communication Model**
The model of advertising communication translates the standard parts of a communication model into the advertising context. It still begins with the advertiser (source) and ends with the consumer or target audience (receiver).

radio, or TV. The message is *decoded*, or interpreted, by the **receiver (R)**, who is the reader, viewer, or listener. **Feedback** is obtained by monitoring the response of the receiver to the message. And the entire process is complicated by what we refer to as **noise**, things that interrupt the sending as well as the receiving of the message, such as a bad connection.

Mass communication is generally a one-way process with the message depicted as moving from the source to the receiver. However, **interactive communication**—the personal conversation Ogilvy wanted to emulate—is a form of two-way communication, a dialogue. The difference between one-way and two-way communication is that the latter communication process is interactive and the source and receiver change positions as the message bounces back and forth between them. Figure 4.1b is a model of how a conversation or dialogue works.

Advertising as Communication

To translate the communication model to advertising, consider that the source typically is the advertiser assisted by its agency, such as the FootJoy company and Arnold Worldwide. Together they determine the *objectives* for the message—the advertisement or commercial—in terms of the effects they want the message to have on the consumer receiver, also known as the target audience. The Advertising Communication Model is shown in Figure 4.2.

Principle
Effective advertising is evaluated in terms of the impact it has on the consumer response to the message.

The advertiser's objectives are focused on the receiver's response; they predict the impact the message will have on the target audience. That impact is what we measure to determine whether the message met its objectives and was effective. It makes good sense to use this yardstick in customer-focused marketing, where *all* communication is evaluated in terms of consumer response. Communicating well with customers is the reason the SignBoy campaign has continued to win awards.

In advertising, as in communication in general, *noise* hinders the consumer's reception of the message. External noise on a macro level includes consumer trends—health trends harm the reception of fast-food messages—and problems with the product's marketing mix (product design, price, distribution, marketing communication). Martha Stewart's trial, for example, created negative noise for her company, Martha Stewart

Living Omnimedia, but it also had a negative effect on business partner Kmart, which carries Martha Stewart–branded products.

On a micro level, external noise could be as simple as bad radio or TV reception, but a more important factor is **clutter**, which is the multitude of messages all competing to get your attention. More specifically, it is all the ads that you see on television and in print media, as well as in unexpected places, such as in imprints on the sand on the beach (see page xxx). The massive number of ads makes it harder and harder for any one ad to get the attention of its audience.

People use many techniques to avoid clutter and information overload. They filter messages they don't want to see, such as turning the page, switching the chan-

■ ■ ■
This ad calls attention to a tiny black New Beetle in the line of cars. The simple copy line "Hey, there's a black one," causes the reader to study the visual to find the new Beetle. This is one of several executions in this campaign that used this same visual technique to intrigue consumers and spark their interest.

nel, hitting the mute button, tossing unopened mail that looks like an ad, and deleting spam without looking at it. Other avoidance techniques such as e-mail filters, "no-call" laws, and direct TV that skips commercials are creating new dilemmas for marketers. Many marketers are experiencing lower response rates to their campaigns as a result of filters and other avoidance techniques. **Viral marketing**, which relies on consumers to pass messages about products among themselves—typically through e-mail—and consumers' direct involvement in product making are possible solutions to the dilemma.[2]

Internal noise includes personal factors that affect the reception of an advertisement, such as the target audience's needs, purchase history, information-processing abilities, and level of avoidance of advertising in general. If you are too tired to listen or your attention is focused elsewhere, then your fatigue creates noise that hinders your reception of the message.

The message, of course, is the advertisement or other marketing communication tool, such as a press release, store sign, brochure, or Web page. The message may be spelled out in the words, but in most advertising the visual elements also carry meaning. In fact, some advertising messages, such as the VW ads for the new Beetle, are primarily visual.

The medium is the vehicle that delivers the message and, in advertising, that tends to be newspapers and magazines in print, radio and TV in broadcasting, the Internet, and other forms of out-of-home vehicles, such as outdoor boards and posters. An example of interesting use of media are the massed iPod posters that Chiat/Day placed on the long walls next to escalators in London tube stations. Other media include the phone, the fax, specialty items (mugs, T-shirts), in-store signs, brochures, catalogs, shopping bags, inflatables, and even sidewalks and toilet doors.

We've talked about the basic parts of a communication model—the source, the message, noise, and the media—in terms of how they relate to advertising. The last category we'll talk about is the receiver, or in advertising terms the consumer, and how the consumer decodes, or responds to, the message, which is what the rest of this chapter will discuss.

In customer-focused marketing and advertising, understanding what motivates the audience is critical to creating effective advertising. The SignBoy character was designed to appeal to golfers of all levels of skill. He also appeared in association with various golf pros and they became part of FootJoy's message reaching golfers who were interested in improving their game.

Adding Interaction to Advertising

Note that this discussion about advertising as communication—and the traditional communication model—is still based on the idea of a one-way model of mass communication with the source (advertiser) sending a message to a targeted audience. In more interactive marketing communication (IMC), these roles switch back and forth with the consumer initiating the message as well as responding to the advertiser's message. Two-way communication is one of the objectives of an IMC-focused program because it leads to a long-term relationship with a brand. If advertisers want to overcome the impersonal nature of mass communication, they need to learn to listen to, as well as send messages to, customers.

In the traditional communication model, customers' response was called *feedback,* and it was gathered primarily through research studies, but in newer approaches to communication feedback occurs in an environment of give-and-take communication. That's achieved by using more interactive forms of marketing communication (personal selling, telemarketing, online marketing) and through response devices such as toll-free numbers and e-mail addresses that encourage dialogue. Figure 4.1 included an Interactive Communication Model that shows the back-and-forth nature of a conversation, and this applies to customer dialogue as well.

Consider This

1. What are the key elements in a communication model, and how do they relate to advertising?
2. How does the communication model change when interactivity is added to it?

THE EFFECTS BEHIND ADVERTISING EFFECTIVENESS

Advertisers have been trying for years to answer the question: How does advertising work? They want to know how it works in order to make it work better. When we ask, "How does it work?," we are talking about the *impact* an advertisement has on the receiver of the message. Message effects, then, are found in the various types of consumer responses produced by the advertising message.

People generally respond to a message in predictable ways, so advertisers try to design advertisements—and think carefully through the strategy behind the ad—in order to create a message that will deliver a desired response. This intended response is the ad's objective. So what are these effects that determine whether an advertisement works or not?

The Simple Answers

The most common and long-standing explanation of advertising effects is one referred to as **AIDA**, which stands for **a**ttention, **i**nterest, **d**esire, and **a**ction. The idea is that first an ad gets attention, then it creates interest, then desire, and finally stimulates action. It's a simple model that identifies four effects and makes a prediction about how they are related in a hierarchy of steps. Because AIDA assumes that consumers start with attention and wind up with a decision, it is referred to as a **hierarchy-of-effects model**.

There are a number of these hierarchical models that advertisers use to plan their advertising.[3] The problem with these models is that advertisers now know that people don't always proceed through steps in this predictable fashion. Sometimes you may just buy something because you're hungry or the product catches your eye at the check-out counter; in other situations, however, you may do research and consider and compare different alternatives before making a decision. This considered purchase is a fairly rational approach and it works for some products, such as major purchases. This rational, information-driven process is what the AIDA model describes. However, with the impulse purchase you almost work the AIDA model backward: You buy the product and then you think about whether you like it or not. And sometimes you may be driven by an emotional need that defies logic and rational thinking. So AIDA isn't adequate as a model of the various types of effects advertising can create.

TABLE
4.1   **Different Paths to a Response**

Path	Goal	Example	Advertising's Objective
think—feel—do	learning, interest	computer game, CD, DVD	provide information, emotion
think—do—feel	learning, understanding	college, a computer, a vacation	provide information, arguments
feel—think—do	needs	a new suit, a motorcycle	create desire
feel—do—think	wants	cosmetics, fashion	establish a psychological appeal
do—feel—think	impulse	a candy bar, a soft drink	create brand familiarity
do—think—feel	habit	cereal, shampoo	remind of satisfaction

Another relatively simple answer to how advertising works, one that tries to get around the hierarchical problem, is the model commonly referred to as **think-feel-do**. The idea here is that advertising motivates people to think about the message, feel something about the product, and do something, such as try it or buy it. This model has been used to identify various patterns of responses (see Table 4.1) depending, again, on the type of product and the buying situation.

When you look at Table 4.1 with all its paths, you realize that maybe the answer to how advertising works is really not all that simple. Your intuition is right, because none of these approaches include several other types of responses that advertisers know are important to effective advertising. One of those is *association,* which explains how brand communication works, and the other is *persuasion.* We'll be exploring each in detail later in this chapter.

We present the AIDA and think-feel-do models here because you'll hear references to both of them in advertising agencies, as well as in advertising classes, and so you should understand what they represent. The problem with both of these, however, is that, because of their simplicity, neither approach really answers the how-advertising-works question very well. The solution, then, is to build on the effects identified in these approaches and add in the missing categories of consumer responses to advertising.

The Facets Model of Effective Advertising

Our objective is to develop a model of advertising effects that does a better job of explaining how advertising creates various types of consumer responses. The effects identified in the AIDA and think-feel-do models are important, but we also need to include other critical objectives that professionals use in their work—such as persuasion and association.

Our answer to the question of how advertising works, then, is to say that effective advertising creates six types of consumer responses. These six effects, and the categories of effects to which they belong, are represented in Figure 4.3. In terms of consumer responses, they are:

1. perceive (perception)
2. understand (cognition)
3. feel (affective/emotion)
4. connect (association)
5. believe (persuasion)
6. act (behavior)

These are facets, polished surfaces like those of a diamond, that come together to make up the unique consumer response to an advertising message. The factors, or aspects, within each effect category in Figure 4.3 give definition to the way that facet is constructed. The effects are holistic, leading to an impression or what Preston calls an "integrated perception."[4] An effective message, then, has a diamond-like quality that represents how the message effects work together to create the desired consumer response.

One of the things you might note about the model is that impact can be created in a number of different ways. For example, a brand message may get attention, explain new

FIGURE
4.3

The Facets Model of Advertising Effects

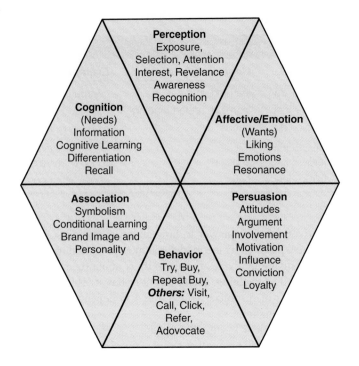

Perception
Exposure,
Selection, Attention
Interest, Revelance
Awareness
Recognition

Cognition
(Needs)
Information
Cognitive Learning
Differentiation
Recall

Affective/Emotion
(Wants)
Liking
Emotions
Resonance

Association
Symbolism
Conditional Learning
Brand Image and
Personality

Behavior
Try, Buy,
Repeat Buy,
Others: Visit,
Call, Click,
Refer,
Adovocate

Persuasion
Attitudes
Argument
Involvement
Motivation
Influence
Conviction
Loyalty

information, and convince consumers to try the brand—in other words, it created impact in the perception, cognitive, persuasive, and behavioral areas of effects. Another message might create awareness, stir up an emotion, and link a product to a lifestyle—which means it created perception, affective, and association effects. Both can be equally effective; they just touched the consumer in entirely different ways.

Let's now explore the six categories of effects in more detail. We'll start with perception, which is where the consumer response begins.

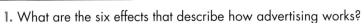

Consider This

1. What are the six effects that describe how advertising works?
2. How does the Facet Model differ from the AIDA and think-feel-do models?

PERCEPTION

Every day we are bombarded with stimuli—faces, conversations, buildings, advertisements, news announcements—yet we actually notice only a small fraction. Why? The answer is perception. **Perception** is the process by which we receive information through our five senses and assign meaning to it. If an advertisement is to be effective, it, first of all, has to get noticed.

The Components of Perception

Advertising creates visibility for a product or brand through exposure. Consumers respond by selecting messages to which they pay attention, a process called **selective perception**. (Some ads for some product categories—condoms, personal hygiene products—have a battle getting attention because people don't choose to watch them.) If the message is selected and attended to, then the consumer may react to it with interest if it is relevant. The result is awareness of the ad or brand, which is filed in memory at least to the point that the consumer recognizes the brand or ad. The key components of perception and their roles in effectiveness are:

Exposure. Making contact

Selection and Attention. Creating stopping power

Interest and Relevance. Creating pulling power

Awareness. Making an impression

Recognition. Making a mental note

Exposure

Exposure, which means being seen or heard, is an important goal of media planners who try to find the best way to expose the target audience to the message. Exposure also is important to IMC planners who consider all contacts a consumer has with a company or brand as a *contact point* where messages are delivered. That goes beyond traditional advertising media to include such things as customer service, delivery trucks and their drivers, the company's lobby and building design, as well as all interactions with employees and other stakeholders. Whereas the impact from exposure to traditional marketing communication messages can be generally predicted, the messages delivered at other contact points may be much harder to control or predict. The effectiveness of media plans is evaluated based on the exposure levels they actually achieve after the advertising has run.

Selection and Attention

The ability to draw **attention**, to bring visibility, to a product is one of advertising's greatest strengths. In advertising novelty or surprise are often used to get attention. A bank in New York used comedian Verne Troyer, who plays Mini-me in the "Austin Power" movies, to promote a home-equity credit line called "Flexline." Because banks rarely use humor in advertising, the advertising not only got a high level of attention, it achieved a huge behavioral response, with participation 85 percent ahead of the bank's previous campaign.[5] One way to evaluate the effectiveness of advertising, then, is to measure the attention level produced by the advertising. (Of course, even more useful to marketers are the business-building results, such as the participation measure, but we'll discuss that later in the section on behavioral impact.)

Would you stop to give someone directions?
If you were walking that way,
would you guide them?
What if it was out of your way?
One mile.
Two miles.

Two thousand miles,
directly inland from the Skeleton Coast,
to a one-room schoolhouse in the foothills of Namibia.
What if you were the teacher in that schoolhouse?
Would you travel that far to teach someone?
To learn something yourself?

Peace Corps.
Life is calling. How far will you go?

Call 800.424.8580 | Visit peacecorps.gov

■ ■ ■

Messages that are relevant speak to a consumer's special interests.

Interest and Relevance

Another factor in perception is **interest**, which means the receiver of the message has become mentally engaged in some way with the ad and the product. Ad messages are designed not only to get but also to hold the audience's interest.

A critical factor in interest is **relevance**, which means the message connects on some personal level. When it appeals to your self-interest, then a message is said to be relevant. For example, the Peace Corps launched a national recruiting campaign with a theme: "Life is calling. How far will you go?" This public-service campaign was introduced in English and Spanish through commercials, print ads, a 15-minute recruitment video, brochures, and a Web site (www.peacecorps.gov). It was designed to address more relevant personal issues for potential volunteers and tell them what they could get back from the volunteer experience.

Awareness

When you are aware of something, you know that you have seen it or heard it before. In other words, **awareness** results when an advertisement initially makes an impression. After the ad has run, do consumers know about the brand? You may not be able to remember much about the product or what the ad said, but you are aware of having seen the ad or heard of the product. Most evaluations of advertising effectiveness will include a measure of awareness as an indicator of perception; but that still doesn't tell us very much about the actual impact of the advertisement, so evaluations of effectiveness usually include other measures beyond simple awareness. Awareness is important, but it is considered to be a relatively low level of response, or a weak response, in comparison to behavioral responses, such as trying or buying a product.

Memory: Recognition   Another factor in perception is memory, which refers to the way people file information away in their minds. Advertisers are interested in two memory factors: **recognition**, which means people remember seeing the ad, and **recall**, which means they remember what the ad said. Recognition is a measure of perception; recall is a measure of understanding and we will talk about that in the next section. When we measure recognition it can be **aided recognition** (or recall); for example, a researcher might page through a magazine (or use some other medium) and ask respondents whether they remember seeing a particular ad. **Unaided recognition** (or recall) means respondents are asked to tell what they remember without being prompted by seeing the magazine (or other medium) to refresh their memories.

The Subliminal Issue

Subliminal advertising is a perceptual issue. Generally, we assume that advertising messages are seen and heard consciously. However, we are largely unaware of some of the ways advertising influences us, such as the use of color in an ad, sound effects in a commercial, or symbols that cue associations. That raises the issue of *subliminal advertising*. So let's distinguish between those influences that we don't think about, and subliminal advertising, which claims to motivate people to do things with messages that you can't see.

Subliminal effects are message cues given below the threshold of perception; in other words, you can't easily perceive them—they are too brief to see or they are disguised in some way. The idea is that they are designed to get past your perceptual filters by talking to your subconscious. People who believe in subliminal advertising presume such messages to be intense enough to influence behavior. Defenders of advertising respond that subliminal perception is not only a joke, it's a contradiction in terms.

The debate began in the 1950s in a movie theater experiment with subliminal effects. The message "Drink Coke" was flashed on the screen in a theater, but it was embedded between frames on the film and passed by so quickly that you couldn't actually see the message unless the film was paused. The original study, which found some suggestion of influence, has been criticized because no one has been able to replicate that effect in subsequent studies.

Most advertising professionals and professors, however, believe that there is no real support for subliminal advertising, as the Matter of Principle box discusses. The idea is that if you can see it, it isn't subliminal; if you can't see it, then the chances of it having an effect are slight. Still there are advertising critics who love to claim that advertising can manipulate people subconsciously and cause them to buy things they don't want and don't need.

COGNITION

Perception is the first effect of an advertising message and occurs before any of the other effects can happen. After that, however, an advertisement may generate any of the other responses: understanding, feeling, association, believing, or acting. For our discussion in this chapter, we'll talk next about the cognitive impact and then the emotional or affective impact; those are the two key effects identified in the think-feel-do model. Note that the order doesn't mean anything; we could just as easily talk about the emotional effects first and then the cognitive effects. The point is: Some messages make us think about the brand; others create a feeling about the brand; and some do both simultaneously. But we do have to talk about one or the other first, so let's begin with cognitive impact.

The Components of Cognition

Cognition refers to how consumers respond to information, learn, and understand something. It's a rational response to a message. A consumer may need something or need to know something, and the information gathered in response to that need leads to under-

A MATTER OF PRINCIPLE
Does Subliminal Advertising Work?

Author Wilson Key maintains in his book *Subliminal Seduction* that subliminal "embeds" are placed in ads to manipulate purchase behavior, most often through appeals to sexuality. For example, he asserts that 99 percent of ads for alcohol use subliminal embeds that are buried so skillfully that the average person does not consciously notice them unless they are pointed out.[6] Since there has been little documentation of such practices in the industry, and no one has been able to replicate Key's studies, most advertising scholars look upon these charges with suspicion.

Professionals just laugh at the notion and say that if such practices existed, then there would be a number of people involved with the production of the message and undoubtedly someone would come forth with stories about it. The stories haven't appeared, because no one in the industry knows of any instances of subliminal messages being used in advertising, other than as a joke. A campaign by one of the liquor companies, for example, showed ice cubes with shapes in them and deliberately called attention to these "subliminal" messages. Of course, they weren't subliminal because you could see the images. The whole campaign was a spoof on Key's theories.

Physiological limitations make it difficult to believe that subliminal messages can affect behaviors, such as causing people to buy, because if they are below the perceptual threshold, any impact they have will be very low-level. Professionals wonder why, when it is so hard to get people's attention and move them to action with messages that *can* be seen, anyone would want to gamble on a message that works below the threshold of perception. Time is also a factor; the impact of any subliminal message is unlikely to last until some later date when a consumer is shopping for a product.

During the 2000 presidential campaign, Democrats accused the Republican National Committee of running a subliminal message. In a TV commercial that attacked Al Gore's plan to add prescription drugs to Medicare, the word RATS appeared on the screen for a split second. The Republicans denied the accusation and explained that the word was just part of the word BUREAUCRATS. Even though the FCC concluded the ad was not subliminal, the Republican National Committee pulled the commercial.

Experts in the ad industry contend that it's silly to think such techniques would work. "I'm not saying it might not have been true," says Stephen A. Greyser, Professor of Marketing at Harvard Business School. "But there is no methodically believable research that supports the notion that it works. Besides, advertising wants to impact on people's consciousness, not their unconsciousness."[7] A *USA*

PEOPLE HAVE BEEN TRYING TO FIND THE BREASTS IN THESE ICE CUBES SINCE 1957.

The advertising industry is sometimes charged with sneaking seductive little pictures into ads.
Supposedly, these pictures can get you to buy a product without your even seeing them.
Consider the photograph above. According to some people, there's a pair of female breasts hidden in the patterns of light refracted by the ice cubes.
Well, if you really searched you probably *could* see the breasts. For that matter, you could also see Millard Fillmore, a stuffed pork chop and a 1946 Dodge.
The point is that so-called "subliminal advertising" simply doesn't exist. Overactive imaginations, however, most certainly do.
So if anyone claims to see breasts in that drink up there, they aren't in the ice cubes.
They're in the eye of the beholder.
ADVERTISING
ANOTHER WORD FOR FREEDOM OF CHOICE.
American Association of Advertising Agencies

The advertising industry considers accusations of subliminal advertising to be both damaging and untrue.

Today column on subliminal advertising described it as a fable from the 1950s,[8] and a Web site that publishes legal cases noted that allegations of subliminal advertising that result in legal cases are "few and far between."[9]

Consider This

1. Why do supporters of Wilson Bryan Key find reason to become alarmed about the way advertising images are presented?

2. Explain the views of critics of Key. Why do they disagree with his concerns?

standing. The information is filed in memory but can be recalled when needed. The key components of cognition and their roles in effectiveness are:

Needs. Matching product features to consumer needs

Information. Facts about products and their features

Learning. Creating understanding

Differentiation. Understanding the differences between competitive products

Recall. Locking information in memory

Needs Advertisers talk a lot about consumer needs and wants. By and large, **needs** are something you think about and **wants** are based on feelings and desires. So when we refer to needs, we are usually talking about the cognitive impact of an advertising message. A cognitive ad will explain how a product works and what it can do for the user, which is the way advertisers address consumer needs. For example, a virus protection program is something computer users need but they still may want an explanation of how the program works and what kind of protection it provides. The objective is to provide information related to a product that meets consumer needs in order to develop their understanding, which is a cognitive response.

Information Advertising often provides information about products, usually facts about product performance and features, such as size, price, construction, design, and so forth. The informative nature of advertising is particularly important for products that are complex (appliances, cars, insurance, computers, software) or that involve a high price or high risk (motorboats, vacations, medical procedures).

Cognitive Learning Consumers learn about products and brands through two primary routes: cognitive learning and conditioned learning. **Cognitive learning** occurs when a presentation of facts, information, and explanations leads to understanding. **Conditioned learning**, however, takes place when the learner links one thing with another. This is a process of *association,* and association, which we'll talk about later, is established through repetition, as in the famous Pavlovian experiment where the dog learned to associate food with the sound of a bell.

The cognitive learning route is used by consumers who are trying to learn everything they can about a product before they buy it. That's typically true of large purchases, such as cars, computers, and major appliances. Advertisements that use demonstrations and comparisons are attempting to help consumers learn by showing how something works and explaining its competitive advantages.

Differentiation A key function of advertising is *differentiation* of one brand from another, which is what happens when consumers understand the explanation of a competitive advantage. In order for that to happen, a consumer has to understand the features of a brand and be able to compare them with the features of competing products. In a major study of effective television commercials, the researchers concluded that one of the most important effectiveness factors was a brand-differentiating message.[10]

Memory: Recall We mentioned that recognition is a measure of perception and recall is a measure of learning or understanding. What that means is that the memory trace goes deeper with a cognitive response to an advertisement. When you remember the ad message, not only do you remember seeing the ad, you remember the *copy points,* which is the information provided about the product. In order to recall information presented in the ad, the consumer must have thought about it either as the information was being presented or afterward. Thinking about it is a form of information processing that helps to anchor the ideas in memory.

When you see an ad for a new product that catches your attention, such as a new music group or CD, and you concentrate on the message, then you have made more of an effort to understand. You may even think about the ad later when you find yourself walking by a music store. So your memory is involved in recalling not just the ad, but the content of the message. That's why we say the impact on memory is deeper with recall than with recognition.

This also explains advertising's **delayed effects**—how messages are seen at one time (at home in front of a TV, in the car on the radio, in the doctor's office in a magazine ad) and come back to mind at a later date when the consumer is in a purchase situation (in a store, at a restaurant). Most advertisements are carefully designed so that these memory traces are easy to recall. That's what sound bites do in political messages, but ads use jingles, slogans, catchy headlines, intriguing visuals, and key visuals in television in order to make this recall process as easy as possible.

Principle

Advertising has delayed effects in that a consumer may see or hear an advertisement but not act on that message until later when in a store.

THE AFFECTIVE OR EMOTIONAL RESPONSE

Affective responses mirror our feelings about something. Affective describes something that stimulates wants, touches the emotions, and creates feelings. Liking the brand or the ad is an important affective response that advertisers monitor. The American Airlines ad shown here demonstrates the difference between a cognitive and an emotional advertising message.

The Components of the Affective Response

The components of the affective response and their roles in effectiveness are:

Wants. Creating desire

Emotions. Affecting feelings

Liking. Creating positive feelings for the ad and the brand

Resonance. Appeal to self-interest

Wants Whereas needs are seen as being more cognitive, wants are depicted as influenced more by emotion or desire. "I want something" implies more of desire, which is based in the emotions, than a rational analysis of a need. Desire is based on wishes, longings, and cravings. Impulse buying is a good example. When you are standing in line at a store and see a display of candy bars, you may want one but that doesn't mean you think about whether or not you need it. Need isn't really relevant in this situation.

Emotions Advertisers have long thought that rational approaches were the most effective in persuasion, and persuasion tests often focus on arguments and how they affect the target audience's beliefs. However, more recent research by advertising scholars has determined that emotion may have more impact than rational approaches on both attitudes and behavior. A similar finding came from a University of Florida study based on analyzing 23,000 consumer responses that found the emotional response is more powerful than cognition in predicting action.[11]

Emotion, which agitates our passions or feelings, appears in a number of forms in advertising, such as humor, love, or fear. Ads that rely on arousing these feelings

To creatively communicate its new seating in coach, American Airlines used a picture of a brain with the left brain representing cognitive thinking and the right brain illustrating an affective response.

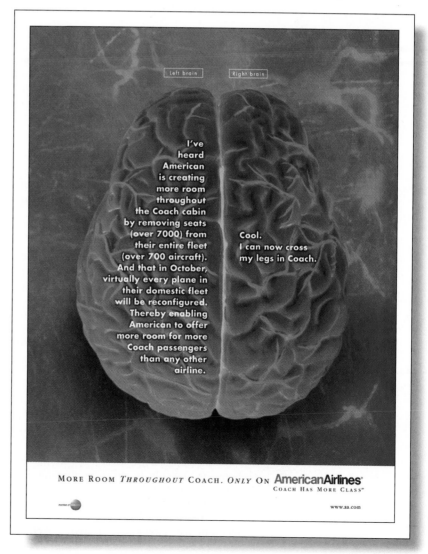

are referred to as **emotional appeals**. Negative ads in political campaigns are an example of an affective strategy that seems to work by putting an opponent on the defensive. Most people dislike them, however, because they sometimes seem unfair or, in the case of political advertising, mean-spirited.

Liking   A major study of advertising testing methods by the Advertising Research Foundation (ARF) found that liking a brand (or ad) was the best predictor of consumer's behavior.[12] *Liking* is measured in terms of two responses: liking the ad or liking the brand. The assumption is that if you like the ad, then that positive feeling will transfer to the brand. It is possible, however, for consumers to like the ad and not even be able to remember the brand, so the positive feeling generated by the ad may not always transfer to the brand. IMC planners argue that brand liking is determined by all the contacts a consumer has with a brand, so the accumulation of positive experiences eventually builds a positive feeling about a brand.

Affective responses, such as "I like it" or "I hate it," also inspire people to share their experiences with their friends and that's how "buzz" happens. The iPod launch benefited from a high level of buzz as people who are computer savvy and into music shared their excitement about iPod, and later iTunes, with their friends.

Resonance   Advertisements that create **resonance** where the message "rings true," help the consumer identify with the brand on a personal level. Resonance is stronger than liking because it involves an element of self-identification. The women's campaign for Nike does a good job of speaking to women in a way that addresses their concerns. If a woman identifies with this message, then it is said to resonate for her. Messages that resonate provide the foundation for an enduring brand relationship.

ASSOCIATION

Association is communication through symbolism. It is the process of making symbolic connections between a brand and characteristics, qualities, or lifestyles that represent the brand's image and personality. For example, you see association at work in advertising in the linking of Mountain Dew with teenage fun. The idea is to associate the brand with things that resonate positively with the customer. It's a three-legged stool: The brand relates to a quality that customers value; then the brand takes on symbolic meaning through such associations. Professor Ivan Preston in his association model of advertising believes that you can explain a lot about how advertising works by just focusing on association.[13]

The Components of Association

Association uses symbolism as well as conditioned learning to make the connections in a consumer's mind between a brand and certain desired qualities that define the brand and make it distinctive. When the connection is successfully established, a brand takes on meaning and is transformed from a generic product to a brand with a unique image. The components of association and their roles in effectiveness are:

Symbolism. Something that stands for something else, such as a quality or value

Conditioned Learning. Creating links and bonds through repetition

Brand Transformation. Creating brand meaning

Symbolism   The association takes on a **symbolic meaning**, which means the brand stands for a certain quality—a Rolex watch, for example, means or symbolizes quality, luxury, and status. In successful branding, a bond or relationship is created between a customer and a brand based on these symbolic meanings. The SignBoy was designed to be a funny, but lovable, brand character who would connect the FootJoy brand with golf pros.

Conditioned Learning   We mentioned earlier that conditioned learning, which is the way association implants an idea in a consumer's mind, is important because it explains much of the impact of advertising. People learn about a product or brand in a largely noncognitive, even nonrational way. Although advertisements sometimes use a cognitive strategy, they frequently are designed to elicit a network of noncognitive associations. Beer advertising directed at a young male audience, for example, often uses images of sporting events, beach parties, and good-looking young women, and those images are repeated so much that the associations become a predictable formula.

Brand Transformation

Several times in the preceding chapters we have mentioned advertising's important role in creating and maintaining a brand image through symbolism and associations. This is a basic principle of branding. Creating brand impression was the goal of the SignBoy campaign for FootJoy golf shoes. The SignBoy campaign uses the antics of the character, as well as his interactions with golf pros, to add an element of excitement and enthusiasm to what might otherwise be seen as a relatively mundane product—golf shoes and other accessories, such as gloves.

Transformation, as explained by DDB Needham's Bill Wells,[14] means a brand takes on meaning when it is transformed from a mere product into something special, something that is differentiated from other products in the category by virtue of its brand identity and image. Nike is more than just an athletic shoe; it rises above the average product in the category and stands out as something unique and special. That transformation in a consumer's mind is a perceptual shift, one that is created almost exclusively by advertising. The "California Avocados" campaign (see the Matter of Practice box) is an example of an attempt to transform a product into a brand.

FootJoy uses the SignBoy as a superfan to call attention to the golf pros, who are FootJoy endorsers.

Principle
Advertising is used to create brand meaning through symbolism and association. These meanings transform a generic product into a specific brand with a distinctive image and personality.

Components of Brand Communication There are many terms used by brand managers to explain how they think a brand works, but there isn't a common set of terms to describe the effects of communication on the branding process. To better understand how this branding process works, the communication dimensions of branding can be outlined using the same six effects that we presented in the Facets Model.

Perceive. Brand identity
Understand. Brand position
Feel. Brand personality
Connect. Brand image
Believe. Brand promise
Act. Brand loyalty

All six of these facets of a brand are driven by communication. Consider the following:

Brand Identity A brand identity must be distinctive. In other words it only represents one particular product within a category, and it must be recognizable and, therefore, memorable. Recognizing the brand means that the consumer knows the brand's identification markers—name, logo, colors, typeface, design, slogan—and can connect those marks with a memory of a message about the brand or a past experience using it.

A MATTER OF PRACTICE
It's Green, It's Squishy, It's Guacamole!

What fruit is black outside and green inside—and why would you want to eat it? The California Avocado Commission is not only trying to convince people to buy and eat avocados (that's called a "generic sell" because it's focused on the category); it also is trying to convince us that the California version is "unlike anything else." Making California Avocados a distinctive brand is important because competitors from Chile, Mexico, and New Zealand are making inroads into the U.S. avocado market.

IS THAT AN AVOCADO FACIAL OR DID YOU RUN OUT OF NAPKINS?
CALIFORNIA AVOCADOS   AVOCADO.ORG

FORGET DESSERT. I'LL JUST HAVE MORE SALAD.
CALIFORNIA AVOCADOS   AVOCADO.ORG

So what's involved in selling the category, as well as the brand? It's not as easy as it sounds because the communication challenge calls for creating multiple types of impact for two different types of audiences: nonusers and light users, as well as frequent users of avocados.

The overall campaign objective was to increase consumption of California avocados. To do that, the campaign sought to maintain the level of use by heavy users, as well as move light and medium users up into the heavy-user category.

The key message for all these consumer groups is a reminder, says Michelle Spelman, marketing director of the avocado commission, telling consumers that avocados are "versatile, and they're good for you." Spelman also explained that, based on consumer research, humor is a good way to deliver the reminder message because "consumers like it, it's catchy, and memorable."

Colby & Partners, the Commission's agency, recommended getting attention and creating liking for California Avocados by using tongue-in-cheek lines, such as "The pit lets you know when to stop eating," "Just tell everyone they're grass stains," and "We also have a support group called A.A."

The campaign was designed to create various types of consumer responses.

On the information front, the California Avocado Commission wanted people to know about the quality of the California variety, as well as its health benefits, and all the different ways it can be used. But that informational approach could be deadly dull, so how do you inform and educate without boring the audience?

By stimulating interest, the campaign planners also hoped to reach light or nonusers and get them to try avocados. For the more important group of users, however, the campaign needed to remind consumers not only that avocados are good, as well as good for you, but also that they should look for the California variety.

The campaign used print, radio, and outdoor advertising to deliver the message. The radio spots, which focused on unlikely locations to grow avocados, such as Alaska and the Sahara, ended with the line that California Avocados are unlike anything else because of the "beautiful sunny weather that makes them so perfect." The California connection resonates with consumers because they know that great agricultural products come from California and recognize it as a badge of quality.

And for those prospective avocado aficionados, the ads also led them to the organization's Web site where information about the health benefits was available, as well as more recipes and tips for using the green fruit.

The list of desired consumer responses, then, included exposure, attention, interest, understanding, liking, brand associations, recognition, recall, and trying and buying the product. All these responses were elicited to significantly increase California Avocado awareness among its various target audiences and create a fun personality for the green fruit, as well as loyalty to the "Genuine California Avocado."

Consider This

1. How many different effects did the "California Avocado" campaign hope to create? Which one do you think is most important?
2. In what way do the headlines quoted in this story deliver the desired effects?

Sources: Adapted from Stuart Elliott, "The Marketing California Avocado's Personality," *New York Times*, February 17, 2004 (www.NYTimes.com); "California Releases Nutrition Study Results," OnRamp Communications Press Room, September 11, 2002 (www.onrampcomm.com/newsroom); California Avocado Commission Web site (www.avocado.org).

Brand Position   Understanding the brand meaning requires the consumer to learn what the brand is and what it stands for relative to its category and its competition. For example, Red Lobster = seafood restaurant, which links the brand to the category. The brand position states what the brand is all about, its essence. However, in many cases, brand position, or essence, moves beyond the category link to include the values the brand represents, such as MTV's connection with the edgy, off-the-wall mind-set of the youth market.

Brand Personality   Brand personality—the idea that a brand takes on familiar human characteristics, such as friendliness, trustworthiness, or snobbery—contributes an *affective* dimension to the meaning of a brand. It reflects how people feel about a brand. Green Giant, for example, built its franchise on the personality of the friendly giant who watches over his valley and makes sure that Green Giant vegetables are fresh, tasty, and nutritious.

Brand Image   Understanding brand meaning involves understanding the symbolism and associations that create **brand image**, the mental impression consumers construct for a product. Meaning is created for a brand by creating associations that connect the brand to lifestyles, types of people who use the product, and other qualities, such as value and status. The richness of the brand image determines the quality of the relationship and the emotional connections that link a customer to a brand.

Brand Promise   A brand is sometimes defined as a promise because it establishes a familiar image and an expectation level based on familiarity, consistency, and predictability. That's what has driven McDonald's to its position as a worldwide leader in the fast-food category. You know what to expect when you walk into a McDonald's store anywhere in the world—quality fast food at a reasonable price.

Brand Loyalty   A personal experience with a brand can develop into a brand relationship, which is a connection over time that results in brand loyalty. People have unique relationships with the brands they buy and use regularly and this is what makes them brand loyal.

Association Networks

In association tests, which are used in planning brand and positioning strategies, people are asked what they think of when they hear a cue, such as the name of a product category. They respond with all the things that come to their mind, and that forms their **network of associations**. Brand perceptions are tested this way to map the structure and logic of these association networks, which lead to message strategies. For example, what do you think of when you think of Taco Bell? Wendy's? Arby's? Each restaurant should bring to mind some things in common (fast food, cheap food), but they also have distinct networks of associations based on type of food (Mexican, hamburgers, roast beef), restaurant design, logo and colors, brand characters, healthfulness, and so forth. Each restaurant, then, has a distinctive profile that can be determined from this network of associations.

PERSUASION

Advertising attempts to develop and change attitudes and behaviors through rational arguments or by touching emotions in such a way that they create belief and a compulsion to act. **Persuasion** is the conscious intent on the part of the source to influence or motivate the receiver of a message to believe or do something. It's central to how advertising works because persuasion can be produced by both rational arguments and compelling emotions.

Principle
Advertising employs both rational arguments and compelling emotions to create persuasive messages.

The Components of Persuasion

Persuasion is designed to change attitudes and behavior and build beliefs. There are many dimensions to persuasion and advertisers identify the following components to explain how persuasion works in advertising:

Attitudes. A state of mind, tendency, propensity, position, inclination

Argument. Reasons, proof

Involvement. Engagement; intensifies brand relationships

Motivation. Incentive or reason to respond

Influence. External people or events that shape attitudes and behavior

Conviction and Preference. Creating agreement and consideration (intend to try or buy)

Loyalty. Repeat purchase; satisfaction; advocate

Attitudes An **attitude** is mental readiness to react to a situation in a given way. Attitudes are seen by many scholars as the most central factor in persuasion.[15] Attitudes can be positive, negative, or neutral. Both positive and negative attitudes, particularly those that are embedded in strong emotions, can motivate people to action—or to lack of action. A negative attitude toward smoking, for example, may keep teenagers from trying cigarettes. Marketing communication is used to establish, change, or reinforce attitudes.

Arguments An **argument** is based on a cognitive strategy. It uses logic, reasons, and proofs to make a point and build conviction. This is a complex process that demands the audience "follow through" the reasoning to understand the point and reach a conclusion. Advertising that deals with problems and their solutions often relies on argument, as does advocacy advertising that presents a company's point of view.

Motivation Another factor in persuasion is **motivation**. The idea is that something, such as hunger or a desire to be beautiful or rich, prompts a person to act in a certain way. How strongly do people feel about acquiring something or about taking a certain kind of action, such as applying to graduate school or signing up for the Peace Corps? In order to intensify the consumer's level of motivation, advertising and other marketing communication areas such as sales promotion use incentives—gifts, prizes, contests—to encourage people to respond.

Conviction and Preference Effective persuasion results in **conviction**, which means consumers believe something to be true. In terms of advertising effects, belief is indicated when consumers develop a **preference** for, or an intention to try or buy a product.

Credibility is an important factor in believing something and that's one of the big advantages of public relations. Publicity stories delivered through a supposedly unbiased news medium are believed to have higher credibility than advertising, which is sometimes seen as self-serving. However, advertising can use a credibility strategy to intensify the believability of its message; using data to support or prove a claim is critical. Another way is to rely on what is called **source credibility**, which means that the person delivering the message, such as a doctor, is respected and believed. The use of brand characters such as the Maytag repairman and Colonel Sanders for KFC, who was a real person and the creator of the famous chicken recipe ("11 herbs and spices"), are designed to give consumers *a reason to believe* in a brand by cementing conviction.

An example of persuasive work designed to create conviction are the ads for the Orlando, Florida, YMCA contributed by Lara Mann, a graduate of the University of Florida who is now a copywriter at FHB Advertising in Orlando. The ads were designed to create conviction and inspire members to commit to the YMCA, as well as to their own health.

Loyalty **Brand loyalty**, which is measured both as an attitude (preference) and by repeat purchases, is an important response that crosses over between thinking, feeling, and doing. It is a response that is built on customer satisfaction. If you try a product and like it, then you will be more likely to buy it again.

Hewlett-Packard promotes its recycling program, which was recognized as "state-of-the-art" practice, to increase the satisfaction of its customers. According to Gary Elliott, HP's Vice President of global branding and marketing communications, this PC-recycling program is "a complete chain of interaction for customer satisfaction." In other words, customers are attracted to HP products because the company assumes responsibility for recycling its old products. That's a benefit for customers and leads to higher customer satisfaction and loyalty to the HP brand.[16]

Loyalty programs, such as frequent flyer or frequent buyer programs, are designed to retain customers, as well as increase their business. "The whole idea of frequent-flyer pro-

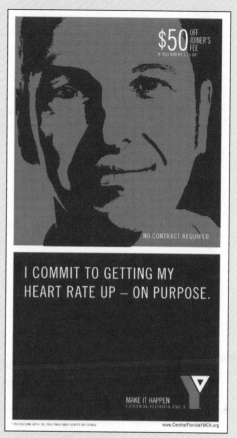

For the Orlando, Florida, YMCA's latest membership drive, the objective was not just to get new members, but to keep them. At the time, the popular perception was that the YMCA was like any other gym. In reality, the YMCA is a family center focused on developing a balanced lifestyle. To resolve these perception issues, the FHB agency developed a campaign highlighting real members' commitments to mind, body, and spirit. With its bold, graphic look, the campaign stood out and was well received.

grams was to artificially induce travelers to change their behavior," says Mark J. Coleman, a longtime airline marketing executive.[17] However, airlines have found such programs to be expensive and sometimes wonder if they are worth it.

Loyalty is of value because it can lead to other behavioral responses, such as advocacy for the brand—that is, speaking out on its behalf—and referrals. (And the opposite—brand aversion—can be disastrous if the dissatisfied customer shares his or her dislike with other people.) In terms of the impact of referrals, the Apple computer's success is credited to some extent to its passionate customers who, as evangelists for the brand, spread the word among their friends and co-workers. This form of word of mouth can be incredibly persuasive, more so than advertising, which is more autonomous.

Involvement's Role in Persuasion

Advertisers can distinguish between products, messages, and media on the basis of the level of involvement they require from the buyer.[18] **Involvement** refers to the degree to which you are engrossed in attending to an ad or making a product decision. Creating a sense of involvement in a marketing communication program is a persuasive tactic because it gets people engaged with a message about a brand. In the case of a special event, participation involves customers with the brand and allows them to have a much more personal contact with the brand. A high level of involvement intensifies the brand–customer relationship.

Involvement is built on relevance—on how much a product message connects with your life and interests. Various types of media are intrinsically more or less involving. Television, for example, is considered to be less involving than print, which demands more concentration from its readers. An advertisement can be more or less involving depending on both the creative strategy used in the message and the medium.[19]

The idea is that you think about some products and reflect on the advertising you see for them; with other products you don't spend much time thinking about them before you buy them. Nor do you pay much attention to their advertising, which you may perceive and file away or even ignore without much thought.

High-involvement products are major purchases, such as cars, computers, and universities to attend, as well as things you care about a lot like clothes and cosmetics. **Low-involvement** products are such things as aspirin, paper napkins, brown envelopes, paper clips, milk, and lettuce.

BEHAVIOR

The behavioral response involving action of some kind is often the most important goal of advertising. In other words, in many campaigns advertising's effectiveness is measured in terms of its ability to motivate people to do something, such as try or buy a product, or respond in some other way, such as visit a store, return an inquiry card, call a toll-free number, or click on a Web site. The "I Want You" poster from World War I is a classic example of an advertising message that was designed to create action.

The Components of the Behavioral Response

Behavior is the action response and it can involve a number of types of action in addition to trying or buying the product. The components of the behavior response are:

Try. Initiating action through trial

Buy. Making it easy to buy

Contact. Responding by visiting, calling, sending back a card, clicking on a Web site, and so forth

Prevention. Discouraging unwanted behaviors

Try and Buy The objective of most marketing programs is sales; the customer view of that is purchase. So in customer-focused marketing programs, the goal is to motivate people to try a product, or buy it. But some marketing programs, such as those for nonprofits, may not be selling goods, so the action response may be to sign up, volunteer, or donate.

Trial is important for new products and expensive products because it lets a customer use the product without investing in its purchase. In other words, the risk is lessened. Sales promotion is particularly good at driving trial through sampling and incentive programs (a free gift when you go to a dealer to test-drive a new car).

Drug advertising is a controversial area precisely because it may lead to action—doctors fear their patients might be so influenced by pharmaceutical advertising that they demand prescriptions even if the drug isn't what the doctor might otherwise prescribe. One

study found that a third of the patients interviewed said they responded with action: They had a discussion with their doctors as a result of seeing a consumer ad. But another study of doctors found that these discussions were more beneficial than problematic because their patients were more informed by the ads and this led them to ask their doctors for more information.[20] In any case, pharmaceutical advertising has been proven to be effective in stimulating action by patients, whether doctors like it or not.

Contact   Trying and buying may be the marketer's dream response, but there are other actions that can also be important measures of an advertisement's effectiveness. Responding by making contact with the advertiser can be an important sign of effectiveness. For example, many ads give a toll-free number, e-mail address, or Web site URL, or contain a response card to send back.

Initiating contact is also valuable, particularly in IMC programs that are designed to maintain brand relationships by creating opportunities for customer-initiated dialogue, such as when a customer contacts a company with a complaint, compliment, suggestion, or referral. Contacting other people is another valued response, particularly when a satisfied customer brings in more business for the brand or company by providing testimonials to friends, family, and colleagues on behalf of the brand.

THE INSIDE STORY

The Curiosity-arousing Function of Antidrug Ads

Carson B Wagner, Ph.D., Assistant Professor, University of Texas

When I first entered graduate school, perhaps the first (and most important) lesson I learned from my mentor was that the best kind of research reveals "differences that make a difference." The more counterintuitive the research finding, the more value it has in the development of knowledge, and small differences that make big differences are better yet. Ideas for studies like this, he said, usually come from everyday observations and from imagining what the implications would be if our assumptions were turned upside down.

Then one weekend, my father, who is an advertising executive, and I got into a conversation about how it seemed every time a news story aired about illicit drugs, a small epidemic of drug use would ensue. Of course, there's been a lot of research done about the ways media can encourage drug use, but most of that is about popular media such as movies and music. News programs and antidrug ads that are meant to show illicit drugs in a negative light, we'd think, shouldn't lead people toward drugs. But, as almost any student of communication has learned, media don't tell us what to think—they tell us what to think about.

So, I decided to test the idea on antidrug ads—the most counterintuitive possibility—in a small experiment for my master's thesis. I scoured prior research, but I couldn't find anything saying such a thing might happen [that antidrug ads would lead to drug use]. Almost all studies showed that drug attitudes became more negative. But, the psychology of curiosity literature suggested something else, for one because if antidrug ads make people think drug use is widespread, they might become curious about experimenting themselves.

The curiosity literature was correct, and oddly enough, I defended my thesis the day after Congress allot-ted $195 million per year to antidrug ads. The following May, I presented my findings at a conference, and the idea seemed to agitate some of those in the crowd. Then, one day in September, I got a call from a radio show in Los Angeles. They wanted me to be a guest and discuss my study. A bit dumbfounded, I then found several e-mails waiting for me asking to send a copy of the thesis. It turns out the Libertarian Party had distributed a press release attacking the federal government for spending taxes to encourage drug use—citing my study.

Over the next few weeks, I was a guest on different talk shows, and a number of news and wire stories appeared. One in particular quoted, "You have to watch your source in studies like this, and you have to watch what people will do to rationalize their findings when you know where they are coming from." Of course, Mr. Weiner, spokesman for U.S. Drug Czar Gen. Barry McCaffrey, didn't know. But Congress called to find out, and they requested the study be presented in their first review of antidrug ad spending. Since then, a large-scale government-sponsored survey examining the first five years of the campaign uncovered similar relationships [between antidrug advertising and drug use], but unfortunately it doesn't seem to have gotten any better reception than mine did.

Carson B Wagner earned his Ph.D. from the University of Colorado at Boulder in 2002, and he received his master's from Penn State in 1998. He grew up with and has worked in his father's ad agency, Orrico & Wagner, and he served with Bill Clinton's advance team in the 1992 presidential primaries. He's now beginning his academic career as Assistant Professor of Advertising at the University of Texas at Austin, where his research continues to receive honors and grant monies.

Nominated by Professor Sandra Moriarty, University of Colorado.

Prevention There are social-action situations where advertising messages are designed to deter behaviors, such as limiting car use due to clean-air campaigns and anti-smoking and antidrug campaigns for teens. This is a complicated process that involves counterarguing by presenting negative messages about an unwanted behavior and creating the proper incentives to stimulate the desired behavior.

Because the effects are so complicated, the impact of such campaigns is not always clear. The national "Just Say No" campaign claims to have had an impact on teenagers' drug use. However, as the Inside Story box explains, sometimes antidrug advertising can boomerang because it *publicizes* the unwanted behavior. The Inside Story author, Carson B Wagner, became a media star when, as a graduate student, he challenged conventional wisdom about the power of antidrug advertising to teenagers.

. . .

Do these ads work? The "Just Say No" campaign believes they do change the behavior
of teens and convince them to avoid drugs. Other researchers believe such ads just make drug taking
more attractive. What do you think?

IT'S A WRAP

SIGNBOY IS A SIGN OF SUCCESS FOR FOOTJOY

. . .

Given the complexity of advertising effects, it's amazing that advertisers can actually prove the effectiveness of their advertising. That's why the EFFIE awards, and other award shows that recognize effectiveness, are so valuable. The "SignBoy" campaign, however, has been deemed to be effective not only by the FootJoy company, but also by EFFIE judges. It has proved to be the most successful campaign in FootJoy's history and has kept the company prominently in front of the golf shoe target audience. Overall sales has continued to increase; but more importantly market share increased from 46 percent in 1998 to 58 percent in 2003.

That market share increase is a huge story for a number of reasons. For one, it's difficult for a market leader to increase share very much, particularly when the market is getting more crowded with competitors. Another reason the market share increase is noteworthy is that FootJoy is a relatively small company, compared to big marketers like Nike who have more visibility and much larger advertising budgets. It takes a breakthrough message to make an impact for a smaller, less-well-known company.

The captivating character of the SignBoy also helped FootJoy capture a much higher percent of the younger market. FootJoy's new shoe use among golfers under 30 increased 10.2 percent after the campaign's first year, while Nike dropped 3.3 percent in the same year. This pattern has continued into 2004 and FootJoy continues to dominate the golf shoe category. Overall, FootJoy was able to widen its market by changing its image to appeal to younger aspiring golfers even as it maintained its leadership position as the shoe of choice for the world's best golfers.

On the perceptual level, the campaign created impact and got the attention of golfers by creating interest in the antics of the SignBoy, a character that was highly memorable. In terms of cognitive effects, the SignBoy created differentiation between FootJoy and other golf shoes and apparel lines and made the FootJoy brand stand out. Through association with the lovable but goofy SignBoy, the campaign transformed the brand and gave it a fun-loving personality. The campaign was persuasive because it highlighted the professional golfers who use FootJoy—and those pros are the models for ordinary golfers who look to them for leadership in golf decisions. So it affected their attitudes and preferences, which ultimately led to the sales and market share results detailed above. The SignBoy campaign is a standard bearer for the industry and that is why is has been recognized with an EFFIE award.

▪▪▪ Summary

1. **Demonstrate why communication is a key factor in advertising effectiveness.** Advertising is, first of all, a form of communication—a message to a consumer about a product. Its effectiveness is determined by its success in following the traditional steps in a communication model: (1) the source (the advertiser and its agencies) effectively encode, (2) a message in the form of an advertisement or other type of marketing communication, which is (3) presented successfully through some channel of communication, and then (4) received by a consumer (a media reader, viewer, listener) who then (5) responds in some way providing feedback (sales, research findings) back to the source. The process can be complicated at any point by noise, which refers to things that distract or impair the communication process.

2. **Explain the Facets Model of Advertising Effects to show how brand advertising works.** Advertising effects are the ways consumers can respond to an advertising message. They can be grouped into six categories: (1) perception, (2) understanding or a cognitive response, (3) feeling or an emotional or affective response, (4) associations that set up connections in the consumer's mind, (5) belief which is the result of persuasion, and (6) action or behavior.

3. **List the six key effects that govern consumer response to advertising messages.** Perception involves how consumers are exposed to a message and how they select information to which they pay attention. This is based on such personal factors as interest and relevance, as well as on how the consumer retains an awareness of a brand or message in memory. Cognition is based on a consumer's needs, particularly for information, and they way that information is learned in order to create a sense of differentiation for a product—something that will be recalled when the consumer needs to make a product decision. The affective response is based on feelings—what consumers want and like and how product messages resonate with their emotions. Association sets up a network of symbols for products that people connect with the brand through conditioned learning—which transforms a product into a distinctive brand with a personality and image. Persuasion is based on attitude change, influenced by arguments, and personal motivation and involvement that leads to conviction and preference. A behavior response involves buying and trying a product, as well as other forms of action such as contacting a company.

▪▪▪ Key Terms

affective responses, 109

AIDA, 102

aided recognition, 106

argument, 114

association, 110

attention, 105

attitude, 114

awareness, 105

brand image, 113	feedback, 100	motivation, 114	resonance, 110
brand loyalty, 114	hierarchy-of-effects model, 102	needs, 108	selective perception, 104
channels, 99	high involvement, 116	network of associations, 113	source, 99
clutter, 101	interactive communication, 100	noise, 100	source credibility, 114
cognition, 106	interest, 105	perception, 104	subliminal, 106
cognitive learning, 108	conditioned learning, 108	persuasion, 113	symbolic meaning, 110
conditioned learning, 108	interest, 105	preference, 114	think-feel-do model, 103
conviction, 114	involvement, 116	recall, 106	transformation, 111
delayed effects, 109	liking, 110	receiver, 100	unaided recognition, 106
emotional appeals, 110	low involvement, 116	recognition, 106	viral marketing, 101
exposure, 105	message, 99	relevance, 105	wants, 108

Review Questions

1. What are the key components of a communication model, and how do they relate to advertising?

2. Explain how the Facets Model of Advertising Effects can be used to describe how brand advertising works. What are the key components of brand messages, and how do they relate to the basic advertising effects?

3. What are the six categories of effects identified in the Facets Model? What does each one represent in terms of a consumer's response to an advertising message?

Discussion Questions

1. What is breakthrough advertising? Give an example and explain how it works. Find an example of an ad that you don't think is breakthrough advertising and explain why you evaluate it that way.

2. This chapter identifies six major categories of effects or consumer responses. Find an ad that you think is effective and explain how it works, analyzing the way it cultivates responses in these six categories.

3. Uma Proctor is a planner in an agency that handles a liquid detergent brand that competes with Lever's Wisk. Uma is reviewing a history of the Wisk theme, "ring around the collar." It is one of the longest-running themes on television, and Wisk's sales share indicates that it has been successful.

What is confusing Uma is that the Wisk history includes numerous consumer surveys that show consumers find "ring around the collar" to be a boring, silly, and altogether irritating advertising theme. Can you explain why Wisk is such a popular brand even though its advertising campaign has been so disliked?

4. You have been asked to participate in a debate in your office about two different approaches to advertising. The question is: Which is most important in creating effective advertising—informing consumers about the product's features or creating an emotional bond with consumers? Take one side or the other and develop an argument in support of that view.

Class Projects

1. From current magazines, identify five advertisements that have exceptionally high stopping power (attention), five that have exceptionally high pulling power (interest), and five that have exceptionally high locking power (memory). Which of these advertisements are mainly information and which are mainly emotional and focused on feelings? Which are focused on building a brand or creating associations? Do them any of them do a great job of creating action? Rank what you believe are the top 5 most effective ads in the collection of 15. Why did you choose those five and what can you learn from them about effective advertising?

2. Organize the class into five teams and refer to the "sticky" Web sites listed in the table. Each team should take one of the five categories of Web sites. Check out those sites that don't require you to subscribe and analyze them in terms of the four categories of effectiveness: perception, learning, persuasion, and behavior. Can you determine from this analysis why these sites are "sticky" Web sites? Which one does your team rate as the most effective? Why?

Sticking around Web Sites	
Automotive	autos.msn.com
	kbb.com
	autotrader.com
	cars.com
	autoweb.com
Shopping	amazon.com
	eBay.com
	barnesandnoble.com
	priceline.com
	cdnow.com
Travel	mapquest.com
	maps.yahoo.com
	travelocity.com
	expedia.com
	travel.yahoo.com
Entertainment	disneygo.com
	windowsmedia.com
	uproar.com
	ticketmaster.com
	webshots.com
Financial	Finance.yahoo.com
	cbs.marketwatch.com
	moneycentral.msn.com
	etrade.com
	quicken.com

Adapted from "Sticking Around." *Brandweek's IQ Interactive Report*, June 15, 2000, p. IQ66.

HANDS-ON 4

C A S E

How Advertising Works

If It Walks Like the Aflac Duck

You've probably never heard of the American Family Life Assurance Co., nor are you likely to be familiar with its primary service: supplemental workplace medical insurance, a type of insurance that is used by people to help cover the many loopholes and deductibles in their primary insurance coverage. Then again, if you are like 90 percent of U.S. consumers, maybe you *have* heard of the company. In its advertising it calls itself "AFLAC."

The four-year AFLAC campaign is the work of Linda Kaplan Thaler, owner of the New York agency that bears her name. Thaler's ads are not known for their subtlety. Among her credits are the Toy's R Us jingle "I don't want to grow up," and the successful campaign for Clairol Herbal Essences, featuring an "orgasmic" hair-washing experience. The Herbal Essences ads strike some as funny, others as quite possibly offensive, but sales of the product have skyrocketed to almost $700 million a year.

In many ways Thaler's ads hearken back to the 1960s, when it was common to feature "sex, schmaltz, chirpy jingles and 'talking' babies and animals," as the *New York Times*'s advertising columnist Stewart Elliott puts it. Industry insiders have been known to snipe at Thaler's work, and few would describe her campaigns as "edgy." But as Maurice Levy, CEO of the giant advertising company Publicis, observes, "There are people who do advertising for what I call the advertising village and people who are doing advertising for the consumer. She is doing advertising much more for the consumer." Thaler herself notes, "We're doing our job when we find ways to get people to buy things."

Thaler's AFLAC ads, by almost any measure, are her best. Almost all feature a white duck desperately screaming "AFLAC!" at people who need supplemental insurance. Unfortunately, the duck's audience never quite seems to hear him. Most of the ads contain a fair amount of slapstick, usually at the expense of the duck, whose exasperated-sounding voice originates with former *Saturday Night Live* cast member Gilbert Gottfried. "He's got the right answer but nobody is listening, and that's a situation that resonates with people," says Kathleen Spencer, director of AFLAC's corporate communications. "There's also just something inherently comical about a duck."

The campaign has been enormously successful. Since the ads first began running, brand name awareness has increased from 15 percent to 90 percent. Over the same period year-to-year sales increases have almost doubled. Dan Amos, CEO for AFLAC, believes that "our name recognition with our advertising campaign and our strong sales force together have combined to truly help our company." In 2003 *Ad Age* named the commercial featuring the duck and the Amazing Kreskin (who hypnotizes a man into thinking he is a chicken) the most-recalled spot in America.

But what makes the AFLAC campaign truly remarkable is how little it has cost the company. The duck has a higher Q score (a measure of a character's familiarity and appeal) than both Ronald McDonald and the Energizer Bunny, but whereas Energizer has spent almost a billion dollars over 15 years on advertising, and McDonald's spends almost $700 million every year, AFLAC's ad budget is only $45 million a year. There is no denying that Thayler's work for AFLAC is a triumph of both effectiveness and value.

Consider This

1. Some viewers don't like the AFLAC ads. Can an ad still accomplish its intended purposes if people find it annoying?
2. The AFLAC campaign is more than four years old. In your opinion, will the campaign stay effective for the foreseeable future?
3. What makes AFLAC ads so effective? Is it something more than their entertainment value? If so, what else contributes to their success?

Sources: "Top Spots," *Advertising Age* (January 13, 2003); Stuart Elliott, "Why a Duck? Because It Sells Insurance: Kaplan Thaler Puts Consumers Ahead of Peer Approval," *New York Times* (June 24, 2002): C11; David Haffenreffer, "AFLAC Inc.—CEO Dan Amos," *CNN Money Morning,* Transcript #102301cb.129, October 23, 2002; Theresa Howard, "AFLAC Duck Gives Wings to Insurer's Name Recognition," *USA Today* (May 17, 2001): 9b.

The Consumer Audience

So What Do You Crave?

Award:
EFFIE® Gold

Company:
White Castle

Agency:
J. Walter Thompson

Campaign:
*"What You Crave—
One of Ours"*

CHAPTER KEY POINTS

After reading this chapter, you will be able to:

1. Assess cultural and social influences on consumer responses.

2. Demonstrate how psychological influences motivate consumers.

3. Explain the behavioral characteristics that describe consumer responses.

4. Describe how the consumer decision process works.

5. Differentiate between segmenting and targeting and trace these planning tools to their sources in cultural, social, psychological, and behavioral factors.

McDonald's has more than 13,000 locations; Burger King has 8,300; Wendy's has 5,300 . . . but White Castle has only 360 restaurants. McDonald's spends more than $660 million on advertising; Burger King spends $300 million; Wendy's spends $230 million. White Castle spends only $10 million. White Castle is outnumbered and outspent by its competition. Its only option, then, is to outsmart them. White Castle limits its menu. White Castle offers a unique, steamy, oniony taste unlike any others in the fast-food hamburger category. Competitors use lots of mainstream television and reach everyone. White Castle's television ads are seen in the odd hours when its devoted fans are craving its burgers.

White Castle succeeds in the increasingly fierce fast-food category because it defies common wisdom and charts its own course for its own special group of customers. The chain's relationship with

125

its customer is different from that of other fast-food chains. Researchers made the discovery that White Castle is more than a full feeling in the stomach; its customers have an emotional attachment to the brand. As one customer explained, "I crave White Castle more than anything else. When I get a craving, I just have to have it." That insight came from an ethnographic study that followed White Castle customers through a day in their lives and observed their behavior. That statement became the source of the White Castle brand idea. The chain's response to its competitive challenge was to leverage this emotional connection its core target audience—the "Craver"—has with the brand.

Under the guidance of the J. Walter Thompson (JWT) agency, White Castle's "Crave" advertising has been a consistent EFFIE winner. In 2003 it was recognized for advertising that delivered higher sales based on improving its level of *purchase intent*—the number of people who say they intend to stop at White Castle. The specific objectives of the campaign were to:

- Improve future purchase intent among the target audience by 10 percent (based on how consumers rate this statement: "It [the advertising] makes me want to go to White Castle.").
- Translate this purchase intention into sales by achieving, on a percentage basis, an annual sales growth 25 percent greater than the average sales growth of McDonald's, Burger King, Wendy's, and Taco Bell combined.

What is it that drives this special brand relationship? One factor is the tiny juicy hamburger smothered with onions that people consider a treat, in spite of onion breath (a result lampooned in some of the chain's commercials). But the real difference is the production of the hamburger, which is cooked with onions on a hot griddle for a short period of time. The result has a distinctive taste that brings its faithful back for sacks of what the chain calls Slyders®. Devoted Cravers, who are the advertising's most important target audience, are a cultlike following with a passion for the steamy Slyders. The success of the "What You Crave" campaign is detailed in the It's a Wrap section at the end of this chapter.

White Castle has an unusual relationship with its customers. In order to better understand that bond, this chapter will look at influences on consumers' behavior—in other words, what motivates them as they make purchase decisions—and then discuss how these factors help define groups of people who might be profitably targeted with an advertising message. The study of influences on consumers helps advertisers design effective campaigns through careful targeting of the message.

HOW DOES CONSUMER BEHAVIOR WORK?

Think about something you bought last week. How did the purchase process happen? Was it something you needed—or just something you wanted? Did you set out to go to a specific store or just go shopping? Or was it something you saw online or in an ad? Had you been planning the purchase for a while? Did somebody tell you about it, or have you talked to someone about it now that you've made the purchase? These are the kinds of questions marketers ask about their customers. And good advertisers also have to be good students of consumer behavior. **Consumer behavior** describes how individuals or groups select,

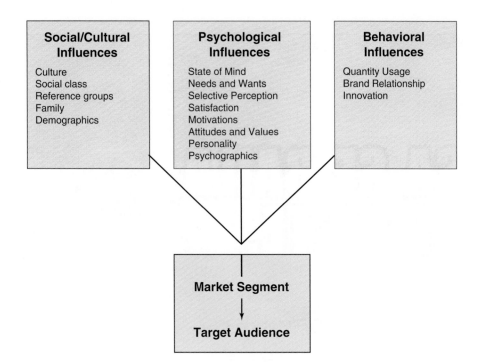

FIGURE 5.1

Influences on Consumer Decision Making

purchase, use, or dispose of products—as well as describing the needs that motivate these behaviors. So as we proceed through this chapter, keep asking yourself questions about your own consumer behavior, as well as that of your friends and family.

The Consumer Audience

In this chapter we look at consumers as the audience for the communication process and we seek to give you more insight into how this consumer response to a message affects their product decision making. *Consumers* are people who buy or use products to satisfy their needs and wants. **Customers** are specific types of consumers; they are people like White Castle's devoted fans who buy a particular brand or patronize a specific store.

There are various ways to categorize consumers. One way is to divide them by the type of market—either business or consumer. As we discussed in Chapter 2, these are usually referred to as business to-business (B2B) or business-to consumer (B2C). Another way to categorize consumers is as either those who shop for and purchase the product (purchasers or customers) or those who actually use the product (users). This distinction is important because purchasers and users can have different needs and wants. In the case of children's cereals, parents (the purchasers) often look for nutritional value and a decent price. In contrast, children (the users) look for a sweet taste and a package with a prize inside or a game on the outside.

In the case of business-to-business (B2B) marketing, customers may be purchasing agents who are professional buyers for their companies; other workers actually use the products that purchasing agents buy. Computers, for example, can be used by everyone in a company for all kinds of specialized jobs, but the computer purchase may be made by the company's purchasing agent. Figure 5.1 is a general model of consumer behavior. It is also a visual roadmap for this chapter.

Principle
Buyers may not be the users and users may not be the buyers. Buyers and users often have entirely different needs.

CULTURAL AND SOCIAL INFLUENCES ON CONSUMER DECISIONS

Many factors affect the way you make product decisions in response to an advertising message. The culture and the society in which you were raised affect your values and opinions. Likewise, you are a product of the family in which you were raised, and many of your habits and biases developed in the family environment. Your friends also are important

■ ■ ■

This ad for Tide exhibits the effective targeting of the Hispanic culture. ("The salsa is something you dance, not what you wear.")

influences on your opinions, as well as your consumer behavior. The cultural and social forces that impact on your behavior as a consumer fall into five major areas: (1) culture, (2) social class, (3) reference groups, (4) family, and (5) demographics.

Culture

Culture is made up of tangible items (art, literature, buildings, furniture, clothing, and music) and intangible concepts (history, knowledge, laws, morals, and customs) that together define a group of people or a way of life. Culture is learned and passed on from one generation to the next, and the boundaries each culture establishes for behavior are called **norms**. Norms are simply rules that we learn through social interaction that specify or prohibit certain behaviors. The source of norms is our **values**, which come from our immersion in a specific culture. Values, particularly cultural values, represent our underlying belief systems. In the United States we value freedom, independence, and individualism; in other countries, particularly some Asian countries, people value families and groups more than individualism. Of course, there are some universals: Most people value good health. Values are few in number and hard to change. They are also internal, and they guide behavior. Advertisers strive to understand the underlying **core values** that govern people's attitudes and refer to them when selecting an ad's primary appeals; the core values of the brand should match the core consumer values. One simplified list consists of nine core values:

1. A sense of belonging
2. Excitement
3. Fun and enjoyment
4. Warm relationships
5. Self-fulfillment
6. Respect from others
7. A sense of accomplishment
8. Security
9. Self-respect

Subcultures   Sometimes, a culture can be further broken down into smaller groups called subcultures. Hispanics living in Southern California, Texas, Miami, and New York City can be quite different, and they are all distinct subcultures of the overall Hispanic culture. **Subcultures** can be defined by geographic regions or by shared human characteristics such as age, values, language, or ethnic background. In the United States there are many different subcultures: teenagers, college students, retirees, southerners, Texans, athletes, musicians, and working single mothers, to name a few.

Corporate Culture   Culture applies to B2B marketing as well as B2C (business-to-consumer). **Corporate culture** is a term that describes how various companies operate. Some are very formal with lots of procedures, rigid work hours, and dress codes. Others are more informal in terms of their operations as well as their communication. The same patterns exist in the way businesses make purchasing decisions: Some rigidly control and monitor purchases; others are loose and easygoing and purchases may be less controlled. Likewise there are norms and values in companies, particularly after the Enron and other scandals, that govern corporate behavior and the buying decisions of agents. Certainly the debates about outsourcing labor and buying from third-world countries where workers may not be treated fairly have become cultural issues for purchasing departments in many corporations.

Social Class

Another influence you experience as a consumer is **social class**, the position you and your family occupy within your society. Social class is determined by such factors as income, wealth, education, occupation, family prestige, value of home, and neighborhood. Every society has a social class structure. In more rigid societies, such as those of India, people have a difficult time moving out of the class into which they were born. In the United States, although people may move into social classes that differ from their families', the country still has a class system consisting of upper, middle, and lower classes. Marketers assume that people in one class buy different goods from different outlets and for different reasons than people in other classes.

Reference Groups

A **reference group** is a group of people we use as a guide for behavior in specific situations. Examples are political parties, religious groups, racial or ethnic organizations, clubs based on hobbies, and informal affiliations such as fellow workers or students—your peers. David Reisman describes individuals in terms of their relationships to other people as *inner-directed* (individualistic) or *outer-directed* (group and society). Advertisers are particularly interested in the role of peers in influencing their outer-directed friends' wants and desires. On the other hand, inner-directed people are more likely to try new things first.

For consumers, reference groups have three functions: (1) they provide information; (2) they serve as a means of comparison; and (3) they offer guidance. Ads that feature typical users in fun or pleasant surroundings are using a reference group strategy. You also may be attracted to a particular reference group and want to be like the members of that group out of respect or admiration. Advertisers use celebrity endorsements to tap into this device.

White Castle "Cravers" recognize that they are part of a unique group. Their sense of being a "Craver" is an important facet of their self-image as an individualist and a fun part of their social lives. They experience life in their own ways; they get it in ways others just don't understand. "Same old, same old" mainstream burgers just don't have the attitude a "Craver" demands. This resonated with the idea of consuming a sack of 10 Slyders almost as a bragging right.

Family

The family is the most important reference group because of its longevity and the intensity of its relationships, as depicted in the Sony ad. Other reference groups such as peers, co-workers, and neighbors tend to change as we age. According to the U.S. Census, a **family** consists of two or more people who are related by blood, marriage, or adoption, and live in the same household. A **household** differs from a family in that it consists of all those who occupy a dwelling whether they are related or not. The family is responsible for raising and training children and establishing a lifestyle for family members. Your **lifestyle** is the way you spend your time and money and the kinds of activities you value.

Advertisers need to understand the structure, changes, and workings of the family in order to communicate effectively. For example, for the first time, one-person households outnumber married couples with children.[1] This reflects a growing trend in America over the past 30 years to marry later in life, divorce, or never get married at all. Marketers and their advertisers have been right on top of this familial trend. Banks have created special

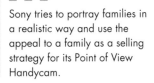

Sony tries to portray families in a realistic way and use the appeal to a family as a selling strategy for its Point of View Handycam.

^{TABLE}
5.1 **Home Ownership by Age**

Householder by Age	% Owing a Home
15–24	18
25–34	46
35–44	66
45–54	75
55–64	80
65–74	81
75–84	77

Source: U.S. Census Bureau, 2000, as reported in "No Place Like It," *American Demographics,* March 2002, p. 48.

mortgages, builders are providing homes and apartments to meet the needs of the single, and food marketers have introduced "single" portions.

Demographics

Demographics are the statistical, personal, social, and economic characteristics used to describe a population including age, gender, education, income, occupation, race, and family size. These characteristics serve as the basis for most advertising strategies and knowing them assists advertisers in message design and media selection for the target market.

Age People in different stages of life have different needs. An advertising message must be geared to the target audience's age group and should be delivered through a medium that members of that group use. How old are you? What products did you use 5 or 10 years ago that you don't use now? Look ahead 10 years. What products might you be interested in buying then? Consider home ownership as a factor of age; the older people are, the more likely they are to own a home. In Table 5.1, note that the largest increase happens when people reach the 25–34 age group.

Age is a key factor in media plans because age usually determines what media you watch, listen to, or read—as Table 5.2 shows. The table breaks down media usage in terms of common age groupings used by advertising planners. Note that young people are hard to reach with any of the traditional media. Young adults 25–34 can be reached best through radio and online. Similar to young adults, midlife adults 35–44 spend more time with radio or online but they are also the most involved with media of all kinds. The predominant media that advertisers use to reach the highly attractive youth market and young adults are the Internet, radio, and magazines that can be delivered via the Internet.

^{TABLE}
5.2 **Media Usage by Age**

Age	Radio	TV	Cable	Magazines	Newspapers	Online
18–24	16%	11%	13%	17%	7%	13%
25–34	23	18	20	21	13	23
35–44	25	19	22	23	21	28
45–54	17	16	17	18	21	22
55–64	9	13	12	10	15	9
65-plus	10	24	15	10	23	5

Overall usage patterns for each medium vary by age group. This table shows the percentage of persons in each age group who are heavy users of the individual medium. For instance, 16 percent of heavy radio listeners are in the 18–24 age bracket.

Source: Reprinted with permission from the February 26, 2001, issue of *Advertising Age.* Crain Communications Inc. 2001.

It's swim or swim.

GUARANTEED INCOME FOR LIFE When you retire, you're not about to sit on the sidelines. Your MetLife advisor can show you how you can continue to do the things you love with an annuity that offers you a safe and secure income. So you'll enjoy financial freedom to explore all life still has to offer. For more information, **call 1-800-MetLife or visit metlife.com**

have you met life today?

MetLife

INSURANCE · INVESTMENTS · BANKING

■ ■ ■

As the baby boomers reach retirement, many companies, such as insurance giant MetLife, are developing new strategies to reach them.

Age is driving a fundamental shift in U.S. marketing. For 50 years, marketers have focused on reaching young people not only because they are in the formative years of making brand choices, but also because the youth market during that era was huge in terms of numbers. Baby boomers, the 76 million consumers born between 1946 and 1964 and now in the final years of their careers, have made a huge population bulge as they have moved through the life cycle. As they grew up, the numbers affected first schools, then the job market, and now retirement programs and health care. The emphasis on youth marketing is changing as proportionately fewer babies are being born and the baby boomers age. Seniors are becoming a much more important target market as these age patterns change.

Gender Gender is an obvious basis for differences in marketing and advertising. The gender breakdown in the 2000 Census was 48.9 percent male, 51.1 percent female. *Primary* gender differences are physical traits that are inherent in males or females, such as a woman's ability to bear children. *Secondary* gender traits tend to be associated with one sex more than the other. Wearing perfume and shaving legs are secondary traits associated with women. The primary gender traits of men and women create demands for products and services directly associated with a person's sex; for example, many consumers consider certain brands to be masculine or feminine. It is unlikely that men would use a brand of cologne called "White Shoulders." The Gillette Company found that the majority of women would not purchase Gillette razor blades, so they introduced brands exclusively for women, such as the Sensor and Daisy disposable razors.

Sexual Orientation In the last decade gay and lesbian consumers have become serious target markets. Because some heterosexuals are still offended by the gay lifestyle, advertisers must determine the best way to target gay consumers. Companies that advertise in gay media, such as GayDish TV network, *Freshmen,* and *Digital Gay World,* include Sony, Apple, Banana Republic, American Express, Hiram Walker, Miller Brewing, Coors, Subaru, and Visa, to name a few. Some companies that target gays run the same ad campaign in both straight and gay media. For a company like furniture retailer IKEA, the risks are great. If its ads are obviously gay in content or visually, they might lose the heterosexual market. Other companies such as Volvo have opted to produce two different campaigns. For these companies, the challenge is to create ads that are an accurate portrayal of the gay lifestyle.

Race and Ethnicity In the United States, ethnicity is becoming a major criterion for segmenting markets. According to the Census Bureau, the number of African Americans will increase by 15 percent during the next 20 years; Asian Americans by almost 68 percent; and Hispanics by about 64 percent; while the Caucasian population will grow by 13 percent. Even so, consumer habits within each ethnic segment will differ, based on factors such as age and income, and in the case of immigrants, how long they have lived in the United States. The 2000 U.S. Census provided the statistics in Table 5.3 on American race and ethnicity.

Few cultures are more important to U.S. marketing than the Hispanic culture. The Hispanic market is becoming a huge opportunity because it is growing faster proportionately than other ethnic groups. Researchers have found that Hispanics spend more per shopping

TABLE 5.3 Race and Ethnicity in the United States

Race and Ethnicity	% of Population*
White	79.2
Black or African American	12.4
American Indian/Alaskan	.2
Asian	.4
Native Hawaiian	.001
Hispanic or Latino	12.3
Other	.01

*Note that the percentages add up to more than 100 percent. This is due to the continuing difficulty the Census Bureau is having in capturing all the elements of race. Simply, some respondents check more than one category. Although the situation is closer to resolution, there are still potential problems with the validity of the data.

Source: U.S. Census Bureau, 2000.

trip than non-Hispanics and that store signage and product labels in Spanish promote stronger brand loyalty.[2] Hispanics also believe in using cash rather than credit cards and are willing to spend proportionately more money on their kids and their clothing than their Anglo-Saxon counterparts. For that reason, Old Navy is launching Spanish-language campaigns to attract the growing Hispanic store traffic.[3] Two-thirds of the U.S. Hispanic population came from Mexico and brought their brand perceptions with them. Colgate outperforms Procter & Gamble brands such as Crest among U.S. Hispanics because Colgate dominates the Mexican market. The same success applies to Coca-Cola and Wal-Mart Stores. Chinese immigrants also have their own preferences for brands based on their family traditions.[4]

There are also media use differences based on ethnicity. For example, a Nielsen study found that 36 percent of Hispanic viewers watch commercials in their entirety compared to an average of 19 percent of non-Hispanic viewers who do so. Nielsen has found that Hispanic audiences are more influenced by advertising than other U.S. consumers. They are more likely to base their purchasing decisions on advertisements; they are less cynical about marketing.[5]

If we look at the African American population, certain additional U.S. demographic information might prove useful to the advertiser:

- The African American population, with a median age of 30, is five years younger than the U.S. population, on average.
- The African American population is expected to grow more than twice as fast as the Caucasian population between 1995 and 2020, reaching 45 million.
- In 1998, 55 percent of African Americans lived in the South, yet the cities with the highest African American population are not in the South.
- In 2000, there were 8.7 million African American households, nearly half of them married.[6]

For Merrill Lynch, all this information, plus its own proprietary information, helped to design an advertising campaign targeting affluent African Americans. The company identified two clear priorities: the need for more community involvement from companies African Americans do business with and the need for more education about financial services. Merrill Lynch developed a series of financial-education programs for affluent African Americans in Chicago and hosted three seminars—one targeted to small-business owners, another for individual investors, and the third designed for clergy and nonprofit organizations.[7] More than 1,300 African Americans participated in the three seminars and Merrill Lynch acquired over $200,000 in new business.

Education The level of education attained by consumers is also an influence on the advertising strategy. According to the 2000 Census (Figure 5.2) statistics show that U.S.

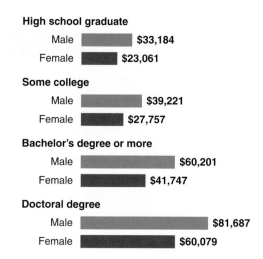

High school diploma or more	2000	1940
All races	84.1%	24.5%
White	88.4	26.1
Black	78.9	7.7
Hispanic	57.0	N/A

Four years of college or more	2000	1940
All races	25.6%	4.6%
White	28.1	4.9
Black	16.6	1.3
Hispanic	10.6	N/A

High school graduate
- Male $33,184
- Female $23,061

Some college
- Male $39,221
- Female $27,757

Bachelor's degree or more
- Male $60,201
- Female $41,747

Doctoral degree
- Male $81,687
- Female $60,079

FIGURE 5.2 Educated Americans

According to the 2000 Census, Americans are better educated than they were in 1940. Also, as the level of education rises, so does salary.

Source: U.S. Census Bureau, 2000.

males attain higher levels of education than U.S. females. Also, income corresponds with gender, regardless of level of education. As far as race is a factor, generally white U.S. consumers attain higher levels of education than blacks and Hispanics.

For advertisers, education tends to correlate with the type of medium consumers prefer, as well as the specific elements or programs within a medium. Consumers with lower education are higher users of television, especially cable. Consumers with higher education prefer print media, the Internet, and selected radio and cable stations. Likewise, education dictates the way copy is written and its level of difficulty. Examine ads in *Fortune* or *Forbes* and you will find words, art, and products different from what you will find in *People* or tabloid publications. Advertisers don't make value judgments about these statistics. Their objective is to match advertising messages to the characteristics of their target markets.

Occupation Most people identify themselves by what they do. In the United States there has been a gradual movement from blue-collar occupations to white-collar occupations during the last three decades. There have also been shifts within white-collar work from sales to other areas, such as professional specialty, technical, and administrative positions. The number of service-related jobs continues to increase, especially in the health care, education, and legal and business service sectors. Much of this transition is a direct result of advanced computer technologies, which have eliminated many labor-intensive, blue-collar occupations. This shift has affected advertising in a number of ways: Today, advertisements seldom portray blue-collar jobs.

Income The most-used demographic indicator for many advertisers is income. You are meaningful to a marketer only if you have the resources to buy the product advertised. Figure 5.3 shows the median household incomes in the United States from the 2000 Census. The median household income (that means half of the households earn more, half earn less) fell from $42,900 in 2001 to $42,409 in 2002, according to a U.S. Census report released in September of 2003. Study the patterns of income distributions in Figure 5.3 and notice which categories tend to make the most money.

Affordability correlates strongly with income: If a marketer knows that an annual income of $125,000 is needed to purchase a BMW, that is important information. It suggests that the setting of the ad should be upscale (country club, executive office tower), and the media employed should match the reading habits of the income group (*Fortune, Money, Wall Street Journal, Town & Country*). Income is correlated with other factors such as education, occupation, and gender. Men, for example, still make more than women in

Principle

Your income is a key demographic factor because you are meaningful to a marketer only if you have the resources needed to buy the product advertised.

comparable jobs. Age is also a factor in income. The mature population in the United States controls 70 percent of all the country's wealth and represents 50 percent of all discretionary spending.[8]

Advertisers track trends in income, especially **discretionary income**, which is the amount of money available to a household after taxes and basic necessities such as food and shelter are paid for. Some industries, such as movie theaters, travel, jewelry, and fashion, would be out of business if people didn't have discretionary income. Discretionary income has found to be a more reliable predictor of spending than income.[9]

Geography   The area in which a target market lives correlates with several demographic characteristics and is important to advertisers. Marketers study the sales patterns of different parts of the country because people residing in different regions need certain products. For example, someone living in the Midwest or the Northeast is more likely to purchase products for removing snow and ice than a Floridian would be. Differences also exist between urban areas and suburban or rural areas. Swimming pools that sell well in a residential suburban neighborhood would not be in demand in an urban neighborhood filled with apartment buildings. To plan advertising, marketers must predict geographic trends and understand how those trends can affect their marketing

Consider This

1. What are the most important cultural and social factors that influence purchase decisions?
2. Why is culture such an important influence?

PSYCHOLOGICAL INFLUENCES THAT MOTIVATE CONSUMERS

We have analyzed cultural, social, and demographic influences on consumer behavior. Now let's look at the internal elements that make you an individual. Advertisers are particularly interested in understanding what psychological factors motivate people to respond as they do. The psychological factors discussed here are the stuff of our motivations. They include state of mind, attitudes and values, and personality.

Perception and State of Mind

Your state of mind affects the way you perceive information as well as determines your particular pattern of consumer behavior. Your past experiences with a brand, as well as what your friends say about it, can color your feelings and make you more or less receptive to a brand message. Other mental states, such as anger, fatigue, hunger, excitement, or lethargy, can also affect your behavior because they can create internal noise that gets in the way of your reception of a message or provide the impetus to drive you to buy something.

Most travel-related companies found their advertising complicated by a negative consumer mind-set after the 9/11 tragedy. Choice Hotels, which includes eight major hotel chains, such as Comfort Inn®, Sleep Inn®, EconoLodge®, and Rodeway Inn®, serves over 16 million guests per year in more than 4,800 hotels across 43 countries. The hotel chain used a "Thanks for traveling" campaign theme to speak to the emotions of its guests and to become a flag waver for the industry.

Needs and Wants   The basic driving forces that motivate us to do something, such as choose a motel when traveling, are called *needs*. Each person has his or her own set of unique needs; some are innate (biological), others are acquired. **Innate needs** include the need for water, food, air, shelter, and sex. Because satisfying these needs is necessary to maintaining life, they are also called *primary needs*. In the case of the needs pyramid developed by psychologist Abraham Maslow (see Figure 5.4), these are called physiological and

The median household income – meaning half earn more, half earn less – rose to $42,148 in 2000 from $40,816 in 1999. Median incomes for various groups:

Household types

Married couples	$59,346

Those living alone:

Male	$26,720
Female	$18,163

Number of persons in household:

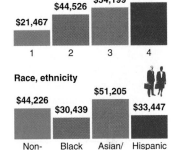

1	2	3	4
$21,467	$44,526	$54,199	$61,852

Race, ethnicity

Non-Hispanic white	Black	Asian/Pacific Islander	Hispanic
$44,226	$30,439	$51,205	$33,447

Geography

Northeast	$45,106
Midwest	$44,646
South	$38,410
West	$44,744
Outside metro areas	$32,837

Age

25–34	$44,473
35–44	$53,240
45–54	$58,218
55–64	$44,992
65 or older	$23,048

FIGURE 5.3

Demographic Medians of Household Income

Because income corresponds with purchase capability, it is an important demographic for advertisers to understand and track.

Source: U.S. Census Bureau, 2000.

A MATTER OF PRACTICE
Choice Hotels Says "Thanks for Traveling"

If you worked for a chain of hotels, how would you have changed your advertising plans after the events of the September 11 tragedy in 2001? What about the following years? The entire country has been consumed by economic uncertainty, security concerns, and the threat of future terrorist acts. This was the marketing problem faced by Choice Hotels International® and its advertising agency Arnold Worldwide.

Choice Hotels is the second-largest hotel franchise in the world. Selecting a hotel is often a combination of rational and emotional needs. Arnold's research found that Choice's core customers have a unique and distinct emotional mind-set. These "True Travelers" are focused on value and quality in their accommodations, without any fancy pretenses or services they will be charged extra for. In the words of the True Traveler, "It's as much about the journey as the destination." Thus the Choice Hotels brand personality had to reflect the same emotional qualities and mind-set of its core audience.

The "Power of Being There" campaign was launched in 2001 to establish Choice Hotels as the "True Traveler" brand. Initial ads titled "Face To Face, Not Fax To Fax" addressed the importance of being there in person for a business meeting. But "Being There" became a lost opportunity after the events of 9/11. The entire travel industry sustained devastating losses as a result of the national tragedy and Choice Hotels wasn't immune to the effects. In spite of its strong rational and emotional connections through its ad campaign, Choice Hotels' occupancy levels plummeted along with the category, making the new marketing challenge twofold:

1. Encourage people to travel again while appearing compassionate and selfless.
2. Provide travelers with a compelling reason to stay at a Choice Hotels property.

Choice market research led to a consumer insight that was particularly appropriate for this new environment: Choice customers and prospects were very patriotic. Arnold's proprietary Mood & Mindset survey established that Americans wanted to maintain the continuity of their everyday lives following 9/11. Thus Arnold's creative direction evolved to position travel as an inherently American freedom that was reinforced by the "Power of Being There" message. The new work elevated the notion of travel as an American right worth sustaining after 9/11, positioning Choice as a natural leader within the industry.

This new strategy came together with the central idea, "Thanks for Traveling," which was emblazoned on 15,000 banners outside Choice Hotel properties and along highways, bridges, and tollbooths. The campaign was officially launched at the reopening of the Reagan National Airport in Washington, D.C., with the involvement of national political figures, including U.S. Secretary of Transportation Norman Mineta. A fully integrated ad

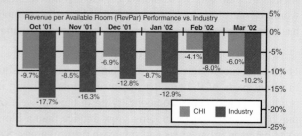

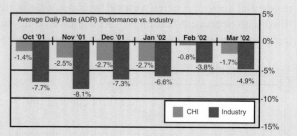

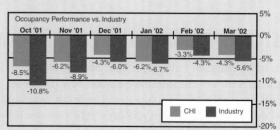

Source: EFFIE brief provided by Choice Hotels and Arnold Worldwide.

campaign followed using TV, print, out-of-home, interactive, point-of-purchase and collateral, direct response, event marketing, and internal communications.

The campaign was effective and its slogan "Thanks for Traveling" became a rallying cry for the entire travel and tourism industry, generating over a $5 million value in consumer and trade PR. Choice Hotels CEO Chuck Ledsinger was invited to appear on Capitol Hill in support of new tourism legislature and the White House invited Mr. Ledsinger to attend the signing of the Airport Security Bill. The success established Choice as the industry leader without making the company appear to be opportunistic. It also united more than 3,500 franchised properties into a single message during a time of crisis. Even other hotels outside the Choice Hotels system were displaying "Thanks for Traveling" banners, posters, and stickers.

In terms of business figures, Choice still experienced major occupancy declines, although at a rate significantly less than the industry. Many competitors tried to lure travelers by drastically cutting rates. Despite widespread deep discounting tactics across the industry, Choice ADR (average daily rate) held up to seasonal norms. Finally, Choice's operating performance (as measured by revenue per available room) experienced declines approximately half as severe as the rest of the industry.

Revelant Products		Example
	SELF-ACTUALIZATION Self-Fulfillment Enriching Experiences	
Hobbies, travel, education		U.S. Army– "Be all you can be."
Cars, furniture, credit cards, stores, country clubs, liquors	**EGO NEEDS** Prestige, Status, Accomplishments	Royal Salute Scotch– "What the rich give the wealthy."
Clothing, grooming products, clubs, drinks	**BELONGINGNESS** Love, Friendship, Acceptance by Others	Pepsi– "You're in the Pepsi generation."
Insurance, alarm systems, retirement, investments	**SAFETY** Security, Shelter, Protection	Allstate Insurance– "You're in good hands with Allstate."
Medicines, staple items, generics	**PHYSIOLOGICAL** Water, Sleep, Food	Quaker Oat Bran– "It's the right thing to do."

FIGURE 5.4 Levels of Needs in the Maslow Hierarchy

Source: Motivation and Personality, 2nd ed., by A. H. Maslow, 1970. Reprinted by permission of Pearson Education, Upper Saddle River, New Jersey.

safety needs. Let's distinguish between needs and wants. Needs are what we feel for more essential items, particularly the primary needs, such as food and shelter. A *want* occurs when we desire or wish for something—we don't die if we don't get it, but it can still provide a strong motivation to try or buy something new. This is particularly true in fashion areas, such as clothing and music. According to Maslow needs must be satisfied before wants can be addressed.

Acquired needs are those we learn in response to our culture and environment. These may include needs for esteem, prestige, affection, power, and learning. Because acquired needs are not necessary to your physical survival, they are considered *secondary needs*. Maslow called them social, egoistic, and self-actualizing. White Castle has built its entire campaign, as well as its continuing sales success, on an understanding of its customers' wants, which it has showcased in its cravings advertising theme. A crave is the ultimate want.

Principle

An item we need is something essential for life; an item we want is something we desire or wish for. Needs must be satisfied before wants come into play as consumer motivations.

Selective Perception: Screens and Filters As we discussed in the previous chapter, ultimately in the perceptual process we select some stimuli and ignore others because we cannot be conscious of all incoming information at one time. The general term for that is *selective perception*. The more clutter there is, the harder it is to sort out those messages that we find relevant to us. Here are the steps in the selection process:

• *Selective exposure* is the way our minds filter incoming information. We naturally tend to notice messages that are pleasant or sympathetic with our views and avoid those that are painful or threatening. Advertising is particularly vulnerable to this filtering process. In fact, one study found that consumers filtered out 96 percent of the advertisements they saw.[10] In other words, they may have been exposed to the message but they didn't pay attention to it. Making messages relevant is the key to getting past this selection and filtering problem.

• *Selective distortion* happens when we are exposed to a message that conflicts with what we believe. We just naturally modify incoming information to fit into our own personal pattern of interests.

• *Selective retention* is the process we go through to save information for future use. A large part of what the brain processes is lost after only an instant. Advertising can aid this process by using repetition, vivid images, easily remembered brand or product names, jingles, high-profile spokespeople, music, and so forth.

Satisfaction   A feeling of satisfaction is only one possible response to selection. More troublesome is dissatisfaction or doubt. People can pay attention to a commercial, buy a product, and be disappointed. One of the reasons is that advertising sometimes raises consumers' expectations. If they actually try or buy the product and it doesn't meet their expectations, they may be dissatisfied. According to the theory of **cognitive dissonance**, we tend to compensate or justify the discrepancies between what we actually received and what we thought we would receive. People engage in a variety of activities to reduce cognitive dissonance. Most notably, we seek out information that supports our decisions and ignore and distort information that does not. Advertising can play a central role in reducing dissonance. For example, IBM uses testimonials by satisfied customers. There is a huge category of automotive service called "aftermarketing," which is designed to keep customers happy after they buy a car.

Motivations

People are complex, dynamic human beings who are suggestible, changeable, often nonrational, and frequently motivated by emotion and habit. Every person's motivations are individual; however, we are influenced by all the social and cultural factors we just discussed, as well as a raft of personal experiences. A *motive* is an internal force that stimulates you to behave in a particular manner. This driving

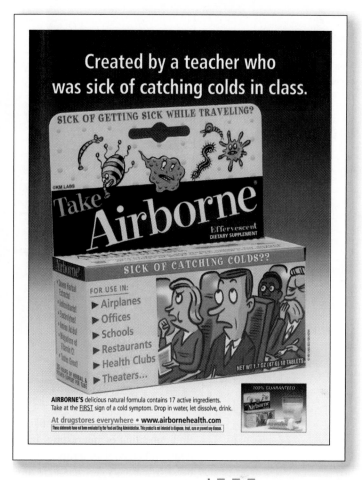

The motivation is obvious for a product that helps you avoid catching a cold when you travel. This ad also features the motivation of the product's creator.

force is produced by the tension caused by an unfulfilled need. People strive to reduce the tension, as the Airborne ad demonstrates. At any given point you are probably affected by a number of different motives. For example, your motivation to buy a new suit will be much higher if you have several job interviews scheduled for the next week.

Research into motivation uncovers the "why" questions: Why did you buy that brand and not another? What prompted you to go to that store? Understanding buying motives is crucial to advertisers because the advertising message and the timing of the ad should coincide with the consumer's motivation priorities. Unfortunately motivations operate largely at an unconscious level. Some of the reasons may be superficially apparent: You go to a restaurant because you are hungry. But what else governs that choice—the location, the interior decorations, a favorite menu item, the recommendation of a friend?

Attitudes and Values

Advertisers are interested in attitudes because of their impact on motivations. Because attitudes are learned, we can establish them, change them, reinforce them, or replace them with new ones. However, most attitudes are deeply set and tend to be resistant to change; you can hold an attitude for months or even years. Attitudes also vary in direction and strength; that is, an attitude can be positive or negative, reflecting like or dislike, or it can be neutral. Attitudes are important to advertisers because they influence how consumers evaluate products, institutions, retail stores, and advertising.

Personality

Who is your best friend and how would you describe that person? We typically describe people—and brands—in terms of their personalities, the distinctive characteristics that

Principle
Strategies that are designed to affect attitudes focus on establishing, changing, reinforcing, or replacing them.

■ ■ ■
The line "interesting life" refers to both the target audience for *Men's Journal* as well as the content of the magazine.

make them individual and unlike anyone else we know. These are also the qualities that you find appealing or interesting. In the psychological literature, **personality** refers to consistency in behavior in terms of how we react to events and situations and behave in various roles. The *Men's Journal* ad is directed at a certain type of personality. The idea of personality traits—old-fashioned, lively, efficient, glamorous, rugged, romantic, helpful, snobbish, sophisticated, warm, dependable—has also been adapted to brands with the idea that brand personalities can be created that will make them distinctive from their competitors.

Psychographic Influences

Psychographics refers to lifestyle and psychological characteristics, such as attitudes, interests, and opinions. The term combines the psychological factors with other consumer characteristics that may have a bearing on how people make decisions. Consumers who have different values, attitudes and beliefs, opinions, interests, motivations, and lifestyles make their product decisions in different ways.[11] Here are some of the major components called AOI (attitudes, opinions, interests) that are used to construct psychographic profiles of consumers:[12]

- *Activities.* Work, hobbies, social events, vacation, entertainment, club membership, community, shopping, sports
- *Opinions.* Self, social issues, politics, business, economics, education, products, future, culture
- *Interests.* Family, home, job, community, recreation, fashion, food, media, achievements

Sometimes these complex psychographic factors are more relevant in explaining consumer behavior than are the simpler demographics. For example, two families living next door to each other with the same general income, education, and occupational profiles may have radically different buying patterns. One family may be obsessed with recycling while their neighbors rarely bother to even keep their newspapers separate from their trash. The differences lie not in their demographics but in their psychographics—their interests and lifestyle.

Advertisers use psychographics in order to understand fairly complex consumer pattern groupings. For instance, there are libraries of psychographic measures that can be

Principle
Often differences in consumer behavior lie in psychographics—consumers' interests and lifestyles—rather than in demographics.

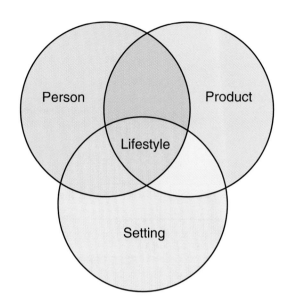

Lifestyle Components
Products are linked to lifestyles in the way they reflect the interests of people and the settings in which the products are used.

purchased from research firms, or a company and its advertising agency can create its own set of psychographic measures to fit its particular product. These psychographic measures can then be used to describe customers (such as heavy users of blended coffee), its advertising message (taste comparison ads), or media choices (heavy users of the Internet).

Lifestyles   One type of psychographics is **lifestyle analysis**, which looks at the ways people allocate time, energy, and money. The *Men's Journal* ad is a good example of a visual that represents a target audience's lifestyle. Some of the most common lifestyle patterns are described by such familiar phrases as yuppies and yuppie puppies (their children). These terms are group identifiers but they also refer to a set of products and the setting within which the products are used. For example, yuppies were characterized as aspiring to an upscale lifestyle, so products associated with this lifestyle might include Rolex watches and BMW cars. Figure 5.5 Illustrates the interactions between the person, the product, and the setting in which a product is used.

The VALS System   Some research firms have taken lifestyle factors one step further by creating lifestyle profiles that collectively reflect a whole culture. One example is the work of SRI International and its Values and Lifestyle System (**VALS**). VALS is a conceptual model that categorizes people according to their values and then identifies various consumer behaviors that go with these values. It then groups consumers according to shared values. Advertisers correlate these VALS groups with their clients' products, and use this information to design ads and select media. SRI has discovered that the relationship between values and purchase is not very strong, so it has developed VALS 2, which groups values and other psychological traits. As we see in Figure 5.6 the system, VALS 2, arranges psychographic groups in a rectangle. They are stacked vertically by resources and horizontally by self-orientation (principle, status, or action oriented). Resources include income, education, self-confidence, health, eagerness to buy, and energy level.

Consumers' positions along the resource and self-orientation axes determines which of eight classifications they fall into: Actualizers, Fulfilleds, Achievers, Experiencers, Believers, Strivers, Makers, or Strugglers. Members of each group hold different values and maintain different lifestyles. Actualizers, for instance, have the highest resources, including income, self-esteem, and energy. Actualizers are difficult to categorize by self-orientation because their high resources allow them the freedom to express many facets of their personalities. Image is important to them. Because of their wide range of interests and openness to change, actualizers' purchases are directed at the finer things in life. Obviously, knowing the psychographic orientation of consumers is a valuable asset to an advertiser in deciding to whom the messages should be targeted.

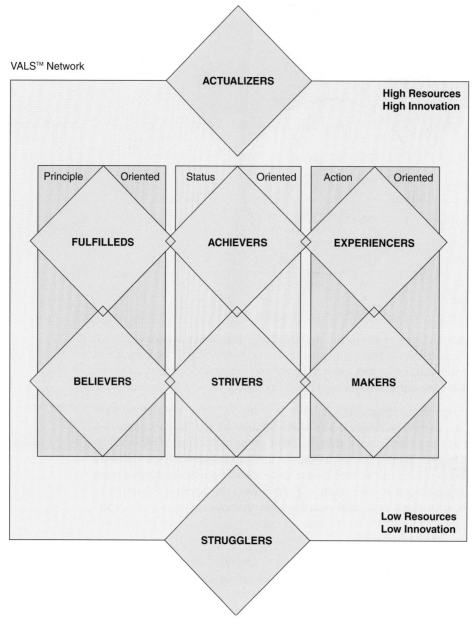

VALS™ Network

ACTUALIZERS

High Resources
High Innovation

| Principle | | Oriented | Status | | Oriented | Action | | Oriented |

FULFILLEDS

ACHIEVERS

EXPERIENCERS

BELIEVERS

STRIVERS

MAKERS

Low Resources
Low Innovation

STRUGGLERS

FIGURE

5.6 **The VALS Network**

VALS 2 is a psychographic model. Advertisers use it when designing targeted advertisements.

One of the leaders in the area of consumer research is SRI Consulting, which created the well-known VALS segmentation system. In the Inside Story, Cheri Anderson describes one of the lessons she's learned working with the VALS data.

A new tool is iVALS, a project that focuses on the attitudes, preferences, and behaviors of online service and Internet users. Early results of iVALS reinforce the idea of a dual-tiered society, but one based on knowledge, not income. Education is the critical factor in who participates in the Internet and to what degree.

VALS is only one of the most highly regarded psychographic models. Another useful model is Yankelovich Partners Inc.'s Monitor MindBase™ that segments consumers by values, attitudes, and mind-sets. In essence, the program uncovers the underlying psychology of consumer behavior on an individual level by segmenting consumers into categories with varying degrees of materialism, ambition, orientation to family life, cynicism, openness to technology, and a host of other elements.[13] Understanding these mind-set segments

THE INSIDE STORY
The Grand Myth of Early Adoption

Cheri L. Anderson, Principal Consultant, SRI Consulting

 Our most creative research assignments come from clients who want to preview the future today. These clients want to know what innovative products to put on the shelf in the future and who is most likely to be the early adopters of their innovative products.

At SRI, we use the VALS psychographic segmentation system to identify consumers most likely to be early adopters in the client's category. In addition, VALS is used as a framework to do primary research on the lifestyle and psychological characteristics of early adopters. Our findings show that early adopters

- are people involved in unusual activities and whose level of activity will disproportionately affect the behaviors of others.
- have many weak social contacts.
- are masters of their own universes.
- are high media users.
- have a more complex history of personal and sexual relationships.

Although there are similarities among early adopters, our VALS research found some important differences. Contrary to popular belief, there is no one innovator or early adopter group. Early adopters are in very different strata and roles in society and cannot be identified by demographics alone.

Using VALS, we have identified three early adopter groups with different psychological characteristics. The "digerati" early adopters seek novelty, are attracted to risk, and tend to be more fashion conscious. They have a desire for emotional and physical excitement, all the way to the extreme. The "ego-oriented" early adopters desire leadership and enhanced personal productivity. These consumers have a need to feel superior within their peer groups. The "sage-tronic" early adopters are intense information seekers and global in perspective. They have a deep need to know and are expertise focused.

We pursue research on early adopters (and other programs of research) with the objective of using psychographics to understand why consumers do what they do. By understanding what motivates and demotivates different early adopter groups, we can help our clients identify targets and steer their brands for successful market entry."

Before joining SRI Consulting's Values and Lifestyles Program, Cheri Anderson was a strategic planner at DDB Needham Worldwide. She earned her doctorate in mass communication/consumer behavior from the University of Minnesota, Twin Cities.

Nominated by Professor Bill Wells, University of Minnesota.

can be helpful in crafting a marketing communication program. For example, a cross-selling opportunity for a financial services product can be improved by understanding the type of message that will grab each recipient.

Trends   The phenomenon of trends and fads is related to lifestyle and psychographic factors, as well as the fascination with choice in a consumer culture. The way teenagers, for example, dress and talk and the products they buy are driven by a constant search for newness and coolness. *Trend spotters* are professional researchers hired by advertisers to identify trends that may affect consumer behavior. *Cool hunters* are trend spotters who specialize in identifying trendy fads that appeal to young people. They usually work with panels of young people in key trend-setting locations, such as New York, California, urban streets, and Japan. Loic Bizel, for example, hunts Japanese super trendy fads as a consultant for many Western companies and designers. Through his Web site, www .fashioninjapan.com, you can have a taste of those cool ideas and fashion in Japan's street and life.[14]

Consider This

1. What are the most important psychological factors that influence consumer decision making?
2. What insights in consumer decision making do you get from psychographics that you don't get from demographics?

BEHAVIORAL INFLUENCES ON CONSUMER DECISIONS

In the previous chapter we used the phrase *think-feel-do* to describe how people respond to a message. The behavioral component of that model is a key factor in describing the relationship consumers have with a product category or a brand and one that is almost always used in profiling consumers.

Usage Behavior

A critical behavior predictor called **usage** refers to how much of a product category or brand a customer buys. Consumers can be described in terms of their relationship with a product category, as well as a brand. There are two ways to look at usage: usage rates and brand relationship, as Table 5.4 illustrates. Usage rates refers to quantity of purchase: light, medium, or heavy. Heavy users typically buy the most of a product category or a brand's share of the market. There's an old rule of thumb called the Pareto Rule that says 20 percent of the market typically buys 80 percent of the products. That explains why the heavy-user category is so important to marketers and why planners will make special efforts to understand this key customer group.

Brand relationship refers to past, present, or future use of the product by nonusers, ex-users, regulars, first-timers, and users of and switchers from—or to—competitive products. People who buy the same brand repeatedly are the ones who display the most brand loyalty. Heavy users and brand-loyal buyers are usually a brand's most important customers and the ones who are most difficult for competitors to switch away from a brand. *Switchers* are people with low levels of brand loyalty who are willing to leave a brand to try another one.

Principle
In many product categories, 20 percent of the users buy 80 percent of the products.

Innovation and Adoption

Another type of behavior has to do with how willing people are to be innovative and try something new. Rogers developed the classification system in Figure 5.7, which he called the Diffusion of Innovation Curve, to identify these behaviors:[15]

This adoption process is identified in terms of the personal behavior of people and how their behavior reflects the speed with which they are willing to try something new. People are grouped based on these behaviors, such as innovators, early adopters, early majority, late majority, and laggards.

The *innovator* category, which is the group of brave souls willing to try something new, only represents about 2.5 percent of the population. Obviously this, and the *early-adopters* category, are important groups for marketers launching new products. What these innovation categories represent are people's willingness to experiment with something new and to take risk. Risk taking is a characteristic of your personality but it combines with behavior in the area of trying a new product. **Perceived risk** is your view of the relationship between what you gain by trying something new and what you have to lose if it doesn't work out. In other words, how important is the consequence of not making a good decision. Price is a huge barrier for high-involvement products; personal status and self-image may be a risk barrier for a fashion product.

TABLE 5.4 **Consumer Categories Based on Product Usage**

Quantity	Brand Relationship	Innovation
Light users	Nonusers	Innovators
Medium users	Ex-users	Early adopters
Heavy users	Regulars	Early majority
	First-timers	Late majority
	Loyal users	Laggards
	Switchers	

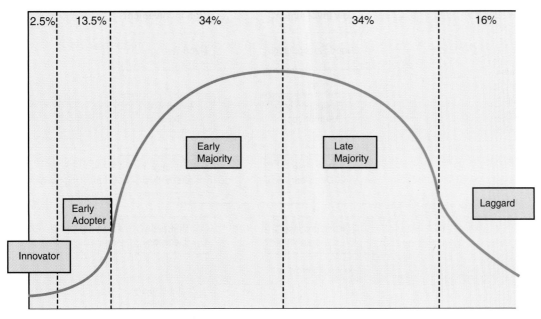

| 2.5% | 13.5% | 34% | 34% | 16% |

FIGURE 5.7 The Diffusion of Innovation

Source: Adapted from Everett Rogers, *Diffusion of Innovations*, 3rd ed. (New York: The Free Press, 1983).

Consider This

1. What are the primary categories of behavior that influence consumer decision making?
2. Why is the adoption-of-innovation model important to advertisers?

THE CONSUMER DECISION PROCESS

Although every consumer makes different decisions in different ways, evidence suggests that most people follow a similar decision process with fairly predictable steps in the decision process: need recognition, information search, evaluation of alternatives, purchase decision, and postpurchase evaluation.

As we discussed in earlier chapters, the process consumers go through in making a purchase can vary somewhat between low-involvement and high-involvement purchase decisions. The generally recognized stages for both are highlighted in Figure 5.8 and the differences noted where appropriate. The stages are (1) need recognition, (2) information search, (3) evaluation of alternatives, (4) purchase decision, and (5) postpurchase evaluation.

1. *Need recognition* occurs when the consumer recognizes a need for a product. This need can vary in terms of seriousness or importance. The goal of advertising at this stage is to activate or stimulate this need.
2. *Information search* can be casual (reading ads and articles that happen to catch your attention) or formal (searching for information in publications such as *Consumer Reports*). Advertising helps the search process by providing information and making it easy to find, as well as remember. For low-involvement products, particularly products purchased on impulse, this stage may not occupy much time or thought or may be skipped altogether. Other ways to describe consumers' behavior in terms of their information needs include such terms as *searchers* and *impulse buyers*. Searchers are people who are driven by a need to know everything they can about a product before making a purchase, particularly for major purchases. People who buy on impulse generally do so without much thought based on some immediate need such as thirst or hunger.

The Low- and High-Involvement Decision Processes

Both high- and low-involvement decision making are part of every consumer's need-satisfying process.

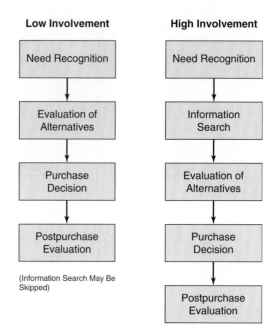

Usually there's not much at stake, so the risk of making a bad decision is small. It is true, however, that some major purchases, such as cars, can be made on the spur of the moment by people who are not dedicated searchers for information.

3. *Evaluation of alternatives* is the stage where consumers compare various products and features and reduce the list of options to a manageable number. They select certain features that are important and use them to judge alternatives. Advertising is important in this evaluation process because it helps sort out products on the basis of tangible and intangible features. Even with low-involvement products there may be what we call an **evoked set** of brands that are all considered permissible. These are the first brands that come to mind when you think of a product category. What are your favorite candy bars? That's your evoked set.

4. *The purchase decision* stage is often a two-part decision. Usually, we select the brand first and then select the outlet from which to buy it. Is this product available at a grocery store, a discount store, a hardware store, a boutique, a department store, or a specialty store? Sometimes we select the outlet first, particularly with impulse purchases. In-store promotions such as packaging, point-of-purchase displays, price reductions, banners and signs, and coupon displays affect these choices.

5. *Postpurchase evaluation* is the last step in the process and the point where we begin to reconsider and justify our purchase to ourselves. As soon as we purchase a product, particularly a major one, we begin to reevaluate our decision. Is the product what we expected? Is its performance satisfactory? This experience determines whether we will keep the product, return it, or refuse to buy the product again. This process may be skipped in a low-involvement decision. Even before you open the package or use the product, you may experience doubt or worry about the wisdom of the purchase. We referred to cognitive dissonance earlier, in the discussion of satisfaction. It is also an important factor in the postpurchase evaluation step. Many consumers continue to read information even after the purchase, to justify the decision to themselves. Advertising, such as copy on package inserts, helps reduce the dissonance by pointing out key features or how to best use the product or how many product users are satisfied.

Influences on B2B Decision Making

Many of the influences that affect consumer buying also are reflected in business-to-business marketing. We mentioned earlier that corporate cultures operate in distinctive ways and affect the way different companies do business. Although some of the consumer factors are relevant in business purchases, there are some differences, as well.

- In organizational buying, many individuals are involved in making the decision, often with a buying committee making the final decision.
- Although the business buyer may be motivated by both rational and emotional factors, the use of rational and quantitative criteria dominates most decisions.
- The decision is sometimes made based on a set of specifications to potential suppliers who then bid on the contract; typically the lowest bid wins.
- The decision may span a considerable time, creating a lag between the initial contact and final decision. On the other hand, once a decision is made it may be in place for a long time and sometimes is supported by a contract.
- Quality is hugely important and repeat purchases are based on how well the product performs.

Personal selling is also important in B2B marketing, so advertising often is used to open the door and generate leads for the sales force. The salesperson may serve as a consultant in helping the buying organization use a product to solve an operations problem. Sometimes the product is custom designed if the organization is a large buyer of the product or service.

Consider This

1. What are the key steps in the consumer decision-making process?
2. How does involvement affect the decision process?

SEGMENTING AND TARGETING

The reason it is important to understand consumer behavior is that advertisers address their messages to certain audiences that they believe will be good prospects for the product or service. We rarely broadcast messages to everyone without any consideration of people's different interests. In other words, advertising that is interesting, relevant, and attention getting is aligned with the audience's interests. So understanding consumer behavior is the first step in identifying a logical target for a brand message.

Most products don't have unlimited funds to spread their messages in all directions. Instead, efficiency—and effectiveness—demands that marketers do two things: segment the market and target the right audience group. **Segmenting** means dividing the market into groups of people who have similar characteristics in certain key product-related areas. **Targeting** means identifying the group that might be the most profitable audience, the one most likely to respond to marketing communication. These decisions are central to both the message and media strategies that are outlined in advertising plans, a topic we'll discuss in Chapter 7.

The idea behind segmenting people into groups is that groups of people to whom advertisers direct their messages are defined by certain key characteristics—usually demographics and psychographics—and these characteristics make them more alike than different. Furthermore, those characteristics also define how they are different from other people who may not be as ideal a market for a product. A motivation researcher explained that "when we are part of a group a whole structure of viewpoints is gradually internalized to become a part of our fundamental psychic system, so that we act and see differently" from people in other groups.

Principle
Segmenting means dividing the market into groups of people who have similar characteristics in common; targeting is identifying the group that is most likely to respond to the brand message.

To Segment or Not to Segment?

The first decision is whether to treat the market as homogeneous (that is, as a single, undifferentiated, large unit) or as heterogeneous (a market composed of separate, smaller groups known as segments). When planners treat the market as homogeneous, they purposely ignore differences in the market and use one marketing strategy that will appeal to as many people as possible. This market strategy is known as an **undifferentiated strategy** or **market aggregation strategy**. At one point in its history, Coca-Cola viewed the U.S. market as homogeneous and used general appeals—such as "Coke is it!"—for all consumers.

But even Coke is sold in different types of places, and people hear about Coke through different types of media. Therefore customers are grouped almost by definition, based on their contact points with the product. And, of course, there are differences in age: There has to be a big difference between an old Coke drinker and a teenager and that difference affects how you address them in advertising, as well as how you reach them in different media.

In other words, few examples of homogeneous markets exist. Often, companies take an undifferentiated approach because they lack the resources to target different market segments. For certain types of widely consumed items, such as gasoline, the undifferentiated market approach may make sense because the potential market is large enough to justify possible wasted resources. At one time, the bottled water industry used this approach. Clearly, that has changed as the market for bottled water has grown and evolved.

Market segmentation is a much more common market approach. It assumes that the best way to sell is to recognize differences within the broad market and adjust marketing strategies and messages accordingly. In a segmentation strategy, marketers divide the larger heterogeneous market into segments that are homogeneous *within* these small markets. From these segments, the marketer identifies, evaluates, and selects a **target market**, a group of people with similar needs and characteristics who are most likely to be receptive to the marketer's product and messages. For White Castle, the JWT team segmented the target audience into several groups. The highest priority groups were termed Ultimate and Committed Cravers. These folks, although only 14 percent of the overall customer base, account for 63 percent of White Castle's annual revenue.

By using a segmentation approach, a company can more precisely match the needs and wants of the customer and generate more sales. That's why soft-drink manufacturers such as Coke and Pepsi have moved away from the undifferentiated approach and have introduced product variations to appeal to different segments, such as diet, caffeine-free, diet caffeine-free, and flavored versions of their basic products. This approach also allows a company to target advertising messages more precisely.

Types of Segmentation   In general marketers segment their markets using five broad categories based on the consumer characteristics that have been described in this chapter. The five approaches, which are illustrated in Figure 5.9, include demographics, geographics, psychographics, behavioral, and benefits (need based). Which approach or combination of approaches is best to use will vary with the market situation and the product category.

- *Demographic segmentation* means dividing the market using such characteristics as gender, ethnicity, income, and so forth. Age is often the first characteristic to be used in defining a market segment.
- *Geographic segmentation* uses location as a defining variable because consumers' needs sometimes vary depending upon where they live—urban, rural, suburb, East, West, and so forth. The most important variables are world or global, region, nation, state, or city. Factors that are related to these decisions include climate, population density, and the urban–rural character. Geography affects both product distribution and its marketing communication.
- *Psychographic segmentation* is primarily based on studies of how people spend their money, their patterns of work and leisure, their interest and opinions, and their views of themselves. It is considered richer than demographic segmentation because it combines the psychological information with lifestyle insights.
- *Behavioral segmentation* divides people into groups based on product category and brand usage.
- *Benefit segmentation* is based on consumers' needs or problems. The idea is that people buy products for different benefits they hope to derive. For example, car buyers might be grouped based on whether they are motivated by concerns for safety, gas mileage, durability or dependability, performance and handling, luxury, or enhancement of self-image.

Sociodemographic Segments   One common approach to demographic segmentation, one that has entered mainstream vocabulary, refers to people in terms of when they were born. Although these categories are age driven, they also refer to lifestyle differences.

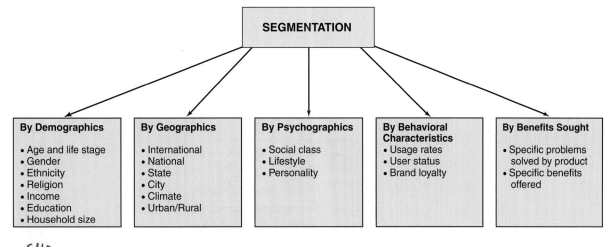

FIGURE 5.9   **Segmentation Approaches**

Market segmentation is based on identifying the factors that best identify the characteristics of people who would be in the market for the product.

The most important of these sociodemographic categories is the baby boomers, who make up the largest age-related category in the United States.

Gen X, also known as the Baby Busters, is the group whose 45 million members were, born between 1965 and 1979. Now adults, they grew up with television and have been described as independent minded and somewhat cynical. They are concerned with their physical health (they grew up during the AIDS outbreak) and financial future (they suffered the most from the dot-com bust).

Born between 1980 and 1996, Generation Y are also known as Echo Boomers because they are the children of baby boomers. They are important to marketers, because they are next in size to the boomer generation. Also described as the Digital Generation because they are seen as more technologically savvy, this group is now the youth and young adult market that marketers want most to reach because they are in the formative years of their brand relationships. They are prime targets for technology, travel, cars, homes, and furniture. The Millennium Generation are those children born around 2000 and in the beginning years of the new century.

Older than the baby boomers, seniors are referred to as the Gray Market and divided into two categories: young seniors (60–74) and older seniors (75 plus). This is another huge market in the United States at least, and also a wealthy one. With baby boomers moving into their retirement years, the senior market will become even larger relative to the rest of the population.

Other fun terms that have been used to describe demographic and lifestyle segments include the following:

- *Dinkies.* Double-income young couples with no kids
- *Guppies.* Gay upwardly mobile professionals
- *Skippies.* School kids with purchasing power
- *Slackers.* This term has been recycled from referring to high school kids in the 1990s (as in the *Slacker* movie) who don't care much and don't do much. More recently the term refers to 20-something burnt-out dot-comers who are unemployed and enjoying a laid-back life.
- *Bling bling generation.* Coined by rappers and hip-hoppers, the term refers to flashy people with a high-rolling lifestyle and costly diamonds and jewelry.

Niche Markets   Although advertising has gone global to reach large markets, many advertisers have moved toward tighter and tighter **niche markets**, which are subsegments of a more general market. Individuals in the niche market, such as ecologically minded mothers who won't use disposable diapers, are defined by some distinctive trait. Instead of

FIGURE
5.10

Narrowing the Target

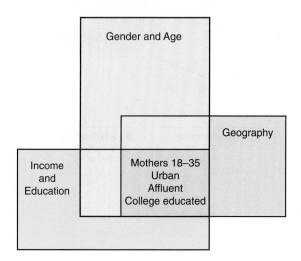

marketing to the masses, they target narrow market segments, such as single women travelers, hockey fans, classical-music enthusiasts, skateboarders, or ethnic business owners. Although large companies may develop niche strategies, niche marketers are companies that pursue market segments that are of sufficient size to be profitable although not large enough to be of interest to large marketers. Elderhostel, for example, markets to seniors who are interested in educationally oriented travel experiences.

Targeting the Right Audience

Through targeting, the organization is able to design specific communication strategies to match the audience's needs and wants and position the product in the most relevant way to match their interests. The target is first of all described using the variables that separate this prospective consumer group from others who probably are not in the market.

Profiling the Target Audience   The target audience is then profiled using descriptive information based on the factors we've discussed in this chapter: What's their age, income, education, and where do they live? What motivates them? **Profiles** are descriptions of the target audience that read like a description of someone you know. These are used in developing media and message decisions. The White Castle target audience is a cultlike following united by their craving for the one-of-a-kind, distinctive, steamed-on-a-bed-of-onions burgers. They share a bond that bridges age—gender, ethnicity, and social status. The taste, the smell, the shape: All are why "Cravers" believe that there is nothing else like a White Castle burger. The target is defined by its multisensory addition.

Pretend you're launching a new diaper service. Mothers of infants, for example, are not all alike. What makes one group different from another set of mothers? Some of them are affluent, others are poor and struggling to get by. Are those important factors for the brand? You build a profile by starting with the most important characteristic. For the diaper service it would be gender, of course, and also age—let's say women 18–35, for example. Then you add other factors, such as income, urban dwellers, education, or whatever are found in research to be the most important predictive variables. As Figure 5.10 illustrates, each time you add a variable you narrow the market as you come closer to the ideal target audience. The objective is to get the largest group that still holds together as a group in such a way that you can direct a message that will speak to all or most of the people in that group. Once these predictor variables have been sorted out, then it should be possible to build an estimate of the size of this target market.

Principle

Each time you add a variable to a target audience definition, you narrow the size of the target audience.

Consider This

1. What is a market segmentation strategy?
2. What kind of information is used is creating a target audience profile?

IT'S A WRAP

MAKING CRAVERS ONE OF OURS

■ ■ ■

In this chapter we identified several key audience traits and behaviors that are relevant to advertisers as they decide how to effectively segment the market and target the audience. Keep in mind that we haven't examined all possible traits and behaviors. Furthermore, those who work on the design and implementation of an advertisement may interpret these traits differently. The point is that the key to effective customer-focused advertising is staying sensitive to the consumer and understanding how they think, act, and feel.

In the White Castle case, the advertising is built on an important consumer insight about how devoted customers crave the hamburger. The idea was expressed in the slogan "What You Crave." The message strategy behind the "Crave" theme focused on the burger's indulgent qualities, the self-indulgence that comes from enjoying a guilty pleasure—such as consuming a sack of 10 burgers smothered with onions. The Craver's self-identity as an individualist who is loyal to a different kind of burger was linked to White Castle's image as a hamburger chain that makes its burgers in a nontraditional way. The goal is to make White Castle Cravers identify themselves with the chain as "one of ours."

In terms of results, the first campaign objective for the "Crave" campaign was to improve future purchase intent by 10 percent. A brand-tracking study by the Millward Brown research company found that the number of individuals who said that the advertising makes them want to go to White Castle increased by 19 percent, which was nearly double the original objective.

The campaign had even more impact on the sales objective, which called for sales growth 25 percent greater than the competition. In fact, the "Crave" campaign delivered a sales growth that was 100 percent greater than competitors, which is four times the goal (an increase of 400 percent). A highly effective campaign, results like these are the reasons White Castle's "Why You Crave" advertising continues to be an EFFIE winner year after year.

■ ■ ■ Summary

1. **Assess cultural and social influences on consumer responses.** The social and cultural influences on consumer decision making include society and subcultures, social class, reference groups, age, gender, family status, education, occupation, income, and race.

2. **Demonstrate how psychological influences motivate consumers.** Psychological influences on consumers include perception, learning, motivation, attitudes, personality, psychographics, and lifestyles. Advertisers identify audiences in terms of demographics and psychographics. Demographic profiles of consumers include information on population size, age, gender, education, family situation, occupation, income, and race. Psychographic profiles include information on attitudes, lifestyles, buying behavior, and decision processes.

3. **Explain the behavioral characteristics that describe consumer responses.** Quantity of usage is an important characteristic of a profitable market. The relationship the consumer has with the brand in terms of use and loyalty is also

important. The innovativeness of people in the group in terms of their willingness to try something new is another important behavioral factor influencing decision making.

4. **Describe how the consumer decision process works.** The decision process involves five stages: need recognition, information search, evaluation of alternatives, purchase decision, and postpurchase evaluation.

5. **Differentiate between segmenting and targeting and trace these planning tools to their sources in cultural, social, psychological, and behavioral factors.** Segmentation involves dividing a market into groups of people who can be identified as being in the market for the product. Targeting is identifying the group that would be the most responsive to an advertising message about the product. Both segmenting and targeting use the social and cultural, psychological, and behavioral characteristics to identify these critical groups of people.

■■■ Key Terms

acquired needs, 138
cognitive dissonance, 139
consumer behavior, 126
core values, 128
corporate culture, 129
culture, 128
customers, 127
demographics, 131
discretionary income, 135
evoked set, 146

family, 130
household, 130
innate needs, 135
lifestyle, 135
lifestyle analysis, 141
market aggregation strategy, 147
market segmentation, 148
niche market, 149
norms, 128

perceived risk, 144
personality, 140
profiles, 150
psychographics, 140
reference group, 129
segmenting, 147
selective distortion, 138
selective exposure, 138
selective retention, 138
social class, 129

subculture, 129
target market, 148
targeting, 147
undifferentiated (market aggregation) strategy, 147
usage, 144
VALS, 141
values, 128

■■■ Review Questions

1. What are the key cultural and social influences that affect consumer responses to advertising?

2. What are the key psychological factors that influence consumer decision making?

3. What are the key behavioral influences on consumer behavior? You want to go out to eat this coming Friday; analyze your decision about where to go in terms of the behavioral factors.

4. Outline the steps in the basic consumer decision-making process.

5. Define targeting. How does it differ from segmenting?

■■■ Discussion Questions

1. Choose four VALS 2 categories and find one or more print advertisements that appear to be targeted to people in each category. Explain why you think the ad addresses that audience. Do you believe that the categories are mutually exclusive? Can consumers (and ads directed to them) be classified in multiple categories? Why or why not?

2. You are working as an intern at the Williams Russell agency and the agency has just gotten a new account, a bottled tea named Leafs Alive. The sale of bottled tea is surging with the industry reaching $5.5 billion in sales in 2003. What consumer trends seem to be driving this product development?

3. What are the stages of the consumer decision process? Give examples of how advertising can influence each stage. Find an ad that addresses the concern of consumers in each stage.

4. Sean McDonnell is the creative director for Chatham-Boothe, an advertising agency that has just signed a contract with Trans-Central Airlines (TCA). TCA has a solid portfolio of consumer research and has offered to let the agency use it. McDonnell needs to decide whether demographic, psychographic, or attitude and motive studies are best for developing a creative profile of the TCA target audience. If the choice were yours, on which body of research would you base a creative strategy? Explore the strengths and weaknesses of each.

5. Consider the social-class segments discussed in this chapter. Select two demographic or psychographic factors that would be most receptive to these product-marketing situations:

   a. Full line of frozen family-style meals (for microwaving) that feature superior nutritional balances

   b. Dairy product company (milk, cheese, ice cream) offering an exclusive packaging design that uses fully degradable containers

   c. A new SUV that is lighter in weight and gets better gas mileage than the average SUV

6. Draw up a target audience profile for students attending your college. How does it differ from another school in your same market area?

■■■ Class Projects

1. Visit one or more stores that sell stereo systems. Report on the sales techniques used (check on advertising, point-of-purchase displays, store design, Web site, and so forth). What beliefs concerning consumer behavior appear to underlie these strategies?

2. Bottled water is an outgrowth of the health and fitness trend. It has recently moved into second place in the beverage industry behind wine and spirits and beating out beer and coffee. The latest twist on bottled water is the "enhanced" category with designer waters that include such things as extra oxygen, vitamins, or caffeine. The emerging brands are Evamor from New Jersey and Trinity Springs from Idaho. Go to the Web site United Business Media (www.unitedbusinessmedia.com). Track down a set of secondary data results. Indicate how you would use this information to design an ad for one of these products.

HANDS-ON

Toyota Goes After Tuners

Young people with limited incomes often look for a great deal on a new car. One way to save some money is to forgo options and upgrades, like a sunroof or a CD player. But when Toyota introduced its funky "Scion" brand, it considered offering a version without something most people assume comes standard: paint. Although they ultimately decided against the idea, at one point Toyota's plan was to sell the brand with just gray primer.

Toyota wasn't really targeting people so cheap they wouldn't spend money on paint. Just the opposite—the car company was going after a group with money to burn, called *tuners*. Tuners are young car buyers who live to customize their cars. The trend really began among young Asian Americans, who typically bought inexpensive Asian import cars and then spent thousands of dollars customizing them. The hobby has spread to other young people, so that today Asian Americans are a minority of tuners. But Japanese brands remain the cars of choice among those dedicated to creating a work of art on wheels. Explaining the idea of a "no paint" option, Jim Farley, Scion general manager, says, "As much as possible, we want to give them [tuners] a blank canvas."

What does a tuner do with his car? He (or she; women make up almost 20 percent of the tuner subculture) might take a basic Honda, add a large and loud exhaust system, paint the intake manifolds, and add ride-lowering springs. Other popular add-ons are technologies that increase vehicle speed, like turbochargers, superchargers, and nitrous kits. And there are some serious bucks involved. The Specialty Equipment Market Association estimates that auto after-market spending (spending on car accessories after the original car purchase) increased from $295 million in 1997 to $2.3 billion in 2002. The motivation? "You build a car for yourself," says one 20-something tuner who plans to one day install an Acura RSX Type-S engine into his Honda Civic. "The satisfaction is in making it your own and knowing that nobody will ever have something that's the same."

The amount of money tuners spend is reason enough to attract the attention of marketers. GM hoped to interest tuners in its Saturn Ion, Chevrolet Cavalier, and Pontiac Sunfire when it launched a "Tuner Tour" of 10 National Hot Rod Association races. GM allowed young car enthu-

siasts to play games and enter contests for prizes, as it in turn collected names and e-mail addresses. GM's focus on relationship marketing makes sense because tuners don't watch a lot of TV. Both Mitsubishi and Ford believe the best way to reach them is with product placements in movies (Mitsubishi bought air time in the popular film "2 Fast 2 Furious"). But even companies selling products unrelated to cars are interested in the tuner lifestyle. Pepsi has hired tuners to customize some of its promotional vehicles.

Which brings us full circle back to Scion. Toyota's goal is to make the new car an immediate hit with tuners. So rather than spend a great deal of money on network television, Toyota decided to sponsor a 22-minute movie *On the D.L.* The movie is a comical docudrama that tells the story of a pair of musicians trying to obtain their first drivers licenses. The stars are musicians from youth-oriented bands: Ahmir "?uestlove" Thompson, from the Roots, and DJ King Britt, who played for the Digable Planets. The film premiered at the Tribeca film festival, after which segments were shared on peer-to-peer networks such as Kaazaa. Toyota hopes that enthusiasts will download the segments and share them with friends.

Consider This

1. Why are tuners so attractive to marketers, even after accounting for their spending power?
2. Evaluate Toyota's strategy of targeting tuners with the Scion campaign. What are the difficulties for a large company in marketing effectively to a youth-oriented subculture? What techniques do you think companies like Toyota are using to try to understand their market?
3. Explain how "tuner" campaigns, such as those by GM and Toyota, work. Analyze these campaigns using the Facets Model to identify the effects they are designed to achieve. How would you determine if these campaigns are effective?

Sources: Jean Halliday, "Tune In, Trick Out Trend Turns On Carmakers," *Advertising Age* (November 3, 2003); Jean Halliday, "Toyota's Scion Goes to Tribeca Film Fest," *Advertising Age* (April 26, 2004); Gail Kachadourian, "What's Hot with Tuners?," *Automotive News* (November 4, 2002); Richard Truett, "Scion Considers a No-Paint Option," *Automotive News* (November 3, 2003).

LeapBaby™

Early learning guide for parents

Discover how music opens
a world of learning.

When should you
**start reading
to your baby?**

How to turn pretend
**into a real
learning experience.**

Learn Something New Every Day.™
www.leapfrog.com

Strategic Research

Leaping Over Learning

Award:
Effie® Grand Prize

Company:
LeapFrog Enterprises

Agency:
Ackerman McQueen, Dallas, Texas; San Francisco, California; and Oklahoma City, Oklahoma

Campaign:
"Learn Something New Every Day"

CHAPTER KEY POINTS

After reading this chapter, you will be able to:

1. Discuss the types of strategic research.

2. Identify the four uses of research in advertising.

3. List the common research methods used in advertising.

4. Explain the key challenges facing advertising research.

Six years ago, Mike Wood, a corporate lawyer at a San Francisco law firm, was searching for a product to help his son learn to read. Mike's son, Mat, was struggling with the relatively complex concept of phonics—the idea that every letter makes its own unique sound. Eventually, Mike stopped looking for the right product and his frustration drove him to simply make one in his garage. Tinkering with gadgets in his spare time, he cobbled together a prototype using voice technology from a talking greeting card. Lo and behold, it worked and Mat began to understand the concept of phonics.

Introduced in 1997, LeapFrog had sales of just $10 million. By 2002, LeapFrog had expanded from one product (Mike's Learn to Read Phonics Desk) to 134 learning products.

Children's learning materials are about as exciting as broccoli on a kid's plate. In contrast, products like Razor Scooters and Yu-Gi-Oh focus solely on fun and have become huge must-have brands for kids. In recent years, licensing has fueled category growth, with items like Harry Potter, SpongeBob, and Spider-Man. So how can educational products compete with the big toy brands?

The preschool section is dominated by a few big, albeit "sleepy," brands such as Fisher-Price, Playskool, and Sesame Street. These names have been fixtures in American families for generations and are rewarded with unaided brand awareness levels above 95 percent. Each of these brands has fostered a strong and emotional bond with consumers—defined by such qualities as "wholesomeness," "trust," and "fun." The challenge to LeapFrog's agency, Ackerman McQueen, was to make LeapFrog competitive against such venerable brands.

To make the situation more challenging, two of the leading preschool brands, Fisher-Price and Playskool, have deep pockets. These brands are owned by the two largest toy manufacturers in the United States—Mattel ($4.9 billion revenue) and Hasbro ($2.8 billion revenue). LeapFrog, an unknown startup with just one product, would have to go head-to-head with these well-funded and entrenched conglomerates.

Consumer Research

The Ackerman McQueen team wanted to uncover what, beyond the conventional demographic data on moms who buy educational materials, really makes LeapFrog moms tick. The team analyzed industry research, as well as conducted an in-home ethnographic study with moms across the country in conjunction with an annual quantitative Brand Tracker study.

The studies determined that LeapFrog moms don't differ much in terms of demographic variables like educational status, income, or where they live. What distinguishes a LeapFrog mom is the fact that she, regardless of her own educational level, consistently values education highly. She understands that stimulating childrens' minds at the earliest age will give them a better chance in life.

The research found that the LeapFrog mom is adventurous, confident, and discerning. In terms of her attitudes and lifestyle, she is different from the typical toy buyer. The purchase of a LeapFrog product is planned, versus the spontaneity of most toy purchases. She will also spend more than five times the industry average ($7) for a LeapFrog product ($40). Lastly, two-thirds (66 percent) of moms will "hand on" or "pass down" LeapFrog products to another child in the household, in contrast to the disposable nature of most toy products.

Ackerman McQueen's qualitative research also found that mom continues to be the primary protector, mentor, and teacher in her child's life. Research revealed that the declining state of the educational system, the pressure to succeed, and the desire to offer her children the best "leg up" all weighed heavy on mom's mind. This is true even at the earliest preschool age. The agency's approach was to play directly to moms' sensibilities, aspirations, and desires to offer her child "only the best." This subtly taps into her fears and needs (plus a tiny dose of guilt) by offering an important solution to teaching young minds.

Walk into any major retailer of children's products today and you'll see that LeapFrog owns the aisle. So how did LeapFrog's research and marketing communication create such a strong brand presence for this upstart company? Check the It's a Wrap section at the end of this chapter to read about the results.

In order to understand consumer response to an advertising message and to plan advertising that has impact on consumers, marketers such as LeapFrog need to do research. This effort, which includes market and competitive research, as well as consumer research, becomes the foundation for the advertising plan, which we discuss in Chapter 7. In this chapter we will discuss some key research concepts, beginning with an explanation of the two most basic categories of research—primary and secondary—and the two categories of research tools—quantitative and qualitative.

RESEARCH: THE QUEST FOR INTELLIGENCE AND INSIGHT

Market and consumer research is usually handled by the advertiser's marketing department. That research, however, is the foundation for many advertising decisions, so discussion of it is included in this chapter. **Market research** compiles information about the product, the product category, and other details of the marketing situation that will impact on the development of advertising strategy. **Consumer research** is used to identify people who are in the market for the product in terms of their characteristics, attitudes, interests, and motivations. Ultimately this information is used to decide who should be the targeted audience for the advertising. In an integrated marketing communication (IMC) plan, the consumer research is enlarged to acquire information about all the relevant stakeholders.

Advertising research focuses on all the elements of advertising, including message development research, media-planning research, and evaluation, as well as information about competitors' advertising. **IMC research** is similar except it is used to assemble information needed in planning the use of a variety of marketing communication tools.

Strategic research uncovers critical information that becomes the basis for strategic planning decisions. In advertising it covers all the factors and steps that lead to the creation of (1) message strategies and (2) media plans. Think of strategic research as collecting all relevant background information needed to make a decision on advertising strategy.

You were engaged in strategic research, for example, when you were looking for an acceptable college to attend. You conducted market research (what information is available?), strategic research (what factors are most important in making a decision and how do the schools stack up?), and evaluative research (how will I know I made the best decision?). An advertising plan goes through similar stages of development with research being the first step.

Types of Research

New advertising assignments always begin with some kind of informal or formal background research into the marketing situation. This is secondary research.

Secondary Research   Background research that uses available published information about a topic is called *secondary research*. When advertising people get new accounts or new assignments, they start by reading everything they can find on the product, company, industry, and competition: sales reports, annual reports, complaint letters, and trade articles about the industry. What they are looking for is important facts and key insights. It's called secondary because it is information that has been collected and published by someone else. Many secondary information sources are available to advertisers doing strategic research.

Government Organizations Governments, through their various departments, provide an astonishing array of statistics that can greatly enhance advertising and marketing decisions. Many of the statistics come from census records on the population's size, geographic distribution, age, income, occupation, education, and ethnicity.

Trade Associations Many industries support trade associations (such as professional organizations whose members all work in the same field) that gather and distribute information of interest to association members. For instance, the American Association of Advertising Agencies (AAAA) issues reports that help ad agencies monitor their own performance and keep tabs on competitors. The Radio Advertising Bureau publishes

■ ■ ■

Demographic information of this kind is fundamental to decision making about advertising targets and market segmentation. An advertiser cannot aim its advertising at a target audience without knowing that audience's size and major dimensions. Figure 6.1 lists some government reports that help advertisers make better decisions.

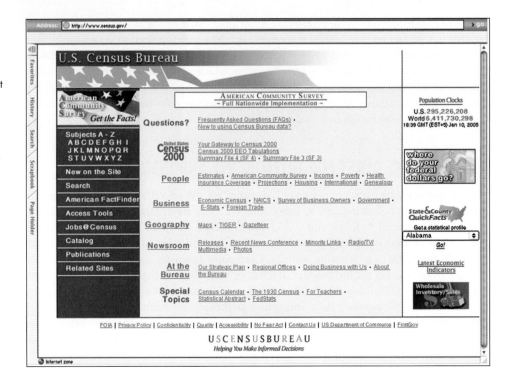

Radio Facts, an overview of the commercial U.S. radio industry, the Account Planning Group (APG) conducts seminars and training sessions for account planners, and the American Association for Public Opinion Research (AAPOR) serves the professional needs of opinion researchers.

Secondary Research Suppliers Because of the overwhelming amount of information available through secondary research, firms called *secondary research suppliers* gather and organize information around specific topic areas for other interested parties. Key secondary research suppliers are FIND/SVP, Off-the-Shelf Publications, Inc., Dialog Information Services, Inc., Lexis-Nexis, Dow Jones News/Retrieval, and Market Analysis Information Database, Inc.

Secondary Information on the Internet For any given company, you're bound to find a Web site where you can learn about the company's history and philosophy of doing business, check out its complete product line, and discover who runs the company. Several sites offer credible information for account planners or others involved in market research. However, it is unlikely that all the needed information will be found on these sites.

Practical Tips

Web Sites for Advertising Research

Here's a sampling of Web sites that contain information that might be useful to you if you are doing background research for an advertising assignment:

• BrandEra (www.brandera.com) offers information by product category.

• Business Wire (www.businesswire.com) is an electronic distributor of press releases and business news.

• Census Bureau (www.census.gov) contains the U.S. Census database, press releases, a population clock, and clips from its radio broadcasts.

• IndustryClick (www.industryclick.com) is a collection of business publications categorized by industry.

• Cluetrain (www.cluetrain.com) is a site that publishes new ways to find and share innovative marketing information and ideas.

United States

Survey of Current Business: Basic operational statistics on U.S. business. (Bureau of Economic Analysis of the U.S. Department of Commerce)

Requirements of Laws and Regulations Enforced by the U.S. Food and Drug Administration: Laws and regulations affecting food and beverage advertising. (U.S. Department of Health and Human Services, Food and Drug Administration)

Children's Information Processing of Television Advertising: How children react to television commercials. (National Technical Information Services, U.S. Department of Commerce)

Canada

Statistical Profile of Canadian Communities. (Office of the Chief Statistician of Canada)

The Economy in Detail. (Statistics Canada)

Canadian Social Trends. (Statistics Canada)

European Union

Shopping around Europe: European Economic Area. (European Union Eurostat Memo)

Key Data on Relations between the EU and Asian ASEM Countries. (European Union Eurostat Memo)

More Babies Born in the EU. (European Union Eurostat Memo)

FIGURE 6.1

A Sample of Government Reports That Interest Advertisers
An advertiser may find government reports to be an invaluable source of research information.

A typical advertising campaign might be influenced, directly or indirectly, by information from many sources, including outside research suppliers, as well as agency research.

Primary Research   Information that is collected for the first time from original sources is called *primary research*. Companies do their own tracking and monitoring of their customers' behavior and they also hire research firms to do this research. Firms that specialize in interviewing, observing, recording, and analyzing the behavior of those who purchase or influence the purchase of a particular good or service are called *primary research suppliers*. The primary research supplier industry is extremely diverse. The companies range from A. C. Nielsen, which employs more than 45,000 workers in the United States alone, to several thousand entrepreneurs who conduct focus groups, individual interviews, prepare reports, and provide advice on specific advertising and marketing problems for individual clients.

■ ■ ■
Some companies either hire outside research firms or do their own tracking and monitoring of consumer behavior.

Many advertising agencies subscribe to large-scale surveys conducted by the Simmons Market Research Bureau (SMRB) or by Mediamark Research, Inc. (MRI). These two organizations survey large samples of American consumers (approximately 30,000 for each survey) and ask questions about the consumption, possession, or use of a wide range of products, services, and media. The products and services covered in the MRI survey range from toothbrushes and dental floss to diet colas, camping equipment, and theme parks.

Strictly speaking, both SMRB and MRI are secondary data sources: They conduct their own original research, but they publish their findings, which are available to their clients. These reports are intended primarily for use in media planning; however, because these surveys are so comprehensive, they also can be mined for unique consumer information, which makes them primary sources. Through a computer program called Golddigger, for example, an MRI subscriber can select a consumer target and ask the computer to find all other products and services and all the media that members of the target segment use. The resulting profile provides a vivid and detailed description of the target as a person—just the information agency creative teams need to help them envision their audiences.

Figure 6.2 shows a sample MRI report of the types of TV programs adults aged 18 to 34 watch. The report breaks down the 18–34 market into four market segments based on size of household and age of children, if any.

Quantitative and Qualitative Research Primary research can be both quantitative and qualitative. **Qualitative research** provides insight into the underlying reasons for how consumers behave and why. Common qualitative research methods include such tools as observation, ethnographic studies, in-depth interviews, and case studies. These exploratory research tools are useful for probing and gaining explanations, insight, and understanding into such questions as:

- What type of features do customers want?
- What are the motivations that lead to the purchase of a product?
- What do our customers think about our advertising?
- How do consumers relate to the brand? What are their emotional links to the brand?

Qualitative methods are used early in the process of developing an advertising plan or message strategy for generating insights, as well as questions and hypotheses for additional research. They are also good at confirming hunches, ruling out bad approaches and questionable or confusing ideas, and giving direction to the message strategy. Because qualitative research is typically done with small groups, advertisers are not able to draw conclusions about or project their findings to the larger population.

Quantitative research delivers numerical data such as number of users and purchases, their attitudes and knowledge, their exposure to ads, and other market-related information. It also provides information on reactions to advertising and motivation to purchase (sometimes called **purchase intent** or intend-to-buy). Quantitative methods that investigate the responses of large numbers of people are useful to test ideas to determine if the market is large enough or if most people really think or behave that way.

Two primary characteristics of quantitative research are (1) large sample sizes (typically from 100 to 1,000 people) and (2) random sampling. The most common quantitative research methods include surveys and studies that track such things as sales and opinions. In contrast to qualitative research, quantitative is usually designed to either accurately count something, such as sales levels, or to predict something, such as attitudes. In order to be predictive, however, this type of research has to follow careful scientific procedures.

Qualitative research should not be used to draw conclusions, which is the province of quantitative research, but instead to better understand a market and generate hypotheses that we can test with quantitative methods.[1] As Sally Reinman, Worldwide Market Planner at Saatchi & Saatchi, observes, research is more than numbers. She explains:

> Research processes are more varied and exciting than ever before. Examples include asking consumers to draw pictures, create collages, and produce home videos to show how they use a product.

Base: Adults Index	Total U.S. 000	Respondent 18–34 1-Person Household				Respondent 18–34 and Married, no children				Respondent 18–34 and Married, Youngest Child <6				Respondent 18–34 and Married Youngest Child 6+			
		A	B	C	D	A	B	C	D	A	B	C	D	A	B	C	D
		000	% Down	% Across	Index	000	% Down	% Across	Index	000	% Down	% Across	Index	000	% Down	% Across	Index
All Adults	184274	5357	100.0	2.9	100	7559	100.0	4.1	100	18041	100.0	9.8	100	4978	100.0	2.7	100
Program-Types: Average Show																	
Adven/Sci Fi/West-Prime	19969	590	11.0	3.0	102	875	11.6	4.4	107	2303	12.8	11.5	118	694	13.9	3.5	129
Auto Racing-Specials	6590	*226	4.2	3.4	118	*242	3.2	3.7	90	634	3.5	9.6	98	*251	5.0	3.8	141
Awards-Specials	16490	397	7.4	2.4	83	514	6.8	3.1	76	1576	8.7	9.6	98	*451	9.1	2.7	101
Baseball Specials	28019	806	15.0	2.9	99	1128	14.9	4.0	98	2671	14.8	9.5	97	*506	10.2	1.8	67
Basketball-Weekend-College	7377	*222	4.1	3.0	104	*244	3.2	3.3	81	531	2.9	7.2	74	*183	3.7	2.5	92
Basketball Specials-College	17096	529	9.9	3.1	106	694	9.2	4.1	99	1459	8.1	8.5	87	*423	8.5	2.5	92
Basketball Specials-Pro.	32470	1057	19.7	3.3	112	1369	18.1	4.2	103	3128	17.3	9.6	98	886	17.8	2.7	101
Bowling-Weekend	16808	312	5.8	1.9	654	744	9.8	4.4	108	1476	8.2	8.8	90	*386	7.8	2.3	85
Comedy/Variety	26254	930	17.4	3.5	122	1150	15.2	4.4	107	3257	18.1	12.4	127	999	20.1	3.8	141
Daytime Dramas	7621	*192	3.6	2.5	87	*287	3.8	3.8	92	845	4.7	11.1	113	*343	6.9	4.5	167
Daytime Game Shows	7747	*97	1.8	1.3	43	*194	2.6	2.5	61	734	4.1	9.5	97	*235	4.7	3.0	112
Documen/Information-Prime	22514	532	9.9	2.4	81	504	6.7	2.2	55	1739	9.6	7.7	79	*454	9.1	2.0	75
Early Morning News	12226	280	5.2	2.3	79	*429	5.7	3.5	86	1065	5.9	8.7	89	*330	6.6	2.7	100
Early Morning Talk/Info/News	14681	258	4.8	1.8	60	580	7.7	4.0	96	1291	7.2	8.8	90	*268	5.4	1.8	68
Early Eve. Netwk News-M-F	25946	596	11.1	2.3	79	836	11.1	3.2	79	1822	10.1	7.0	72	*594	11.9	2.3	85
Early Eve. Netwk News-Wknd	11338	*197	3.7	1.7	60	*208	2.8	1.8	45	795	4.4	7.0	72	*187	3.8	1.6	61
Entertainment Specials	19630	408	7.6	2.1	71	701	9.3	3.6	87	1719	9.5	8.8	89	*494	9.9	2.5	93
Feature Films-Prime	17232	371	6.9	2.2	74	*538	7.1	3.1	76	1209	6.7	7.0	72	*475	9.5	2.8	102
Football Bowl Games-Specials	13322	369	6.9	2.8	95	*381	5.0	2.9	70	1512	8.4	11.3	116	*245	4.9	1.8	68
Football Pro.-Specials	44804	1471	27.5	3.3	113	1766	23.4	3.9	96	4555	25.2	10.2	104	1104	22.2	2.5	91
General Drama-Prime	19880	581	10.8	2.9	101	571	7.6	2.9	70	2095	11.6	10.5	108	*555	11.1	2.8	103
Golf	5161	*102	1.9	2.0	68	*152	2.0	2.9	72	*324	1.8	6.3	64	*15	.3	.3	11
Late Evening Netwk News Wknd	5146	*146	2.7	2.8	98	*114	1.5	2.2	54	*293	1.6	5.7	58	*104	2.1	2.0	75
Late Night Talk/Variety	9590	313	5.8	3.3	112	*297	3.9	3.1	75	1009	5.6	10.5	107	*198	4.0	2.1	76
News-Specials	14508	234	4.4	1.6	55	510	6.7	3.5	86	1297	7.2	8.9	91	*212	4.3	1.5	54
Pageants-Specials	22025	439	8.2	2.0	69	952	12.6	4.3	105	2503	13.9	11.4	116	547	11.0	2.5	92
Police Docudrama	23575	726	13.6	3.1	106	1179	15.6	5.0	122	2309	12.8	9.8	100	731	14.7	3.1	115
Pvt Det/Susp/Myst/Pol.-Prime	28183	673	12.6	2.4	82	763	10.1	2.7	66	1739	9.6	6.2	63	*493	9.9	1.7	65
Situation Comedies-Prime	19097	598	11.2	3.1	108	919	12.2	4.8	117	2737	15.2	14.3	146	688	13.8	3.6	133
Sports Anthologies-Weekend	4847	*218	4.1	4.5	155	*232	3.1	4.8	117	*403	2.2	8.3	85	*108	2.2	2.2	82
Sunday News/Interview	5809	*70	1.3	1.2	41	*116	1.5	2.0	49	*214	1.2	3.7	38	*97	1.9	1.7	62
Syndicated Adult General	10444	*271	5.1	2.6	89	462	6.1	4.4	108	766	4.2	7.3	75	*221	4.4	2.1	78
Tennis	10033	338	6.3	3.4	116	380	5.0	3.8	92	826	4.5	8.2	84	*105	2.1	1.0	39

FIGURE 6.2 Sample of an MRI Consumer Media Report

A report such as this one from Mediamark Research can be a source of primary data.

Source: Mediamark Research, Inc.

As consumers around the world become better informed and more demanding, advertisers that target different cultures need to find the "commonalities" (or common ground) among consumer groups from these cultures. Research for Toyota's sport-utility vehicle (SUV), the RAV 4, showed that consumers in all the targeted countries had three common desires: They wanted an SUV to have style, safety, and economy.

To find these commonalities, I work with experts to learn the cultural meaning of codes and symbols that people use to communicate. The experts I work with include cultural and cognitive anthropologists, psychologists, interior decorators, and Indian storytellers. Anyone who can help me understand consumers and the consumer decision-making process is fair game.

THE USES OF RESEARCH

In the 1950s, major advertising agencies began developing large, well-funded, highly professional research departments. Some large advertisers, as well as big agencies, still have in-house research departments. These departments collect and disseminate secondary research data and conduct primary research that ultimately finds its way into advertising.

As markets have become more fragmented and saturated, and as consumers have become more demanding, there has been an increased need for research-based information in advertising planning. There are five ways research is used in advertising planning:

1. Market Information
2. Consumer Insight Research
3. Media Research
4. Message Development
5. Evaluation Research

Market Information

Marketing research is formal research, such as surveys, in-depth interviews, observational methods, focus groups (which are like in-depth interviews with a group rather than individuals), and all types of primary and secondary data used to develop a marketing plan and, ultimately, provide information for an advertising plan. A subset of marketing research, known as *market research,* previously discussed, is research used to gather information about a particular market—consumers, as well as competitive brands.

Market information, then, includes everything a planner can uncover about consumer perceptions of the brand, product category, and competitors' brands. Planners sometimes ride with the sales force and listen to sales pitches, tour manufacturing plants to see how a product is made, and work in a store or restaurant to evaluate the employee interaction with customers. In terms of advertising, planners test the brand's and its competitor's advertisements, promotions, retail displays, packaging, and other marketing communication efforts.

Brand information includes an assessment of the brand's role and performance in the marketplace—is it a leader, a follower, a challenger, or a subbrand of a bigger and better-known brand? This research also investigates how people perceive brand personalities and images.

Consumer Insight Research

Both the creative team (which creates messages) and the media planners (who decide how and when to deliver the messages) need to know as much as they can, in as much depth and detail as possible, about the people they are trying to reach. Demographic and psychographic information is used to describe the target audience.

The objective of most consumer research is to puzzle out a key consumer insight that will help move the target audience to respond to the message. Through qualitative and quantitative research, for example, LeapFrog's agency found that there was tremendous "confusion" at retail when moms shopped the LeapFrog Learning Center. The brand's rapid growth

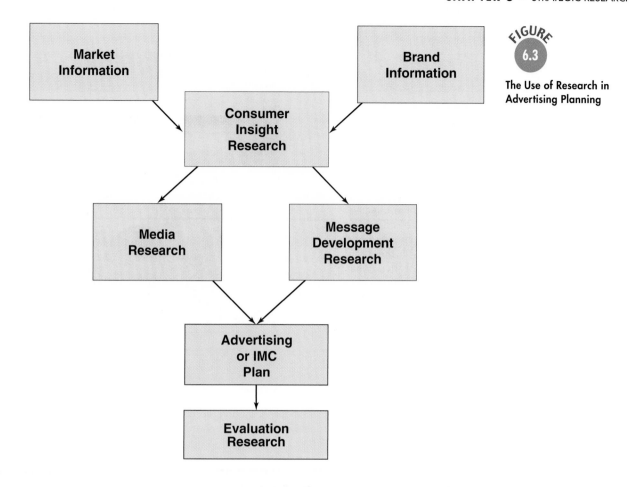

FIGURE
6.3

The Use of Research in Advertising Planning

was the primary culprit. In the last six years, LeapFrog had grown from one platform to seven (and 134 products total), targeting different age groups. To codify this for the consumer and the retailer, the agency spearheaded a new "systems" approach called "LeapLevels: The right stage for the right age." This made it possible to simplify age grading of platforms and integrate the products into a cohesive "total learning system." This program is communicated through point-of-sale signage, floor graphics, shelf blades, and retailer circulars.

Identifying the consumer insight is the responsibility of the account planner, and that role and process will be described in more detail in the planning chapter. For example, the Matter of Principle box describes the research conducted by and for the Army that provided the justification for moving from the "Be all you can be" campaign to the "Army of one."

Media Research

Media planning begins with media research that gathers information about all the possible media and marketing communication tools that might be used in a campaign to deliver a message. Media researchers then match that information to what is known about the target audience. Figure 6.3 illustrates the type of information media researchers consult and how they use that information to make recommendations.

Message Development and Evaluation Research

As planners, account managers, and people on the creative team begin the development of an advertisement, they involve themselves in various types of informal and formal research. They read all the relevant secondary information provided by the client and the planners to become better informed about the brand, the company, the competition, and the product category.

Furthermore, as writers and art directors begin working on a specific creative project, they almost always conduct at least some informal research of their own. They may do

A MATTER OF PRACTICE
The Army Marches to a Different Drummer

A basic principle of advertising is that you need to understand your target audience before changing a successful strategy. The Army faced that challenge is assessing the future of its well-known "Be all you can be" campaign theme.

The 1990s started out with the Army in good shape—meeting its recruitment goals and riding on the effectiveness of the highly successful "Be all you can be" campaign theme. By the end of the decade things had changed and the recruitment numbers started to fall—with the Army missing its recruitment goals three out of five times between 1995 and 1999.

In response, Congress called for "aggressive, innovative experiments" to find new soldiers. A study by Defense Secretary William Cohen sought to find out why the recruiting effort was failing. A new agency, Leo Burnett, was assigned to the account; it undertook a major study to identify the barriers to recruiting and the consumer insights that would lead to a new recruitment strategy. In response to this research, the Army created a new marketing division and embraced a consumer-driven philosophy.

The Burnett team had a difficult decision: Should it keep the 20-year-old "Be all you can be" campaign that had such huge visibility and awareness or should it reinvent the Army through a new campaign? It was, after all, one of the most successful and recognizable campaigns ever created. The Army's research uncovered some insights about the "Be all you can be" campaign. Highly memorable and successful in the past, the message no longer seemed to resonate with the Army's target audience.

Burnett's Research

The Burnett agency conducted a full-scale research project to uncover the barriers to recruitment, using numerous quantitative and qualitative research methods including a detailed segmentation study. Its findings pointed to the following problems, some of which mirrored the results of the Army's own study.

- *Perceptions of the Army.* The Army didn't have a strong brand identity; it was seen as faceless and a place for losers. The target market didn't understand how the Army was different from the other services.
- *The "Be all you can be" theme.* The theme was wearing out and losing its power. The target market didn't understand what it meant.
- *The current "$50,000" ads.* The current advertising, which focused on the value of military service, was seen as providing money for college and didn't appeal to many of the target market who weren't considering college.

Analysis of the Research

Both the Army's and Burnett's research concluded that the target market, as well as the Army and its competitive envi-

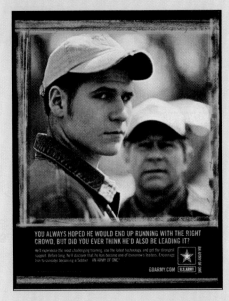

ronment, had changed and a new message strategy was needed. In terms of changes in the Army, the new military relied on high-tech weaponry—and that meant a need for a very specialized force with highly trained individuals, not just raw recruits who could easily be trained to carry guns and do other low-skilled jobs.

In terms of the target audience, a different mind-set was driving the recruitment decisions of new service members. Although the Burnett team still considered the "Be all you can be" theme to be an important truth about the Army, it had lost its power to speak to contemporary youth, who were concerned about giving up their individuality to become an anonymous cog in the Army's machinery. The old theme offered its target audience a chance to improve themselves, which is an important value. However, Burnett's research found that today's youth wanted a job that allowed some degree of individualism and empowered them as take-charge individuals. Burnett's planners translated these insights into what they called the "Me. Now." philosophy. Young people want to live in a world where they are "in control—doing things [they] want to do, not things [they're] told to do."

This became a key insight: The target's need for empowerment paralleled the Army's need for highly trained individuals who could think for themselves as they operated the sophisticated new technology. Having uncovered this truth, Burnett's next challenge was to translate that into a theme that would resonate with this market.

Sources: Jacob Hodes and Emma Ruby-Sachs, "America's Army Targets Youth," *The Nation* (August 23, 2002); U.S. Army, "U.S. Army Recruiting Command: Advertising and Public Affairs Overview for Students 2002," October 12, 2001; James Dao, "Ads Now Seek Recruits for 'An Army of One,'" *New York Times* (January 10, 2001); Steven Lee Myers, "Army, Its Recruiting Not All It Could Be, Decides to Overhaul Its Advertising," *New York Times* (January 8, 2000).

their own personal observational research and visit retail stores, talk to salespeople, and watch people buy. They may visit the information center, browse through reference books, and borrow subject and picture files. They will look at previous advertising (especially the competition's) to see what others have done, and in their hearts they will become absolutely convinced that they are able to create something better than, and different from, anything that has been done before. This informal, personal research has a powerful influence on what happens later in the advertising process.

Research is also used in development of the message strategy to evaluate the relative power of various creative ideas, which is called **concept testing**, and the relative effectiveness of various approaches to the sales message, which is called **copy testing**.

Strategic and evaluative research share some common tools and processes, which we will briefly describe in this chapter, although a formal discussion of advertising evaluation and its role in determining effectiveness will be the focus of Chapter 19.

RESEARCH METHODS USED IN ADVERTISING PLANNING

This section focuses on the use of research in message development. We'll bring together the research situations with the types of methods typically used. The three stages in message development where research is used are preparation research, consumer research, and development research.

Background Research

Background research of a variety of types is used to familiarize advertising planners with the market situation. Secondary research includes reading everything that is published or reported on the market, the competition, and consumers. Primary research involves, among other things, personally buying and using the product.

The Brand Experience When an agency gets a new client, the first thing the agency team has to do is learn about the brand. That means, if possible, going through all the experiences that a typical consumer has buying and using the product. If you were taking on a pizza restaurant account, for example, you might try to work in the store, as well as visit it as a customer. It's also a form of commitment: The parking lots of agencies that have automotive accounts are usually full of cars of that make.

Competitive Analysis It's also important to do a competitive analysis. If you handle a soap account, you obviously want to use that brand of soap, but you may also buy the competitors' and do your own personal comparative test just to add your personal experiences to your brand analysis.

An Advertising Audit Either formally or informally most advertising planners will begin an assignment by collecting every possible piece of advertising and other forms of marketing communication by the brand, as well as its competitors', and other relevant categories that may have lessons for the brand. This include a historical collection, as well. There's nothing more embarrassing than proposing a great new advertising idea only to find out that it was used a couple of years ago by a competitor.

Content Analysis The advertising audit might include only informal summaries of the slogans, appeals, and images used most often, or it might include more formal and systematic tabulation of competitors' approaches and strategies called a **content analysis**. By disclosing competitors' strategies and tactics, analysis of the content of competitive advertisements provides clues to how competitors are thinking, and suggests ways to develop new and more effective campaigns. Planners also try to determine what mental territories or positions are claimed by competitors and which are still available and relevant to the brand.

Semiotic Analysis Another technique used to analyze advertisements is **semiotic analysis**, which is a way to take apart the signs and symbols in a message to uncover layers and types of meanings. The objective is to find deeper meanings in the symbolism and meanings, particularly as they relate to different groups of consumers. Its focus is on determining the meanings, even if they are not obvious or highly symbolic, that might relate to consumer motivations.

For example, the advertising that launched General Motors' OnStar global positioning system (GPS) used a Batman theme. The commercial featured a conversation between Batman and Alfred, his trusty butler, during which most of the features and uses of the OnStar system were explained. By looking at this commercial in terms of its signs and symbols, it is possible to determine if the obvious, as well as hidden, meanings of the message are on strategy. For example, the decision to use a comic book hero as the star created a hero association for OnStar. However, Batman is not a superhero, but rather more of a common person with a lot of great technology and cool gadgets (remember Jack Nicholson as the Joker and his famous comment: "Where does he get all those wonderful toys?"). The "bat beacon" then becomes OnStar for the average person. Batman is also ageless, appealing to young people who really read comic books, as well as older people who remember reading them in their youth.[2] A highly successful effort, this "Batman" OnStar campaign won a David Ogilvy Research Award.

Consumer Research

Consumer research is used to better understand how users, prospects, and nonusers of a brand think and behave using both qualitative and quantitative methods. From this research, segments and targets can be identified, and profiles can be drawn. An example of how this works comes from the Forrester Research company and is called "design personas." Harley Manning, research director for Web site design, explains the concept in The Inside Story.

Ways of Contact   Before moving to a discussion of specific types of consumer research methodologies, let's talk about ways to contact consumers when conducting advertising research. The contact can be in person, by telephone, by mail, through the Internet or cable TV, or by a computer kiosk in a mall or store. In a personal interview the researcher poses questions to the consumer directly. These interviews are often conducted in malls and downtown areas where there are lots of people. With telephone contacts the concept is described or the copy is read and the consumer is asked several questions about the ad via a phone call. Mail contacts are similar but in this method the test ad is mailed to the consumer along with a set of questions, which the consumer is expected to return promptly. Contacts through the Internet require access to the consumers via e-mail or instructions on how to click through to a research site in order to view the test ad. Concurrently, consumers are sent a set of questions about the ad, which they can return electronically.

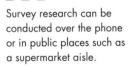

Survey research can be conducted over the phone or in public places such as a supermarket aisle.

THE INSIDE STORY
The Power of Design Personas

Harley Manning, Research Director, Site Design and Development, Forrester Research

In 1999, software inventor Alan Cooper introduced the concept of *personas* in his book *The Inmates Are Running the Asylum*. Forrester first referenced this idea in a 2001 report on design methodologies. We quickly realized that the concept had captured the imaginations of both designers and their clients. So in 2003 we began research for a report focused on best practices for creating and using personas.

What is a persona? It's a model of a customer's goals, needs, attitudes, and behaviors distilled from interviewing and observing real people in a market segment. The end result guides designers and their clients by replacing dry data about "the customer" with a vivid profile of a person.

Well-crafted personas are crisp, accurate, and sound like a description of someone you know. As a result, they're easy to both understand and relate to. For example, "Stanley" is a persona used by J.P. Morgan to model its active, savvy investors who won't be satisfied by a simple account summary and instead want advanced portfolio details, such as net liquidating value. Software giant SAP created three personas to inform the design of its call center software, including "Tina Ferraro-Smith," a telesales agent with personal goals that include putting clients first and going home in a decent mood.

We began our research by contacting a variety of agencies to find out which ones used personas. We followed up with hour-long interviews of creative directors, researchers, and account managers at firms ranging from interactive specialists like R/GA to diversified agencies like ZIBA Design, which creates everything from marketing strategies to physical environments like the FedEx Retail Service Centers. We also interviewed the agencies' clients—such as American Express, Ford, Reuters, and Travelocity—to determine why they bought into personas, how they used them, and what results they achieved.

We found that personas are getting very popular, very quickly. Although they started out as a tool for software designers, they're now being used to create marketing campaigns, sales training, Web sites, products, and even call center scripts. We also found that companies that use them correctly report compelling results. This led us to conclude that personas are here to stay and will be increasingly important for all types of design efforts.

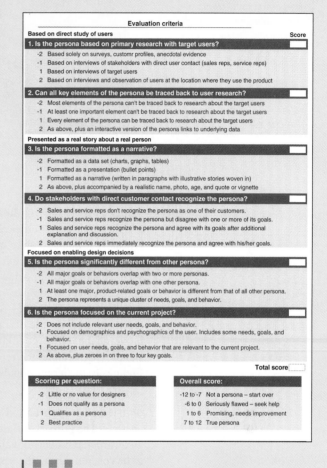

This is an example of the coding sheet used by Forrester Research to evaluate the strength of the personas they uncover for various types of consumers.

Leading the Site Design and Development group at Forrester Research, Harley Manning's work focuses on interactive media. Manning came to Forrester after 18 years of designing and building interactive services for Dow Jones, AT&T, MCI, Prodigy, and Sears. He received a Master of Science degree in Advertising from the University of Illinois, Urbana, in 1977.

Nominated by the late Kim Rotzell, former dean, University of Illinois College of Communication

■ ■ ■

In-depth interviews are conducted one-on-one with open ended questions that permit the interviewee to give thoughtful responses. The informal structure of the questions also allows the interviewer to follow up and ask probing questions to dig deeper into attitudes and motivations.

Survey Research   In a survey, questionnaires are used to obtain information about people's attitudes, knowledge, media use, and exposure to particular messages. **Survey research** is a quantitative method that uses structured interviews to ask large numbers of people the same set of questions. The questions can deal with personal characteristics, such as age, income, behavior, or attitudes. The surveys can be conducted in person, by phone, by mail, or online.

The people interviewed can be from an entire group, or **population**, or they can be a representative **sample** of a much larger group, a subset of the population that is representative of the entire population.[3] Careful scientific procedures are used in drawing the sample to guarantee the representativeness of the group in order to be able to project the findings to the larger population.

In-depth Interviews   An **in-depth interview** is a qualitative method conducted one-on-one using **open-ended questions** that require the respondents to generate their own answers. The primary difference between an interview and a survey is the interview's use of an unstructured questionnaire.[4] Interviews use a discussion guide, which outlines the areas to be covered during the session; they tend to be much longer than surveys, with questions that are usually very broad. An example is: "What do you like or dislike about this product?" or "What type of television programs do you like to watch?" Interviewers probe by responding to the answer with "Why do you say that?" or "Can you explain in more detail?" Interviews are considered qualitative because they typically use smaller sample sizes than surveys and their results are not generalizable and subject to statistical tests.

Focus Groups   Another qualitative method is a **focus group**, which is a group of 8 to 10 users or even up to 15 potential users of a product who are gathered around a table to have a discussion about some topic, such as the brand, the product category, or advertising. The objective is to get them talking in a conversational format so researchers can observe the dialogue and interactions among the participants. It's a directed group interview.[5] A moderator supervises the group providing direction through a set of carefully developed questions that stimulate conversation and elicit the group members' thoughts and feelings in their own words. Other qualitative tools can also be used with groups such as verbal and nonverbal exercises, having participants create things such as posters, diaries, or day mapping (mapping a day's activities), poems, and memory associations (what comes to mind when you think of something, such as a brand, situation, or location).

Focus groups can be used at any step in the planning process but they are often used early in the information-gathering process to probe for patterns of thought and behavior

■ ■ ■
Focus groups are conducted around a conference table with a researcher as the moderator who has prepared discussion questions. The session is usually held in a room with one-way glass so the other team members from the agency and client can observe the way the respondents answer the questions.

that are then tested using quantitative research tools, such as surveys. They are also useful in testing advertising ideas or exploring various alternatives in message strategy development. For example, when Kellogg Co. wanted to test the idea of "Corn Flakes as a high-fiber alternative," it conducted nearly a hundred focus groups of people from 40 to 55 years old throughout the United States.

Friendship focus groups[6] are used in a comfortable setting, usually people's homes, where the participants have been recruited by the host. This approach is designed to break down barriers and save time in getting to more in-depth responses. For example, one study of sensitive and insensitive visuals used in advertising to black women found that a self-constructed friendship group was easier to assemble and yielded more honest and candid responses.[7]

Observation Research   Like anthropologists, observation researchers study the actual behavior of consumers in naturalistic settings where they live, work, shop, and play, acting as what Sayre refers to as "professional snoops."[8] A qualitative form of research, direct **observation research** is closer and more personal than quantitative research. It takes researchers into natural settings where they note the behavior of consumers using video, audio, and disposable cameras to record consumers' behavior at home (with consumer consent), in stores, or wherever people buy and use their products.

A marketer will often use observation in the aisles of grocery, drug, and discount stores to watch people making their product selection. The observer is able to watch how people walk the aisle, where they stop, how much effort they make in reading labels, and so forth.

An example of a major observational research project that opened the door for this type of research in marketing was the Consumer Behavior Odyssey that put a team of researchers in a Winnebago on a trip from Los Angeles to Boston. Along the way, the team used a variety of observational techniques to watch and record people behaving as consumers.[9]

Ethnographic Research   Related to observation, **ethnographic research** involves the researcher in living the lives of the people being studied. Ethnographers have elevated people watching to a science. In ethnographic research in anthropology, which is the home of this research method, observers "go native" and immerse themselves in a culture in order to study the meanings, language, interaction, and behavior of the people in the group.[10] Sometimes the observations are supplemented by field interviews. This method is particularly good at deriving a picture of a day in the life of a typical consumer.

Major companies like Harley-Davidson and Coca-Cola now use ethnographic research to get close to their customers. These companies hire marketing professors trained in social science research to observe and interpret customer behavior at rallies. These participant observers then meet with the company's managers, planners, and marketing staff to discuss their impressions.[11]

The case of Best Western International provides an example. In the spring of 2000, the company paid 25 couples who were over age 55 to tape themselves on their travels across the United States. The purpose of the research was twofold. First, the hotel chain wanted to learn how seniors decide when and where to stop for the night. Second, based on this information, the company wanted to determine whether it should increase its 10 percent senior discount. The tapes certainly were revealing. Seniors who talked the hotel clerk into a better deal didn't need the lower price to afford the room; they just liked making the deal. Best Western marketers concluded that increasing the senior discount was not a good idea.[12]

Today, virtually all major agencies offer their clients the opportunity to conduct ethnographic research. In fact, at Averett, Free & Ginsberg, 9 out of 15 large clients have opted for the service. "Ethnography is the intimate connection to the consumer," says Bill Abrams, founder of Housecalls, a New York consultancy that worked on the Best Western effort.[13]

Direct observation and ethnographic research have the advantage of revealing what people actually do, as distinguished from what people say they do. It can yield the correct answer when faulty memory, desire to impress the interviewer, or simple inattention to details would cause an interview answer to be wrong. The biggest drawback to direct observation is that it shows what is happening, but not why. Therefore, the results of direct observation often are combined with the results of personal interviews to provide a more complete and more understandable picture of attitudes, motives, and behavior.[14]

Diaries   Sometimes consumers are asked to record their activities through the use of diaries. These **diaries** are particularly valuable in media research because they tell media planners exactly what programs and ads the consumers watched. If comment lines are provided, then the activities can also be accompanied by thoughts. Beeper diaries are used as a way to randomize the recording of activities. In other words, consumers participating in the study will grab the diary and record what they are doing when the beeper goes off. Diaries are designed to catch the consumer in a more realistic, normal life pattern than you can derive from surveys or interviews that rely on consumers to remember accurately their activities. This can also lead to the re-creation of a day in the life of a consumer.

Other Qualitative Methods   Advertising planners are always probing for reasons, feelings, and motivations behind behaviors and what people say. To arrive at useful consumer insights, they use a variety of interesting and novel research methods. In particular, they use stories and pictures.

Cognitive psychologists have learned that human beings think more in images than words. But most research has to use words to ask questions and obtain answers, so the object with visual-based research opens up new avenues of expression that may be better able to uncover people's deep thoughts. To overcome this problem, researchers try through pictures to uncover mental processes that guide consumer behavior.

Harvard Business School professor Gerald Zaltman believes that the conventional wisdom about consumer research, such as using interviews and focus groups that rely on talking to people and grilling them about their tastes and buying habits, is only good for getting back predictable answers. If you ask people what they think about Coke, you'll learn that it is a "high-energy, thirst-quenching, fun-at-the-beach" kind of drink. But that may not be an adequate description of how people really feel about the soft drink.[15]

Here is a collection of some of the more imaginative ways qualitative researchers are getting insights about people's relationships to the brands they buy.

- *Fill-in-the-Blanks.* A form of attitude research in which people fill in the blanks in a story or balloons in a cartoon. Their perceptions will sometimes come to the surface in the words they use to describe the action or situations depicted in the visuals.
- *Purpose-driven Games.* These are used by researchers to see how people solve problems and search for information.[16] Games can make the research experience more fun and involving for the participants. It also uncovers problem-solving strategies that may

mirror their approach to information searching or the kinds of problems they deal with in certain product situations.

- *Story Elicitation.* Consumers are asked to explain the artifacts of their lives—what you see in photos of their homes, as well as the things in their lives that they treasure. These stories can provide insights into how and why people use or do things.
- *Artifact Creation.* This technique uses such ideas as *life collages, day mapping,* and the *construction of instruction books* as ways to elicit stories that discuss brands and their role in daily life. These projects are also useful later in explaining to others—clients, the creative team, other agencies—the triggers behind the consumer insights.[17]
- *Photo Elicitation.* Similar to artifacts, visuals can be used to elicit consumer thoughts and opinions. Sometimes consumers are asked to look at a set of visuals or they are instructed to visually record something with a camera, such as a shopping trip. Later, in reviewing the visuals, they are asked what the photo brings to mind or to explain what they were thinking or doing at the time the photo was taken.
- *Photo Sorts.* Another visual technique is called a photo sort where consumers are asked to sort through a deck of photos and pick out visuals that represent something, such as typical users of the product, or situations where it might be used. In identifying typical users, they may be asked to sort the photos into specific piles, such as happy, sad, angry, excited, or innovative people.

L'original

◼ ◼ ◼
This ad equating evian sparkling water with a mermaid tries to add a touch of originality to the evian brand image.

- *Metaphors.* Some researchers believe that metaphors can enrich the language consumers use to talk about brands. A metaphor says one thing—a brand, for example—is like something else, as in the evian ad shown here. The insight into how people perceive brands through such connections comes from exploring the link between the two concepts. Metaphor games are used in creativity to elicit new and novel ideas, but they can also be used to analyze cognitive patterns in people's thinking. Harvard professor Gerald Zaltman is the creator of ZMET (pronounced ZEE-MET), the Zaltman Metaphor Elicitation Technique, which uses metaphors and visual images to uncover patterns in people's thinking.[18] For Coca-Cola in Europe, for example, Zaltman asked volunteers to spend a week collecting at least a dozen pictures that captured their feelings about Coca-Cola from magazines, catalogs, or other printed materials. Then they discussed the images in personal interviews. Finally, the volunteers created a summary image—a digital collage of their most important images—and recorded a statement that explained its meaning. The ZMET team found that Coke is not just about feelings of high energy and good times, but that it also has an element of calm, solitude, and relaxation.

Choosing a Research Method

Determining the appropriate research method to use is an important planning decision. It might help to understand two basic research criteria: validity and reliability, which are derived from what researchers call the "scientific method." **Validity** means that the research actually measures what it says it measures. Any differences that are uncovered by the research, such as different attitudes or purchasing patterns, really reflect differences among individuals, groups, or situations. **Reliability** means that you can run the same test again and get the same answer.

Quantitative researchers, particularly those doing experiments and surveys, are concerned about being faithful to the principles of science. Selecting a sample that truly represents its population, for example, increases the reliability of the research. Poorly worded questions and talking to the wrong people can hurt the validity of surveys, and of focus groups.

The problem is that experiments are limited by the small number of people in the experimental group and the sometimes artificial conditions in which they are conducted. The information you get from surveys of a broad cross section of a population is limited to your ability to develop good clear questions that everyone can understand and answer. This tight control makes it harder to ask questions around the edges of a topic or elicit unexpected or unusual responses. On the other hand, focus groups and in-depth interviews, which permit probing, are also limited by small numbers and possible problems with representativeness.

In other words, there are three big objectives in advertising research: (1) test hypotheses, (2) get information, and (3) get insights. Each has strengths and weaknesses. Generally quantitative methods are more useful for gathering data (how many do this or believe that?) and qualitative methods are better at uncovering reasons and motives (why do they do or believe?). For these reasons, most researchers believe in using a variety of research methods—quantitative, as well as qualitative.

RESEARCH CHALLENGES

Advertising researchers face five key challenges: globalization, new media technology, Internet and virtual research, embedded research, and insightful analysis. We examine each challenge briefly.

Globalization

Advertisers are becoming increasingly redemdant global. Multinational advertisers and their marketing communication agencies are expanding all over the world. In-depth understanding of the economic and cultural conditions, government regulations, and communications media of each country is more important than ever before. The key issues that global researchers face include how to manage and communicate global brands in different local regions and how to shift from studying differences to finding similarities around the world. The biggest problem is cross-cultural communication and how to arrive at an intended message without cultural distortions or insensitivities. Researchers are becoming more involved in puzzling out cultural meanings and testing advertising messages for cultural sensitivity in different countries.

New Media Technology

The expansion from three on-air television networks to a plethora of cable channels changed television programming, television program audiences, and television advertising throughout the United States. The merger of the telephone, the TV, and the home computer will also change advertising. Wireless phones are now operating like personal data assistants (PDAs), as well as cameras and text-messaging sytems.

Changes in media technology will alter the meaning and consequences of almost all of our most familiar research constructs: involvement, brand equity, attitude toward the ad, emotional processing, and cognitive processing, to name a few. Advertising research today focuses largely on full-page print ads, 30-second television commercials, and more recently Web sites. As technology changes in the media unfold, the old research measures will become increasingly invalid. Multimedia research, for example, allows automated

testing of concepts, storyboards, and designs in multiple markets. That's a lot simpler and cheaper than having staff develop actual prototypes or multiple sets of storyboards.

Because of media fragmentation, researchers and planners must strive to develop message strategies as well as new research methods that enable media planners to reach consumers most effectively. That includes using multiple product messages in multiple media vehicles: Internet for interactivity, print for details, direct mail for personalization, and TV for creating an emotional connection. New media technology is also opening the door to new ways to do and test permission and relationship marketing.

Another factor is the emergence of genuine two-way communication opportunities. Advertising and marketing communication has always been focused on the design and measure of one-way communication from a source (company) to the receiver (target audience), but all that is changing. As consumers take charge of more of their exposure opportunities through new media, how will researchers undertake developmental research designed to open up opportunities for interactivity? What measures are appropriate for developing message strategies designed to generate consumer-initiated messages?

Internet and Virtual Research

Another aspect of new media is the feasibility of **virtual research** that gathers real-time information through online media and streaming video. The low cost and quick speed of gathering research data online has made the Internet a popular survey tool with companies. Hershey's uses online research to test its new products, as well as its marketing and advertising concepts, an award-winning project that has been recognized by the industry.[19]

Even in a more traditional one-way communication model, creating effective ads for the new interactive media is a particular challenge. Numerous companies provide information about Internet use, but some sources are more valid than others. Some companies use true random surveying to generate figures. Other companies depend on information provided voluntarily by Internet users or industry sources (which often have a vested interest in promoting good news). Those who want to plan or evaluate Internet ads must stay abreast of the latest developments in research on this interactive medium because the methods are still in their infancy.[20]

Embedded Research

The development of **embedded research** is related to virtual research. In this case, the research methods are embedded directly into real purchase and use situations, so that the consumer is a recipient and direct beneficiary of the information. A non-Internet example of embedded research comes from Nordstrom's Personal Touch Program, which uses a team of *personal shoppers* who are fashion consultants on one level, but on another level they are trained to gather information from their clients to feed back into the company's business planning and marketing.

Call centers, both inbound (customer calls to complain or get assistance) and outbound (telemarketing), can also be used as research centers to gain real-time feedback about the brand and its marketing and advertising strategies. In other words, whenever a call is made, for whatever purpose, that contact provides an opportunity to ask a brand-related question.

The most common Internet approach is to use this method for **product reviews**, where customers enter the Web site and select from an array of product categories they would like to know about. The opinions of reviewers can be accessed with a click. You see this on the Amazon.com site where reviews of music and books are posted on the page with the product information. Reviews come from other customers, who report their own experience.

Insightful Analysis

Marketers are inundated with information, so getting information is less of a problem than is making sense of it. The challenge is not information but rather *intelligence*. Information overload is a fact in marketing and advertising and it complicates planning. In analysis, data from one source often take on new meaning when compared with data from other sources. For example, the Army could look at the awareness levels of its "Be all you can be" theme and conclude that the advertising is working. But when those data are compared with relevance scores, then a gap may be seen between what is promised and what the target audience perceives the meaning to be.

The magic in research, then, lies in the interpretation of the findings to uncover unexpected or unrealized insights into consumers, products, and the marketplace situation. That's the gift of people called account planners; these we will discuss in the next chapter.

IT'S A WRAP

LEAP INTO A TOTAL LEARNING SYSTEM

In a short six years, LeapFrog established a strong brand presence as a leader in children's learning materials. Its objectives were to continue increasing sales at a 25 percent rate, increase its brand awareness by 20 percent, and, in general, own the educational brand position by building an emotive, focused brand.

Its marketing communication surpassed all three of the measurable objectives. By 2003 sales were increasing at a 37 percent rate, making LeapFrog the third-largest toy manufacturer in the United States. At the same time, brand awareness increased 21 percent. In terms of dominance, three of the best-selling toys in the United States were from LeapFrog (LeapPad Books, LeapPad, and My First LeapPad). More importantly, the top-rated "toy" was actually a book and it beat out established favorites like Hot Wheels, Bratz, and Spider-Man.

Not only did the research effort, as well as the marketing communication program developed by Ackerman McQueen, make LeapFrog dominant in children's educational materials; it also became a dominant player in the larger toys category, elevating the entire concept of educational materials. That's why LeapFrog was named an EFFIE® winner in 2003.

▪▪▪ Summary

1. **Discuss the types of strategic research.** Secondary research is background research that gathers already published information, and primary research is original research of information that is collected for the first time from original sources. Quantitative research is statistical and uses numerical data to investigate how people think and behave; qualitative research is exploratory and uses probing techniques to gain insights and identify questions and hypotheses for further quantitative research.

2. **Identify the four uses of research in advertising.** Research is used to (1) develop an analysis of the marketing situation; (2) acquire consumer information and insights for making targeting decisions; (3) identify information about available media in order to be able to match the media to the target audience; (4) develop message strategies and evaluate their effectiveness.

3. **List the common research methods used in advertising.** Survey research is used to amass quantities of responses from consumers about their attitudes and behaviors. In-depth interviews probe the reasons and motivations consumers give to explain their attitudes and behavior. Focus groups are group interviews that operate like conversations directed by a researcher. Observation is research that happens in the store or home where researchers watch how consumers behave. Ethnographic research is an anthropological technique that involves the researcher in participating in the day-to-day lives of consumers. Diaries are records of consumers' behavior, particularly their media use. A number of other qualitative methods are used to creatively uncover patterns in the way consumers think and act.

4. **Explain the key challenges facing advertising research.** Globalization complicates the way research is conducted for global products because it adds a cultural dimension, as well as legal restrictions. New research techniques are being created as a result of new media technology, as well as the Internet, which offers opportunities for virtual interviews. Embedded research is a way to get immediate feedback that comes from the process of buying or using the product. Beyond the accumulation of numbers and information, the search for insight is a driving force in advertising research.

▪▪▪ Key Terms

advertising research, 157
concept testing, 165
consumer research, 157
content analysis, 165
copy testing, 165
diaries, 170
embedded research, 173

ethnographic research, 169
focus groups, 168
friendship focus groups, 169
IMC research, 157
in-depth interview, 168
market research, 157
marketing research, 162

observation research, 169
open-ended questions, 168
population, 168
product reviews, 174
purchase intent, 160
qualitative research, 160
quantitative research, 160

reliability, 172
sample, 168
semiotic analysis, 165
strategic research, 157
survey research, 168
validity, 171
virtual research, 173

▪▪▪ Review Questions

1. Explain the value of strategic research. How is it used in advertising?

2. What are the four uses of research in advertising? Give an example of each one.

3. Describe the most common research methods used in advertising.

4. Explain how advertising is changing and the challenges it faces.

▪▪▪ Discussion Questions

1. Every year Copper Mountain must decide how much emphasis to put on front-range day skiers, skiers from the Denver market who stay overnight, and skiers from outside Copper Mountain's geographic area. What research information would help Copper Mountain's managers make those decisions? Where would they get that information?

2. Suppose you are developing a research program for a new bookstore serving your college or university. What kind of exploratory research would you recommend? Would you propose both qualitative and quantitative studies? Why or why not? What specific steps would you take?

3. The research director for Angelis Advertising always introduces her department's service to new agency clients by comparing research to a roadmap. What do maps and research studies have in common? How does the analogy of a map reveal the limitations of research for resolving an advertising problem?

4. Research professionals recommend using focus groups to help develop a campaign strategy or theme, but many are opposed to using focus groups to choose finished ads for the campaign. Is this advice self-contradictory? Why or why not?

5. A new radio station is moving into your community. Management is not sure how to position the station in this market and has asked you to develop a study to help them make this decision.

   a. What key research questions must be asked?

   b. Outline a research program to answer those questions that uses as many of the research methods discussed in this chapter as you can incorporate.

▪▪▪ Class Projects

1. Run a focus group. Brainstorm to come up with something the class would like to advertise, such as new audio equipment. Divide into researchers and the consumer group (you can run two groups and trade roles, if you'd like). Meet to decide on questions and format. Make assignments for note taking, facilitating, and collecting and organizing feedback. Write a one- to two-page report on the process and the group's findings.

2. Assume you are working for Gerber Baby Foods. Your assignment is to identify the relevant trends that are forecasted for U.S. birth rates between 2003 and 2010. Identify Internet sources that would provide that information. Select one and write a one-page report on the trends you find.

HANDS-ON CASE

What Lies Beneath? Making a Choice

"If you have a 'buy button' in your brain," the *New York Times* headline asked, "what pushes it?" The *Times* article summarized a recent study in which neurologists monitored the brain activity of participants as they sampled unmarked cups of Coke and Pepsi over several trials and indicated their preference. The scientists observed that participant brain activity was confined to "reward centers" associated with reactions to the pleasurable taste of the beverages. The scientists also observed that the participant preferences were evenly split between Coke and Pepsi.

Then the scientists changed the procedure a bit by clearly marking the samples as Coke or Pepsi. Different regions of the participants' brains were now activated and "overrode" the reward center responses that the researchers had observed earlier. And this new pattern of activity seemed to change the participants' sensory experience of the samples, because at the end of the second wave of trials respondents showed a decided preference for Coke, choosing it 75 percent of the time.

These results are viewed with great interest by scientists and advertisers alike, because they are a clear testa-

ment to the power of brands. "At issue," wrote the *Times* reporter, "is whether marketers can exploit advances in brain science to make more effective commercials."

Advertisers have long been fascinated with technologies that promise richer and deeper insights into how people think and feel than do focus groups and surveys, which may fail to capture key aspects of how consumers choose. These traditional methods may fall short not because consumers won't tell marketers what they think, but rather because they *can't*. This intriguing claim is offered by Harvard Business School professor Gerald Zaltman, who believes that most thinking occurs below our level of consciousness. In Zaltman's view, what we understand as conscious thought represents only about 5 percent of all cognitive processes. The other 95 percent, which is a more important influence on consumer decision making, occurs outside our awareness. In Zaltman's view, "the unconscious mind represents a significant frontier where marketers may establish secure beachheads of competitive advantage. Certainly no firm can claim to understand consumers without colonizing this land of opportunity."

But tapping into the subconscious is not easy. Zaltman believes marketers should consider abandoning traditional techniques for new methods, including the technologies for measuring brain activity described earlier—as well as less expensive approaches such as metaphor elicitation and response latency techniques. In metaphor elicitation, such as Zaltman's ZMET technique, consumers are asked to bring a photograph or other symbol of a concept (such as the perfect home) to a depth interview. The interviewer's role is to try, in a nondirective way, to help the consumer explore and articulate the meaning of the picture.

In response latency approaches, mental relationships and links are explored by measuring the relative speed of word recognition. Cognitive psychology has demonstrated that people recognize a word faster when the word follows a related concept or idea (for instance, people recognize the term *cream cheese* faster when it appears after *bagel* than when it appears after *Kansas.*). Advertising researchers can use this phenomenon to determine whether a brand name or symbol speeds recognition of attributes believed to be associated with the brand. For instance, they might test whether showing people *Honda,* speeds up recognition of the word *reliable.*

Consider This

1. A great deal of current research assumes that people can consciously describe why they do things and what they intend to do in the future. Do you think Zaltman is correct in criticizing this assumption?

2. The *New York Times* article mentioned above also presented views from a strong critic of this kind of research. The critic believes that it is dangerous for companies to learn how to affect consumer subconscious thinking because future campaigns could then be used to affect consumers without their recognition. For the critic, this is a violation of the consumers' free will. What do you think? What limits, if any, should there be on campaigns developed from this new knowledge?

3. How do research methods, such as the "brain science" methods discussed here, help advertising planners gain insights into consumer attitudes and behavior? How would you determine if the research helped create more effective advertising?

Sources: Sandra Blakeslee, "If You Have a 'Buy Button' in Your Brain, What Pushes It?" *New York Times* (October 19, 2004); Gerald Zaltman, *How Customers Think: Essential Insights into the Mind of the Market* (Cambridge, MA: Harvard Business School Press, 2004).

Indifferent

CITIZE
Not your

Member FDIC

We don't take money from strang

CITIZE
Not your

Member FDIC

Service

CITIZE
Not your

Member FDIC

Strategic Planning

CHAPTER 7

The Legendary Service of Citizens Bank

Award:
EFFIE® Silver

Company:
Citizens Bank

Agency:
Arnold Worldwide

Campaign:
"Legendary Service"

CHAPTER KEY POINTS

After reading this chapter, you will be able to:

1. Differentiate between objectives, strategies, and tactics in strategic planning.

2. Identify the six basic decisions in an advertising plan.

3. Explain how account planning works.

4. Outline the key factors in an IMC plan.

When Citizens Bank, the second-largest bank in New England, announced its purchase of Mellon Bank, a 150-year-old Pennsylvania bank, it faced a serious loss of customers. Mellon's customers had been dissatisfied for years and were more likely to switch banks than the customers of any other bank in the region.

The good news was that Citizens Bank had a strong reputation for outstanding customer service in its home market, although this reputation hadn't reached the Mellon market. The problem then was to stabilize Mellon's vulnerable, dissatisfied customer base long enough for Citizens to demonstrate its superior customer service.

The Arnold Worldwide agency restated that challenge as objectives for a new image-building campaign for the bank. The objectives were:

1. Minimize customer attrition during the acquisition keeping it under 10 percent.

179

2. Quickly build awareness through advertising.

3. Reduce customers' intentions to leave the bank.

The Mellon customer was described as adults 35–54 with a household income of $50,000–$150,000. Arnold's research found a general indifference among these customers, a sense that the acquisition was just another in the long drumbeat of takeovers in the banking industry. With nearly a quarter of the customers "likely" or "highly likely" to switch, it was clear many were ready to leave at the next sign of trouble. Interestingly, some consumers mixed their negative expectations of fee increases and branch closures with a "wait and see" attitude. "How much worse can it get?" many asked.

Arnold's strategy was to make the Citizens brand promise so irresistible and different that customers would be compelled to give the bank a try. Here's how they stated the bank's new customer-focused philosophy:

Citizens Bank is "Not your typical bank." It's a bank
that believes in quality customer service, quick response,
and treating its customers with a uniquely high level of respect.

This message was communicated in stages, first with a series of TV ads that re-created true incidents of great service by Citizens bankers, with a humorous, self-deprecating twist. This stage was designed to build awareness and set customer expectations high.

Given the boldness of the "not typical" promise, the next stage was to make the promise real and tangible. It was important to have as many people as possible experience this level of customer service, as soon as possible. So as opening day approached, an extensive promotion was developed in Philadelphia and Pittsburgh. On opening day, commuters in each market experienced Citizens' "Legendary acts of service" firsthand with free transit rides, coffee, pastries, even meter feeders and squeegee squads.

Citizens' opening day was an event, one that included filming and editing four documentary-style TV spots in time to air on that evening's news. Unlike slick, traditional bank advertising, Citizens' reality-TV approach captured actual customers and employees reacting to the opening-day events. They were surprising and fresh and clearly reinforced that Citizens was setting a new standard of customer service.

The promotion was advertised via radio, newspaper, and transit posters. The events themselves also gained media coverage, as well as becoming material for use in subsequent television ads.

The Results

The "Not Typical" campaign was highly successful in taking Citizens and Mellon customers through the transition and successfully protected the value of the customer franchise Citizen was acquiring. Here is the evaluation of the campaign's three objectives:

1. Minimize customer attrition keeping losses under 10 percent: During the six-month period of the merger, Mellon Bank and Citizens experienced vir-

tually no customer attrition and the bank enjoyed a net increase in deposits, a response that is nearly unheard of in a bank acquisition.

2. Quickly build advertising awareness: During this period, the integrated communication efforts helped drive Citizens' awareness in the new market from zero to 31 percent in just a few short weeks, and to 60 percent by opening day.

3. Reduce customers' intentions to leave the bank: During the three-month period leading up to opening day, the proportion of Mellon customers likely to switch banks was cut in half (from 24 percent to 12 percent) and continued to drop through the next six months.

Sources: 2003 EFFIE Awards Brief provided by Citizens Bank and Arnold Worldwide; "Citizens Bank's Legendary Service Campaign Wins EFFIE Award for Arnold Worldwide," PR Newswire, July 20, 2002, http://www.prnewswire.com.

Marketing and advertising strategies are chosen from an array of possible alternatives. Often in advertising there is no completely right way, but if you understand how advertising works, you may be able to identify the best strategy to accomplish the objectives. This chapter will explain strategic planning, as well as basic planning decisions used in business, marketing, and IMC and advertising plans. It will also introduce the concept of account planning and explain its critical role in determining the consumer insights that lead to message and media strategies.

STRATEGIC PLANNING

Strategic planning is the process of determining *objectives* (what you want to accomplish), deciding on **strategies** (how to accomplish the objectives), and implementing the **tactics** (which make the plan come to life). This process occurs within a specified time frame.

Even those experienced in advertising sometimes have a hard time telling the difference between an objective and a strategy. Remember, *an objective* is a goal to be accomplished, and in advertising they are determined by the effects you want to achieve, which were explained in Chapter 4. A *strategy* is the means, the design, or the plan by which the objective is accomplished—the advertising message and media strategies, for example. In advertising the *tactic*s are the way the ads (and other marketing communication efforts) are executed—how they are designed and what they say.

In the Citizens Bank case, the objective was to use advertising to make the acquisition as successful as possible without losing a lot of the Mellon customers. The strategy was to focus on Citizens' high level of customer satisfaction. The tactics were to demonstrate the customer focus in initial ads that featured true examples of Citizens' personal service, then in reality-TV ads shot and run on opening day, and by personal experiences of Citizens service that were tied in with the opening-day celebration.

To sort out the difference between objectives, strategies, and tactics consider a hypothetical situation. If a marketer's objective is to reinforce brand loyalty for its product, its planners could use any number of strategies. They could set up a frequent buyer club; they could use direct marketing to reach customers individually; they could use advertising to remind customers to repurchase the brand; or they could use sales promotion to encourage buyers to repurchase. For each strategy a different set of tactics would be needed to implement the strategy. Before we develop the idea of advertising planning in more depth, let's review the basics of business and marketing planning, which are also concerned with objectives, strategies, and tactics.

Strategic Planning from Top to Bottom

Strategic planning reaches all levels of an organization, from the corporate level to tactical daily operations.

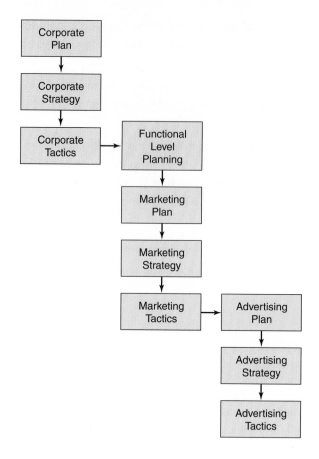

The Business Plan

Strategic planning is a three-tiered process that starts with the business plan, then moves to functional areas of the company such as marketing where a marketing plan is developed that outlines objectives, strategies, and tactics for all areas of the marketing mix. As illustrated in Figure 7.1, both the business plan and the marketing plan contribute direction to specific plans for specialist areas, such as advertising and other areas of marketing communication.

A business plan may cover a specific division of the company or a **strategic business unit (SBU)**, such as a line of products or all the offerings under a single brand name. These divisions or SBUs share a common set of problems and factors. Figure 7.2 depicts a widely used framework for the strategic planning process in business. The objectives for planning

The Business Strategic Planning Process

For most organizations, strategic planning starts by formulating a business mission statement.

Source: Philip Kotler, *Marketing Management*, 10th ed. (Upper Saddle River, NJ: Prentice Hall, 2000), 76.

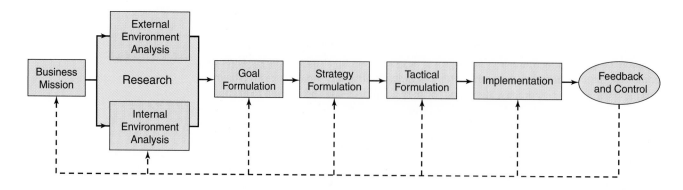

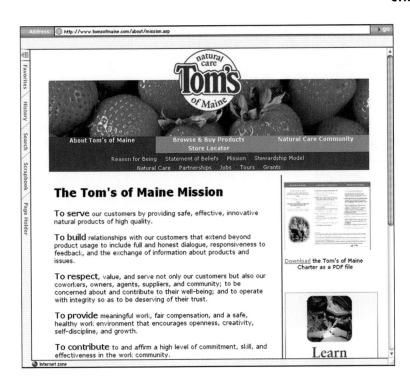

at this level tend to focus on maximizing profit and **return-on-investment (ROI)**. ROI means that, in general, the costs of conducting the business—the investment—should be more than matched by the revenue produced in return. The revenue above and beyond the costs is where profit lies.

Note that the business planning process starts with a business **mission statement** that is unique, focused, and differentiating, one that supports the broad goals and policies of the business unit. Tom's of Maine states its mission clearly on its Web site.

*Through the years, we have been guided by one simple notion—do what is right, for our customers, employees, communities, and environment. We call this **Natural Care**—a philosophy that guides what we make and all that we do.*

The Marketing Plan

A **marketing plan** is developed and evaluated annually, although sections dealing with long-term goals might operate for a number of years. To a large extent, the marketing plan parallels the business strategic plan and contains many of the same components, as we see in Figure 7.3, which illustrates the steps involved in creating a marketing plan.

Steps in the Marketing Plan
The marketing plan parallels the business strategic plan and contains many of the same steps.

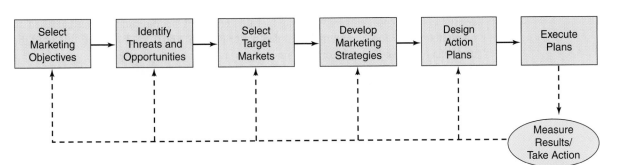

Rockport

I'M COMFORTABLE BEING WRONG SOMETIMES

james j. cramer,
financial guru,
founder of the street.com

be comfortable. uncompromise: start with your feet.

■ ■ ■
This ad for Rockport's shoes
determined that consumers were
interested in comfort. This
became the focus of the ad and
a key product attribute that loyal
users appreciate.

A *market situation analysis* assesses the external and internal environments that affect the marketing operations. This analysis looks at the company's history, products, and brands, as well as the competitive environment, consumer trends, and other marketplace trends that affect the product category. A set of "What's going on?" questions help structure this market analysis. Answers to these questions help define the marketing problem and, ultimately, the area of message opportunity.

- What is happening with the brand and the category?
- How is it happening?
- Where is it happening?
- When is it happening?
- To whom is it happening?

We could answer those questions for Citizens Bank by summarizing the market situation as a difficult merger with a set of unhappy customers who have been disappointed in the service received from their original bank. The new bank wants to address this dissatisfaction by bringing its own high level of customer service to their attention.

The objectives at the marketing level tend to be focused on *sales levels* and *share of market,* which refers to the percentage of the category purchases that are made by the brand's customers. Other objectives deal with specific areas of the marketing mix, such as distribution, where an objective might detail how a company is going to open a new territory.

For advertising managers, the most important part of the marketing plan is the *marketing mix strategy.* It links the overall strategic business plan with specific marketing programs, including advertising and other IMC areas. The brand loyalty problem discussed earlier is an example of strategies that a marketing manager might consider in solving the objective of increasing loyalty. Using a frequency club in an advertising campaign or a sales promotion reflects marketing communication decisions that come under the review of the marketing manager.

The Advertising or IMC Plan

Advertising planning operates with the same concern for objectives, strategies, and tactics that we've outlined for business and marketing plans. An example of a company that effectively brought all these elements together is Rockport, which has been making comfortable walking shoes since 1971. After doing research on existing customers, the company concluded that Rockport users are actively seeking comfort on every level: physical, emotional, and spiritual. The core Rockport strategy emphasized the need for comfort by challenging the consumer: If you compromise your comfort, you compromise yourself. To challenge consumers, Rockport's agency invented a rallying cry: "Uncompromise," and launched an integrated marketing communication plan featuring print and TV advertising that used the umbrella theme of "Be comfortable, uncompromise. Start with your feet."[1]

Consider This

1. What is strategic planning, and how is it used in marketing and advertising?
2. How does an advertising plan relate to a marketing and a business plan?

BASIC STRATEGIC PLANNING DECISIONS

A firm may operate with an annual advertising or IMC plan that outlines all the advertising or marketing communication activities. In addition to or instead of an annual plan, a firm may develop a **campaign plan** which is more tightly focused on solving a particular marketing communication problem. A campaign plan, which we will focus on in this chapter, typically includes a variety of messages carried in different media and sometimes targeted to different audiences. Below is an outline of the sections, and the decisions they represent, in a typical advertising campaign plan.

Typical Advertising or IMC Plan Outline

I. Situation analysis
   - Background research
   - SWOTs: strengths, weaknesses, opportunities, threats
   - Key advertising problem(s) to be solved

II. Key strategic decisions
   - Advertising/IMC Objectives and Strategies
   - Target audience (or stakeholder targets in an IMC Plan)
   - Brand position: product features and competitive advantage
   - Brand image and personality
   - Budget

III. Media strategy (or Points of Contact in an IMC Plan)
   - Media objectives
   - Vehicle selection and budget allocation
   - Scheduling

IV. Message strategy
   - Key consumer insight (Brand Relationship Insight in IMC)
   - Selling premise
   - Big idea
   - Executions

V. Other tools (in an IMC Plan)
   - Sale promotion
   - Public relations
   - Direct marketing
   - Personal selling
   - Sponsorships, merchandising, packaging, point-of-purchase
   - Integration strategy

VI. Evaluation of effectiveness

To illustrate how one concept can be carried across different media and message strategies in a campaign, consider how the Gander Mountain campaign is developed under the slogan "We live outdoors." Trent Walters, account supervisor at The Richards Group in Dallas, Texas, explains the campaign as follows:

Gander Mountain is a hunting, fishing and camping retailer located in the upper Midwest that carries a wide selection of supplies and gear at great prices. The employees at the stores are outdoor experts. They don't just sell gear; they also use it as they participate in outdoor activities themselves. However, few people knew this about the brand.

After conducting initial research, management interviews and meetings with Gander Mountain's marketing team, we determined that the Gander Mountain brand was all about "creating outdoor memories." All our future communication efforts should tell customers about the "great gear at great prices" and "employees who are outdoor experts" and who can help make the customer's outdoor experiences "more fulfilling." From this new strategy we developed television, radio and print executions.

SHOWCASE

■ ■ ■
Gander Mountain used this campaign to establish its brand identity and differentiate itself among the other outdoor retailers in the marketplace.

Situation Analysis

The first step in developing an advertising plan, just as with a marketing plan, is not planning but *backgrounding*—researching and reviewing the current state of the business that is relevant to the brand and gathering all relevant information. As discussed in Chapter 6, advertising planning is preceded by research of market, product and company, and likely consumer. After the research is compiled, analysis begins; it is sometimes referred to as a **situation analysis**. Planners collect and analyze information about the company, the brand, the competition, as well as consumers in general and the brand's customers specifically.

SWOT Analysis The primary tool used to make sense of the information is a **SWOT analysis**, which stands for **s**trengths, **w**eaknesses, **o**pportunities, and **t**hreats. The strengths and weaknesses are *internally focused* and the opportunities and threats lie in the *external* marketing environment. In strategic planning the idea is to *leverage* the strengths and opportunities and *address* the weaknesses and threats, which is how the key problems and opportunities are identified.[2]

Principle
Analysis of SWOTS means finding ways to address the weaknesses and threats and leverage the strengths and opportunities.

- The *strengths* of a business are its positive traits, conditions, and good situations. For instance, being in a growth industry is a strength. Planners ask how they can leverage this strength in the brand's advertising.
- The *weaknesses* of a business are traits, conditions, and situations that are perceived as negatives. Losing market share is a weakness and planners ask how they can address it with advertising.
- An *opportunity* is an area in which the company could develop an advantage over its competition. Often, one company's weakness is another company's opportunity. Planners strive to identify these opportunities and leverage them in the brand's advertising.
- A *threat* is a trend or development in the environment that will erode business unless the company takes action. Competition is a common threat. Advertising planners ask themselves how they can address this threat if it is a critical factor affecting the success of the brand.

In the Citizens Bank case, the strength of the new bank would lie in its customer service, although the weakness is the customer dissatisfaction that lingers in the minds of the Mellon customers. The opportunity exists to transfer Citizens Bank's excellent reputation for customer service to the new merged bank. The threat is the high level of switching that the Mellon customers report and the fact that they might switch before Citizens Bank has time to establish its reputation and business operations among the Mellon customers.

Key Problems and Opportunities   The key word in the title of this section is *analysis,* and that means making sense of all the data collected and figuring out what the information means for the future success of the brand. Advertising planners must analyze the market situation for any communication problems that affect the successful marketing of a product, as well as opportunities that advertising can create or exploit. Analyzing the situation and identifying the problem that can be solved with an advertising message are at the heart of strategic planning.

For example, DDB Needham searches for "Barriers to Purchase."[3] These barriers are reasons why people do not buy any or enough of a product. The American Dairy Association asked DDB Needham to find out why cheese consumption was declining. A study identified one barrier that was most easily correctable through an advertising message: the absence of simple cheese recipes for homemakers. Ads as well as the Association's Web site (ilovecheese.com) offer many such recipes.

Advertising can solve only message-related problems such as image, attitude, perception, and knowledge or information. It cannot solve problems related to the price of the product, availability, or quality. However, a message can speak to the perception that the price is too high. It can portray a product with limited distribution as exclusive. In other words, advertising can affect the way consumers perceive price, availability, and quality.

Principle
Advertising can solve only message-related, or perception, problems.

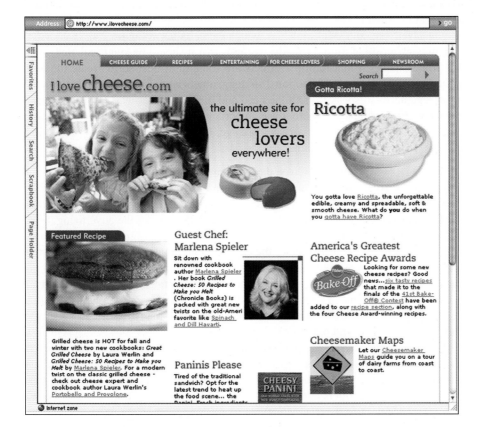

■ ■ ■
DDB Needham agency found that a "barrier to purchase" cheese was the lack of good recipe ideas using cheese products. The American Dairy Association responded by getting more recipes out there through advertising and by posting them on its Web site.

Effects-based Advertising Strategies

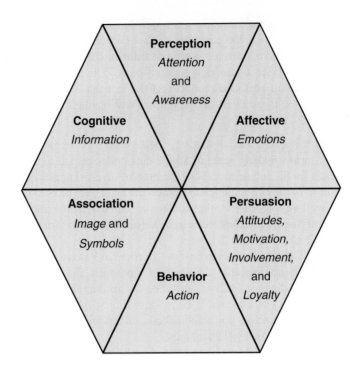

Advertising Objectives and Strategies

After the planners have examined the external and internal environment and defined the critical areas that need to be addressed, they can develop specific objectives to be accomplished during a specified time period. Remember from Chapter 4 that there are six categories of effects in the Facets Model of Message Effectiveness (see a summary in Figure 7.4). These main effects are perception, cognition, affective or emotional, association, persuasion, and behavior. These main categories of effects can be used to identify the most common advertising and IMC strategies, which are in italics in Figure 7.4.

Although a rule of thumb for advertising is that it should be single-minded, we also know from Chapter 4 that multiple effects are sometimes needed to create the desired impact. Some ads may use an emotional strategy; others are informational. But sometimes the message needs to speak to both the head and the heart. That was particularly true for the Citizens Bank campaign where it was important that Mellon customers become aware of and understand the customer service message, but more than that, they needed to feel that they were respected as customers.

The Logic of Objectives   Given the huge amounts of money spent on advertising, it is important for advertisers to know what to expect from a campaign or an ad. The categories of main effects also can be used as a template for setting advertising objectives, as Table 7.1 shows. Objectives are formal statements of the goals of the advertising (or other marketing communication) and outlines what the message is designed to achieve and how it will be measured. Note that some of the objectives are tightly focused on one particular effect, but others, such as brand loyalty, call for a more complex set of effects. In order to create brand loyalty, for example, an advertising campaign must have cognitive and affective effects, as well as move people to repeat buying. That's one reason brand loyalty is a type of long-term impact that is developed over time from many experiences that a consumer has with a brand and brand messages.

The advertiser's basic assumption is that advertising works if it creates an impression, influences people to respond, and separates the brand from the competition. Note also that communication objectives may be important, even if they aren't focused directly on a sale. For example, Expedia.com is a travel consulting company and it views its advertising as a way to draw attention to itself, create name recognition, and create understanding of the products and services it sells.

TABLE 7.1 Analyzing Advertising Objectives

The objective is this advertising message is to	Percp	Cog	Aff	Asoc	Beh	Rers
grab attention and create awareness	•					
establish brand identity	•	•			•	
establish or cue the brand position		•				
establish or cue the brand personality, image				•	•	
create links to associations				•	•	
cue the emotional or psychological appeal			•	•		
stimulate interest	•					
deliver information		•				
aid in understanding features, benefits, differences		•				
explain how to do something		•				
touch emotions			•			
create brand liking			•			
stimulate recognition for the brand	•					
stimulate recall of the brand message		•				
stimulate desire; brand preference, intent to buy						•
create conviction, belief		•				
stimulate change of opinion or attitudes						•
stimulate behavior (buy, call, click, visit, etc.)						•
stimulate repeat purchases						•
stimulate brand loyalty		•	•			•
remind of brand	•	•		•		
create buzz, word of mouth						•
create advocacy and referrals						•

Measurable Objectives   We cannot overstate the importance of delineating specific advertising objectives. Every advertising campaign, and the ads in it, must be guided by specific, clear, and measurable objectives. We say *measurable objectives* because that's how the effectiveness of the advertising is determined. It is critical that an objective statement be specific, quantified, and **benchmarked**, which means using a comparable effort to predict a logical goal. There are five requirements for a measurable objective:

1. A specific effect that can be measured
2. A time frame
3. A baseline (where we are or where do we begin)
4. The goal (a realistic estimate of the change the campaign can create; benchmarking is used to justify the projected goal)
5. Percentage change (subtract the baseline from the goal; divide the difference by the baseline)

Segmenting and Targeting

As we know from Chapter 5, a *market segment* is a group of consumers having similar characteristics. The segments the planner selects become the target audience. In the Citizens Bank case, the Mellon customers could be identified with demographics—

The new organizer

NOKIA
6200

■ ■ ■
Nokia is known as a leader in the cell phone market but this ad demonstrates how it is trying to reposition the product as a personal organizer, as well as a phone.

Principle
The point of positioning is to establish a location in the consumer's mind based on the product's features and its advantages relative to its competition.

adults 35–54 with a household income of $50,000–$150,000—but the critical group to reach was those people who were in the "likely to switch" category. The Citizens planners estimated that was one-quarter of the Mellon customer base.

But there is more to targeting than just identifying a possible audience and profiling them. Advertising planners want to know what's going on in people's heads and hearts—what motivates them to attend to a message and respond to it. Getting deeper insight into consumers is the responsibility of the account planning function. We'll return to that role later in this chapter and explain how account planners use research to add depth to the understanding of what motivates consumers to think and act as they do.

Positioning Strategy

Another key area in the advertising plan is the analysis of the product in comparison to competing products. Determining what place a product should occupy in a given market is called **positioning**. The objective is to establish a location in the consumer's mind based on what the product offers and how that compares with the competition, as the Nokia ad illustrates. Before we explain positioning strategy in more depth, you need to understand some other concepts related to how we define the competitive situation: product features and attributes, differentiation, and competitive advantage.

Product Features   The first step in crafting a position is to identify the features of your brand, as well as the competition to determine where the brand has an advantage over its competitors. That means a marketer carefully evaluates the product's tangible features (such as size, color, ease-of-use) and other intangible attributes (such as quality, status, value, fashion, safety) in order to identify the relevant dimensions of the product that make it different from its competitors. The opening story provides an example of a bank taking advantage of its strength in customer service to overcome the potential problems of a merger.

A technique called **feature analysis** helps structure this analysis. First, you make a chart of a client's product and competitors' products, listing each product's relevant features as Table 7.2 illustrates. For example, taste is important for sodas, and trendiness is important for fashion watches. Then evaluate how well the product and the competitors' products perform on that feature. Is it a strong point or a weak point? Next, evaluate how important each feature is to the target audience based on primary research. In other words, do consumers care about these various features, and which ones are most important to them?

Competitive Advantage   Using the two factors of *importance* and *performance,* **competitive advantage** lies where the product has a strong feature in an area that is important to the target and the competition is weaker. So if the product in Table 7.2 was tableware, then it would compete well on both price and style against competitor X, on price against competitor Y, and on style against competitor Z. Competitor X seems the most vulnerable on the two features, price and style, that consumers rate as most important decision points.

Differentiation   Most markets contain a high level of competition. How does a company compete in a crowded market? It uses **product differentiation**, a strategy designed to create product differences that distinguish the company's product from all others in the

TABLE
7.2   **Feature Analysis**

Feature	Importance to Prospect	Product Performance			
		Yours	X	Y	Z
Price	1	+	–	–	+
Quality	4	–	+	–	+
Style	2	+	–	+	–
Availability	3	–	+	–	–
Durability	5	–	+	+	+

eyes of consumers. *Branding,* the creation of a unique image for a product, is the most obvious way to differentiate one product from another. Those perceived differences may be tangible (design, price) or intangible (quality). We refer to products that really are the same (examples include milk, unleaded gas, and over-the-counter drugs) as *undifferentiated* or *parity products*. For these products marketers often promote intangible, or psychological, differences. The popular Swatch watch differentiates itself as a fashionable watch at a modest price.

Locating the Brand Position   Let's return now to the concept of a position. A company or brand's position is the first thing that comes to mind when you think about a product based on a particular feature or attribute. Volvo owns the safety position, while ESPN owns the sports information position. A **position**, then, is a location in a consumer's mind where the product or brand is placed relative to its competitors on the basis of the key factors the consumer uses to make a decision, such as fashion (high, low) or price (high, low). Think of a map; in fact, the way planners compare positions is by using a technique called a *perceptual map* that plots all the competitors on a matrix. Figure 7.5 illustrates how positions can be mapped for automobiles.

Many ad campaigns are designed to establish the brand's position by giving the right set of cues that will help locate the brand in someone's mind. Another common objective for advertising is to reposition a brand. That's the challenge explained in the Inside Story feature about an advertising campaign in Iceland. After nine successful years of branding Rubin as an upscale coffee the brand seemed to have tapped out.

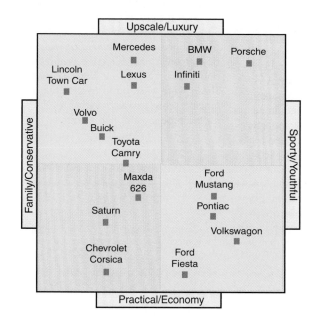

FIGURE
7.5

A Perceptual Map for Automobiles

THE INSIDE STORY

Exploiting the Dot—Repositioning a Luxury Coffee Brand

Ingvi Logason, Principal, HÉR & NÚ Advertising, Reykjavik, Iceland,

I always remember this one exercise we did back in college in advertising class. It was called "exploiting the dot," the objective being to reposition a brand of your choice. It was always good for a few laughs but little did I know then how useful it would be in repositioning the Rubin brand.

The market was stagnant and coffee drinking was transferring from homes to cafés. To increase sales and infuse the brand with new life, a risky strategic decision was made to transfer the brand image of Rubin coffee from the upscale to the daily market—in other words, to go "downmarket." At the same time it was important to attract more men to the brand, without losing women buyers (the existing majority) as research showed that men were the driving force in the daily market

With just two-thirds distribution of the competition and only a fraction of their shelf space, it was clear that advertising would have to carry the load of increasing the sales. The marketing objective was set at 55 percent sales increase within a two-year time period. Three ambitious communication objectives were set:

- Transfer the brand image of Rubin to correspond better with the daily market.
- Increase brand awareness and trial of Rubin among heavy coffee drinkers.
- Put more emphasis on men in the execution to increase usage proportionally more among men from 48 percent to 50 percent[+].

After researching the coffee market, we decided to direct our message at heavy coffee drinkers since we would need to convert fewer people that way to increase sales. This decision was made even though these users were generally more brand loyal than other coffee drinkers, thus making the work even more challenging.

The strategic solution had to overcome one big challenge: It had to change the brand image, which had been Rubin's biggest selling point so far, without scaring away existing buyers. Our solution was to create micromarkets within the coffee market and our target groups and tie our brand to them. Then we would steer those micromarkets and combine them in a larger market until we had one big target market—big enough to bring us economies of scale in advertising.

The media buy would start in media with small specific reach, and then gradually move upward to media with high reach. This would allow us to tailor-make advertisements early on and transform the groups until we had a big enough market to send out a single message. Still it was important to have one big idea that could be fitted to any special interest.

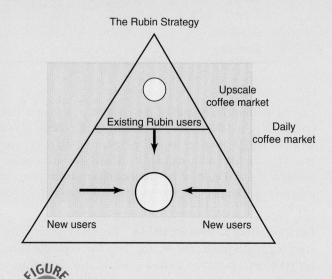

The Rubin Strategy

FIGURE 7.6

The Rubin Strategy
Shift existing Rubin users along with the brand from the upscale coffee market to the daily coffee market and attract new users.

The big idea "Without Rubin?" hit home with the execution of the strategy. It connected on an emotional level, with the target group pairing Rubin coffee to everyday scenes where you would want a coffee. All ads asked the question "Without Rubin?" for various interesting situations, hinting that you would not want that without Rubin.

The results of the campaign were beyond expectations. After only 18 months sales had already gone up 69 percent (the objective was 55 percent in two years). Over 85 percent of the increased usage came from heavy users and male usage went from 48 percent to 57 percent. These were very good overall results that contributed to making those two years some of the most profitable ever for the producers of Rubin coffee.

A principal in his own agency, HÉR & NÚ Advertising, in Reykjavik, Iceland, Ingvi Logason graduated with a degree in advertising from Western Florida University.

Nominated by Professor Tom Groth, Western Florida University

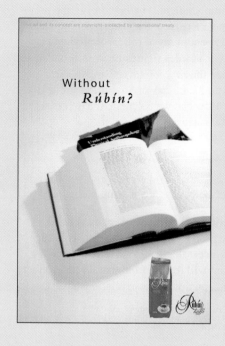

The advertising shapes the position, but personal experiences *anchor* it in the target audience's mind. The role of the advertising strategy, then, is to relate the product's position to the target market's life experience and associations. In fact, positioning represents one of advertising's most critical tasks.

Budgeting

The budget is a critical part of planning an advertising campaign. A $50,000 budget will only stretch so far and probably will not be enough to cover the costs of television advertising in most markets. The budget also determines how many targets and multiple campaign plans a company or brand can support and the length of time the campaign can run.

Determining the total appropriation allocated to advertising is not an easy task. Often a dollar amount, say $370,000, is budgeted for advertising during the budget planning process (just before the end of the fiscal year). The big budgeting question for both the marketing mix and marketing communication-mix is: How much do we need to spend? Let's examine five common budgeting methods to help answer that question.

- *Historical Method.* Historical information is the source for this common budgeting method. A budget may simply be based on last year's budget, with a percentage increase for inflation or some other marketplace factor. This method, though easy to calculate, has little to do with reaching advertising objectives.
- *Objective-Task Method.* The **objective-task method** looks at the objectives for each activity and determines the cost of accomplishing each objective: What will it cost to make 50 percent of the people in the market aware of this product? This method's

advantage is that it develops the budget from the ground up so that objectives are the starting point.

- *Percentage-of-Sales Method.* The **percentage-of-sales method** compares the total sales with the total advertising (or marketing communication) budget during the previous year or the average of several years to compute a percentage. This technique can also be used across an industry to compare the expenditures of different product categories on advertising. For example, if a company had sales figures of $5 million last year and an advertising budget of $1 million, then the *ratio* of advertising to sales would be 20 percent. If the marketing manager predicts *sales* of $6 million for next year, then the ad budget would be $1.2 million. How can we calculate the percentage of sales and apply it to a budget? Follow these two steps:

$$\text{Step 1: } \frac{\text{past advertising dollars}}{\text{past sales}} = \% \text{ of sales}$$

$$\text{Step 2: } \% \text{ of sales} \times \text{next year's sales forecast} = \text{new advertising budget}$$

- *Competitive Budgets.* This method uses competitors' budgets as benchmarks and relates the amount invested in advertising to the product's share of market. This suggests that the advertiser's share-of-advertising voice—that is, the advertiser's media presence—affects the share of attention the brand will receive, and that, in turn, affects the market share the brand can obtain. Here's a depiction of these relationships:

$$\frac{\text{Share of}}{\text{media voice}} = \frac{\text{Share of}}{\text{consumer mind}} = \frac{\text{Market}}{\text{share}}$$

    Keep in mind that the relationships depicted here are only a guide for budgeting. The actual relationship between share-of-media voice (an indication of advertising expenditures) and share of mind or share of market depends to a great extent on factors such as the creativity of the message and the amount of clutter in the marketplace.

- *All You Can Afford.* When a company allocates whatever is left over to advertising, it is using the "all-you-can-afford" budgeting method. It's really not a method, but rather a philosophy about advertising. Companies using this approach don't value advertising as a strategic imperative. For example, a company that allocates a large amount of its budget to research and has a superior product may find the amount spent on advertising is less important.

Evaluation: Determining Effectiveness

Evaluation is an important section in an advertising plan because it is the process by which the effectiveness of the campaign is determined. All of these procedures and techniques will be discussed in more detail in Chapter 19.

Consider This

1. What are the six categories of strategic decisions found in most advertising and IMC plans?
2. How do strategies and objectives relate to what we know about advertising effects?

ACCOUNT PLANNING: WHAT IS IT?

In general, an advertising plan matches the right audience to the right message and presents it in the right medium to reach that audience. These three elements are at the heart of an advertising plan and the agency's planner is responsible for making the following decisions:

- *Consumer Insight.* Whom are you trying to reach and what insight do you have about how they think, feel, and act? How should they respond to your advertising message?

- *Message Strategy.* What do you say to them? What directions come from the consumer research that are useful to the creative team?
- *Media Strategy.* How and where will you reach them? What directions come from the consumer research that are useful to the media team?

The account planning function develops the advertising strategy and guides its implementation in the creative work. **Account planning** is the research-and-analysis process used to gain knowledge and understanding of the consumer, understanding that is expressed as a key *consumer insight* into how people relate to a brand or product. An *account planner,* then, is a person in an agency who uses this disciplined system to research a brand and its customer relationships in order to devise advertising (and other marketing communication) message strategies that are effective in addressing consumer needs and wants. The KFC story in the Matter of Practice box illustrates how one account planner approached a client's image problem. We've featured the EFFIE awards in most of these chapters, but this story is an Account Planning Group (APG) award winner.

Account planners are often described as "speaking for the consumer" or "speaking with the voice of the consumer." As London's Account Planning Group (APG) explains it, "Their job is to ensure that an understanding of consumer attitudes and behavior is brought to bear at every stage of communications development via continuous involvement in the process."[4]

An account planner doesn't solely design the creative strategy for an ad—this is usually a team process—but instead evaluates consumers' relationships with the brand and with media to determine what kind of message they might respond to and when and how they would be most likely to respond favorably to an ad. Ultimately the objective is to help the creative team come up with a better idea—making their discovery process easier and faster. Susan Mendelsohn, a leader in the U.S. account planning industry, explains the account planner's task as follows:[5]

1. Understand the meaning of the brand.
2. Understand the target audience's relationship to the brand.
3. Articulate communication strategies.
4. Prepare creative briefs based on understanding of consumer and brand.
5. Evaluate the effectiveness of the communication in terms of how the target reacts to it (so that planners can keep learning more about consumers and brand communication).

Account planning was designed to bridge the client perspective and the consumer perspective. Account planners, then, became the voice of the consumer or the consumer advocate within the agency and the campaign planning process.

Principle
The account manager is seen as the voice of the client and the account planner is seen as the voice of the consumer.

The Research Foundation

Consumer research is at the core of all account planning. Account planners use research to get inside the consumers' heads, hearts, and lives. Research and the analysis of its findings is used in three phase of the advertising planning process: strategy generation, creative development, and campaign evaluation.[6] As discussed in the previous chapter, planners use a wide variety of research tools to do "insight mining" including secondary sources, as well as primary research. They are particularly interested, however, in developing innovative qualitative research tools that provide methods for deep probing into consumer attitudes and motivations. In a sense they are social anthropologists who are in touch with cultural and social trends and understand how they take on relevance in people's lives. To do that the account planner is an integrator (bringing all the information together) and synthesizer (what does it all mean in one startlingly simple statement?).

Consumer Insight

Advertising is sometimes thought to be an idea factory but account planners look at advertising as an *insight* factory. As Mendelsohn explains, "Behind every famously great idea, there is a perhaps less flashy, but immensely powerful insight." Insights are the fuel that

A MATTER OF PRACTICE
Everybody's Favorite Soul Food

How do you sell American-style southern fried chicken to Brits? That was the assignment the London-based Bartle Bogle Hegarty agency took on when it won the Kentucky Fried Chicken account.

Although KFC was a major player in the fast-food market, research into its loyalty profile uncovered what Alistair Green, the planner on the KFC account, described as "suspicious" findings: The majority of KFC's users were light users and a high percentage of them were lapsed users, which means it may be months between KFC visits. The KFC profile was considerably different from that of other fast-food brands, all of which exhibited much higher levels of loyalty. So why were there so many lapsed KFC customers?

The consumer insight that Greene discovered was a lack of "brand regard," which meant that when customers were asked to describe the brand meaning, they had very little to say about it. In contrast, when asked to describe McDonald's, consumers gave lots of responses rich in imagery and brand values. Green not only asked for descriptions of the brand, he also asked consumers to create a "brand world" using images they cut out of magazines. Again the competitors' "brand worlds" were rich with imagery but there was very little that the consumers found to paste on a KFC poster. Greene's conclusion was that most KFC users related to KFC with little emotion, empathy, or feeling.

The BBH research into the legend of Colonel Sanders found a rich historical legacy but the details were not particularly relevant to the British market. What Green did spot was the cultural environment in which the Colonel developed his cuisine—the social spirit and soul-satisfying flavors of dishes that originally developed in the American Deep South. Referred to colloquially as "soul food," it means "comfort food" that satisfies not just the stomach, but also the head, heart, and soul.

Although the "soul food" phrase in the United States is more linked to American black culture, Green determined that in the United Kingdom the essence of soul food is not limited to America, black culture, or the South. In fact, most cultures contain something equivalent to soul food and many are composed of chicken: Jamaican Jerk Chicken, French Coq au Vin, Indian Chicken Korma, Ukranian Chicken Kiev, and the proverbial Jewish mother's chicken soup. And that multicultural map of chicken-based "soul food" also was a good reflection of British society. In other words, the meaning of soul food could easily travel and have relevance to U.K. consumers.

So that became the heart of the brief given to BBH creatives: to use the strong emotional component of soul food, which was derived directly from the roots of Colonel Sanders's chicken, to build a new brand world for KFC.

Did the "soul food" campaign for KFC in the United Kingdom work? In terms of key objectives, the brand's share of the fast-food market grew while competitors' shares fell. Advertising awareness, which is a precursor to loyalty, reached the highest levels that the KFC brand had seen for the previous 18 months. But more importantly, the BBH tracking research confirmed that the "soul food" campaign had grown its heavy-user base. The ad tracking data also showed KFC gaining market share, outperforming all of its competitors in the fast-food category, which is why it was recognized as an APG winner.

Source: APG brief provided by KFC and Bartle Bogle Hegarty; personal interview with Alistair Green, November 2003.

fires the ideas. A great insight always intersect with the interests of the consumer and the features of the brand, as the Crest Whitestrips ad illustrates. It identifies the value that the brand has for the consumer.

Through the process of strategic and critical thinking, the planner interprets the consumer research in terms of a key consumer insight that uncovers and showcases the relevance factor, the reason why a consumer cares about a brand message. Consumer insights reveal the inner nature of a consumer's thinking—including such things as mind-sets, moods, motivations, desires, aspirations, and motives that trigger their attitudes and actions.

Insight Mining Insight mining—finding the "Aha!" in a stack of research reports, data, and transcripts—is the greatest challenge for an account planner. The London-based Account Planning Group (APG) describes this process as "peering into nooks and crannies without losing sight of the big picture in order to identify a key insight that can transform a client's business."

Mendelsohn describes insight mining as "a deep dive" into the meaning of a brand looking for "major truths." She explains that the planner engages in unearthing the relationship (if any) a target audience has with a brand or product—and what role that brand plays in their lives. Understanding the brand–consumer relationship is important because account planners are taking on the position of the agency's brand steward. Abigail Hirschhorn, chief strategic planning officer at DDB Needham, explains that "Our work puts our clients in touch with the souls of their brands."[7] The emphasis on brand building is one reason account planning is moving beyond advertising and being used in IMC campaign planning. Jon Steel, author of a book on advertising and account planning, says that planning works best when it is integrated into the entire communication mix.[8]

The account planning toolkit is made up of questions that lead to useful insights that are culled from research. Here is a set of questions that can lead to useful insights:

- What is a realistic response objective (perception, knowledge, feelings, attitudes, symbolic meanings, behavior) for this target group?
- What are the causes of their nonresponse?
- What are the barriers to the desired response?
- What could motivate them to respond in the desired way?
- What is the role of each element in the communication mix to motivate them or remove a barrier?

Here's an example of how data analysis works: Imagine you are working on a cookie account. Here's your brand share information:

■ ■ ■
Crest Whitestrips claims that it whitens teeth in 7 days and equates that to a consumer's wish to take off 14 years of staining.

	2003 share (%)	2004 share (%)
Choco Nuts (your brand)	50	40
Sweet 'n Crunchy (your main competitor)	25	30

What's the problem with this situation? Obviously your brand is losing market share to your primary competitor. So one of your goals might be to use a marketing communication mix that could drive higher levels of sales. But that goal is so broad that it would be difficult to determine whether communication is sufficient to solve the problem. So let's dig deeper and consider another set of data about household (HH) purchases in a year.

	2003 HH purchases	2004 HH purchases
Choco Nuts	4	3
Sweet 'n Crunchy	2.5	3

What's the problem identified here? It looks like your loyal brand users are reducing their purchases at the same time Sweet 'n Crunch customers are increasing their purchases, although only slightly. It may even be that some of your customers are switching over to Sweet 'n Crunchy. So a strategy might be to convince people that your brand tastes better and also to remind your loyal customers of the reasons they have preferred your brand. Those are goals that can actually be accomplished by marketing communication.

But when you combine the two pieces of information and think about it, another insight might explain this situation. Perhaps people are simply eating fewer cookies. If that's a problem, then the communication opportunity lies in convincing people to return to eating cookies. That is more of a "category sell" problem (sell cookies), rather than a competitive sell (set the brand against the competition). Here's a summary of these two different strategic approaches. Which do you think would be more effective?

	Competitive Sell	**Category Sell**
What?	Challenger brand	Leader brand
Who?	Loyal buyers	Medium/light/lapsed buyers
What effect?	Compare cookie brands	Compare against other snacks
Objective?	Increase share of wallet	Increase total category sales
Message?	"Our cookies are better than theirs"	"Cookies are better than candy, or salty snacks"

The important dimensions that account planners seek to understand in planning brand strategies are the brand relationship, the perceptions, the promise, and the point of differentiation. Most importantly, planners are looking for clues about the brand's meaning, which is usually phrased in terms of the brand essence (core, soul), personality, or image, as the Pacific Life ad illustrates.

The Communication Brief

The outcome of strategic research usually reaches agency creative departments in the form of a strategy document called a **communication brief** or **creative brief**, which explains the consumer insight and summarizes the basic strategy decisions (position, targeting, objectives, brand strategy). Although the exact form of this document differs from agency to agency and from advertiser to advertiser, most have six major parts: the marketing objective, the product, the target audience, the promise and support, the brand personality, and the strategy statement.

The brief is an outline of the message strategy that guides their work and helps keep their creative ideas strategically sound. It is the planner's main product and it should be clear, logical, and single focused. It's strategic, but it also should be creative. It is designed to ignite the creative team and give a spark to their idea process. A good brief doesn't set up limitations and boundaries, but rather serves as a springboard. It is the first step in the creative process. Here is an outline of a typical communication brief.

Communication Brief Outline*

*   *Problem.* What's the problem that communication can solve? (establish position, reposition, increase loyalty, get people involved, increase liking, etc.)
*   *Target Audience.* Who do we want to speak to? (brand loyal, heavy users, infrequent users, competition's users, etc.)
*   *The Brand Position.* What are the important features? What's the point of competitive advantage? What's the brand's position relative to the competition?
*   *Brand Imperatives.* Brand essence, brand personality and image. Ogilvy & Mather says, "What is the unique personality for the brand? People use products, but they have relationships with brands."
*   *Communication Objectives.* What do we want them to do in response to our messages? (perception, knowledge, feelings, symbolic meanings, attitudes and conviction, action)
*   *Consumer Insight.* What motivates the target? What are the "major truths" about the target's relationship to the product category or brand?
*   *The Proposition or Selling Idea.* What is the single-minded thought that the communication will bring to life in a provocative way?
*   *Support.* What is the reason to believe the proposition? Ogilvy & Mather explains, "We need to give consumers 'permission to believe'—something that allows them to rationalize, whether to themselves or others, what is in reality an emotionally driven brand decision. The support should be focused on the insight or proposition, the truths that make the brand benefit indisputable."

---

*This outline was compiled from one contributed by Susan Mendelsohn, as well as from the creative brief outline developed by the Ogilvy and Mather advertising agency and presented on its Web site.

- *Creative Direction.* How can you best stimulate the desired response? How can we best say it?
- *Media Imperatives.* Where and when should we say it?

Personal Characteristics of a Planner

What makes a good account planner? Obviously that person has to be proficient in research and strategic thinking, but some also argue that an account planner has to be a creative thinker as well because the job demands an ability to do problem solving. The APG Web site has a hypothetical job description for account planner recruitment. It includes the personal characteristics identified in the Practical Tips. Test yourself against these qualities and figure out if account planning would be a good job for you.

Practical Tips

Test Yourself: Would You Make a Good Account Planner?

- Curiosity about what makes people act and think the way they do.
- Questioning—accepting nothing at face value.
- Ability to look at a problem from different angles without losing sight of the big picture—a creative, as well as critical, thinker.
- Eclectic information searcher—desire to draw on all types and sources of information. An information sponge. Wide range of interests.
- Capable of taking a creative idea and making a reasonable guess its intended effects and its effectiveness.
- Able to describe a target audience without relying on demographics.
- Ability to numerate—to use numbers, visualize the meaning of numbers, and generate hypotheses and draw conclusions from numbers.
- Team player: can appreciate and use inputs from others; knows when to push and when to relax.
- Must like an informal, loosely structured work environment.
- Must be able to handle criticism and disagreement; not territorial, defensive, or paranoid.

Source: Adapted from "The ideal Account Planner—Recruitment Specs," Account Planning Group Web site (http://www.apg.org.uk).

■ ■ ■
Pacific Life has used the image of a leaping whale to reflect its image of a confident insurance company that works with other great companies.

Consider This

1. What is account planning?
2. What is a communication brief and what information is usually included in it?

PLANNING FOR IMC

An IMC plan follows the same basic outline as an advertising plan. The difference, however, lies with the scope of the plan and the variety of marketing communication areas involved in the effort. The more tools used, the harder it is to coordinate them and maintain consistency across a variety of messages. The objective in IMC planning is to make the most effective use of all marketing communication functions and to influence or control

TABLE
7.3 **Types of Stakeholder Audiences**

Corporate Level	Marketing Level	Marketing Communication Level
Employees	Consumers	Target audiences
Investors, financial community (analysts, brokers, and the financial press)	Customers	Target stakeholders
	Stakeholders	Employees
	Market segments	Trade audiences
Government bodies and agencies	Distributors, dealers, retailers, and others in the distribution channel	Local community
		Media (general, special interest, trade)
Regulatory bodies	Suppliers and vendors, including agencies	Consumer activist groups
Business partners	Competitors	General public
		Opinion leaders

the impact of other communication elements. Effective IMC plans are the ones that lead to profitable long-term brand relationships.

Differences in IMC Strategic Decisions

There are three main areas where an IMC plan is different from an advertising plan: stakeholders, contact points, and objectives.

Stakeholders The target market in an IMC plan includes more than just consumers. *Stakeholder* refers to any group of people who have a stake in the success of a company or a brand. These audiences include all those who might influence the purchase of products and the success of a company's marketing program, as Table 7.3 shows. Employees are particularly important and their support or "buy in" for marketing, advertising, and marketing communication programs is managed through an activity called **internal marketing**.

The important thing to remember is that stakeholders overlap. Employees, for example, may also be customers, as well as shareholders and members of the local community, perhaps even elected officials. That complicates message strategy and demands that there be a certain core level of consistency in all messages.

Contact Points IMC programs are designed to maximize all the various types of contacts that a consumer and other stakeholders might have with a company or brand. **Contact points**, also called **touch points**, are all the ways and places where a person can come into contact with a brand; all the points where a message about the brand is delivered. The point to remember is that everything a brand does—and sometimes what it doesn't do—delivers a message.[9]

IMC Objectives IMC objectives are tied to the effects created by the various forms of marketing communication. All the various marketing communication tools have strengths and weaknesses. You use public relations, for example, to announce something that is newsworthy and sales promotion to drive immediate action. Therefore an IMC plan operates with a set of interrelated objectives that specify the strategies for all the various tools. Each area will have a set of objectives similar to those outlined in Table 7.1 (see page 189) for advertising; those will be presented in more detail in later chapters. But for discussion at this point, let's just consider the main areas in terms of their primary effects, as outlined in Table 7.4.

TABLE
7.4   Area Objectives

Marketing Communication Area	Typical Objectives
Public Relations	Announce news; affect attitudes and opinions; maximize credibility and likability; create and improve stakeholder relationships
Consumer Sales Promotion	Stimulate behavior; generate immediate response, intensify needs, wants, and motivations; reward behavior; stimulate involvement and relevance; create pull through the channel
Trade Sales Promotion	Build industry acceptance; push through the channel; motivate cooperation; energize sales force, dealers, distributors
Point-of-Purchase	Increase immediate sales; attract attention at decision point; create interest; stimulate urgency; encourage trial and impulse purchasing
Direct Marketing	Stimulate sales; create personal interest and relevance; provide information; create acceptance, conviction
Sponsorship and Events	Build awareness; create brand experience, participation, interaction, involvement; create excitement
Packaging	Increase sales; attract attention at selection point; deliver product information; create brand reminder
Specialties	Reinforce brand identity; continuous brand reminder; reinforce satisfaction; encourage repeat purchase

IT'S A WRAP

PROVING THAT A BANK IS NOT TYPICAL

Advertisers don't create messages by relying on whimsy or a sudden flash of inspiration. They formulate messages to achieve specific objectives that will overcome real problems that are hurting an organization's marketing program. Then they develop strategies to achieve those objectives and tactics that implement the strategies. It's a process designed to help advertising planners make intelligent decisions.

The strategic decisions—researching and analyzing the marketplace, setting objectives, targeting the right audience and uncovering consumer insights, identifying a competitive advantage and creating a brand position, budgeting, and implementing and evaluating the strategy—are the foundation for the development of effective advertising messages and media plans. Here is the evaluation of the campaign's three objectives:

1. *Minimize customer attrition keeping losses under 10 percent*. During the six-month period of the merger, Mellon experienced virtually no customer attrition and the bank enjoyed a net increase in deposits, a response that is nearly unheard of in a bank merger.
2. *Quickly build advertising awareness*. During this period, the integrated communication efforts helped drive Citizens' awareness in the new market from zero to 31 percent in just a few short weeks, and to 60 percent by opening day.
3. *Reduce customers' intentions to leave the bank*. During the three-month period leading up to opening day, the proportion of Mellon customers likely to switch banks was cut in half (from 24 percent to 12 percent) and continued to drop through the next six months.

The "Legendary Service" merger campaign plan was highly successful in taking Citizens and Mellon customers through the transition and successfully protected the value of the customer franchise Citizens was acquiring.

Summary

1. **Differentiate between objectives, strategies, and tactics in strategic planning.** Objectives are what you want to accomplish, a goal; strategies are how you will accomplish the objectives, the design or plan; and tactics are the ways you implement the strategies, the executions.

2. **Identify the six basic strategic areas in an advertising or IMC plan.** An advertising or IMC plan summarizes the strategic decisions in the following areas: situation analysis (background research, SWOTs, key problem); key strategic decisions (objectives, targeting, positioning, brand image, budget level); media strategy (objectives, vehicle selection, budget allocation, scheduling); message strategy (consumer insight, selling premise, big idea, execution ideas); other IMC tools; and evaluation of effectiveness.

3. **Explain how account planning works.** Account planning matches the right message to the right audience and identifies the right media to deliver that message. The three key factors are: consumer insight, message strategy direction, and media strategy direction.

4. **Outline the additional key factors in an IMC plan.** The three additional factors that you find discussed in an IMC plan are the stakeholders, the contact points, and a wider set of objectives that identify the interwoven effects of the various marketing communication tools.

Key Terms

account planning, 195
benchmarked, 189
campaign plan, 185
communication brief, 198
competitive advantage, 190
contact points, 200
creative brief, 198

feature analysis, 190
internal marketing, 200
marketing plan, 183
mission statement, 183
objective-task method, 193
percentage-of-sales method, 194

position, 191
positioning, 190
product differentiation, 190
return on investment (ROI), 183
situation analysis, 186

strategic business unit (SBU), 182
strategic planning, 181
strategies, 181
SWOT analysis, 186
tactics, 181
touch points, 200

Review Questions

1. Define objectives, strategies, and tactics, and explain how they differ.

2. Explain the six basic strategic planning decisions in an advertising plan.

3. What is account planning, and what does the account planner bring to an advertising plan?

4. What is the difference between an advertising plan and an IMC plan?

Discussion Questions

1. Think of a product you purchased recently. How was it advertised? Which strategies can you discern in the advertising? Did the advertising help to convince you to purchase the product? Why or why not?

2. In Luna Pizza's situation analysis for 2005, we find: Luna is a regional producer of frozen pizza; its only major competitor is Brutus Bros. Estimate the year 2005 advertising budgets for Luna under each of the following circumstances:

   a. Luna follows a historical method by spending 40 cents per unit sold in advertising, with a 5 percent increase for inflation.

   b. Luna follows a fixed percentage of projected sales method, using 7 percent.

   c. Luna follows a share-of-voice method. Brutus is expected to use 6 percent of sales for its advertising budget in 2003.

	Actual **Last Year**	**Estimates** **Next Year**
Units sold	120,000	185,000
$ Sales	420,000	580,000
Brutus $ Sales	630,000	830,000

3. Using resources such as the *Wall Street Journal* online, find an example of a company whose strategy matches its mission. What leads you to believe its strategy matches its mission? Next, find an example of a company whose strategy does not seem to match its mission. What leads you to

believe its strategy does not match its mission? Support your arguments with points from this chapter.

4. You are assigned to the account for a new hybrid automobile. Use the Communication Brief outline and list the research that you need to conduct for each step in the strategic decision-making process. What do you need to do in order to put together a useful brief for the creative team?

5. Pick one of your favorite brands. Analyze its strategy using the Facets Model of Advertising Effectiveness.

▪▪▪ Class Projects

1. With some classmates, select two print ads, one for a consumer product and one for a business-to-business product. Working from the ads, determine the selling premise, the product position, the product image, the competitive advantage, and the specific target audience. What were the objectives? Were they achieved? Determine where the strategy was clear and where it was unclear.

2. Examine the following Web sites: fordvehicles.com/suvs, hondasuv.com and cadillacsuv.com. Based on what you find on these sites, compare the positioning strategies for their top-of-the-line SUV models. Analyze the product features, their competitive advantage, and their points of differentiation.

HANDS-ON ⑦
CASE

Unscrambling the NASCAR Fan

What's America's favorite sport, at least in terms of attendance? That's easy, football. How about the second biggest? Would you guess baseball? Basketball?

How about car racing? There are about 35 million NASCAR enthusiasts in the United States, and a large percentage of them are avid fans. That's why lots of companies pony up big bucks to be NASCAR sponsors, including Nextel, which has committed $700 million over the next 10 years as sponsor of the sport's championship cup. In 2004 more than 100 Fortune 500 companies were NASCAR sponsors; together they spent almost a billion dollars.

Small wonder, then, that NASCAR is anxious to keep its sponsors happy. One way to do that is to help sponsors better understand the fans that turn out each weekend to watch the races. But obtaining data on fans is not easy. Companies sometimes learn about lifestyle segments by purchasing readership data from lifestyle-relevant media, but no existing magazine targets the NASCAR audience (Time Inc. is readying one to launch, however, titled *Racing Fan*).

Enter Josh Linkler and his decoder. Make that his e-decoder. Linkler's company makes an e-decoder that looks nothing like the rings kids used to get out of Cracker Jack boxes. This one looks like a square, bearing the phrase "Race to Win. Grand Prize $10,000 cash." Owners of the e-decoder are instructed to go to a special Web site and hold the device against their screen to see whether they have won NASCAR prizes. Prizes are awarded every day during the NASCAR season. But there is a catch: Fans have to give a small amount of personal information each time they play. Someone who plays regularly can end up giving responses to more than 150 questions, and not all the questions deal with racing. Some deal with race fan hobbies such as camping and others are meant to find out where fans shop.

In the first two months Linkler's company had distributed more than a million decoders, and almost 26,000 fans had gone to the Web site to play. The race promoters are thrilled with the results and plan to put the data to good use. NASCAR marketing spokesperson Keith Karbo gives an example, "If we know that a race fan likes to fish, then one way to reach that fan is to use outdoor media." He adds, "If we have data on that, we can approach fishing-related companies and ask them to become sponsors." Future plans also include targeted e-mails sent to fans on the basis of responses to lifestyle questions.

Consider This

1. Do you see any drawbacks to obtaining fan data this way? How can NASCAR avoid alienating some of its fans, who might be worried about privacy or who might not wish to receive e-mail advertisements?

2. What is attractive about NASCAR sponsorship to companies? How can a decision to sponsor a race team or NASCAR be justified as a part of a company's marketing mix?

3. Evaluate NASCAR's strategy for getting data about its fans. Why might this data be so appealing to sponsors? How can it be used in planning an advertising campaign?

Source: Jon Fine, "Time Breaks into NASCAR Territory", *Advertising Age* (November 29, 2004). Kris Oser, "Speedway Effort Decodes NASCAR Fans," *Advertising Age* (May 17, 2004); Rich Thomaselli, "Sponsors Sweat New NASCAR Scoring System," *Advertising Age* (February 2, 2004); Rich Thomaselli, "Nextel Antes Up $70 million to Leverage NASCAR," *Advertising Age* (February 9, 2004).

Part 2
Planning and Strategy

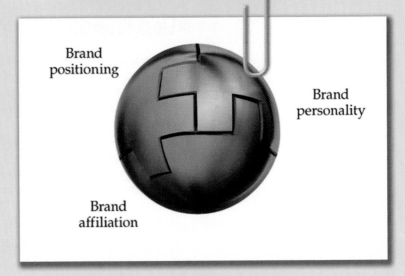

There are three key components to building a powerful brand—positioning, personality, and affiliation.

Building the Chick-fil-A brand is a top priority for both Chick-fil-A and its advertising agency, The Richards Group. Agency and client agree that of all the things Chick-fil-A owns, nothing is as important as its brand. Its brand is its future, and great brands have the potential to continue forever.

The Richards Group defines a brand as a promise made to consumers through everything they can observe about a product, like logos, the color of a package, signage, the store appearance, and the employees. To fully understand a client's brand, the agency uses a tool it developed called Spherical® Branding.

The first step in the Spherical Branding process is to accurately identify the client's business and formulate a brand vision—an ongoing goal that a brand should continually strive to achieve. Here is the brand vision by which Chick-fil-A measures itself:

"To be America's best quick-service restaurant at winning and keeping customers."

The next step is to identify three branding strategies that work together: brand positioning, brand personality, and brand affiliation. The development of a brand-positioning strategy is not done by mere consensus. It requires thorough data analysis and primary research. It must define the target audience, a competitive frame of reference, and the most meaningful point of difference for the brand. Here is how Chick-fil-A defines its brand:

Chick-fil-A Brand Positioning: **To choosy people in a hurry,**

↑

(target audience)

Chick-fil-A is the premium **fast-food restaurant** brand

↑

(frame of reference)

that **consistently serves America's best-loved chicken sandwiches.**

↑

(point-of-difference)

Next is the task of identifying the brand personality. What are the human traits your brand portrays to the consumer? To illustrate, Chick-fil-A's personality is:

Caring, genuine, clean-cut, dependable, and unexpectedly fun.

The final branding strategy is brand affiliation. In essence, brand affiliation answers the question, "How are other people going to perceive me as a result of my using this brand?" Chick-fil-A brand answers it this way:

"I don't mind paying a little more because it's worth it. I appreciate a nicer, better experience. I like associating with a company that has good values."

These three strategies affect the mind (positioning), heart (personality), and ego (affiliation) of the consumer. All three strategies are necessary in order for consumers to build conviction for a brand. Spherical Branding provides everyone in the company, no matter what the department, with a framework for developing consistent communication to the consumer.

After all, it's not just the marketing and advertising departments that are responsible for communicating to consumers and building the brand.

Source: Information courtesy of Mike Buerno, The Richards Group.

Consider This

1. Although the brand is very important, do you feel the definition offered by Chick-fil-A is clear and concise?
2. How do employees represent the brand and what is their role in accomplishing the Spherical Branding plan?

Finding Creative Ways to Connect

The previous section discussed planning and strategy. The next two sections focus on how advertising is done—both through the creation as well as the delivery of an advertising message. Even though we examine media planning before creative planning, they are parallel processes that constantly influence one another.

Media decisions and message decisions are interdependent. The creative people planning the advertising message must understand the media opportunities before they are able to develop their creative plans. For example, is television going to be used or not? There's a big difference between developing an advertising message for print and television, so there has to be some sense of what media are going to be used before the creative people can even begin their work.

Likewise, some of the media decisions are based on the nature of the message, therefore creative decisions also influence media strategies. In other words, media and message planning are two strategic tracks that have to be planned simultaneously recognizing that these decisions are interdependent.

Creativity is also important to the media side, as well as the creative side. Media planners are creative problem solvers. As the media landscape becomes more complex and customers become more resistant to traditional advertising, innovative new media are being designed that open up unexpected ways to deliver messages that are appropriate and sensitive to consumer interests.

Another key change is the reframing of media planning as *connection planning*. Modern media planning philosophy sees media as more than a delivery system but rather as a way to connect with consumers. To carry that out, a new breed of planners closely related to account planners is being added to media staffs. Called a connection planner (or context planner in some agencies), these strategists bring the account planner's dedication to consumer insight to media planning. Their role is to understand the basis for the media connection by evaluating consumers' relationships with media.

Media planners must understand the context within which brand messages connect with consumers—how, where, and when consumers experience products, as well as experience messages about the product. The emphasis is on finding contact points where a message is welcomed by consumers, and then connecting with the hearts and minds of that audience. Media planners are moving beyond just attracting eyeballs. If a positive connection is established between the brand and the consumer, then the brand relationship will be strengthened.

Source: Aaron, Barr, "A New Face at Media Shops: The Account Planner," *Adweek* (March, 31, 2003): 10.

Print and Out-of-Home Media

Apple Tops the Charts with Digital Music

Award:
*Advertising Age's
Marketer of the Year*

*Magazine Publishers
of America Kelly Award
Grand Prize*

Company:
Apple

Agency:
TBWA/Chiat/Day

Campaign:
iPod and iTunes

CHAPTER KEY POINTS

After reading this chapter, you will be able to:

1. Explain the key concepts of media planning and buying.

2. Identify the strengths and weaknesses of newspapers as an advertising medium.

3. Describe the key factors that advertisers should know to make effective decisions about advertising in magazines.

4. Analyze why packaging is such an important advertising opportunity.

5. Discuss factors that advertisers should consider in making out-of-home media decisions.

6. Outline the factors that advertisers use to make decisions about using directory advertising.

The iPod is cool. That's why hip DJs in cool clubs are holding iPod parties where lucky participants are selected to design iPod playlists. In effect, the DJs—without any incentive from Apple, iPod's maker—are conducting iPod seminars for their clubbers. And as the trendy clubbers twist and shout, Apple dances to meet the demand for the sleek digital music players that have been flying off the shelves.

The iPod holds the largest share of the fragmented portable digital MP3 music player market at 50 percent, but giant competitors such as Wal-Mart, Sony, and Microsoft are also entering the market. Paired with the revolutionary iTunes Music Store, however, Apple offers the only holistic digital music system combining both player and song delivery. With an easy-to-use iPod plugged into a computer (PC or Mac), songs automatically transfer from iTunes.

iTunes, iPod's dance partner, solves a huge Napster-created downloadable music problem—giving the troubled music industry a new lease on life. For a reasonable 99 cents per tune, iTunes Music Store customers can legally download and copy the songs from Apple's enormous music library. There's no monthly fee or hidden charges. Once you buy your song, it's yours to burn onto a CD, load onto an MP3 player like iPod, or transfer to some other computer.

The iPod/iTunes partnership also is a vehicle to expand the Apple brand into entirely new space occupied by the music-obsessed youth market. The portable players, which can store between 2,500 and 10,000 downloaded songs, were only a beachhead for Apple. Starting with its loyal Macintosh base, Apple then launched a PC version of its iTunes. The music delivery system, however, was priced cheaply enough so that it could build a new generation of Apple enthusiasts for the more profitable iPod and the newer, more colorful iPod mini.

Apple CEO Steve Jobs announced the new product news and created the initial buzz that started an effective word-of-mouth campaign among music and computer fans. This public relations effort was phenomenally successful with more than 6,000 iPod and iTunes stories in major publications around the world. (Buzz marketing is a great tool for Apple, which has achieved incredible brand loyalty and an army of passionate advocates who spread the word on Apple's behalf.)

Apple then launched a combination of iconic print advertising and posters. The ads creatively present the digital player, and its player, as cool. It uses silhouettes of people dancing against brightly colored neon backgrounds.

The print campaign was followed by an equally interesting television campaign using the same graphic image that featured iPod's distinctive silhouetted dancing figures. Most importantly, these ads needed to sell the idea that iPods and iTunes would work with PCs, as well as Macs.

Total spending for the iPod print ads in the first half of 2003 was $9 million, according to TNS Media Intelligence/CMR, up from $4 million in all of 2002. Overall Apple spent $125 million in 2003 advertising iTunes and iPod on billboards, TV shows, and in mainstream print magazines.

The distinctive ads got attention and built awareness by creating buzz and by resonating with the interests and lifestyles of its target audience.

IPod and iTunes—a big hit on the pop charts.

Sources: Adapted from Jefferson Graham, "Music Moves Apple Up Charts," *The Denver Post* (December 29, 2003): 5L; Michelle Kessler, "Wal-Mart to Challenge iTunes Store," *The Denver Post* (December 29, 2003): 5L; Alice Z. Cuneo, "Marketer of the Year: Apple," *Advertising Age* (December 15, 2003): 1; "Apple Emerges from the Pod," *BBC News Magazine*, December 16, 2003, http://news.bbc.co.uk/go/pr/fr/-/hi/magazine/3321943.stm; "Prophet's List of 2003 Branding Hits Topped by Apple on Digital Music Front," *PR Newswire*, December 1, 2003, http://www.findarticles.com/cf_0m4PRN/2003_Dec_1/110672217/p1/article.jhtml.

IPod and iTunes used space in magazines and posters to create attention-getting images that connected with the trendy buyers of its products. This chapter and the three that follow will explain the side of the media advertising story that you don't see: how the advertising gets placed and why you see the ads that you do when you watch, listen, or read your favorite kinds of mass media. In particular, this chapter will present the world of print advertising in all its varied forms—from newspaper and magazine ads to

TABLE
8.1   **Ad Spending by Medium**

Media	2002 (in million $)	2003 (in million $)	% Change	% of Media
Newspapers	**$45,341**	**$46,256**	**2.0**	**23.8**
Local newspaper	20,994	$21,341	1.7	
National newspapers	7,210	7,797	8.1	
Free-standing inserts	1,239	1,317	6.3	
Classifieds	15,898	15,801	−0.6	
Magazines	**26,047**	**27,280**	**4.7**	**14.0**
Consumer magazines	17,254	18,347	6.3	
B-to-B magazines	7,227	7,277	0.7	
Sunday magazines	1,264	1,331	5.3	
Local magazines	311	325	4.6	
Directories	**13,776**	**14370**	**4.1**	**7.3**
Television	**52,666**	**54,462**	**3.4**	**28.0**
Network TV	20,016	20,375	1.8	
Spot TV	17,165	16,244	−5.4	
Cable TV	10,593	12,251	15.6	
National syndication	2,946	3,396	15.3	
Spanish-language network TV	1,946	2,196	12.8	
Radio	**9,993**	**10,368**	**3.8**	**5.3**
Local radio	6,575	6,732	2.4	
Network radio	966	1,001	3.6	
National spot radio	2,452	2,635	7.5	
Outdoor	**2,475**	**2,673**	**8.0**	**1.3**
Internet	**5,613**	**6,495**	**15.7**	**3.3**
Other	**30,730**	**32,320**	**4.9**	**16.6**
Total:	**$165,144**	**$175,048**	**6.0**	

Sources: Adapted from Noreen O'Leary, "'03 a Bumper Year for Ads," *Adweek* (March 15, 2004): 14; "Media," *2003 Marketing Fact Book* (July 7, 2003): 17; Newspaper Association of America Web site, May 2004, www.naa.org.

packages on the grocery store shelf, outdoor boards, posters, and ads that you look up in phone directories. But first we will start with a quick review of the media industry and basic media concepts.

THE MEDIA INDUSTRY

People in contemporary society live in a web of **media**-delivered news, information, and the advertising that makes the news and information possible. Advertising media is a huge industry with almost $195 billion in spending, as Table 8.1 shows. Although media ad spending has been slumping during the economic downturn in the early 2000s, it began to show a turnaround in 2003 with an overall spending increase of 6 percent from the previous year. Note that the Internet, cable TV, syndicated TV programming, and directory advertising led this resurgence. Newspapers and network television stayed even, but local (spot) television continued to decline.

This chapter is focused on print media, which includes newspapers, magazines, packaging, out-of-home media, and directories. Let's first consider some of the basic concepts that drive the media advertising industry.

BASIC MEDIA CONCEPTS

A **media mix** is the way various types of media are strategically combined in an advertising plan, such as using newspapers and posters to announce a new product as the iPod managers did, followed by television advertising that shows how to use the product, and billboards that remind people to look for it when they go to the store. A **media vehicle** is a specific TV program (*60 Minutes, The Simpsons*), newspaper (*USA Today, Wall Street Journal*), magazine (*Woman's Day, GQ*), or radio station or program (NPR's *All Things Considered*, Rush Limbaugh's talk show).

Planning and Buying

The iPod launch campaign is a great example of creative use of media opportunities to connect with people who might be in the market for an MP3 player. A *media plan*, which identifies the best media to use to deliver an advertising message to a targeted audience, is a subsection within an advertising plan. The media plan will have its own objectives, strategies, and tactics; the challenge is to determine the best strategy for delivering a message. The execution of the media plan is done through media buying. **Media planning** is the way advertisers identify and select media options based on research into the audience profiles of various media; planning also includes scheduling and budgeting. **Media buying** is the task of identifying specific vehicles, such as TV programs or Web sites, negotiating the costs to advertise in them, and handling the details of billing and payment.

Reach and Frequency

The goal of most media plans is to reach as many people in the target audience as often as the budget allows. **Reach** is the percentage of the media audience exposed at least once to the advertiser's message during a specific time frame. When we say that a particular media vehicle, such as the Super Bowl, has a wide reach, that means a lot of people are watching the program. When we say it has a narrow reach, such as a cable program on oil painting, we mean that a smaller percentage of the TV viewing audience is watching that show.

Principle
The goal of a media plan is to reach as many people in the target audience as often as the budget allows.

The idea for the iPod launch was to reach not just everyone who likes music, but those technologically sophisticated people who would know how to assemble a music playlist on a computer for use on the iPod. They also would need to have enough discretionary income that the initial cost of the iPod would not be a negative factor. That audience profile leads to a young-adult target of innovators, people who are into cool things and love music.

As important as reach is **frequency**, which refers to the number of times a person is exposed to the advertisement. Different media have different patterns of frequency, as well as of reach. Radio commercials, for example, often are able to achieve high levels of frequency because they can be repeated over and over to achieve impact.

Impressions

An **impression** is one person's opportunity to be exposed *one time* to an ad in a broadcast program, newspaper, magazine, or outdoor location. Impressions can be added up as a measure of the size of the audience either for one medium (one announcement in broadcast or one insertion in print) or for a combination of vehicles in a media mix as estimated by media research.

The idea of impressions is different from **circulation**, because impressions (at least in print) estimate the actual readership, rather than just the circulation, which refers to copies sold. In broadcast media, impressions estimate viewers for television and listeners for radio. Television **exposure**, which is similar to circulation, measures households with sets turned on, called **HUT** (households using television). For example, a magazine may have a circulation of 1 million but it might be read, on the average, by 2.5 people per issue. That means impressions for that issue would be 2.5 million. If the ad ran in three consecutive issues, then the estimate of total impressions, or **gross impressions**, would be 7.5 million. Similarly, the impressions from television, or the number of viewers watching a program, might be greater than the number of households reached since there may be more than one viewer watching.

These gross impression figures become very large and difficult to work with, which is why the television industry uses **ratings** (percentage of exposure), which is an easier measurement to work with because it converts the raw figure to a percentage of the population or households. We'll work with these concepts later when we talk about media objectives.

Media Key Players

In the media industries, there are professionals who both sell and buy advertising. **Media salespeople** work for a medium, such as a magazine or local television station, and their objective is to build the best possible argument to convince media planners to use the medium they represent. A media salesperson is responsible for putting packets of information, or *sales kits,* together on the medium he or she represents, which usually means compiling profile information about the people who watch, listen, or read the medium, along with the numbers describing audience size and geographical coverage.

There are also **media reps**, who are people or companies that sell space (in print) and time (in broadcast) for a variety of media. If an advertising agency wants to buy space in all the major newspapers in the West, for example, the agency's buyer would not need to contact every newspaper individually, but instead could contract with a media rep firm that handles national sales for all those newspapers. That allows the media buyer to place the buy with one order.

On the agency side, media planners, buyers, and researchers work primarily for agencies, although they can also be found working for marketers who handle their own media work in house. *Media planners* make the strategic decisions outlined in the media plan. *Media buyers* implement the media plan. They are in regular contact with the media suppliers with whom they do business on behalf of the client or agency. Media buyers are expected to maintain good media supplier relations to facilitate a flow of information about the dynamic media marketplace. This means there should be close working relationships between planners and buyers so media planners can tap this source of media cost information to better forecast media price changes. *Media researchers* compile audience measurement data, as well as media costs and availability data for the various media options being considered by the planners.

As was mentioned in Chapter 2, *media-buying services* are independent companies that specialize in doing media research, planning, and buying. These agencies are taking over the media role that used to be the responsibility of advertising agency media staff. In many cases, they are the media department that spun off from a full-service agency. They consolidate the media buying in order to get maximum discounts from the media for the volume of their buys. They then pass on some of this saving to their clients. Now let us turn to our review of the print media.

Consider This

1. What are the basic concepts in advertising media use?
2. Some ads work best when marketers maximize their frequency. Are there other kinds of advertising that do not lend themselves to a high-frequency schedule? What are they, and why are they effective at low frequency?

PRINT MEDIA

Print advertising includes printed advertisements in newspapers, magazines, brochures, and on other printed surfaces, such as posters and outdoor boards. Readers find that reading a publication is more flexible than watching or listening to broadcast because they can stop and reread, read sections out of order, or move through the publication at their own speed. Because the print message format is less fleeting than broadcast and more concrete, people tend to spend more time with print and absorb its messages more thoroughly. Print provides more detailed information, rich imagery, and a longer message life. That's why advertisers trying to reach an audience of adult women with an ad about food or health may find magazines such as *Country Home* or *Family Circle* to be useful.

These ads for *Country Home* and *Family Circle* ran in *Advertising Age* as a way to promote the publication to media planners and buyers and make a statement about the kind of people who read the magazine.

NEWSPAPERS

Newspapers are used by advertisers trying to reach a local market because most newspapers, other than *USA Today,* are identified by the city or region they serve. Newspapers' primary function is to carry news, which means that advertisers with news to announce, such as a special sale or sale price, may find them a comfortable environment. Studies have consistently found that people consider ads—commercial information—to be news, too, and they read newspapers as much for the ads as for the news stories.

Newspaper readership has been declining for years, although it remains a fairly healthy advertising medium. If you just look at local newspapers and compare them to network TV, then newspapers continue to be the largest single medium, as Table 8.1 showed. However, when you summarize the categories, the newspaper category appears to be losing ground to television when you add in cable and all the other TV options. The two largest U.S. newspapers, *USA Today* and the *Wall Street Journal,* saw circulation increases in 2004, although circulation continues to erode for many local newspapers.[1]

Principle
A basic principle of newspaper publishing is that people read newspapers as much for the ads as for the news stories.

Although newspapers go to a mass audience, they do have **market selectivity** that allows them to target specific consumer groups using these methods. Examples of market selectivity are special interest newspapers, special interest sections (business, sports, lifestyle), and advertising inserts delivered only to particular zip codes or zones.

The Structure of the Newspaper Industry

Newspapers can be classified by three factors: frequency of publication (daily, weekly, and so on), format and size, and circulation. Each factor helps the media planner to better fit newspapers into the overall media mix.

Frequency of Publication Most newspapers are published either daily or weekly. About 1,530 dailies and 8,000 weeklies currently exist in the United States. Daily newspapers usually are found in cities and larger towns, and have morning editions, evening editions, or all-day editions. Daily papers printed in the morning deliver a record of the previous day's events, including detailed reports on local and national news, and on business, financial, and sports events. (Some daily newspapers also have morning editions, as well as editions that come out later in the day.) Evening papers follow up the news of the day and provide early reports of the events of the following day. Evening papers tend to depend more on entertainment and information features than do morning papers. The *San Francisco Examiner* is an example of a daily evening paper.

Approximately 30 percent of the dailies and a few of the weeklies also publish a Sunday edition. Sunday newspapers are usually much thicker and contain a great deal of news, advertising, and special features. For a media planner, matching the timing of the advertising message with the time the target audience is available is crucial. Knowing, for example, that your target audience spends twice as much time with the Sunday edition as with the daily edition suggests the best placement for many local advertisers is in the Sunday paper. There is a trade-off, however, as the Sunday paper is also more cluttered with competitive advertising.

Weekly papers appear in towns, suburbs, and smaller cities where the volume of hard news and advertising is insufficient to support a daily newspaper. These papers emphasize the news of a restricted area; they report local news in depth but tend to ignore national news, sports, and similar subjects. *Beverly Review* is an example of a weekly circulated in a Chicago neighborhood. National advertisers often shun weeklies and are not heavy advertisers in daily papers. They use local papers indirectly through advertising placed by local retailers, dealers, or franchisees. Another type of weekly paper is the *advertiser* or *penny saver* publications that are distributed free. These are usually found in suburban areas and they contain mostly classified advertising.

Business, trade, and organizational newspapers, such as *Advertising Age,* may be published weekly, monthly, or on some other schedule such as quarterly, bimonthly (every other month), or semimonthly (twice a month).

Format and Size   Newspapers typically are available in two sizes. The first, called the **tabloid**, consists of five or six columns, each of which is about 2 inches wide and has a length of approximately 14 inches. The *Chicago Sun-Times* uses this size, as does the *New York Daily News,* the *National Enquirer,* and the *Star.* The standard size, or **broadsheet** newspaper, is twice as large as the tabloid size, usually eight columns wide and 300 lines deep, or 22 inches deep by 14 inches wide. More than 90 percent of all newspapers, including the *New York Times* and the *Los Angeles Times,* use this standard size.

The success of *USA Today* indicates that newspapers can and will adjust to changing consumer tastes in order to compete for consumer attention. *USA Today* stories are brief and breezy, dressed up with splashy graphics and full color in every section, and they include an array of charts and graphs to simplify the day's events for readers. *USA Today* was designed with jazzy graphics to be more attention getting because it relies heavily on newsstand sales, rather than subscription.

Apart from the size and publishing schedule of a newspaper, advertisers pay close attention to newspapers' required advertisement format. Until the 1980s national advertisers shied away from using newspapers because each paper had its own size guidelines for ads, making it impossible to prepare one ad that would fit every newspaper. In the early 1980s, however, the American Newspaper Publishers Association and the Newspaper Advertising Bureau introduced the **Standard Advertising Unit (SAU)** system to solve this problem. The latest version of the SAU, shown in Figure 8.1, made it possible for newspapers to offer advertisers a great deal of choice within a standard format. An advertiser can select one of the 56 standard ad sizes and be assured that its ad will work in every newspaper in the country.

Circulation   For the most part, newspapers are a local mass medium and their primary advertising revenue comes from local retail advertising and classified advertising. Other sources of revenue include reader subscriptions and single-copy sales at newsstands. The word *circulation* refers to the number of copies a newspaper sells and is the primary way newspapers' reach is measured and compared with the reach of other media.

A few newspapers have a national circulation, such as the *Wall Street Journal* and *USA Today,* which is the largest newspaper in the United States. *USA Today* is different

Depth In Inches	1 col. 2-1/16"	2 col. 4-1/4"	3 col. 6-7/16"	4 col. 8-5/8"	5 col. 10-13/16"	6 col. 13"
			13"			
FD	1 × FD	2 × FD	3 × FD	4 × FD	5 × FD	6 × FD
18%	1 × 18	2 × 18	3 × 18	4 × 18	5 × 18	6 × 18
15.75"	1 × 15.75	2 × 15.75	3 × 15.75	4 × 15.75	5 × 15.75	
14"	1 × 14	2 × 14	3 × 14	4 × 14	5 × 14	6 × 14
13"	1 × 13	2 × 13	3 × 13	4 × 13	5 × 13	
10.5"	1 × 10.5	2 × 10.5	3 × 10.5	4 × 10.5	5 × 10.5	6 × 10.5
7"	1 × 7	2 × 7	3 × 7	4 × 7	5 × 7	6 × 7
5.25"	1 × 5.25	2 × 5.25	3 × 5.25	4 × 5.25		
3.5"	1 × 3.5	2 × 3.5				
3"	1 × 3	2 × 3				
2"	1 × 2	2 × 2				
1.5"	1 × 1.5					
1"	1 × 1					

1 Column 2-1/16"
2 Columns 4-1/4"
3 Columns 6-7/16"
4 Columns 8-5/8"
5 Columns 10-13/16"
6 Columns 13"

Double Truck 26-3/4" (two pages)
There are four suggested double-truck sizes:
13 × FD 13 × 18 13 × 14 13 × 10.5
*FD (full depth): Can be 21" or deeper.
Depths for each broadsheet newspaper are indicated in the Standard Rate and Data Service (SRDA). All broadsheet newspapers can accept 21" ads, and may float them if their depth is greater than 21".

Tabloids: Size 5 × 14 is a full page tabloid for long-cut-off papers. Mid cut-off papers can handle this size with minimal reduction. The N size measuring 9-3/8 × 14 represents the full-page size—the size for tabloids such as the *New York Daily News* and *Newsday* and other short cut-off newspapers. The five 13-inch-deep sizes are for tabloids printed on 55-inch wide presses such as the *Philadelphia News*. See individual SRDS listings for tabloid sections of broadcast newspapers.

FIGURE 8.1 The Expanded Standard Advertising Unit System
The Standard Advertising Unit system offers a number of choices in sizing within a standardized format, which makes it easier for national advertisers to plan their ads and buy space.

Source: Guide to Quality Newspaper Reproduction, joint publication of the American Newspaper Publishers Association and Newspaper Advertising Bureau, 1986.

from other daily newspapers in that it is targeted to travelers and its primary sales is either single-copy sales, rather than subscriptions, or to hotels that buy a million copies a day in bulk to give to their guests.[2] Table 8.2 illustrates the difference in circulation patterns between *USA Today,* the *Wall Street Journal,* and the *New York Times.*

Some newspapers try to reach certain target audiences in other ways. Publishers are trying to build circulation by publishing Spanish-language editions, such as *El Nuevo Herald,* a Spanish daily published in Miami. *Hoy* is an attempt by the Tribune Company to build a national Spanish-language brand by launching dailies in major Hispanic cities under the *Hoy* name (*Hoy* is Spanish for today).[3] More than 200 newspapers in the United States are aimed primarily at African Americans. In New York City alone, there are Chinese, Spanish, Russian, Yiddish, German, and Vietnamese newspapers.

Special newspapers also exist for special interest groups, religious denominations, political affiliations, labor unions, and professional and fraternal organizations. For exam-

TABLE 8.2 Newspaper Circulation Patterns

Distribution Method	USA Today	Wall Street Journal	New York Times
Circulation	2,162,454	1,820,600	1,130,740
Home delivery	14%	75%	63%
Single copies	40%	8%	29%
Hotel/guest copies	23%	4%	—
Third Party (restaurants, airlines, etc.)	20%	9%	1%

Source: "A Snapshot of USA Today," Time (July 21, 2003): 50.

ple, *Stars & Stripes* is the newspaper read by millions of military personnel. The *Wall Street Journal* and the *Financial Times* are considered specialty newspapers because they concentrate on financial business information.

Types of Newspaper Advertising

Mirroring the circulation patterns, advertising can also be categorized as national or local. Table 8.3 breaks out these categories in terms of sources of ad revenue. Note that the declining state of revenues from 2000 to 2001 reversed in 2002 and 2003.[4]

The pricing for newspaper advertising is sold based on the size of the space used. The charges are published on **rate cards**, which is a list of the charges for advertising space and the discounts given to local advertisers and to advertisers who make volume buys. There are three types of advertising found within the local newspaper: classified, display, and supplements.

Classified   There are two types of **classified ads**: advertising by individuals to sell their personal goods and advertising by local businesses. These ads are arranged according to their interest to readers, such as "Help Wanted," "Real Estate for Sale," and "Cars for Sale." Many business advertisers use classifieds to sell their business or hire new employees. Classified ads represent approximately 40 percent of total newspaper advertising revenue. Many analysts feared that classified advertising would move from print to online media, and that classified spending will shrink. What seems to be happening, however, is that newspapers have taken their own classified ads online themselves and thus have participated in the switch to online.

Display   The dominant form of newspaper advertising is **display advertising**. Display ads can be any size and can be placed anywhere in the newspaper except the editorial page. Display ads can even be found in the classified section. Display advertising is further divided into two subcategories: local (retail) and national (general). Local businesses, organizations, and individuals that use local display advertising pay a lower, local rate.

Advertisers who don't care where their ads run in the newspaper pay the **run-of-paper (ROP) rate**. If they want more choice over the placement, they can pay the **preferred-position rate**, which lets them select the section in which the ad will appear. Sometimes local advertisers are also able to specify a position on a page, such as near the top or near a special feature, such as the weather box.

Some newspapers discount for frequency or as an incentive to attract certain categories of advertising. To retain current profitable customers, some newspapers offer hybrid rates to regular national advertisers (such as airlines, car rental companies, and hotels) that are lower than the national rate but higher than the local rate.

One alternative that allows the national advertiser to pay the local rate is cooperative (co-op) advertising with a local retailer. **Co-op advertising** is an arrangement between the advertiser and the retailer whereby the retailer buys the ad and then the manufacturer pays half—or a portion depending on the amount of space the manufacturer's brand occupies.

In South Florida, journalistic excellence in *español* means...

El Nuevo Herald is proud to be recognized as the best Spanish-language newspaper in the United States, reaching more than a half million readers over the course of a week.

Your advertisement in any of our award-winning sections is the sure way to be on the spotlight of the nation's third and most affluent Hispanic market with a whopping buying power of $13 billion plus a year!

The fact is, no other daily newspaper has a higher penetration in a Hispanic market nationwide!

For current rates and information call our **Advertising Department at (305) 376-4951.**

El Neuvo Herald is one example of a successful newspaper targeted at a specific ethnic group, in this case the Spanish-speaking consumer.

TABLE

8.3   Newspaper Advertising Expenditures (in millions $)

Type	2001	% change	2002	% change	2003	% Change
National	$7,004	−8.5	$7,210	2.9	7,797	8.1
Local/Retail	20,679	−3.4	20,994	1.5	21,341	1.7
Classified	16,622	−15.2	15,898	−4.4	15,801	−0.6

Source: "Media," 2003 Marketing Fact Book (July 7, 2003): 17; Newspaper Association of America Web site, May 2004, www.naa.org.

A newer system designed to avoid the rate differential and ease the difficulty of making a national newspaper buy is known as *one-order, one-bill*. Essentially, media rep firms sell newspaper advertising space to national advertisers on behalf of many different newspapers. This company handles all rate negotiation and billing with the individual newspapers. Because the rep firm has so many newspaper clients, it can offer lower rates for newspaper ad space. The advertisers not only benefit from lower rates, but they also do not have to deal with the hassle of placing orders in many single newspapers. In the past, national advertisers buying space from 150 newspapers would receive as many as 150 pieces of paper using 150 different accounting methods.

Supplements   Newspaper supplements can carry both national and local advertising. **Supplements** are syndicated, which means an independent publisher sells its publications to newspapers throughout the country, or they are local full-color advertising inserts that appear throughout the week and especially in the Sunday edition of newspapers. Independent publishers create and distribute syndicated supplements to newspapers throughout the country. The logo for the publisher and the local paper appear on the flag (usually at the top of the page). The best-known syndicated supplements are *Parade* and *USA Weekend*. Whether syndicated or locally edited, magazine supplements resemble magazines more than newspapers in content and format.

A **free-standing insert (FSI)** is the set of advertisements, such as the grocery ads, that are inserted into the newspaper. These preprinted advertisements range in size from a single page to more than 30 pages and may be in black-and-white or full color. This material is printed elsewhere and then delivered to the newspaper. Newspapers charge the advertiser a fee for inserting the supplement into the newspaper. FSI advertising is growing in popularity with retail advertisers for three reasons: (1) It allows greater control over the reproduction quality of the advertisement; (2) it commands more attention than just another ad in the paper; and (3) advertisers can place free-standing inserts in certain newspapers that are delivered to certain neighborhoods, or even certain people. The *Houston Post* does this for retailers such as Arby's and Kohl's by distributing a Spanish-language insert to neighborhoods where Spanish is the dominant language.

Newspaper Readership

By all demographic standards, the newspaper is a solid mass-market medium, reaching about 68 percent of the adult population.[5] Nearly half of all adults receive home delivery of a Sunday or weekend newspaper; delivery levels are highest in medium-size cities and lowest in rural locations and larger metropolitan areas. Frequent readers of daily newspapers tend to be the most regular readers of the Sunday paper. Historically, newspaper reading tends to be highest among older people and people with a higher educational level. It is lowest among people in their late teens and early twenties. Newspaper readership tends to be selective, with a greater percentage reading specific sections rather than the whole paper. Figure 8.2 shows more information about newspaper readership for one particular age group.

Measuring the Newspaper Audience   Newspapers measure their audiences to assess their performance and to spot growth opportunities. They also use readership data to attract advertisers who want to reach their readers. This type of information facilitates the media planner's ability to match a certain newspaper's readership with the target audience. Newspapers obtain objective measures of newspaper circulation and readership by subscribing to one or both of the following auditing companies:

• *The Auditing Bureau of Circulations (ABC)*. The ABC is an independent auditing group that represents advertisers, agencies, and publishers. This group verifies statements about newspaper circulation statistics and provides a detailed analysis of the newspaper by state, town, and county. ABC members include only paid-circulation newspapers and magazines. Newspapers that do not belong to an auditing organization such as the ABC must provide prospective advertisers with something official, such as a publisher's statement about the number printed or a Post Office statement about the number mailed.

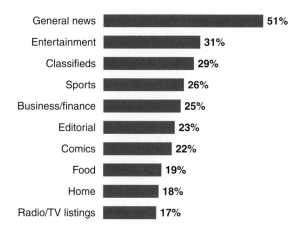

Selective Readership Patterns (for Baby Boomers)
Like most adults, baby boomers (ages 38–57) read newspapers selectively. Only 21 percent of those surveyed read every section of the newspaper. Shown here is section or page readership data for this age group.

- *Simmons-Scarborough.* Simmons-Scarborough Syndicated Research Associates provides a syndicated study that annually measures readership profiles in approximately 70 of the nation's largest cities. The study covers readership of a single issue and the estimated unduplicated readers for a series of issues. Simmons-Scarborough is the only consistent measurement of audiences in individual markets.

The Advantages and Disadvantages of Advertising in Newspapers

The newspaper medium has numerous advantages, which is why newspapers are still the number-one medium in respect to ad billings.

- *Range of Market Coverage.* Advertisers can reach local or metro markets, special-interest groups, and racial and ethnic groups in a cost-efficient manner.
- *Comparison Shopping.* Consumers use newspapers for comparison shopping, so they are especially useful for advertisers that have products with an obvious competitive advantage.
- *Positive Consumer Attitudes.* Readers generally perceive newspapers, including the advertisements, to be current and credible information sources.
- *Flexibility.* Newspapers offer geographic flexibility: Advertisers can choose to advertise in some markets and not in others. Newspapers also offer production flexibility. Unusual ad sizes, full-color ads, free-standing inserts, different prices in different areas, sample products, and supplements are all newspaper advertising options.
- *Interaction of National and Local.* Newspapers provide a bridge between the national advertiser and the local retailer. A local retailer can easily tie in with a national campaign by using a similar advertisement in the local daily. In addition, quick-action programs, such as sales and coupons, are implemented easily through local newspapers.

Like every other advertising medium, newspapers also have disadvantages. The most problematic issues in newspaper advertising include:

- *Short Life Span.* People tend to read newspapers quickly and only once. The average life span of a daily newspaper is only 24 hours, so the life span of the ad is limited.
- *Clutter.* Most newspapers are cluttered with ads, particularly on supermarket advertising days and on Sundays, when information overload reduces the effect of any single advertisement. Even supplemental inserts are now so thick that they represent additional newspaper clutter.
- *Limited Coverage of Certain Groups.* Although newspapers have wide market coverage, certain market groups are not frequent readers. For example, newspapers traditionally have not reached a large part of the under-20 age group. Newspapers often cannot provide total market coverage for national advertisers because of cost and the fact that there are few national newspapers.

• ***Poor Reproduction.*** Despite the introduction of new production technology, with the exception of special printing techniques and preprinted inserts, the reproduction quality of newspapers is poor, especially for color advertisements, compared to magazines, brochures, and direct mail. In addition, the speed necessary to compose a daily newspaper prevents the detailed preparation and care in production that is possible with weekly or monthly publications.

The Future of the Newspaper Industry

The increased costs of newspaper production have resulted in a general consolidation in the newspaper industry. This consolidation has helped the industry implement new technologies and delivery mechanisms. Some technology advances include online circulation information systems, electronic libraries, and database publishing. The emergence of the Internet as a mechanism for delivering a newspaper, or part of a newspaper, has had a tremendous impact on the newspaper industry. Virtually every major newspaper and many medium-size newspapers are now online. In addition to conventional Internet sites, stories are now being distributed through Web-enabled phones, pagers, e-mail, and Palm Pilots. Busy executives are now able to download stories from the *Wall Street Journal* and the *New York Times* via a cell phone anytime and anywhere.

Newspapers are by no means obsolete. The traditional benefits to an advertiser are obvious, but today's customers expect more. Whether the industry as a whole can deliver on these expectations remains to be seen, but there is potential for positive change. Now let's look at magazines.

Consider This

1. What are the key advantages of using newspapers as an advertising medium?
2. Does it surprise you that younger people are less likely to read a newspaper? Why or why not?

MAGAZINES

There are thousands of magazine titles and a few of them today—*Time, Newsweek, Reader's Digest*—reach a general audience. But most magazines today are special interest publications aimed at narrower target markets. There are magazines for every hobby, every sport, every age group, every business category, and every profession. These special interest publications, however, are not necessarily small. The number-one magazine in terms of circulation is *Modern Maturity* with a circulation of almost 18 million, followed by *Reader's Digest* at 12.5 million.

As Table 8.4 illustrates, specialty magazines, such as the brides' magazines, seem to have an edge over more general publications in terms of maintaining their growth. The business publications, such as *Forbes* and *Fortune,* were clearly hurt by the economic downturn of the 1990s and early 2000s. Upscale magazines provide an ideal place for the image advertising of luxury products. For example, magazines such as *Gourmet, Architectural Digest*, and *Condé Nast Traveler* have increased their ad pages in the last 10 years. In terms of advertising revenue and ad pages, *People* is the leader followed by the *New York Times Magazine* according to *Advertising Age*. Note that a special interest publication for brides is in the third position. Table 8.4 rank-orders these publications, using the 2003 ad pages total as the primary leadership indicator.

Historically, more than half of all new publications fail. Despite the high risks associated with the magazine business, new ones do continue to emerge, especially those that target business markets and growing market segments such as computer users and skateboarders. The teen market, which was seen as a growth area, has begun to slump because of too much competition even as the number of titles proliferates. Within this changing environment, publishers are investing more money than ever in existing titles to hold on to

Principle
If you want to start a successful magazine, create a special interest publication aimed at a narrow or niche target audience.

TABLE
8.4 **Magazine Advertising Leaders**

Magazine	03 Pages	% Change	03 Revenue	% Change
1. People	3,705	.2	$744,245,218	4.3
2. The New York Times Magazine	3,363	1.5	234,703,794	10.4
3. Bridal Guide	3,128	35.1	56,869,011	5.2
4. Forbes	3,124	−10.8	246,102,559	−12.4
5. Fortune	3,054	−8.3	279,204,933	−4.9
6. In Style	3,045	0.5	292,756,724	10.7
7. Business Week	3,034	−9.0	336,112,450	−4.4
8. Vogue	2,958	2.4	274,944,082	13.2
9. Bride's Magazine	2,956	5.4	161,840,483	3.4
10. Transworld Skateboarding	2,496	−13.5	24,786,585	−5.6
11. New York Magazine	2,457	−2.2	64,165,120	−10.1
12. TV Guide	2,453	−0.2	381,603,743	8.4
13. Time	2,350	0.8	604,865,803	6.3
14. Sports Illustrated	2,338	−6.4	644,468,454	−0.4
15. The New Yorker	2,280	2.2	175,886,753	15.4

Source: "Data Center: Magazine Ad Page Leaders," *Advertising Age* (January 26, 2004).

market share. One growth area, however, is the business publication market. The International Truck case in the Matter of Practice box illustrates how this category works as an advertising medium.

Types of Magazines

Advertisers that want to target their ads to specific audiences use many types of magazine classifications when planning and buying print media and when creating print ads.

Audience Focus   The three main types of audiences that magazines target are consumer, business, and farm audiences. **Consumer magazines**, directed at consumers who buy products for personal consumption, are distributed through the mail, newsstands, and stores. Examples are *Reader's Digest, Lear's, Time,* and *People.* Business magazines target business readers; they include the following types:

* *Trade papers* aimed at retailers, wholesalers, and other distributors. *Chain Store Age* is an example.
* *Industrial magazines* aimed at manufacturers. One example is *Concrete Construction.*
* *Professional magazines* aimed at physicians, lawyers, and other professionals. *National Law Review* targets lawyers, for instance.

Business magazines are also classified as vertical or horizontal publications. A **vertical publication** presents stories and information about an entire industry. *Women's Wear Daily,* for example, discusses the production, marketing, and distribution of women's fashions. A **horizontal publication** deals with a business function that cuts across industries—such as *Direct Marketing.* Farm magazines, the third audience category, targets farmers and those engaged in farm-related activities. *Peanut Farmer* is an example of a farm magazine.

Other Classifications   The following factors also explain how magazines are classified.

* *Geography.* Many magazines cover certain sections or regions of the country or have regional editions. The area covered may be as small as a city (*Los Angeles Magazine* and *Boston Magazine*) or as large as several contiguous states (the southwestern

A MATTER OF PRACTICE
International Truck Delivers the Goods

How do you sell a delivery truck? More importantly, how do you reach owners of medium-size businesses who buy delivery trucks—such as commercial bakers, furniture store owners, landscapers, or beverage distributors? That was the problem Fallon Worldwide faced in handling advertising for its client International Truck.

Delivery trucks are a major capital investment and operating cost for International's business customers. If the truck is off the road for repairs, it's not delivering the goods and that cuts into profits. But few business owners are experienced buyers.

The medium-size business owner is International's bread and butter, but increased competition from bigger truck manufacturers, such as GMC and Ford, have created bumps in International's road. The big boys offered the reassurance of scale and a huge network of distributors. They also have deep pockets for business-to-business advertising, as well as a halo effect from their consumer advertising.

International knew it needed to improve awareness of its products among truck buyers. Furthermore, it had to differentiate International on three key factors that drive customer reassurance: having the right trucks, the best service, and immediate parts availability.

The problem was to reach a diverse audience. Previous advertising had been in truck trade magazines, but International's customers—business owners from florists to bakers—aren't professional truckers, so they were unlikely to be reading trade magazines. Fallon media planners sorted out the trade publications to find the most profitable business segments for delivery trucks. By significantly reducing duplication in the truck industry magazines, they freed up the budget to fund media beyond the trucking trade publications.

The media budget was flat from the previous year, but this broader approach to targeting created greater impact, as well as reach. Even though International was outspent by up to 3:1 by key competitors, it achieved its objectives.

The new advertising helped International increase its awareness by 20 percent. In fact, International moved to second-highest unaided awareness in the category, second only to Ford, and closing that gap.

In terms of the reassurance message, the creative approach connected to consumers with a commonsense approach focused on trucks that got the job done in a straightforward and honest way. No chest beating and "glamour chrome." This approach vaulted International past its chief competitors on all three measures.

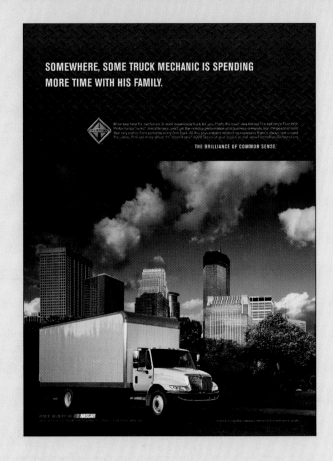

Consider This

1. What were International's points of differentiation?
2. Why did International's agency recommend magazines, and what was the primary switch in the strategy for using trade magazines?

Source: Adapted from "International," *Fallon Effies 2004* (Minneapolis: Fallon Advertising, 2004), 45–47.

edition of *Southern Living Magazine*). Geographic editions help encourage local retail support by listing the names of local distributors in the advertisements. Most national magazines also offer a zone edition that will carry different ads—and perhaps different stories—depending on the region of the country.

- *Demographics.* Demographic editions group subscribers according to age, income, occupation, and other classifications. Some magazines for example, publish a special "ZIP" edition for upper-income homes that is sent to subscribers who live in a specific zip code and typically share common demographic traits, such as income. *Newsweek* offers a college edition and *Time* sends special editions to students, business executives, doctors, and business managers.

- *Editorial Content.* Each magazine emphasizes a certain type of editorial content. The most widely used categories are general editorial (*Reader's Digest*), women's service (*Family Circle*), shelter (*House Beautiful*), business (*Forbes*), and special interest (*Ski*).

- *Physical Characteristics.* Media planners and buyers need to know the physical characteristics of a magazine because ads containing various elements of words and pictures require a different amount of space. The most common magazine page sizes are 8½ × 11 inches and 6 × 9 inches. Ads run in *Reader's Digest,* which is a 6 × 9-inch format, allow for fewer visuals and little copy.

- *Ownership.* Some magazines are owned by publishing companies (*Glamour, Gourmet, Vanity Fair,* and *The New Yorker* are owned by Condé Nast), and some are published by organizations, such as the AARP's *Modern Maturity*. There are also magazines published by consumer companies, such as Kraft's *Food & Family,* that sell ads plus carry stories and ads for many of their own products. *surf & turf* is a publication jointly sponsored by athletic company REI and *Shape* magazine.

Magazines reach a carefully defined target audience with a special interest. This publication by Kraft (*Food & Family*) is produced in partnership with *Shape* magazine to reach women who are interested cooking and baking.

Distribution and Circulation

Media planners and buyers also pay attention to a magazine's distribution so they can assess circulation potential and determine whether the correct audiences will be reached. Traditional delivery is through newsstand purchases or home delivery via the U.S. Postal Service. Nontraditional delivery methods include hanging bagged copies on doorknobs, inserting magazines in newspapers (such as *Parade* magazine), delivering through professionals (doctors' and dentists' offices), direct delivery (company magazines or those found on airplanes), and electronic delivery, which is being used by organizational publications, such as university alumni magazines. Nontraditional delivery is referred to as **controlled circulation**, meaning the magazine is distributed free to specific audiences.

Magazine Advertising

By their nature, magazines must fill a niche with unique editorial content to satisfy specific groups of readers. Readers also tend to spend more time reading a magazine than they do reading a newspaper, so there is a better opportunity to provide in-depth information. Quality of reproduction is one of the biggest strengths of magazine advertising because it allows the advertiser's products to be presented in a format superior to newspapers. In deciding in which magazines to place ads, advertisers need to consider factors such as format and technology.

Format   Although the format may vary from magazine to magazine, all magazines share some format characteristics. For example, the inside and back cover pages are the most costly for advertisers because they have the highest level of exposure compared to all the other pages in a magazine. The inside back cover is also a premium position.

Normally, the largest unit of ad space that magazines sell is the **double-page spread**, in which two ad pages face each other. A double-page ad design must bridge or jump the **gutter**, the white space (needed in the printing process) running between the inside edges of the pages, meaning that no headline words can run through the gutter and that all body text is on one side of the spread or the other. A page without outside margins, in which the color extends to the edge of the page, is called a **bleed** page.

Magazines can sometimes offer more than two connected pages (four is the most common number) that fold in on themselves. This kind of ad is called a **gatefold**. Car manufacturers often use four- to six-panel gatefolds inside the front cover of major magazines. The use of multiple pages that provide photo essays is really an extension of the gatefold concept.

Another popular format for advertisers is a special advertising page or section that looks like regular editorial pages but is identified by the word "advertisement" at the top. The content is usually an article about a company, product, or brand that is written by the advertiser. The idea is to mimic the editorial look in order to acquire the credibility of the publication's articles.

Photo essay ads also are becoming more common in magazines such as *Fortune* and *Business Week;* these magazines may present a 20-page ad for a business in a foreign country. Finally, a single page or double page can be broken into a variety of units called *fractional page space* (for example, vertical half-page, horizontal half-page, half-page double spread, and checkerboard in which ads are located on double-page upper left, lower right, on both pages).

Technology   New technologies have enabled magazines to distinguish themselves from one another. For example, selective binding and ink-jet imaging allow publishers to personalize issues for individual subscribers. *Selective binding* combines information on subscribers kept in a database with a computer program to produce magazines that include special sections for subscribers based on their demographic profiles. Ink-jet imaging allows a magazine such as *U.S. News & World Report* to personalize its renewal form so that each issue contains a renewal card already filled out with the subscriber's name, address, and so on. Personalized messages can be printed directly on ads or on inserts ("Mr. Jones—check our new mutual fund today").

Satellite transmission, along with desktop publishing technology, allows magazines to print regional editions with regional advertising. This technology also permits publishers to close pages (stop accepting new material) just hours before press time (instead of days or weeks as in the past) so that advertisers can drop up-to-the-minute information in their ads. Sophisticated database management lets publishers combine the information available from subscriber lists with other public and private lists to create complete consumer profiles for advertisers. This process has come under close scrutiny with the public's increasing concern for personal privacy.

Magazine Readership Measurement

For the media planner and buyer it is critical to know whether magazine readers have unique characteristics and, if so, whether there is a way to verify these facts. We know, for instance, that 92 percent of all American adults read at least one magazine per month, and 80 percent of these readers consider magazine advertising "helpful as a buying guide." In general, media planners know that people tend to pay more attention to magazine advertising than to television advertising because they are concentrating more on the medium.

Several companies attempt to verify the paid circulation of magazines, along with demographic and psychographic characteristics of specific readers. Media planners and buyers rely heavily on this information when making choices.

Magazine rates are based on the circulation that a publisher promises to provide, or the guaranteed circulation. Magazine circulation is the number of copies of an issue sold, not the readership of the publication. A single copy of a magazine might be read by one person or by several people, depending on its content. As with newspapers, the ABC is responsible for verifying circulation numbers. The ABC audits subscriptions as well as newsstand sales and also checks the number of delinquent subscribers and rates of renewal.

MediaMark, which provides a service called MRI, is the industry leader in readership measurement. MRI measures readership for many popular national and regional magazines (along with other media). Reports are issued to subscribers twice a year and cover readership by demographics, psychographics, and product use. The Simmons Market Research Bureau (SMRB) provides psychographic data on who reads which magazines and which products these readers buy and consume. Other research companies, such as Starch, Gallup, and Robinson, provide information about magazine audience size and behavior.

One problem with these measurement services is their limited scope. MRI, for example, measures only about 210 magazines, although there are thousands in the marketplace. That leaves media buyers in the dark regarding who is actually seeing their ads in those other magazines. Without an objective outside measurement company, advertisers must rely on the data from the magazines themselves, which may be biased.

One interesting change in magazine measurement is the move, which is supported by the Magazine Publishers Association (MPA), to quantify the "experience" of reading the magazine, rather than just the circulation of the title. A major study to pilot test this concept was conducted by the Northwestern University Media Management Center, the Magazine Publishers Association, and the American Society for Magazine Editors (ASME). The study identified a set of 39 types of experiences that people report having with their magazines. More importantly, the study found that the more engaged people were in the magazine experience, the more impact the advertising had.[6]

Advantages and Disadvantages of Advertising in Magazines

The benefits of magazine advertising include the ability to reach specialized audiences, audience receptivity, a long life span, format, visual quality, and the distribution of sales promotion devices.

- *Target Audiences.* The ability of magazines such as *Men's Health, Fast Company,* and *Seventeen* to reach specialized audiences is a primary advantage of magazines. For example, *B-to-B* would be very effective in reaching people interested in business-to-business Internet marketing.
- *Audience Receptivity.* Magazines have a high level of audience receptivity. The editorial environment of a magazine lends authority and credibility to the advertising. Many magazines claim that advertising in their publication gives a product prestige.
- *Long Life Span.* Magazines have the longest life span of all the media. Some magazines, such as *National Geographic* and *Consumer Reports,* are used as ongoing references and might never be discarded. (Other publications, such as *TV Guide,* are used frequently during a given period of time.) In addition, magazines have high reach potential because they are passed along to family, friends, customers, and colleagues. People also tend to read magazines at a comparatively slow rate, typically over a couple of days, so they offer an opportunity to use detailed copy.
- *Format.* The magazine format also allows creative advertising variety through multiple pages, inserts, and other features.
- *Visual Quality.* The visual quality of magazines tends to be excellent because they are printed on high-quality paper that provides superior photo reproduction in both black-and-white and color as fashion advertisers, in particular, appreciate.
- *Sales Promotions.* Advertisers can distribute various sales promotion devices, such as coupons, product samples, and information cards through magazines. A 1987 U.S. Post Office ruling allowed magazines to carry loose editorial and advertising supplements as part of the publication if the magazine is enclosed in an envelope or wrapper.

Magazines are limited by certain factors. The most prominent disadvantages are limited flexibility, lack of immediacy, high cost, and difficult distribution.

- *Limited Flexibility.* Ads must be submitted well in advance of the publication date. In some instances advertisers must have camera-ready full-color advertisements at the printer more than two months before the cover date of a monthly publication. As noted earlier, magazines that have adopted desktop publishing and satellite transmission can allow advertisers to submit ads just hours before press time. Magazines also limit the choices for ad locations. Prime locations, such as the back cover or inside front cover, may be sold months in advance.

* *Lack of Immediacy.* Some readers do not look at an issue of a magazine until long after it comes to them, so the ad may take a long time to have an effect on the reader. Even if you might keep a *National Geographic* for many years, advertisers hope you will read it immediately.
* *High Cost.* The third disadvantage of magazine advertising is its high cost. For a general-audience magazine such as *Newsweek,* advertising rates are quite high, and magazines of this type do not compare favorably with other media such as network TV in terms of the cost to reach a broad mass audience. However, magazines with carefully segmented audiences, such as *Byte,* can be cost efficient because they reach a tightly targeted audience.
* *Distribution.* The final disadvantage of magazines is their limited distribution. With the exception of magazines such as *Woman's Day* and *People,* which are distributed on newsstands throughout the United States, many of the 2,500 different magazines that exist typically are not distributed to a broad spectrum of potential audience members.

The Future of Magazine Advertising

Magazine editors are under constant pressure to include product placements in their editorial content. That means marketers would pay the magazine for running an article that features a product, usually just seen in a visual, as part of the story. The Magazine Editors Association is against this but has conceded that it will probably happen soon.

As with newspapers, emerging technology—particularly online technology—is changing the magazine industry. For example, *Salon* is a virtual magazine distributed only on the Internet. These virtual magazines do not rely on paper or postage, and have no length limitations.[7] There are also questions by circulation experts who doubt Internet subscription sales will be large enough to supplant more traditional methods.

An interesting irony about magazines going into the Web has been the reversal of that pattern since the dot-com bust in 2000–2001. Not long ago the Internet was supposed to ruin print media. However, at least seven Web sites have created a print magazine, including Nerve.com, Space.com, and the travel site Expedia.

Magazines and newspapers have existed for several years in their current format because they provide interesting writing that's portable. The Web is most certainly not that yet, which begs the question: Will people really want their newspapers and magazines online after the novelty has worn off?[8] The question is not the inherent superiority of the Internet over traditional print. The question is which works better as part of an intelligently developed media strategy.

Consider This

1. What are the key reasons for using magazines as an advertising medium?
2. How are publishers attempting to personalize their publications for individual subscribers, and do you think this is an effective practice?

PACKAGING

Principle
A package is the last ad a customer sees before making a decision on which brand to buy.

In today's marketing environment, a package is both a container and a communication vehicle. In particular, it is the last ad a customer sees before making the decision to buy a product and once on the shelf at home or in the office it is a constant brand reminder. That's the reason we include it in this chapter. An article in *Advertising Age* explained the importance of the package as a communication medium: "Even if you can't afford a big advertising budget, you've got a fighting chance if your product projects a compelling image from the shelf."[9]

Impact on the shelf is the goal of packaging strategy. In an attempt to win over undecided consumers at the point of purchase many manufacturers are focusing on creating innovative, eye-catching packages. A prominent example is Heinz's attempt to win over kids by offering ketchup in a range of colors in brightly decorated squeeze bottles. Although the industry has never developed a standard for measuring impressions from a shelf, advertisers are aware of the "billboarding" effect of a massed set of packages, a practice that Pepperidge Farm uses to good effect.

The package serves as a critical reminder of the product's important benefits at the moment the consumer is choosing among several competing brands. Sometimes, the package itself is the focus of the advertising, particularly if there is a new size or innovation, such as Coca-Cola's introduction of a plastic bottle in its classic curved shape. In sum, packaging is a constant communicator, an effective device for carrying advertising messages, and a strong brand reminder.

Pepperidge Farm, with its consistent design and distinctive brand image, dominates the cookie shelf because of the power of its repeated design across all the brand's variations.

When the package works in unison with consumer advertising it catches attention, presents a familiar brand image, and communicates critical information. The packages can also deliver customer benefits. For example, recipes for Quaker Oats famous Oatmeal Cookies, Nestle's Tollhouse Cookies, Chex Party Mix, and Campbell's Green Bean Bake all started as promotional recipes on the product's packaging and turned into long time favorites in homemakers' recipe boxes. There is even a Web site for these classic recipes (www.backofthebox.com), which features more than 1,500 packaging-related recipes.[10]

OUT-OF-HOME ADVERTISING

Out-of-home advertising includes everything from billboards to hot-air balloons. That means ads on buses, posters on walls, telephone booths and shopping kiosks, painted semi-trucks, taxi signs, transit and rail platforms, airport and bus terminal displays, shopping mall displays, in-store merchandising signs, grocery store carts, shopping bags, public restroom walls, skywriting, in-store clocks, and aisle displays. And don't forget blimps and airplanes towing messages over your favorite stadium. The only thing that's standard is that the image is applied using some form of printing process.

Today total spending on out-of-home media is estimated to be more than $5 billion. Out-of-home advertising is situational: It can target specific people with specific messages at a time when they are most interested. A sign at the telephone kiosk reminds you to call for reservations at your favorite restaurant; a sign on the rail platform suggests that you enjoy a candy bar while riding the train; and a bus card reminds you to listen to the news on a particular radio station.

Outdoor Advertising

One of the growth areas in the out-of-home category is **outdoor advertising**, which refers to billboards along streets and highways, as well as posters in other public locations. In 2003 outdoor advertising increased 5.7 percent from the previous year.[11] Total outdoor ad revenue increased during the 1990s and leveled off in the early 2000s, as Figure 8.3 illustrates. Of the $5.2 billion spent on outdoor advertising, billboard ads accounted for approximately 60 percent, while street furniture, which is signs on benches and the like, and transit ads brought in the rest.[12]

■ ■ ■
The sides of buses and
semi–tractor trailers can be
highly effective moving
billboards when they are
painted with attention-getting
graphics.

Size and Format   In terms of size and format, there are two kinds of billboards: poster panels and painted bulletins. **Printed posters** are a type of billboard created by designers (provided by the advertiser or agency), printed, and shipped to an outdoor-advertising company. They are then prepasted and applied in sections to the poster panel's face on location, much like applying wallpaper. They come in two sizes based on the number of sheets of paper used to make the image: 8 sheet (5 × 11 feet) and 30 sheet (12 × 25 feet).

The other kind of billboard is the **painted bulletin**. Painted bulletins differ from posters in that they are normally created on site and are not as restricted as billboards in size or shape, although their standard size is 14 × 48 feet. They can be painted on the sides of buildings, on roofs, and even on natural structures, such as the side of a mountain.

Designers can add **extensions** to the painted billboards to expand the scale and break away from the limits of the long rectangle. These embellishments are sometimes called **cutouts** because they present an irregular shape.

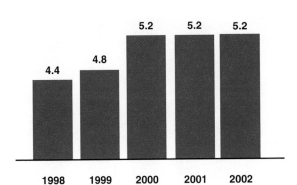

FIGURE
8.3

**Total Outdoor Ad Revenue
(in billions)**

Source: "Media," *2003 Marketing Fact Book*
(July 7, 2003): 17.

An advertiser would use a billboard for two primary reasons. First, it would supplement a mass-media strategy by providing reminders to the target audience. A second use for billboards is to act as primary medium when the board is in close proximity to the product. Most common are billboards directing travelers to hotels, restaurants, resorts, and gas stations.

Because of the very short time consumers are normally exposed to a billboard (3 to 5 seconds), the message must be short and the visual must have "stopping power." No more than 8 to 10 words is the norm. An example of an unusual billboard with immense attention-getting power is the Adidas "Football (Soccer) Challenge."

Buying Outdoor Space The outdoor advertising industry has increased its professional standards and become more competitive with other media. The industry uses a system based on **showings**, which refers to a standard unit for space sales based on the opportunity a person has to see a particular outdoor board. This is typically based on a *traffic count*, that is, the number of vehicles passing a particular location during a specified period of time. If an advertiser purchases a 100 showing, the basic standard unit is the number of poster boards in each marketing that will expose the message to 100 percent of the market population every day. If three posters in a community of 100,000 people achieve a daily exposure to 75,000 people, the result is a 75 showing. Conversely, in a small town with a population of 1,200 and one main street, two boards may produce a 100 showing.

Advertisers can purchase any number of units (75, 50, or 25 showings daily are common quantities). The number of boards required for a 100 showing varies from city to city. Boards are usually rented for 30-day periods, with longer periods possible. Painted bulletins are bought on an individual basis, usually for one, two, or three years.

Advantages and Disadvantages of Outdoor Advertising Although it is rare for a media strategy to be built around outdoor advertising, it does offer several advantages. Most notably, it is a high-impact medium offering larger-than-life visuals, on a hard-to-ignore structure. It is valued as a directional medium because it tells someone how to find a business establishment. It can also serve as a brand reminder and it can reinforce a creative concept employed in other media. Finally, outdoor boards and signs are the least expensive of all major media, especially in light of their long life.

There are some disadvantages to using outdoor advertising. As previously noted, because consumers pass on-premise

Two live players play a game of vertical soccer in the Adidas "Football challenge" outdoor board that captivated audiences in Japan.

Las Vegas is the home of many highly creative on-premise signs.

signs and outdoor boards very quickly and are often distracted, the message could fail to be seen or have any impact. Outdoor advertising is a very passive medium, which means that if the billboard is some distance away from the road, it can be very easy to miss.

Historically, many people have been critical of outdoor advertising because it creates visual pollution. Several states, such as Oregon and Hawaii, have banned billboards, while other states have restricted locations. Both outdoor and on-premise signs may also be regulated by local or federal laws depending on their location.

On-Premise Signs

Retail signs that identify stores have been with us throughout recorded history and are today the most ubiquitous form of advertising. Signs are found on small independent businesses, restaurants and chains like Starbucks, hospitals, movie theaters, and other public facilities like zoos, and large regional shopping centers. In this complex environment an effective sign may be relatively simple—like McDonald's giant M—or more complex—like those found on the strip in Las Vegas with their large illuminated and animated visual extravaganzas. Signs that are mounted on a store or its property are described as directional, as well as informational. The Signage Foundation describes them as "The Speech of the Street." Without signs consumers would find it difficult to locate the shops they patronize and, likewise, businesses would become largely invisible to their prospective customers. For some businesses, a sign along with an ad in the local phone directory may be the most important forms of advertising. For businesses that serve travelers, such as fast-food restaurants, gasoline stations, and motels, the sign is their primary way to attract business.[13]

Posters

Posters are used on the sides of buildings and vehicles, as well as on bulletin boards and kiosks. In London, daily hand-lettered posters are used to announce newspaper headlines and the walls of the subway or tube stations are lined with posters advertising all kinds of products, but particularly theater shows. The iPod was launched in London with the walls that tube riders encounter coming up or down the exit stairs being papered with the distinctive silhouetted images against their neon backgrounds. The repetition of the images created a strong billboarding effect.

Posters more enduring than the hand-lettered London newspaper signs are printed by lithography, which is a high-quality color printing process. Lithography created the "golden age" of the poster beginning in the late 1880s when posters were the work of serious artists. These posters are now considered art and valued as collector items, as are movie posters both historic and contemporary.

Obviously the impact of a poster is derived primarily from its striking design. In most cases there are few words, although posters designed for places where people wait, such as transit stops and kiosks, may carry longer messages, as well as take-along materials such as tear-off coupons. The impact of a poster is also determined by its location. The Special K story in the Inside Story is an example of an award-winning media idea that was recognized as Media Plan of the Year by the *MediaWeek* trade magazine.

Kiosks   Special structures called *kiosks* are designed for public posting of notices and advertising posters. Some of these locations are high-traffic places such as a many-sided structure in a mall or near a public walkway; others are places where people wait. The location has a lot to do with the design of the message. Some out-of-home media serve the same function as the kiosk, such as the ad-carrying bus shelter.

Transit Advertising

Transit advertising is mainly an urban advertising form that places ads on vehicles such as buses and taxis that circulate through the community. Some of these graphics are striking, such as the designs on the sides of the Mayflower moving trucks. Transit advertising also includes the posters seen in bus shelters and train, airport, and subway stations. Most of these posters must be designed for quick impressions, although posters on subway platforms or bus shelters are often studied by people who are waiting, so they can present a more involved or complicated message than a billboard.

There are two types of transit advertising: interior and exterior. *Interior transit advertising* is seen by people riding inside buses, subway cars, and some taxis. *Exterior transit advertising* is mounted on the sides, rear, and tops of these vehicles, so pedestrians and people in nearby cars see it. Transit advertising is reminder advertising; it is a high-frequency medium that lets advertisers get their names in front of a local audience at critical times such as rush hour and drive time.

The Transit Audience   Transit messages can be targeted to specific audiences if the vehicles follow a regular route. Buses that are assigned to a university route will expose a higher proportion of college students, while buses that go to and from a shopping mall will expose a higher population of shoppers. Mercedes-Benz busboards were used in a local market although they were designed to have a national look and feel.

Transit media, in all their various forms, offer the same advantages and disadvantages as outdoor media. The strategic rationale is much the same as well. Used primarily as a reminder or supplement to other media, it would be a minor part of the media mix unless the product and the ad are in close proximity. Also, transit media do not have the size advantage of outdoor media, but the consumer has more time to view the message.[14]

Consider This

1. What are the key reasons for using out-of-home media?
2. Why do you think it is difficult to measure the effectiveness of outdoor advertising? Can you think of any ways to improve the measurement process?

THE INSIDE STORY

Kellogg's Special K 2-Week Challenge

Amy Hume, Associate Media Director, Kellogg's Cereal Starcom Worldwide, Chicago

Each year, Kellogg's supports its Special K cereal with marketing efforts during the New Year's Resolution time frame, capitalizing on consumers' goals to lose weight after the holidays. In January 2002 Special K had promoted a 2-Week Challenge event with a campaign touting "lose up to 6 pounds in 2 weeks by replacing two meals with Kellogg's Special K or Special K Red Berries cereal and eating a sensible third meal."

It was a *very* successful effort when launched that year, and thus Kellogg had even higher goals for the effort in 2003. As an agency we were challenged with generating awareness and trial among both consumers who had participated in 2002 and those who hadn't been interested in the program previously. While the message itself can be one way to attract new consumers, our goal at Starcom was to come up with a different way to contact and connect with consumers via ad placement.

As consumers are typically bombarded in TV with weight-loss messages around the New Year's Resolution time period, our idea was to reach them in targeted locations where they are conscious of their weight and appearance and therefore are most receptive to our message. To further strengthen the communication, the media plan drove the creative, with Kellogg's tailoring the message to each location.

The subsequent communication surrounded the consumer on wallboards positioned within locations where people were actively thinking about their weight and appearance—in the department store dressing room, health club, doctor's office, hair or nail salon, and bridal salon. The message was tailored to each location through tag lines such as "The doctor will see (less of you) now." Believing that the medium *is* the message, we wanted consumers to think: "If the entire diet can be communicated on a board, it must be easy enough for me to follow." This contrasted with

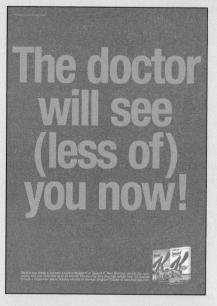

competitors' complicated diets that utilized only traditional vehicles to ensure consumer understanding. The wallboards also distributed a take-home brochure that the dieter used to keep track of his or her results.

The total plan was a $7 million effort that included television, magazines, and online advertising, but the wallboards were only $250,000. The schedule included 924 wallboard postings across 15 markets. The plan reached 17 percent of U.S. households but because of its careful targeting, it reached 22 percent of the Special K high-volume users. The following summarizes the placements for the wallboards:

- Doctors' offices: 325 per month for 3 months
- Hair and nail studios: 125 per month for 1 month
- Bridal stores: 125 per month for 1 month
- Health clubs: 319 per month for 1 month
- Department stores: 30 per month for 1 month

National TV also was utilized in support of the wallboards to generate quick, mass reach with magazines extending reach further within relevant Resolution/Weight Loss editorial. Additionally we had an Internet component that established an online community where consumers could interact to discuss the 2 Week Challenge and receive daily tips on sticking with it.

Reaching consumers at the moment they are in need of a weight-loss solution and delivering a simple diet in the context of their environment was very effective: Business results show an overall lift in wallboard markets of 20 percent over nonwallboard markets.

Amy Hume graduated from University of Colorado, Boulder, in 1988 with a BS in Journalism with an emphasis in Advertising. She has been with Starcom Worldwide, Chicago, since January 1993, starting as Media Buyer/Planner (*Nintendo, Amurol Confections*) and moving to Supervisor (*Walt Disney World, Kellogg*) and then to Associate Media Director (*Kellogg*).

Nominated by Professor Sandra Moriarty, University of Colorado

SHOWCASE

RICH UNCLE WON'T DIE?

Mercedes-Benz of Portland and Wilsonville

C-Class. Under $30K.

Mercedes-Benz

WIN THE LOTTERY LATER.

Mercedes-Benz of Portland and Wilsonville

C-Class. Under $30K.

Mercedes-Benz

■ ■ ■

Mercedes-Benz is often seen as elite and unapproachable. This campaign is promoting the safe and affordable nature of the C-Class. The tone and humor of the copy help make the dealerships seem like a group of nice people with a fun personality. These busboards were contributed by Karl Schroeder, a copywriter at Coates Kokes in Portland, Oregon, and a graduate of the University of Oregon advertising program.

DIRECTORY ADVERTISING

Directories are books like the Yellow Pages that list the names of people or companies, their phone numbers, and their addresses. In addition to this information, many directories publish advertising from marketers who want to reach the people who use the directory. This is a prime audience and one of the biggest advantages of advertising in directories; because people have taken the initiative to look for a business or service, the listing is reaching an audience already in need of something. Directory advertising doesn't have to create a need because it is the number-one shopping medium.

Directory advertising is described as *directional advertising* because it tells people where to go to get the product or service they want. There is a key difference between directional advertising and brand-image advertising. Directory advertising reaches *prospects,* people who already know they have a need for the product or service; brand-image advertising seeks to create a need. If you are going to move across town and you want to rent a truck, you will consult the local phone book. Directory advertising is the main medium that prospects consult once they have decided to buy something they need or want.

The most common directories are those that a community's local phone service produces. The listings and ads in the Yellow Pages are a major advertising vehicle, particularly for local retailers. National advertisers such as Pizza Hut also use them extensively. In fact, the Yellow Pages is Pizza Hut's second-largest media expenditure after TV. A single line for each Pizza Hut store is considered a unique ad.

Principle
The principle behind directory advertising is that it is directional—it tells people who already are in the target market where to go to get the product or service they are looking for.

Yellow Pages   The **Yellow Pages**, which lists all local and regional businesses that have a telephone number, is a $14 billion industry.[15] In addition to the phone number listing, retailers can buy display space and run a larger ad. The industry's core advertisers are service providers (restaurants, travel agents, beauty parlors, and florists, for example). For some small businesses, the Yellow Pages is the only medium of advertising, because it's where customers find out about them and it's affordable.

Because AT&T never copyrighted the name "Yellow Pages," any publisher can use it. As recently as 1995, the local phone companies controlled around 96 percent of Yellow Pages, but now they control only around 86 percent and are losing share because, in many cities, there are competing directories.[16] In fact, there are so many competing directories in some areas that publishers of Yellow Pages advertise their directories to build customer loyalty.

Almost 90 percent of those who consult the Yellow Pages follow up with some kind of action. Because a Yellow Pages ad is the last step in the search for a product or service by a committed consumer, the ads are not intrusive. Consequently, Yellow Pages users spend more per year than most advertisers' average customers do.[17]

Since the Yellow Pages are filled with ads, the level of clutter is quite high. Finding that breakthrough concept or graphic image is really the key to creating impact. Other decisions are driven by the budget and competition, such as decisions about ad size, use of color, and listings in several sections of the directory.

Other Directories   In addition to the Yellow Pages, an estimated 7,500 directories exist that cover all types of professional areas and interest groups. For example, the *Standard Directory of Advertisers and Advertising Agencies* (known as the Red Books) not only lists advertisers and agencies; it also accepts advertising targeted at those who use the directory. *The Creative Black Book,* another directory used by advertising professionals, also takes ads for photographers, illustrators, typographers, and art suppliers.

The ads in trade and professional directories usually are more detailed than those in consumer directories because they address specific professional concerns, such as qualifications and scope of services provided. Trade directories also use supplemental media such as inserts and tipped-in cards (glued into the spine) that can be detached and filed or sent back.

Most of the directories can be transformed into an electronic version accessible through the Internet. Electronic directories provide convenience and speed to customers who have the right technology. The dominant directory remains the Yellow Pages, which can be either an area-wide or a neighborhood directory, as well as electronic.

Advantages and Disadvantages of Directory Advertising   Like all the media we have discussed so far, directories offer certain advantages to advertisers. Most prominent is the fact that directories are a shopping medium, meaning that consumers initiate the search process when they have a need or want. If done correctly, therefore, a directory ad can be a very effective selling tool. Directories are inexpensive and provide a return on investment of 1:15; every dollar spent on a directory ad produces $15 in revenue. Directories also offer a great deal of flexibility in respect to size, colors, and formats. Finally, directories have a long life.

The primary weakness of directories is competitive clutter. Literally hundreds of look-alike ads are listed on a single page, often forcing advertisers to purchase larger ads they cannot afford. Ads cannot be changed for several months, meaning that if a business changes location or phone number, its ad may be wasted, so there's a flexibility problem. Finally, there are consumers, such as non-English speakers or the illiterate, who cannot easily use directories.

Consider This

1. Based on what you have read in this section on directory advertising, what are the key reasons for using this type of media?

2. Some local businesses advertise only in the Yellow Pages. When might this be a sufficient form of advertising?

USING PRINT ADVERTISING

Now that we have explored the main types of print media and their strengths and weaknesses, we can determine how to use these media effectively. Advertisers should always ask their media planner the cost of each medium, its ability to meet their advertising objectives, its ability to accommodate the style of message, and how targeted the audience is. The Practical Tips box provides guidelines for print media decision makers.

Practical Tips

When to Use Print

Use Newspapers If . . .	Use Magazines If . . .	Use Out-of-Home If . . .	Use Directories If . . .
You are a local business	You have a well-defined target audience	You are a local business that wants to sell locally	You are a local business or can serve local customers
You want extensive market coverage	You want to reinforce or remind the audience	You are a regional or national business that wants to remind or reinforce	You want to create action
You sell a product that is consumed in a predictable manner	You have a product that does not have to be demonstrated, but must be shown accurately and beautifully	You have a product requiring little information and little demonstration	You want to allow comparisons or provide basic inquiry and purchase information
You do not need to demonstrate the product	You need to relate moderate to extensive product information	You have a small to moderate budget	You have a small to moderate budget
You have a moderate to large budget	You have a moderate to large budget		

IT'S A WRAP

I P O D   D A N C E S   T O   I T U N E S

Over the years, Apple has struggled to move from its niche position in the computer market into the mainstream of the computer industry. It was the success of iPod and iTunes in opening a new market for Apple that brought recognition by Prophet, a leading management consulting firm, as well as *Advertising Age*, which named Apple Marketer of the Year. Prophet CEO Michael Dunn says about the Apple beachhead strategy, "We're betting this will fuel substantial growth for Apple and may even increase the chances of some PC users considering Apple for their next purchase." It's only a short step from the elegantly designed iPod to the grown-up Macintosh. Lee Clow, chairman of TBWA Worldwide, Apple's longtime ad agency, notes that "We all understood strategically that iPod is a window for the whole world to come to an Apple product."

Since it was first introduced in October 2001, Apple sold more than 1.5 million iPods, or about 300,000 by 2003. In two years, Apple achieved the sales rate for the iPod that it took 25 years to achieve with its PCs. It's become the top-selling MP3 player, with a 50 percent market share, according to market research NPD Group.

iTunes was launched in late April 2003 and by the end of the year, more than 25 million songs had been purchased and downloaded off Apple's site. As iTunes moved out beyond its Mac base, more than 1 million tracks were sold in the first week the service became available to Windows users. In recognition of its highly successful launch, *Time* magazine hailed iTunes as the "Coolest Invention of 2003."

■■■ Summary

1. **Explain the key concepts of media planning and buying.** A media mix is the way various types of media are strategically combined in an advertising plan. A media plan, which is prepared by a media planner, is a document that identifies the media to be used to deliver an advertising message to a targeted audience. Media buying is the identification of specific vehicles and the negotiation of costs and details to advertise in them. Reach is the percentage of the media audience exposed at least once to the advertiser's message during a specific time frame and frequency is to the number of times a person is exposed to the advertisement.

2. **Identify the strengths and weaknesses of newspapers as an advertising medium.** The strengths of newspapers include local market coverage with some geographic flexibility plus an interaction with national news and the ability to reach shoppers who see the paper as a credible source. Weaknesses include a relatively short life span, clutter, limited reach to some groups, and rather poor reproduction of images.

3. **Describe the key factors that advertisers should know to make effective decisions about advertising in magazines.** Magazines reach special interest audiences who have a high level of receptivity to the message. People read them slowly and they have long life and great image reproduction. They have long lead times, a low level of immediacy, limited flexibility, and generally do not reach a broad mass market.

4. **Analyze why packaging is such an important advertising opportunity.** Packaging is the last ad a customer sees before making the decision to buy. It can provide a critical reminder of the product's important benefits at the moment the consumer selects a product. The package is a good brand reminder.

5. **Discuss factors that advertisers should consider in making out-of-home media decisions.** Out-of-home advertising includes everything from billboards to hot-air balloons. A type of out-of-home advertising is outdoor advertising, which refers to billboards along streets and highways, as well as posters. Outdoor is a high-impact and directional medium; it's also good for brand reminder and relatively inexpensive with a long life. Other forms of out-of-home advertising include on-premise signs, posters, and transit advertising.

6. **Outline the factors that advertisers use to make decisions about using directory advertising.** Directories are a shopping medium for consumers who are searching for a product or service. They are inexpensive with a long life but are inflexible once printed. They are also a highly cluttered environment in which it is difficult for an advertisement to stand out.

■■■ Key Terms

bleed, 224
broadsheet, 215
circulation, 212
classified ads, 217
consumer magazine, 221
controlled circulation, 223
co-op advertising, 217
cutouts, 228
display advertising, 217
double-page spread, 224
exposure, 212
extensions, 228

free-standing insert (FSI), 218
frequency, 212
gatefold, 224
gross impressions, 212
gutter, 224
horizontal publication, 221
HUT (households using television), 212
impression, 212
market selectivity, 214
media, 211
media buying, 212

media mix, 212
media planning, 212
media reps, 213
media salespeople, 213
media vehicle, 212
out-of-home advertising, 227
outdoor advertising, 227
painted bulletins (outdoor), 228
preferred position rate, 217
printed posters (outdoor), 228
rate card, 217

ratings, 213
reach, 212
run-of-paper rate, 217
SAU (Standard Advertising Unit), 215
showings, 229
supplements, 218
tabloid, 215
vertical publication, 221
Yellow Pages, 234

▪▪▪ Review Questions

1. What is the difference between media planning and buying? What are the key concepts that guide their decisions?
2. What are the key advantages and disadvantages of using newspapers as an advertising medium?
3. What are the key advantages and disadvantages of using magazines as an advertising medium?
4. Why is packaging such an important advertising opportunity?
5. What are the advantages and disadvantages of outdoor advertising?

▪▪▪ Discussion Questions

1. You are the media planner for an agency handling a small chain of upscale furniture outlets in a top-50 market that concentrates most of its advertising in the Sunday supplement of the local newspaper. The client also schedules display ads in the daily editions for special sales. Six months ago a new, high-style metropolitan magazine approached you about advertising for your client. You deferred a decision by saying you'd see what reader acceptance would be. Now the magazine has shown some steady increases (its circulation is now about one-quarter of the newspaper's). If you were to include the magazine on the ad schedule, you'd have to reduce the newspaper use somewhat. What would be your recommendation to the furniture store owner?
2. Petra Wilcox, a display ad salesperson for the *Daily Globe,* thought she had heard all the possible excuses for not buying newspaper space until she called on the manager of a compact-disc store that sold new and used discs. "I heard about newspaper reader studies that prove how wrong the audience is for me. Readership is too adult—mostly above 35 years of age," he said. "And besides, readers of newspapers are families with higher incomes—the wrong market for our used disc business," he continued. If the *Globe* is a typical metropolitan daily, could the store manager be correct? In any event, how should Wilcox try to counter the manager's views?
3. Since his freshman year in college, Phil Dawson, an advertising major, has waited tables at Alfredo's, a small family-operated restaurant featuring excellent food and an intimate atmosphere. A Yellow Pages representative approaches the owner to run a display ad. The owner asks Phil for advice on whether such an ad would help, and if so, what the ad should look like. What should Phil recommend?

▪▪▪ Class Projects

1. As a class make a decision on where advertising should be placed for a new restaurant in town that specializes in low-carb menus. Have different members of the class contact as many media as possible in the community: Consider a medium-to-large newspaper, magazines, outdoor, or directory advertising business. Collect all the relevant information on services provided to advertisers. Ask as many questions as you need to. Compare the types of information and services available. Was the customer service helpful? Is this the right media choice for your company? Analyze the results in a brief report; begin by stating your advertising goals, then state what you might or might not accomplish by advertising in the publication.
2. Collect Web site versions of three online newspapers or magazines. Write a one- to two-page report on how these vehicles could be better advertising mechanisms. What might they do to reach potential advertisers?

HANDS-ON

Next Month's Magazine Issue: Credibility

At most newspapers and magazines there is a boundary that cannot be crossed—the one that exists between the news or feature stories created by the publication's writers (sometimes called the editorial matter) and the advertising. The separation of these two is so strict it has been called "the church-state rule." Publications work hard to convince readers (though not always successfully) that advertising revenue does not drive story selection, the flavor or scope of news coverage, or critical reviews and recommendations. That independence has long been viewed as a lynchpin for the credibility of a publication's articles.

Some savvy TV viewers realize that no such independence exists for many TV shows, where product placements are more and more common. To cite just one example, in 2004 ESPN2, a subsidiary of the Walt Disney Company, broadcast a biography of the boxer Roy Jones Jr. The program itself had actually been created by Wieden NY, an ad agency, for its most important client, Nike. Jones receives sponsorship money from Nike, and he was interviewed wearing Nike clothes and hats from its Jordan line. Nike claims to have promoted its products judiciously during the show. "We did not want to develop a 60-minute Jordan ad—we felt like that would harm us," claims Roman Vega, a Nike senior advertising manager. "Teenagers are finicky—they don't like to be marketed to."

In fact, the relationship between advertisers and TV networks frequently includes greater collaboration than viewers realize. For example, ABC and media-buying agency MindShare have an agreement to jointly develop several series of programs. This type of agreement reduces the program development costs and risks for ABC and assures Mindshare of a program that will be advertiser friendly (translation: family oriented and not too controversial).

In fact, this type of entanglement between advertisers and television networks is nothing new. In the early days of TV, almost every program was sponsored by a single key advertiser that paid for all production costs associated with the show and frequently had a strong say in the development of scripts.

Unlike TV networks, newspapers and magazines have fought to maintain the independence of their product from the influence of advertising, but that independence may be weakening. Consider these examples:

- *Country Living Magazine* runs an eight-page insert advertisement for Expo Design Center. On the facing page, before the insert begins, is a story describing how the "help and careful planning" of Expo have helped to turn "a dreary kitchen" into "an efficient workspace."

- *Rolling Stone* places movie star Angelina Jolie on its cover. Jeep takes advantage by buying a cover fold-out ad featuring the actress (as Lara Croft) in a Jeep.
- *Playboy* runs ads for Tommy Hilfiger featuring "Playmates" modeling the designer's clothes.

Each of these cases raises some concerns about whether the practices in question follow guidelines of the American Society of Magazine Editors (ASME) for separating ads from content. Jann Wenner, publisher of *Rolling Stone*, apologized for his magazine's ad and promised *Rolling Stone* would not do it again. But advertiser Jeep saw nothing wrong. Jeff Bell, a Jeep vice president of marketing, denied the ad implied that the company had any influence over *Rolling Stone* or its Jolie interview. "Did we tell them, 'No, please ask her if she likes Jeep'? It's an interview. She's going to say what she wants to say."

Jeep is not alone in wanting to leverage its ad dollars and many advertisers are pressuring print vehicles, especially magazines, to be more accommodating. In a competitive marketplace in which advertisers can place ads in a wide variety of media, magazines may have a hard time saying no. And some may ask, why should they? Perhaps the best answer comes from Mark Whitaker, ASME president and *Newsweek* editor. In an interview with the *Wall Street Journal*, Whitaker offered this rationale for why magazines should avoid offering advertisers "branded entertainment and product placement" opportunities:

> One of the great things about magazines is the very personal relationship that readers have with them. That's one of the things that advertisers should want. On the other hand, to my mind, that relationship depends in part on magazines having independence and credibility with their readers, as being produced by editors for readers primarily. I think that the problem with product placement is that it runs the risk of undermining that special relationship.

Consider This

1. Evaluate Whitaker's rationale for the "wall" between editorial content and advertising in magazines. Do you agree with his argument? Consider the issue from the perspective of each of these groups: consumers, magazine publishers, and advertisers.

2. What are advertisers trying to get from the blending of product promotion and magazine content? What are some long-term effects that are likely to result from this blending?
3. Is there some other way, besides pressuring magazines to blur content and advertising, that advertisers can achieve the same goals? What other print tools might be used?

Sources: Brian Steinberg, "Blurring the Line? Magazines Face New Pressure as Marketers Seek to Blend Advertising with Content," *Wall Street Journal* (Eastern edition) (August 9, 2004): B1; Brian Steinberg, "Taking a Stand as Lines Blur between Editorials and Ads," *Wall Street Journal* (Eastern edition) (August 18, 2004): 1; Brian Steinberg and Emily Nelson, "Unit of WPP Will Own Stake in ABC Shows," *Wall Street Journal* (Eastern edition) (December 1, 2003): B1; Suzanne Vranica, "Advertising: Hollywood Goes Madison Avenue; Television Shows Have Met the Sponsor: It Is them," *Wall Street Journal* (Eastern edition) (December 15, 2003): B5.

Broadcast Media

CHAPTER 9

A Drugstore Goes Online

Award:
*EFFIE® Gold,
Health Care category*

Company:
drugstore.com™

Agency:
Fallon Worldwide

Campaign:
*"A Very Healthy Way
to Shop"™*

CHAPTER KEY POINTS

After reading this chapter, you will be able to:

1. Describe the structure of radio, how it is organized, its use as an advertising medium, its audience, and the advantages and disadvantages of radio advertising.

2. Explain the structure of television, how it is organized, its use as an advertising medium, the TV audience, and the advantages and disadvantages of TV advertising.

3. Outline how advertisers use film and video.

4. Identify advantages and disadvantages of using product placements.

The dot-com bust in the early years of the 2000s saw a number of Internet businesses come unplugged. One that survived was drugstore.com, the leading online drugstore and information site for healthy, beauty, wellness, personal care, and pharmacy products. It wasn't easy, however, and the company didn't have a profitable quarter until 2004. So how did drugstore.com weather the economic storms that accompanied its startup?

Although drugstore.com™ was the first Internet drugstore when it was introduced in 1999, it soon faced ferocious competition from a variety of dot-coms looking to hit it big offering drugs via the Internet. With most of them stocking many of the same products, it became clear that online drugstore retailing was becoming a high-cost, inventory management nightmare, and that drugstore.com

241

would have to become an expert in customer service if it was going to survive. Its strategic partnerships with amazon.com, Rite Aid, GNC, and Cigna® helped it deliver on its promise.

Furthermore, it had to reach a fairly broad audience in order to build the volume of sales needed to make the company viable. Based on research, drugstore.com targeted head-of-household women, known as gatekeepers because they make most purchase decisions for the entire family. Also, unlike men, women actually enjoy shopping for drugstore products, but they hate the long lines and the medical environment.

So drugstore.com positioned itself as a comfortable way for women to buy pharmaceuticals online. This position was based on research that indicated that women prefer not to make multiple trips to the drugstore. A second round of research showed that this need to limit shopping trips was very much tied to their greater concern for saving time.

On the basis of these two rounds of research, the company's agency, Fallon Worldwide, designed a campaign around the tagline "A very healthy way to shop."™ The agency positioned drugstore.com as a premier online shopping alternative, less taxing and more convenient than driving to a drugstore.

The initial campaign identified eight top Internet markets including New York, Chicago, and San Francisco. The campaign placed television commercials in those cities in conjunction with the Academy Awards telecast. The first 30-second spot featured a woman who runs her entire life while relaxing in her bathtub. Ads that followed during the next four months showed a series of vignettes highlighting how a woman can solve her problems as well as those of others by using drugstore.com.

These spots also had a secondary purpose. Customers and potential customers were not quite sure what drugstore.com did and how it worked. Drugstore.com management thought that the slice-of-life vignettes would indirectly provide this information as well as support the ease-of-use positioning strategy. The ads showed what products drugstore.com carried. How the company delivered them and the reliability of product quality were demonstrated in a variety of creative ways through the television commercials.

How did drugstore.com's new campaign do? Check the It's a Wrap section at the end of this chapter.

Source: EFFIE brief provided by Fallon Worldwide and drugstore.com, as well as the drugstore.com Web site, www.drugstore.com, December 2004; Tom Taulli, "Drugstore.com Cowboy, The Motley Fool, October 12, 2004, www.Fool.com; Rick Aristotle Munarriz, "Drugstore Now, Boy," The Motley Fool, January 21, 2004, www.Fool.com; Kevin Newcomb, "Drugstore.com Offers Best Site Search," Jupiterimages, October 21, 2004, www.clickz.com/news/article.php/3424911; "First Data and Drugstore.com Offer 'Paperless' Purchases," First Data press release, October 4, 2004, http://news.firts data.com/media/ReleaseDetail.cfm?ReleaseID=148306.

Television delivered a powerful message to a mass audience for drugstore.com and helped the company position itself as a convenient way to shop. In this chapter, we explore the uses, structure, audiences, and advantages and disadvantages of radio and television as advertising media. We will also review film and video formats that use advertising, as well as the use of product placement in film and television.

BROADCAST MEDIA

Broadcast media, which transmit sounds or images electronically, include radio and television. Print is a static medium bought by amount of space, such as column inch; broadcast media are dynamic and bought by amount of time (seconds, minutes). Broadcast media messages are also fleeting, which means they may affect the viewer's emotions for a few seconds and then disappear, in contrast to print messages that linger and can be revisited and reread.

Broadcast media messages differ from print advertising messages in large part because broadcast engages more senses than reading and adds audio as well as motion for television.

RADIO

Even with the advent of television there are still more than 10,000 commercial radio stations. And the industry remains healthy with a 27 percent increase in ad revenues in the five-year period between 1998 and 2003.

The Structure of the Radio Industry

The basic structure of radio is shown in Figure 9.1. The traditional radio stations are found on the AM/FM dial and serve a primarily local market, but that's only the beginning of the radio listener's options, which also include public radio, cable and satellite radio, low-powered stations, and Web radio.

AM/FM Stations with a broadcast range of approximately 2.5 miles are considered local stations. Regional stations may cover an entire state or several states. The most powerful stations are called "clear channel" stations and can deliver signals for long distances.

Radio stations are delivered by two different ranges of **signals** or radio wave frequencies: AM or FM. The strength of an AM signal depends on the transmitting power the FCC grants the station, but AM signals tend to be stronger, sometimes reaching as far away as 600 miles. An FM station typically sends a signal that travels 50 miles. The tonal quality of an FM signal is superior to that of AM, which is why music stations prefer FM and talk radio and stations that broadcast sporting events are often found on AM. An advertiser can achieve better targeting by knowing the advantages and disadvantages of AM and FM radio and determining the technical quality needed for the transmission of the radio commercial.

Public Radio Public radio is very much like its television counterpart and must abide by the same rules and regulations. Local public radio stations are usually affiliates of National Public Radio (NPR) and carry much of the same programming, although they

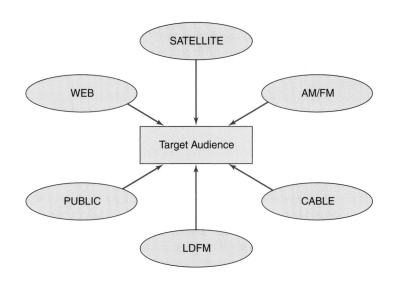

The Structure of Radio

As seen here, the structure of the radio industry has expanded to include cable, public, Web, and satellite radio.

have to buy or subscribe to the NPR services. For that reason, some local public radio stations carry a full range of NPR programming and some that are less well funded may carry only a partial list of NPR programs.

These stations are considered noncommercial in that they rely on listener support for most of their funding. In recent years, however, they have slowly expanded their corporate sponsorship messages.

Although public television is losing market share to the many new cable competitors, public radio is growing relative to its competitors. Public radio audience size increased by nearly 60 percent during the 1990s.

Likewise, corporate underwriting (sponsorship) has increased along with the audience size because public radio is one of the few media that can deliver the well-educated, affluent consumer. "It's a desirable audience that's difficult to find in a lot of commercial broadcasting," says James Harman, manager of corporate giving for General Electric, which underwrites *Marketplace,* a PBS show that discusses business trends and issues.[1]

There are a number of other ways that the radio industry is configured in the United States.

- *Cable Radio.* Launched in 1990, cable radio technology uses cable television receivers to deliver static-free music via wires plugged into cable subscribers' stereos. The thinking behind cable radio is that cable television needs new revenue and consumers are fed up with commercials on radio. The service typically is free of commercials and costs $7 to $12 per month. An example of cable radio is Digital Music Express, which offers CD-quality sound in 30 music formats (rock, classical, etc.) around the clock.
- *Satellite Radio.* The newest rage in radio technology is satellite radio. It can deliver your favorite radio stations, regardless of where you are in the continental United States. New York City–based Sirius Satellite Radio and Washington, D.C.–based XM Satellite Radio introduced their systems in 2002. For $12.95 a month, the system allows you to access 100 stations. A few car manufacturers offered three-band radios (AM/FM/SAT) in several of their high-end models. The retailers Circuit City, the WIZ, and others are beginning to market satellite-compatible car radios.[2]
- *LPFM.* If you're a college student, you probably have a **low-power FM (LPFM)** station on your campus. These nonprofit, noncommercial stations serve a small market, with a reach of 3 to 5 miles. Although the FCC has not allowed these stations to carry advertising, many have positioned themselves in case this ruling is changed. Advertising would provide revenue to the stations, and local advertisers would enjoy a new, affordable outlet. Often, these stations provide unusual programming unavailable through other radio venues.[3]
- *Web Radio.* Web radio provides **Webcasting**, which is audio streaming through a Web site. Webcasting station operators, from giant Clear Channel Communications down to smaller station groups such as Buckley Broadcasting and Emmis Communications, all provide radio programming through the Web. Still, Web radio does offer thousands of stations as well as highly diverse radio shows that play mostly to small select audiences. Moreover, Web-based radio could offer advertisers spots that run only in certain parts of a city, something impossible with broadcast radio. Such localization would open up new opportunities for smaller advertisers and help them handle their budgets more efficiently.

Radio Advertising

The radio listening experience is unlike interaction with any of the other media, which creates both challenges and opportunities for radio advertisers. It can be a more intimate experience, because we tend to listen to it alone, particularly for those people wearing headphones. It can also engage the imagination more because it relies on the listener's mind to fill in the visual element. That means radio dramas and ads can involve the audience on a more personal level. And radio can deliver a high level of frequency because radio commercials, particularly **jingles**, which are commercials set to music, lend themselves to repetition.

Principle

Radio advertising has the power to engage the imagination and communicate on a more personal level than other forms of media.

SHOWCASE

ANNCR:	If you want an easy, fast and convenient way to buy, sell, job-hunt or hire, nothing works better than the Register-Guard Classifieds. Well, actually, there is maybe one easier way:
SFX:	Knocking. Door opens.
NEW GUY:	Hello, I'm your new neighbor. I brought you an apple pie.
WOMAN:	Well, come in! I'll give you a tour of the house!
NEW GUY:	Oh lovely! Say, hard wood floors!
WOMAN:	Upstairs and downstairs. 3 bedrooms, two baths. Care to take it off my hands?
NEW GUY:	What?
WOMAN:	Buy it. It's for sale.
NEW GUY:	But I just bought the house next door.
WOMAN:	Do you have an out-of-state mother-in-law?
NEW GUY:	Good point. I'll take it– Oooh, a gazebo!
ANNCR:	Yes, they could walk right up to your doorstep, ready to buy, but, really, how many rich, apple-pie toting neighbors can you expect in a month? 3, tops, right? Yes, better to stick with the premiere marketplace of Western Oregon. With more listings and readers than all the competition combined, nothing connects buyers with sellers better than the Register-Guard Classifieds, with fresh listings in print and online every day.
SFX:	Knock, knock. Door opens.
NEW GUY:	Sorry, deal's off. The other neighbors have a pool!
WOMAN:	Darn it! Those Johnsons!
ANNCR:	The Register-Guard. Get more out of it. Move those homes and make some money! Call 342-twelve-twelve today!

■ ■ ■

Karl Schroeder, copywriter at Portland, Oregon–based Coates Kokes and a graduate of the University of Oregon advertising program, contributed this script. He explained that the strategy development began with research to compare The *Register-Guard's* perception of itself with consumers' perceptions. One insight the agency gained is that people will say they don't read the newspaper and then admit they read certain sections, such as the TV section. The campaign's objectives were to make the newspaper more approachable by using humor and to remind the one-section readers that the paper also had a useful Classifieds section.

Radio can be effective at creating humorous minidramas that capture the listener's attention. It can also be used in a local market to reach people who aren't reading the newspaper, which is why local newspapers frequently advertise on radio as the script for the (Portland, Oregon) *Register-Guard* newspaper Classifieds illustrates.

One problem is that radio also plays in the background for many of our activities. So although the radio is on, the multitasking listener may not really be listening to, or concentrating on, the message. Listeners tend to tune in and tune out as something catches their attention, which is why effective radio advertising is designed to "break through" the surrounding clutter.

Radio advertising is available on national networks and in local markets. Its revenue is divided into three categories: network, spot, and local. Network revenues are by far the smallest category accounting for approximately 5 percent of total radio revenues. Local advertising revenues account for 77 percent, and national spot advertising makes up the remaining 18 percent.[4] We will now examine network, syndicate, and spot radio advertising.

Network Radio Advertising Radio advertising can be bought from national networks who distribute programming and advertising to their affiliates. **Network radio** is a group of local affiliates connected to one or more national networks through telephone wires and satellites. There are five major radio networks: Westwood One, CBS, ABC, and Unistar. The largest network, however, is Clear Channel with more than 1,200 stations. Satellite transmission has produced important technological improvements that also make it easier to distribute advertising to these stations. Many advertisers view network radio as a viable national advertising medium, especially for food and beverages, automobiles, and over-the-counter drugs. The growth of network radio has contributed to the increase in syndicated radio, creating more advertising opportunities for companies eager to reach new markets. In fact, syndication and network radio have practically become interchangeable terms.

Spot Radio Advertising In **spot radio advertising** an advertiser places an advertisement with an individual station rather than through a network. Although networks broadcast blocks of prerecorded national advertisements, they also allow local affiliates open time to sell spot advertisements locally. (Note: National media plans sometimes buy spots at the local level rather than through the network, so it is possible to have a national spot buy.) Thanks to the flexibility it offers the advertiser, spot radio advertising makes up nearly 80 percent of all radio advertising. With so many stations available, spot messages can be tailored for particular audiences. In large cities such as New York, Chicago, and Los Angeles, 40 or more radio stations are available. Local stations also offer flexibility through their willingness to run unusual ads, allow last-minute changes, and negotiate rates. Buying spot radio and coping with its nonstandardized rate structures can be very cumbersome, however.

Syndicated Radio Advertising Program **syndication** has benefited network radio because it offers advertisers a variety of high-quality, specialized, and usually original programs. Both networks and private firms offer syndication. A local talk show, such as Rush Limbaugh, may become popular enough to be "taken into syndication." Here we're not talking about reruns of *Seinfeld,* which is the kind of programming that makes up syndicated television, but original radio programming playing on a large number of affiliated stations. Advertisers value syndicated programming because of the high level of loyalty of its audience.

The Radio Audience

Principle
Media planners use radio for tight targeting of narrow, highly segmented markets.

Because radio stations are so tightly targeted based on special interests (religious, Spanish language, talk shows) and musical tastes, radio is a highly segmented advertising medium. Program formats offered in a typical market are based on music styles and special interests including hard rock, gospel, country and western, top-40 hits, soft rock, golden oldies, and other nonmusic programs such as talk radio and advice, from car repair to finances to dating. Virtually every household in the United States (99 percent) has at least one radio and most have many sets.[5]

Radio listeners can be separated into four segments: station fans, radio fans, music fans, and news fans. Station fans make up the largest segment of radio listeners. They have a clear preference for one or two stations and might spend eight hours or more each day listening to their favorites. Most station fans are women between the ages of 25 and 44. Radio fans represent a third of the listeners. They may listen to four or five different stations per week, and they show no preference for one particular station. Most are under 35 years of age, although many women aged 55 and older are radio fans.

Only 11 percent of the audience is classified as music fans—people who listen exclusively for the music being played. Men between the ages of 25 and 45 are most likely to be music fans, although many elderly adults fit into the profile. Finally, a percentage of radio listeners choose their stations based on a need for news and information. They have one or two favorite stations, listen in short segments, and are almost exclusively aged 35 or older.

Experts contend that much of the future success of radio comes from its ability to reach kids and teens. Recent research has provided some findings that bode well for radio.

Measuring the Radio Audience   Advertisers considering radio are most concerned with the number of people listening to a particular station at a given time. Radio audiences are grouped by the time of day when they are most likely to be listening. The typical radio programming day is divided into five segments called **dayparts** as follows:

6–10 A.M.

10 A.M.–3 P.M.

3:00–7:00 P.M.

7:00 P.M.–midnight

midnight–6 A.M.

The 6–10 A.M. segment is called **morning drive time** and it is the period when the most number of listeners are tuned in to radio. This drive-time audience is getting ready for work or commuting to work and radio is the best medium to use to reach them.

The radio industry and independent research firms provide several measures for advertisers, including **coverage**, which is similar to circulation for print media. The most basic measure is the station's coverage. This is simply the number of homes in a geographic area that are able to pick up the station clearly, whether those homes are actually tuned in or not. A better measure is a station or program's **ratings**, which measures the percentage of homes actually tuned in to the particular station. Factors such as competing programs, the types of programs, and the time of day or night influence the circulation figure.

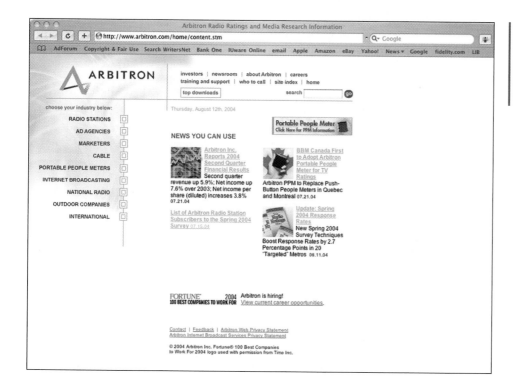

Arbitron is one of several major audience-rating services in the advertising industry. It estimates the size of radio audiences for over 250 U.S. markets.

Several major audience-rating services operate in the advertising industry.

- *Arbitron.* The Arbitron Ratings Company estimates the size of radio audience for more than 250 markets in the United States. Arbitron uses a seven-day self-administered diary that the person returns to Arbitron at the end of the week. Editors check that each diary has entries for every day and that the postmark shows the diary wasn't mailed before the week was over.
- *RADAR.* A second audience-rating service is Radio's All-Dimension Audience Research (RADAR). This company (owned by Arbitron) deals with both local and network radio. For RADAR, Statistical Research calls 12,000 respondents for seven consecutive days and asks about network radio listening done the day before. The company contacts respondents before beginning data collection, asking them to pay close attention to their listening habits.

Advantages and Disadvantages of Advertising on Radio

Radio is not for every advertiser, and it is important to understand its advantages and disadvantages.

- *Target Audiences.* The most important advantage radio offers is its ability to reach specific audiences through specialized programming. In addition, radio can be adapted for different parts of the country and can reach people at different times of the day. For example, radio is the ideal means of reaching people driving to and from work. Pizza Hut, for instance, reached out to its target audience of women making dinner choices by using radio during the 4:00–7:00 P.M. time slot.
- *Affordability.* Radio may be the least expensive of all media. The costs of producing a radio commercial can be low, particularly if a local station announcer reads the message. Radio's low cost and high reach of selected target groups make it an excellent supporting medium.
- *Frequency.* Because radio is affordable, it's easier to build frequency through repetition. Media plans that use a lot of radio are designed to maximize high levels of frequency. (Planners use buys on multiple stations in order to build any kind of reach at all.) Another reason why radio is a good frequency medium is the nature of the radio message. Reminder messages, particularly jingles and other musical forms, are easier to repeat without becoming irritating.
- *Flexibility.* Radio offers advertisers flexibility. Of all the media, radio has the shortest closing period: Copy can be submitted up to airtime. This flexibility allows advertisers to adjust to local market conditions, current news events, and even the weather. For example, a local hardware store can quickly implement a snow shovel promotion the morning after a snowstorm. Radio's flexibility is also evident in the willingness of stations to participate in promotional tie-ins such as store openings, races, and so on.
- *Mental Imagery.* Radio allows the listener to imagine. Radio uses words, sound effects, music, and tone of voice to enable listeners to create their own pictures. For this reason, radio is sometimes called the *theater of the mind*.
- *High Level of Acceptance.* The final advantage is radio's high acceptance at the local level. Radio is not normally perceived as an irritant. People have their favorite radio stations and radio personalities, which they listen to regularly. Messages delivered by these stations and personalities are likely to be accepted and retained.

Radio is not without its drawbacks as an advertising medium. Here are five key disadvantages:

- *Listener Inattentiveness.* Because radio is strictly a listening medium, radio messages are fleeting, and listeners may miss or forget commercials. Many people think of radio as pleasant background and do not listen to it carefully.
- *Lack of Visuals.* Developing radio ads that encourage the listener to see the product is a difficult challenge, and clearly, products that must be demonstrated or seen to be appreciated are inappropriate for radio advertising. Experts believe that humor, music, and sound effects may be the most effective way to create visualization.

- *Clutter.* The number of radio stations has increased, and so has the heavy repetition of some ads. The result is tremendous clutter in radio advertising.
- *Scheduling and Buying Difficulties.* Advertisers seeking to reach a wide audience often need to buy time on several stations, complicating scheduling and ad evaluation. The bookkeeping involved in checking nonstandardized rates, approving bills for payment, and billing clients can be a staggering task. Fortunately, computers and large-station representatives have helped to ease much of this burden.
- *Lack of Control.* Most of radio's recent growth has come from talk shows. There is always the risk that a radio personality will say something that offends the audience, which would in turn hurt the audience's perception of an advertiser's product.

Using Radio Effectively

We have seen that radio is highly targeted and inexpensive. Although radio may not be a primary medium for most businesses, it does have excellent reminder and reinforcement capability. To maximize the impact of a radio spot, timing is critical. Restaurants run spots before meals; auto dealerships run spots on Friday and Saturday, when people are usually free to visit showrooms; jewelry stores run them before Christmas, Valentine's Day, and Mother's Day. For a company like Pizza Hut, radio buys at the local level supplement national television and cable. Radio acts as a reminder, with 30-second spots concentrated from 11:00 A.M. to noon and 4:00 to 7:00 P.M. The messages focus on the location of local Pizza Hut restaurants and any special promotions.

■ ■ ■
Lids can be CDs. Used to promote new music albums, the "enhanced" multimedia CDs can not only sample songs, but also provide video clips and other content viewable on computers. In case you're wondering, the straw fits through the hole in the middle of the disk.

Trends in Radio/Audio Advertising

Exciting new opportunities for audio advertising are showing up in novel new formats. For example, mini-CDs are now being embedded in the lids of soft drink cups at movie theaters and theme parks.[6] In an entirely different area of audio surprises, supermarket shoppers may be caught off guard when they walk down an aisle and a voice addresses them from the shelf. Narrowly targeted laserlike sound beams can pinpoint individual shoppers with prerecorded messages encouraging them to try or buy some product. The audio messages also can be combined with plasma screens carrying electronic visual messages.[7]

Consider This

1. Why does radio continue to be a viable advertising medium?
2. From a strategic viewpoint, when would you be inclined to include radio in a media plan?

TELEVISION

Television advertising is embedded in television programming, so most of the attention in media buying, as well as in the measurement of television advertising's effectiveness, is focused on the performance of various shows and how they engage their audiences. Some programs are media stars and reach huge audiences: The Super Bowl is a good example

■ ■ ■

When people are engaged in watching a program, advertisers assume that concentration carries over to the commercials that surround the program.

with its 130 million viewers. Others reach small but select audiences, such as *The News Hour with Jim Lehrer* on PBS.

It's become popular to measure the size of the final viewing audience for well-loved programs such as *M*A*S*H, Cheers, Seinfeld, Friends,* and *Frasier* as a gauge of the program's popularity. Table 9.1 gives you not only program comparisons, but also an indication of how the size of viewing audiences has changed over the years. Three of every five homes tuned in to the final episode of *M*A*S*H,* for example, which set the record for final episodes. As the television audience has fragmented, audiences that size are increasingly difficult to attract. Note also that the price of a 30-second ad has increased as the size of the audience has gotten smaller.

In order to better understand how television works, let's first consider its structure and programming options. Then we'll look at television as an advertising medium and the way it connects with its audience, as well as its advantages and disadvantages.

Structure of the Television Industry

The key types of television delivery systems are wired and unwired network, local stations, public stations, cable and subscription. Specialty, syndicated, interactive television, and TiVo offer different types of programming and ways to manipulate the programming. Figure 9.2 shows these options.

Network Television   A broadcast **network** exists whenever two or more stations are able to broadcast the same program that originates from a single source. Networks can be over-the-air or cable. The FCC (Federal Communications Commission) defines a network as a program service with 15 or more hours of **prime-time** programming per week between the hours of 8 and 11 P.M.

TABLE
9.1 **Final Episodes**

Show	Date Aired	Viewers (in thousands)	Av Price/ 30 sec ad
M*A*S*H CBS	February 1983	105,467	$450,000 *846,000
Cheers NBC	May 1993	80,401	650,000 *843,000
Seinfeld NBC	May 1998	76,260	1.5 million *1.72 million
Friends NBC	May 2004	50,000	2 million

*Adjusted for inflation

Source: Suzanne Vanica, "'Friends' Costly Farewell," *Wall Street Journal,* (April 27, 2004): B1.

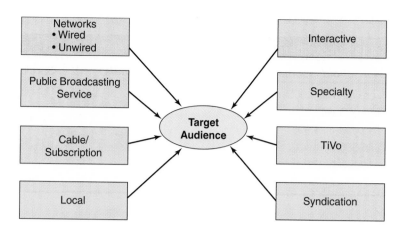

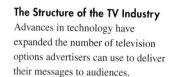

The Structure of the TV Industry
Advances in technology have expanded the number of television options advertisers can use to deliver their messages to audiences.

Currently, there are four national, over-the-air television networks in the United States: the American Broadcasting Company (ABC), the Columbia Broadcasting System (CBS), the National Broadcasting Company (NBC), and Fox Broadcasting. ABC, CBS, and NBC own 15 regional stations. The remaining 600 regional stations are privately owned **affiliates** that have a contractual relationship with the broadcasting company (each network has about 150 affiliates). The cost of the network and station operations are paid for from the local and national advertising carried on these channels. WB and UPN are cable-delivered networks and their operational costs are supported in part by advertising and in part by subscriptions.

The major networks originate their own programs and provide the programming to the local affiliates who, in return, provide the audience. The affiliate station signs a contract with the national network agreeing to carry network-originated programming during a certain part of its schedule. Some of the commercial time is sold by the network to national advertisers, and some is left open for the affiliates to fill with local advertising. Affiliates pay their respective networks 30 percent of the fees they charge local advertisers. In turn, affiliates receive a percentage of the advertising revenue (12 to 25 percent) paid to the national network. This advertising is the primary source of affiliate revenues.

In over-the-air network scheduling the national advertiser contracts with a national network to show commercials on a number of affiliated stations. Sometimes an advertiser purchases only a portion of the network coverage, known as a *regional leg*. This type of purchase is common with sports programming, in which different games are shown simultaneously in different parts of the country.

The problem facing network TV is that its audience—at least the audience for the big networks like NBC, CBS, and ABC—continues to erode as other viewing opportunities make inroads on their audiences. As Bob Garfield, ad critic for *Advertising Age,* observes, "Television networks are in a panic, because a decade-long erosion of audience has become more like a tectonic shift." Some 1.5 million men aged 18–24 simply disappeared from the television audience in 2003, throwing off the television ratings industry and puzzling media buyers, as well as television sales reps.[8]

Others speculate that these young male viewers, who are a critical target audience for a number of product categories such as as MTV, Pepsi, Coke, or Sony Playstation, are now playing videogames or surfing the Internet.[9] Although young people, on the average, devote four hours to media consumption, the consumption patterns are switching away from television.

Cable and Subscription Television The initial purpose of *cable television* was to improve reception in certain areas of the country, particularly mountainous regions and large cities. However, cable systems have grown rapidly because they provide highly targeted special-interest programming options. Cable is the most familiar example of **subscription television**, which means that people sign up for service and pay a monthly fee. Currently, two out of three homes subscribe to cable through traditional cable delivery

TABLE 9.2 Cable Subscribers and the Services They Select

Household Income	Premium Channels	Satellite Dish
Less than $25,000	23%	9%
$25,000–$49,999	33%	14%
$50,000–$74,999	40%	15%
$75,000 or more	44%	17%
All households average	34%	13%

Source: "I Want My MTV," *American Demographics* (March 2003): 8.

systems. Research has also determined that subscription levels increase with household income, as Table 9.2 illustrates.

Cable is also stealing ad revenue from network TV. The data show that network television had increased its ad dollars by 2.5 percent from 1998 to 2003 but cable increased 82 percent during the same five-year period. Clearly cable is a significant threat to the financial health of the networks. One reason is that cable stations have started to develop programs that get high viewership, such as *The Sopranos* on HBO. Viewing time for cable also is increasing. The average American watches cable or satellite for nearly as many hours as network TV.

Some cable stations develop and air their own programs in addition to programs initiated by other stations. Pay programming, available to subscribers for an additional monthly fee, offers movies, specials, and sports under such plans as Home Box Office, Showtime, and The Movie Channel. Pay networks do not currently sell advertising time.

Another form of subscription television is *satellite TV*. Launched in 1994, DirectTV offers the equipment, including the satellite dish, to access some 125 national and local channels. Satellite television is particularly useful for people who live in rural areas without local service.

About 8 percent of cable programming comes from independent cable networks and from independent *superstations*. These networks include Cable News Network (CNN), the Disney Channel, the Entertainment and Sports Programming Network (ESPN), and a group of independent superstations whose programs are carried by satellite to cable operators (for example, WTBS-Atlanta, WGN-Chicago, and WWOR-New York).

■ ■ ■

The highly successful show *The Sopranos* has brought new power and visibility to cable station HBO.

The two categories of cable scheduling are network and local. **Network cable** scheduling runs commercials across the entire subscriber group simultaneously. With **local cable** scheduling, advertisers can show their commercials to highly restricted geographic audiences through **interconnects**, a special cable technology that allows local or regional advertisers to run their commercials in small geographic areas through the interconnection of a number of cable systems. Interconnections offer small advertisers an affordable way to reach certain local audiences through television.

Local Television Most local television stations are affiliated with a network, as explained above, and carry both network programming and their own programs. There are also local stations called *independent stations* because they are not affiliated with a network. Costs for local advertising vary, depending on the size of the market and the demand for the programs carried. For example, a major station in Houston may charge local advertisers $2,000 for a 30-second spot during network prime time. This same time slot may cost $50 in a smaller town. The local television market is substantially more varied than the national market. Most advertisers for the local market are local retailers, primarily department stores or discount stores, financial institutions, automobile dealers, restaurants, and supermarkets. Advertisers buy time on a station-by-station basis.

National advertisers sometimes buy local advertising on a city-by-city basis, using **spot buys**. They do this to align the buy with their product distribution, to "heavy-up" a national schedule to meet competitive activities, or to launch a new product in selected cities.

Public Television   Although many people still consider public television to be commercial-free, in 1984 the FCC liberalized its rules and allowed the public broadcasting system (PBS) stations, of which there are approximately 350, some leeway in airing commercial messages, which are called **program sponsorships**. The FCC says these messages should not make a **call to action** (ask for a purchase) or make price or quality comparisons. PBS is an attractive medium for advertisers because it reaches affluent, well-educated households. It also attracts households with children as the *Sesame Street* ad demonstrates. In addition, PBS still has a refined image, and PBS advertisers are viewed as good corporate citizens because of their support for noncommercial TV.

Current FCC guidelines allow ads to appear on public television only during the local 2.5-minute program breaks. Each station maintains its own acceptability guidelines. Some PBS stations accept the same ads that appear on paid programming. However, most PBS spots are created specifically for public stations. Some PBS stations will not accept any commercial corporate advertising, but they do accept noncommercial ads that are "value neutral"—in other words, ads that make no attempt to sell a product or service.

Television programs advertise in other media in order to build their audiences. This ad for *Sesame Street* was placed in *USA Weekend*. To acknowledge PBS's reluctance to advertise, the ad also functions as a poster.

Programming Options

Different types of programming options and distribution formats are available to stations, as well as advertisers.

Specialty Television   The FCC has licensed *low-power television (LPTV)* to provide programming outlets to minorities and communities that are underserved by full-power stations. LPTV stations have signals that cover a radius of 15 miles. (*Full-power stations* reach viewers in a 70-mile radius.) Homes pull in LPTV signals through special antennas and LPTV carries advertising for local retailers and businesses. Hotels and restaurants use multipoint distribution systems (MDS) to provide guests with movies and other entertainment. Although specialty systems like these can carry ads, they are a minor delivery system.

Principle

If you want to reach an otherwise difficult-to-reach target—the well-educated, affluent household—one way to do it is to use public television program sponsorships.

Pay-per-view   This is another type of special television programming delivered by satellite. Usually used for major sporting and music events, commercial customers, such as bars, as well as home viewers subscribe for live delivery of the events without any commercials. Some experts predict that this business will increase because people who are irritated by the blizzard of commercials on regular television will change over to pay-cable and satellite channels and rely less on "free" television.[10]

Program Syndication   Independent TV and cable stations have grown to fuel the syndication boom. Table 8.1 in the previous chapter showed that syndication was one of the biggest growth areas in the media industry. Syndicated programs are television

■ ■ ■
*"Everybody Loves Raymond"
went into off-network syndication in the summer of 2001.
That means local TV stations
can purchase the program.*

programs purchased by local stations to fill time in open hours. **Off-network syndication** includes reruns of network shows, like *M*A*S*H, The Bob Newhart Show, Star Trek, ER,* and *Seinfeld.*

Seinfeld went into syndication in 1998. Each episode was sold for $6 million, meaning that the 160 episodes generated nearly $1 billion, $50 million of which went directly to Jerry Seinfeld as producer. *Everybody Loves Raymond* went into syndication during the summer of 2001, and also has been a huge success. Sometimes network shows that did not meet the minimal number of episodes, such as *Too Close for Comfort, It's A Living,* and *Rescue 911,* are purchased from the networks by syndication distributors, such as Starcom Worldwide or Viacom, and moved into syndication even as the shows' owners continue to produce new episodes. This process is called **first-run syndication**.

Interactive Television   An interactive TV set is basically a television with computer capabilities. With some systems it is possible to do everything you can do online, except that the monitor is either the TV screen or a picture-in-picture configuration that lets you watch one or more television programs while surfing the Internet. **Interactive television** development appears to be taking off, thanks to **broadband**. Simply defined, broadband has more capacity to send data and images into a home or business through a cable television wire than does the much smaller capacity of a traditional telephone wire or television antenna system.

Time Warner took the plunge into interactive television in 2000. It provided 5,000 homes in Oahu, Hawaii, with video-on-demand. By the fall of 2001, the Ocean Cable system had more than 30,000 subscribers, who each paid $52 a month. While the current system provides movies-on-demand, program blocking, and banner ads, there is the promise that features such as high-speed Web browsing, e-mail, and digital storage are on the horizon. The new medium's big advantage is that it is two-way. Audience measurement can be based on a census, not a sample. And programs that require viewers to log in can contain highly targeted messages, since the sender will know the recipient. A sponsor could theoretically "buy" a specific audience.

High-Definition TV (HDTV)   Like interactive TV, *high-definition TV (HDTV)* has been slow to build demand, although that seems to be changing. HDTV is a type of TV set that can play back movie-quality, high-resolution images. Of course, the station or network has to broadcast the program in an HDTV format. It's been a struggle getting enough programming to build demand on the consumer side. As stations upgrade their equipment, however, they are moving to HDTV and the availability of programming is now making it more desirable for consumers who are buying new TV sets. Advertisers have been watching this development and will provide HDTV ads as demand builds.

Digital Video Recorders (DVR)   Another new technology that is expected to have a profound effect on television programming and the way people watch television are *digital video recorders (DVRs).* Introduced by Replay TV and TiVo in 1999, DVR systems allow users to record favorite TV shows and watch them whenever they like. Users get a TiVo "box" and subscribe to a service that distributes programming. The revolutionary technology makes it possible to record the programming without the hassles of videotape, letting users pause, do instant replays, and begin watching programs even before the recording has finished. This is known as **time-shifting**. More than 3.5 million U.S. households had DVR technology by the end of 2003. Devoted users of DVR describe it as "life-changing."[11]

Here's the rub for advertisers: The owner need not fast-forward through a commercial because the viewer can set the recording to program out commercials as the shows are recorded. TiVo is a substantial threat to marketers because it allows consumers to skip commercials completely. Advertisers are alarmed over the increasing popularity of the technology, as are television executives. It calls into question audience measurement numbers: If 20 percent of the audience is recording *West Wing* on Wednesday night only to watch it Saturday morning commercial-free, then is the Wednesday night measurement accurate?

It also raises the issue of how advertisers should respond. Should they seek legislation to block such technology? After all, ads are what keep television (relatively) free, at least on network TV. Or should they seek new ways to send messages? Coca-Cola, for example, has created ads that appear on screen when a DVR user pauses a program for a few minutes.

Television Advertising

Television is used for advertising because it works like the movies: It tells stories, engages the emotions, creates fantasies, and can have great visual impact. Because it's an action medium, it is also good for demonstrating how things work. It brings brand images to life and adds personality to a brand.

Forms of Television Advertising   The actual form of a television commercial depends on whether a network, local, or cable schedule is used, as we see in Figure 9.3. Networks allow sponsorships, participations, and spot announcements through their affiliates. In turn, local affiliates allow local sponsorships, spot announcements, and national spots. Cable systems allow system (national) spots and local spots. Finally, interactive television allows (national) spots and local spots.

Sponsorships   In program **sponsorships**, the advertiser assumes the total financial responsibility for producing the program and providing the accompanying commercials. The *Hallmark Hall of Fame* is an example of a sponsored program. Sponsorship can have a powerful effect on the viewing public, especially because the advertiser can control the content and quality of the program as well as the placement and length of commercials.

DVR technology poses a challenge for advertisers since it enables consumers to bypass commercials.

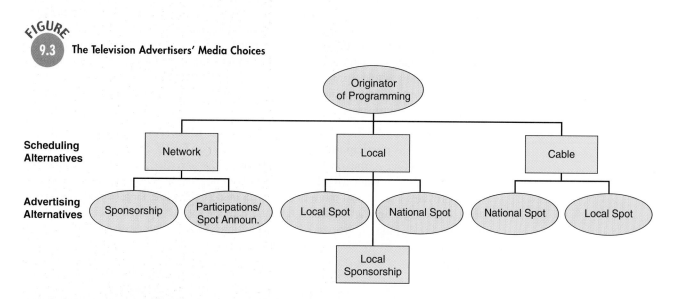

FIGURE 9.3   The Television Advertisers' Media Choices

A MATTER OF PRACTICE
Starbucks Makes TV Less Intrusive

Starbucks coffee is now sold in grocery stores but how many people realize it? To get that message out, the well-known coffee house chain needed to reach its customers nationwide with that message.

Television commercials would be the obvious way to reach those people, but Starbucks' management knew that their customers are not big fans of television commercials and resent the interruption of their favorite program. That's why Starbucks has been such an infrequent advertiser on TV. Its on-air promotional activities have been limited primarily to radio and its only previous use of TV had been support announcements on public TV.

That was the problem facing Starcom's MediaVest group. The agency used a creative solution: It recommended a partnership with the Bravo cable network. Bravo would run four Independent Film Channel (IFC) movies on Friday nights for a month and Starbucks would buy all the commercial time surrounding the movie airings.

The MediaVest team knew that Bravo's "IFC Friday" night films would be a good way to reach the stakeholder audience because research had described that customer base as people who are up on the latest trends, like to attend live performances of the arts, are apt to see a movie during the weekend it opens, and generally are interested in cutting-edge things. MediaVest calls this customer "the attuned explorer."

Even though Starbucks bought all the commercial time, the MediaVest team recommended letting the movies run uninterrupted. Starbucks' advertising message was delivered in supporting Bravo promotions of the movies during each week leading up to the Friday night telecast. About 40 seconds of each 60-second preview spot showed scenes from the movie and 20 seconds promoted Starbucks as the movie sponsor.

Other promotional activities were also used in support of the campaign. One month before the movies aired, a $1-off coupon for a bag of Starbucks Coffee was sent to 3 million targeted consumers around the country, along with a viewer guide introducing the Starbucks-sponsored independent movie festival.

Starbucks billboards also appeared during the movie month coinciding with the Independent Spirit Awards, the independent film industry's annual telecast, which aired on both Bravo and IFC.

The innovative Bravo partnership wound up not only increasing sales of Starbucks Coffee by 15 percent for the month the campaign ran, but also increased viewership on Bravo by 33 percent. These results led the campaign to be named a Media Plan of the Year by *Adweek* magazine.

Consider This

1. What was the problem Starbucks wanted to overcome in order to effectively advertise that its coffee brand was available in supermarkets?
2. How did the partnership work? Is there anything you could recommend that would extend the reach of this campaign?

Source: John Consoli, "MediaVest Media Plan of the Year: Best Use of Cable TV," *Adweek Media Plan of the Year Special Report* (June 17, 2002): SR18–20; "EyeballNYC's Packages 'IFC'," January 2003 Friday's on Bravo," May 2002, www.eyeballnyc.com/recentwork/archive_index.html; Eugene Hernandez, "The IFC? Sundance Channel?—It's Up to You New York, New York," indieWIRE (July 2002),

Principle

If you are going to use television, design a message that takes advantage of its visual and emotional impact.

However, the costs of producing and sponsoring a 30- or 60-minute program make this option too expensive for most advertisers. Several advertisers can produce a program jointly as an alternative to single sponsorship. This plan is quite common with sporting events, where each sponsor receives a 15-minute segment. The Starbucks story in the Matter of Practice box explains another way to maximize TV sponsorship opportunities, while addressing a television problem. In order to make television commercials more effective, advertisers must connect with people in ways they appreciate—and that often means being less intrusive.

Participations   Sponsorships represent less than 10 percent of network advertising. The rest is sold as **participations**, where advertisers pay for 10, 15, 20, 30, or 60 seconds of commercial time during one or more programs. The advertiser can buy any time that is available. This approach, which is the most common one used in network advertising today, provides a great deal more flexibility in market coverage, target audiences, scheduling, and budgeting. Participations do not create the same high impact as sponsorships, however. Finally, the *"time avails"* (available time slots) for the most popular programs are often bought up by the largest advertisers, leaving fewer good time slots for small advertisers.

TABLE
9.3 | **Standard Television Dayparts**

Early morning	M–F 7:00 A.M.–9:00 A.M.
Daytime	M–F 9:00 A.M.–4:30 P.M.
Early fringe	M–F 4:30 P.M.–7:30 P.M.
Prime access	M–F 7:30 P.M.–8:00 P.M.
Prime time	M–Sa 8:00 P.M.–11:00 P.M.
	Su 7:00 P.M.–11:00 P.M.
Late news	M–Su 11:00 P.M.–11:30 P.M.
Late night	M–Su 11:30 P.M.–1:00 A.M.
Saturday morning	Sa 8:00 A.M.–1:00 P.M.
Weekend afternoon	Sa–Su 1:00 P.M.–7:00 P.M.

Note: All times are Eastern Standard Time (EST).

Spot Announcements   The third form a television commercial can take is the **spot announcement**. (Note that the word *spot* is also used in conjunction with a time frame, such as a 30-second spot, but don't confuse those with spot announcements.) Spot announcements are commercials that appear in the breaks between programs, which local affiliates sell to advertisers who want to show their ads locally. Commercials are sold on a station-by-station basis to local, regional, and national advertisers. However, local buyers dominate spot television. The commercial breaks between programs are not always the best time slots for advertisers because there is a great deal of clutter from competing commercials, station breaks, and public service announcements. Commercial breaks also tend to be the time when viewers take a break from their television sets.

The price of a spot or set of spots is based on the rating of the surrounding program (note the rating is for the program, not the commercial) and the daypart during which the commercial is shown. Table 9.3 shows the Television Standard Dayparts. The most expensive time block is prime time.

The Television Audience

Television has become a mainstay of American society, with 98 percent of American households having one or more television sets, although this audience is highly fragmented, tuning in to a hundred or more different channels in the United States. A great number of advertisers consider television their primary medium. Can television deliver a target audience to advertisers effectively? What do we really know about how audiences watch television? Is it a background distraction? Do we switch from channel to channel without watching any single show? Or do we carefully and intelligently select what we watch on television? Television viewers are often irritated by what they see, particularly the advertising, and are not reluctant to switch channels, zip through commercials, or avoid them altogether using TiVo. Clutter is part of the problem and the audience has become very good at avoidance, unless the ads are highly engaging.

Measuring the Television Audience   Several independent rating firms periodically sample a portion of the television viewing audience, assess the size and characteristics of the audiences watching specific shows, and then make these data available (for a fee) to advertisers and ad agencies, who use them in their media planning. Currently, A. C. Nielsen dominates this industry and provides the most commonly used measure of national and local television audiences.

Nielsen measures television audiences at two levels: *network* and *spot*. Nielsen uses two measuring devices for local measurement, one of which is the **audiometer**. This instrument records when the TV set is used and which station it is tuned to, but it cannot identify who is watching the program. The second measurement device is the *viewing diary,* which provides data on who is watching which shows. Diaries are mailed each week during survey months to sample homes in each of the 211 television markets, amounting to approximately 1 million diaries returned per year.

Ratings   When you read about a television show having a rating of 20.0 that means that 20 percent, or one-fifth of all the households with television, were tuned in to that program. Note: One rating point equals 1 percent of the national's estimated 1,084,000 TV homes; that's why planners describe this program as having 20 **rating points**, or percentage points. A 20 rating is actually a huge figure, since the fragmentation of cable has diversified television watching and made it very difficult to get 20 percent of the households tuned to any one program. It's also a bit misleading, since media planners are more concerned about the number of people watching rather than merely the number of households with televisions turned on, the HUT estimate.

Share   A better estimate of impressions might be found in a program's **share of audience**, which refers to the percentage of viewers based on the number of sets turned on. The share figure is always larger than the rating, since the base is smaller. For example a Super Bowl might get a rating of 40 (40 percent of all households with television) but its share might be 70 (70 percent of all televisions turned on were tuned to the Super Bowl). As this was written the 2000 Super Bowl held the ratings record with a 43.3 rating. In 2004, the game was seen by 143.6 million viewers and recorded a rating of 41.3, which was the percentage of the 1.084 million TV homes with sets on.[12]

To illustrate how the concepts of viewers, ratings, and share are calculated for use by media planners, consider the data in Table 9.4. This Nielsen data are for a few of the programs shown on one Tuesday evening at 8:00 and 9:00 in December in 2003. Note how the share figure is larger than the rating.

Gross Rating Points   The sum of the total exposure potential (i.e., total ratings) expressed as a percentage of the audience population is called **gross rating points (GRPs)**. GRPs are calculated by dividing the total number of impressions by the size of the audience and multiplying by 100. GRPs are used by media planners to compare the impact of various alternative media schedules.

To demonstrate GRP calculations, consider a program as having 100,000 viewer impressions. Suppose there were a total of 500,000 possible viewers (total number of households with televisions, whether the sets are on or off) at that hour. The 100,000 viewers watching the show out of the possible 500,000 would represent 20 percent of viewers,

TABLE 9.4   Viewers, Ratings, and Share Data

	Viewers (in millions)	Rating (HH)	Share (HH)
8:00			
8 Simple Rules (ABC)	9.4	6.0	11
Tracy Morgan Show (NBC)	7.0	4.3	8
That '70s Show (Fox)	6.5	4.0	7
A Home for the Holidays (CBS)	6.2	4.1	7
One on One (UPN)	3.0	1.9	3
Gilmore Girls (WB)	2.9	1.9	3
9:00			
According to Jim (ABC)	9.4	5.6	10
Frasier (NBC)	7.6	4.9	8
American Idol Christmas (Fox)	7.3	4.4	8
The Guardian (CBS)	6.4	4.0	7
Rock Me Baby (UPN)	2.2	1.3	2

Source: Adapted from "Nielsen Ratings," USA Today (December 31, 2003): 4D.

or a 20.0 rating. The gross rating point total for four telecasts would be 80 (20 rating × 4 telecasts). Planners can use the sum of rating points to calculate the total gross rating points for any schedule, whether actual or proposed.

People Meters   In 1987 Nielsen Media Research began to measure not only what is being watched but who is watching which shows nationally. It replaced its audiometer and supplemented the diary system with 5,000 **people meters**, which record what television shows are being watched, the number of households that are watching, and which family members are viewing. The recording is done automatically; household members indicate their presence by pressing a button.

Nielsen continues to add people meters in its top markets to track local viewing patterns. Currently, people meters determine audience demographics on only a national basis. On a local basis meters are used only to determine what show is being watched, and not the specific demographics of who is watching it. Instead diaries are relied on. The new locally based meter system will also allow Nielsen to identify the age, race, and gender of viewers on a nightly basis, which is a significant improvement over the old measuring system, and it will make the viewing audience measurements more reliable at the local level.[13]

Advantages of Advertising on Television

Television has three key advantages.

- *Pervasiveness.* Television is in almost every home and some homes have televisions in almost every room. Furthermore, these televisions are turned on for a great part of the day. Consequently television can have an influence on the kinds of topics we think about, the fashions we wear, the homes we live in, and the way we raise our kids. This social impact was discussed in Chapter 3.
- *Cost-Efficiency.* Many advertisers view television as the most cost-effective way to deliver a mass-media message because it has such a wide reach. Even though a television buy is expensive in sheer dollars, this mass coverage can be extremely cost-efficient because the costs are spread across so many viewers. For an advertiser attempting to reach an undifferentiated market, a 30-second spot on a top-rated show may cost a penny or less for each person reached.
- *Impact.* Television makes a strong impact. The interaction of sight, sound, color, motion, and drama creates a strong emotional response. Television is also good for delivering demonstrations and dramas, as the Inside Story illustrates, showing how it is easier for people to buy their own home.

Principle
Network television is an expensive medium, but because of its traditionally high reach to a mass audience it is considered cost-efficient.

Disadvantages of Television Advertising

Despite the effectiveness of television advertising, it has four problems: the cost of production, clutter, nonselective targeting, and inflexibility.

- *Production Costs.* The most serious limitation of television advertising is the extremely high cost of producing and running commercials. Although the cost per person reached can be relatively low, the absolute cost can be restrictive, especially for small and even midsize companies. Production costs include filming the commercial (several thousand to several hundred thousand dollars) and paying the talent—writers, directors, and actors. For celebrities, the price tag can be millions of dollars. Media time for 30-second prime-time spot averages about $185,000. Special shows, such as the Super Bowl, World Series, or Academy Awards, charge much more. Table 9.5 shows the ad rates for the top TV shows from 1980 to 2004. The 2004 Super Bowl charged $2.25 million for 30-second commercial, which was a new record. For that charge, advertisers had the opportunity to reach an estimated 131.7 million viewers.
- *Clutter.* Television suffers from commercial clutter. In the past, the National Association of Broadcasters (NAB) restricted the allowable commercial time per hour to approximately six minutes, but the Justice Department overturned this restriction and the number of commercials has increased. As the number of commercials increases, the visibility and persuasiveness of television advertising diminishes.

THE INSIDE STORY
Selling a Political Party with Humor

Ingvi Logason, Principal, HÉR&NÚ, Reykjavik, Iceland

Advertising for political parties in an election campaign process is one of the most challenging assignments in the advertising business. The window of opportunity is very narrow; the competition is far more fierce and ruthless than in any consumer category; and the media is saturated with political ads making it hard to stand out. That's true in the U.S. political arena, but it's also true in elections in other countries as well.

That job befell the HÉR&NÚ agency (in close cooperation with SagaFilm and Dixil) for the Icelandic parliamentary election in 2003 (in Iceland there is a multiparty system where usually two parties join in an alliance to form the government). The campaign for the Framsokn political party was hugely successful and won a gold EFFIE award in 2003, which is highly unusual for political commercials.

Framsokn, historically one of the three largest political parties in Iceland, found itself in a downward spiral in popularity for the parliamentary election in 2003. According to research, the party's image was old, "heavy," negatively conservative, rural, and out of sync with what the true party was. Even though it had been a successful government for 12 years running, it received no credit for the positive economic and social changes in the country. Opinion polls showed that the party registered an all-time low in among voters.

Furthermore, Framsokn received more negative publicity and had more negative stories written and broadcasted about it than any other Icelandic political party. To make matters worse, the party was in the forefront of various unpopular issues supported by the government such as industrial and environmental issues and supporting the invasion of Iraq.

The objective as defined by HÉR&NÚ marketing communication was to correct the image problem, inspire voters with a vote of confidence in the party, aim for 17 percent of voters' support (up from 10 percent), and obtain an increased number of seats in parliament.

So what do you do to completely turn around the voters' image of a political party?

You do humor with a serious selling point. You do "product advertising" for a political race and you support it with a top-notch communication program. And you use engaging television ads.

The agency's mission was to break the mold of political advertising with a new, fresh approach to politics: Political ads don't have to be boring, serious, and "gloomy." With a fully integrated, multilayered campaign, we took more of a "consumer advertising" approach. All advertisement had to pass the "what's in it for me" test and have a strong selling point.

Analysis of the party's research resulted in a targeting strategy based more on lifestyle than demographics. The objective was skewed to acquiring new voters from the ranks of young people and women, at the same time holding on to existing followers.

One of the strategic decisions was to focus on TV advertising as the cornerstone of the campaign because of its ability to reach a broad target audience, as well as to deliver the image message and resonate in a gently humorous way with the concerns of voters. TV counted for 65 percent of the media budget.

Not only was the party a winner, the campaign was recognized as having turned around the party's image and as the best political campaign that year—and possibly ever in Iceland.

Source: Contributed by Ingvi Logason, principal in HÉR&NÚ Marketing Communications. A graduate of Western Florida University, his work was nominated by Professor Tom Groth.

<table>
<tr><td colspan="2">**TABLE 9.5   Time Is Money: The Top Shows by Ad Rates**</td></tr>
<tr><td>2004</td><td>$/:30</td></tr>
<tr><td>*Friends*</td><td>$473,500</td></tr>
<tr><td>*Will & Grace*</td><td>$414,500</td></tr>
<tr><td>2001</td><td>$/:30</td></tr>
<tr><td>*ER*</td><td>$425,400</td></tr>
<tr><td>*Friends*</td><td>$353,600</td></tr>
<tr><td>1998</td><td>$/:30</td></tr>
<tr><td>*Seinfeld*</td><td>$575,000</td></tr>
<tr><td>*ER*</td><td>$560,000</td></tr>
<tr><td>1992</td><td>$/:30</td></tr>
<tr><td>*Murphy Brown*</td><td>$310,000</td></tr>
<tr><td>*Roseanne*</td><td>$290,000</td></tr>
<tr><td>1987</td><td>$/:30</td></tr>
<tr><td>*The Cosby Show*</td><td>$369,500</td></tr>
<tr><td>*Cheers*</td><td>$307,000</td></tr>
<tr><td>1980</td><td>$/:30</td></tr>
<tr><td>*M*A*S*H*</td><td>$150,000</td></tr>
<tr><td>*Dallas*</td><td>$145,000</td></tr>
</table>

Sources: Joe Mandese, "The Buying and Selling," *Advertising Age* (Spring 1995): 20; "Top 10 Shows by Ad Rates," *Advertising Age* (September 15, 1997): S2.

- *Wasted Reach.* Television advertising includes a great deal of **wasted reach**: communication directed at an unresponsive (and often uninterested) audience that may not fit the advertiser's target market characteristics. Cable television is much more targeted than network and spot television, so it has less waste.
- *Inflexibility.* Most network television is bought in the spring and early summer for the next fall season. If an advertiser is unable to make this up-front buy, only limited time slots remain available. Also, it is difficult to make last-minute adjustments in copy and visuals. Production of a TV commercial takes weeks for local spots and sometimes months for national network commercials.
- *Intrusiveness.* Television commercials intrude into the programs and are therefore more irritating than other forms of advertising. The high irritation level is what has led viewers to mute and zap commercials and use DVRs that make it possible to eliminate the advertising altogether.

Principle
As the number of commercials increases, the visibility and persuasiveness of television advertising diminishes.

Changes and Trends in Broadcast Television

New forms of television advertising are increasing with sponsorships, product placements, and advertiser-controlled programming. Wieden & Kennedy, the agency for Nike, is actively developing itself into an entertainment company with the goal to make its client a content provider on television, rather than just an advertiser or sponsor. Similarly in London, the MindShare media unit of advertising conglomerate WPP is developing shows for its clients. With clutter and the rising cost of network TV, media and advertising planners are finding that they need to offer clients a very different way of marketing brands.[14]

Second, the telecommunication industry and the cable industry are battling over who will control digital TV technology. Digitization (the transfer of analog pictures, text, and video into a series of ones and zeros) will allow information to flow into households just as electricity does today. As a result, tomorrow's viewers may see only what they want to see. Switching channels will be a thing of the past because TVs will be programmed to send only programs preselected by the viewer. The question is then which medium (telephone or cable) is better able to deliver this new technology.

The implications of these changes for the media planner are significant. Most notably, the advantage of traditional network television to deliver a message to a mass audience is quickly disappearing. Instead, television is becoming an increasingly fragmented medium, which means that reaching a mass audience will be increasingly difficult.

Consider This

1. How are television audiences measured?
2. From a strategic viewpoint, when would you be inclined to include television in a media plan?

FILM AND VIDEO

The Cinema Advertising Council (CAC) is an organization devoted to advertising in movies. This ad was placed in *Advertising Age* to reach media buyers and remind them of the power of cinema advertising to reach moviegoers.

Movie theaters, particularly the large chain theaters, sell time at the beginning of their film showings for commercials, called **trailers** that are movie previews. Most of these trailers are advertising upcoming films, but some are national commercials for brands or local commercials for local businesses. These ads can be targeted to a certain extent by the nature of the film and the rating, such as G or PG. Some films, such as *The Calendar Girls,* drew an audience that was heavily female, while other action films, such as the *Matrix* series, draws more males. The cost of the trailer is based on the number of theaters showing the spot and their estimated monthly attendance. Generally the cost of a trailer in a first-run theater is about the same as the cost of a 30-second television spot in prime time

Videocasette and DVD distributors are also placing ads before their movies, as well as on the packaging cases. The targeting strategy is the same as that for theater ads where the ad is matched to the movie audience. Unlike the theaters, rental videos tend to carry more brand advertising than movie previews. Even some billboards are now equipped to run minimovies and ads electronically. The job-search company Monster.com has been successful with trailers that replay as electronic signboard messages.

There are also promotional video networks that run programs and commercials, such as the channels you see in grocery stores, doctor's offices, and truck stops that distribute commercials by video or satellites. The Kmart in-store channel, for example, is sent by satellite to 2,300 stores.[15]

Advantages and Disadvantages of Movie Advertising

The reason trailers are valued by advertisers is that they play to a captive audience, one that is not able to do other things, like read or talk to other people. The attention level is higher for these ads than for almost any other form of commercials. But the captive-audience dimension is

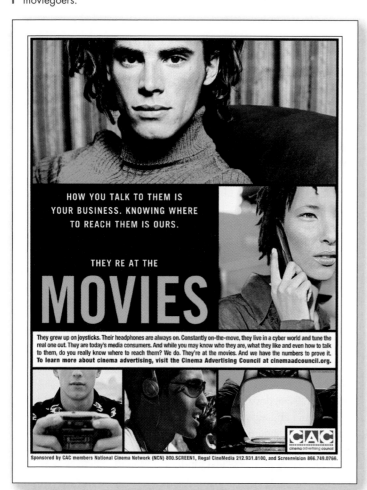

HOW YOU TALK TO THEM IS YOUR BUSINESS. KNOWING WHERE TO REACH THEM IS OURS.

THEY'RE AT THE

MOVIES

They grew up on joysticks. Their headphones are always on. Constantly on-the-move, they live in a cyber world and tune the real one out. They're today's media consumers. And while you may know who they are, what they like and even how to talk to them, do you really know where to reach them? We do. They're at the movies. And we have the numbers to prove it. To learn more about cinema advertising, visit the Cinema Advertising Council at cinemaadcouncil.org.

CAC
cinema advertising council

Sponsored by CAC members National Cinema Network (NCN) 800.SCREEN1, Regal CineMedia 212.931.8100, and Screenvision 866.749.0766.

also the biggest disadvantage of movie advertising because people who have paid $6–$10 for a ticket resent the intrusion. They feel they paid for the ticket so they shouldn't have to pay with their time and attention to watch commercials.

PRODUCT PLACEMENT

What was the company that was featured in the Tom Hanks's, movie *Castaway*? In that story, as you may remember, Hanks played a Federal Express deliveryman who wound up on a desert island and ultimately, after his rescue, delivers the package. Some movie critics joked that the whole movie was really a FedEx commercial. In fact, it's a good example of a practice known as **product placement**, in which a company pays to have verbal or visual brand exposure in a movie or television program.

Product placement is becoming popular because it isn't as intrusive as conventional advertising and audiences can't zap the ads, as they can for television advertising using the remote control or a DVR like TiVo. At the same time, it makes the product a star.[16] Sometimes the product placement is subtle, as when a particular brand of aspirin is shown in a medicine chest or a character drinks a particular brand of beverage. In other cases, like FedEx, the brand is front and center. That happened with the prominent role of BMW Z28, which became a star in the James Bond movie *The World Is Not Enough*. The movie placement, in fact, was the car's launch vehicle.

Television programs have also gotten into the product placement game. An example is the use of well-known stores and products in the Fab Five makeover series, *A Queer Eye for the Straight Guy*. Both the Coca-Cola brand and the Ford Motor brand have been embedded into the successful talent show *American Idol*. And the Target bull's-eye is frequently seen as part of the action sets and props on *Survivor*.

Advantages and Disadvantages of Product Placements

The greatest advantage of product placement is that it demonstrates product use in a natural setting ("natural" depending upon the movie) by people who are celebrities. It's also unexpected and catches the audience when their resistance to advertising messages may be dialed down. It's also good for engaging the affections of other stakeholders, such as employees and dealers, particularly if the placement is supported with its own campaign.

The biggest problem is that the placement may not be noticed. There is so much going on in most movies that you need to call attention to the product in order for its appearance to register. A more serious problem occurs when there is not a match between the product and the movie or its audience. But equally serious is the problem that the success or failure of a movie is not known when the contract for the placement is being negotiated. If the movie is a dud, what does that do to the brand's image?

Consider This

1. What are the opportunities for advertising using movies?
2. From a strategic viewpoint, when would you be inclined to include product placement in a media plan?

USING BROADCAST ADVERTISING EFFECTIVELY

Now that we have reviewed television and radio media and their strengths and weaknesses, we can now determine how to use broadcast media effectively. The Practical Tips box provides guidelines for broadcast media decisions.

Practical Tips

When to Use Broadcast Media for Advertising

Use radio if . . .	*Use television* if . . .	*Use movie ads* if . . .	*Use placement* if . . .
You are a local business	You want to reach a wider mass audience	You are advertising a national brand and have the budget to do high-quality commercials	You want your brand to be associated with the movie's story and stars
You need a highly targeted local audience	Your audience's interests align with a certain type of cable television program	You want your brand to be associated with the movie's story and stars	The people in the audience match your brand's target audience
You have a relatively small advertising budget	You have a relatively good advertising budget	The people in the audience match your brand's target audience	There is a natural fit between the product and the movie's storyline
You want to build frequency	You have a product that needs both sight and sound, such as an emotional message, a demonstration, or a drama	Your commercial has enough visual impact and quality production that it will look good next to the movie previews	There is an opportunity for the brand to be a star
You know the timing when your audience is considering the purchase	You want to prove something so the audience can see it with their own eyes		The placement will appeal to the brand's stakeholders
Your audience's interests align with certain types of music, advice programs, or talk shows	You want the halo effect of a big TV ad to impress other stakeholders, such as dealers and franchisees		You have the budget for a campaign to support the placement
You have a personal message that uses the power of the human voice	You need to create or reinforce brand image and personality		
You have a message that works well in a musical form or one that is strong in mental imagery			
You need a reminder message			

IT'S A WRAP

USING TV TO DEMONSTRATE CONVENIENCE

■ ■ ■

Throughout this chapter we have described the benefits and problems attached to the two primary broadcast media: television and radio. One of the most prominent drawbacks is the actual cost of producing and sending broadcast advertising. In the case of drugstore.com, the company spent far less on its television-based campaign compared to what its competitors spent on advertising at the same time. Yet, the company's objectives were quite ambitious and readily met because the media buy made it possible to effectively reach the relatively broad target audience of women.

In the case of each goal outlined in the EFFIE brief, drugstore.com reached or exceeded its goals. In fact, the majority of the goals were reached within six months. With the help of the campaign, drugstore.com increased brand awareness in the various target markets and average weekly visits to the site increased from the previous year. The most satisfying surprise was the leap in the number of consumers who perceived the site as a convenient place to shop for their drugstore items.

Convenience is definitely one of the site's strengths. In addition to winning a Gold EFFIE, drugstore.com was also recognized in 2004 as having the best site search experience by the prestigious Jupiter Research, an Internet research company. Also in 2004, drugstore.com partnered with electronic commerce and payment leader First Data Corp. to create a more simplified shopping and bill-paying process.

Most importantly, however, drugstore.com survived in terrible economic times, led the industry in innovation, educated its customers about online shopping and health care products, and provided a convenient way to shop for drugstore and personal-care products.

▪▪▪ Summary

1. **Describe the structure of radio, how it is organized, its use as an advertising medium, its audience, and the advantages and disadvantages of radio advertising.** The traditional radio stations are found on the AM/FM dial and serve a primarily local market, but that's only the beginning of the radio listener's options, which also include public radio, cable and satellite radio, low-powered stations, and Web radio. It is used primarily to reach a local audience. Listeners can have a very intimate relationship with radio and can be quite loyal to their favorite stations, but radio also serves as background.

2. **Explain the structure of television, how it is organized, its use as an advertising medium, the TV audience, and the advantages and disadvantages of TV advertising.** The key types of television delivery systems are: wired and unwired network, local stations, public stations, cable, and subscription. Specialty, syndicated, interactive television, and TiVo offer ways to manipulate the programming. Television is useful as an advertising medium because it works like a movie with story, action, emotions, and visual

impact. TV audiences are fragmented and often irritated by advertising and prone to avoidance. Audiences are measured in terms of ratings share and gross rating points. TV's greatest advantage is that it is pervasive and cost-efficient when reaching a large number of viewers. Because of the special-interest aspect of cable programming, it is also becoming good at reaching more narrow target audiences.

3. **Outline how advertisers use of film and video.** Movie theaters sell time for advertisements before their films. Advertising is also carried on videocassettes and DVDs, as well as in the lobbies. Video-generated commercials can also be seen in other environments, such as in supermarkets, transit stations, and waiting rooms for professional services such as in doctor's offices.

4. **Identify advantages and disadvantages of using product placements.** Product placement, which shows a product embedded in a movie or TV program, is popular because it isn't as intrusive as conventional advertising.

▪▪▪ Key Terms

audiometer, 257
broadband, 254
broadcast media, 243
call to action, 253
coverage, 247
dayparts, 247
first-run syndication, 254
gross rating points (GRPs), 258
interactive television, 254

interconnects, 252
jingles, 244
local cable, 252
low-power FM (LPFM), 244
morning drive time, 247
network, 250
network cable, 252
network radio, 246
off-network syndication, 254
participations, 256

people meters, 259
prime-time, 250
product placement, 263
program sponsorships, 253
rating points, 258
ratings, 247
share of audience, 258
signals, 243
sponsorship, 255
spot announcement, 257

spot buy, 253
spot radio advertising, 246
subscription television, 251
syndication, 246
time-shifting, 254
trailer, 262
wasted reach, 261
Webcasting, 244

▪▪▪ Review Questions

1. What are the advantages and disadvantages of advertising on radio?

2. What are the four types of television delivery systems, and how are they different?

3. In what ways are film and video used by advertising (other than TV commercials)?

4. What is product placement, and why has it become popular as an advertising medium?

▪▪▪ Discussion Questions

1. You are a major agency media director who has just finished a presentation to a prospective client in convenience food marketing. During the Q-and-A period a client representative says: "We know that network television viewers' loyalty is nothing like it was 10 or even 5 years ago because so many people now turn to cable and VCRs. There are smaller audiences per program each year, yet television-time costs continue to rise. Do you still believe we should consider commercial television as a primary medium for our company's advertising?" How would you answer?

2. Message clutter affects both radio and television advertising. Advertisers fear that audiences react to long commercial groupings by using the remote control for the television set or the tuner on the radio to steer to a different channel. Some have proposed that advertisers should absorb higher time costs to reduce the frequency and length of commercial interruptions. Others argue that broadcasting should reduce the number of commercials sold and also reduce program advertising even if it means less profit for broadcasters. Which of these remedies would be better?

3. You are the media planner for a cosmetics company introducing a new line of makeup for teenage girls. Your research indicates that television advertising will be an effective medium for creating awareness about your new product line. How do you design a television advertising strategy that will reach your target market successfully? What stations do you choose? Why? What programs and times do you choose? Why? Do you consider syndicated television? Why or why not? What advertising forms do you use and why?

▪▪▪ Class Projects

1. Each student should make a chart for five radio stations. List the type of station (easy listening, top 40, classical, and so on), the products commonly advertised, and the probable target markets for these products. Note the time of the day these products are advertised. Now put all of the products in a hat and, in teams of three, have each team draw one out. Each team is now responsible for choosing the radio stations for its product. Each team needs to allocate a budget of $2,500 among the five stations for a week's worth of programming. Assume 30 seconds of air time costs $250. Have the teams present their work and as a class compare the different patterns of radio use.

2. Examine the various ads found on www.nike.com, www.IBM.com, and www.Sears.com. Which ads did you find most appealing? engaging? motivating? Which ones do you think could easily be used as television commercials? as radio commercials? Write a one- to two-page report on your assessment.

HANDS-ON

Will Radio Listeners Finally Get Sirius with Howard Stern?

There has been no shortage of excitement for communications company Sirius during its short history. Sirius is trying to change the way people listen to radio by convincing them to pay a monthly fee (around $13) for almost 200 channels of radio, much of it commercial free. But Sirius is not alone in the satellite radio business, and the first two years of competition have largely favored competitor XM Satellite Radio Holdings Inc., which claims 2.5 million subscribers to Sirius's 600,000. In 2003 Sirius almost went under before finding investors willing to help the company pay off its substantial debt. And from 2000 to 2004 shares of Sirius stock fell from a high of $66.50 to under $5.

Sirius is hardly out of the picture, however. It has inked partnerships with DaimlerChrysler and Ford to offer satellite radio as an option for new car models. In 2004 the company announced it would pay close to $200 million for the rights to carry NFL football telecasts. And in possibly its biggest move to date, Sirius announced that in January 2006 radio personality Howard Stern would leave the radio airwaves and bring his program to Sirius.

The signing is an audacious gamble for Sirius. The original "shock jock," Howard Stern describes himself somewhat tongue-in-cheek as the "King of Media." His daily audience of close to 8 million loyal listeners attracts enough advertising to bring current employer Viacom between $80 and 90 million in ad revenue annually. So Sirius knew the bidding would be high, and the deal with Stern is expected to cost it up to half a billion dollars over five years.

Sirius executives say that for the deal to be profitable Stern must bring 1 million new subscribers to the network. Can such a large number of people, who currently listen to the show for nothing on inexpensive radios, be convinced to pay a monthly fee and buy equipment that can cost a couple of hundred dollars? Sirius claims their research shows an even greater number of Stern's current audience will follow him to satellite when his contract with Viacom expires. And that may happen sooner rather than later. Stern has used his morning show to announce the "end of broadcast radio," and suggests that Sirius may buy out the remainder of his Viacom contract.

Former Viacom executive and Stern fan Mel Karmazin thinks attracting talent like Stern is just what satellite radio should do. Karmazin points to Fox's expensive acquisition of the rights to broadcast NFL games as the moment it became a major network. But even if Stern brings listeners to Sirius, the deal is not without risk. Stern's raunchy show received unwanted attention from the FCC when it fined Viacom for broadcast indecency. The move to largely unregulated satellite will bring less federal scrutiny, but it may raise the ante for Stern to push the limits of taste even further. And XM, with its larger subscriber base, is still in the picture. Shortly after the Stern signing, XM announced it had acquired the rights to broadcast Major League Baseball games beginning in summer 2005.

Consider This

1. Stern is one of the highest-paid and highest-profile entertainers in radio. What are the implications of his signing for Sirius and for satellite radio in general? Has the signing meant that satellite radio has entered a new phase in its development?

2. Assume Stern does bring in excess of a million new listeners to Sirius. Can you think of other ways that the deal might still be risky for Sirius? For Stern?

3. Cable television changed the face of television broadcasting. In your opinion, does satellite radio offer the same possibility for the radio industry? How would you determine its effectiveness?

Sources: Krysten Crawford, "Howard Stern: I May Be Out Soon," CNN/*Money*, November 11, 2004; Emmanuel Legrand, "The World According to Karmazin," *Billboard* (November 10, 2004); Jube Shiver, "With Howard Stern, Sirius Hopes to Make Waves," *Los Angeles Times* (October 10, 2004).

Manual. Automatic.

Whatever it is you're looking for, do it eBay.

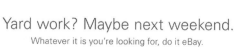

Yard work? Maybe next weekend.

Whatever it is you're looking for, do it eBay.

You can't stop time. But you sure can try.

Whatever it is you're looking for, do it eBay.

Interactive and Alternative Media

eBay Reinvents the Marketplace

Award:
Number 2 on Business 20's "Fastest Growing Companies"

Company:
eBay

Agency:
Goodby, Silverstein & Partners

Campaign:
"Do it eBay"

KEY POINTS

After reading this chapter, you will be able to:

1. Determine the difference between interactive media and more conventional mainstream media.

2. Explain how the Internet works as a business and as marketing communication.

3. Discuss how Internet advertising works.

4. Describe how e-mail advertising works.

5. Show how the different forms of interactive and alternative new media are changing the way advertising works.

eBay® is more than just a dot-com auction. The powerhouse Web merchant has become the world's largest online marketplace—a worldwide bazaar of individual buyers and sellers—and it has invented a new form of doing business. There are no shops, no booths, no displays, just a phone line and a computer screen.

It started as an online flea market or garage sale—a way to clean out garages, basements, and attics. Then it began attracting collectors looking for a specific brand or item, such as Zippo lighters, Pez dispensers, antique toys, Beanie Babies, cigar boxes, or Star Trek memorabilia.

eBay began its business in 1995 through word of mouth and didn't start advertising until 2002. In total contradiction to the free-spending glory days of the dot-com boom when e-businesses were throwing money at big-budget advertising media such as the Super

269

Bowl, eBay built its business from the ground up through the testimonies of its passionate users.

Using a campy rewrite of the Sinatra standard, "My Way," the company began its television advertising with a brand-building effort. The "Do It eBay" commercials feature a balding Sinatra look-alike belting out an eBay version of the song as he dances through various scenes and croons funny lines about mainstream retailers.

The objective was to move eBay from being seen as an online flea market to a broad-based Web marketplace. The campaign also was designed to remind users of the entertainment value of eBay, what the company calls "the gaming aspect of it." This campaign's budget of $51.3 million wasn't a big effort when compared to the company's extensive press coverage. A little more than half—$28 million—went to magazines and another $15 million to television.

Even eBay's approach to advertising is nontraditional and honors the company's customer-focused core values. Using the eBay live event, which brought 10,000 faithful eBay users to Orlando, Florida, for a live auction, eBay's advertising agency, Goodby, Silverstein & Partners, presented the advertising concept and its storyboards to the auction participants for their review and critique. The participants were pleased to be consulted, as well as pleased with the campaign idea.

Staying true to its collaborative nature, eBay also partners with other companies in its advertising, such as UPS, which offers shipping services to sellers. The eBay Entertainment section, which sells DVDs, CDs, and other memorabilia, is promoted jointly with E! Entertainment.

In addition to its consumer advertising campaign, eBay also has a B2B advertising effort for its eBay Business, which was launched as a subsite in 2003 (www.ebaybusiness.com). The first ads targeted the restaurant, metalworking, office technology, and test and measurement industries. By monitoring its searches eBay determined that these categories have been pulling a great deal of business from B2B marketers. The integrated effort includes ads aimed at business decision makers run in print, direct mail, online, and e-mail. eBay is running a more general version of the B2B campaign in *Entrepreneur Magazine* and regional business journals.

So what is the secret to eBay's success as an online retailer? Check the It's a Wrap feature at the end of the chapter for a discussion of eBay's phenomenal growth, as well as the factors that have led to the company's success, and the role advertising is now playing in maintaining that growth.

Sources: Ed Finkel, "eBay's Old-School Business Wisdom," *Kellogg World,* Summer 2004, http://www.Kellogg.Northwestern .edu/kwo/sum04/indepth/ebay2.htm; Chip Bayers, "Growth Dispenser," *Business 2.0* (October 2003): 107; Catharine Taylor, "The eBay Way: Brand It Now," *Brandweek* (October 20, 2003): PM20; Tobi Elkin, "4 with Vision: eBay," *Ad Age Special Report: Marketer of the Year* (December 15, 2003): S-4; Alice Cuneo, "Latest Campaign Casts eBay as Daily Destination," *Advertising Age* (November 11, 2002): 4; Kate Maddox, "eBay Makes Big b-t-b Push," *B to B* (May 5, 2003): 3–4.

eBay is an example of a company conducting its business totally online, taking advantage of the Internet's ability to create personal interaction between buyers and sellers. In this chapter we will discuss a number of interactive media, including the Internet and e-mail. We'll also talk about alternative and new media—formats that open up novel ways to deliver advertising messages and connect with consumers.

INTERACTIVE MEDIA

Interactive media refers to communication systems that permit two-way communication, such as a telephone call or an e-mail message. There is a range of interactivity, however. Some people consider a television commercial with a toll-free number or e-mail address to be interactive. Contact information like that does open up the door for interactivity, but the television ad itself is not interactive (although that's changing with new advances in interactive TV technology).

The point is: The closer the medium is to a dialogue, or the more a user is able to manipulate the content, the more it can properly be described as interactive communication. Two-way communication is believed to be the most persuasive type of communication available to marketers. With interactive media, such as the Internet or the phone, it is possible for a consumer to use the medium to contact the company and get a personal answer, as well as interact with the information provided on a Web site.

The Internet is interactive because users are involved in selecting the information they attend to and they can contact the company and other users directly. The Internet bridges print and broadcast media. Newspapers, magazines, and other print forms, such as direct mail, can be delivered online and their messages still look like print stories. Since the Internet delivers messages to audiences electronically and has the capability to present moving images, it also fits the broadcast description. So the Internet blurs the distinction between print and broadcast.

But *interactive* describes media other than the Internet, such as the phone and e-mail, both of which are used as advertising vehicles. The phone is the most interactive of all media, the one that most lends itself to conversation and dialogue. It is used for direct-marketing purposes, a practice called telemarketing that will be described in Chapter 15.

Principle

The more interactive a medium and the closer it is to a dialogue, the more personal and persuasive the communication experience.

THE INTERNET

The U.S. Census Bureau reported, based on the data it collected in the 2000 census, that more than 50 percent of U.S. households owned a computer and 42 percent went on the Internet at least once a day.[1] Although the number continues to increase, the Internet is still a long way from the penetration levels of newspapers, TV, and radio and remains just one choice in the media mix. Technically the **Internet** is a linked system of international computer networks. The **World Wide Web** is the information interface that allows people to access the Internet through an easy-to-use graphical format. Most people use these terms interchangebly.

E-Business and Marketing Communication

IBM has been focusing its marketing efforts on e-business since the late 1990s. In IBM's advertising, which focuses on its connectivity services, **e-business** refers to all the hardware, software, and computer know-how that provides a platform for businesses that use the Internet to sell products, as well as to manage their accounting, distribution, production, advertising, customer service, personal sales, internal communication to employees, and external communication to outside stakeholders.

The most familiar form of e-business is companies, such as Amazon.com, that sell products online. Amazon.com's Web site contains complete information about the product offerings, as well as a way to place an order, pay for it, and contact customer service if there is a problem. The Web site operates like a direct-mail catalog except it is interactive.

THE INSIDE STORY

Entertaining the User Through Web Site Redesign

Eric Telchin, designer, Washingtonpost.com Entertainment Guide

Redesigning an award-winning online Entertainment Guide is not about rearranging entertainment content in an interesting way. It's about what our users want.

As designer for Arts and Entertainment at washingtonpost.com, I was charged to redesign the Entertainment Guide—the definitive guide to local entertainment information in the metropolitan D.C. area. The Guide is a database-driven site with over 12,000 searchable restaurants, movies, performances, places, and events.

My task was to collaborate with editors, information architects, and programmers to create a fluid online experience—leveraging the database with vast editorial content.

We learned through both qualitative and quantitative research—focus groups, usability testing, and surveys specifically—that our users wanted more flexibility in our site. Users told us they wanted to experience the guide in a more natural manner, to bounce around the site in a way that makes most sense to them.

To provide this fluid experience, we decided to allow the user to search all entertainment subjects from any page in our site. We created a navigation system referred to as "the core tool," which empowers the user to find a movie theater in their neighborhood from any restaurant review, or locate a nearby Irish pub from a museum profile.

To achieve our goal, we combined navigation with search functionality. The user can use the core tool as navigation, either by clicking on the word "restaurants" to visit the restaurants index page, or by rolling over the word "search" next to "restaurants" to explode a restaurant-specific search box.

As simple as our solution was, it was the most complicated aspect of the entire redesign process. The success of the redesign hinged on the success of the core tool, so we needed to ensure its efficiency and ease-of-use.

As the design process began with our user, soliciting user feedback was an integral aspect of the final design solution. By employing usability testing—moderated one-on-one interviews—we were able to see the effectiveness of our tool and modify it to better suit the needs of our users.

Because of our commitment to provide value to users of our site, the market research we conducted was essential. As we continue to learn more about our users' needs, we will undoubtedly improve the way in which we meet those needs and incorporate them into the next version of the Entertainment Guide.

Consider This

1. What was the consumer problem that the Web designer was trying to solve with this Web site redesign?

2. How does the redesign of this Web site provide a competitive advantage to the electronic publisher, and how might that feature be the focus of an advertising campaign?

Eric Telchin studied Visual Communications and marketing as a Presidential Arts Scholar from the George Washington University in Washington, D.C. He has worked for major print, television, and Web organizations, and is currently the designer for washingtonpost.com's Entertainment Guide.

Nominated by Professor Lynda Maddox, George Washington University

Customers can make inquiries and the company can use its databases to personalize customer communication.

Providing Information   But there are other ways the Internet has helped bring interactivity to customer communication, such as providing information. Web publishers, who are media providers using the Internet to deliver news, features, and programs, also need to advertise these services. An example is the Web page for the *Washington Post* online entertainment guide, which delivers basic information about programs as well as about the newspaper, and also carries advertising and other sales messages. It is both a form of advertising and a way to sell advertising space to other advertisers.

Collecting Customer Information   In addition to providing information, e-businesses also capture information and use it to direct their marketing communication efforts to make messages more personal and relevant to consumers.. Every time you order something from Amazon.com, for example, the company keeps track and starts building a profile of your interests. When you go to Amazon the next time, the site will probably open with an announcement about some new book or CD that might interest you. If you have given Amazon permission, it will also send these announcements to you by e-mail. In other words, companies that collect data about the behavior of their customers are able to better target them with advertising messages and personalize special promotional offers.

The Internet and Privacy Some people see problems with the collection of such information. Their concern is with how it is used and whether its use violates people's privacy. AOL, for example, assembles a huge database of customer information, some of which it sells to other direct marketers. It admits this practice in its privacy policy, which is published on its Web site. It also buys information about its subscribers from other outside database suppliers, which it can use to better target its customers interests. And that's the primary reason companies collect this type of information: It lets them better target their advertising messages.

Companies try to maintain a responsible position by posting their **privacy policy** on their Web sites, which details, among other things, how or whether the site is collecting data on its visitors and how that data are used. Sometimes this information is easy to find, sometimes it is buried on the site and difficult to access, and in some instances the Web site doesn't have any published privacy statement at all.

A number of consumer activists follow this issue; if you want to learn more about their activities, check the watchdog site Junkbusters (www.junkbuster.com). The government also has an Electronic Privacy Information Center (www.epic.org), which monitors information-collecting practices and privacy issues. This privacy issue is the focus of the discussion in the Matter of Principle box, which looks at the principle of respectful use of personal information.

Principle

Companies that keep track of their customers' online behavior are better able to personalize their advertising messages.

A MATTER OF PRINCIPLE
Cookies and G-Mail

One principle of database-driven communication is that the collection of personal information should be done with sensitivity and not violate principles of privacy.

When the giant search engine company Google™ announced that it was going to offer free e-mail, called G-mail, apprehensive privacy experts voiced their concerns. The problem was that G-mail had a built-in feature that allowed its computers to search for certain keywords in its e-mail users' messages and display ads related to those words. Civil liberties groups worried that Google would be able to assemble user profiles in the process of matching ads to their interests.

Tracking information is a common practice on the Internet and customer-savvy businesses make sure their customers know when they are using such tools. But there are other tracking mechanisms that you may not be aware of, such as **cookies**, which are little electronic bugs that can be placed on your computer by a Web server to track your movements online. They don't do anything bad, like a virus does, but they do report back to their owners what sites you visited and from that can build an online profile about you and your interests. On the good side, cookies let companies store information about your registration, as well as your preferences, so you don't have to retype

everything every time you go to that site.

So, are cookies a bad practice or good? Critics say they are an invasion of privacy, but marketers say they are just a way to gather marketing information without the tedious survey process. In fact, many people recognize the trade-off: If they provide a company information, they will get a more personalized service in return.

For more information about how you can get your Internet service provider to remove cookies, check out the Web site www.Webwasher.com.

Consider This

1. What is the problem the critics worry about with Google's free e-mail service?
2. Do you think the exchange of personal information for a more personalized or free service is a good idea? How do you feel about having cookies collect information on your computer?

Source: Kevin J. Delaney, "Will Users Care If Gmail Invades Privacy? *Wall Street Journal* (April 7, 2004): B1; Nand Mulchandani, "The Truth Behind Web Cookies," TechTV Web site, www.techtv.com; Jane Bryant Quinn, "Fighting the Cookie Monster," *Newsweek* (February 28, 2000): 63.

In addition to providing information on a product and collecting information to target customers, the Internet is also useful in handling other important forms of e-business communication, such as customer service and technical support. *Customer service* is the department customers contact when they have problems, questions, complaints, or suggestions. In high-technology companies, a specific type of customer service is called *technical support,* which refers to departments with highly trained staff who are available to answer customer questions about a product's use.

The Internet and Marketing Communication

The marketing communication dimensions of the Internet vary. Some Web-based tools are used for stakeholder communication (employees, suppliers, distributors) and some are for advertising and other types of promotion.

The Internet has the capability to deliver inexpensive internal communication, which is an important part of integrated marketing communication (IMC). IMC programs try to coordinate marketing communication activities. **Intranets** are internal communication systems that connect employees. As an example, consider how an intranet is used within an advertising agency. A concept for an ad can be roughed out and distributed to a number of people within the agency for critiquing. These people can be located anywhere in the world, so the communication is instantaneous and not limited to the vagaries of the mail system. **Extranets** are similar communication systems that connect a company and its employees to key external stakeholders, such as clients, photographers, producers, artists, and other suppliers involved in producing an ad.

The Internet has also become a major internal communication source with password-protected Web sites for employees, vendors and suppliers, dealers and distributors, and sales representatives. For the sales staff, in particular, the B2B Web page can carry the same information as an advertisement or printed sales literature, as well as other corporate information. Its advantage is that it can provide more in-depth information than printed materials.

Web sites   Sometimes called a "home page," a company's **Web site** is the online face it presents to the public. In some cases, the Web site is the business. The Web site is a communication tool that sometime blurs the distinction between common forms of marketing communication, such as advertising, direct marketing, and public relations. In some cases it looks like an online corporate brochure or it may function as an online catalog. It can also be an information resource with a searchable library of stories and data about products, product categories, and related topics. More recently, as advertisers have searched for more effective ways to connect with their audiences, some of these sites have become more entertaining with games and contests, interviews with celebrities, even musical performances.

Web site redesign is often tied to an IMC program with the objective to unify all marketing materials. The Showcase work illustrates how one agency, Ohio-based Nova Creative, redesigned the Web site for one of its clients, the accounting firm Battelle (www.battellecpas.com), as part of a brand identity program.

Advertising Resources   Most Internet users depend upon **search engines**, such as Google, Yahoo!, or Ask Jeeves, to find information. These Internet tools use *keywords,* such as topics or company or brand names, to compile a collection of information relating to that word. For marketers, an important first step in creating a viable Web site is getting it registered with popular search engines so that it begins building visibility and shows up early on the list provided by the search engine.

Another search engine role is to provide a site on which advertisers can place ads. The phrase **search marketing** describes an approach that relies on actions initiated by consumers. Since they are searching for a particular topic, Web sites and the ads on them are not perceived to be as intrusive as other forms of advertising. Business-to-business marketing find these ads to be particularly high in impact. For example, when Corrugated Metals, a small sheet-metal company in Chicago, needed to build its business, it spent $200 a month to get an ad for its business to pop up on Google when anyone searched for "roll forming," a process that shapes metal. The firm reported that within days, the ad generated millions of dollars of sales.[2]

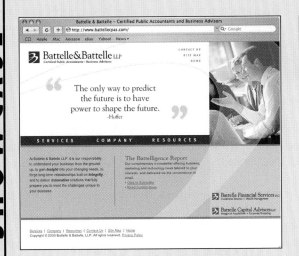

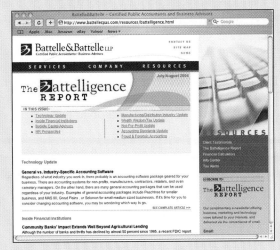

In this Web site redesign, Nova restructured the information on the existing Web site to fall into three main categories making the new site easier to navigate. The site was given a clean, professional look for a more contemporary corporate image. This Web site redesign was contributed by Amy Niswonger, at the Nova Group, an advertising graduate of the Miami University (Oxford, Ohio) program, where she was named Most Promising Student by the American Advertising Federation (AAF).

Beyond search engine ads, B2B marketers rely on the Internet in other ways. **B2B ad networks**, the oldest of which (B2B Works) appeared in early 2000, link B2B Web sites vertically (through an industry) and horizontally (across a mass market). These networks produce something akin to a custom directory of B2B Web sites for each advertiser, helping the advertiser target a precise business audience with the right message. The networks then track the response to ads on different Web sites and adjust the campaign as appropriate.

Chat Rooms Groups of people with a special interest can contact one another and exchange their opinions and experiences through **chat rooms**, which are sites located online, sometimes as part of an organization's Web site, but sometimes completely independent of any company. For example, numerous chat rooms are organized around various computer systems and topics (Linux, Apple, ThinkPad, Sega), as well as topics (1:1 marketing, guerilla marketing, virutal marketing).

On these sites people can post notes and respond to other people's postings. The communication is so fast that announcements, rumors, and criticisms can circulate worldwide within a matter of minutes. These Web discussion sites have become a major tool for customers to talk about their brand experiences both before and after they make a purchase. Chat rooms are good information sources regarding customer and industry perspectives, as well as competitive information.

Blogs A new communication form is the **blog** (short for Web log), which is a personal diary-like Web page that is created by an individual. These personal publishing sites also contain links to other related sites that the writer feels are relevant. There are thousands of these sites and most are read by only a few people, but a popular blog can attract more than a million readers a month. Once derided as the ramblings of self-important nobodies, these sites have become more valued by advertisers as their readership climbs. This success has led corporations to consider blogs as an alternative to their traditional Web sites. It is a way to keep employees and other stakeholders informed, particularly of changing news. Microsoft has several hundred staffers blogging on their personal sites.[3]

Advertisers are in the experimental stage with this new "blogosphere." A typical blog is Dailykos, a liberal political Web site run by Markos Moulitsas Zuniga. Initially he wanted to keep his blog ad-free but when he needed to buy new servers to keep up with the growing traffic on his site, he started taking ads to pay the bills. In three months he doubled his ad rates and brought in $4,000 a month. Another popular political blog, TalkingPointsMemo, also began taking ads and now brings in more than $5,000 a month.[4] The new media form has developed to the point that there is a media rep company, Pressflex LCC, that connects advertisers with a network of blogs. It charges 20 percent for its efforts and has about 200 blogs in its network.

Consider This

1. What is e-business, and how does it relate to marketing communication?
2. Which Internet-based communication tool seems to be of most use to marketing communication programs?

INTERNET ADVERTISING

Internet advertising, although still the new baby on the advertiser's block, is a growing industry. Advertisers see it as a relatively low-cost alternative to mainstream advertising media. It is also a form that reaches people who aren't watching much television or reading newspapers. It skyrocketed in the 1990s with the dot-com boom and then fell back after the Internet bust in the early 2000s. Observers believe that the industry is bouncing back: In 2004 ad spending on the Internet was estimated a + $6.5 billion, a 15.7 percent increase from the previous year.[5]

Table 10.1 tracks this performance over a six-year period. Note the high rate of increase in the initial years of 142 and 78 percent was followed by a huge drop in 2001 and 2002 when advertising revenues bottomed out. The following year, however, the industry was happy to see that the advertising revenues were beginning to recover, although the total spending was still less than the banner year of 2000.

More than 90 percent of Internet advertising is found on a small group of large, established news media sites that operate as electronic publishers, such as NYtimes.com, WSJ.com, and ESPN.com, as well as on major search engines and service providers, such as Google and Yahoo!.[6] Because the media organizations have established reputations and know how to sell advertising, they have been pioneers in the development of Internet advertising. Advertisers get access to an Internet site through providers, such as DoubleClick, an Internet advertising service that places more than 60 billion online ads per

10.1 The Boom, Bust, and Rebuilding of Web Advertising

Year	Spending (in billions)	% change
1998	$1.9	
1999	$4.6	142
2000	$8.2	78
2001	$7.2	−12
2002	$5.6	−22
2003	$6.5	16

Source: Ann Mack, "A Building Year," *Adweek Special Report* (September 29, 2003): SR18; "'03 a Bumper Year for Ads," *Adweek* (March 15, 2004): 14.

month. DoubleClick provides reports on the placement and performance of these ads to both publishers and advertisers.

Purpose of Internet Advertising

Online advertising serves three primary purposes. First, it provides a brand reminder message to people who are visiting a Web site. Second, it works like an ad in traditional media and delivers an informational or persuasive message. The third purpose, however, is most critical in that it provides a way to entice people to visit the advertiser's site by clicking on a banner or button on the Web site. This is called *driving traffic* to the Web site.

Some people may find an advertiser's Web site after doing a search using a search engine; others may come across the site address in some other communication, such as an ad or brochure. But another way is to encounter an ad on a related site, an ad that has enough impact that it will entice the visitor to leave the original site and move to this new one. Internet strategists are keenly aware of the difficulty of driving people to Web sites.

Types of Internet Advertising

What kinds of Internet advertising are available today? The industry is moving so quickly that by the time you read this passage, other categories may replace or supplement those we discuss here. Essentially, Internet advertising can be delivered as a traditional ad just like you see in print advertising in a magazine or it can be presented in the following formats that are new forms of Web advertising.

Banner Ads   IBM introduced banner ads in 1994. **Banner ads** are small ads on other Web pages on which people can click to move to the advertised Web site, such as the one featured here for Zippo lighters. They are easy to create and are usually placed on a Web site featuring complementary products or related topics. While banner ads were very popular when they first appeared, the overall click-through rate has dropped to 0.3 percent. For a collection of funny banners, check the Web site www.valleyofthegeeks.com.

Other Formats   The design of Internet advertising is constantly changing as the industry advances. Here are some common formats:

- *Skyscrapers.* The extra-long, skinny ads running down the right or left side of a Web site are called **skyscrapers**. The financial site CBSMarketWatch.com, for instance, regularly runs this kind of ad. Response rates for skyscrapers, which began to be used aggressively by more companies in 2000, can be 10 times higher than for traditional banner ads.
- *Pop-Ups and Pop-Behinds.* Pop-up ads burst open on the computer screen either in front of or behind the opening page of the Web site. Companies like Volvo and GlaxoSmith-Kline (for its Oxy acne medicine) use these forms to present games and product information.

■ ■ ■
This series of banners for the Zippo lighter develops a message as it unfolds. The message takes off on the blackouts urban areas sometimes experience in the summer when electrical use is high.

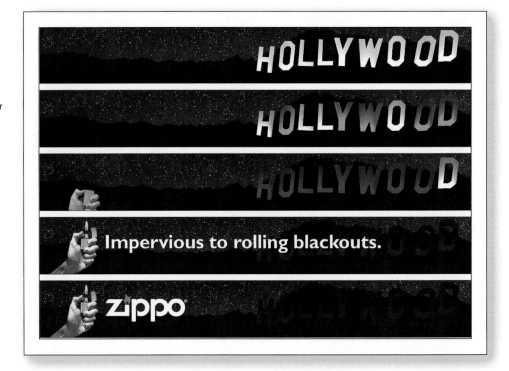

- *Minisites.* Minisites allow advertisers to market their products without sending people away from the site they're visiting. The General Motors minisite will appear on the Shell Oil site, and the consumer can access and enlarge it later. This type of advertising gets a higher click rate: Around 5 percent of the people who see the sites click on them, estimates portal About.com.
- *Superstitials.* Unveiled by online marketer Unicast in 1999, these are thought of as "the Internet's commercial," designed to work like TV ads. When you go from one page on a Web site to another, a 20-second animation appears in a window. These ads now run on more than 350 Web sites.

Interactive Formats   Originally banner ads were jazzed up using relatively simple animation techniques to make elements move. New technologies—including plug-ins, Java script, Flash, and media streaming—provide even more active components. A recent study by Greg Interactive, New York, and ASI Interactive Research found that the click-through rate nearly doubles when an interactive element is added to a banner ad. Newer interactive ads that deliver multimedia effects using sound, still images, and full-motion video are referred to as **rich media**. The phrase **streaming video** is used to describe moving images that can be transmitted online and received through most computers and their modems.

Off-line Advertising for Web Sites

One of the most difficult problems facing Internet marketers is driving traffic to their sites. One way to do this is to use **off-line advertising**, which appears in conventional media to drive traffic to a Web site. Print is particularly useful because it offers the opportunity to present the URL in a format that makes it possible for the reader to note the address. It's harder to present that information in broadcast media, where the message is here and gone.

The Internet Audience

Principle
The primary use of the Internet by people of all demographic categories is for information searching.

The early Internet users, mostly young and male, were high-tech innovators who rushed to be the first to experiment with online communication. In the 20 years since, the new medium has become a standard communication tool in both business and personal use. It is now the leading tool for information searching by all ages. Travel sites, such as the one shown here for *Budget Travel,* are particularly popular.

The Internet is particularly good at reaching teens, who spend more time online than any other age group. A study by Yahoo! and the online company Carat Interactive, found that 13- to 24-year-olds spend an average of 16.7 hours a week online and that excludes time spent on e-mail. That's why Procter & Gamble is advertising its Always sanitary napkins on Yahoo!'s teen sites. The ads drove an increase in traffic to P&G's BeingGirl.com Web site.[7]

Measuring Internet Audiences   The advantages of the Internet as a potential advertising vehicle are tremendous, with rapid, near instantaneous feedback and results chief among them. Rather than wait weeks or months to measure the success of an advertising campaign, marketers can instead run tests online, measure meaningful results within days, and quickly invest in the best performers with minimal switching costs. The problem, however, is that there is a lack of standards to measure Internet effectiveness. At the heart of the problem is the question of what exactly is to be measured—readers, viewers, visitors?—and how it equates to the reach of other media.

Consider **hits** (the number of times a particular site is visited), viewers (the number of viewers to a site), unique visitors (the number of different viewers during a particular time period), and page views (the number of times viewers view a page). These measures track a consumer through a Web site, but they offer no insights as to motivation, nor do they tell us whether a visitor paid any attention to the surrounding ads.

The primary method currently used to measure consumer response to Internet advertising is **click-through** (the number of people who click on a banner ad). This measure is considered insufficient by many Internet advertisers; a host of private research providers have emerged to expand on that measure. For example, Denver-based Match Logic identifies for its clients what viewers do next after *not* clicking on a banner ad.

Having the ability to quantitatively measure audiences is particularly important to media buyers, who need to show what the click-through, page view, or total traffic means to their clients. It would also be meaningful for advertisers or media buyers to obtain similar information from comparable sites so that they could see if they were getting a fair deal. This information about audience measurement is good for companies who want to structure their advertising rates based on the actual activity on their Web sites. Accurate audience measurement also helps advertisers determine the effectiveness of their ads.

This ad claims that Budget Travel is the fastest and easiest way to find the best travel deals. The Web site is a partnership between Arthur Frommer's *Budget Travel* magazine and the MSNBC channel.

Advantages and Disadvantages of Internet Advertising

One reason Internet advertising is growing in popularity is that it offers distinct advantages over other media. Most notably, it is relatively inexpensive. It can also deliver business, such as the pop-behind ads that motivate people to respond by offering a special price deal.

Advertisers can also customize and personalize their messages over the Internet. Thanks to database marketing, an advertiser can input key demographic and behavioral variables, making the consumer feel like the ad is just for him or her. For an example, check out classmates.com. Ads appearing on a particular page are for products that would appeal to a particular age group. Someone who graduated from high school in 1960 would see banner ads for investments that facilitate early retirement as opposed to someone graduating in 2000 who might see career ads.

For the B2B advertiser, Internet advertising can provide excellent sales leads or actual sales. Users of a typical B2B site, for example, can access the product catalogs, read the product specifications in depth, request a call from a salesperson, and make a purchase online.

The Internet can level the playing field for small and medium-size companies that compete against larger organizations. The cost of creating a Web site, a set of ads, and a database is affordable for virtually every marketer. Undoubtedly, the most serious drawback is the inability of strategic and creative experts to consistently produce effective ads and to measure their effectiveness. Consider, too, that clutter is just as much a problem with the Internet as it is in other media. In fact, because multiple ads may appear on the same screen—many moving or popping up—the clutter may be even worse.

The Web in International Advertising

The Web is an international marketing and advertising medium but it faces access, legal, linguistic, currency, and technological barriers. First, not everyone around the globe has the access or ability to use the Internet via computer, but the number of Internet users is growing exponentially. The Internet audience is growing faster internationally than it is in the United States, particularly in developing countries, such as China and India.

Second, advertising and sales promotion laws differ from country to country. Differences in privacy laws between Europe and the United States are expected to force American companies to change the way they collect and share consumer information.

Language is another factor. Although English is the dominant language on the Internet, some advertisers who want to provide different Web sites for different countries have trouble ensuring consistency across all sites. Another issue is exchange rates. Companies must decide whether to offer prices in their own currency or in the local currency. For example, one Canadian shopper reported that books on a Canadian Web site were cheaper than the same books on Amazon.com. In addition, some companies make different offers available in different countries.

Marketers must also keep in mind the technological differences among the worldwide Internet audiences. Users in some countries have to pay per-minute charges and therefore want to get on and off quickly, which precludes sophisticated graphics that take a long time to load. In other countries, users have access to fast lines and may expect more sophisticated Internet programming.

One company that uses Internet advertising to drive its store sales is Waterford Crystal of Ireland. Waterford does not sell its products to customers directly online, but instead uses its Web site to offer images and descriptions of its full product line, as well as information about local retailers who offer its products. Waterford's goal is to channel potential customers to its retailers in various countries from whom the customer can make a final purchase. Such an approach overcomes many of the overwhelming challenges to conducting business internationally on the Internet that we just discussed. And it is appreciated by the retailers, who benefit from the increased customer exposure and traffic.

Changes and Trends in Internet Advertising

One of the biggest problems faced by Internet advertisers is the varying levels of technological sophistication viewers have available. Some use a high-speed DSL line, which is a form of broadband that makes connections and delivers data rapidly. Most people, however, are using slow dial-up modems and narrow-band width systems, which make online access and transmission tedious. *Bandwidth* refers to the amount of digital information that can be sent through a phone line or fiber optic line. As the technology has improved, and many users now have appropriate software, a high-speed modem, and broadband line (such as DSL), it is becoming easier to download the images of rich media.

Other changes that accompany the upgraded technology include the new willingness of online publishers, such as NYTimes.com and ESPN.com, to accept various types of advertising other than banners on their pages. Bigger spaces, such as that provided by skyscrapers, and rich media make it easier for advertisers to design messages with impact. But the publishers benefit as well: They have seen dramatic increases in their advertising revenue after opening up their sites to bigger and more interactive formats.

The biggest changes, however, will happen in the area of measurement as the Internet becomes more like mainstream television. Media planners and buyers hope to be able to use the same daypart data, as well as reach and frequency tools to evaluate the effectiveness of online advertising. Planners believe Web site clicks will eventually be audited the same way viewership and readership are for traditional media.[8]

Consider This

1. What are the purposes and types of Internet advertising?
2. If an outdoor store in your community wanted to move into online advertising, how would you describe the strengths and weaknesses of this medium?

E-MAIL ADVERTISING

One of the attractive things about e-mail advertising is that it is so inexpensive. All it takes is a list of e-mail addresses, a computer, and an Internet connection. Today's improved databases allow marketers to target prospects with unsolicited e-mail. In fact, the response rate for an unsolicited e-mail campaign is many times higher than for a banner ad campaign. Unfortunately for e-mail advertisers, people generally do not welcome unsolicited e-mail, even if the response rate is higher than for banners. *Permission marketing* attempts to address this problem by asking potential consumers for their permission to send them e-mail.

Spam

Blasting millions of unsolicited e-mail messages to e-mail in-boxes for everything from loans to computer cartridges to pornographic sites is called *spamming*. Consumers who are irritated by the avalanche of solicitations that clutter their in-boxes may think of **spam** as "junk e-mail," but providers prefer to call it "bulk e-mail." They see bulk e-mail as an exciting new business opportunity—and bulk e-mailing as a legitimate commercial activity.

Critics—and that's most of the rest of us—would like to see the government close down these operations. There are technological problems to controlling these practices, however, and spammers have proven very creative in finding ways to get through filters installed by service providers and host corporations, such as companies and universities.

There is a register of spammers known as Rokso, or Register of Known Spam Operations. It's kind of a "most wanted" list maintained by Internet hosts and service providers, like AOL, whose computers strain to handle the huge bulk e-mails[9] and are quick to kick off known spammers. An antispam Web site called spam.abuse.net is also available, and Congress is getting into the debate with various proposals for regulating spam.

Does spam bring in revenue? Spammers solicit business from sources like AOL's profiles where people indicate their interests and activities. A spammer might send out 100,000 e-mails and get only two to five clients, which seems like a totally unacceptable number of responses. But a spammer who charges $300 to send out 100,000 messages or $900 for a million might make $14,000 to $15,000 on those few responses. That's not a bad return when you consider the cost of getting into the business: a computer and an Internet connection.

Opt-In and Opt-Out Proposed solutions to the spam problem usually incorporate one of two permission marketing strategies for consumers to control their inclusion on e-mail lists. **Opt in** means that all bulk e-mailers have to get your permission before sending any e-mail. This is the form used by legitimate e-mail advertising businesses and one that is both tougher for spammers to abuse and more sensitive to consumer rage when they do. **Opt out** means that e-mailers can send a first e-mail, but they have to have an option that

Principle
Opt-in and opt-out strategies make mass e-mail campaigns more acceptable because customers give permission to marketers to contact them.

makes it possible for you to say no to any further e-mails from that business. Either way, spammers will probably find a way to get around the regulation.

Viral Marketing

A practice designed to deliver a groundswell of opinion or marketplace demand for a product is called *viral marketing*. It uses e-mail to circulate a message among family and friends. For example, to launch a new brand of beer named Blowfly from a small Australian microbrewery called Blowfly, one of the owners sent e-mails to some 140 people he knew. He asked them to register as members on the brand's new Web site (www.blowfly.com.au). In exchange they would get the chance to vote on every aspect of the beer and its advertising, plus when it launched, they would get a single share of stock in the company for each six-pack they purchased. He also told them to share the news with their friends and family. By the end of the third week, the site had more than a thousand members, ultimately growing to 10,000.[10]

Consider This

1. How is e-mail advertising used by marketers, and what is its biggest problem?
2. Describe viral marketing, and explain where it would or would not be appropriate for an advertiser to use.

ALTERNATIVE AND NEW MEDIA

Mainstream media of all types are hurting. This is particularly true of network television, which is under assault from cable and TiVo. A New York–based financial analyst company specializing in media companies reported declines over the past five years in the time consumers spend with traditional media. But in the same period, it reported double-digit annual increase in the time spent with video games, home video and, of course, the Internet.[11]

The search for new media is particularly important for advertisers trying to reach the youth market, since teens are often the first to experiment with new media forms—and that's true for girls as well as boys. A vice president of programming at Channel One, the TV channel beamed into high schools, explains that, "When it comes to traditional media, teen girls today want it interactive and responsive." He explains that the most popular features are ones that allow teens to express their own voice and influence the outcome of a plot or event.[12]

In some ways, this search for new ways and places to deliver messages is just as creative as the message concepts developed on the creative side of advertising. That's why one of the principles of this book is that the media side can be just as creative as the creative side of advertising. These new media forms are called either **new media**, a phrase that has been used to refer to new electronic forms such as the Internet, or **alternative media**, which refers to nontraditional or unexpected communication tools and events. This section will discuss the trends in both these areas.

Principle
The media person's search for new ways to deliver messages is just as creative as the creative person's search for new advertising ideas.

Advertainment

In an attempt to stand out among the media clutter, several companies have begun integrating brands into the content of television shows—known as **advertainment** or **branded entertainment**.[13] Similar to the presence of FedEx in *Castaway,* these shows use the product as a prop or central feature of the program. Further examples would be a plan by Mattel and Columbia Pictures to make films based on Hot Wheels and the backing of a short-film cable channel by Anheuser-Busch. The show *Extreme Makeover: The Home Edition* promotes Sears products. Branded entertainment more aggressively promotes a product than product placement. Described as *situational ads* because they are embedded in specific programs, they are harder for viewers to dismiss immediately as ads because the product is a character in the program.

■ ■ ■
In the continual search for new ways to reach audiences, innovative media placements are being explored in the form of ads on conveyer belts at airports and stenciled messages in the sand on beaches.

New Internet Practices

Of course, not only is the Internet itself a new advertising form, it is also a catalyst for new thinking about how advertising should be handled. We'll talk about two approaches that are particularly innovative: *brand experiences* and *webisodes*.

Brand Experiences on the Web   Many consumers consider pop-ups, banner ads, and superstitials not only annoying but also ineffective. So many companies instead are making their Web sites more engaging and entertaining. Web sites for Nike and the Gap are excellent examples of the practice of providing **brand experiences**. The Nike site features engaging subsites within the main site, each dedicated to a different sport. For example, NikeBasketball outlines Nike's 30 years of marketing basketball shoes and NikeGoddess provides targeted content and shopping to women.[14]

Burger King has developed an interactive Web site that lets visitors make a human being in a chicken suit dance, jump, watch TV, or do pushups. The crazy chicken that responds to viewers' commands is featured on the site, www.subservientchicken.com, and appeals to the zany side of Web surfers. It also experiments with a dimension of virtual interactivity: The chicken seems to interact with its viewers through what appears to be a Web-cam window.[15] The chicken also relies on viral marketing for its visibility, recognizing that the young Web surfer audience is likely to share the site with friends. Originally only 20 people who were friends and co-workers of the staff at Burger King's agency, Crispin Porter + Bogusky, knew about the site. Since then the site has received 15 to 20 million hits and visitors spend an average of six minutes playing with the chicken.

Jerry Seinfeld starred in a four-minute "Webisode" for American Express.

Webisodes Similar to television programs with recurring episodes in a developing story, **Webisodes** have created a new form of Web advertising. This follows the "advertainment" trend in television advertising that blends advertising and entertainment in order to attract audiences turned off by traditional mainstream media.[16] The original experiment with this new format was created by Fallon Worldwide for its client BMW. Known as the "BMW films," the series consisted of high-action minimovies by well-known action movie directors (John Woo, Guy Ritchie, and Ang Lee) all of which featured various BMW models in starring roles. The films can only be seen online at www .bmwfilms.com. Randall Rothenberg, an advertising critic, wrote that the highly entertaining films reinvented advertising.[17]

American Express has sponsored a four-minute humorous online commercial featuring comedian Jerry Seinfeld and an animated Superman. The two sidekicks play the role of neurotic New Yorkers complaining about such earth-shaking topics as the amount of mayonnaise on their tuna sandwiches. They also discover the benefits of using an American Express card. The message is soft sell and followed by a gag, which makes the commercial feel more like cinema than advertising. The minifilm, directed by Academy Award–winning director Barry Levinson, has generated much buzz, which extends its impact through the power of word of mouth. In explaining the new format, Seinfeld jokes that it isn't going to be interrupted with a commercial because it is a commercial.[18]

Video Games

Marketers and ad executives have been frustrated trying to reach young people with traditional ads on mainstream media. That has led to an increased focus on Internet advertising, but also on unusual media that are clearly the province of young people, such as video games. Now a global $16 billion industry, the video game business is developing as a major new medium for advertisers to target males aged 12–34, although girls are getting into the act as well.[19] There are more than 220 million computer and video games sold in the country every year.

Opportunities will be mined by both creating online games as well as placing products within games.[20] For example, Activision games feature product placements for Puma athletic shoes and Nokia mobile phones, and Skittles candies star in *Darkened Skye,* a Simon & Schuster game. Volkswagen of American bought a placement on Sony Computer Entertainment's *Gran Turismo 3,* a car-racing game. The advertisement may be a simple product placement or make the product the star. Chester Cheetah, the Chee-tos cheese snack mascot, stars in several games of his own. Just as advertisers are sponsoring their own TV shows, their brand characters may soon be stars in video games.

As video games develop as an advertising medium, planners and buyers are asking for standardized independent data that prove their effectiveness. Nielsen Media Research is developing a system that will track how many gamers see the ads in the console-based video games. The new service will probably use a device like the set-top boxes used to monitor TV viewing, supplemented by follow-up phone surveys.[21]

Wireless Communication

The mobile cell phone has exploded as a popular form of telecommunication and *wireless communication* that links the common phone to a computer is possibly the most important change in communication systems so far in the new millennium. Some places, like the Scandinavian countries and Japan, are highly advanced in wireless communication and their consumers are far more accustomed to using smart phones, videophones, and instant messaging than those in the United States.

Cell phones have also introduced new product lines such as graphic faceplates and specialty ring tones. The fact that there is a market for these products demonstrates that young people use their phones as fashion accessories and to make personal style statements. Adults, in contrast, look to cell phones for convenience. Young people also consider their phones to be part of their entertainment environment, and that opens up promotional opportunities similar to those being used by more conventional advertising media that are exploring the edge of advertainment.

Instant Messaging Young people are also more adept at exploring connection opportunities with new communication systems than are older people. Teens, particularly girls, use their cell phones constantly to chat with their friends both by phone and by **instant messaging (IM)**, which allows them to keyboard brief messages into a cell phone screen. A firm that researches the youth market found in 2003 that 49 percent of younger teen girls use instant messaging daily to reach their friends, far more than do adults.[22] As teens have mastered this skill, they also have developed an abbreviated code or new language that lets them communicate rapidly. An example comes from a headline on a story about instant messaging that reads: "Wot R They Up 2?"

The problem is that teens hate IM advertising because they see it as invasive. As in other forms of advertising, the way to be less intrusive is to be more relevant and offer opt-in options. Teens may permit advertising if it offers them information they want, such as news about music, games, sports, cosmetics, and fashion.

Click-and-dial systems use wireless phones to access Web sites. For example, if it is your mother's birthday, a reminder note may come through on your phone and you can respond by clicking a button that sends you to your favorite florist where you can place an order. These are interesting and innovative uses of wireless communication, but the industry is so new that we haven't begun to explore all the possibilities this technology offers for advertising and permission marketing.

Hybrid Technologies *Convergence* is a big word in the traditional media industries where the differences between television, print, and the Internet media seem to be blurring. The potential of interactive media is that they may combine the advantages of broadcast (high-impact visuals), print (the ability to inform), and the Internet (personalization and interactivity). Convergence is also creating opportunities in the wireless environment where companies like Nokia are offering cell phones that are not only cameras, but also gaming devices and MP3 players.

Nonelectronic New Media

Ads have been appearing in unexpected places, such as the back of toilet stall doors, for some time. One idea comes from NASA, which has considered printing emblems and logos alongside NASA's on space shuttles and the space station. McDonald's, for example, might put its golden arches on the kitchen "galley," in return for promoting space exploration to kids in its restaurants.[23]

Guerilla Marketing

Guerilla marketing is unconventional marketing communication activities that are intended to get buzz on a limited budget. The idea is to use creative ways to reach people where they live, work, and walk to create a personal

■ ■ ■

These painted stairs at the Denver Pavillions, an entertainment complex in downtown Denver, advertise membership in the nearby Colorado Athletic Club. Called a "captive ad," it is unavoidable for people walking up or down the stairs.

connection and a high level of impact. If it works, the encounter gets talked about by word of mouth rather than through the media. More about matching wits than matching budgets, guerilla marketing does have limited reach. For example, Sony Ericsson Mobile Communications Ltd. hired actors to create buzz about a new mobile phone that is also a digital camera. The actors pretended to be tourists who wanted their picture taken, thus allowing consumers to try the product.

Guerilla marketing has even reached into the political realm. Before the 2004 election, Ben Cohen, co-founder of Ben & Jerry's Ice Cream, created a pink van shaped like a piggy bank that pulls two other smaller pigs on trailers. The largest was labeled Iraq and $200 billion; the two little ones were labeled education $34 billion and poverty & hunger $10 billion. The Pig Mobile toured critical states with volunteers at the wheel.[24] Whether you agree with the sentiment or not, you have to admit it's a creative way to get attention and make a statement.

Consider This

1. Why are alternative, nontraditional, or new media useful to advertisers?
2. Do you think guerilla marketing is an effective way to reach consumers? What are its advantages and disadvantages?

IT'S A WRAP

EBAY REWRITES THE RULES FOR E-MARKETERS

This entire chapter on interactive and alternative new media is about changes in the media industry so there's no need to wrap up this chapter by trying to figure out what's next. The changes are coming so fast that it's impossible to predict what new media forms are on the horizon. It is important to realize, however, that some of the most creative ideas in advertising are seen in the areas of interactive and alternative new media. The Internet has revolutionized the media industry just as eBay is revolutionizing retailing.

eBay's formula for success—one part commerce, one part entertainment, and one part town meeting all rolled together—is based on a commitment to business fundamentals. For example, it is one of the few companies that can boast that it has made a profit every year since it was a startup. And profits continue to be the focus of all its marketing initiatives. One reason for its enviable balance sheet is that it resisted using extensive advertising during its startup days, as so many companies did during the dot-com boom days in the early 2000s. Instead, the company focused on maintaining its profit level and relied on word of mouth from its dedicated users. eBay didn't start advertising until late 2002 in the United States and 2003 in its international markets, and now it is used as a reminder, as well as to tease new business from people who may have been slow to venture into the world of online auctions.

The recent advertising effort, however, has helped fuel the company's continued growth. eBay is not only a dominant Internet marketer in the United States; it has expanded to 20 countries since its founding in 1995. It recorded $1.7 billion in revenue in 2003 and by mid-2004 the company's high gross margins resulted in $3 billion in cash on hand. The bottom line-focused business strategy has made it not only a survivor of the dot-com bust, but also a model e-business company. That's why it was named number two on *Business 2.0*'s "fastest growing companies" list for 2003.

Summary

1. **Determine the difference between interactive media and more conventional mainstream media.** Interactive media permit interaction with the source of the message, as well as with the message itself. Conventional forms of advertising media, such as print and broadcast media, do not engage their audiences in conversations. It can be used to both provide and collect information. The structure includes corporate Web sites, as well as online communication networks. External activities and sources, such as chat rooms, blogs, and search engines, can also provide information that impact on the way business is conducted.

2. **Explain how the Internet works as a business and as marketing communication.** The phrase *e-business* refers to all the hardware, software, and computer know-how that provides a platform for businesses that use the Internet to sell products, as well as manage their communication systems.

3. **Discuss how Internet advertising works.** Most Internet advertising is found on established news media sites that operate as electronic publishers, such as NYTimes.com, WSJ.com and ESPN.com, as well as on major search engines and service providers, such as Google and Yahoo!. Advertisers place ads on the Internet through providers such as DoubleClick, an Internet advertising service.

4. **Describe how e-mail advertising works.** E-mail advertising is a way to send an advertising message to a list of e-mail addresses. Unsolicited e-mail is called spam and is generally disliked; permission marketing asks potential customers to opt in and put themselves on the list.

5. **Show how the different forms of interactive and alternative new media are changing the way advertising works.** Because of the problems faced by traditional media, there is a continual search for new and novel ways to reach consumers. That's particularly true for the youth market. Video games, Internet Webisodes, instant messaging, and guerilla marketing are being used to create new forms of communication. The new media also open up opportunities for new types of personal brand experiences.

Key Terms

advertainment, 282
alternative media, 282
banner ads, 277
blog, 276
branded entertainment, 282
brand experiences, 283
B2B ad networks, 275
chat rooms, 275
click-through, 279

cookies, 273
e-business, 271
extranet, 274
guerilla marketing, 285
hits, 279
instant messaging (IM), 285
interactive media, 271
Internet, 271

intranet, 274
new media, 282
off-line advertising, 278
opt in, 281
opt out, 281
privacy policy, 273
rich media, 278
search engines, 274

search marketing, 274
skyscrapers, 277
spam, 281
streaming video, 278
superstitials, 278
Webisodes, 284
Web site, 274
World Wide Web, 271

Review Questions

1. From what you have read in this chapter, how are interactive media defined? How do these media differ from traditional advertising media?

2. Identify and explain the key communication-related components of e-business.

3. What are the primary purposes of Internet advertising?

4. How does e-mail advertising work?

5. What are some of the new forms of Internet practices that advertisers are experimenting with? Explain how they work and what advantages they provide.

Discussion Questions

1. One interesting way to combine the assets of print and broadcast is to use the visuals from a print ad or a television commercial in an Internet ad. Why would an advertiser consider this creative strategy? What limitations would you mention? Would you recommend doing this?

2. You are the media planner for a cosmetics company introducing a new line of makeup for teenage girls. Your research indicates that the Internet might be an effective medium for creating awareness about your new product line. How do you design an Internet advertising strategy

that will reach your target market successfully? What Web sites would you choose? Why? What advertising forms would you use on these sites and why?

3. How can Internet sites entice companies to advertise on them? What competitive advantage, if any, does Internet advertising provide? If you are a sales rep working for a college newspaper that has an online version, how would you attract advertising? What companies would you recommend contacting? What are the arguments that the sales rep might present to a prospect?

■■■ Class Projects

1. Your small agency works for a local retailer (pick one from your community) that wants to create buzz and get people talking about it. The retailer has very little money to use on advertising. Your agency team agrees that guerilla marketing would be a solution. Brainstorm among yourselves and come up with a list of at least five ideas for guerilla marketing that would get people talking about the store. Write the ideas as a proposal to the store owner and prepare a presentation to share your ideas with your class.

2. This chapter briefly discussed the concept of rich media. Visit various sites related to Internet marketing and find out what is being said about this new form. Start with the Interactive Advertising Bureau (IAB), which you can find at www.iab.com, and DoubleClick at www.doubleclick.com. Then find several other sites that have discussions on this topic. Put together a report titled "New Trends in Rich Media" for your instructor.

HANDS-ON CASE

BMW Knows the ABC's of C to B

Advertisers are starting to realize that they have to communicate with prospects in a way that does not increase privacy fears or irritate viewers. This thinking is behind the new buzz in the industry, C to B, or consumer to business. The idea is to create advertising messages that consumers *want* to see, so the consumer will come to the marketer rather than the other way around.

One showcase for C to B is an innovative campaign sponsored by BMW. Responding to research indicating that nearly half of all consumers considering a new-car purchase search the Internet before buying, the luxury-car manufacturer developed a series of highly polished, action-filled movie "shorts" that can be viewed at its Web site (watch them yourself at http://usa.bmwfilms.com). BMW spent over a million dollars on each of the shorts. Big-name directors (John Woo, John Frankenheimer, Tony Scott, Ang Lee, Guy Ritchie) and actors (Madonna, Gary Oldham, Mickey Rourke, F. Murray Abraham, Don Cheadle) helped to ensure that each film plays like a miniaturized Hollywood action picture. The star of the series, playing a character named "the Driver," is British actor Clive Owen, but the consistent scene stealers are the various BMW cars, which are central to each story and help create much of the action.

BMW's effort appears to be paying big dividends. Through 2004 the film site has been viewed by an astonishing 45 million visitors, each of whom has registered with a name and e-mail address. And BMW did pretty well in the sales department too, recording record U.S. sales in 2001 of 213,127 vehicles, up 12.5 percent from 2000.

When something works, people take notice. The shorts received a great deal of media attention, some positive, some less so. *New York Times* film critic Elvis Mitchell wrote that the series appears to be "a marriage of commerce and creativity, straddling the ever-dwindling line between art and merchandising." But others praised BMW and its agency, Fallon Worldwide in Minneapolis (a subsidiary of French holding company Publicis Groupe), for its creativity and imagination. The shorts are cool, the cars look great, and star Owen has the glamour and looks one expects from an A-list movie star.

And it wasn't just critics who took notice. The series sparked "me-too" efforts from Mercedes, Volvo, even American Express, which promoted 15-minute Web movies featuring cartoon hero Superman and Jerry Seinfeld. During the 2004 Christmas season Amazon.com ran shorts with top-notch Hollywood talent at its site. TV ads, which in the past have done most of the heavy lifting in creating brand value, are now being used by several of these advertisers to drive traffic to the Internet. Advertisers get prospects who willingly go to their sites, register, and watch brand messages. Consumers get free, high-quality entertainment and a chance to receive special offers and promotions. All of which proves that BMW really does know the ABC's of C to B.

Consider This

1. After viewing the shorts at the BMW Web site, what is your reaction? Does the entertainment overshadow the brand, or do the films simultaneously entertain and create brand value?

2. How can manufacturers of less glamorous brands, such as Ford and Chevrolet, use the Web to build partnerships with potential buyers?

3. In your opinion, is the BMW "films" campaign an effective way to increase consumer interactivity with a brand?

Sources: Bill Britt, "Volvo Sets Plans for BMW-like Net Film," *Advertising Age* (October 6, 2003); "Direct Gets Respect; Budgets Swell as Marketers Seek Accountability," *Advertising Age* (August 30, 2004): 1: Jefferson Graham, "Original Programming Smiles on Dot-coms Again," *USA Today* (October 21, 2002). Updated 10/21/2002; Jean Halliday, "Study Claims TV Advertising Doesn't Work on Car Buyers," *Advertising Age* (October 13, 2003); Stefano Hatfield, "In BMW'S Wake, Mercedes In U.K. Tries Its Own 'Movie,'" *Advertising Age* (July 22, 2002); Anthony Vagnoni, Jean Halliday, and Catharine P. Taylor, "Behind the Wheel," *Advertising Age* (July 23, 2001).

Archipelago's THE **OPEN** SHOW

Archipelago's THE **OPEN** SHOW

Archipelago's THE **OPEN** S

Media Planning and Buying

CHAPTER 11

**Archipelago Rings
the Bell**

Award:
Adweek's Media Plan
of the Year; 2004 Gold
EFFIE®; Media Grand Prix
at Cannes 2003

Company:
The Archipelago Exchange

Agency:
Fallon Worldwide

Campaign:
"The Open Show"

CHAPTER KEY POINTS

After reading this chapter, you will be able to:

1. Outline the basic media concepts used by planners and buyers.

2. Describe the types of information compiled by media researchers

3. Analyze how media planners set media objectives.

4. List the key media strategy decisions.

5. Identify the responsibilities of media buyers.

Have you ever made an appointment to watch an ad? Actually scheduled your TV viewing around a commercial?

With all the programming choices TV viewers have today, there is not much on the air that can be considered "appointment" television. That's why an ad campaign for the Archipelago Exchange, the Chicago-based electronic stock market, was so unique. Instead of airing traditional 30-second spots, Fallon Minneapolis created and produced a TV program that would air in 1-minute increments every morning at 7:59 A.M., one minute before the opening of the Archipelago stock exchange. The program featured two characters that Fallon created and a developing storyline that stock traders watched like a regular TV program, only this one was just 1 minute long.

Archipelago had been around since 1997 as an electronic trading platform for professional stock traders. However, in mid-2002, the SEC approved Archipelago's application to operate a stock exchange in competition with premier marketplaces such as the New York Stock Exchange (NYSE) and NASDAQ. The challenge to Fallon was to find a creative way to launch the new exchange.

Fallon's primary objective was to redefine Archipelago and connect it to the idea of a stock exchange. Other objectives included increasing interest and referrals, establishing the image of the new exchange as viable, and increasing its level of use among professional traders. In addition, Fallon wanted to build awareness, increase the level of interaction with traders, and involve them more in the launch of the new exchange.

The solution was found in an innovative media idea. Although stock exchanges are famous for their ritualistic daily opening ceremonies, the Archipelago Exchange is fully electronic and isn't confined to a single trading-floor location; that meant it could open its trading floor from anywhere. Since the Archipelago Exchange starts trading at 8:00 A.M. Eastern, it also had a 90-minute advantage on the big exchanges.

The idea was an episodic, 60-second TV program called *The Open Show,* which featured two guys traveling the world looking for the best way to signal the opening of the new exchange. A different episode would run every morning from a different location. Through the storyline of the journey, Fallon creatives were able to weave in the benefits of trading over the Archipelago Exchange.

The secret was the complementary impact of a media idea and a creative idea used synergistically. The media scheduling was designed to create and maintain loyal viewers. The Fallon media team negotiated a 60-second time slot every trading day on CNBC at precisely 7:59 A.M. To keep *The Open Show* positioned as a program, rather than a commercial, the team also asked CNBC to guarantee that it wouldn't run in a pod of ads but in a stand-alone time slot.

The Open Show was then promoted as if it were a new series with "coming soon" teasers on CNBC. Manhattan was blanketed with posters announcing the opening. The exchange's Web site provided background stories about the characters, as well as past episodes that could be downloaded.

The media plan was so successful that Archipelago was named "Media Plan of the Year" in 2003 and the launch campaign for the new exchange received an EFFIE award in 2004.

Sources: "Archipelago," Fallon EFFIES 2004 (Minnesota: Fallon Worldwide, 2004): 4–7; "Media Plan of the Year: Best Use of National Television and/or Cable," *Adweek Special Report* (June 23, 2003): 18–20.

As Archipelago and the media planners at Fallon know, media planning is a problem-solving process. The problem: How can media choices help meet the marketing and advertising objectives? The ultimate goal is to reach the target audience with the right message in the best possible way at the best possible time. In this chapter, we review how a media plan is developed—how media planners set objectives and develop media strategies—and we illustrate that by explaining how one company developed a media plan. We then explore the media-buying function and explain how media buyers execute the plan.

MEDIA PLANNING AND BUYING

Traditionally, the advertising agency has been responsible for developing the media plan, which is usually devised jointly by the agency's media department, the account and creative teams, and the marketer's brand management group. Once the plan is formed, a media-buying unit, sometimes attached to the ad agency or sometimes a separate company, executes it.

Media planning and buying have gone through a technical and structural revolution during the last 25 years. In the late 1980s media gained access to the computer, and buyers could check prices and place orders electronically. Today, the media-buying process has moved online. Media-buying services have come on the scene along with *unbundling,* which refers to moving the media-buying function outside the agency. The media-planning field also has undergone a metamorphosis because of the fragmentation of mainstream media, particularly television, and the proliferation of new media such as interactive and alternative media. This has made media planning and buying more challenging—and more creative.

Although we talk about advertising media, media are used in all the other areas of marketing communication as well. Public relations, for example, places stories, as well as corporate and advocacy ads, in print and broadcast media and uses the Internet, other print forms such as brochures, and activities such as special events. Sales promotion also relies on ads in various media to deliver the announcement about the promotion. Regardless of area, finding the right moment to deliver a message is the key challenge to media planners, a concept called the media *aperture.*

The Aperture Concept

Prospective customers for a product or service have one or more ideal times and places at which they can be reached with an advertising message. For example, when it's rainy, you think about umbrellas; when it's sunny, you think about sunglasses. This ideal point is called an **aperture**. The goal of the media planner is to expose the target audience to the advertiser's message at the critical point when a consumer is receptive to the brand message. *Aperture,* referring to the opening of a camera lens, is here used as a metaphor: It illustrates the idea that media planners need to focus tightly on their target audience using all the details they can find about these people in order to reach the target audience—no more, which leads to waste, and no less, which leads to missed opportunities. Regardless of whether a company is spending a few hundred dollars on one medium or millions of dollars on a variety of media, the goal is still the same: to reach the right people at the right time with the right message. So let's look at how a media plan is constructed to maximize the right moment for a message.

Principle
Advertising is most effective when it reaches the right people at the right time with the right message.

THE MEDIA PLAN

The *media plan,* as we saw in Chapter 8, is a written document that summarizes the objectives and strategies pertinent to the placement of a company's advertising messages. The goal of a media plan is to find the most effective ways to deliver messages at every important *contact point,* the point where a consumer has an opportunity to connect with a brand and respond in some way to a brand message. To see where media buying and planning fit into the advertising process, look at Figure 11.1, which outlines the primary components of a media plan.

Media Research: Information Sources

Some people believe that media decisions are the hub in the advertising wheel, the central point where all campaign elements (that is, the spokes of the wheel) are joined. Not only are media decisions central to advertising planning, but media research is central to media planning. That realization stems from the sheer volume of data and information that media planners must gather, sort, and analyze before media decision making can begin, which are

FIGURE
11.1

The Components of a Media Plan

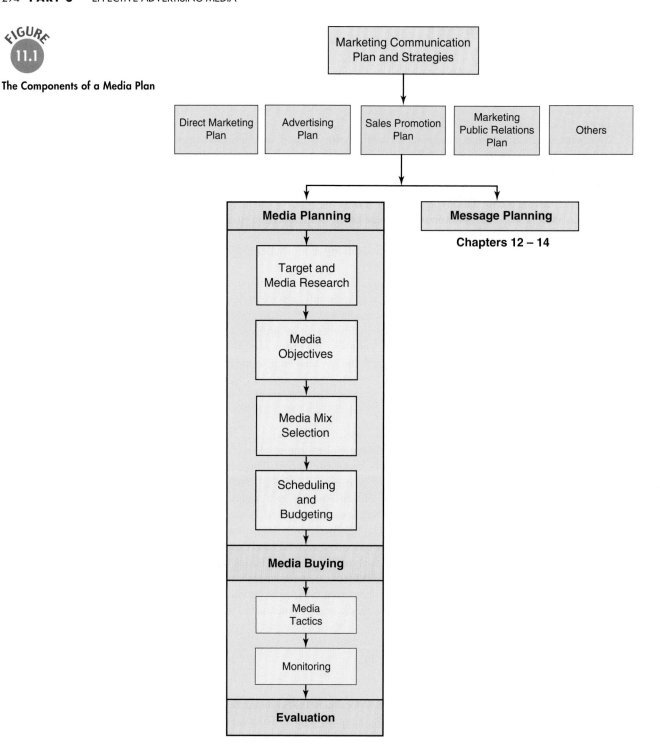

discussed below. Figure 11.2 illustrates the wide range of media information sources and the critical role media research plays in the overall advertising planning process.

• *Client Information.* The client is a good source for various types of information media planners use in their work, such as targeted markets, previous promotions and their performance, product sales and distribution patterns, brand plans, and, most importantly, the budget. *Sales geography* is a critical set of information. Although companies may distribute goods and services in many cities and states, sales are seldom consistent across all areas, no matter how popular the brand. Sales differences affect the decision about which markets the advertiser should reach for the campaign and how many dollars are allocated to each geographic region.

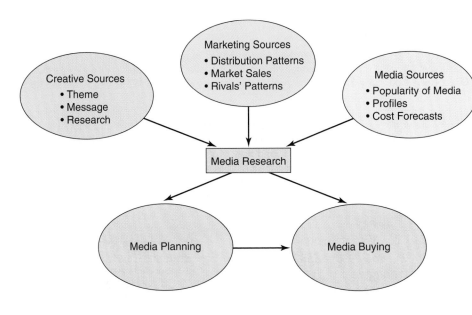

The Central Role of Media Research

Media planners look for data from sources, including creative, marketing, and media sources. All this information is used in both media planning and buying.

• **Market Research.** Also valuable to media planners is independently gathered information about markets and product categories, such as that provided by Mediamark Research Inc. (MRI), Scarborough (local markets), and Mendelsohn (affluent markets). This information is usually organized by product category (detergents, cereals, snacks) and cross-tabulated by audience groups and their consumption patterns. Accessed online, this wealth of information can be searched and compared across thousands of categories, brands, and audience groups. Although the reports may seem intimidating, they are not that difficult to use. Figure 11.3 is a page from an MRI report showing how to read MRI data. Media planners use MRI data to check which groups (based on demographics and lifestyles) are high and low in category use, as well as where they live, and what media they use.

• **Competitive Advertising.** In crowded product categories (household products, food, and durable goods) few advertisers ignore competitors' advertising activity. In such situations media planners make scheduling decisions based on the amount of competitive traffic. The objective is to find media where the advertiser's voice is not drowned out by competitors' voices. This concept is called **share of voice**, which measures the percentage of total advertising spending by one brand in a product category relative to the competition; it gives media planners an idea of how much their advertising will stand out.

• **Media Information.** The various media all provide information about the size and makeup of their audiences. Although useful, this information is also suspect because it is assembled to make the best possible case for advertising in that medium. For that reason outside research sources, such as media rep companies (see the MNI ad) and the Nielsen reports, also are used. As discussed in previous chapters, Nielsen Media Research audits national and local television and Arbitron measures radio. Other services, such as the Audit Bureau of Circulations (ABS), Simmons, and Mediamark Research (MRI) monitor print

■ ■ ■

Information about media vehicles is available from the media themselves, but also from media rep firms, such as MNI, that sell ads to be placed in multiple vehicles in a category. MNI, for example, sells ads for newsmagazines in 170 markets.

How to Read an MRI CrossTab

The CrossTab format is a standard research display format that allows multiple variables of related data to be grouped together. Below is a screen capture of an MEMRI² CrossTab, complete with explanations of key numbers. Please note that all the numbers are based on the 2004 Spring MRI study, and that the projected numbers (000) are expressed in thousands.

> Unit labels: these describe each one of the variables in the stacked format — e.g.: the top number in each cell is the unweighted count, and the bottom number in each cell is the index.

> Base counts: in the MRI Spring 2004 study weighted to Population (000), there were 25,639 MRI respondents, and they represent 211,845,000 adults (18+) in the 48 contiguous United States

		All	A 18-34	A 35-54
All	Unwgtd	25639	6654	10787
	(000)	211845	66588	84359
	Horz %	100.00	31.43	39.82
	Vert %	100.00	100.00	100.00
	Index	100	100	100
Energy Drinks: Red Bull: All users: Drank in Last 6 Months	Unwgtd	1149	638	424
	(000)	10126	6341	3260
	Horz %	100.00	62.62	32.19
	Vert %	4.78	9.52	3.86
	Index	100	199	81

> Unweighted Count: 424 MRI Respondents, Adults age 35–54, who drank Red Bull in last six months.

> Projected Count (000): projected to the full population, 3,260,000 Adults 35–54, who said they drank Red Bull in last six months.

> Index: people who are 18–34 are 99% more likely to drink Red Bull in the last six months, than the A 18+ population. (9.52%/4.78% = 199)

> Vertical Percent: out of all people 35–54, only 3.86% said they drank Red Bull in the last six months.

> Horizontal Percent: out of all people 18+ who drank Red Bull in the last six months, 32.19% were 35–54

How the Numbers are Derived

Unwgtd=424	The number of MRI respondents who meet the qualifications specified (in this case, A 35–54 who drank Red Bull in the last six months).
(000)=3,260	After applying each respondent's weight, the "(000)" value is the number of thousands of adults in the 48 contiguous United States represented by the MRI respondents who met the qualifications specified. Expressed in terms of individuals, this means 3,260,000 people.
Horz %=32.19	The percent calculated by dividing the "(000)" value in the cell by the "(000)" value in the base column=3260/10126=32.19%.
Vert %=3.86	The percent calculated by dividing the "(000)" value in the cell by the "(000)" value in the base row=3260/84359=3.86%.
Index=199	The percent calculated by dividing either the horz % in the cell by the horz % in the base row (62.62/31.43) or by dividing the vert % in the cell by the vert % in the base column (9.52/4.78). Either calculation generates the same result, because, when the horz % numbers and vert % numbers are expressed in terms of "(000)", the relationship is identical.

FIGURE 11.3

How to Read MRI Cross Tabs

The MRI market research service provides information on 4,090 product categories and services, 6,000 brands, and category advertising expenditures, as well as customer lifestyle characteristics and buying style psychographics.

Source: Courtesy of Mediamark Research Inc. All rights reserved.

audiences and Media Metrix measures Internet audiences. All of these provide extensive information on viewers, listeners, and readers—both the size of the audience, as well as their profiles.

One type of media-related information about markets is the broadcast coverage area for television, which is called a **designated marketing area (DMA)** and is referred to by the name of the largest city in the area. This is a national market analysis system and every county in the United States has been assigned to a DMA. The assignment is based on where most of the residents receive their television signals, which generally reach a 50- to 60-mile radius. Even though this system is based on TV broadcast signals, it is universally used in doing local market planning.

• *Consumer Information.* We mentioned in Chapter 5 some of the consumer research sources that are used in developing segmentation and targeting strategies. They are also useful in planning media strategies. For example, media planners use such services as the Claritas PRIZM system, Nielsen's ClusterPlus system, and supermarket scanner data to locate the target audience within media markets.

Consider This

1. What are the key components of a media plan?
2. What kinds of information are collected through media research?

MEDIA OBJECTIVES

Media planners must consider three critical elements in setting specific media objectives: the degree of exposure (impressions), the number of different people exposed to the message (reach), and repetition needed to reach those people and make an impression on them (frequency).

Exposure and GRPs

We explained the concept of exposure in Chapter 8. In order to better understand how media objectives are constructed, let's consider how planners work with impressions in calculating the exposure of their plans. If *The David Letterman Show* has an audience of 100,000 viewers, for example, then each time the advertiser buys time on that program, the value in impressions is 100,000. If the advertiser uses a 30-second commercial in each of four consecutive broadcasts, the total viewer impressions would be 100,000 times 4, or 400,000. If the commercial played twice on each of those shows, the total impressions would be estimated at 800,000.

In practice, media planners use gross impressions as a primary measure for total impressions. As mentioned earlier, gross impressions are the sum of the audiences of all the media vehicles used during a certain span of time. The summary figure is called "gross" because the planner has made no attempt to calculate how many different people were in the audience or whether the same person saw the same ad several times; it ignores duplication of exposure. Here's how it is calculated: To get the sum of gross impressions, the media planner finds the audience figure for each vehicle used, multiplies that figure by the number of times the vehicle was used, and adds the vehicle figures. The table below provides an example of how gross impressions would be calculated, assuming an ad was run four times on *Jeopardy,* in two issues of *People,* and in two issues of *USA Today.*

Total Target Impressions Calculation

Media Vehicle	Target Impressions	Number of Messages	Total Target Impressions
TV: *Jeopardy*	3,270,000	4	13,080,000
Magazine: *People*	8,620,000	2	17,240,000
Newspaper: *USA Today*	1,700,000	2	3,400,000
			33,720,000

To avoid the huge numbers, media planners convert impressions to *gross rating points, as* the table below illustrates, in order to compare the efficiency of different media schedules. The problem is determining how much is enough: Is 36.2 GRPs a good number—is it high enough or too high? The answer is, there's no good rule of thumb. Based on experience, intelligent guessing, and computer models, planners have a general idea how many GRPs are necessary to effectively impact a particular market. So, for example, it might take 1,000 GRPs per month to be sufficient for San Diego, but 850 GRPs per month for Richmond, Virginia, as the level of brand development and competitive situations vary by market.

National Audience Gross Rating Points

Media Vehicle	Rating	Number of Messages	Total GRPs
Jeopardy	3.5	4	14.0
People	9.1	2	18.2
USA Today	2.0	2	4.0
			36.2

It should be noted that media objectives for a campaign are always stated in terms of some time frame, often weekly or a four-week period, but it may also be a quarter, six months, or a year. That's true for exposure, but even more so for reach and frequency. Reach and frequency measures are the basis for most media planning and are terms familiar to everyone who works in advertising.

The Reach Objective

An important aspect of an advertising campaign is how many different members of the target audience can be exposed to the message in a particular time frame, which is a measure of the campaign's reach. Different or **unduplicated audiences** are those that have at least one chance of being exposed to a message. Most advertisers realize that a campaign's success is due in part to its ability to reach as many of the targeted audience as possible. Consequently, many planners feel that reach is the most important objective and that's the place to start in figuring out a media plan.[1]

As we explained in Chapter 8, *reach* is the percentage of a medium's audience that is exposed at least once to the advertiser's message during a specific time frame. The media planner calculates the reach of a media schedule according to research estimates that forecast the unduplicated audience. To see how the reach calculation could work in television, we use a simplified scenario. Our fictional television market of Hometown, U.S.A., has only 10 television households. The table below reports a television survey that shows home viewing for *The David Letterman Show.* The viewing survey is for four weeks, during which the commercial ran once each week.

Principle

Reach is the first place to start in setting objectives for a media plan.

Viewing Homes/Week for *The David Letterman Show*

Home	Week 1	Week 2	Week 3	Week 4	Total Household Viewing
1	TV	–	TV	TV	3
2	–	TV	–	TV	2
3	TV	–	–	–	1
4	–	TV	–	–	1
5	–	TV	TV	TV	3
6	–	–	–	–	0
7	–	–	–	TV	1
8	TV	TV	TV	–	3
9	TV	–	TV	–	2
10	–	–	–	–	0
Viewing/week	4	4	4	4	16

Each week four homes viewed *The David Letterman Show*. Because there are 10 homes in Hometown, the average program rating per week was 4 of 10, or 40 percent. To be counted as "reached," a household only has to have the opportunity to view (the set is on and tuned to the right channel) one episode, and 8 of the 10 homes did that during the week. The reach during the four-week period, therefore, is 8 of 10, or 80 percent.

The Frequency Objective

While the reach estimate is based on only a single exposure, *frequency,* the rate of exposure, estimates the number of times the exposure is expected to happen. To estimate the frequency of a schedule, planners use two methods: a shorthand summary called **average frequency** and the **frequency distribution** method, which shows the percentage of audience reached at each level of repetition (exposed once, twice, and so on).

Average Frequency   To figure the average frequency, you need only two numbers: the gross rating points (GRPs) of a schedule and the reach estimate. (Media planners can also calculate the average frequency from the gross impressions and the unduplicated impressions if ratings are not available.) The table below shows readership measures used to plan the purchase of space in three magazines, including rating and impression values.

Average Frequency Calculation Magazine Schedule (One Insertion Each)

Magazine Readers = Reach	Reader/Issue	Rating (GRP)	Unduplicated
Today's Happiness	50,000	50.0	30,000
News Round-Up	40,000	40.0	15,000
Fast-Paced Life	18,000	18.0	11,000
Totals	108,000	108.0	56,000

Target population: 100,000 [100,000 represents the total target audience]
Total gross impressions: 108,000
Gross rating points: 108.0
Unduplicated readers: 56,000
Reach: 56.0 (56,000/100,000)
Average frequency: 1.9 issues seen (108,000/56,000 = 1.9) or (108 GRP/56 Reach = 1.9)

The schedule involves three magazines: *Today's Happiness, News Round-Up,* and *Fast-Paced Life.* Each magazine is listed by its total readership, readers expressed as a percentage (rating), and the number of unduplicated readers (those who do not read either of the other two magazines). Note that the formula calculations are at the bottom of the table. Here is the formula that derived the 1.9 average frequency.

$$\text{Average frequency} = \frac{\text{Gross rating points}}{\text{Reach (\%)}}$$

or

$$\text{Average frequency} = \frac{\text{Gross audience impressions}}{\text{Unduplicated impressions}}$$

Frequency Distribution   Average frequency can give the planner a distorted idea of the plan's performance. Suppose you had a schedule that meant that the ad could be seen a maximum of 20 times. If we figured the average from one person who saw 18 and another who saw 2 exposures, the average would be 10. But 10 exposures aren't close to the experience of either audience member. Most planners who consider frequency tend to calculate frequency distribution whenever possible. The table on page 300 shows the importance of frequency distribution for a schedule of three newsmagazines: *Time, Newsweek,* and *U.S. News & World Report.* Each publication is to receive two ad insertions for a total of six advertising placements. The minimum exposure would be one insertion, and the maximum would be six.

**Magazine Frequency Distribution Table
(Based on Three Magazines, Two Issues Each)**

Issues Read	Readers	Target Population (%)
0	44,000	44.0
1	7,000	7.0
2	6,500	6.5
3	20,000	20.0
4	10,600	10.6 ⎫
5	8,200	8.2 ⎬ 22.5
6	3,700	3.7 ⎭
Totals	100,000	100.0

56,000 read at least one issue. Reach = 56.0.

The planner who evaluates this distribution might consider changing this schedule for two reasons: (1) 44 percent of the target audience would not be exposed, and (2) only 22.5 percent would read more than half the scheduled issues (that is, four, five, or six issues). The frequency distribution method is more revealing, and thus more valuable, than the average frequency method of reporting repetition.

Effective Frequency

As we have just seen, the reach of an audience alone is not a sufficient measure of an advertising schedule's strength. Because of the proliferation of information and clutter, many media planners believe there should be a threshold, or minimum frequency level, before they consider an audience segment to have been exposed to the advertising message. This theory essentially combines the reach and the frequency elements into one factor known as **effective frequency**. The idea is that you add frequency to reach until you get to the level where people respond. Some planners call this *effective reach* because it is making the reach level more effective—but it does this by increasing frequency. That's the reason why we call it effective frequency in this book. Even though this approach is widely used by the industry, there is still concern about the most appropriate method of calculating effective frequency.[2]

Consider This

1. How are reach and frequency objectives calculated?
2. What is effective frequency, and why is it important?

MEDIA STRATEGIES

Through **media strategy** media planners determine the most cost-effective media mix that will reach the target audience and satisfy the media objectives. Strategic thinking in media involves a set of decision factors and tools that help identify the best way to deliver the advertising message.

Delivering on the Objectives

Strategies are designed to deliver on the media objectives, to deliver the right level of exposure in terms of reach and frequency. In terms of a media strategy, some plans might emphasize reach while others emphasize frequency, but it's also possible to work for a balance of both. A high-reach strategy, for example, might be used to deliver a reminder message for a well-known mass-marketed brand or to launch a new product, particularly if it is a fairly easy-to-understand product extension of an existing brand. The wider the market, the greater the need for a high-reach strategy, but regardless of the breadth of the market, reach is the first and most important objective. If you don't reach the right people, then it doesn't matter how many times the ad runs.

In terms of frequency, a general rule of thumb is that it takes three to four exposures for a message to sink in. However, that varies with the type of product and marketing situation. Low-frequency strategies are used with well-known brands and simple messages. Some argue that advertising for established brands need only be seen once in the immediate prepurchase period to have an effect.[3] High-frequency strategies might be used because you want to build excitement about a new product or an upcoming event. More complex messages also may need more repetition. If you are advertising Coke at 99 cents you don't need to repeat it a lot, but if you are trying to explain something new like how TiVo works, then you may need more frequency. Frequency is also used to counter competitive offers, as well as build the brand's share of voice in a highly cluttered category.

The strategic thinking challenge is to come up with ideas about how the objectives will be accomplished. If the objective is a reach of 80 percent and a weekly frequency of 15, then how can you best accomplish that? These strategies generally include decisions that focus on who (target audience), what (the media used), when (time frame), how long (duration), and how big (size). In this section on media strategy, we'll discuss these strategies in terms of the target audience, the media mix, and scheduling.

Target Audience Strategies

The media plan implements the targeting strategy by findings ways to reach the target audience in the most efficient way possible. Consider all the different types of audiences that can be reached just with magazines. Now add the varieties of cable channels, network programs, newspapers, and so forth. You can see how important it is to effectively match a medium's audience to the target audience.

For the new Archipelago exchange, the Fallon media planners had a fairly specific profile—one that suggested the target audience would be difficult to reach with conventional media. They don't sit around and watch a lot of television. They do talk a lot to one another, so anything that can get them to talk about Archipelago would help make the brand hard to ignore. The breadth of the target, as defined in the advertising plan, determines whether the media planner will be using a broad mass-media approach or a tightly targeted and highly focused approach, as in the Archipelago case. For Archipelago the early morning *Open Show* on CNBC, supplemented with posters in the Wall Street area, were enough to reach the audience. The tighter the focus, the easier it is to find appropriate media to deliver a relevant and focused message.

Assessing the media for target audience opportunities is a major challenge for media planners. The evening news on television, for example, reaches a broad mass-market audience, but if your target is women age 25–49, then you have to consider the **targeted reach** of that news program. Obviously both men and women watch news, so if you find that a news program has a rating of 6 (households with sets on), then you know that your audience would probably be half of that. (It's probably less than half if you consider that there are older and younger women also included in that rating.) So maybe the evening news isn't a very good option to reach this target because there would be so much waste in the viewing audience.

That's why planners consult research services like MRI to find programs that reach a large proportion of the target audience. In most cases, no one program or publication will reach the target perfectly (although the CNBC morning show came close to reaching all of the targeted audience for Archipelago). Finding connections like this based on matching consumer insights and media information is one of the creative aspects of the media planner's role, a challenge that is discussed in the Matter of Practice box.

Principle
The tighter the focus on a target market, the easier it is to find appropriate media to deliver a relevant message.

■ ■ ■

Advertisers look at the audience, geographic coverage, demographics, and editorial diversity of magazines as criteria for advertising feasibility in a media plan.

A MATTER OF PRACTICE
Polaroid Zones In

When Polaroid cameras came on the scene years ago, everyone loved them. They provided instant gratification—just shoot and watch the photograph develop. While the traditional 600-series instant camera remains the company's cornerstone, Polaroid made a decision that it needed to target new users and introduce new products if it was going to grow.

Its marketing objective was to target Generation Y (21 and under) with a new image-creation technology. The strategy began in Japan in late 1997 as a low-cost plastic camera that was an instant hit with females age 12–26. Still, research indicated that that version of the camera was not ready for a global market. Most notably, it could shoot in focus at only 2.5 feet. Polaroid hired an industrial de-sign firm to redesign the camera. The result was a pocket-size camera called the I-Zone that takes instant photo booth–size pictures that you can stick anywhere—on phones, T-shirts, and so on. At a cost of $17.99, it comes in four funky colors (see www.i-zone.com).

Polaroid's biggest challenge was reaching the targeted teenagers (primarily girls) at the optimal time. The company knew that teenagers used a host of electronic devices, including cell phones, pagers, and e-mail. These devices satisfied the teens' needs for independence and social interaction. Now the question was how to tell these teenagers that the I-Zone fit into their world.

The initial media strategy used both traditional and nontraditional media. It was also quite systematic. Initially, five TV spots were produced. The nontraditional strategy was to use e-mails, instant messaging, and Web advertising before the TV campaign hit. The TV campaign was a series of 30-second spots on programs with a high teen viewership, such as *Dawson's Creek* and *Sabrina the Teenage Witch*. Complementing the broadcast TV, the company used Channel One television to reach teens at school.

Polaroid courted teen celebrity endorsements before the I-Zone was released by sending complimentary cameras to Christina Aguilera, Britney Spears, and the Backstreet Boys. Polaroid also sponsored tours by the Backstreet Boys, Britney Spears, and a mall tour with Nobody's Angel—all of this to get cameras into the hands of teenage girls while providing a link between product and stars.

i-Zone pocket camera and sticky film from Polaroid.

How well did the campaign work? Overall, the initial campaign was highly successful, selling 1.49 million I-Zone cameras and 3.1 million I-Zone films the first year. It became America's best-selling camera and had built a 7.9 percent market share with the nearest competitor having a 3.8 percent share. Most importantly, 83 percent of sales were among females 13 to 17 years old. With this kind of success, you can see why the I-Zone campaign was an EFFIE award winner.

Consider This

1. Explain what made this media plan effective.
2. Polaroid has learned that its target audient has a short attention span and it needs new media strategies to efficiently reach this market. What would you recommend?

Additional target information used by media planners includes consumer media use, geography, and their consumption patterns.

• *Media Use.* The consumer research used in targeting and segmenting almost always asks for information about what media people use, as well as what other activities engage their time. Media planners have realized for some time that people are moving away from traditional media, such as broadcast TV, daily newspapers, and consumer magazines, and spending more time with cable TV, home video, video games, and the Internet. They also

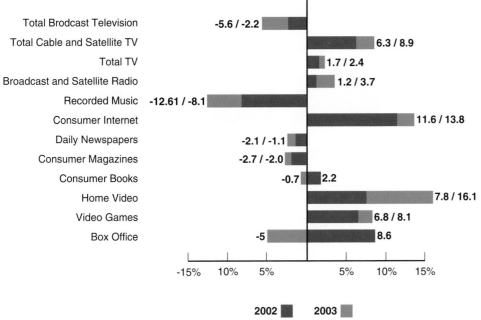

**Changes in Consumer Media Use
(2001–2003)**

Source: "Media Blitzed," *American Demographics,* February 2004, p. 41. © Veronis Suhler Stevenson. Reprinted with permission of American Demographics.

are concerned that people seem to be spending more time traveling and enjoying such leisure-time activities as cruises, both of which limit media use. Figure 11.4 summarizes how consumer media use changed from 2001 to 2003.

- *Geography.* Another factor planners use in analyzing the target audience is geography. Are potential customers found all over the country (therefore calling for a national campaign), and does the client have the budget to afford such an extensive media plan? In most cases, the media plan will identify special regions or cities to be emphasized with a **heavy-up schedule**, which means proportionately more of the budget is spent in those areas. The company's sales geography is one factor used to make this decision; there's no sense advertising in areas where the product isn't available. Most national or regional marketers divide their market geographically. The amount of sales produced in each geographic market will often vary, and marketers try to match advertising investment with the amount of forecasted sales.

- *Consumption Patterns.* If General Mills were to bring out a new line of grits, it wouldn't advertise nationally as most of the consumption of grits occurs in the South. A **category development index (CDI)** is calculated for various categories, which is an index of the relative consumption rate of a product in a particular market. Similarly a **brand development index (BDI)** is an index of the consumption rate of a brand in a particular market. The CDI tells you where the *category* is strong and weak and the BDI tells you where a particular *brand* is strong and weak. There are different strategies for dealing with these levels and they have implications for the media mix and schedule. Planners typically don't make heavy allocations in weak sales areas unless strong marketing signals indicate significant growth potential. Conversely, strong sales markets may not receive proportional increases in advertising unless clear evidence suggests that company sales can go much higher with greater advertising investment.

Media Mix Selection

We mentioned earlier that you rarely can reach your entire target audience with just one medium. Perhaps a small-business owner may find a directory ad to be sufficient, but most organizations need a variety of ways—a *media mix*—to get their messages out to their customers. Why bother with a media mix—why not just pick the best medium and use it? Using a number of media distributes the message more widely because different media tend to have different audience profiles. Some people even reject certain media: Television adver-

Consumer Attitudes and Advertising Spending

Consumers consider print and television advertising to be most trustworthy.

Source: S. Lawrence, "Numbers: The Medium Shapes the Message," Business 2.0 (July 2003): 32.

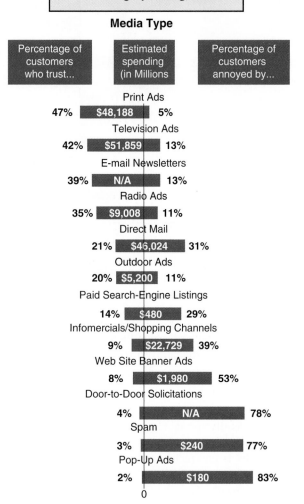

tising, for example, is considered intrusive and Internet advertising is irritating to some people.[4] Believability is a factor. Print and television, for example, are considered more trustworthy,[5] as Figure 11.5 shows, so they might be used by a media planner for a campaign that seeks to establish credibility for a product. Different media also have different strengths in terms of reach and frequency. For example, a media planner may use television to build reach and radio to build frequency. Planners also try to create a synergistic effect between the messages delivered in different media. This is called **image transfer** and refers to the way radio, in particular, reinforces and recreates the message in a listener's mind.

In general, however, media selection is based on message needs. Here is where media planning and message planning overlap. Brand reminders, for example, are often found in television commercials and on billboards. More complex information-laden messages are more likely to be found in magazines, direct mail, or publicity releases. If you want to stimulate immediate action, you might use newspapers, radio, or sales promotion offers.

Media Weighting   Media planners often use a decision criterion called **weighting** to help them decide how much to budget. For example, if a media planner is advertising disposable contact lenses, there might be two segments to consider: the consumer and the eye doctor who makes the recommendation. If the strategy is to encourage the consumer to ask the doctor about the product (a pull strartegy), the planner might recommend putting more emphasis on consumer publications than on professional journals for eye doctors. A weighting strategy, then, might be to put 60 percent of the budget on consumers and 40 percent on doctors. Weighting strategies can be designed to show the relative proportion of media activity in terms of any number of factors, such as seasonality, geography, or audience segment.

Computer Optimization Modeling   Media mix modeling is a computer technique that enables marketers to determine the precise impact of the media plan on product sales and optimize the efficiency of the media mix.[6] The development of this *optimization* software began in the packaged goods sector as a result of the supermarket scanner systems. An example of one optimization model came about through the partnering of McCann-Erickson Worldwide and Media Plan, a developer of media planning software and systems. They created a media allocation software system code named MediaFX. The system can create an unlimited number of media combinations and then simulate the sales produced by each. The media planner can then make intelligent decisions, given factors such as budget, timing, and so forth.

Size, Length, and Position   In addition to selecting the media to use, a media planner also identifies the appropriate size and length that the message will run in each medium. This question of scope and scale applies to all media—even transit advertising. The size or length chosen should relate to the advertising objectives. If the objective is to educate the target audience through a great deal of technical information, a full-page ad or a 60-second spot might be necessary. However, a 10-second spot might be sufficient to create name recognition. Positioning research (where to place an ad on a page or in a pod or group of TV spots) suggests that within a print medium the inside cover and first few pages have slightly better readership, placement of compatible stories adjacent to an ad may enhance its effect, and having many competing ads on the same page detracts from its effectiveness.

■ ■ ■
This photo illustrates the use of transit advertising—in this case a panel on the top of a taxi— to promote the *Wall Street Journal*. The media plan would give direction to the decisions about the size of the sign and the duration of its appearance.

Cost Efficiency: CPM and CPP

Advertisers don't always evaluate the media mix in terms of audience impressions. Sometimes the decision comes down to cold, hard cash. The advertiser wants prospects and not just readers, viewers, or listeners; therefore, advertisers should compare the cost of each proposed media vehicle with the specific vehicle's ability to deliver the target audience. The cheapest vehicle may not deliver the highest percentage of the target audience, so the selection process is a balancing act.

The process of measuring the target audience size against the cost of that audience is based on calculations of efficiency—more popularly referred to as **cost per thousand (CPM)**, which is an estimate of the cost to expose 1,000 audience members, and **cost per point (CPP)**, which is a method of comparing media vehicles by relating the cost of the message to the audience rating. Typically, media specialists make these calculations and provide them to the account executive or the advertiser. Anyone working in advertising should understand what CPM or CPP represents.

• *Cost Per Thousand.* It is best to use CPM analysis to compare vehicles within one medium (one magazine with another or one television program with another). It is also important to base it only on the portion of the audience that has the target characteristics, such as women between the ages of 25 and 34. This is called the *targeted cost-per-thousand*. To calculate the CPM you need only two figures: the costs of the unit (say time on TV or space in a magazine) and the estimated target audience reached by the program. We divide the cost of the unit by the target audience's gross impressions to determine the advertising dollars needed to expose 1,000 members (because it's cost per thousand) of the target.

$$\text{CPM} = \frac{\text{Cost of message unit}}{\text{Gross impressions}} \times 1{,}000$$

Here are two examples that show how to calculate CPMs for magazines and television programs.

• *Magazines.* An issue of *You* magazine has 10,460,000 readers who could be considered in the target audience. The advertising unit is a four-color page and its rate is $42,000. To calculate the CPM:

$$\text{CPM} = \frac{\text{Cost of page or fractional page unit}}{\text{Target audience readers}} \times 1{,}000$$

$$= \frac{\$42{,}000 \times 1{,}000}{10{,}460{,}000} = \$4.02$$

• *Television.* The show *Inside Gossip* has 92,000 target viewers. The cost of a 30-second announcement during the show is $850.

$$\text{CPM} = \frac{\$850 \times 1{,}000}{92{,}000} = \$9.24$$

• *Cost per Point.* Some planners prefer to compare media on the basis of rating points (ratings) instead of impressions. Although both efficiency calculations are used, planners favor the CPP because of its simplicity. The calculation is parallel to CPM with one exception: The denominator is the rating percentage rather than the total impressions. (Note: Because CPP is not calculated on a per-thousand basis, we do not multiply by 1,000.) If the target audience rating for the program *Inside Gossip* was 12.0 and the cost was still $850, the CPP would be 850/12, or $70.83.

$$\text{CPP} = \frac{\text{Cost of message unit}}{\text{Program or issue rating}}$$

Both the CPM and the CPP are relative values. Planners would not know whether *Newsweek*'s CPM of $27.89 was good or bad unless they have comparable figures for *Time* and *U.S. News & World Report*. Although we can use these efficiency analyses across media (comparing one medium to another), we make such comparisons carefully. When comparing the CPMs for radio and television, for example, we are comparing very different audience experiences, and since the experience is totally different, it is difficult to say that one medium is more efficient than the other. CPM and CPP are more valid when used to compare vehicles within a medium. For example, compare the age 18–49 audience watching television on a Thursday night in 2004. The top-rated *Friends* costs about $34 per 1,000 viewers to reach that audience. Or you could pay $11 and reach the same audience watching the *WWE Smackdown* show. Obviously the top-rated show is more expensive for its upscale audience, but maybe wrestling fans are closer to your target audience. In that case, then, the CPM tells you that you've found a bargain using *WWE Smackdown*.[7] It all depends on how you've defined the target audience.

Scheduling Strategies

If advertising budgets were unlimited, most companies would advertise every day. Not even the largest advertisers are in this position, so media planners manipulate schedules in various ways to create the strongest possible impact given the budget. Three scheduling strategies involve timing, duration of exposure, and continuity of exposure.

Timing Strategies   When to advertise can be based on seasons, months, or parts of the day or week. Timing decisions relate to factors such as seasonality, holidays, days of the week, time of day, how often the product is bought, whether it is used more in some months than in others, the consumer's best aperture, and competitors' advertising schedules. There are two critical questions to consider: duration and continuity.

• *Duration: How Long.* For how many weeks of the year or the campaign should the advertising run? If there is a need to cover most of the weeks, the advertising will be spread

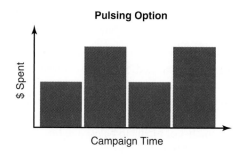

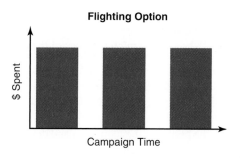

FIGURE 11.6

The Continuity Strategies of Pulsing and Flighting

Pulsing continuity strategies means ads run all the time, sometimes more often than not. A flighting continuity strategy means ads alternate between running intensely for a period and then not at all for a period.

rather thin. If the amount of time to cover is limited, advertising can be concentrated more heavily. Message scheduling is often driven by consumer use cycles, especially for products and services that demand high usage rates, such as candy and gum, fast-food restaurants, and movies. In general, if you cannot cover the whole year, you should heavy up the schedule in higher-purchase periods. For example, movie marketers do most of their newspaper advertising on the weekends, when most people go to movies.

Another question is how much is enough: At what point does the message make its point? If the advertising period is too short or there are too few repetitions, then the message may have little or no impact. If the period is too long, then the ad may suffer from *wearout,* which means the audience gets tired of it and stops paying attention.

The concept of **lead time** is also relevant. It has two meanings of interest to us. It refers to the amount of time allowed before the beginning of the sales period to reach people when they are just beginning to think about seasonal buying. Back-to-school advertising is an example. Advertising typically starts in July or early August for a school calendar that begins in late August or September. Lead time also refers to the production time needed to get the advertisement into the medium. There is a long lead time for magazines, but it is shorter for local media, such as newspapers and radio.

• *Continuity: How Often.* **Continuity** refers to the way the advertising is spread over the length of a campaign. A **continuous strategy** spreads the advertising evenly over the campaign. Planners who cannot afford or do not want continuous scheduling have two other methods to consider: pulse patterns and flight patterns, as shown in Figure 11.6.

A **pulsing strategy** is designed to intensify advertising before an open aperture and then to reduce advertising to much lower levels until the aperture opens again. The pulse pattern has peaks and valleys, also called bursts. Fast-food companies such as McDonald's and Burger King use pulsing patterns. Although the competition for daily customers suggests continuous advertising, chains of such restaurants will greatly intensify activity to accommodate special events such as new menu items, merchandise premiums, and contests. Pulsed schedules cover most of the year, but still provide periodic intensity.

A **flighting strategy** is the most severe type of continuity adjustment. It is characterized by alternating periods of intense advertising activity and periods of no advertising (hiatus). This on-and-off schedule allows for a longer campaign without making the advertising schedule too light. The hope in using nonadvertising periods is that the consumers will remember the brand and its advertising for some time after the ads have stopped. Figure 11.7 illustrates this awareness change. The jagged line represents the rise and fall of consumer awareness of the brand. If the flight strategy works, there will be a *carryover*

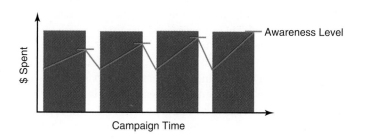

FIGURE 11.7

Consumer Awareness Levels in a Flighting Strategy

By using a flighting strategy, advertisers hope that there will be a carryover effect, meaning consumers will remember the product during advertising downtimes.

effect of past advertising that means consumers will remember the product across the gap until the next advertising period begins. The critical decision involves analyzing the *decay* level, the rate at which memory of the advertising is forgotten.[8]

The Media Flowchart   The strategy for meeting time and duration requirements calls for a balance between the available advertising dollars and the length of the campaign. After the schedule has been worked out in terms of what media run when and for how long, these decisions are plotted on a *media flowchart*. Across the top is the calendar for the period of the campaign and down the side is the list of media to be used in this campaign. Bars are then drawn across the calendar that identify the exact timing of the use of various media. When the chart is complete, strategies such as pulsing and flighting are easy to observe.

The Media Budget

Media planning begins and ends with the budget. An initial assessment of the amount of money available (small budget, large budget) determines what kinds of media can be used. A small-budget campaign, for example, may not be able to afford television as it is the most costly of all media. A small budget may also dictate that the campaign be local or limited to a few areas, rather than trying to be national. As the Inside Story explains, small budgets are a creative challenge for media planners.

At the end of the planning process, after the media mix has been determined, the media planner will allocate the budget among the various media chosen. The most common format used to present the media allocation decisions is a pie chart that clearly shows the various media being used in proportion to the amount being spent on each medium.

Global Media Planning

Advertising practitioners can debate global theories of advertising, but one fact is inescapable: Global media do not currently exist. Television can transmit the Olympics around the globe, but no one network controls this global transmission. The closest we come to that is CNN, but even it doesn't reach everywhere and other national and regional news channels, such as BBC, challenge it for dominance. An advertiser seeking global exposure, therefore, must deal with different networks in different countries.

Satellite transmission now places advertising in many homes, but its availability is not universal because of the footprint (coverage area of the satellite), the technical limitations, and the regulations of transmission by various governments. Satellites beam signals to more than one country in Europe, the Asian subcontinent, North America, and the Pacific, but they are regional, not global, in coverage.

Despite its regional limitation, satellite transmission is still an enormous factor in the changing face of international advertising. The reach of satellite stations is based on a foundation of shared language, which is making national borders increasingly irrelevant in international markets.

The North American, European, Asian, and Latin American markets are becoming saturated with cable TV companies offering an increasing number of international networks. Such broadcasters include the hugely successful Latin American networks of Univision and Televisa, whose broadcasts can be seen in nearly every Spanish-speaking market, including the United States. One of Univision's most popular programs, Sabado Giganta, is seen by tens of millions of viewers in 16 countries.

Star TV, with an audience spanning 38 countries including Egypt, India, Japan, Indonesia, and Russia's Asian provinces, was the first to reach this market of an estimated 2.7 billion people. It was closely followed by CNN and ESPN. Sky Channel, a U.K.-based network, offers satellite service to most of Europe, giving advertisers the opportunity to deliver a unified message across the Continent. The expansion of satellite television makes it possible to distribute a standardized message to extensive audiences, the potential of which presents international advertisers with new and unique challenges and powerfully enticing rewards.

THE INSIDE STORY

The Reality of Budget Cuts

Heather Beck, Media Coordinator Stern, Advertising, Cleveland, Ohio

It is common to hear about budget cuts in today's economy, but that doesn't make it any easier to plan accordingly. It's also commonly true that one of the first areas to lose money is the advertising budget.

Recently, we had a client cut their budgets significantly (about 30 percent off an already minimal figure). To top it off, they did so at the last possible minute to get the year's media plans in order. This left us with the seemingly impossible task of putting together an all-new media plan with only a fraction of the money to work with. We had one week to do what normally would take at least two months.

The first and probably most important factor we had on our side was research. We had already done most of the research for the year during our regular planning schedule. To keep the information organized, we have flowcharts set up for all of the markets that our client is in (about 150 major markets, plus some smaller submarkets). On those flowcharts, we list the major advertising options (TV, radio, newspaper, direct mail, etc.), as well as their costs. Using Excel, we can enter formulas that will automatically add costs together and subtract from the budget so that we can easily keep track of the money spent and/or still available.

The next thing we had to think about was what media our client could realistically afford with the new budget. Although they had done a good deal of TV and radio in the past, we had to explain to them that it would just not be feasible with little money. We had to weigh the options. They could either waste the money running a TV campaign for only a few weeks out of the year, with nothing to back it up, or they could advertise in a more affordable medium, such as newspapers, and be able to spread their advertising dollars a little more throughout the year. We had to refer back to the data gathered in previous years on the effectiveness of newspaper advertising for this particular client. We also had to see whether a market's main large newspaper was effective, or if the smaller but more afford-

able suburban papers were a better choice. How many of our client's customers would we reach? It turned out that newspaper advertising would be effective in most of the client's markets. We also found that radio could be relatively affordable and effective in some smaller markets.

Another key is maintaining relationships with all media vendors so that we can negotiate contracts. Almost all newspapers have "bulk contracts" that give a lower cost per inch rate if the client agrees to run a certain amount of advertising throughout the year. However, when you have a strong relationship with a sales representative of a paper, he or she can sometimes offer a bulk rate, even if you will not run enough advertising to cover the minimum. This can sometimes save enough money to run a few extra ads that the client might not have been able to afford otherwise. Every dollar counts. The same thing goes for other media. Having a client who advertises in several markets will benefit contracts with national vendors, such as Valassis or Advo, who send out the sales paper packets you often see in the middle of newspapers or on their own in the mailbox. If you buy in bulk for several markets, you can send out inserts for a low average cost per thousand.

There are various ways to cut costs and get the most advertising for each dollar. You should always be prepared, however, for drastic budget cuts and having very little time to change media plans. Stay up-to-date on all research, including customer response to previous ads and vendor changes (rates, circulation, etc.). Keep all this information well organized, and use a program like Excel to track and access the data quickly and easily.

A graduate of the advertising program at Middle Tennessee State, Heather L. Beck has been a media coordinator since March 2001 with Stern Advertising, a Cleveland-based agency, which is a member of the Integer Group, an Omnicom company. Some accounts handled by the agency include McDonald's (regional), Pearle Vision, Things Remembered, Ohio Lottery, and Kay Jewelers.

Nominated by Professor Edd Applegate, Middle Tennessee State University

After this review of media planning, let's stop for a moment and look at how a media plan comes together, focusing on a plan constructed for Pizza Hut. After this discussion, we'll turn our attention to media buying and explain how a plan is executed.

Consider This

1. What are the key media strategy decisions found in a media plan?
2. If a media planner wants to reach a person like you (that is, you are in the target audience), plot out the media research needed in order to make key media strategy decisions. In other words, what does the media planner need to know about people like you?

A SAMPLE MEDIA PLAN FOR PIZZA HUT

Media plans do not have a universal form, but there is a common (and logical) pattern to the decision stages. To illustrate a style of presentation in a real-life setting, we use an actual media plan (excerpted with disguised numbers) from a Pizza Hut national media plan. Let's briefly explore each major section in this plan.

Situation and Consumer Analysis

The background and situation analysis is the marketing perspective we discussed at the beginning of the chapter. Pizza Hut's overview discusses media options and opportunities to narrowly target consumers using niche channels and programs. It also describes the target audiences, their psychographics, and the best way to reach these audiences. This overview is an analysis that sees media ownership consolidation as a marketing opportunity.

Pizza Hut Media Plan Overview

- **Pizza Hut's Background/Situation Analysis.** The turn of the century saw an explosion of media choices for consumers. On the positive side, Pizza Hut can now narrowly target its consumers using these niche channels and programs.

- **Occasion-based Marketing.** Research shows that Pizza Hut is a strong brand with the 40-plus age group, who make "food-focused" dinner decisions. The groups where Pizza Hut has not maximized its share of occasions are the Echo Boomers and Generation X groups, age 20 to 40, who make decisions based on functional needs. These needs are reflected predominantly by two types of occasions.

  "Pressure Cooker" occasions are driven by impulse orders, dominated by moms who are looking for a dinner solution that appeals to kids (cheese pizza) with a good price point. They make dinner decisions between 4 and 8 P.M. with 56 percent of decisions made within one hour of dinner. Solutions to the meal dilemma should be presented during dinnertime broadcast TV and family-focused cable. Because mom is also found in her car coming home from work, going to soccer practice or piano lessons, or running her errands, radio can put Pizza Hut in her mind at the right time.

  The "Hanging Out" occasion skews heavily toward the 18 to 24 age group, who think of eating pizza as part of a social occasion. High-profile programming such as late-night television, MTV, ESPN, and sports capture the heart of the need-state. Alternative rock and young country radio stations are also important pieces of the media makeup of these young adults.

Media Objectives and Aperture Strategies

The Pizza Hut advertising objectives concentrate on brand awareness, reaching the target audience, and integrating national and local media plans.

The Media Mix

The strategy section of the media plan explains why a single medium or set of media is appropriate for the campaign objectives. For the television portion of the Pizza Hut campaign, shown in Figure 11.9, the planner cannot be assured of program availability or specific pricing in television except for major events such as an NFL Pregame Super Bowl sponsorship. As a result, the strategies deal with specifics where possible and omit detail when the specific media vehicle hasn't been identified. For simplicity's sake, we show excerpts from the TV and Internet media strategies and omit the print and co-op radio strategies with local franchisees.

Pizza Hut Media Plan
Research findings are a part of Pizza Hut's media plan specifics.

Pizza Hut National Media Objectives

- **Establish a Pizza Hut Presence.** Maintain top-of-mind awareness.

- **Create Highly Visible Launch Platforms.** Build broad research for new products/big events.

- **Reach Heavy Pizza Users Target.** Ensure important male targets are reached, and balance age 18–34 and 35–49 demographic deliveries.

- **Integrate National and Local Media Plans.** Provide option windows to address local needs.

   Pizza Hut's Media Plan Objectives spotlight research findings about media apertures that shaped its media plan, as we see in Figure 11.8. Other aperture strategies include the following:

- Launches that will build broad reach for new products and big events using a strategy of 80 percent reach with a frequency of four times per week.

- Using national media covering the NFL and the NCAA, which ensures that male targets are reached.

- A balanced delivery between adults aged 18 to 35 and 35 to 49 through focus on net-work broadcast media and programs that target the echo boomers (children of baby boomers).

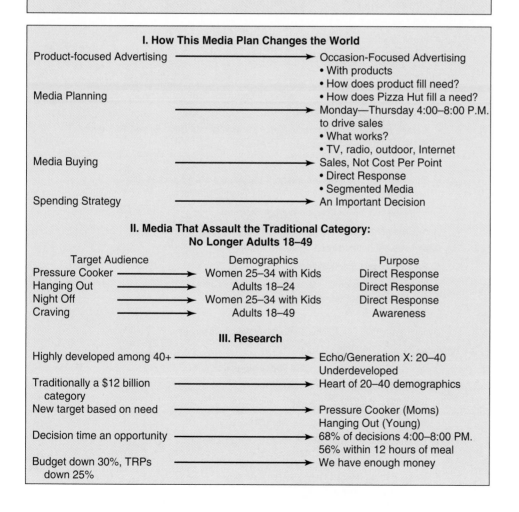

The Flowchart: Scheduling and Budgeting Allocation

Figure 11.10 illustrates most of the media recommendations. It uses graphics to show the month-by-month placement of messages, detail the anticipated impact through forecasted levels of GRPs, and illustrate how the campaign budget is allocated by medium and by month. In a concise fashion, the flowchart is the template for the media mix.

Pizza Hut TV and Internet Media Strategies
Here Pizza Hut lays out how it plans to advertise on TV and Internet media.

I. National TV Media Strategy

A. Establish a Pizza Hut Presence
- Own the SCAA: Basketball 15 Weeks
- Own Fox NFL: Pregame Sponsorship 20 Weeks
- ESPN and Fox Cable Sports: Sports Show Feature 32 Weeks
- Cable Stretch: Own Tuesday Night Pizza Occasions 32 Weeks

Enhancement
- CBS NFL Pregame Sponsorship 10 Weeks
  - Shared with KFC, but *locks out* Domino's!

B. Create Highly Visible Launch Platforms for *Big New Yorker* and *Star Wars* Event
- Roadblocks
- Network Strips
- Highly Visible Programming
- 1 Week Reach 80% with a 4 Frequency

Enhancement
- Leverage Tricon Partners Inventory to Achieve These Goals for Star Wars

C. Reach Heavy Pizza User Target
- Continue Leveraging Sports to Ensure Male/Female Balance and Target Key Pizza Consumption Occasions

Enhancement
- Target Echo Boomers/Generation X to Balance 18–24 and 25–34 with 35–49
  - Increased mix of Fox and Warner Brothers
  - Cable focus on USA, TNT, F/X, E!, and Comedy Central

D. Integrate National and Local Media Plans
- Provide Local Option Windows
- When on Air Nationally Have Sufficient Prime/Sports/Cable So That Co-ops Do Not Have to Buy Premium Programming

II. The Brave New World: Internet

America's Online: 70.5 Million Adults

USA Today, August 27, 2000

ESPNet SportsZone: A Toe in the Water
- 300 Million E-mailed Coupons
- Special Coupon Offer Just for Internet?

Pizza Hut Must Become More Active
- Using Our Website
- Investments That Facilitate Internet Ordering
- Advertising More Effectively

1999 PLANNING TEMPLATE

	1st Quarter			2nd Quarter			3rd Quarter			4th Quarter		
	Period 1	Period 2	Period 3	Period 4	Period 5	Period 6	Period 7	Period 8	Period 9	Period 10	Period 11	Period 12	Period 13
	De January	February	March	April	May	June	July	August	September	October	November	December
Monday Dates	21 28 4 11 18 25	1 8 15 22	1 8 15 22	29 5 12 19 26	3 10 17 24 31	7 14 21	28 5 12 19 26	2 9 16 23 30	6 13 20 27	4 11 18 25	1 8 15 22	29 6 13 20
Key Events	Xmas Bowl NFL Sup / Gms POs Bowl			Fnl Estr / 4 Chmp / AA		Mem / Day	Jul / 4th		Lbr / Day		Hwe	Tks Xmas / gvn
National Topic		Big NY	Big NY	TBD		Star Wars	Star Wars		Big NY		TBD	TBD
NETWORK												
Product :30;15		630	475	440		530	420		445		600	425	3,965
Promo :30 Only	160				30			25		85		35	335
Kids 6–11 (A18–49 20 index)				500		600			500				320 / 4,620
SPOT TV												
Product		800	600	400	400	700	600	500	700	400	700	400	400	6,600
TOTAL TV		960	1230	875	940	730	1202	968	725	845	885	1000	825	35	11,220
SPOT RADIO		400	400		300			300		300			300	2,000
Monday Dates	21 28 4 11 18 25	1 8 15 22	1 8 15 22	29 5 12 19 26	3 10 17 24 31	7 14 21	28 5 12 19 26	2 9 16 23 30	6 13 20 27	4 11 18 25	1 8 15 22	29 6 13 20
	De January	February	March	April	May	June	July	August	September	October	November	December

FIGURE 11.10

Pizza Hut Media-Planning Template
Pizza Hut's media-planning template maps out month-by-month placement of ads, as well as their expected gross rating points.

Consider This

1. What is the key problem and opportunity this media plan grapples with?
2. Explain how the specific media plan decisions deliver on the objectives.

MEDIA BUYING

The media plan is a recommendation that the client must approve before any further steps are taken. In fact, planning is only the first stage in advertising media operations. Once the plan directions are set, media buyers convert objectives and strategies into tactical decisions. They select, negotiate, and contract for the time and space in media. In this section we explain how the media buyer makes the media plan come to life. A media buyer has distinct responsibilities as outlined in Figure 11.11.

Media Buying Specifics

Buying is a complicated process. The American Association of Advertising Agencies (AAAA) lists no fewer than 21 elements in the authorization for a media buy. In this section, we examine the most important buyer functions: providing information to media planners, selecting the media, negotiating costs, billing and payment, monitoring the media choices, evaluating the media choices after the campaign, and handling billing and payment.

• *Providing Inside Information.* Media buyers are important information sources for media planners. They are close enough to day-to-day changes in media popularity and pricing to be a constant source of inside information. For example, a newspaper buyer discovers that a key newspaper's delivery staff is going on strike; or a magazine buyer's source reveals that the new editor of a publication is going to change the editorial focus dramatically. All of these things can influence the strategy and tactics of current and future advertising plans.

Principle
Media buyers should be consulted early in planning as they are a good source of information on changes in media.

The Functions of a Media Buyer
Media buyers have six main responsibilities.

■ ■ ■

Physical characteristics of a magazine can affect its ability to deliver the desired message. For example, the V8 ad, which appeared in *Readers' Digest*, uses simple visuals and minimal copy to accommodate the smaller page size. *Readers' Digest* may not be the best choice for a complex ad.

• *Selecting Media Vehicles.* The key function of media buying is choosing the best media vehicles that fit the target audience's aperture. The media planner lays out the direction, but the buyer is responsible for choosing the specific vehicles. Armed with the media plan directives, the buyer seeks answers to a number of difficult questions: Does the vehicle have the right audience profile? Will the program's current popularity increase, stabilize, or decline? How well does the magazine's editorial format fit the brand and the message strategy (see the V8 ad example)? The answers to those questions bear directly on the campaign's success.

• *Negotiation.* Just as a labor union negotiates with management for pay raises, security, and work conditions, so does a media buyer pursue special advantages for clients. The key questions are whether the desired vehicles can be located and whether a satisfactory schedule and rates can be negotiated and maintained.

Aside from finding the aperture of target audiences, nothing is more crucial in media buying than securing the lowest possible price for placements. Every medium has a published rate card but media buyers negotiate special prices with discounts for volume buys. The buyer must understand the trade-off between price received and audience objectives. For example, a media buyer might be able to get a lower price for 30 commercials on ESPN, but part of the deal is that half the spots are scheduled with programs that don't reach the primary target audience. So the price may not be a good deal in the long run. Here are some other negotiation areas:

- *Preferred Positions.* Media buyers must bargain for *preferred positions:* the locations in print media such as magazines that offer readership advantages. Imagine the value a food advertiser would gain from having its message located in a special recipe section that the homemaker can detach from the magazines for permanent use. How many additional exposures might that ad get? Because they are so visible, preferred positions often carry a premium surcharge, usually 10 to 15 percent above standard space rates.

- *Extra Support Offers.* With the current trend toward using other forms of marketing communication in addition to advertising, buyers often demand additional promotional support. These activities, sometimes called **value-added media services**, can take any number of forms, including contests, special events, merchandising space at stores, displays, and trade-directed newsletters. The "extra" depends on what facilities each media vehicle has and how hard the buyer can bargain. The ad for Meredith Company promotes a number of its available media service options.

- *Billing and Payment.* Bills from the various media come in continuously. Ultimately, it is the responsibility of the advertiser to make these payments. However, the agency is contractually obligated to pay the invoice on behalf of the client. Keeping track of the invoices and paying the bills is the responsibility of the media buyer in conjunction with the accounting department.

- *Monitoring the Media Buy.* A media buyer's responsibility to a campaign does not end with the signing of space and time contracts. The media buyer is responsible for tracking the performance of the media plan as it is implemented, as well as afterward as part of the campaign evaluation. Buys are made in advance, based on forecasted audience levels. What happens if unforeseen events affect scheduling? What if newspapers go on strike, magazines fold, or a television show is canceled? Buyers must fix these problems. Underperformance and schedule problems are facts of life. Poorly performing vehicles must be replaced or costs must be modified. Buyers also check the publication issues to verify whether advertisements have been placed correctly. Buyers make every attempt to get current audience research to ensure that schedules are performing according to forecast.

Temporary snags in scheduling and in the reproduction of the advertising message usually are unavoidable. Buyers must be alert for missed positions or errors in handling the message presentation and ensure that the advertiser is compensated appropriately when they occur. A policy of compensating for such errors is called "making good on the contract" known as **make-goods**. Here are some examples.

Program preemptions. Special programs or news events often interrupt regular programming and the commercial scheduled is also interrupted. In the case of long-term interruptions (for example, war coverage), buyers may have difficulty finding suitable replacements before the schedule ends.

Missed closings. Magazines and newspapers have clearly set production deadlines, called **closings**, for each issue. Sometimes the advertising materials do not arrive in time. If the publication is responsible, it will make good. If the fault lies with the client or the agency, there is no restitution by the publication.

Technical problems. Technical difficulties are responsible for numerous goofs, glitches, and foul-ups that haunt the advertiser's schedule. Bleed-throughs and out-of-register colors for newspapers, torn billboard posters, broken film, and tapes out of alignment are typical problems.

Meredith is a large magazine publishing company. In order to make the sale more attractive, the company's sales literature explains all the ways Meredith can support the advertising with additional sales and merchandising promotions.

• *Postcampaign Evaluation.* Once a campaign is completed, the buyer's duty is to compare the plan's expectations and forecasts with what actually happened. Did the plan actually achieve GRP, reach, frequency, and CPM objectives? Did the newspaper and magazine placements run in the positions expected? Such analysis is instrumental in providing guidance for future media plans.

Global Media Buying

The definition of global media buying varies widely, but everyone agrees that few marketers are doing it at this time. However, many are thinking about it, especially computer and other information technology companies that are being pursued by media such as CNN International. Today, the growth area is media buys across a single region. But as media become more global, some marketers are beginning to make the leap between regions. About 60 percent of ad buys on CNN International are regional and 40 percent are global.

In Europe, the rise of buying "centrals" came about with the emergence of the European Union and the continuing globalization of trade and advertising. Buying centrals are media organizations that buy across several European countries. Their growth also began with the development of commercial broadcasting and the expansion of media choices. These firms have flourished in an environment of flexible and negotiated rates, low inflation, and a fragmented advertising market. The buying centrals have nearly three-fourths of the media market in France, nine-tenths in Spain, and about two-fifths in Britain, Holland, Italy, and Scandinavia.

Consider This

1. What are the primary functions of a media buyer, and how do they differ from the role of a media planner?
2. In what ways is a media buy monitored?

MEDIA PLANNING CHANGES AND CHALLENGES

The entire area of media is dynamic and changing so fast, it's hard to keep track of how business is practiced. All of these changes create new ways of operation and new opportunities for innovative media planners and buyers.

Unbundling Media Buying and Planning

We've mentioned the growth of media buying services, such as the media megashop Starcom MediaVest, as separate companies that specialize in media buying. This shift in the way the media industry is organized is referred to as **unbundling media services**. Being able to aggregate the buying function across many different clients enables media companies to negotiate better rates for their clients. Because these companies control the money, they have become a powerful force in the advertising industry, leading to a tug of war over control of planning. That is why, faced with competition from these independent media companies, many large agencies have set up or bought their own buying services to compete with the independents and go after outside business.

Some of these media companies are now offering *consolidated services,* which means bringing the planning and buying functions back together. To take advantage of this consolidation argument, some media companies are also adding special planning teams for other related areas such as events, product placement, Internet, and guerilla marketing programs. WPP's MindShare has created an agency-within-the-agency called the "Wow Factory" to develop ideas for nontraditional media.[9] For a major presentation to Coca-Cola, Starcom MediaVest pulled together a team that represented basic media planning and buying, research, consumer insights, programming, product placement, entertainment marketing, and integration solutions.[10] At this point, these big media companies begin to look more like traditional agencies.

Online Media Buying

At one time, GM set up GMTradeXchange.com for its vendors to buy and sell their goods and services online. A comparable system to GM's has been set up by more than 50 consumer goods companies, including Procter & Gamble, Coca-Cola, and Unilever. Today, many companies rely on Covisint (www.covisint.com) to handle these requests, allowing them to buy billions of dollars in advertising through Internet technology.

New Forms of Media Research Needed

One challenge media planners face is the lack of reliable audience research on new media. But the problem is deeper than that as the industry continues to challenge the validity of the traditional media monitoring systems, such as the Nielsen ratings. According to *Advertising Age,* "as the industry confronts change, it is increasingly clear that the tools and key metrics used as the basis for hundreds of billions of dollars spent on media, especially TV and print, may no longer be adequate to the task."[11] Calls for reform, which include better metrics on all media, are needed to reflect the different ways consumers are using media, as well as new forms of media such as TiVo and interactive TV.

SaveonTv.com is an example of a media buying service on the Internet.

Some experts are calling for innovative media monitoring systems that measure outcomes and results instead of simply delivery. In other words, media measures should recognize advertising response functions, as well as program delivery.[12]

Another problem is that media research is based on each medium as a *silo*—separate studies for separate media. Most of the research services are unable to tell you much about the effectiveness of combined media, such as seeing the same message on television and then reading about it in a newspaper story or ad. One British company, Knowledge Networks/Statistical Research (KN/SR), is trying to develop a tool for measuring a multimedia, consumer-centric approach to media, one that also offers uniform measurements across media.[13]

IT'S A WRAP

THE OPEN SHOW OPENS THE DOOR FOR ARCHIPELAGO

Media planning is about delivering a message but it's also about making connections with a consumer in a way and at a time that engages that person in a positive brand interaction. It takes into consideration the feelings that the target audience has about the contact point—both traditional and nontraditional—as well as their involvement with and response to the message.

The success of the Archipelago *Open Show* can be measured in terms of business measures, as well as advertising response indicators. The campaign successfully launched Archipelago with total trading volume increasing 54 percent during the campaign. Market share also increased during that same period by 40 percent.

Advertising results determined that the campaign was successful at its first objective, which was redefining Archipelago as an exchange and building its business:

- The campaign increased interest among stock traders with many saying that they were more interested in the new exchange as a result of the advertising.
- There was an increase in buzz with referrals increasing by 82 percent.
- Most importantly, the image of Archipelago as a viable exchange was established, with traders saying that Archipelago was "viable and had staying power." That was an improvement of 36 percent from before the campaign.
- In terms of business, there was an increase of 67 percent in the number of professional traders who said they had used Archipelago.

The awareness objective was met, with unaided awareness of the campaign achieving a level of 52 percent, which was the highest in the category. The awareness level was achieved even though the NYSE outspends Archipelago 4 to 1.

Another set of objectives focused on trader interaction with the new exchange and *The Open Show.* A total of 408 contest entries to be on the show were received from traders, who are typically a non-promotion-oriented group. Hundreds of traders sent e-mails with suggestions for locations and plot lines for the episodes. The Archipelago *Open Show* is a good example of a great award-winning media idea that connected with its audience at the same time it built business for its client.

Summary

1. **Explain the concept of media aperture.** Aperture is a media concept that says advertising should be delivered and is most effective when are people are receptive to the product information.

2. **Describe the types of information compiled by media researchers.** Media research is a step in the media planning process that involves collecting audience data about the marketplace, consumers, and various media vehicles that might be used to reach the target audience. A situation analysis is constructed based on client, market research, competitive advertising, media vehicles, and consumer information.

3. **Analyze how media planners set media objectives.** Media planners consider three critical elements in setting specific media objectives: the degree of exposure (impressions), the number of different people exposed to the message (reach), and the amount of repetition needed to reach those people and make an impression on them (frequency).

4. **List the key media strategy decisions.** Media strategies are designed to find media opportunities that will deliver on the media objectives and reach the appropriate target audience. The key strategies include geographical selection, media mix selection, cost-efficiency decisions, and scheduling and budgeting decisions.

5. **Identify the responsibilities of media buyers.** Media buyers have inside information about the media industries that they feed back into the planning. Their responsibilities as buyers include selecting media vehicles, negotiating the rates, handling the billing and payment, and monitoring the effectiveness of the media buy.

Key Terms

aperture, 293
average frequency, 299
brand development index (BDI), 303
category development index (CDI), 303
closing, 315
continuity, 307

continuous strategy, 307
cost per point (CPP), 305
cost per thousand (CPM), 305
designated market area (DMA), 297
effective frequency, 300
flighting strategy, 307
frequency distribution, 299

heavy-up schedule, 303
image transfer, 304
lead time, 307
make-goods, 315
media strategy, 300
pulsing strategy, 307
share of voice, 295
targeted reach, 301

unbundling media services, 316
unduplicated audience, 298
value-added media services, 315
weighting, 304

Review Questions

1. What is aperture, and how is it used in media planning?
2. What are the five sources of information compiled by media researchers, and how are they used in media planning?
3. Give some examples of strategic decisions that deliver the reach and frequency objectives.
4. How do consumer media use, geography, and consumption patterns affect a media plan?
5. What are the six primary functions of a media buyer?

▪▪▪ Discussion Questions

1. The Pioneer account has accepted your recommendation for 10 one-page insertions (10 issues) in a magazine known as the *Illustrated Press.* Your total target audience is 30 million people. The magazine reaches an estimated 3 million of your target audience per month, or, we could say, a 10 percent rating per issue. The cost per page of the publication is $20,000. What is the total GRP delivered by this schedule? What are the CPM and the CPP?

2. If you were doing a frequency analysis composed of two magazines, a radio network schedule, and a national newspaper, would you rather use the average frequency procedure or a frequency distribution analysis? Explain your choice.

3. Explain why media planners try to balance reach, frequency, and continuity of proposed media schedules. What considerations go into this decision?

4. You have just begun a new job as a media planner for a new automobile model from General Motors. The planning sequence will begin in four months, and our media director asks you what data and information you need from the media research department. What sources should you request? How will you use each of these sources in the planning function?

5. The marketing management of McDonald's restaurants has asked you to analyze the aperture opportunity for its breakfast entrees. What kind of analysis would you present to management? What recommendations could you make that would expand the restaurant's nontraditional, as well as traditional, media opportunities.

6. Your client is a major distributor of movie videotapes. Its early media plan for magazines has been settled and you are in negotiation when you learn that a top publishing company is about to launch a new magazine dedicated to movie fans and video collectors. Although the editorial direction is perfect, there is no valid way to predict how the magazine will be accepted by the public. Worse, there won't be solid research on readership for at least a year. The sales representative offers a low charter page rate if the advertiser agrees to appear in each of the first year's 12 issues. To use it you will have to remove one of the established magazines from your list. Is the risk worthwhile? Should you bother the client with this information, considering that the plan is already set? The new magazine will also be available online. Should you take advantage of this opportunity? Make some recommendations to your client and explain your reasoning.

▪▪▪ Class Projects

1. In performing an aperture analysis, consider the following products: video games (Nintendo, for instance), men's cologne (such as Davidoff's "Cool Water"), computer software (such as Lotus), and athletic shoes for aerobics (Reebok, for example). For each of these products, find the answers to these questions:
   a. Which media should be used to maximize aperture leverage?
   b. How does aperture work in each of your recommendations?
   c. Explain how the timing and duration of the advertising improve the aperture opportunity.

2. Go to www.overture.com. Indicate how you would use the information provided by this site in developing your media plan for a new reality TV show. Focus on the Internet as a primary medium. Write a one- to two-page report.

HANDS-ON

CASE

P&G Puts the Medium Before the Message

To borrow and slightly modify an old ad slogan, when Proctor & Gamble speaks, people listen. At least, people in the advertising business do, because P&G is one of the biggest spenders on advertising and promotions in the world. You know the brands: Crest toothpaste, Tide detergent, Charmin toilet paper, Pringles potato chips, and dozens of others.

In early 2004, P&G was speaking. The company was saying that it intended to revolutionize the process by which advertising is developed. Its new approach, called *communications planning*, puts the medium before the message. The idea is to strategically select media first, then to develop creative messages that best take advantage of each channel. This approach is, of course, a reversal of the tried-and-true method of developing what you want to say before you decide where to say it.

To make P&G's idea a bit less abstract, imagine creating a campaign for a P&G brand the old way. The agency creatives working for Charmin, P&G's toilet tissue brand, would start with the message strategy; for example, they might decide that the Big Idea for a campaign should be the softness and comfort of the tissue. After coming up with the creative strategy, they would then consider the best way to communicate it. Charmin's agency creatives might decide, for example, that consumers should see a demonstration of the brand's softness (Charmin's old commercials featured store manager "Mr. Whipple," who was constantly trying to stop consumers from impulsively squeezing rolls of Charmin). The creatives' decision to illustrate the Big Idea via a demonstration would strongly increase the likelihood that television will be an important medium for the campaign, since TV is very effective for product demonstrations.

The message-then-medium approach described above seems logical, so why has P&G abandoned it? The answer can be found in changes occurring in the media world. For years large advertisers have been questioning the wisdom of spending massive amounts of money on network TV. Fewer people watch the networks, network TV ads are regularly zipped or zapped, and the networks have a difficult time delivering segmented audiences, and yet network ad rates have increased far faster than the rate of inflation. You might expect agencies to have walked away from network TV buys a long time ago, but they haven't, in part because creative work for large brands tends to be developed for broadcast, and perhaps in part because buying network ad time is what everybody else does.

How might the Charmin campaign described above develop under a *communications-planning* approach? In *communications planning* the initial work is done by media specialists. They might conclude that television is a poor choice for reaching Charmin's desired audience, perhaps because of its expense or because some other medium better segments the desired audience. The specialist would then work on selecting media and other promotional channels that more efficiently and effectively reach the target. Once these choices were made, the campaign would be sent to the creatives, who would be asked to develop creative strategies best suited to the chosen media. The whole idea is to choose effective media before creating the messages.

In 2004 the company announced it was choosing two media agencies, Starcom MediaVest (a subsidiary of the Publicis Groupe) and the Aegis Group (a subsidiary of PLC Carat), to direct more than $3.5 billion in media buys. Starcom and Aegis would help P&G decide how to allocate spending across various media, including television, but also including less traditional media, such as radio, the Web, promotions, events, public relations, and direct-to-consumer advertising. The very clear mandate was to broaden advertising away from traditional vehi-

cles. The way its new approach might change the way P&G reaches its consumers was reported by Suzanne Vranika in a recent issue of *Advertising Age*:

> One P&G marketing ploy involves a 53-foot truck that houses 27 individual sweet-smelling bathrooms equipped with air conditioning, hardwood floors and Charmin Ultra toilet paper. The vehicle, called Charmin's Ultra Potty Palooza, travels to state fairs and other outdoor events, offering people the chance to use a clean restroom.
>
> "The consumer has changed; he or she uses a whole host of communications that didn't exist in the past," says Cindy Tripp, P&G's associate director of media and marketing. "Because of the fragmentation, we need to be better at connecting with them."

Will P&G revolutionize the way advertising is done? As Paul Woomirigton, CEO of MDC Partner's Media Kitchen, points out, radical changes of this type are "easier said than done." One big challenge is comparing different media in terms of effectiveness. But lots of industry insiders think it would be unwise to bet against P&G's leadership. The trend "is not on the same pace as brand or global [marketing strategies] are," according to John Dooner, McCann WorldGroup CEO. "If [acceptance of] brand advertising is at 97 percent and global is at 85 percent, then maybe total communications probably hasn't reached 20 percent. But that doesn't mean it isn't key to the future—it is." Dooner's point: What P&G does today will be industry practice tomorrow.

Consider This

1. Evaluate the marketplace realities that seem to be driving *communications planning*. Is P&G's approach a sensible response to those realities? Why or why not?
2. How will major players in the advertising world, including media companies, agencies, and advertisers, likely be affected if the *communications-planning* approach becomes dominant?
3. Explain how the *communications-planning* approach will affect traditional media planning and buying. How would you determine if this is an effective approach?

Sources: Jonah Bloom, "P&G's Public Commitment to Planning Marks a Watershed," *Advertising Age* (August 2, 2004); John Consoli, "Post Mortem: Big Six Got Their Way," *MediaWeek* (June 21, 2004): 4; Jack Feuer, "Who Will Follow P&G into Communications Planning?" *Adweek* (April 12, 2004); Jack Feuer, "Team Spirit Marks SMG's McCann," *Adweek* (August 9, 2004); Suzanne Vranica, "Publicis and Aegis Win Big with P&G," *Wall Street Journal* (Eastern Edition) (July 15, 2004): B6; Paul Woolmington, "Unbundled Bundling," *Adweek* (July 26, 2004).

Part 3
Effective Advertising
Media

Chick-fil-A is not your typical quick-service restaurant chain, and nowhere is the difference more evident than in its media plans. First of all, Chick-fil-A is dramatically outspent by its competition, which allows its competition to buy more media. Second, a majority of Chick-fil-A competitors use broadcast media as their primary vehicle. Chick-fil-A focuses its media dollars on outdoor advertising. Third, the competitors buy national advertising to promote their brands and sell products. Conversely, Chick-fil-A spends its dollars at the local level where it knows it can have an impact. Besides, a national campaign for a chain located predominantly in the southern part of the country would be a waste. Finally, Chick-fil-A customizes each plan by market, where its competitors take more of a one-size-fits-all approach.

The company's planning process is similar to other companies', however. It sets media objectives and develops strategies. It reviews and analyzes media opportunities within each individual market. What may be a breakthrough idea in one market might fall short in another. Again, Chick-fil-A customizes its media mix based on the needs and competitive factors in each market. It completes and reviews preliminary plans, and after several discussions and revisions, a media plan is finally approved.

A typical media plan for a larger Chick-fil-A market might include 50 percent outdoor, 20 percent radio, 20 percent TV, and 10 percent local marketing. However, there are several Chick-fil-A markets whose media plans might include 70 percent outdoor and 30 percent local marketing.

Chick-fil-A is patient in its approach to media planning and buying. If a market has not reached a 30 showing (daily TRPs) delivered by an outdoor board, which is the medium of choice for the campaign, media planners are strongly encouraged to improve those results before moving dollars into radio or TV.

Chick-fil-A uses radio primarily to drive traffic during key promotional periods. Local area marketing directors for Chick-fil-A use the radio buys as an opportunity to receive value-added promotions, which provide additional exposure for the Chick-fil-A brand. Television is the place where everyone wants to be, but, again, Chick-fil-A is patient and waits for markets to mature to the point when a consistent TV schedule is cost-effective.

Source: Information courtesy of Mike Buerno, The Richards Group.

Consider This

1. How could the Internet be added to the Chick-fil-A media plan?
2. Why do you think outdoor has been so successful for Chick-fil-A?

Clutter Busting with Breakthrough Advertising

The new century brought unprecedented competition for the attention of customers and a different kind of challenge for people who create advertisements.

There are hundreds of television channels that seem to show advertising all of the time. The number of TV advertisements the average person sees each week increased 20 percent from 2002 to 2004.

The problem is that the more commercials that appear, the less effective they are. Customers respond to commercial message overload by rationing their attention and avoiding ads—they are saying no to telemarketers, taking their names off direct mail lists, zipping and zapping TV commercials, and installing TiVo.

One solution is to redefine advertising. Viral marketing is gaining because the voices of opinion leaders and trendsetters are heard more than traditional advertising. Guerilla marketing and alternative media are being used because it is easier to reach people where they are, which is often not in front of a TV.

Breakthrough advertising is advertising that breaks through the clutter. It does so by being creative, by getting attention, and by delivering a message people want to watch and read.

As clutter increases, the creative stakes get higher. That's the challenge creative people are facing today.

Microsoft

WEEKENDS
Made better with MSN

Fitness & Recreation

MSN Search   Photo E-Mail

                Life's better with the Butterfly

Calendar   Entertainment   Golf Gear

MSN Hotmail

msn

The Creative Side and Message Strategy

···

CHAPTER 12

MSN Takes Wing

Award:
EFFIE® Gold

Company:
Microsoft®

Agency:
*McCann-Erickson,
San Francisco*

Campaign:
*"Learn Something
New Every Day"*

CHAPTER OBJECTIVES

After reading this chapter, you will be able to:

1. Define creative advertising and explain how it leads to a Big Idea.

2. Describe the characteristics of creative people and their creative process.

3. Discuss key creative strategy approaches.

4. Outline the key parts of a creative brief.

f you were asked to create a mascot for an online search engine, what would come to mind? What kind of creature could you use that darts, flies, flits, and moves with grace and beauty?

The Microsoft Network (MSN) and its agency McCann-Erickson of San Francisco created a colorful butterfly character to represent the network of Internet services. Under the slogan "It's better with the Butterfly," the campaign's strategy was designed to inform consumers, especially those with high-speed broadband connections, about the launch of a new version of MSN that featured rich information services, advanced communication tools, and comprehensive security solutions.

Microsoft faced a real challenge establishing MSN because of the entrenched position of AOL with its domination of the category and strong awareness. There was also a serious problem with consumer inertia: It's a lot of trouble to switch Internet providers. The target audience may not want to change, but if it believes that a better

Internet experience is out there, it is open to the promise of a more useful Internet service. Furthermore, there was consumer confusion since consumers didn't know if MSN was a portal, a search engine, or an access provider. The objectives of the campaign were to clearly define MSN's offering as an Internet service provider and to motivate subscribers to switch from AOL. The specific objectives were to:

* Generate switching momentum from AOL to MSN
* Substantially increase MSN Internet subscriptions
* Clarify the MSN brand and increase unaided awareness
* Increase perception that MSN is the chief competitor, or alternative, to AOL

Richard Bray, MSN vice president, explained why a butterfly is a great icon for the promise of MSN: "The Butterfly resonates with consumers as fun, friendly, and approachable and it's quickly become the personification of MSN."

During the initial days of the campaign launch, MSN visitors were entertained by a butterfly flitting around the home page and then landing on the link to a preview site, which featured highlights of the new home page, as well as other new services. Customers were also invited to download a free butterfly cursor to use on their computers. The campaign included print, outdoor, radio and television ads, direct mail, public relations, as well as ads on other partner Web sites. A new format included five 15-second spots that could be seen online via the new MSN Video, a free streaming video service (see http://new.msn.com/prss/).

In the television commercials, the butterfly loiters in the background of everyday scenarios—situations in which MSN can help people do more things online than they might have thought possible. Michael McLaren, executive VP with Mc-Cann, explains, "As we continue to extend and develop the MSN Butterfly, we are building a lasting and memorable brand identity that people relate to and believe in." The commercials showcase MSN as a world of answers. In one commercial that features MSN's search function, expectant parents are choosing names for the baby when the Butterfly interjects a wry comment:

He:	"How about Cassandra?"
She:	"That's pretty. I wonder what it means."
Butterfly:	"That's Greek for prophet of doom."
He:	"Catherine?"

The campaign has been recognized for the strength of its creative idea. As *Advertising Age*'s ad critic, Bob Garfield, observed, "The real genius of the campaign lies in its limitless opportunities for new executions—one of the principal characteristic of a bona fide Big Idea." So did it work? The results will be presented in the It's a Wrap section at the end of this chapter.

Sources: EFFIE brief provided by McCann-Erickson, San Francisco, and Microsoft; "The MSN Butterfly Is Back to Kick Off the New MSN Multimedia Marketing Campaign—And Now It Has Something to Say," Microsoft news release, http://www.msn.com/.

Effective advertising is both an art—the creative dimension—and a science—the strategic dimension. In this chapter, we focus first on the creative aspect and then we'll discuss the strategic dimension. We'll investigate how creative advertising is defined, the creative concept or Big Idea, the characteristics of creative people, and the process of creative thinking. Then we'll turn to creative strategy and explain the logic behind the message and how the strategy works with creative ideas to deliver on the message objectives. We'll end with a discussion of a planning tool called a creative brief, and explain how it provides direction for the execution of the Big Idea, as well as for the evaluation of the creative strategy.

THE ART AND SCIENCE OF CREATIVE ADVERTISING

In the book *Creative Strategy in Advertising,* the authors say that an ad "needs to contain a persuasive message that convinces people to take action." To be creative, however, they suggest that an ad "must make a relevant connection with its audience and present a selling idea in an unexpected way."[1] This definition of creative advertising supports the principle that there is both a science (the way a message is persuasive, convincing, and relevant) and an art (the way a message is an unexpected idea) driving effective advertising.

Principle
Effective advertising is a product of both science (persuasiveness) and art (creativity and originality).

The ROI of Effective Advertising

According to the DDB Needham agency, an effective ad is relevant, original, and has impact—which is referred to as **ROI**.[2] In other words, ideas have to be *relevant,* to mean something to the target audience. An advertising idea is considered *creative* when it is novel, fresh, unexpected, and unusual. *Original* means one of a kind. Because it is novel, it is surprising and gets your attention.[3] To be effective, the ideas also must have *impact.* Many advertisements just wash over the audience. An idea with impact breaks through the clutter, gets attention, and sticks in memory. An advertisement with impact has stopping power that comes from an intriguing idea, something you have never thought about before, as the Microsoft campaign demonstrated with its use of the Butterfly idea to represent online searching.

■ ■ ■
The idea that some moments, such as eating cupcakes and cookies, require a glass of milk is the creative concept behind the award-winning "Got Milk?" campaign.

The Big Idea   Behind every effective advertisement is a **Big Idea**, a **creative concept** that implements the advertising strategy so that the message is both attention getting and memorable. This is the "art" side of creative advertising. In the award-winning California Milk Board campaign "Got Milk?" the Big Idea is that people drink milk with certain foods such as cookies. If milk is unavailable to drink with those foods, they are—to say the least—frustrated. A Big Idea is one that is expressed visually and verbally. "Got Milk?" is the question, but in most of the campaign's ads, it is reinforced in the picture of someone (or sometimes something) with a white milk mustache. In getting the great idea, sometimes the visual idea comes first; sometimes it's the words. The important thing is that they work together to complete the thought.

According to advertising legend James Webb Young, a founder of the Young & Rubicam agency, an idea is a new combination of thoughts. In his classic book on creative thinking, Young claims that "the ability to make new combinations is heightened by an ability to see relationships."[4] An idea, then, is a thought that comes from placing two previously unrelated concepts together. Metaphors and analogies are great ways to create such juxtapositions, as the Harley "Steak for your ears" ad demonstrates.

But what makes the idea creative? Any idea can seem creative to you if you have never thought of it before, but the essence of a creative idea is that no one else has thought of it either. In an industry that prides itself on creativity, **copycat advertising**—that is, using an idea that someone else has originated—is a concern.

■ ■ ■

The Harley-Davidson ad equates the taste of a steak with the throaty roar of a Harley engine.

TREAT YOUR EARS
TO A THICK JUICY STEAK.

Advertising expert John Eighmy estimates that about 50 percent of the advertising in the United States falls into this category.[5]

The challenge in advertising is to come up with novel, interesting ideas for products that might appear to be rather boring. Karl Schroeder, copywriter at Portland-based Coates, Kokes agency, explains how he dealt with a client assignment for Shel Lab, an industrial products company:

> Vacuum ovens. Anaerobic chambers. Incubator shakers. Who needs Nike when you can sell sexy products like these? The truth is, you're going to have a few clients with products that aren't as exciting as others. And chances are these products will be in the business-to-business category. But why let the products appear boring in advertising? I've found with our client, Shel Lab, there is still room for a little humor and good design.
>
> I have to admit, when we first started the project I was not too excited. But after some account-planning workshops and a tour of the manufacturing plant, I realized Shel Lab is actually very cool. The company had a ton of "firsts" in its industry, and the tour revealed how enthusiastic Shel Lab is about its products—or rather, how enthusiastic people at Shel Lab are about their products. Both of those things were very energizing for me creatively.

The Practical Tips box provides more advice for creating original ideas that get attention and stick in memory.

Practical Tips

Tips for Creating Original Ideas

To create an original and unexpected idea, use the following techniques:

- **An unexpected twist.** An ad for Amazon.com used the headline, "460 books for Marxists. Including 33 on Groucho."
- **An unexpected association.** An ad for Compaq used a visual of a chained butterfly to illustrate the lack of freedom in competitors' computer workstations.

- *Catchy phrasing.* Isuzu used "The 205 Horsepower Primal Scream" for its Rodeo headline.
- *A play on words.* Under the headline "Happy Camper," an ad for cheese showed a picture of a packed sports utility vehicle with a huge wedge of cheese lashed to the rooftop.
- *Analogy and metaphor.* Harley-Davidson compared the legendary sound of its motorcycles to the taste of a thick, juicy steak.
- *Familiar and strange.* Put the familiar in an unexpected situation: UPS showed a tiny model of its familiar brown truck moving through a computer cord.

To prevent unoriginal ideas, avoid the following:

- *The common.* Avoid the obvious or the predictable, such as a picture of a Cadillac on Wall Street or in front of a mansion.
- *The look-alike.* Avoid copycat advertising that uses somebody else's great idea.
- *Clichés.* They may have been great ideas the first time they were used, but phrases such as "the road to success" or "the fast track" become trite when overused.
- *The tasteless.* In an attempt to be cute, a Subaru ad used the headline, "Put it where the sun don't shine."

The Creative Leap   A Big Idea that expresses an original advertising thought involves a mind-shift. Instead of seeing the obvious, a creative idea looks at something in a different way, from a different angle, such as in an ad for 76 automotive oil that associates the brand with various symbols of Americana. It doesn't matter how dull the product might appear to be; there is always an opportunity to move it beyond its category through a creative Big Idea. But how is that done?

SHOWCASE

These 76 ads ran in national trade publications for the trucking industry. The creative team wanted to remind the target audience that 76 has been a symbol of Americana for a long time. The imagery speaks to trucking fleet owners who authorize the purchase of such commodities as oil. These ads were contributed by Chris Hutchinson, art director at Weiden + Kennedy, who graduated from the advertising program at the University of Oregon.

Another safe delivery.
Michelin. Because so much is riding on your tyres.

Michelin's dependability and durability surround and protect a car's precious cargo.

Finding the brilliant creative concept entails what advertising giant Otto Kleppner called "the creative leap"[6]— a process of jumping from the strategy statement to an original idea that conveys the strategy in an interesting way. Since the creative leap means moving from the safety of a predictable strategy statement to an unusual idea that hasn't been tried before, this leap is often referred to as the creative risk: If it hasn't been tried before, then it's a gamble. All creative ideas in advertising involve this element of risk, and that's why **copy-testing** is used to test the idea before it runs, to try to determine whether it works.

Creative Thinking

So how do you make the creative leap and get creative ideas? A common technique advertisers use to force the leap is to make an unusual association. For example, Michelin's tire advertising is driven by the strategic idea that the tire is durable and dependable—language that would make a pretty boring ad. The creative idea, however, comes to life in the long-running campaign that shows a baby sitting in a tire. The visual is reinforced by the slogan, "Because so much is riding on your tires." The creative concept, then, "leaps" from the idea of a durable tire to the idea of protecting your family, particularly precious members like tiny children, by surrounding them with the dependability of a Michelin tire.

Creativity is a special form of problem solving and everyone is born with some talent in that area. In advertising, as in all areas of business, creativity is not limited to the writers and art directors. Media planners and market researchers are just as creative in searching for new ideas and innovative solutions. The most common techniques that creative thinkers use to stimulate new ideas are free association, divergent thinking, analogies and metaphors, and right-brain thinking. Let's look at these techniques:

- *Free Association.* Creates the juxtaposition of two seemingly unrelated thoughts. In free association you think of a word and then describe everything that comes into your mind when you imagine that word.
- *Divergent Thinking.* Differs from the rational, linear thinking that we use to arrive at the "right" conclusion. Divergent thinking, which is the heart of creative thinking, uses exploration (playfulness) to search for all possible alternatives.
- *Analogies and Metaphors.* Used to see new patterns or relationships. William J. J. Gordon, a researcher who founded the Synectics school of creative thinking, discovered that creative thinkers often expressed new ideas as analogies.
- *Right-brain Thinking.* Intuitive, nonverbal, and emotion-based thinking (in contrast to left-brain thinking, which is logical and controls speech and writing). A left brain–dominant person is presumed to be logical, orderly, and verbal. A right brain–dominant person tends to deal in expressive images, emotion, intuition, and complex, interrelated ideas that must be understood as a whole rather than as pieces.

Another approach is called *creative aerobics.* Creative aerobics is a thought-starter process that works well in advertising because it uses both the head and the heart, which we refer to in strategy development as rational and emotional appeals. Developed by Linda Conway Correll, a professor at Southeast Missouri State, it is a four-step, idea-generating process, which is explained here in terms of finding a creative idea for selling oranges:[7]

1. *Facts.* The first exercise is left brain and asks you to come up with a list of facts about a product (an orange has seeds, is juicy, has vitamin C).

2. *New Names.* In the second exercise you create new "names" for the product (Florida, a vitamin supplement, a kiss of sunshine).

3. *Similarities.* The third exercise looks for similarities between dissimilar objects. (What are the similarities between the new names and the product—for instance, Florida sunshine and oranges both suggest warmth, freshness, sunshine, the fountain of youth.)

4. *New Definitions.* The fourth exercise, a cousin of the pun, creates new definitions for product-related nouns. Peel (face peel, peel out), seed (seed money, bird seed), navel/naval (naval academy, contemplating one's navel), pulp (pulp fiction), C/see/si/sea (C the light). Headlines derived from those definitions might be: "Seed money" (the money to purchase oranges), "Contemplating one's navel" (looking at oranges), "Peel out" (when your grocer is out of oranges), "Navel intelligence" (information about an orange), "Pulp fiction" (a story about an orange), "C the light" (the orange is a low-calorie source of vitamin C). These new definitions stimulate the flowering of a new Big Idea.

Creative Roles   All agencies have copywriters and art directors who are responsible for developing the creative concept and crafting the execution of the advertising idea. They often work in teams, are sometimes hired and fired as a team, and may work together successfully for a number of years. Broadcast producers can also be part of the team for television commercials. The creative director manages the creative process and plays an important role in focusing the strategy of ads and making sure the creative concept is strategically on target. Because advertising creativity is a product of teamwork, copywriters and art directors work together to generate concept, word, and picture ideas. Their writing or design specialties come into play in the execution of the idea.

The Creative Person   Creative ideas, such as the award-winning Microsoft "Butterfly" campaign, aren't limited to advertising. People such as Henry Ford, the father of the Model T; Steven Jobs, the co-founder of Apple Computer; and Lucille Ball of *I Love Lucy* fame are or were highly creative. They are idea people, creative problem solvers, and highly original thinkers. Creative people are found in business, science, engineering, advertising, and many other fields. But in advertising, creativity is both a job description and a goal. Figure 12.1 is a minitest to evaluate your own creative potential.

You probably know people who are just naturally zany, who come up with crazy, off-the-wall ideas. Creative advertising people may be zany, weird, off-the-wall, and unconventional, but they can't be eccentric. They still must be very centered on creating effective advertising. Coming up with a great idea that is also on strategy is an emotional high. According to Derek Clark, a copywriter at Detroit's Campbell-Ewald agency, "Creative advertising at the national level has to be one of the biggest emotional rollercoasters in the business world. When it's bad, you feel like fleeing the country. When it's good, there's nothing better. I love it."

Research by the Center for Studies in Creativity and the Creative Education Foundation, both in Buffalo, New York, has found that most people can sharpen their skills and develop their creative potential. First, let's explore the characteristics of a creative person. Then let's see how people develop creative skills.

Principle
Creative probelm solvers are risk takers with a high tolerance for ambiguity.

Research indicates that creative people tend to be independent, assertive, self-sufficient, persistent, and self-disciplined, with a high tolerance for ambiguity. They are also risk takers with powerful egos that are internally driven. They don't care much about group standards and opinions and typically have inborn skepticism and strong curiosity. Here are a few of the key characteristics of creative people who do well in advertising:

- *Problem Solving.* Creative problem solvers are alert, watchful, and observant, and reach conclusions through intuition rather than through logic. They also tend to have a mental playfulness that allows them to make novel associations.
- *The Ability to Visualize.* Most of the information we accumulate comes through sight, so the ability to manipulate visual images is crucial for good copywriters, as well as designers. They can see products, people, and scenes in the mind's eye, as well as visualize a mental picture of the finished ad while it is still in the talking, or idea, state.

 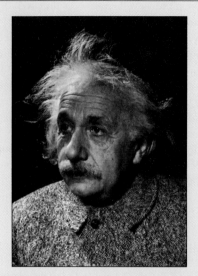 

■ ■ ■
Leonardo DaVinci, Albert Einstein, and Georgia O'Keefe excelled in different fields, but all three qualify as geniuses.

Do you ever wonder whether you are creative? Does creativity have anything to do with your personality? Your personality is your own distinctive and consistent pattern of how you think, feel, and act. A current view of creativity suggests that the area of personality most related to creativity is how open you are to new experiences. According to researchers McCrae and Costa, how open you are to new experiences can be measured by survey questions that ask if you agree or disagree with the following statements:

1. "I enjoy working on 'mind-twister'-type puzzles."

2. "Once I find the right way to do something, I stick to it."

3. "As a child I rarely enjoyed games of make-believe."

4. "I enjoy concentrating on a fantasy or daydream and exploring all its possibilities, letting it grow and develop."

FIGURE 12.1 **The Creative Personality**
How Creative Are You? If you said "I agree" to 1 and 4, you.re thinking like a creative person.

Source: Information provided by Sheri J. Broyles, University of North Texas; R. R. McCrae and P. T. Costa Jr., "Openness to Experience" in *Perspectives in Personality,* Vol. 1, R. Hogan and W. H. Jones, eds. (Greenwich, CT: JAI Press), 145–72.

- *Openness to New Experiences.* Over the course of a lifetime, openness to experience may give you many adventures from which to draw. Those experiences would give a novelist more characters to write about, a painter more scenes to paint, and the creative team more angles from which to tackle an advertising problem.[8]
- *Conceptual Thinking.* It's easy to see how people who are open to experience might develop innovative advertisements and commercials because they are more imaginative.[9] Such imagination led to a famous Nike commercial in which Michael Jordan and Larry Bird play an outlandish game of horse—bouncing the ball off buildings, billboards, and places that are impossible to reach.

Principle
Emphasize concepts. Worry about executions later.

As important as creative thinking is for advertising professionals, strategic thinking is just as important. In taking a peek into the minds of those who hire new creative people, researchers found repeated verbatim comments from creative directors concerning the importance of strategic thinking and Big Ideas. "Emphasize concept," said one creative director. "Teach them to think first and execute later."[10]

The Creative Process: How to Get an Idea

Only in cartoons do light bulbs appear above our heads from out of nowhere when a good idea strikes. In reality, most people who are good at thinking up new ideas will tell you that

An art director works on a graphic solution to a visual probelm.

it is hard work. They read, study, analyze, test and retest, sweat, curse, and worry. Sometimes they give up. The unusual, unexpected, novel idea rarely comes easily—and that's as true in science and medicine as it is in advertising.

Steps and Stages   The creative process usually is portrayed as a series of steps. English sociologist Graham Wallas was the first to outline the creative process followed by others, including Alex Osborn, one of the founders of the BBDO agency and the Creative Education Foundation.[11] Let's summarize these approaches with the steps outlined below:

Step 1: Immersion. Read, research, and learn everything you can about the problem.

Step 2: Ideation. Look at the problem from every angle; develop ideas; generate as many alternatives as possible.

Step 3: Brainfog. You may hit a blank wall and want to give up.

Step 4: Incubation. Try to put your conscious mind to rest to let your subconscious take over.

Step 5: Illumination. There is that unexpected moment when the idea comes, often when your mind is relaxed and you're doing something else.

Step 6: Evaluation. Does it work? Is it on strategy?

Brainstorming   As part of the creative process, some agencies use a thinking technique known as **brainstorming**, where a group of 6 to 10 people work together to come up with ideas. One person's idea stimulates someone else's, and the combined power of the group associations stimulates far more ideas than any one person could think of alone. The secret to brainstorming is to remain positive and defer judgment. Negative thinking during a brainstorming session can destroy the playful atmosphere necessary to achieve a novel idea. To stimulate group creativity against a deadline, some agencies have special processes for brainstorming with walls that can be covered with sheets of paper on which to write ideas and no distractions and interruptions (such as telephones and access to e-mail). Some agencies rent a suite in a hotel and send the creative team there to get away and immerse themselves in the problem. When the GSDM agency was defending its prized Southwest Airlines account, president Roy Spence ordered a 28-day "war room" death march that had staffers working around the clock, wearing Rambo-style camouflage, and piling all their trash inside the building to keep any outsiders from rummaging around for clues to their pitch.

CREATIVE STRATEGY

The art and science of advertising come together in the phrase *creative strategy*. A Big Idea must be both *creative* (original, different, novel, unexpected) and *strategic* (right for the product and target; meets the advertising objectives). It's not just about coming up with a novel idea that no one has thought of before; advertising creativity is about coming up with an idea that solves a communication problem in an original way. In its section on advertising, the *Encyclopedia of Creativity* points out that effective advertising creativity is measured not only by its originality, but also by its strategic contributions.[12]

People who create advertisements also make a distinction between creative strategy and creative executions. **Creative strategy**, or **message strategy**, is what the advertisement says and *execution* is how it is said. This chapter is focused on creative strategy and the two chapters that follow will explore the writing, design, and production of advertising executions.

Message Objectives

In planning creative strategies, it is important to have an idea of what you want that message to accomplish. In previous chapters on how advertising works (Chapter 4) and planning (Chapter 7), we introduced the concept of the Facets Model of Advertising Effects (Figure 4.5) and how the facets lead to advertising objectives. The advertising objectives that relate to the six facets of effectiveness are:

1. **Perception:** Objectives—create attention, awareness, interest, recognition and recall.
2. **Cognitive:** Objectives—deliver information and understanding.
3. **Affective:** Objectives—touch emotions and create feelings.
4. **Persuasion:** Objectives—change attitudes, create conviction and preference.
5. **Transformation:** Objectives—establish brand identity and associations.
6. **Behavior:** Objectives—stimulate trial, purchase, repurchase, or some other form of action.

Head and Heart Strategies

Once you have an objective or set of objectives to guide the advertising message, how do you go about translating that into strategy? Two basic approaches are sometimes referred to as *head and heart strategies*. Remember the discussion in Chapter 4 on the three types of effects, and how *think* (cognitive) and *feel* (affective) drive the do, or *action* decision. The think and feel dimensions are sometimes referred to as rational and emotional, or what we are calling the head and heart factors. In the Facets model (page 104) the cognitive and persuasion objectives generally speak to the head, and the affective and transformational objectives are more likely to speak to the heart. In the strategy statement for VW and its "Drivers Wanted" campaign, which was discussed in Chapter 1, the Arnold agency identifies both rational and emotional dimensions to VW's brand essence:

VW's rational brand essence: "The only brand offering the benefits and 'feeling' of German engineering within reach."

VW's emotional brand essence:
- Exciting
- Different driving feeling
- Different way of living
- More feeling, fun, alive, connected

The decision to use a head or a heart strategy is also affected by the product situation, particularly by the involvement factor. The Foote, Cone & Belding (FCB) agency has been a leader in creating strategies that combine logic and emotion with an understanding that some decisions may demand a lot of thought (high involvement), while others are made with little or no thought or even on impulse. We described the FCB Grid in Chapter 4; if you go back and look at page 00 you will see how different kinds of message strategies emerge from an analysis of thinking and feeling for low- and high-involvement products.

SHOWCASE

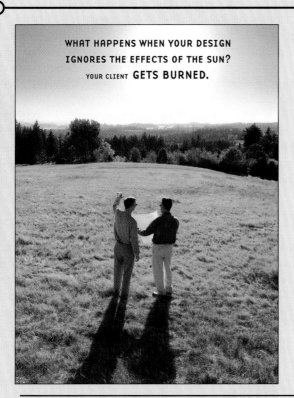

■ ■ ■

This campaign, aimed at professionals in the building trades, was designed to be educational in presenting the consulting company's services. Rather than lofty or preachy (like a "Save the planet" ad), the creative strategy called for the message to be practical (good for business), emotional (good for the environment), and rational (make a good business decision). In addition, the strategy emphasized how those three factors were a win-win-win decision that added up to a sustainable, high-performance building. These ads were contributed by Karl Schroeder, copywriter at Coates, Kokes in Portland Oregon, who is a graduate of the University of Oregon advertising program.

Hard- and Soft-Sell Strategies   Related to head and heart strategies are hard- and soft-sell approaches. A **hard sell** is an informational message that is designed to touch the mind and create a response based on logic. The assumption is that the target audience wants information and will make a rational product decision. The approach emphasizes tangible product features and benefits. We'll talk more about the rational approach in the section that follows on selling premises. A **soft sell** uses emotional appeals or images to create a response based on attitudes, moods, dreams, and feelings. The assumption with soft-sell strategies is that the target audience has little interest in an information search and will respond more favorably to a message that touches their emotions or presents an attractive brand image.

Some ads, such as the BetterBricks ads, combine both a hard and a soft sell. The company helps building professionals construct and maintain buildings that work better for business, people, and the environment. However, focusing on the company is less effective than talking about what the business does and what that means to people. The strategy decision was to present BetterBricks as a cheerleader for sustainable, high-performance buildings.

Lectures and Dramas   Most advertising messages use a combination of two basic literary techniques to reach the head or the heart of the consumer: lectures and dramas.[13] A *lecture* is a serious instruction given verbally. The speaker presents evidence (broadly speaking) and uses a technique such as an argument to persuade the audience. The advantages of lectures are many: They are (relatively speaking) not expensive to produce and are compact and efficient. A lecture can deliver a dozen selling points in seconds, get right to the point, and make the point explicitly. In advertising we use the phrase "a talking head" to refer to an announcer who delivers a lecture about a product. This can also be a celebrity spokesperson or an authority figure, such as a doctor or scientist.

Drama, however, relies on the viewer to make inferences. Through dramas, advertisers tell stories about their products; the characters speak to each other, not to the audience. Like fairy tales, movies, novels, parables, and myths, advertising dramas are essentially stories about how the world works. They can be funny as well as serious. Viewers learn from these commercial dramas by inferring lessons from them and by applying those lessons to their everyday lives. When a drama rings true, viewers join in, draw conclusions from it, and apply those conclusions to their product decisions. The Leo Burnett agency built a creative philosophy around "Inherent Drama," which was the storyline built into the agency's archetypal brand characters, such as the Marlboro Man, Charlie the Tuna, the Jolly Green Giant, and Tony the Tiger.

FACETS OF CREATIVE STRATEGY

It's important to understand the difference between emotional and rational strategies, but actually this distinction may be too simplistic to describe the varieties of messages used in advertising. The idea behind creative strategy is that there are a number of different ways to deliver a message. Which approach to use will vary with the target audience, the marketing situation, the product itself, and its category. The goal is to match the objective with the best possible way to deliver the message. To better understand how these creative strategies deliver more effective advertising, we'll look at these facets one at a time and describe the advertising techniques that deliver these effects.

Messages That Drive Perception

To be effective, advertisements need to get exposure through the media buy. The message, however, needs to get attention and build awareness. It also needs to get consumers' interest, which it tries to do by being relevant. Then advertisers hope consumers will remember the message. Here are some suggestions on how to do that.

Attention and Awareness   Getting consumers' attention requires *stopping power.* Ads that stop the scanning and break through the clutter are usually high in originality. Intrusiveness is particularly important in cluttered markets and media and for products that have a small **share of mind**—those that are not very well known or not very interesting, such as toilet paper, canned vegetables, or motor oil. In many cases there is little difference between competing brands, so the product interest is created solely by the advertising message.

Principle
To get attention, an ad has to have stopping power.

What can you do to create this kind of breakthrough impact? The function of originality is to capture attention. People will notice something that is new, novel, or surprising. Creative advertising breaks through the old patterns of seeing and saying things; the unexpectedness of the new idea creates stopping power. Unexpected media is also good at breaking through clutter, which is why guerilla marketing and the use of alternative (unexpected) media has become so popular. Many clutter-busting ads are intrusive and use loud, bold effects to attract viewer attention; they work by shouting. Others use captivating ideas or mesmerizing visuals. In print ads, for instance, research indicates that *contrast* can attract viewer attention. If every other ad in the medium is big and bold, then try one that is small, quiet, and simple; use a lot of white space. If everything else is tiny and gray (like type), then be big and bold or use color. If everything else is colorful, then use black-and-white.

Interest   Getting attention is the stopping power of an advertisement; keeping attention is the *pulling power* of an ad: It keeps pulling the reader or viewer through to the end of the message. Advertisers stimulate interest by speaking to the personal interests of their target audience. We pay attention to topics that are relevant to us, that reflect our personal interests in such areas as hobbies, concerns and issues, trends, fashion, improvements, news, and so forth. Another way is to elicit curiosity, such as using a **teaser** campaign where the

This teaser ad is for a car's Web site. Its deliberate ambiguity is intended to excite curiosity about the site and the car.

message unfolds over time. Ads that open with questions or dubious statements are designed to create curiosity. New information is often greeted by phrases such as "Can you believe it?" This confrontation of curiosity with doubt means you have entered the interested state. Buick used a teaser strategy to announce the new Buick Regal Web site.

The sequencing of the ad message elements affects its pulling power: Does the copy pull the reader or viewer through to the end? For example, if we start with a question, then readers tend to continue through the ad to find the answer. Storytelling is another good technique for holding the audience. Most people want to know how a story ends. Suspense, drama, and narrative are good tools for maintaining interest.

Memory   Not only does advertising have to *stop* (get attention) and *pull* (create interest), it also has to *stick* (in memory). One technique to ensure memorability is repetition. Psychologists maintain that people need to hear or see something a minimum of three times before it crosses the threshold of perception and enters into memory. Jingles are valuable memorability devices because the music allows the advertiser to repeat a phrase or product name without boring the audience.

Clever phrases are useful not only because they catch attention, but also because they can be repeated to intensify memorability. Advertisements use slogans for brands and campaigns (a series of ads run under an umbrella theme). An example of a slogan is "Get Met. It Pays" (Met Life), or Nike's slogan, "Just Do It." *Taglines* are used at the end of an ad to summarize the point of the ad's message in a highly memorable way, such as "Nothing outlasts the Energizer. It keeps going and going and going." When a tagline is used consistently on all marketing messages, it becomes a *slogan.* Both slogans and taglines are written to be highly memorable, often using mnemonic devices (techniques for improving memory) such as rhyme, rhythmic beats, and repeating sounds.

Color can be a memory cue, as well. Wrigley's Doublemint gum uses green and Juicy Fruit uses yellow in the same way. Shape is another memory cue: The Absolut vodka campaign has used a thousand different visual images to reinforce the shape of the product's bottle—to the point that the bottle shape is recognizable even without a label.

In addition to verbal memory devices, many print and interactive ads and most television commercials feature a *key visual* (or *key frame* in television). This visual is a vivid image that the advertiser hopes will linger in the viewer's mind. Because television is mainly a visual medium, an effective commercial relies on some dominant scene or action that conveys the essence of the message and can be remembered easily, as in the Proflowers key frame.

Memorability also depends on the ad's structure. The beginning of an advertising message is the most important part for attracting attention, and the end or closing of a message is the most important part for memorability. Most print ads end with a *logo* (a distinctive mark that identifies the product or company) or a *signature* (the name of the company or brand, written in a distinctive type style). Television commercials often conclude with a memorable tagline and superimpose the product name on the last visual, accompanied by the announcer repeating the brand name.

Principle

Not only does advertising have to stop (get attention) and pull (create interest), it also has to stick (in memory).

SHOWCASE

■ ■ ■

Proflowers wanted a commercial that would reach its target audience of middle-aged people. The nostalgic hairstyle and setting in this key frame is a nod to a simpler time that would appeal to the target audience. The brand name is clearly visible, even if upside down. This commercial was contributed by Chris Hutchinson.

Messages That Drive Cognition

Now let's look at effective creative strategies to get consumers to learn about products. In general, informational strategies are focused on a product's features. The BetterBricks ads on page 335, for example, were designed to be educational, to help the target audience learn about the company's consulting services. To have a practical effect on customers, managers must identify the product characteristics or **features** (also called **attributes**) that are most important to the target audience. In addition to importance to the consumer, the advertising might also point to the product's **point of differentiation** relative to the competition, which reflects its position.

Automotive advertising is particularly interesting to analyze because there are so many different features that can be the focus of the strategy. An article compared various types of cars to find the best model in the class and their distinguishing features. In explaining the evaluations, the raters noted spaciousness and firm ride for the small sedan agile handling and comfortable ride for the small SUV, luxury interior for the midsize SUV, silky smooth engine and powertrain for the luxury sedan, superb cornering and lively acceleration for the "fun to drive" category, spirited performance and seating for the three-row SUV, handling for the minivan, and spacious size for the "green car" hybrids.[14] You can see how challenging it is to decide which feature of all these possibilities should be mentioned.

Attributes can be both tangible and intangible (see Figure 12.2). The ads for Sunkist oranges and Gander Mountain focus on tangible and intangible features. Attributes can also be category based. An ad that is focused on the product, rather than the brand, may be designed to build the use of the category. It's called a *generic strategy* and it makes sense when a particular brand, such as Campbell's Soup, dominates the category, so increased category sales will automatically lead to increased brand sales. DeBeers used a generic strategy to sell rings for the other hand, the right hand, in an attempt to promote the use of diamonds for rings other than wedding rings.[15]

One type of informational strategy is a **claim**, which is a product-focused strategy that is based on a statement about how the product will perform. Proof statements that

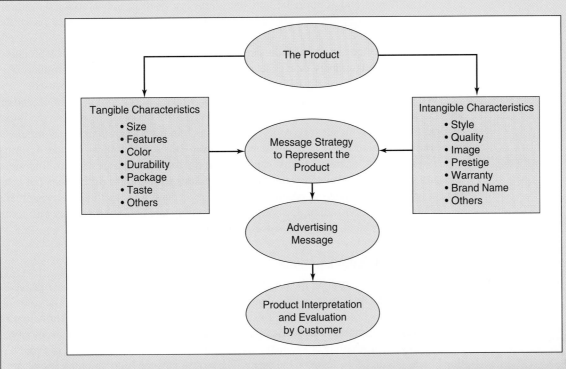

FIGURE
12.2

Tangible and Intangible Features

The Sunkist ad compares its oranges to candy but in the comparison it identifies tangible product characteristics. The key frame from a Gander Mountain commercial explains how the company and its employees understand cold weather. The understanding of the employees is an intangible benefit shoppers get from patronizing the store.

give the rationale and support behind the claim are used to substantiate the claim. Torture tests, comparisons, and before-and-after demonstrations are used to prove the truth of a claim.

Companies often use news announcements to provide information about new products, to tout reformulated products, or even let consumers know about new uses for products. The news element, which is usually delivered by publicity stories, is information focused.

When designing an advertising message for which understanding is an objective, advertisers present the facts in a way that makes it easy for people to assimilate the information. Sometimes this means a *long-copy approach* in print or an *infomercial* in television, both of which provide detailed information. Basic techniques include defining terms—particularly technical terms—and explaining concepts and ideas, as well as steps and procedures. Companies use product comparisons to highlight differences between their products and competing products. In terms of explaining something, television ads will often use a demonstration. Demonstrations not only add believability; they also teach how to solve a problem, how to do something, or how something works.

Messages That Touch Emotions

Emotional strategies highlight the psychological attraction of the product to the target audience through such responses as love, fear, anxiety, envy, or sexual attraction. These are all soft-sell strategies because they aren't using a rational approach to present information or reasons. A soft-sell strategy can be used for hard products. NAPA auto parts ran an emotional ad that showed a dog sitting at a railroad crossing, forcing a truck to brake hard to avoid hitting him as a train bears down on the scene. The slogan puts the heart-stopping visual story into perspective: "NAPA because there are no unimportant parts." Creating a feeling of involvement is another good way to connect with people on a personal level. Events, such as fairs, contests, grand openings, and exhibits, are particularly good at doing this.

A general emotional goal is to deliver a message that people like in order to create liking for the product. That's a popular justification for the use of entertainment as a message strategy. Entertainment uses drama, humor, and song-and-dance messages to reward the audience with an engaging message. Advertisers have found that commercials that look like TV shows and provide high entertainment value seem to be better liked by audiences than ads with high levels of information. Using entertainment to sell is an issue that advertising experts debate because although entertainment may get and keep attention, some people believe that it doesn't sell products very well. However, the creative directors who participated in the study of creative concepts felt that entertainment, particularly humorous entertainment, was of paramount importance.

Are emotional strategies manipulative? They can be, if they play too strongly on fears. However, most advertising that uses an emotional strategy is trying to connect with an emotion that is a natural response to a situation. In other words, they aren't trying to get you to feel something you're not feeling but rather to connect with that feeling.

Messages That Persuade

Persuasive advertising is designed to affect attitudes and create belief. Strategies that are particularly good are testimonials and messages that generate word of mouth about the product. A referral from someone who is not affiliated with the product will have more persuasiveness than an ad that everyone knows is paid for by its sponsor. That's why Oprah's book club had such an impact on the sales of popular books and why creative strategy uses testimonials and endorsements by celebrities or experts.

Appeals   Persuasion sometimes uses the psychological appeal of the product to the consumer as the focus of a message strategy. An **appeal** connects with some emotion that makes the product particularly attractive or interesting, such as security, esteem, fear, sex, and sensory pleasure. Although emotion is at the base of most appeals, in some situations appeals can also be logical, such as saving money for retirement. Appeals generally pinpoint the anticipated response of the audience to the product and the message. For example, if the price is emphasized in the ad, then the appeal is value, economy, or savings. If the product saves time or effort, then the appeal is convenience. Advertisers use a status appeal to estab-

The appetite appeal of the trail mix bar is dramatized by an extremely close-up visual that shows all the nuts and raisins larger than life.

lish something as a high-quality, expensive product. Appetite appeal using mouth-watering visuals is found in food advertising, such as the one for Quaker Chewy Trail Mix.

Selling Premises   Advertising has developed a number of approaches that speak to the head with a sales message. A **selling premise** states the logic behind the sales offer. A premise is a proposition on which an argument is based or a conclusion is drawn. It is usually a rational approach—an appeal to the head. A rational, prospect-centered selling premise identifies a reason or argument that might appeal to prospects and motivate them to respond. Here is a summary of these rational customer-focused selling premises.

- *Benefit.* The **benefit** emphasizes what the product can do for the user by translating the product feature or attribute into something that benefits the consumer. For example, a GM electric car ad focuses on the product feature (the car doesn't use gas) and translates it into a benefit: lack of noise (no pistons, valves, exhaust).
- *Promise.* A **promise** is a benefit statement that looks to the future and predicts that something good will happen if you use the product. For example, Dial soap has promised for decades that if you use Dial, you will feel more confident.
- *Reason Why.* A type of a benefit statement that gives you the **reason why** you should buy something, although the reason sometimes is implied or assumed. The word *because* is the key to a reason-why statement. For example, an Amtrak ad tells you that travel on Amtrak is more comfortable than on a plane because Amtrak is a more civilized, less dehumanizing way to travel.
- *Unique Selling Proposition (USP).* A **USP** is a benefit statement that is both unique to the product and important to the user. The USP is a promise that consumers will get this unique benefit by using this product only. For example, an ad for a camera states, "This camera is the only one that lets you zoom in and out automatically to follow the action."

An important part of a selling premise is the proof given for the claim or benefit statement. The proof, or substantiation needed to make a claim believable, is called **support**. In some cases this calls for research findings. Most selling premises demand facts, proof, or explanations to support the sales message.

Conviction   The end result of persuasion is conviction, which means the consumer is committed to something, prefers it, and probably intends to buy it or respond in some way. Conviction is often built on strong, rational arguments that use such techniques in their creative strategies as test results, before-and-after visuals, testimonials by users and experts,

This is what losing up to 6 lbs.
in 2 weeks looks like.

There's a new way to jump-start your healthy lifestyle. A leading university has discovered that eating Kellogg's *Special K®* and Kellogg's *Smart Start®* cereals can help you lose up to six pounds in just two weeks. Here's how:

✓ Start with a serving of cereal and skim milk with fruit for breakfast.
✓ Replace either lunch or dinner with the cereal meal.
✓ Have a third meal as you normally would.
✓ Snack on fruits and vegetables between meals.
✓ In two weeks, strut your stuff.

Consult your physician before starting any diet or exercise program. A registered dietician can help you plan a healthy diet. Results may vary. Average weight loss 4.2 pounds.

■ ■ ■
Kellogg's uses 28 cereal bowls to demonstrate the amount of Special K and Smart Start it would take to help a person lose six pounds in two weeks.

Principle
When advertising gives consumers permission to believe in a product, it establishes the platform for conviction.

and demonstrations to prove something. The Kellogg's ad shown here is an example. Publicity that generates news stories in the media is more believable than ads and thus rates higher in credibility.

Celebrity endorsements are also used to intensify conviction in the target audience (as well as get attention, cue the brand personality, and stick in memory). Celebrities get handsome fees for appearing in most commercial messages. Rookie NBA star Lebron James, for example, gets $90 million for appearing in Nike advertisements. The National Park Service uses a public service campaign featuring Jerry Seinfeld, the comedian, Walter Cronkite, the television journalist, and Allan Houston, the New York Knicks guard, all of whom donated their services to deliver a message about restoring and renewing the national parks. Other celebrities who have been involved include Julia Louis-Dreyfus, Richard Dreyfuss, Morgan Freeman, and Tom Hanks. The idea is that celebrities draw attention, but they also carry a strong message of conviction when they speak with passion about something they believe in.[16]

Product placements can be persuasive because they show a product in use in the context of a movie and in use by stars. Celebrities, product placements, and other credibility techniques are used to give the consumer **permission to believe** a claim or selling premise. It's easier to make people aware of a brand than it is to convince them that the brand is better than its competitor's. That's why conviction is one of the last steps in the persuasion process and one of the hardest objectives to accomplish with an advertising message.

Messages That Transform a Product into a Brand

The transformative power of *branding,* where the brand takes on character and meaning, is one of advertising's most important functions. **Image advertising** is used to create a representation in a consumer's mind. The image takes on a particular meaning based on the ideas, feelings, and attitudes that a consumer has about a product, as well as the consumer's past experiences with the product and its advertising. Advertising's role is to provide the cues that make these meanings and experiences come together as a coherent image of the brand. Note in the Inside Story how Wrigley, a familiar brand, is positioned for a new target market where it is less well known.

Associations   An **association message strategy** delivers information symbolically by connecting a brand with a certain type of person, lifestyle, or other characteristics. This link is often created through visuals. A car in front of a mansion says luxury without having to state that message in words. The Sunkist ad associated oranges with candy to convey the message of sweetness. Gorilla Glue has its association embedded in the name of the product, but it also uses a gorilla on the label and the product shot in the ad shows a gorilla hand holding the bottle. A consumer gets a feeling about the product—who uses it and how and where they use it—through these symbolic undertones.

The megastore SuperTarget used a commercial that featured the brand characters of the brands it sells, such as Tony the Tiger, Mr. Peanut, the Kool-Aid pitcher man, and the Hamburger Helper Glove. The ad strategy was to polish the store's image by associating it

THE INSIDE STORY

How Does a Quintessentially American Brand Introduce Itself en Español?

Sonia Montes, Leo Burnett/Lápiz, Chicago

The William Wrigley, Jr. Company was faced with a challenge when one of its key brands, Doublemint, was experiencing a declining sales trend, year on year. Lack of innovation and news in a mature category was setting this trend. The solution was very specific: Wrigley would target Hispanics, a market segment that was not yet saturated. It would create relevance to consumers with the traditional, iconic American brand in various ways. First, Doublemint's brand objective was to stem the declining situation and reestablish the brand as a prominent competitor. Doublemint's relaunch also included a new, longer-lasting formula, revamped packaging, and a relevant message directed toward Hispanics.

However, there were some barriers to overcome since Doublemint did not have a relationship with the growing Hispanic target. The William Wrigley, Jr. Company had never developed specific Spanish-speaking marketing strategies or tactics for this market. Hispanics recognized the product via packaging (especially color) and distribution, but brand recognition and linkage to product attributes were low, due in part to the brand's low development in Latin America. And finally, brand recognition for competitive products leveraged a halo effect as the brands had a much stronger equity and distribution in Latin America.

Based on the insight that Latinos know how to enjoy even the simplest of moments (such as watching a *telenovela* with family or having friends over for dinner) and that gum is, after all, just gum, Doublemint was positioned as one of life's simple pleasures—the everyday gum with an unexaggerated smooth mint flavor that one doesn't need an excuse to chew. This created a clear personality for the brand and linked the product attributes to the brand name. The "Simple Pleasures" campaign depicted simple, slightly misleading situations that capture the sensorial experience of chewing Doublemint. . . . But ultimately, the consumer was always reminded that it's just gum—one of life's simple pleasures and nothing more.

TV executions of 30 and 15 seconds on Spanish-language TV, combined with print and out-of-home vehicles in markets with a high Hispanic penetration were key drivers in making sure the message was correctly delivered. The combination of a smart media strategy and strong positioning statement that correctly captured a key target insight proved to be a valuable combination. Doublemint increased brand awareness by +14 percent, ad awareness rose by 38 percent, and future purchase intent escalated by 63 percent! These are results to chew on!

Sonia graduated from Michigan State University in 2000 with a BA in advertising. While at MSU, she was president of American Advertising Federation (AAF), the largest student chapter in the country at that time, and she was named one of the 25 Most Promising Minority Students in Communications 2000 by *Advertising Age* and AAF. She began her career at FCB Chicago and has worked on such brands as S.C. Johnson and Kraft. She is currently a Senior Account Executive at Leo Burnett/Lápiz.

with well-known and well-loved spokescharacters. Sponsorships are also used by companies to link themselves and their brands to events, such as the Olympics, or good causes, such as the Breast Cancer "Race for the Cure."

The objective of many branding campaigns is to create a brand relationship, which gives a sense of ownership or affiliation to the user. Loyalty programs, such as frequent flyer and frequent buyer clubs, are *relationship marketing programs* that lock customers into an ongoing brand relationship. The Harley Owners Group (HOG) is a customer-initiated club that has endured for years among loyal Harley riders. Self-mage appeals are also delivered through symbolism and association. Some advertising strategies want you to identify with the user of the product or see yourself in that situation. Fashion products invite you to project yourself into the ad and make a fashion statement when you wear or use the product. If you buy and wear Oakley sunglasses or Doc Marten boots, you are making a statement about your own taste and fashion sense because of the image these brands project.

Messages That Drive Action

Even harder to accomplish than conviction is a change in behavior. Sometimes an advertising message can drive people to act by offering something free or at a discounted sales price, as in retail advertising. Many of the strategies advertisers use to encourage behavior come from other marketing communication areas, such as direct marketing and sales promotion. Sales promotion, for example, works in tandem with advertising to stimulate immediate action using sampling, coupons, and free gifts as incentives for action. Advertising plays a role in delivering information about these promotions.

Most ads end with a signature of some kind that serves to identify the company or brand, but it can also serve as a **call to action** if it gives direction to the consumer about how to respond. Gorilla Glue ads have a call to action ("Request your free information kit!") along with contact information. Most ads have response information, such as a toll-free phone number, Web site URL, or e-mail address to make it easier for people to respond. Gorilla Glue gives both a Web site URL and a toll-free phone number.

Another challenge is to find interesting and original ways to generate word of mouth and get people talking about the product. Trade shows can do this. This is sometimes called **viral marketing**, or **buzz**, and it takes advantage of the fact that personal communication is generally seen as more persuasive than mass-media advertising and more likely to motivate action. Viral marketing, which refers to messages being passed through an online network, is another way to create buzz.

Ultimately, advertisers want loyal customers who purchase and repurchase the product as a matter of habit or preference. Advertising can, in a number of ways, foster loyalty leading to repeat purchases. Distributing coupons or introducing a continuity program (such as a frequent flyer program) is effective in keeping customers. Simply keeping the brand name in front of customers goes a long way toward reinforcing continued use of that brand by customers who have had a positive brand experience. That's what **reminder advertising strategies** are designed to do.

Message Approaches

There is no one right way to do advertising. In addition to the basic categories of creative strategies, there are some common message formats or "formulas." We referred to some of these when we talked about ways to deliver different types of effect. Here are some common formats used by a planner to give direction to the creative team.

* *Straightforward.* A straightforward factual or informational message conveys information without any gimmicks, emotions, or special effects. For example, in an ad for www.women.com, the Web site advertises that "It's where today's educated, affluent women are finding in-depth coverage on issues they care about" and that more than 2 million women visit each month.
* *Demonstration.* A *demonstration* focuses on how to use the product or what it can do for you. For example, an ad for Kellogg's Special K and Smart Start uses cereal bowls to demonstrate how a daily regimen of healthy cereal would help a dieter lose six pounds.

- *Comparison.* A *comparison* contrasts two or more products finding the advertiser's brand superior. The comparison can be *direct,* with competitors mentioned, or *indirect,* with just a reference to "other leading brands." In comparison, as in demonstration, seeing is believing, so conviction is the objective. When people see two products being compared, they are more likely to believe that one is better than the other.
- *Problem Solution/Problem Avoidance.* In a **problem solution format**, also known as **product-as-hero**, the message begins with a problem and the product is the solution. A variation is the *problem avoidance* message format, in which the product helps avoid a problem.
- *Humor.* Advertisers use *humor* as a creative strategy because it gets attention; they hope that people will transfer the warm feelings they have as they are being entertained to the product. Humor is hard to handle because some people will think it's funny but others may hate it. For a humorous ad to be effective, the selling premise must reinforce the point of the humor.
- *Slice of Life.* The **slice-of-life format** is an elaborate version of a problem solution staged in the form of a drama in which "typical people" talk about a common problem and resolve it.
- *Spokesperson.* In the *spokesperson* (spokescharacter) or **endorser format**, the ad uses celebrities we admire, created characters (the Aflac duck), experts we respect, or someone "just like us" whose advice we might seek out to speak on behalf of the product to build credibility.
- *Teasers.* *Teasers* are mystery ads that don't identify the product or don't deliver enough information to make sense, but they are designed to arouse curiosity. These are often used to launch a new product. The ads run for a while without the product identification and then when curiosity is sufficiently aroused—usually at the point when the product is officially launched—a concluding ad runs with the product identification.
- *Shockvertising.* Advertising that tries to grab attention and generate buzz by using outlandish creative ideas or provocative visuals is referred to as shock advertising or **shockvertising**. Bennetton has used this strategy for years. Pushing the envelope in terms of taste is a risky strategy but may appeal to younger target markets.[17]

Delivering on the Objectives and Strategies

We've talked about objectives and strategies and this last section has reviewed techniques that deliver on the strategies. Table 12.1 pulls all this information together as a set of basic strategies that describe most advertising messages. The underlying logic is the same as the original Facets model from Chapter 4.

You'll also notice that there are other marketing communication tools besides traditional advertising in Table 12.1. As Rick Boyko, former co-president of Ogilvy and now managing director of the VCU AdCenter, explains, "There is almost no limit to what can be considered advertising. Because the fact is, virtually everything the consumer experiences that has anything to do with a brand will play a role in defining that brand."[18]

PLANNING AND MANAGING CREATIVE STRATEGY

We've talked about creative strategy and how it is developed, as well as the types of effects advertising creates and the message strategies that deliver on these objectives. Now let's look at the process and planning document creative teams use to express their ideas. We'll end this chapter with a discussion of how executions follow from the creative brief and how the creative strategy is evaluated.

The Creative Brief

The creative strategy and the key execution details are spelled out in a document called a **creative brief** (or *creative platform, worksheet,* or *blueprint*). The brief is the document prepared by the account planner to summarize the basic marketing and advertising strategy. It

TABLE

12.1 **Message Strategy Objectives and Techniques**

Strategies	Objectives	Techniques
Awareness strategy	Grab and stick—attention, memory, clutter busting, interest	Novelty and originality; intrusiveness; shockvertising, guerilla marketing, curiosity, teasers, personal or self-interest, key visuals and sound bites, repetition through campaigns, slogans and taglines, jingles, brand characters, reminder ads
Information strategy	Understanding	Claims, news announcements, features, point of differentiation, generic category ads, long-copy ads, problem-solution, direct marketing, public relations, infomercials
Emotion strategy	Emotions, psychological appeals	Feel good (or feel anxiety) appeals, humor, sex and fear appeals, fantasy, song-and-dance commercials, advertainment, events
Persuasion strategy	Attitudes—conviction, preference	Selling premises, comparison, demonstration, testimonials or endorsements, slice-of-life commercials, publicity, advocacy ads, product placements
Brand strategy	Brand identity, associations	Image ads, brand characters, brand identity cues, high-impact imagery, lifestyle ads, association ads, ads that link to self-image, sponsorships, relationship marketing (frequent buyer and other clubs)
Action strategy	Trial, purchase, other actions	Call to action, price ads, incentives, sales promotion (sampling), direct marketing, buzz-building programs, viral marketing, trade shows and exhibits, reminder ads

gives direction to the creative team as they search for a creative concept. The formats of these briefs vary, but most combine the basic advertising strategy decisions:

1. the problem to be solved
2. the objectives
3. the target market
4. the positioning strategy
5. the type of creative strategy
6. the selling premise
7. suggestions about the ad's execution, such as tone of voice

The briefs typically are in outline form, to be filled in by account planners and given to the creative team, as you can see from the examples in Table 12.2.

Consider how a creative brief was developed for a university football team. Even though the University of Minnesota Golden Gophers play in the Metrodome, an off-campus, indoor stadium, over the years the stadium has rarely been filled because few fans come to home games. During the six losing seasons old traditions linked to better days in Gopher football began to die as losses overshadowed the wins. Minnesota fans who had never experienced Gopher football as a tradition-rich event had no reason to invest in season tickets. Local sportswriter Jim Caple wrote, "There's only one marketing method that will recover the lost generation of Gopher football fans. It's called winning." It sounds like a pretty hopeless challenge, doesn't it? But the Minneapolis-based Fallon advertising agency hoped to attract people to Gopher games even if the team wasn't winning, just for the fun of it. The "Gopher Talk" creative brief (Figure 12.3) sets up the strategy behind this EFFIE award–winning campaign.

TABLE
12.2 **Creative Strategy Briefs**

Young & Rubicam

Key Fact (the key piece of information that will be used in the campaign—i.e., a product point of difference, a consumer need, etc.)

Consumer Problem the advertising will solve

Advertising Objective

Creative Strategy

Prospect Definition

Competition

Consumer Benefit

Reason Why

Ogilvy & Mather

Product

Key Issue/Problem

The Promise

The Support

Our Competition

Target Consumer: Who are we talking to?

Desired Behavior: What do we expect?

Target's Net Impression

Tone and Manner

Leo Burnett

Convince: Target audience—current belief re: brand/category

That: Desired belief (benefit)

Because: Focus of sale or proposition (key drama)

Support: Reasons why

DDB Needham

Marketing Objective

Advertising Objective

Position

Target

Key Insight

Reward and Support

Execution: Personality or Tone

Tracy-Locke

Target Audience

User Benefits

Reason Why

Brand Character

Focus of Sale

Tone

The Phelps Group

Client/Product

Target: Demographics and Psychographics

Positioning (In the mind of our client)

Objectives (What we want the prospect to do)

Ad Strategy (What we are saying)

Tactical Strategy (Where/How we say it)

Support

Message Execution

There are many ways to execute any ad. An *execution* is the form in which the ad's message is presented. Creative teams will spend hours comparing and testing various approaches to arrive at the one version they feel best delivers on the strategy. The execution details are the specifics about how the message will look, read, and sound in its finished form. Although general decisions about how the creative message is to be executed are suggested in a creative brief, as you can see in Table 12.2, the brief also contains entries for such things as tone and attitude. (We will discuss the production of ads in more detail in Chapters 13 and 14.)

Because ad copy is written as if it were a conversation, it can also be described in terms of **tone of voice**. Most ads are written as if an anonymous announcer were speaking. Even with anonymity, however, the tone of voice may be identifiable. Some ads are angry, some are pushy, some are friendly. Message tone, like your tone of voice when you speak to someone, reflects the emotion or attitude behind the ad. Recently, *attitude* has become a synonym for a style of advertising that is in-your-face, outrageous, or even abrasive. Although most of the 1980s and early 1990s advertising was fairly serious, in the late 1990s and 2000s, attitude began creeping into advertising as a way to reach a younger generation.

Gopher Football Creative Brief

Problem to Be Solved?

The Gophers are coming off six consecutive losing seasons. They play in the Metrodome and struggle to draw large groups of students. During the losing seasons, old traditions linked to Gopher Football as a tradition-rich event began to die.

Who Are We Talking To?

Primary Target: *Students*

Many of these students have attended Gopher Athletics and probably even a football game, but for some, interest is still only latent. They have a positive disposition and respect tradition, but don't necessarily see anything attracting them to Gopher football games.

Secondary Target: *Recent Alumni and the Lost Generation of Gopher Fans*

These groups represent the people who have become disillusioned with Gopher football. "The team doesn't win and the games aren't fun anymore." These fans want to support the team, but are waiting for something to change their perceptions.

What We Expect the Advertising to Accomplish

Compel students to rediscover Gopher Football by demonstrating that everything about Gopher Football (the games, the pregame events, the parties) is an exciting, entertaining and unpredictable source of fun.

Key Idea

On the field or off the field, with Gopher Football, *anything can happen!*

Why Should They Believe This?

- U of M will sponsor events and activities that make the game a three-day event (on-campus treasure hunts, Maroon & Gold nights at local bars, band and Alumni band events, pregame parties, tailgating parties on Metrodome Plaza).
- With a new coach, the Gophers are committed and could start winning.
- Students and season ticket purchases are the highest since Lou Holtz was coach.

Brand Personality?

Enthusiastic. Unpredictable. Slightly Irreverent.

Executional Considerations

The administration is committed to Coach Mason and his vision for the team. Fortunately, Coach Mason understands that students and their traditions help make games more exciting. The advertising needs to be edgy enough to appeal to students, but cannot be offensive to the general public. "Anything Can Happen" should not be used as a tagline.

12.3 Creative Strategy Brief

An example of a completed creative brief comes from an EFFIE-winning campaign designed to sell season tickets for a university football team, the Minnesota Golden Gophers, a team that rarely wins and whose fans say the team "has little appeal to anyone born after the Truman administration." The Big Idea focused on two smart-mouth, football-crazed grandmothers named Marge and Barb who parodied the blue-hair stereotype of the typical Gopher fan.

Managing the Global Creative Strategy

Global campaigns, like domestic campaigns, require ad work that addresses the advertising objectives and reflects the product's positioning. The opportunity for standardizing the campaign across multiple markets exists only if the objectives and strategic position are essentially the same. Otherwise a creative strategy may call for a little tweaking of the message for a local market or even major revision if there are many cultural and market differences.

In the case where the core targeting and positioning strategies remain the same in different markets, it might be possible for the central creative idea to be universal across markets. For Starbucks the central idea is high-quality products in a relaxing atmosphere. Although the implementation of this idea may vary from market to market, the creative concept is sound across all types of consumers. Whiskas, for example, tries to build on universal truths about cats as explained in the Matter of Principle box.

Even if the campaign theme, slogan, or visual elements are the same across markets, it is usually desirable to adapt the creative execution to the local market. Adaptation is especially important if the advertiser wants its products identified with the local mar-

A MATTER OF PRINCIPLE
Finding a Universal Truth About Cats

Whiskas is the number-one global catfood brand and its management team wanted to find an advertising strategy that could be used across its various markets. A basic principle of global marketing is that globalized strategies work only if they are based on some universal truths about the product that lead to a standardized positioning strategy. Research by Whiska's agency, TBWA, and the Waltham Center for Pet Nutrition in Britain revealed that cats, not surprisingly, have a strong innate drive to eat what is good for them.

Understanding cats' instinctive behavior led the agency to dismiss standard creative approaches that portray cats in cute, unnatural ways or present them as surrogate children. In reality, the agency realized, cats are closer to their wild feline cousins than are dogs or other domesticated animals. TBWA's commercials use special effects to show pet cats as if they live the in wild, stalking herds of water buffalo and zebra. "Your cat has an inner beast," the announcer says. "Feed it."

The creative team used this approach to appeal to cat owners who appreciate their cats' weird, quirky behavior and understand where it comes from. Understanding this universal truth about cats has turned around the category of cat food, according to John Hunt, Worldwide Creative Director at TBWA, the agency behind the campaign.

Consider This

1. What is the primary requirement for a global advertising campaign?
2. How did TBWA use that basic principle to develop a creative strategy for Whiskas?

Source: Stuart Elliott, "Whiskas Lets Cats Roam Wild," NY Times Direct, July 1, 2003, NYTDirect@nytimes.com; "TBWA's Dru: 'Disruption Is in Our DNA,'" Adforum Worldwide Summit, October 9, 2003, http://www.adforum.com/ specialevents/summit/tbwa.asp.

ket rather than as a foreign import. Advertisements may be produced centrally, in each local market, or by a combination of both. With a standardized campaign, production usually is centralized and all are advertisements produced simultaneously to reap production cost savings.

The Go/No-Go Decision

An important part of managing creative work is *evaluation,* which happens at several stages in the creative process. Chapter 19 focuses on this component, but we'll introduce some basics here to help you understand this important role in the creative process. Although evaluation is based on research, at some point there is a personal go/no-go decision, by either the creative team or the client. Craig Weatherup, president and CEO of PepsiCo, explained, "You must have a clear vision and have the nerve to pull the trigger." BBDO's president Phil Dusenberry says, "On Pepsi, the kill rate is high." He explains, "For every spot we go to the client with, we've probably killed nine other spots."[19]

A particular problem that Big Ideas face is that the message is sometimes so creative that the ad is remembered but not the product. That's called **vampire creativity** and it is one of the reasons some advertisers shy away from really novel or entertaining strategies. One method is to assess the effectiveness of the ad's creative features. Research firm McCollum Spielman determined the characteristics of effective creative messages based on 25 years of research and 25,000 copy-tests, as Table 12.3 shows. Insights such as these are very useful to advertising professionals who are making go/no-go decisions.

Structural Analysis   The Leo Burnett agency has an approach for analyzing the logic of the creative strategy as it is being developed. The Burnett creatives use it to keep the message strategy and creative concept working together, as well as the head and the heart appeals. This method, called **structural analysis**, relies on these three steps:

1. Evaluate the power of the narrative or story line (heart).
2. Evaluate the strength of the product claim (head).
3. Consider how well the two aspects are integrated—that is, how the storyline brings the claim to life.

TABLE

12.3   Twelve Tested Creative Hot Buttons

What makes a creative message effective? Here are the 12 recurring qualities found in the most sales-effective advertising as measured by research firm McCollum Spielman.

1. Brand rewards/benefits are highly visible through demonstration, dramatization, lifestyle, feelings, or analogy.
2. The brand is the major player in the experience (the brand makes the good times better).
3. The link between the brand and execution is clear (the scenario revolves around and highlights the brand).
4. The execution has a focus (there's a limit to how many images and vignettes the consumer can process).
5. Feelings (emotional connectives) are anchored to the needs and aspirations of the targeted consumer.
6. Striking, dramatic imagery is characteristic of many successful executions, enhancing their ability to break out of clutter.
7. An original, creative signature or mystique exists in many of the best commercials to bond the consumer to the brand and give it a unique personality.
8. In food and beverage advertising, high taste appeal is almost always essential.
9. The best creative ideas for mature brands often use fresh new ways of revitalizing the message.
10. Music (memorable, bonded tunes and lyrics) is often a key to successful executions for many brands.
11. When humor is used, it is relevant, with a clear product purpose.
12. When celebrities are used, they are well matched to brands and have credibility as users/endorsers, and their delivery is believably enthusiastic.

Source: McCollum Spielman Worldwide, *Topline* (October 1993): 2, 32.

Burnett creative teams check to see whether the narrative level is so high that it overpowers the claim or whether the claim is strong but there is no memorable story. Ideally, these two elements will be so seamless that it will be hard to tell whether the impact occurs because of the power of the story or the strength of the claim. Such an analysis keeps the rational and emotional sides of an advertisement working together.

Copy-testing   A more formal method of evaluating the effectiveness of an ad, either in a draft form or after it has been used, is called *copy-testing*. To evaluate the results of the advertising, the objectives need to be measurable—which means they can be evaluated to determine the effectiveness of the creative strategy. The last chapter in this book will concentrate on the evaluation of effectiveness.

IT'S A WRAP

MSN'S BUTTERFLY EMERGES AS A WINNING BIG IDEA

No matter how much the creative people or the client or the account executive may like an idea, if it doesn't communicate the right message or the right product personality to the right audience at the right time, then it is not effective. That's the science of advertising messages; the art side comes from creative Big Ideas that have stopping power and break through the competitive clutter.

MSN's "Butterfly" campaign is a good example of both the art and science of advertising. It was designed to motivate consumers to consider MSN as an alternative to AOL and to sign up for the new service. By tapping into what consumers truly want from their Internet service provider—a more useful experience—the McCann team developed an impactful advertising campaign. It has been recognized as effective because it delivered on its objectives:

- Generate switching momentum from AOL to MSN: The campaign resulted in 715,000 AOL users switching to MSN.
- Increase Internet subscriptions: The total MSN subscriptions grew 31 percent with a significant increase during the six-week online campaign.

- Increase unaided awareness: Unaided brand awareness jumped 42 percent from 17 percent before the campaign to 24.2 percent a year later.
- Increase perception of MSN as AOL competitor: After the campaign 53 percent of respondents rated MSN as AOL's chief competitor, up from 38 percent before the campaign. That's an increase of 39 percent.

The campaign not only put a serious chink in AOL's armor, it also elevated MSN to a top-of-mind position in the consumers' decision making. With results like these, you can understand why the MSN Butterfly was recognized for an EFFIE award.

▪▪▪ Summary

1. **Define creative advertising and explain how it leads to a Big Idea.** To be creative an ad must make a relevant connection with its audience and present a selling idea in an unexpected way. There is both a science (the way a message is persuasive, convincing, and relevant) and an art (the way a message is an unexpected idea). A Big Idea is a creative concept that makes the message attention getting and memorable.

2. **Describe the characteristics of creative people and their creative process.** Creative people tend to be independent, assertive, self-sufficient, persistent, and self-disciplined, with a high tolerance for ambiguity. They are also risk takers with powerful egos that are internally driven. They don't care much about group standards and opinions and typically have inborn skepticism and strong curiosity. They are good problem solvers with an ability to visualize and do conceptual thinking. They are open to new experiences. A typical

creative process involves immersing yourself in background research, developing alternatives through ideation, brainfog where you hit the wall and can't come up with anything, and illumination where you get the great idea.

3. **Discuss key creative strategy approaches.** Creative strategies are often expressed as appeals to the head, the heart, or both. The six facets of creative strategy are perception, cognitive, affective, persuasion, transformation, and behavior. These can be rephrased as awareness, information, emotion, persuasion, brand image, and action strategies.

4. **Outline the key parts of a creative brief.** From the advertising strategy comes the problem statement, the objectives, the target market, and the positioning strategy. The message strategy decisions include the appropriate type of creative strategy, the selling premise, and suggestions about the ad's execution, such as tone of voice.

▪▪▪ Key Terms

appeal, 340
association message strategy, 342
attributes, 338
benefit, 341
Big Idea, 327
brainstorming, 333
buzz, 342
call to action, 344
claim, 338
copycat advertising, 327

copy-testing, 330
creative brief, 345
creative concept, 327
creative strategy, 334
endorser format, 345
features, 338
hard sell, 335
image advertising, 342
message strategy, 334
permission to believe, 342
point of differentiation, 338

problem solution format, 345
product-as-hero, 345
promise, 341
reason why, 341
reminder advertising strategies, 344
ROI, 327
selling premise, 341
share of mind, 336
shock vertising, 345
slice-of-life format, 345

soft sell, 335
structural analysis, 349
support, 341
tone of voice, 347
teaser, 336
unique selling proposition (USP), 341
vampire creativity, 349
viral marketing, 344

▪▪▪ Review Questions

1. What is a Big Idea and what are its characteristics?
2. List five characteristics of creative people. How do you rate yourself on those factors?
3. Describe the six steps in the creative process.
4. What are the six facets of creative strategy?

5. What is the role of originality in driving perception?
6. What are the seven general types of information found in a creative brief?

■■■ Discussion Questions

1. Find the ad in this book that you think is the most creative. Analyze it in terms of the ROI formula for evaluating effective creative advertising.

2. Peter Madison, a sophomore in advertising, is speaking informally with a copywriter from a local advertising agency following the writer's class presentation. Peter states his strong determination to be some sort of creative professional once he gets his degree. "My problem is that I'm a bit shy and reserved. I'm interested in all sorts of stuff, but I'm not really quick in expressing ideas and feelings. I'm not sure my personality is suited for being an advertising creative. How do I know whether I've picked the right career direction?" What advice should the writer give Peter?

3. What are some of the major traits of creative people? Which characteristics of the advertising world do you think enhance creativity? Which discourage it? How do you rate yourself on these traits?

4. Find a newspaper or magazine advertisement that you think is bland and unexciting. Explain how you might rewrite it, first to demonstrate a hard-sell approach, and then to demonstrate a soft-sell approach.

5. Explain how creative advertising relates to advertising effectiveness. Find an ad you think is good and one that you think doesn't work very well. Analyze them in terms of their creativity (art) and strategy (science). If you were a professional working on these accounts, how would you go about evaluating the effectiveness of these two ads to test your intuitive judgment?

■■■ Class Projects

1. The class should be divided into groups of 8 to 10, with each group working in a separate area. Here's the problem: Your community wants to encourage people to get out of their cars and use alternative forms of transportation. How many different creative concepts can your team come up with to express that idea in an advertisement? Brainstorm for 15 minutes as a group, accumulating every possible idea regardless of how crazy or dumb it might initially sound. Appoint one member to be the recorder who lists all the ideas as they are mentioned. Then go back through the list as a group and put an asterisk next to the ideas that seem to have the most promise. When all the groups reconvene in class, each recorder should list the group's ideas on the blackboard. Cover the board with all the ideas from all the groups. As a class, pick out the three ideas that seem to have the most potential. Analyze the experience of participating in a brainstorming group and compare the experiences of the different teams.

2. Consult the BrandEra.com Web site and open up the "Creative" or "Advertising" topics in the Department section. Find an article that discusses the creative strategy behind an ad or campaign. Summarize the discussion and relate it to things you have learned in this chapter about how creative strategies are developed.

HANDS-ON

CASE 12

How Do You Put a Price on Great Creative? Ask McCann-Erickson

The McCann-Erickson advertising agency was hungry for fresh talent when it hired a young copywriter named Joyce King Thomas. It was the mid-1990s and McCann was in a creative slump. Its biggest and most famous client, Coca Cola, had fired the agency after decades of collaboration on some of the greatest ads in history. McCann's creative director Nina DiSesa had liked King Thomas's work at another agency and thought she could help lead a creative revival at McCann.

McCann got its chance when credit card giant MasterCard became a client in 1997. MasterCard wanted something fresh that could help it regain lost ground against top-competitor Visa. "Visa was the aspirational, globe-trotting card, and MasterCard was the everyday, hardware-store card. We needed to take the ordinariness of the card and glorify it," recalled executive creative director Jonathan Cranin. Eric Einhorn, McCann's head of strategic planning, put it this way. "We considered it a travesty that you could use your MasterCard wherever you could use your Visa—and in more places around the world. But Visa was it and MasterCard was just another card."

King Thomas, Einhorn, and Cranin thought they should avoid a benefits focus and shoot for ads that would strike an emotional chord. The ideas did not come easily, but after days of brainstorming, false starts, and lots of crumpled paper, Cranin came up with "There are some things money can't buy. For everything else, there's MasterCard." That was good, everyone agreed, but how to present it? King Thomas suggested a "shopping list" approach. She described a father and son attending a baseball game. As the two enjoy food and souvenirs together an announcer checks off the dollar costs (Two tickets: $28; two hot dogs, two popcorns, and two sodas: $18; one autographed baseball: $45) leading up to the emotional close: "Real conversation with 11-year-old son: priceless."

The group believed they had a winner but were taking no chances. When they presented their ideas to MasterCard the ads were encased in blue-velvet-covered books. Most of pitching was done by King Thomas, who backed up the creative with clips taken of the enthusiastic focus groups that had watched the ads. "It was choreographed beautifully," recalls a McCann executive. "Joyce took us through the work, and she had such passion for it."

The client's reaction? "Without naming names, there were a few tears at the presentation," says Cranin.

And thus a hit was born. The long-running Master-Card campaign has led to large gains in both consumer awareness and card usage. The ads are cultural icons, inspiring parodies on *Saturday Night Live* and the HBO program *Arliss*. And McCann is back on top, with a strong roster of new clients, including Verizon Wireless ($300 million), Staples ($60 million) and *USA Today* ($10 million). The agency has almost $3 billion in yearly billings. As for King Thomas? She has just been named to succeed DiSesa as creative director, placing her in charge of about 150 people.

The McCann story holds some important lessons for agencies: Fancy reputation? Good. Impressive roster of past clients? Noteworthy. The best creative talent in the business? Priceless.

Consider This

1. Campaigns that seek an emotional connection are difficult to pull off. Joyce King Thomas put it this way. "One thing we were worried about was that people would think we were telling them they would have to spend money to have a close relationship. But that hasn't come up." King Thomas worried from the start that the campaign might be deemed manipulative or sappy by the consumer. "This kind of work can easily slip into bad Hallmark advertising." What in McCann's work has helped MasterCard to avoid this problem?

2. When the HBO program *Arliss* used the "Priceless" tagline in one episode, MasterCard sued for trademark and copyright infringement. Would you have advised MasterCard to protect its slogan this way? Why or why not?

3. What makes the MasterCard "Priceless" theme a winning creative idea? How would you determine if it is truly effective?

Sources: Hank Kim, "Mastercard Moments." *Adweek* (April 12, 1999); Mallorre Dill, "Creative Briefs," *Adweek* (July 17, 2000); Kathleen Sampey, "King Thomas Takes Over Creative at McCann Flagship," *Adweek* (October 25, 2004); Todd Wasserman, "Credit Cards," *Adweek* (April 26, 2004).

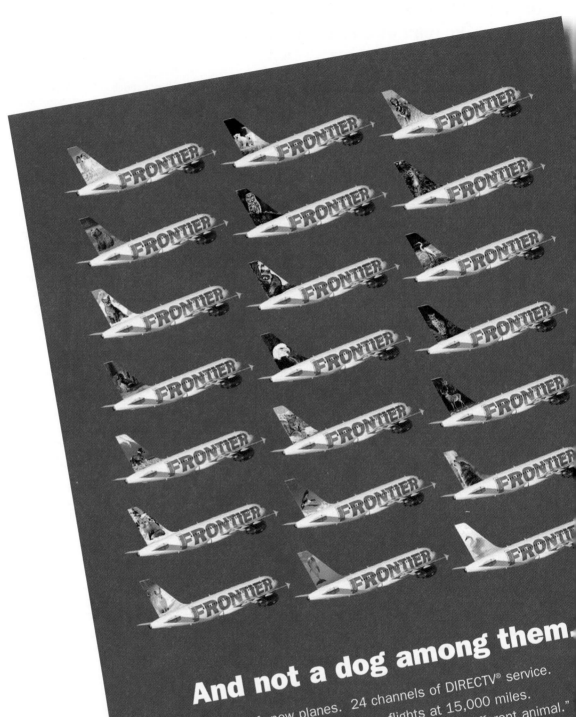

And not a dog among them.

Comfy new planes. 24 channels of DIRECTV® service.
First-run movies. Free flights at 15,000 miles.
Just a few things that make us "a whole different animal."

Copywriting

Frontier's
Tales About Tails

Awards:
*ADDY; New York Festivals
International Awards;
Mobius Awards (Television
Commercials Festival);
Cresta Creative Standards
Award; Denver Advertising
Federation "Fame and
Fortune" Award*

Company:
Frontier Airlines

Agencies:
*Sticky Grey (a division of
Grey Worldwide); Sterling-
Rice Group; Genesis, Inc.*

Campaign:
"A Whole Different Animal"

CHAPTER OBJECTIVES

After reading this chapter, you will be able to:

1. Explain the basic style of writing used for advertising copy.

2. Describe the various copy elements of a print ad.

3. Explain the message characteristics and tools of radio advertising.

4. Discuss the major elements of television commercials.

5. Discuss how Web advertising is written.

Frontier Airlines, a low cost carrier that started up in 1994, took off with animals emblazoned on the tails of its planes. Frontier's distinctive aircraft tails, all of which depict wildlife images, have made the Frontier brand name synonymous with the airline's western heritage.

The idea of using animals on the tail, according to Diane Willmann, Frontier's director of advertising, came from Jim Adler, who heads up the brand-identity company Genesis, Inc. She explains, "We had virtually no advertising budget in the early years. We needed our aircraft to communicate for us and emotionally connect with the public. In fact, the challenge was to create a livery that was so different and compelling that we would have people lined up at the airport with their noses pressed against the glass just to catch a glimpse of the plane."

The animals have helped bring the Frontier brand to life as its advertising brought them to life as talking characters on the tarmac. Every aircraft in Frontier's fleet of 40-plus Airbus planes has a different

355

animal on its tail, and these creatures have become stars in radio and television commercials that feature their conversations as they line up at the gate.

Willmann explains, "They are attention getting, visually appealing and connote a different kind of airline . . . one that is as individual as the passengers it carries, and one that is warm, alive, and 'human.' No single animal represents Frontier. The diversity of the animals is essential to the character and personality of the airline." And the diversity comes out in their commentaries on life at the gates.

Flip the dolphin complains because he's always getting sent to frigid Chicago even though Frontier has a number of flights to Florida. Larry the lynx, who sounds like he's seen too many Don Rickles routines, tells him to "chill out," saying "Your blowhole is leaking."

Foxy, a sultry red fox that is being pursued by lovesick Jack the Rabbit, smirks that she would rather eat a rabbit for dinner than have dinner with a rabbit. Larry knows why Foxy won't go out with the big white bunny when Jack asks "How's my breath?" Larry responds, "It smells like carrots."

Griswald the Buddy Hackett–like bear gloats about his Florida routes and says he has his suitcase filled with sunscreen, a beach ball, and a thong. Larry replies about the thong, "That'll clear the beach."

In one scene Larry brags on Frontier's new LiveTV feature. Jack responds, "I prefer the old-fashioned technology." "What, cable?" growls the lynx. "No, rabbit ears," retorts the rabbit.

Other characters include Klondike and Snow, who were polar bear cubs born at the Denver Zoo; Sal the Cougar; Mo and Jo, the twin red fox pups; Montana the elk; Ozzy the Orca whale; Carl the coyote; Hamilton the hummingbird; and Lucy the Canadian goose—to name just a few of the tail gang. The award-winning advertising created by Sticky Grey, a division of Grey Worldwide, can be viewed on Frontier's Web site at http://www.frontierairlines .com.

Part of a massive rebranding campaign, the slogan "A whole different animal," developed by Sticky Grey, was used to signify Frontier's growth and new routes, low fares, customer service, and onboard amenities such as its LiveTV satellite service. It also became the focal point in an awareness-building campaign in Denver and ultimately in other major markets. Frontier flies to some 47 cities in 30 states, as well as 5 resorts in Mexico.

The ads are fun, but the message strategy is a hard-nosed business-building effort. When you say you're "a whole different animal" in a highly competitive business like airlines, you're making "an enormous customer promise," explained Buddy Ketchner, managing partner at Sterling-Rice, a Boulder-based branding agency that conducted the research to define the message strategy.

The advertising works not only because it delivers on the brand promise, but also because customers like the airline more because of the campaign and follow the stories of the cast of characters. They write in with suggestions for storylines; some have sent photos of their own pets gracing a Frontier tail. Little kids want to know which animal they are flying with and you'll see them in waiting rooms trying to catch sight of their favorite animal tail.

Sources: Diane Willman Interview, September 28, 2004; David Kesmodel, "Tale of the Tails," *Rocky Mountain News* (June 12, 2004): 1C, 6C; Amy Bryer, "Frontier's Animal Ads Proving Popular, Attention-getters," *Denver Business Journal* (March 15, 2004), http://denver.bizjournals.com/denver/stories/2004/03/15story8.html; "Frontier Airlines' 'Talking Animals' Ad Campaign Receives Critical Praise from Around the Country," April 22, 2004, Frontier press release, www.frontierairlines.com; Barry Janoff, "What Do You Call a Funny Airplane? A One Liner," *Brandweek* (August 18, 2003): 28 Flight information based on 6/2005 schedule.

Words and pictures work together to produce a creative concept. However, the idea behind a creative concept in advertising is usually expressed in some attention-getting and memorable phrase. Finding these "magic words" is the responsibility of copywriters, who search for the right way to warm up a mood or soften consumer resistance. This chapter will describe the role of the copywriter and then explain the practice of copywriting in print, broadcast, and Internet advertising.

COPYWRITING: THE LANGUAGE OF ADVERTISING

Some creative concepts are primarily visual; however, intriguing thoughts can also be expressed through language. A long-running NYNEX campaign for its Yellow Pages illustrates a word-oriented creative concept. The campaign used a visual play on words to illustrate some of the headings in its directory, but the pun doesn't make sense until the visual is married with the heading from the directory. One commercial in the series included three train engineers with overalls, caps, and bandannas sitting in rocking chairs in a parlor and having tea to illustrate the "Civil Engineering" category; a picture of a bull sleeping on its back illustrates the category "Bulldozing."

■ ■ ■
NYNEX's ads have featured puns based on its category headings. This ad, which was directed to media buyers, used that same creative technique with a visual pun on the heading.

Although advertising is highly visual, there are four types of advertisements in which words are crucial.

1. If the message is complicated, words can be more specific than visuals and can be read over and over until the meaning is clear.
2. If the ad is for a high-involvement product—meaning the consumer spends a lot of time considering it—then the more information the better, and that means using words.
3. Information that needs definition and explanation, like how a new wireless phone works, is better delivered through words.
4. If a message tries to convey abstract qualities, such as justice and quality, words tend to communicate these concepts more easily than pictures.

Words are powerful tools in advertising and the person who understands their beauty and power, as well as how best to use them is the copywriter.

The Copywriter

The person who shapes and sculpts the words in an advertisement is called a **copywriter**. *Copy* is the text of an ad or the words that people say in a commercial. In most agencies, copywriters work in teams with art directors, who design the way the ad will look. A successful advertising copywriter is a savvy marketer and a literary master, sometimes described as a "killer poet." Copywriters love words and they search for the clever twist, the pun, the powerful description, the punch, the nuance—for words that whip and batter, plead, sob, cajole, and impress. They are experts on words, or, rather, students of them, as the YMCA ad demonstrates. They know meanings and derivations, as well as the moods and feelings of words and the reverberations and vibrations they create in a reader's mind.

Many copywriters have a background in English or literature. In addition to having an ear for the right or clever phrase, they listen to the way people talk and identify the tone of voice that best fits the target audience and advertising need. Versatility is a common trait of copywriters. They can move from toilet paper to Mack trucks and shift their writing style to match the product and the language of their target audience. Like poets, copywriters

SHOWCASE

■ ■ ■

Part of a membership drive campaign, this ad demonstrates how a copy-writer plays with language to deliver a selling point with style. Lara Mann, a graduate of the University of Florida advertising program, and copywriter at FHB Advertising in Orlando, contributed this ad.

spend hours, even days, crafting a paragraph. After many revisions others read the copy and critique it. It then goes back to the writer, who continues to fine-tune it. Copywriters have to have thick skins as there is always someone else reading their work, critiquing it, and making changes.

Advertising Writing Style

Advertising has to win its audience—no small task given that it usually competes in a very cluttered environment. For that reason, the copy should be as simple as possible. It is succinct and single-minded, meaning it has a clear focus and usually tries to convey only one selling point. Advertising writing is tight: Every word counts because both space and time are expensive. Ineffective words—such as *interesting, very, in order to, buy now and save, introducing, nothing less than*—waste precious space. Copywriters revise copy a hundred times to make it as concise as possible. The tighter the copy, the easier it is to understand and the greater its impact. Simple ads avoid being gimmicky because they may come off as too cute; they don't try too hard or reach too far to make a point.

Principle
Effective copy is succinct and single-minded.

Copywriters try to write the way the target audience thinks and talks. That often means using direct address. For example, an ad for Trojan condoms makes a pointed argument on a touchy subject for its young, single-person target audience. Combining headline with body copy, it reads as a dialogue:

I didn't use one because I didn't have one with me.
Get Real.
If you don't have a parachute, don't jump, genius.

The Practical Tips feature summarizes some characteristics of effective copy.

Practical Tips

Writing Effective Copy

- **Be succinct.** Use short, familiar words, short sentences, and short paragraphs.
- **Be single-minded.** Focus on one main point.
- **Be specific.** Don't waste time on generalities. The more specific the message, the more attention getting and memorable it is.
- **Get personal.** Directly address your audience whenever possible as "you" and "your," rather than "we" or "they."
- **Keep a single focus.** Deliver a simple message instead of one that makes too many points. Focus on a single idea and support it.
- **Be conversational.** Use the language of everyday conversation. The copy should sound like two friends talking to one another, so don't shy away from incomplete sentences, thought fragments, and contractions.
- **Be original.** To keep your copy forceful and persuasive, avoid stock advertising phrases, strings of superlatives and brag-and-boast statements, and clichés.
- **Use variety.** To add visual appeal in both print and TV ads, avoid long blocks of copy in print ads. Instead, break the copy into short paragraphs with subheads. In TV commercials, break up television monologues with visual changes, such as shots of the product, sound effects, and dialogue. The writer puts these breaks in the script while the art director designs what they will look like.
- **Use imaginative description.** Use evocative or figurative language to build a picture in the consumer's mind.

The pompous overblown phrasing of many corporate statements doesn't belong in ads. We call it **your-name-here copy** because almost any company can use those words and tack their signature on the end. It isn't attention getting and it doesn't contribute to a distinctive and memorable image. That's always a risk with company-centered copy. A broadband company named Covad started off an ad with copy that could be used by any company:

Opportunity. Potential. These are terms usually associated with companies that have a lot to prove and little to show for it. But on rare occasion, opportunity can be used to describe a company that has already laid the groundwork, made the investments, and is well down the road to strong growth.

Tone of Voice   To develop the right tone of voice, copywriters write to the target audience. If they know someone who fits the audience profile, then they write to that person as if they were in a conversation. If they don't, then they may go through a photo file, select a picture of the person they think fits the description, and write to that person. Molson Beer won awards for a commercial it created, called "The Rant," that mirrored the attitude of many Canadians. The commercial started softly with an average-Joe character disassociating himself from Canadian stereotypes. As he talks, he builds up intensity and at the end, he's in a full-blown rant. The commercial was so successful it was played at events all around the country:

> *Hey. I'm not a lumberjack or a fur trader. And I don't live in an igloo or eat blubber or own a dogsled. And I don't know Jimmy, Sally or Suzy from Canada, although I'm certain they're really, really nice. I have a Prime Minister, not a President. I speak English and French, not American. And I pronounce it 'about' not 'aboot.' I can proudly sew my country's flag on my backpack. I believe in peace-keeping, not policing. Diversity, not assimilation, and that the beaver is a truly proud and noble animal. A toque is a hat. A chesterfield is a couch, and it is pronounced 'zed,' not 'zee.' Zed! Canada is the second largest land mass, the first nation in hockey, and the best part of North America. My name is Joe, and I am Canadian.*

Grammar   Copywriters also are attuned to the niceties of grammar, syntax, and spelling, although sometimes they will play with a word or phrase to create an effect, even if it's grammatically incorrect. The Apple Computer campaign for the Macintosh that used the slogan "Think different" rather than "Think differently" caused a bit of an uproar in Apple's school market, which is the reason copywriters think very carefully about playing loose with the language even if it sounds right.[1]

Adese   Formulaic advertising copy is one problem that is so well-known that comedians parody it. This type of formula writing, called **adese**, violates all the guidelines for writing effective copy that we described in the Practical Tips. It is full of clichés, superlatives, stock phrases, and vague generalities. For example, can you hear yourself saying anything like the following to a friend? "Now we offer the quality that you've been waiting for—at a price you can afford," and "Buy now and save."

Another type of adese is **brag-and-boast copy**, which is "we" copy written from the company's point of view with a pompous tone. Consider a print ad by Buick. The ad starts with a stock opening, "Introducing Buick on the move." The body copy includes superlatives and generalities such as "Nothing less than the expression of a new philosophy," "It strikes a new balance between luxury and performance—a balance which has been put to the test," and "Manufactured with a degree of precision that is in itself a breakthrough." Because people are so conditioned to screen out advertising, messages that use this predictable style are the ones that are the easiest to ignore.

Now that we've discussed the basics of advertising style, let's look at how copy is written for print and broadcast media.

COPYWRITING FOR PRINT

A print advertisement is created in two pieces: a copy sheet and a layout. We discuss the copy in this chapter and the layout in the next. The two categories of copy that print advertising uses are **display copy** and **body copy** (or text). Display copy includes all elements that readers see in their initial scanning. These elements—headlines, subheads, call-outs, taglines, and slogans—usually are set in larger type sizes than body copy and are designed to get attention and to stop the viewer's scanning. Body copy includes the elements that are designed to be read and absorbed, such as the text of the ad message and captions. Table 13.1 summarizes the primary copy elements that are in the copywriter's toolkit.

How to Write Headlines

The **headline** is a key element in print advertising. It conveys the main message so that people get the point of the ad. It's important for another reason. The headline works with the visual to get attention and communicate the creative concept. This clutter-busting Big Idea breaks through the competitive messages. It comes across best through a picture and words working together, as the DuPont ad illustrates. The headline carries the theme ("To

TABLE 13.1 The Copywriter's Toolkit

No one ad uses all of the copy elements: however, they are all used in different ads for different purposes. Here are the most common tools in the copywriter's toolkit:

Headline: A phrase or a sentence that serves as the opening to the ad. It's usually identified by larger type or a prominent position and its purpose is to catch attention. In the Corporate Angel Network ad, for example, the headline is "Cancer Patients Fly Free."

Overlines and **underlines:** These are phrases or sentences that either lead into the headline or follow up on the thought in the headline. They are usually set in smaller type than the headline. The purpose of the overline is to set the stage, and the purpose of the underline is to elaborate on the idea in the headline and serve as a transition to the body copy.

Body Copy: The text of the ad. It's usually smaller-sized type and written in paragraphs or multiple lines. Its purpose is to explain the idea or selling point.

Subheads: Used in longer copy blocks, subheads begin a new section of the copy. They are usually bold type or larger than the body copy. Their purpose is to make the logic clear to the reader. They are useful for people who scan copy and they help them get a sense of what the copy says. The Corporate Angel Network ad uses subheads.

Call-outs: These are sentences that float around the visual, usually with a line or arrow pointing to some specific element in the visual that they name and explain. For example, Johnson & Johnson once ran an ad that used call-outs as the main pieces of the body copy. The head read: "How to bathe a mommy." Positioned around a picture of a woman are short paragraphs with arrows pointing to various parts of her body. These "call outs" describe the good things the lotion does for feet, hands, makeup removal, moisture absorption, and skin softening.

Captions: A sentence or short piece of copy that explains what you are looking at in a photo or illustration. Captions aren't used very often in advertising because the visuals are assumed to be self-explanatory; however, readership studies have shown that, after the headline, captions have high readership.

Taglines: A short phrase that wraps up the key idea or creative concept that usually appears at the end of the body copy. It often refers back to the headline or opening phrase in a commercial. For example, see the line, "Need a lift? Just give us a call. We'll do the rest," in the Corporate Angel Network ad.

Slogans: A distinctive catch phrase that serves as a motto for a campaign, brand, or company. It is used across a variety of marketing communication messages and over an extended period of time. For example, see "The Miracles of Science" line that serves as a corporate motto for the DuPont company.

Call to Action: This is a line at the end of an ad that encourages people to respond and gives information on how to respond. Both ads—Corporate Angel Network, and DuPont—have response information: either an address, a toll-free phone number, an e-mail address, or Web address.

Do List for the Planet") and the **underline** ("Find food that helps prevent osteoporosis") makes a direct connection with the visual. People who are scanning may read nothing more, so advertisers want to at least register a point with the consumer. The point has to be clear from the headline or the combination of headline and visual. Researchers estimate that only 20 percent of those who read the headline go on to read the body copy.

Headlines need to be catchy phrases, but they also have to convey an idea and attract the right target audience. Tobler chocolates has won EFFIE® awards for a number of years for its clever headlines and visuals. For Tobler's Chocolate Orange, the creative concept showed the chocolate ball being smacked against something hard and splitting into slices. The headline was "Whack and Unwrap." The next year the headline was "Smashing Good Taste," which speaks to the candy's British origins and to the quirky combination of chocolate and orange flavors. The headline and visual also tell consumers how to "open" the orange into slices—by whacking it.

Agencies will copy-test headlines to make sure they can be understood at a glance and that they communicate exactly the right idea. **Split-run tests** (two versions of the same ad) in direct mail have shown that changing the wording of the headline while keeping all other elements constant can double, triple, or quadruple consumer response. That is why the experts, such as ad legend David Ogilvy, state that the headline is the most important element in the advertisement.[2] Because headlines are so important, some general principles guide their development and explain the particular functions they serve:

* A good headline will attract only those who are *prospects;* there is no sense in attracting people who are not in the market. An old advertising axiom is, "Use a rifle, not a shotgun." In other words, use the headline to tightly target the right audience.
* The headline must work in combination with the visual to stop and grab the reader's attention. An advertisement by Range Rover shows a photo of the car parked at the edge of a rock ledge in Monument Valley with the headline "Lots of people use their Range Rovers just to run down to the corner."
* The headline must also identify the product and brand, and start the sale. The selling premise should be evident in the headline.
* The headline should lead readers into the body copy. For readers to move to the body copy, they have to stop scanning and start concentrating. This change in mind-set is the reason why only 20 percent of scanners become readers.

Headlines can be grouped into two general categories: **direct-** and **indirect-action headlines.** Direct-action headlines are straightforward and informative, such as "The Power to Stop Pain." It links the brand to the benefit. Direct headlines are highly targeted, but they may fail to lead the reader into the message if they are not captivating enough. Indirect-action headlines are not as selective and may not provide as much information, but they may be better at drawing the reader into the message.

Types of Direct-Action Headlines

* *Assertion.* An assertion is a headline that states a claim or a promise that will motivate someone to try the product.
* *Command.* A command headline politely tells the reader to do something.
* *How-To Heads.* People are rewarded for investigating a product when the message tells them how to use it or how to solve a problem.
* *News Announcements.* News headlines are used with new-product introductions, but also with changes, reformulations, new styles, and new uses. The news value is thought to get attention and motivate people to try the product.

Types of Indirect-Action Headlines

* *Puzzles.* Used strictly for their curiosity and provocative power. Puzzling statements, ambiguity, and questions require the reader to examine the body copy to get the answer or explanation. The intention is to pull readers into the body copy.
* *Associations.* These headlines use image and lifestyle to get attention and build interest.

The "Help, I Think I Need A Tourniquet" headline draws us into the Motorola Talk About ad. Headlines like this one, which also plays on the sounds of words, are provoca-

tive and compel people to read on to find out the point of the message. Sometimes these indirect headlines are called "blind headlines" because they give so little information. A **blind headline** is a gamble. If it is not informative or intriguing enough, the reader may move on without absorbing any product name information, but if it works as an attention getter, it can be very effective.

How to Write Other Display Copy

Next to the headline, **captions** have the second-highest readership. In addition to their pulling power, captions also serve an information function. Visuals do not always say the same thing to every person; for that reason, most visuals can benefit from explanation. In addition to headlines, copywriters also craft the **subheads** that continue to help lure the reader into the body copy. Subheads are considered display copy in that they are usually larger and set in type (bold or italic) different from the body copy. Subheads are sectional headlines and are also used to break up a mass of "gray" type (or type that tends to blur together when one glances at it) in a large block of copy.

    Taglines are short, catchy, and particularly memorable phrases used at the end of an ad to complete or wrap up the creative idea. An ad from the Nike women's campaign used the headline "You are a nurturer and a provider. You are beautiful and exotic" set in an elegant script. The tagline on the next page used a rough, hand-drawn, graffiti-like image that said, "You are not falling for any of this." **Slogans**, which are repeated from ad to ad as part of a campaign or a long-term brand-identity effort, also may be used as taglines. To be successful, these phrases have to be catchy and memorable, yet many corporate slogans fall back into marketing language or clichés and come across as leaden ("Total quality through excellence," "Excellence through total quality," or "Where quality counts").[3] Consider the distinctiveness and memorability of the slogans in Table 13.2. Which ones work and which ones don't?

    Copywriters use a number of literary techniques to enhance the memorability of subheads, slogans, and taglines. These are other techniques copywriters use to create catchy slogans:

- *Direct Address.* "Have it your way; "Think small."
- *A Startling or Unexpected Phrase.* The NYNEX campaign used the phrase, "If it's out there, it's in here," which is an example of a twist on a common phrase that makes it unexpected.

TABLE 13.2 Test Yourself: Identify the Company

Match the company with its slogan:

1. It's What Your Family Deserves.	a. Nissan
2. Communication Without Boundaries	b. Tyson
3. Our Challenge is Life	c. Delta
4. Know How.	d. Avaya
5. A Business of Caring	e. Hitachi
6. On top of the World	f. Cigna
7. Inspire the Next	g. Hertz
8. Enjoy the Ride	h. Canon
9. Where winners rent	i. Chrysler
10. Inspiration Comes Standard	j. Aventis

Answers to Companies: 1:b Tyson; 2:d Avaya; 3:j Aventis; 4:h Canon; 5:f Cigna; 6:c Delta; 7:e Hitachi; 8:a Nissan; 9:g Hertz; 10:i Chrysler.

Source: Jayne Clark, "It's Hard to Love Those Tourism Slogans," *USA Today* (May 7, 2004): 5D; A1 Ries, "Wasting Money on Bad Advertising Slogans," January 2004, Adage.com.

- *Rhyme, Rhythm, Alliteration.* Uses repetition of sounds, as in the *Wall Street Journal's* slogan—"The daily diary of the American Dream."
- *Parallel Construction.* Uses repetition of the structure of a sentence or phrase, as in Morton Salt's "When it rains, it pours."
- *Cue for the Product.* Folgers' "Good to the last drop;" John Deere's "Nothing runs like a Deere," Wheaties' "Breakfast of Champions;" "Beef. It's What's for Dinner."
- *Music.* "In the valley of the Jolly, ho-ho-ho, Green Giant"

How to Write Body Copy

Principle
Good body copy keeps people's interest so they continue reading past the headline.

The *body copy* is the text of the ad and its primary role is to maintain the interest of the reader. It develops the sales message, states the argument, summarizes the proof, and provides explanation. It is the persuasive heart of the message. You excite consumer interest with the display elements, but you win them over with the argument presented in the body copy, assuming the ad uses body copy.

There are as many different kinds of writing styles as there are product personalities, but there are also some standard approaches:

- *Straightforward.* Factual copy usually written in the words of an anonymous or unacknowledged source.
- *Narrative.* Tells a story in first person or third person.
- *Dialogue.* Lets the reader "listen in" on a conversation.
- *Explanation.* Explains how something works.
- *Translation.* Technical information, such as that written for the high-tech and medical industries, must be defined and translated into understandable language.

Two paragraphs get special attention in body copy: the **lead** and the **close**. The lead, the first paragraph of the body copy, is another point where people test the message to see whether they want to read it. An example comes from Nike's women's campaign. Notice how the first line works to catch the attention of the target audience:

> *A magazine is not a mirror.*
> *Have you ever seen anyone in a magazine who*
> *Seemed even vaguely like you looking back?*
> *(If you have, turn the page.)*
> *Most magazines are made to sell us a fantasy of what we're supposed to be.*
> *They reflect what society deems to be a standard,*

However unrealistic or unattainable that standard is.
That doesn't mean you should cancel your subscription.
It means you need to remember
That it's just ink on paper.
And that whatever standards you set for yourself,
For how much you want to weigh,
For how hard you work out,
Or how many times you make it to the gym,
Should be your standards.
Not someone else's.

Closing paragraphs in body copy serve several functions. Usually, the last paragraph refers back to the creative concept and wraps up the Big Idea. Direct-action messages usually end with a **call to action** with instructions on how to respond. A Schwinn bicycle ad that is headlined "Read poetry. Make peace with all except the motor car" demonstrates a powerful and unexpected ending, one that is targeted to its youthful audience:

Schwinns are red, Schwinns are blue.
Schwinns are light and agile too.
Cars suck. The end.

Print Media Requirements

There are a variety of media in the print category—everything from newspapers and magazines to outdoor boards and product literature. They all use the same copy elements, such as headlines and body copy; however, the way these elements are used varies with the objectives for using the medium.

Newspapers   Newspaper advertising is one of the few types of advertising that is not considered intrusive because people consult the paper as much to see what is on sale as to find out what is happening in City Hall. For this reason, the copy in newspaper advertisements does not have to work as hard as other kinds of advertising to catch the attention of its audience. Because the editorial environment of a newspaper generally is serious, newspaper ads don't have to entertain, as television ads do. As a result, most newspaper advertising copy is straightforward and informative. The writing is brief, usually just identifying the merchandise and giving critical information about styles, sizes, and prices.

Magazines   Magazines offer better-quality ad production, which is important for brand image and high-fashion advertising. On the other hand, consumers may clip and file advertising that ties in with the magazine's special interest as reference information. This type of magazine ad can be more informative and carry longer copy than do newspaper ads. Copywriters also take care to craft clever phrasing for the headlines and the body copy, which, as in the Nike women's campaign, may read more like poetry.

Directories   Publications that provide contact information, such as phone numbers and addresses, often carry display advertising. In writing a directory ad, copywriters advise using a headline that focuses on the service or store personality unless the store's name is a descriptive phrase such as "Overnight Auto Service" or "The Computer Exchange." Complicated explanations don't work well in the Yellow Pages, because there is little space for such explanations. Putting information that is subject to change in an ad can become a problem because the directory is published only once a year.

Posters and Outdoor Advertising   Posters and outdoor boards are primarily visual, although the words generally try to catch consumers' attention and lock in an idea, registering a message. An effective poster is built around a creative concept that marries the words with the visual. For the Coffee Rush chain, Karl Schroeder created a series of posters to change consumers' perceptions that the shop was merely a drive-through for fast, cheap coffee. Schroeder's team did this by promoting a line of cold drinks with captivating names such as Mango Guava and Wild Berry.

One of the most famous billboard campaigns ever was for a little shaving cream company named Burma Shave. The campaign used a series of roadside signs with catchy little

SHOWCASE

LIKE MOM
USED TO MAKE.
REMEMBER,
WHEN SHE'D BOIL
MANGO AND
WILD BERRY
LEAVES.

— Mango Guava
Wild Berry —
TEA FREEZES

ANY MORE FRUIT IN THESE
SMOOTHIES AND WE'D HAVE TO
SELL THEM
BY THE
POUND.

Strawberry Banana —
Blueberry
Mango Pineapple —
Banana
SMOOTHIES

HONEY,
YOUR COFFEE
IS MELTING.

— White Chocolate
Chocolate Raspberry —
Rush Slush

■ ■ ■

These posters for the Coffee Rush group of small, drive-through coffee shops told newcomers that Coffee Rush sold more than just "a cup of joe." The copy, which had to be simple, to be read by people in a car, was designed to tease people into tasting these fun drinks. These posters were contributed by Karl Schroeder, a graduate of the University of Oregon and a copywriter at Coates Kokes in Portland, Oregon.

poems—a most unlikely format for a highway sign. There were some 600 poems and they worked well for nearly 40 years, from 1925 to 1963, until the national interstate system made the signs obsolete.[4] The product was always a hero:

> *If you think*
> *she likes*
> *your bristles*
> *walk bare-footed*
> *through some thistles*
> *Burma Shave*

> *My job is*
> *keeping faces clean*
> *And nobody knows*
> *de stubble*
> *I've seen*
> *Burma Shave*

More recently, Albuquerque used the Burma Shave format to encourage drivers to reduce their speeds through a construction zone. Today, a construction zone is about the only place where traffic moves slowly enough to use a billboard with rhyming copy.

> *Through this maze of machines and rubble*
> *Driving fast can cause you trouble*
> *Take care and be alert*
> *So no one on this road gets hurt.*

The most important characteristic of copywriting for outdoor advertising is brevity. Usually, there is one line that serves as both a headline and product identification. Often the phrase is a play on words. A series of black-and-white billboards in the Galveston-Houston area, recruiting priests for the Roman Catholic diocese, features a Roman collar with witty wording such as, "Yes, you will combat evil. No, you don't get to wear a cape." Others are more thoughtful, "Help wanted. Inquire within yourself." Some experts suggest that copywriters use no more than six to seven words. It must catch attention, but it also must be memorable. For example, a billboard for Orkin pest control showed a package wrapped up with the word Orkin on the tag. The headline read, "A little something for your ant."

Product Literature   Sometimes called **collateral materials** because they are used in support of an advertising campaign, brochures and pamphlets and other materials provide details about a product, company, or event. They can be as varied as hang tags in new cars or bumper stickers. Taco Bell's little messages on its tiny taco sauce packages is an example of clever writing in an unexpected place with messages like: "Save a bun, eat a taco," "Warning! You're about to make a taco very happy," "and "My other taco is a Chalupa."

Typically, product literature is a heavy-copy format, or at least a format that provides room for explanatory details along with visuals; the body copy may dominate the piece. For a pamphlet with folds, a writer must also consider how the message is conveyed as the piece is unfolded. These pieces can range from a simple three-panel flyer to a glitzy full-color brochure.

Consider This

1. What are the key pieces of print copy, and what roles do they play?
2. What would you expect to see in clutter-busting copy for a print ad? How would it work?

HOW TO WRITE RADIO COPY

Ads that are broadcast on either radio or television are usually 15, 30, or 60 seconds in length, although 10- and 15-second spots may be used for brand reminders or station identification. This short length means the commercials must be simple enough for consumers to grasp, yet intriguing enough to prevent viewers from switching the station. That's why creativity is important to create clutter-busting ads that break through the surrounding noise and catch the listener's attention.

Because radio is a transitory medium, the ability of the listener to remember facts (such as the name of the advertiser, addresses, and phone numbers) is difficult. That's why copywriters repeat the key points of brand name and identification information, such as a phone number or Web address. Radio is pervasive in that it surrounds many of our activities, but it is seldom the listener's center of attention and usually in the background. Radio urges the copywriter to reach into the depths of imagination to create a clutter-busting idea that grabs the listener's attention.

Radio's special advantage, referred to as **theater of the mind**, is that the story is visualized in the listener's imagination. Radio copywriters imagine they are writing a musical play that will be performed before an audience whose eyes are closed. The copywriter has all the theatrical tools of voices, sound effects, and music, but no visuals. How the characters look and where the scene is set come from their listener's imagination.

As an example of theater of the mind, consider a now-classic commercial written by humorist Stan Freberg for the Radio Advertising Bureau. Using sound effects and the voice of an announcer, the copy describes the fantasies you can create in audio, such as draining Lake Michigan, filling it with hot chocolate, and dropping in a 10-ton cherry from an Air Force plane.

The Radio Advertising Bureau has used the slogan "I saw it on the radio" to illustrate the power of radio's ability to evoke rich images in the mind of the listener. Research indicates that the use of imagery in radio advertising leads to high levels of attention and more positive general attitudes toward the ad and its claims.[5] Even though we're talking about imagery, it is produced by the copywriter's masterful use of the tools of audio: voice, music, and sound effects.

Tools of Radio Copywriting

Print copywriters use a variety of tools—headlines, body copy, slogans, and so forth—to write their copy. In radio advertising, the tools are the audio elements that the copywriter uses to craft a commercial: voice, music, and sound effects.

Voice   The most important element in radio advertising are voices, which are heard in jingles, spoken dialogue, and announcements. Most commercials have an announcer, if not as the central voice, at least at the closing to wrap up the product identification. The voices the copywriter specifies help listeners "see" the characters in the commercial. The copywriter understands that we imagine people and what they are like based on their voices. Dialogue uses character voices to convey an image of the speaker: a child, an old man, an executive, a Little League baseball player, or an opera singer. Copywriters specify voices for commercials based on the evocative qualities they contribute to the message. Radio announcer Ken Nordine's voice was once described as sounding like warm chocolate; Ray Charles was described as having a charcoal voice.

Radio advertising relies on conversational style and vernacular language. A good radio copywriter also has an ear for the distinctive patterns of speech for the target audience. Spoken language is different from written language. We talk in short sentences, often in sentence fragments and run-ons. We seldom use complex sentences in speech. We use contractions that would drive an English teacher crazy. Slang can be hard to handle and sound phony, but copy that picks up the nuances of people's speech sounds natural. In radio advertising, speaking style should match the speech of the target audience. Each group has its own way of speaking, its own phrasing. Teenagers don't talk like 8-year-olds or 50-year-olds.

Principle
Radio copywriters try to match the conversational style of the target audience.

Music   Similar to movie scriptwriters, radio copywriters have a sense of the imagery of music and the role it plays in creating dramatic effects. Music can be used behind the dialogue to create mood and establish the setting. Any mood, from that of a circus to that of a candle-lit dinner, can be conveyed through music. Advertisers can have a piece of music composed for a commercial or can borrow it from a previously recorded song. Numerous music libraries sell stock music that is not copyrighted.

The primary use of music is in support of **jingles**, which are commercials in song. Radio copywriters understand the interplay of catchy phrases and "hummable" music that creates little songs that stick in our minds. Anything consumers can sing along with helps them remember, as well as get involved with, the message. The campaign for Boston-based Bertucci's restaurants was successful because of music. The infectious jingle is based on a Cab Calloway song, "Everybody Eats When They Come to My House," sung in a bouncy, swinging jazz style reminiscent of Harry Connick Jr. The words, however, have been changed to feature menu items with lines like: "Try the scaloppini, Jeannie," "More mozzarella, Stella," "Pass the parmigiana, Donna," and "Brick oven's flamin', Raymond."[7]

Jingle houses are companies that specialize in writing and producing commercial music, catchy songs about a product that carry the theme and product identification. A custom-made jingle—one that is created for a single advertiser—can cost $10,000 or more. In contrast, many jingle houses create "syndicated" jingles made up of a piece of music that can be applied to different lyrics and sold to several different advertisers in different markets around the country for as little as $1,000 or $2,000.

Sound Effects   The sound of seagulls, automobile horns honking, and the cheers of fans at a stadium all create images in our minds and cue the setting, as well as the action. **Sound effects** are described in a radio script, and are important in making a commercial attention-getting and memorable. Sound effects can be original, but more often they are purchased from sound effect libraries.

The Practice of Radio Copywriting

The following guidelines for writing effective radio commercials address the distinctive characteristics of radio advertising:

- *Keep It Personal.* Radio advertising has an advantage over print: the ability to use the human voice. The copy for radio ads should use conversational language—as if someone is "talking with" the consumer rather than "selling to" the consumer.
- *Speak to Listeners' Interests.* Radio allows for specialized programming to target markets. Listeners mostly tune in to hear music, but talk radio is popular, too. There are shows on health, pets, finance, politics—whatever people are interested in. Copywriters should design commercials to speak to that audience interest and use the appropriate tone of voice. If the station plays heavy-metal music, then the style and tone of the commercial might be raucous and spirited.
- *Wake Up the Inattentive.* Most people who are listening to the radio are doing something else at the same time, such as jogging or driving. Radio spots must be designed to break through the inattention and capture attention in the first three seconds with sound effects, music, questions, commands, or something unexpected.
- *Make It Memorable.* To help the listener remember what you are selling, commercial copy should mention the name of the product emphatically and repeat it. An average of three mentions in a 30-second commercial and five mentions in a 60-second commercial may not be too frequent, as long as the repetition is not done in a forced and/or annoying manner. Copywriters use taglines and other key phrases to lock the product in consumers' memories.
- *Include Call to Action.* The last thing listeners hear is what they tend to remember, so copywriters make sure the product is it. They phrase the Big Idea in a way that serves as a call to action and reminds listeners of the brand name at the close of the commercial. For example, a commercial about the wonderful things that happen when people eat Edy's Grand Ice Cream ends with the line: "It's creamy, it's rich, it's wonderful. It's Edy's Grand Ice Cream."
- *Create Image Transfer.* Radio advertiesments are sometimes designed to link to a television commercial. Called **image transfer**, the visuals from the TV version are re-created in a listener's mind by the use of key phrases and ideas from the TV commercial.

Planning the Radio Commercial: Scripts

Copywriters working on a radio commercial use a standard *radio script* format to write the copy to certain time blocks—including all the words, dialogue, lyrics, sound effects, instructions, and descriptions. The instructions and descriptions are to help the producer tape the commercial so that it sounds exactly as the copywriter imagined. The *script* format usually has the source of the audio written down the left side, and the content—words an announcer reads, dialogue, and description of the sound effects and music—on the right. The instructions and descriptions—anything that isn't spoken—are in capital letters. The Inside Story explains how one creative team approached a radio advertising problem and gives an example of radio scripts from this campaign.

Consider This

1. What are the key characteristics of effective radio ads?
2. What would you expect to see in clutter-busting copy for a radio ad? How would it work?

HOW TO WRITE TELEVISION COPY

Television copywriters understand that it is the moving image, the action, that makes television so much more engaging than print. The challenge for the writer is to fuse the images with the words to present not only a creative concept, but also a story, as the Frontier

THE INSIDE STORY

Selling Newspaper Classifieds on the Radio

Karl Schroeder, copywriter, Coates Kokes, Portland, Oregon

The Register-Guard, Oregon's second largest newspaper, needed to boost classified ad sales. Before doing any work for *The Register-Guard*, our agency interviewed people at the paper and conducted a couple of focus groups with people from the area. This allowed our strategy team to compare *The Register-Guard's* perception of itself with consumers' perceptions. One insight we discovered was that if you ask someone, "Do you read *The Register-Guard?*" they most likely will answer, "No." But if you ask that same person whether she looks at the TV section or the entertainment section of the paper, she will say, "Yes." So what does this mean? One: It suggested that people who read one or two sections don't see themselves as "reading the paper." Two:

(and obvious) A lot of people just get the paper for a section or two, not the whole thing.

Taking what we learned and applying it to classifieds, it made sense to make the paper more approachable by using humor in the advertising (maybe they'll buy the paper more often if it seems less stuffy). We thought it also made sense to remind those one-section users that the paper has a useful classifieds section. In addition, we wanted to reinforce the message that the classifieds will reach more people in Lane County than any other selling tool.

Karl Schroeder went to the University of Oregon where he majored in Advertising and minored in Fine Arts and English. He interned at a small agency in Portland called Big Ads during his junior year. After graduating in 2000, he started working for Coates Kokes in Portland.

Nominated by Professor Charles Frazer, University of Oregon

Register-Guard script

ANNCR:	If you want an easy, fast and convenient way to buy, sell, job-hunt or hire, nothing works better than the Register-Guard Classifieds. Well, actually, there is maybe one easier way:
SFX:	Knocking. Door opens.
NEW GUY:	Hello, I'm your new neighbor. I brought you an apple pie.
WOMAN:	Well, come in! I'll give you a tour of the house!
NEW GUY:	Oh lovely! Say, hard wood floors!
WOMAN:	Upstairs and downstairs. 3 bedrooms, two baths. Care to take it off my hands?
NEW GUY:	What?
WOMAN:	Buy it. It's for sale.
NEW GUY:	But I just bought the house next door?
WOMAN:	Do you have an out-of-state mother-in-law?
NEW GUY:	Good point. I'll take it—Oooh, a gazebo!
ANNCR:	Yes, they could walk right up to your doorstep, ready to buy, but, really, how many rich, apple-pie toting neighbors can you expect in a month? 3, tops, right? Yes, better to stick with the premiere marketplace of Western Oregon. With more listings and readers than all the competition combined, nothing connects buyers with sellers better than the Register-Guard Classifieds, with fresh listings in print and online every day.
SFX:	Knock, knock. Door opens
NEW GUY:	Sorry, deal's off. The other neighbors have a pool!
WOMAN:	Darn it! Those Johnsons!
ANNCR:	The Register-Guard. Get more out of it. Move those homes and make some money! Call 342-twelve-twelve today!

commercials do so well. One of the strengths of television, then, is its ability to reinforce verbal messages with visuals or reinforce visuals with verbal messages. As Ogilvy's Peter Hochstein explains, "The idea behind a television commercial is unique in advertising. The TV commercial consists of pictures that move to impart facts or evoke emotion, and selling words that are not read but heard. The perfect combination of sight and sound can be an extremely potent selling tool."[8]

In Frontier's advertising (see photoboard on next page) the words and pictures work seamlessly to deliver the idea of "It's a whole different animal." The slogan is a brand promise that comes alive in the execution of the talking animal friends. The animal characters in the Frontier advertising bring a touch of levity and a gentle humor to an experience that's a source of anxiety for many passengers. But the appeal goes deeper than just the curiosity effect of what will they say next. Graham Button, the creative director, explains that when the animals gather at the gates and catch up with each other like friends do, it creates a sense of community. The animals humanize the often cold and rushed experience of flying; it is a new way for an airline to do business.

Viewers watching a program they enjoy often are absorbed to a degree only slightly less than that experienced by people watching a movie in a darkened theater. Effective television commercials, like the Frontier talking animals, can achieve this level of audience absorption if they are written to maximize the dramatic aspects of moving images and storytelling. To build on the interest the commercials have created, Frontier keeps the ads coming because they have their own following. Like a successful sitcom, fans of the ads watch for new stories and new characters. Fans of the talking animals include former U.S. Secretary of Transportation Norman Mineta, who, when talking to a Frontier official, wondered if Jack would ever get a date with Foxy.

Storytelling is one way that copywriters can present action in a television commercial more powerfully than in other media. Television's ability to touch our emotions, and to show us things—to demonstrate how they look and work—makes television advertising highly persuasive. (See Table 13.3.) These are just a few of the techniques used in television advertising. Let's look at others.

Principle
In great television commercials, words and pictures work together seamlessly to deliver the creative concept.

TABLE 13.3 Characteristics of Television Copy

Characteristic	Message Design
• **Action:** When you watch television you are watching a walking, talking, moving world that gives the illusion of being three-dimensional.	• Good television advertising uses the effect of action and motion to attract attention and sustain interest. Torture tests, steps, and procedures are all actions that are easier to present on TV than in print.
• **Demonstration:** Seeing is believing. Believability and credibility—the essence of persuasion—are high because we believe what we see with our own eyes.	• If you have a strong sales message that lends itself to demonstration, such as "how-to" messages, then television is the ideal medium for that message.
• **Storytelling:** Most of the programming on television is narrative so commercials use storytelling to take advantage of the medium's strengths.	• TV is our society's master storyteller because of its ability to present a plot and the action that leads to a conclusion in which the product plays a major role. TV can dramatize the situation in which a product is used and the type of people using it. Stories can be riveting if they are well told, but they must be imaginative to hold their own against the programming that surrounds them.
• **Emotion:** The ability to touch the feelings of the viewer makes television commercials entertaining, diverting, amusing, and absorbing. Real-life situations with all their humor, anger, fear, pride, jealousy, and love come alive on the screen. Humor, in particular, works well on television.	• Emotional appeals are found in natural situations that everyone can identify with. Hallmark has produced some tear-jerking commercials about the times of our lives that we remember by the cards we receive and save. Kodak and Polaroid have used a similar strategy for precious moments that are remembered in photographs.

VISUAL		AUDIO
Fade in on several Frontier planes chilling out on the tarmac at Denver Int. Airport.		*SFX: Airport noise. Planes landing and taking off ...*
Cut to a close up of **Larry the Lynx**. He talks...		**LARRY:** So Flip, you get that Florida gig?
Cut to a close up of **Flip the Dolphin**. He responds... They continue to chat... Flip is obviously annoyed. *SFX: Pregnant pause...*		**FLIP THE DOLPHIN:** Nope. Chicago again. **LARRY:** Sorry, bud. **DOLPHIN:** We got a *zillion* flights to Florida and where do they send me? The Windy City! I'm a dolphin, Bob. Dolphins *belong* in Florida. **LARRY:** I hear ya, man. So...who IS going to Florida?
Cut to a 3rd plane rolling by with **Billy & Bobby Klondike** on the tail. Cut to close up...		*SFX: Plane rolling past.* **BILLY:** Sunscreen? **BOBBY:** Check. **BILLY:** Beachball? **BOBBY:** Check. **BILLY:** Speedo? **BOBBY:** Check.

■ ■ ■

This is an edited version of a photoboard for a Frontier commercial that illustrates how a copywriter brings the "A Whole Different Animal" theme to life.

VISUAL		AUDIO
Flip is shocked at the thought of Klondikes in a Speedo.		**DOLPHIN:** Did he say Speedo? *Please* tell me he didn't say Speedo.
Cut to **Larry**. He nods his head.		**LARRY:** Yeah, he said Speedo. *SFX: Dolphin grunts off-camera.*
Cut to graphic map treatment. Animated "trails" launch from Denver to all 36 cities. Super pops onto frame... Two other supers appear and disappear in sucession.		*SIGNATURE MUSIC....* **SUPER:** Over 60 nonstops daily. **SUPER:** ...to America's top destinations.

Super **logo** and **tagline**		**SUPER:**
		      FRONTIER
		  A Whole Different Animal.
		
		frontierairlines.com

Tools of Television Copywriting

Television copywriters have two primary tools: their audio and visual toolkits. Both words and pictures are designed to create exactly the right impact. Because of the number of video and audio elements, a television commercial is one of the most complex of all advertising forms.

Video When we watch a commercial, we are more aware of what we're seeing than anything else. Copywriters keep in mind that visuals and motion, the silent speech of film, should convey as much of the message—the Big Idea—as possible. Likewise, emotion, which is the effect created by storytelling, is expressed convincingly in facial expressions, gestures, and other body language. Because television is theatrical, many of the copywriter's tools, such as characters, costumes, sets and locations, props, lighting, optical and computerized special effects, and on-screen graphics, are similar to those you would use in a play, television show, or movie.

Audio As in radio, the three audio elements are music, voices, and sound effects, but they are used differently in television commercials because they are connected to a visual image. The copywriter, for example, may have an announcer speak directly to the viewer or engage in a dialogue with another person, who may or may not be on camera. The copywriter has to block out on paper how this "talk" happens, as well as write the words they will say. A common manipulation of the camera–announcer relationship is the **voice-over**, in which an announcer who is not visible describes some kind of action on the screen. Sometimes a voice is heard **off camera**, which means you can't see the speaker and the voice is coming from the side, behind, or above. A commercial for Geico insurance won a John Caples International award for its engaging use of a voice. The copywriter was responsible for both the words and the way they were delivered. In a spot titled "Collect Call," which was set in a hospital waiting room, a man places a collect call to his parents. To save on the costs of the call, he states as his name:

> "Bob Wehadababyitsaboy."

The message is delivered, but the call is refused by his parents who didn't understand the message. So the next scene shows him trying to cram even more information into his name:

> "Bob WehadababyitsaboyeightpoundssevenouncesMomsfine."

The voice-over at the end advises the audience that they don't have to cheat the phone company to save money. A 15-minute call to Geico can save them up to 15 percent on their insurance.

Music is also important in most commercials. Sometimes it is just used as background, other times the song is the focus of the commercial. In recognition of the role of music in advertising, Universal Music in 2001 released a CD called "As Seen on TV: Songs from Commercials," a collection of tunes that have become popular—or resurrected—thanks to their use in TV commercials. Included among the 20 songs are "Mr. Roboto" by Styx, "Right Here, Right Now" by Fatboy Slim, "Lust for Life" by Iggy Pop, and "Got to Give It Up" by Marvin Gaye. All of these songs have been used effectively in a television commercial. Clash's "London Calling" song became the theme for a highly successful sales event for Jaguar, as illustrated in the Matter of Practice box.

Other TV Tools The creative tools examined next are the setting, casting, costumes, props, and lighting—all of which the copywriter must describe in the script. The setting, or *set,* is where the action takes place. It can be something in the studio, from a simple tabletop to a constructed set that represents a storefront. Commercials shot outside the studio are said to be filmed **on location**, which means the entire crew and cast are transported somewhere away from the studio.

A MATTER OF PRACTICE

"Hello. London Calling with a Jaguar Just for You."

Jaguar is a classy, expensive, upscale British motorcar. Ask car fanatics and they will also tell you its quality isn't as good as German and Asian cars and it only sells to conservative, snobby older persons. So how do you market such a car to a younger car-savvy audience that has money and a sense of style, but holds a somewhat tarnished perception of Jaguar?

To complicate the assignment, the third quarter of the year is typically a year-end close-out period in which *heavy* automotive advertising promotes price discounts to clear out inventory. So how does a car company like Jaguar, one that believes price discounting would only damage the brand's upscale image, survive this distressing period? That was the assignment given to Young & Rubicam. The objectives were to drive traffic to dealers during the six-week period of the third quarter, deliver on aggressive sales goals, and attract a younger buyer who would contribute to long-term brand health.

The Y&R team recommended a cultural event ("The Jaguar London Calling Sales Event") with an inviting creative theme that would tap directly into the target's passion for culture by making "Britishness" cool. The key was the use of punk rock group Clash's title song "London Calling," which was paired with images of London's stylish, lively streets to link the cool, very modern Jaguar to its distinctive British roots. In the world of popular culture, Britain was climbing the charts of "coolness," as a hotbed of up-and-coming musicians, designers, hotels, and restaurants. The campaign was designed to reflect this "Cool Britannia" phenomenon.

The London image was appealing to the target audience, which research determined was fascinated by British fashion, architecture, design, travel, art, and performances. And this fascination with British culture was reinforced in Jaguar's longtime slogan, "The Art of Performance."

The copy in the print advertising simply linked the car to the song with the headline, "London Calling. Will you answer the call?" The visual icon of a red British telephone booth paired with this message invited consumers to "answer London's call" by visiting a Jaguar dealer. In television commercials, the phone is ringing in the background.

The intergrated campaign reached the target at home with upscale magazines, national and spot TV, and a direct-mail piece designed as an airline travel itinerary. It reached them at work with a *Wall Street Journal* polybag wrap, and newspaper inserts. It reached them online with a dedicated campaign Web site. It reached them on the road with city phone-booth wraps, bus shelter posters, and outdoor boards. It reached them as they traveled with a variety of airport displays. And it reached them in the

dealership with a red phone booth kiosk and other point-of-sale materials.

Promotions were a central part of the campaign's theme. One popular idea was a compilation CD giveaway featuring modern British artists. A partnership promotion with British Airways featured a contest with a trip to London as the prize.

The Jaguar "London Calling" campaign achieved all of its sales objectives. It changed the perception of Jaguar from "the stuffy old Brit" to "Cool Britannia," while at the same time it produced sales in a difficult selling period. In other words, even without special price offers, the "London Calling" campaign successfully drove traffic to dealers during the six-week period. Dealers reported traffic was up more than 28 percent. Not only did it receive praise from dealers and customers; the campaign also won a silver EFFIE award.

Source: EFFIE brief provided by Jaguar and Young & Rubicam.

For many commercials, the most important element is the people, who are called **talent**. Finding the right person for each role is called *casting*. People can be cast as:

- *Announcers* (either onstage or offstage), presenters, introducers
- *Spokespersons* (or "spokesthings"—such as talking butter dishes)
- *Character types* (old woman, baby, skin diver, police officer)
- *Celebrities*, such as Shaquille O'Neal, who came to the NBA with a complete marketing plan in hand outlining his endorsement strategy

Costumes and makeup can be an important part of the story depending upon the characterizations in the commercial. Of course, historical stories need period costumes, but modern scenes may also require special clothing such as ski outfits, swimsuits, or cowboy boots. Makeup may be important if you need to change a character from young to old. All of these details have to be specified by the copywriter in the script. The director usually manipulates the lighting, but the copywriter might specify special lighting effects in the script. For example, you might read "Intense bright light as though reflected from snow," or "Light flickering on people's faces as if it were reflecting from a television screen."

Copywriters might also have to specify the commercial's *pace*—how fast or slowly the action progresses. Some messages are best developed at a languid pace; others work better when presented at an upbeat and fast pace.

Planning the TV Commercial

Copywriters must plan how long the commercial will be, what shots will appear in each scene, what the key visual will be, and where and how to shoot the commercial. Other key decisions the copywriter has to consider in planning a commercial are the length, number of scenes, and *key frames*. The common lengths of commercials are 10, 15, 20, 30, and 60 seconds. The 10-, 15-, and 20-second lengths are used for reminders and product or station identification. The 60-second spot, which is common in radio, has almost disappeared in television because of the increasing cost of airtime. The most common length for a TV commercial is 30 seconds.

A commercial is planned in **scenes**—segments of action that occur in a single location. Within a scene there may be several shots from different angles. A 30-second commercial usually is planned with four to six scenes, but a fast-paced commercial may have many more. Because television is a visual medium, the message is often developed from a key visual that contains the heart of the concept. A **key frame** is that visual that sticks in the mind and becomes the image that viewers remember when they think about the commercial.

Copywriters need to answer many questions when planning a television spot. How much product information should there be in the commercial? Should the action be fast or slow? Is it wise to defy tradition and do unusual ads that create controversy? How intrusive should the ad be? Every producer and director will respond to these questions differently, depending on personal preferences and advertising objectives. Nevertheless, these general principles as outlined by Jewler and Drewniany in their creative strategy book, are relevant for most effective television commercials:[9]

- *What's the Big Idea* you need to get across? In 30 seconds you barely have time to do much more than that. Alternative concepts are also tested as key visuals in the development of the idea for the commercial. For each idea, a card with the key visual drawn on it is given to a respondent, along with a paragraph that describes the concept and how it will be played out in the commercial.
- *What's the Benefit* of that Big Idea, and who does it benefit? Connect the Big Idea back to the target audience.
- *How can you turn that benefit into a visual element*? This visual is what sticks in people's minds.
- *Gain the interest* of your viewer at the beginning; the first 3 seconds are critical.
- *Focus on a key visual,* a scene that encapsulates your entire selling message into one neat package.

WESTWAYNE

BellSouth Advertising & Publishing: TV
The *Real* Yellow Pages® "Bedroom"

VIDEO	AUDIO
SUPER: Dixie Relaxes in Bedroom.	TITLE: The *Real* Yellow Pages® from BellSouth.
OPEN ON DIXIE SITTING IN YOGA POSITION ON BED, FULLY CLOTHED.	DIXIE: Now that the bedroom's finished, I can finally relax!
SHE CONTENTEDLY PATS COVER OF BOOK LYING NEXT TO HER ON BED.	Fortunately, with The *Real* Yellow Pages®, I can do all the work on my new living room right from here!
DIXIE IN 2ND YOGA POSITION.	DIXIE: Delivery at twelve. GREAT.
FINGER POINTS TO "DONNA'S GLASS" IN THE BOOK.	DIXIE: Cobalt blue glasses . . .
DIXIE IN 3RD YOGA POSITION.	DIXIE: . . . lovely!
FINGER POINTS TO "D.J. SMITH RUGS" IN THE BOOK.	DIXIE: Carpet? No . . .
DIXIE IN 4TH YOGA POSITION.	DIXIE: A big area rug.
DIXIE HOLDING BOOK.	DIXIE: Isn't it amazing how much you can do with this trusty, dependable book?
SFX: (DOORBELL)	DIXIE: Except open the door.
CUT BACK TO DIXIE ON BED.	
SUPER: Next Living Room.	

FIGURE
13.1 BellSouth "Bedroom" TV Script

- *Be single-minded.* Tell one important story per commercial. Tell it clearly, tell it memorably, and involve your viewer.
- *Observe the rules of good editing.* Make it easy for the viewer to get into the idea of the commercial.
- *Try to show the product* in close-up at the end.

Scripts and Storyboards   Commercials are planned with two documents: a television script prepared by the copywriter and a storyboard drawn by the art director. Similar to a radio script, a *TV script* is the written version of the commercial's plan. It contains all the words, dialogue, lyrics (if important to the ad message), instructions, and descriptions of the details we've been discussing—sets, costumes, lighting, and so forth. The **storyboard**, which is the visual plan or layout of the commercial, shows the number of scenes, the composition of the shots, and the progression of the action. (See BellSouth example above.)

For television commercials that use dialogue, the script is written in two columns, with the audio on the right and the video on the left. The BellSouth "Bedroom" script featuring Dixie Carter is an example of a television script. Note how the video includes descriptions of key frames from the commercial. The key to the structure of a television script is the relationship between the audio and the video. The audio is typed opposite the corresponding video. Sometimes these audio and visual segments are numbered to correspond to the frames on the storyboard.

Consider This

1. What are the key characteristics of effective television commercials?
2. What would you expect to see in clutter-busting copy for a television commercial? How would it work?

WRITING FOR THE WEB

The Web is more interactive than any other mass medium: Not only does the viewer initiate the contact; viewers can send an e-mail on many if not most Web sites. This makes Web advertising more like two-way communication, and that's a major point of difference from other advertising forms. So not only is the Web copywriter challenged to attract people to the site, but also to manage a dialogue-based communication experience. Web advertisers have to listen and respond, as well as target messages to audiences. That's a major shift in how Web marketing communicators think about advertising.

In this complicated, fast-changing medium, there aren't a lot of rules. For banners and other formats that look like advertising and seek to attract someone to a company's Web site, verbosity is a killer. In that situation, no one wants to read a lot of type online. However, the Web is an information medium and users come to it, in some cases, for extensive reference information; formats look a lot like catalog, or even encyclopedias. The challenge for Web advertisers, then, is to understand the user's situation and to design messages that fit the user's needs. That means Web copywriters have to be able to write everything from catchy phrases for banners to copy that works like traditional advertisements, or brochures, or catalog. A basic principle, however, is that good writing is good writing, whether it be for traditional advertising media or for the Web. The Matter of Principle box demonstrates that with a striking campaign about scuba diving.

Principle
To write great copy for the Web, copywriters must think of it as an interactive medium and open up opportunities for interaction with the consumer.

Banners

The most common form of online advertising are small banner ads containing text, images, and perhaps animation. Banners in this extremely small format have to be creative to stand out amid the clutter on a typical Web page and, similar to outdoor advertising, they have to grab the surfer's attention with few words. Effective banners must arouse the interest of the viewer, who is often browsing through other information on the computer screen. The key to stopping surfers is vivid graphics and clever phrases. To grab the surfer,[10] the copywriter must think about:

- *Offering a deal* that promises a discount or a freebie as a prize.
- *Using an involvement device* such as a challenge or contest.
- *Changing the offer frequently,* perhaps even daily. One of the reasons people surf the Net is to find out what's happening now. Good ads exploit "nowness" and "newsiness."
- *Keeping the writing succinct* because most surfers have short attention spans and get bored easily.
- *Focusing surfers' attention* by asking provocative questions or offering knowledge they can use.
- *Using the advertisement* to solicit information and opinions from users as part of the research. Reward surfers for sharing their opinions by offering them three free days of a daily horoscope or something else they might find fun or captivating.

Sometimes banners provide brand reminder information only, like a billboard, but they usually also invite viewers to "click" on the banner to link to an ad or the advertiser's home page. The effectiveness of such efforts is monitored by the number of click-throughs. Their creators make banners entertaining by using multimedia effects such as animation and sound, interactivity, emotional appeals, color, and provocative headlines. One mistake copywriters sometimes make, however, is to forget to include the company name or brand in the banner or ad. Surfers should be able to tell immediately what product or brand the banner is advertising. A study of the most effective banner ads found that although they

A MATTER OF PRINCIPLE

The Ocean Speaks

The scuba-diving industry wanted to revive interest in the sport of scuba, with both current divers and potential newcomers. The objective of this striking campaign was to build a relationship with diving and move people from print to the industry's Web site.

Art director Chris Hutchinson explains, "We created a campaign in the literal voice of the ocean. The Ocean irreverently compares itself to the dull world up above, and invites people to come down for a visit. Instead of using traditional beauty shots of scuba diving, we commissioned surreal organic underwater scenes. The ads were recently featured in *Archive*. The creative idea is that the ocean not only has a personality, it speaks in the body copy."

Read the copy from these ads, and then consider how that style of writing has been transferred to the Web site.

> **Dear Hollywood,**
> You're blowing this whole shark thing out of proportion.
> Not every shark becomes a ravenous lunatic at the scent of a paper cut.
> Most of them would rather eat fish than divers anyway. The neoprene gets stuck in their teeth.
> —the Ocean

> **Excuse me Mr. Jobs.**
> This whole iMac thing—distinctly shell-like.
> I think you ripped those colors from me too.
> Let's give credit where credit is due, huh?
> —the Ocean

The ocean also speaks on the Web site (time2dive .com). Once on the home page, visitors identify themselves as either new divers or experienced divers. Each page has its own message from the ocean at the top, followed by a sign-up sheet. This is from the new-diver page:

> **About this weekend.**
> I have 15,000 unidentified species down here all waiting to be classified.
> But if you have to help somebody move or something, I'll understand.
> —the Ocean

And this is from the old-timers' page:

> **Haven't seen you in a while. So what's up?**
> It's come to my attention that you haven't been diving in what, 6 months?
> Did I do something wrong? Was it that rip tide when you were body surfing? Lighten up.
> —the Ocean

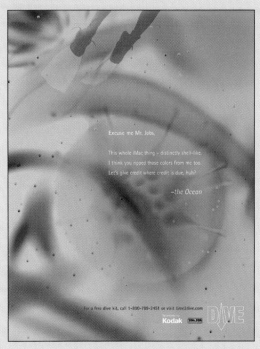

Source: Ads contributed by Chris Hutchinson, art director for Portland, Oregon–based Weiden + Kennedy. Before that he worked at Bulldog Drummond in San Diego where he designed these ads. A graduate of the University of Oregon, he and his work were nominated for this feature by Professor Charles Frazer.

satisfy the need for entertainment, information, and context (a link to a product), they seldom use promotional incentives, such as prizes or gifts, to motivate visitors to click through to the sponsor's Web site[11] to drive action.

Web Ads

Similar to traditional advertising, Web ads are designed to create awareness and interest in a product and build a brand image. In terms of creating interest, good copywriting works well in any medium, including the Internet. These ads aren't focused as much on attracting attention as they are on maintaining interest. Burton Snowboards (http://www.burton.com/company) uses copy that speaks in the voice of the product's user:

> *We stand sideways.*
> *We sleep on floors in cramped resort hotel rooms.*
> *We get up early and go to sleep late.*
> *We've been mocked.*
> *We've been turned away from resorts that won't have us.*
> *We are relentless.*
> *We dream it, we make it, we break it, we fix it.*
> *We create.*
> *We destroy.*
> *We wreck ourselves day in and day out and yet we stomp that one trick or find that one line that keeps us coming back.*
> *We progress.*

And then its closes with the following corporate copy:

> *Burton snowboards is a rider-driven company solely dedicated to creating the best snowboarding equipment on the planet.*

Other Web Formats

Many marketers are experimenting with new forms of Web advertising such as games, pop-up windows, daughter windows, and side frames. For example, one Procter & Gamble site supports the Scope "Send-a-Kiss" campaign, where visitors can send an electronic kiss to the special people in their lives. The site is customized for special holidays such as Valentine's Day and Mother's Day. P&G has found that of those who visit the site, 20 percent actually send e-mail kisses to mom on Mother's Day. Ultimately, these marketers want Web ads that are totally interactive. An Internet approach that uses broadcast media as a model may be the answer. They want to make Internet advertising better than television advertising—offering all the visual impact of traditional broadcast with the additional value of interactivity. The creative team comes up with the ideas for such Web formats and it's up to the copywriter to put the idea in words and explain how the user's experience with this Web site will work.

Consider This

1. What are the key characteristics of effective Internet ads?
2. What would you expect to see in clutter-busting advertising on the Web? How would it work?

COPYWRITING IN A GLOBAL ENVIRONMENT

Language affects the creation of the advertising. English is more economical than many other languages. This creates a major problem when the space for copy is laid out for English and one-third more space is needed for French or Spanish. However, English does not have the subtlety of other languages such as Greek, Chinese, or French. Those languages have many different words for situations and emotions that do not translate precisely into English. Standardizing the copy content by translating the appeal into the language of the foreign market is fraught with possible communication blunders. It is rare to find a copywriter who is fluent in both the domestic and foreign language and familiar with the culture of the foreign market.

Headlines in any language often rely on a play on words, themes that are relevant to one country, or slang. Because these verbal techniques don't cross borders well, copywriters must remove them from the advertising unless the meaning or intent can be re-created in other languages. For this reason, international campaigns are not literally translated. Instead, a copywriter usually rewrites them in the second language. How a poor translation can send the wrong message is shown in an ad for a Rome laundry:

Ladies, leave your clothes here and spend the afternoon having a good time.

Although computer words and advertising terms are almost universally of English derivation, some languages simply do not have words equivalent to other English expressions. Since 1539 the French have had legislation to keep their language "pure" and now have a government agency to prevent words, especially English words, from corrupting the French language. The words *marketing* and *weekend,* unacceptable to the French government agency, are translated literally as "study the market" (or "pertaining to trade") and "end of the week," respectively.

Experience suggests that the most reasonable solution to the language problem is to use bilingual copywriters who understand the full meaning of the English text and can capture the essence of the message in the second language. It takes a brave and trusting international creative director to approve copy he or she doesn't understand but is assured is right. A **back translation** of the ad copy from the foreign language into the domestic one is always a good idea, but it never conveys a complete cultural interpretation.

IT'S A WRAP

TALKING ANIMALS ON THE TARMAC

■ ■ ■   Good creative ideas like Frontier's "A Whole Different Animal" advertising campaign work, not just because they are funny or touch the emotions, but because they stick in the memory and move people to respond. Frontier's primary objective was to build awareness in the Denver market as a first-step in increasing its visibility in all of the cities to which it flies.

Five months into the campaign, a survey in Denver found that 57 percent of the adults interviewed mentioned Frontier when asked to name an airline serving Denver International, an improvement of 20 percent. In terms of brand awareness, before the animals started their chats, fewer than 40 percent of Frontier's Denver home base consumers were aware of the airline. After five months, unaided awareness of Frontier's advertising was 72 percent. In comparison, United was only 58 percent. Frontier's advertising director, Diane Willmann, points out that this is an enormous jump in unaided awareness. In addition, 90 percent of the respondents said it was likable and entertaining; 88 percent said it held their attnention; and 44 percent said they were more likely to fly Frontier.

■ ■ ■ Summary

1. **Explain the basic stylistics of advertising copy.** Words and pictures work together to shape a creative concept; however, it is the clever phrases and "magic words" crafted by copywriters that make ideas understandable and memo-

rable. Copywriters who have an ear for language match the tone of the writing to the target audience. Good copy is succinct and single-minded. Copy that is less effective uses adese to imitate the stereotyped style of advertising.

2. **Describe the various copy elements of a print ad.** The key elements of a print ad are the headlines and body copy. Headlines target the prospect, draw the reader's attention, identify the product, start the sale, and lure the reader into the body copy. Body copy provides persuasive details, such as support for claims, as well as proof and reasons why.

3. **Explain the message characteristics and tools of radio advertising.** Radio commercials are personal and play to consumers' interests. However, radio is primarily a background medium. Special techniques, such as repetition, are used to enhance retention. The three audio tools are voice, music, and sound effects.

4. **Discuss the major elements of television commercials.** The elements of TV commercials are audio and video tools. Television commercials can be characterized as using action, emotion, and demonstration to create messages that are intriguing as well as intrusive.

5. **Discuss how Web advertising is written.** Web advertising is interactive and involving. Web advertising has primarily focused on banners, although advertisers are using new forms that look more like magazine or television ads. Banners and other forms of Web advertising have to stand out amid the clutter on a typical Web page and arouse the interest of the viewer.

▪▪▪ Key Terms

adese, p. 360	collateral materials, p. 367	jingles, p. 368	storyboard, p. 377
back translation, p. 381	copywriter, p. 357	key frame, p. 376	subheads, p. 363
blind headline, p. 363	direct-action headline, p. 362	lead, p. 364	taglines, p. 363
body copy, p. 360	display copy, p. 360	off camera, p. 374	talent, p. 376
brag-and-boast copy, p. 360	headline, p. 360	on location, p. 374	theater of the mind, p. 367
call to action, p. 365	image transfer, p. 369	scenes, p. 376	underline, p. 362
captions, p. 363	indirect-action headline,	slogans, p. 363	voice-over, p. 374
close, p. 364	p. 362	sound effects, p. 368	your-name-here copy, p. 359
		split-run tests, p. 362	

▪▪▪ Review Questions

1. Why is it so important that advertising copy be succinct? What are other characteristics of advertising copy?

2. Describe the various copy elements of a print ad.

3. Explain the message characteristics of radio advertising.

4. Describe the tools of television commercial copywriting.

5. What are the characteristics of Web advertising?

▪▪▪ Discussion Questions

1. Creative directors say the copy and art must work together to create a concept. Of all the ads in this chapter, which ones do you believe demonstrate that principle? Explain what the words contribute and how they work with the visual.

2. One principle of print copywriting is that the headline catches the reader's eye, but the body copy wins the reader's heart. Find an ad that demonstrates that principle and explain how it works.

3. Professor Strong has set up a debate between the advertising sales director of the campus newspaper and the manager of the campus radio station, which is a commercial operation. During the discussion the newspaper representative says that most radio commercials sound like newspaper ads, but are harder to follow. The radio manager responds by claiming that radio creativity works with "the theater of the

mind," and is more engaging than newspaper ads. Explain what these media selling points mean. Would you rather write for a newspaper or radio?

4. Jingles are a popular creative form in radio advertising. Even so, there are probably more jingles that you don't want to hear again than ones that you do. Identify one jingle that you really dislike and another one that you like. Write an analysis of why these jingles either don't work or do work effectively for you.

5. A principle of TV message design is that television is primarily a visual medium. However, very few television commercials are designed without a vocal element (actors or announcers). Even the many commercials that visually demonstrate products in action use an off-screen voice to provide information. Why is there a need to use a voice in a television commercial?

▪▪▪ Class Projects

1. Select a product that is advertised exclusively through print using a long-copy format. Examples might be business-to-business and industrial products, over-the-counter drugs, and some car and appliance ads. Now write a 30-second radio and a 30-second TV spot for that product. Present your work to the class along with an analysis of how the message design changed when you moved from print to radio and then to TV.
2. Surf the Web and find one banner ad that you think works to drive click-throughs and one that doesn't. Print them out, then write an analysis that compares the two banner ads and explains why you think one is effective and the other is not.

HANDS-ON 13

CASE

Beautiful Just the Way You Are, Finds Ogilvy

Beauty ads have offered to help women look and feel more attractive ever since there have been ads for beauty products. Isn't that why women buy the product—to look better? Of course, the constant barrage of messages suggesting that women should improve their looks invites criticism from some that the ads, which typically feature young, thin, impossibly beautiful models, cultivate a beauty ideal that is impossible for most women to match.

Critics within the advertising industry might raise another objection to such ads: Does anyone believe them? Who really thinks that a particular brand of soap or shampoo will help them look like a model? These thoughts were probably on the minds of the creatives at the Ogilvy & Mather ad agency when they began thinking about the Big Idea for Dove Firming, a skin cream product from European consumer products giant Unilever that is sold in England. Ogilvy copywriters doubtless considered that the brand could benefit from a fresh approach. And a fresh approach is what they came up with.

The central theme of the campaign Ogilvy created was "normal is beautiful." The ads featured unretouched photographs of ordinary women appearing in white underwear. The women appearing in the ads were older and heavier than the models that more typically appear in beauty product ads. A good example is TV researcher Linda di Maria, who stands 5 feet 9 inches and weighs about 168 pounds. Encouraging readers to rethink, or at least broaden, their standards of beauty, the copy printed in one ad exclaimed: "Let's face it, firming the thighs of a size 8 supermodel wouldn't have been much of a challenge."

The campaign generated a good deal of attention, especially in the British press. According to one media outlet, British women responded to the appeals by discussing whether they preferred the "more realistic" models to those normally found in print ads. The brand got lots of attention too, the kind of attention Ogilvy and Unilever were hoping for. Sales of Dove Firming rose from 280,000 units to 2.3 million units from 2003 to 2004.

In 2004 Unilever and Ogilvy began using the theme in ads directed at American women. The U.S. ads, like those from the England campaign, also feature ordinary women

(in fact, one model selected for the campaign was Tabatha Roman, an account coordinator at Ogilvy, who was noticed by the campaign's celebrity photographer Ian Rankin on a visit to Unilever). Not all the models are overweight; some have freckles, others have less-than-curvy figures.

The U.S. campaign is supported by a number of supplementary promotions, including a Web site announcing that Dove "aims to change the status quo and offer in its place a broader, healthier, more democratic view of beauty." In addition, Unilever created a "Dove Fund for Self-Esteem," intended to support women's groups such as "Uniquely Me!" a self-esteem program for Girl Scouts. Among its other initiatives, Unilever has funded research into ways that mass media support the unrealistic beauty standard, and the company funded an endowment at Harvard to create a Program for Aesthetics and Well-Being that examines pop culture depictions of beauty and its effects on women.

Consider This

1. Will the Dove campaign be as big a success in the United States as it was in England? Do you think American women will respond the same way English women did? Why or why not?
2. Does Dove leave itself open to criticisms that its campaign is manipulative?
3. Why do you think English women responded so positively to the Dove Firming campaign? What in the language of the ads appealed to these women? How would you determine the effectiveness of the copywriting in this campaign?

Sources: Jack Neff, "In Dove Ads, Normal Is the New Beautiful," *Advertising Age* (September 9, 2004); Alexandra Jardine, "Dove Plans More 'Real Women' Ads," *Advertising Age* (August 9, 2004); Ken Wheaton and Jack Neff, "Adages," *Advertising Age* (October 18, 2004); BBC News World Edition, "Waif Goodbye: Women Yearning in Despair for the Perfect Figure Are Hitting Back," Monday, March 29, 2004, http://news.bbc.co.uk/2/hi/programmes/breakfast/3577763.stm; Yahoo! India news. "'Real Women' Replace Air-brushed Models for Beauty Ad!" March 30, 2004, http://in.news.yahoo.com/040330/139/2cahq.html; Erin White, "Dove 'Firms' with Zaftig Models; Unilever Brand Launches European Ads Employing Non-supermodel Bodies," *Wall Street Journal* (April 21, 2004): B3.

Hemingway had a tremendous appetite for life.

The Ernest Hemingway Collection by Thomasville. An eclectic mix of home furnishings inspired by the passionate lifestyle and writings of one of the twentieth century's greatest authors. A collection equally at home in a formal setting or a cozy breakfast nook. A line of beautifully crafted furnishings that is truly a feast for the eyes. 1-877-370-2146 www.thomasville.com

A quality we also bring to the t

Design and Production

CHAPTER 14

The Work of a Lifetime

Award:
EFFIE® Silver, household furnishings category

Company:
Thomasville Hemingway and Bogart Collection

Agency:
Long Haymes Carr

Campaign:
"Collection of a Lifetime"

CHAPTER OBJECTIVES

After reading this chapter, you will be able to:

1. Explain how visual impact is created in advertising.

2. List the principles of layout and explain how design is affected by media requirements.

3. Describe how art and color are reproduced.

4. Explain how the art director creates TV commercials.

5. Identify the critical steps in planning and producing broadcast commercials.

6. Summarize the techniques of Web design.

magine sitting in Ernest Hemingway's study or Humphrey Bogart's living room. Look around. What kind of furniture comes to mind? Both of these legendary figures have inspired a line of furniture for the Thomasville furniture company that carry on the style and elegance of the 1940s and 1950s.

Ernest Hemingway was a writer, but when you think of him, you also think of bullfighting, foreign wars, deep-sea fishing, hunting, and safaris—of Barcelona, Paris, Kenya, Cuba, Key West, and Ketchum, Idaho. The Hemingway mystique is rich in imagery that reflects an exotic, adventurous lifestyle. And that was the reason North Carolina–based Thomasville Furniture chose to launch a collection of furniture called the Ernest Hemingway Collection from its

Collection of a Lifetime line, which was designed with rugged leather, dark woods, and masculine detailing.

More recently, the Humphrey Bogart Collection was introduced with its images of Hollywood's masculine hero who is romantic, refined, relaxed, and inherently classy. The furniture line isn't straight out of *Casablanca* or *African Queen*, but rather reflects the feeling of what a party at Bogart's house would have felt like. The line carries names like Bel Air, El Morocco, Melrose, and Romanoff's.

The challenge to the creative team at the Long Haymes Carr agency in North Carolina was to create advertising that reflected the craftsmanship of both the furniture and these legendary figures. Two insights from an ethnographic study helped the creative team frame the strategy: (1) New items of furniture tended to be seen as devoid of meaning and viewed from a purely utilitarian or stylistic perspective; and (2) men were reluctant shoppers for furniture. A successful campaign, then, had to use the Hemingway and Bogart lifestyles to make an emotional connection with the target audience, men as well as women.

In addition, although Thomasville had a healthy brand loyalty among an older (age 50+), more traditional market, this retro lifestyle collection was an opportunity to reach the younger, affluent baby boomer homeowners. These homeowners are more eclectic in their decorating tastes and want to make their homes an expression of their own creativity and style. The designs used settings that reflected these retro lifestyles, archival black-and-white photos of the men, and color photos of the contemporary furniture.

The Hemingway furniture collection—and campaign—were so successful, they brought in a record $100 million in the first year, the reason the campaign was an EFFIE-award winner. The new Bogart campaign started out equally as successful.

Source: Adapted from the EFFIE brief provided by Long Haymes Carr and Thomasville Furniture, and from Stuart Elliott, "Bogart the Salesman," The New York Times Direct, February 25, 2003, NYTDirect@nytimes.com; Sandra Dolbow, "Brand Builders," *Brandweek* (July 24, 2000): 19; Sandra Dolbow "Literary License," *Brandweek* (July 24, 2000): 3; Beth Snyder, "Thomasville Moves Hemingway into TV Ads," *Advertising Age* (August 23, 1999): 8.

The richness of the imagery in the Thomasville Furniture campaign goes far beyond the ability of words to describe things. The images also communicate ideas about the lives of Hemingway and Bogart, as well as feelings about nostalgia and the lifestyles they connote. This chapter is about the visuals used in advertising—how they are designed and what they contribute to the meaning of the ad. First we'll review some basic ideas about visual impact and the role of the art director. Then we'll consider print art direction and production, followed by sections of television art direction and production. We'll end with a discussion of the design of Internet advertising.

VISUAL COMMUNICATION

In effective advertising, it's not just the words that need to communicate ideas and feelings; it's the visuals, too. The visuals normally work together with the words to present the creative concept. How would you demonstrate the smallness of something like a computer chip or a new miniature hard drive? IBM did it through a visual analogy: The new IBM hard disk drive is as small as an egg or a newborn chick.

Words and pictures accomplish different message effects. The visuals in the Thomasville ads, for example, create associations. They link the image of Hemingway and the exotic places he liked with a style of furniture. Even radio can evoke mental pictures through suggestive or descriptive language and sound effects. Designers focus on six key reasons for the effective use of visuals in advertising:

1. *Grab Attention.* Generally visuals are better than words at getting and keeping attention.
2. *Stick in Memory.* Visuals stick in the mind because people generally remember messages as visual fragments, as key images that are filed easily in their minds.
3. *Cement Belief.* Seeing is believing, as the IBM chick ad demonstrates, so visuals that demonstrate add credibility to a message.
4. *Tell Interesting Stories.* Visual storytelling is engaging and maintains interest.
5. *Communicate Quickly.* Pictures tell stories faster than words, as the Handgun Control ads (on the next page) demonstrate. A picture communicates instantly, while consumers have to decipher verbal/written communication word-by-word, sentence-by-sentence, line-by-line.
6. *Anchor Associations.* To distinguish undifferentiated products with low inherent interest, advertisers often link the product with visual associations representing lifestyles and types of users, as the Hemingway and Bogart campaigns for Thomasville Furniture demonstrate.

IBM used a chick and an egg to demonstrate the smallness of its hard disk drive, which is about the size of a large coin.

Visual Impact

In most advertising the power to get attention primarily lies with the visual. In general, designers have found that a picture in a print ad captures more than twice as many readers as a headline does. Furthermore, the bigger the illustration, the more the advertisement grabs consumers' attention. Ads with pictures also tend to pull more readers into the body copy; initial attention is more likely to turn into sustained interest with the help of a strong visual.

Principle
The visual's primary function in an advertisement is to get attention.

People not only notice ad visuals, they remember those with pictures more than those composed mostly of type. The believability factor, as well as the interest-building impact of a visual story, also are reasons why visuals are anchored so well in memory. An example of an intriguing story idea told totally through visuals is a British campaign for Volkswagen, which won the Best of Show award in a One Show award competition. It featured a gently humorous 30-second commercial built around the low price of the VW Polo. Fallon's Bob Barrie, who was president of The One Club (an association for people in the creative side of advertising), explained that it was possibly the quietest, most understated TV spot entered in the show. The idea was simple: A woman sits at her kitchen table. Her scanning of the newspaper, as well as her hiccups, are stopped dead by an ad for the VW Polo with its "surprisingly ordinary" price.[1]

Attention, interest, memorability, believability—these are the factors that help explain the visual impact of messages such as the Handgun Control ads. The art director for this **pro bono campaign** (which means all services, as well as time and space, are donated) explained that the objective was keeping guns out of the hands of children. Note the dramatic visuals and the way the words work to reinforce the impact of the visual.

The Art Director

The person most responsible for creating visual impact is the art director. The art director is in charge of the visual look of the message, in both print and TV, and how it communicates mood, product qualities, and psychological appeals. Specifically, art directors make decisions about whether to use art or photography in print—or film or animation in television—and what type of artistic style to use. They are highly trained in graphic design,

SHOWCASE

The pro bono Handgun Control campaign was designed as a wakeup call following the Columbine High School shootings. Chris Hutchinson, art director at Weiden + Kennedy, explained that "Children killing children with guns is a very real issue and we wanted to communicate the horror of this. The visuals are meant to shock, juxtaposing toys with gun violence." Hutchinson graduated from the advertising program at the University of Oregon.

including art, photography, typography, the use of color, and computer design software. Although art directors generally design the ad, they rarely create the finished art. If they need an illustration, they hire an artist. Newspaper and Web advertising visuals are often **clip art**, images from collections of copyright-free art that anyone can use who buys the clip-art service.

One of the most difficult problems that art directors—and those who work on the creative side of advertising—face is transforming a concept into words and pictures. During the brainstorming process, both copywriters and art directors are engaged in **visualization**, which means they are imagining what the finished ad might look like.

In addition to advertising, art directors may also be involved in designing a brand or corporate logo, as well as merchandising materials, store or corporate office interiors, and other aspects of a brand's visual presentation, such as shopping bags, delivery trucks, and uniforms. A *logo*, which is the imprint used for immediate identification of a brand or company, is an interesting design project because it uses typography, illustration, and layout to create a distinctive and memorable image, as the Falling Rock logo demonstrates. Think of the cursive type used for Coca-Cola, the block letters used for IBM, and the rainbow-striped apple for Apple computers.

munising, mi

FALLING ROCK
cafe & bookstore™

■ ■ ■

A logo needs to be simple enough to provide immediate recognition and yet convey the personality and meaning of the brand. That was the design problem solved by Mike Dattolico (www.brokenroses.com), a freelance art director who graduated from the advertising program at the University of Florida.

Consider This

1. In what ways do visuals add impact to advertising?
2. How good are you at visualization? If you were asked to participate in visual-association brainstorming for the word *bank,* how many different images come to mind? Make a list and include a brief description of the images you see in your mind.

PRINT ART DIRECTION

The art director's toolkit for print advertising includes the photos, illustrations, typefaces, color, and layout of the proposed ad. Let's look at these and other elements of print ad design.

Illustrations and Photos

When art directors use the word *art,* they usually mean photographs and illustrations, each of which serves different purposes in ads. For instance, photography has an authenticity that makes it powerful, a dimension skillfully employed by the Hemingway and Bogart

■ ■ ■

A simple photograph of the top of a can takes on new meaning when the can's rings are associated with the rings in water from a fishing bobber.

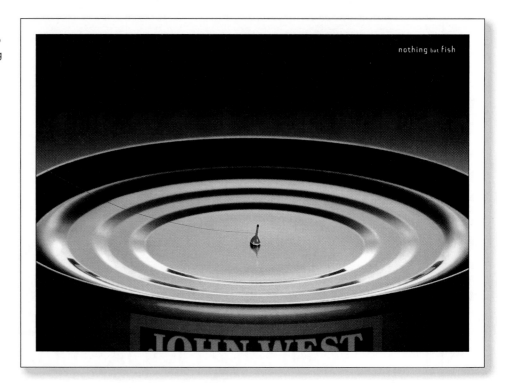

nothing but fish

JOHN WEST

campaigns. Most people feel that pictures don't lie (even though they can be altered). For credibility, then, photography is a good medium. A photograph is more realistic and an illustration (or animation in television) is more fanciful. Illustrations, by definition, eliminate many of the details you see in a photograph, which can make it easier to understand since what remains are the "highlights" of the image that we use most often in recognizing what it represents. This ease of perception can simplify the visual message but it can also focus attention on key details of the image. It can also intensify meanings and moods, making illustrations ideal for fantasy (think about comic books and animated films).

The decision to use a photograph or an illustration is usually determined by the advertising strategy and its need for either realism or fanciful images. The Thomasville ads use what we call a "beauty shot" of the furniture to establish the quality of the product. The historical photos of Hemingway and Bogart are treated with a technique that makes it more artful, symbolizing its historical qualities. The distinction between the images is a visual statement of the strategy behind the ad campaign, which links these historical figures with the new furniture line. Photographs, of course, can also evoke fanciful images. For example, the billboard art for British canned fish brand John West is given a dramatic touch by making the rings on the can's top look like rings of rippling water cast from a fishing bobber.

Color in Print

In addition to photos and illustrations, another important visual element that art directors manipulate is color, which they use to attract attention, provide realism, establish moods, and build brand identity. Art directors know that print ads with color, particularly those in newspapers, get more attention than ads without color. Many ads are in full color, especially when art directors use photographs, such as the furniture shots in the Hemingway and Bogart collections. However, note how the historical photo in black-and-white appears in contrast to the full-color photo. Black-and-white also lends a dignity and sophistication to the visual, even if it's a boot, as the Dunham ad demonstrates. Ads can also use **spot color**, in which they use a second color in addition to black (a black-and-white photo or illustration with an accent color) to highlight important elements. The use of spot color is highly attention getting, particularly in newspaper ads. The ACG ad uses red spot color to accent the product and brand name.

■ ■ ■
The layout for the Dunham boot ad shown here speaks in a quiet voice about the beauty of nature. Even though it's a boot ad, it projects an elegance that reflects an appreciation for nature and a serene outdoor scene (footprints in the snow).

When it is important to convey realism in an ad, full-color photographs may be essential. Some products and ad illustrations just don't look right in black-and-white: pizza, flower gardens, and nail polish, for instance. Color also can help an ad convey a mood. Warm colors, such as red, yellow, and orange, convey happiness. Pastels are soft and often bring a friendly tone to a print ad. Earth tones are natural and no-nonsense. Cool colors, such as blue and green, are aloof, calm, serene, reflective, and intellectual. Yellow and red have the most attention-getting power. Red may symbolize alarm and danger, as well as warmth. Black communicates high drama and can express power and elegance.

■ ■ ■
This ad, with an asymmetrical layout, uses spot color effectively as an accent to identify the product and the brand. Note how the layout "shouts," in contrast to the soft tone of the Dunham boot ad.

Typography

Not only do art directors carefully choose colors, they also design the ad's **typography**—the appearance of the ad's printed matter in terms of the style and size of typefaces. In most cases, good use of type does not call attention to itself because its primary role is functional: to convey the words of the message. Type, however, also has an aesthetic role and the type selection can, in a subtle or not so subtle way, contribute to the impact and mood of the message. The Petersen magazine group ad is an example of the use of typography as art. In this case, the heavy, bold, hand-drawn type has an attitude that reflects the readers of the Petersen's RAW Sport Group, which includes such publications as *Dirt Rider, Mountain Biker, MX Racer, BMX Rider, Inline,* and *sNoBoard.*

Print ad designers choose from among thousands of typefaces to find the right one for the ad's message. Designers are very familiar with type classifications, but it is also important for managers and other people on the creative team to have some working knowledge of typography in order to understand what designers are talking about and to critique the printed material and make suggestions.

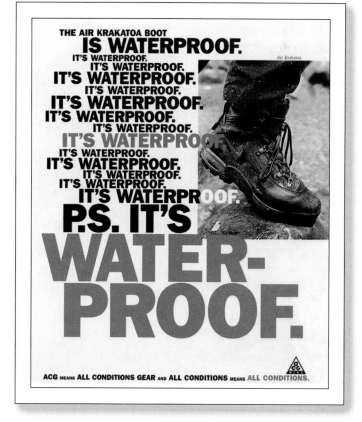

THE AIR KRAKATOA BOOT
IS WATERPROOF.
IT'S WATERPROOF.
IT'S WATERPROOF.
IT'S WATERPROOF.
IT'S WATERPROOF.
IT'S WATERPROOF.
IT'S WATERPROOF.
IT'S WATERPROOF.
IT'S WATERPROOF.
IT'S WATERPROOF.
IT'S WATERPROOF.
IT'S WATERPROOF.
IT'S WATERPROOF.
P.S. IT'S
WATER-
PROOF.

ACG MEANS **ALL CONDITIONS GEAR** AND **ALL CONDITIONS** MEANS **ALL CONDITIONS.**

Principle
Type has a functional role in the way it presents the letters in words so they can be easily read, but it also has an aesthetic role and can contribute to the meaning of the message through its design.

Families and Fonts   The basic set of letters in a particular typeface is known as the **font**. A font contains the alphabet for one typeface, such as Times Roman, plus the numerals and punctuation that go with that typeface, as Figure 14.1a shows. Each font represents one size of that alphabet style. There are two major typeface families: serif and sans serif. **Serif** means that the end of each stroke of a letter has a little flourish. A **sans serif** typeface is one that is missing this detail and the ends of the stroke tend to be more blocklike. Serif letters are most often used for formal effects—invitations, for example—and when there is a lot of copy to be read; most books, for example, are basically set in serif faces (as is this one). Sans serif faces are used for copy that is consulted, rather than read—think about a phone book, or type in a diagram, because the look is "clean"—or as purposeful contrast to the serif type.

Designers must work with the following aspects of typeface selection:

- *Uppercase* refers to the use of a capital letter, as in the capital U in the word Uppercase.
- *Lowercase* means small letters used without capitals.
- *All caps* is a design in which *every* letter in a word is a capital letter.
- *U&lc* (upper- and lowercase) is a design in which the first letter of every important word is capitalized and the others are lowercase (prepositions and conjunctions are usually lowercase).
- *Weight, posture, and width* of a typeface can vary using such elements such as light, bold (weight), italic (posture), expanded, and condensed (width).

Justification   How the lines align at the end is another design choice (see Figure 14.1b). With **justified type**, the ends align on both the right and left sides of the column of type (they are **flush right** and **flush left**). With **unjustified type**, also called **ragged right**, the line endings on the right side of the column fall where they will. The opposite, which is rarely used, is **ragged left** (more often known as *flush right* where the lines are aligned on the right but the beginnings of the lines vary. A final option is to center the type.

Type Measurement   There are several measurement systems used in graphic design. The smallest system of measurement units is called **points**, which designers use to indicate the size of typefaces (see Figure 14.1c). There are 72 points in an inch. Display copy is usually 14 points or larger. Body copy in newspaper and magazine ads is usually 12 points or smaller. (The body copy of this text is 12 point Times.) Designers also measure the width and length of columns in **picas**. The pica is a bigger unit of measurement with 6 picas in an inch and 12 points in a pica. So 12-point type is exactly 1 pica high, or one-sixth of an inch. The column width used for the captions in this book is 10 picas. The text of the book is set on a 30-pica line length.

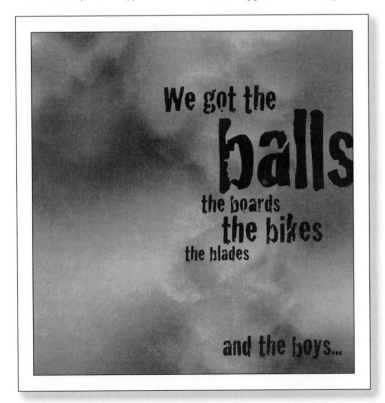

■ ■ ■
This is the cover for a four-page ad for Petersen Publications inserted into advertising trade publications to dramatize that the group's magazines can deliver a youthful male udience. The message is in words, but it's also in the style of the type.

Legibility   The *legibility* of type refers to how easy it is to perceive the letters. Research has discovered a number of typographic practices that can hinder the reading process.[2] Figure 14.1d demonstrates some of these legibility concerns. For example, **reverse type**, white letters reversed out of a dark surrounding area, is hard to read because people are accustomed to reading type as black or dark shapes on a white or light background. Reverse works best for headlines and is more problematic for body copy. The same thing is true for **all capitals**. We identify words by their distinctive

a)

A Font

14 pt

ABCDEFGHIJKLMNOPQRST
abcdefghijklmnopqrstuvwxyz
1234567890

Serif (top) and
Sans Serif (bottom)

ABCDEFGHIJKLMNOPQRSTUVWXYZ ABCD
ABCDEFGHIJKLMNOPQRSTUVWXYZ ABCD

All caps (top),
lower case (middle),
and u&lc (bottom)

THIS IS TIMES ROMAN IN ALL CAPS.
this is times roman in lower case.
This is Times Roman in Upper and Lower Case.

Typeface variations

This is set in a light typeface.
This is set in a normal weight.
This is set in a boldface.
This is set in italic.
This is set in an expanded typeface.
This is set in a condensed typeface.

Type has an aesthetic role in an ad. Art directors choose a serif or sans serif font, as well as a font's size and style, to support the tone of the advertising message.

b)

This is justified text. This is justified text. This is justified text. This is justified text. This is justified text. This is justified text. This is justified text. This is justified text. This is justified text. This is justified text.

This is centered text. This is
centered text.

This is left aligned text. This is
left aligned text.

This is right aligned text. This
is right aligned text.

Where the type sits on the ad and how it relates to the margin has an effect on the ad's overall look.

c)

6 Point

ABCDEFGHIJKLMNOPQRSTUVWXYZABCDEFGHIJKLMNOPQRSTUVWXYZABCDEFGHIJKLMNOPQRSTUVWXYZ
abcdefghijklmnopqrstuvwxyzabcdefghijklmnopqrstuvwxyzabcdefghijklmnopqrstuvwxyzabcdefghijklmnop   1234567890

12 Point

ABCDEFGHIJKLMNOPQRSTUVWXYZABCDEFGHIJKLM
abcdefghijklmnopqrstuvwxyzabcdefghijklmnopqr 1234567890

18 Point

ABCDEFGHIJKLMNOPQRSTUVWXYZ
abcdefghijklmnopqrstuvwxyz 1234567890

Here is a set of different sizes for the Times Roman typeface.

d)

THIS IS CAPITAL LETTERS.   This is reverse type letters.

This is ornamental type letters.

Research has shown that some typography presentations, such as those shown here—all cap letters, reverse type, overly ornamental type, and surprinted type—hinder the reading process.

FIGURE

14.1 **The Art of Typefaces**

The Legibility of Vertical Type

I	L	M
N	I	A
F	F	N
O	E	A
R	C	G
M	Y	E
A	C	M
T	L	E
I	E	N
O		T
N		

shapes, and when they are set in all caps, then the word's distinctive shape is obscured. It is less of a problem for headlines but slows down the reading of body copy. **Surprinting**, which means running the type over another image, is difficult to read because the letters can be confused with the background pattern.

Another practice that harms legibility is printing letters vertically (see Figure 14.2) one on top of another. It's almost impossible to decipher words printed like this. For example, a full-page ad for EMC^2, an information management company, used the headline in Figure 14.2. It's an interesting puzzle but a busy reader scanning a newspaper like the *Wall Street Journal* may not want to play the game to figure it out.

Layout and Design

Once art directors have chosen the images and typographic elements, they manipulate all the visual elements on paper to produce a layout. A **layout** is a plan that imposes order and at the same time creates an arrangement that is aesthetically pleasing. Here are some common types of ad layouts the art director might use:

- *Picture Window.* One of the most common layout formats is one with a single, dominant visual that occupies about 60 to 70 percent of the ad's space. Underneath it is a headline and a copy block. The logo or signature signs off the message at the bottom. The "Dive" ad in Chapter 13 is an example.
- *All Art.* The art fills the frame of the ad and the copy is embedded in the picture. The "Lost Innocence" ad for the Handgun Control campaign (page 388) is an example.
- *Panel or Grid.* A layout can use a number of visuals of matched or proportional sizes. If there are multiple panels all of the same size, the layout can look like a window pane or comic strip panel. The Thomasville Hemingway ads use two panels of different size side by side to contrast Hemingway and his historical period with the contemporary furniture.
- *Dominant Type or All Copy.* Occasionally, you will see layouts that emphasize the type rather than the art, or even an all-copy advertisement in which the headline is treated as type art, such as the ACG ad (page 391). A copy-dominant ad may have art, but it is either embedded in the copy or placed in a subordinate position, such as at the bottom of the layout.

This ad for Schwinn bicycles uses a plumbing drain motif to convey the industrial-strength features of the bike. It is a nonlinear design in that it doesn't matter where you start and what you read next. The text is carried in call-outs that point to different visual elements in the layout.

- *Circus.* A layout combines lots of elements—art, type, color—to deliberately create a busy, jumbled image. This is typical of some discount store ads or ads for local retailers, such as tire companies.
- *Nonlinear.* A contemporary style of layout that can be read starting at any point in the image. In other words, the direction of viewing is not ordered, as in the "What a Ride" ad for Schwinn. This style of ad layout works for young people, who are more accustomed to nonlinear forms; they are not as effective for older generations.
- *Grunge.* A style of layout that shows what is presumed to be a Generation X–inspired lack of concern for the formalities of art, design, type styles, and legibility. The Petersen magazine ad (page 392) is in that style.

Different layouts can convey entirely different feelings about a product. For example, look at the two ads for work boots. The ACG "Air Krakato" ad (page 391) screams "waterproof!" to signal the boots' ability to stand up to the most serious weather conditions. In contrast, the ad for the Dunham boot looks like a work of fine art. The difference between the two campaigns clearly lies with the visual impact that comes from the layouts, as well as the imagery.

Design Principles   A layout begins with a collection of miscellaneous elements: a headline and other display copy, one or more pieces of art, captions, body copy, a brand or store signature, and perhaps a trademark, slogan, or tagline. Local retail advertising also includes reminder information such as address, hours, telephone number, and credit cards accepted. Arranging all these elements so that they make sense and attract attention is a challenge. The design has both functional and aesthetic needs. The functional side of a layout makes the message easy to perceive; the aesthetic side makes it attractive and pleasing to the eye. Here are eight design principles that guide designers as they lay out an ad:

- *Direction.* Usually, designers create a visual path for the eye as it scans the elements. In Western countries most readers scan from top to bottom and from left to right. Most layouts work with these natural eye movements, although a layout can manipulate directional cues to cause the eye to follow an unexpected path. Figure 14.3 shows how the layout for one ad guides the eye.
- *Dominance.* Normally, the dominant element, which is point of emphasis or a focal point, is a visual, but it can be a headline if the type is big and bold enough to dominate other elements. By definition there can be only one dominant element, one focal point; everything else must be subordinate. Dominant elements, such as the picture of the car in Figure 14.3, are larger, more colorful, bolder, or positioned in a more prominent spot, such as at the top of the page.
- *Unity.* With unity, all the elements in an ad fuse into one coherent image and the pieces become a whole, as in the Crane & Company "Banknote" brochure on page 398. Neighboring elements that touch and align add unity and help with direction. An old axiom states the importance of grouping things: "Keep things together that go together."
- *White Space.* Areas of the layout that aren't covered by art or type are called **white space** or **negative space**. White space can be a design element in itself—either to frame an element or to separate elements that don't belong together.
- *Contrast.* Contrast makes one element stand out from another and indicates importance. Contrast is created by size (larger versus smaller) and tone (light versus dark).
- *Balance.* When artists decide where to place an element, they are manipulating balance. There are two types of balance: formal and informal. Formal balance is symmetrical, centered left to right. It is conservative, suggests stability, and is used in more upscale product ads. Informal balance is asymmetrical and creates a more visually dynamic layout, counterbalancing visual weights around an imaginary optical center. The Handgun Control ad is an example of informal balance.
- *Proportion.* Equal proportions of elements in a print ad are visually uninteresting because they are monotonous. Two visuals of the same size fight with one another for attention, and neither provides a point of visual dominance. Copy and art should be

FIGURE
14.3

Porsche Ad with Tissue Overlay
The tracing on the tissue identifies the starting point and the visual path the eye takes when scanning this ad.

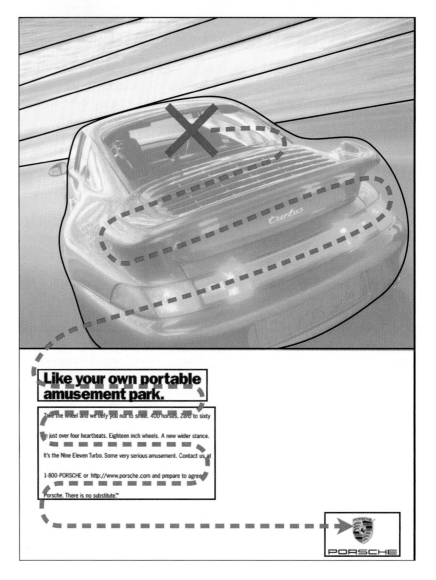

Like your own portable amusement park.

Take the wheel and we defy you not to smile. 400 horses. Zero to sixty

in just over four heartbeats. Eighteen inch wheels. A new wider stance.

It's the Nine Eleven Turbo. Some very serious amusement. Contact us at

1-800-PORSCHE or http://www.porsche.com and prepare to agree.

Porsche. There is no substitute.™

PORSCHE

Principle
Design is usually improved by simplifying the number of elements. "Less is more."

proportionately different. Usually, the art dominates and covers two-thirds to three-fifths of the page area (if the ad is not meant to be text-heavy).

- *Simplify, Simplify, Simplify.* This is a truism but most art directors realize that less is more. Generally, the more elements that are crowded into a layout, the more the impact is fragmented. The fewer the elements, the stronger the impact. Clutter is the opposite of simplicity. It comes from having too many elements and too little unity. However, like all rules, this one is made to be broken. Art directors know that to create the effect they want in a nonlinear discount store layout, they have to sacrifice simplicity.

Layout Stages The stages in the normal development of a print ad may vary from agency to agency or from client to client. Figure 14.4 shows the six-stage development of an Orly nail polish ad that agency Wiley & Associates created. This ad went through **thumbnail sketches**, which are quick, miniature preliminary sketches; **rough layouts**, which show where design elements go; **semicomps** and **comprehensives**, which are drawn to size and used for presentation either inside or to the client; and **mechanicals**, which assemble the elements in their final position for reproduction. The final product is a high-resolution computer file used for the actual production of the ad.

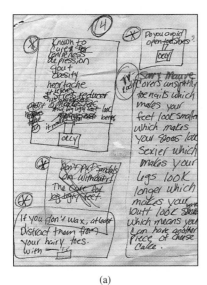

(a)   (b)   (c)

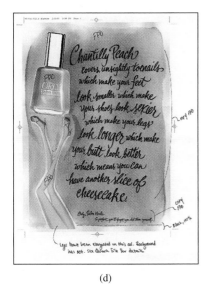

(d)   (e)   (f)

FIGURE 14.4

Orly "Chantilly Peach" Creative Process

(a) **Thumbnail Sketches.** These ideas for Orly were developed by the Wiley creative team late at night over Diet Coke and Chinese chicken salad. (b) **Rough Layout.** Transitioning to legs and painted toenails, the layout begins to give some glamour and personality to the product. (c) **Semicomps.** Type, color, and tagline still not finalized, but layout is more complete. (d) **Comprehensives.** Tagline approved. Illustrator has added more glitz to the layout. (e) **Mechanicals.** Quark file before retouching. Client still made small changes at this stage, but had approved the ad's layout and copy. (f) Final **High-Resolution Film.** The film house had to retouch, creating separate files for the legs and background image so that the proportion of the leg illustration would be correct.

Consider This

1. What's the difference in the way photos and illustrations contribute meaning to an ad? When would you use one or the other?
2. Find an ad that you think does a great job of using the basic design principles. Explain how the layout works.

SHOWCASE

■ ■ ■

This beautifully designed brochure by Peter Stasiowski, art director at Gargan Communication in Dalton, Massachusetts, promotes the durability of Crane & Company's banknote paper. A business-to-business piece, it demonstrates how great design is not limited to consumer marketing. The impact of the message comes from the unity of creative concept, selling premise, and the visual elements. Stasiowski is a graduate of the advertising program at the University of West Florida.

PRINT PRODUCTION

Art directors need to understand print ad production not only because it affects the look of the ad, but also because it affects costs.

Print Media Requirements

Different media put different demands on the design, as well as the production, of advertising. Newspapers, for example, are printed at high speed on an inexpensive, rough-surfaced, spongy paper called **newsprint** that quickly absorbs ink on contact. Newsprint is not a great surface for reproducing fine details, especially color photographs and delicate typefaces. Most newspapers offer color to advertisers, but because of the limitations of the printing process, the color may not be perfectly in **registration** (aligned exactly with the image). For that reason, ads such as the Oklahoma City ads are specifically designed for high-contrast black-and-white printing.

Magazines have traditionally led the way in graphic improvements because their paper is better than newsprint. Excellent photographic and color reproduction is the big difference between newspapers and magazines. Magazine advertisements are also turning to more creative, attention-getting devices such as pop-up visuals, scent strips, and computer chips that play melodies when the pages are opened. The design of Yellow Pages ads has changed as advertisers design their ads to be not just listings but to stand out in a cluttered environment. The Practical Tips shows some guidelines that designers follow when creating Yellow Pages ads.

■ ■ ■
High-contrast graphics are the key to good reproduction in a newspaper. The art in these ads simulates an old wood engraving.

Practical Tips

Creating a Yellow Pages Ad

- **Size.** The larger the ad, the more consumers notice it.
- **Image.** Graphics signal the reputation or image of the store. If possible, the headline, the illustration, the layout, and the use of type all should communicate the store's personality. A beauty shop ad will look different from an ad for auto parts.
- **Simplicity.** Keep the number of design elements to a minimum.
- **Art.** Illustrations work better than photographs.
- **Map.** If using a map, keep it simple to make the location clear.
- **The business.** Use graphics to convey the product category. Spell out the scope of service or product lines in the body copy.
- **Convenience Cues.** Give prominence to location and hours because people look for stores that are open and easy to reach.
- **Critical Information.** In addition to location and hours, the phone number must be included. Many consumers will call to see whether the product they want is available before making a trip. Note the multiple phone numbers listed in the IBM ad.

The key to an effective poster or outdoor board is a dominant visual with minimal copy. Because billboards must make a quick and lasting impression from far away, their layout should be compact with a simple visual path. The Institute for Outdoor Advertising (IOA) recommends these tips for designers.

- **Graphics.** Make the illustration an eye-stopper.
- **Size.** Images in billboards are huge—a 25-foot-long pencil or a 43-foot pointing finger. The product or the brand label can be hundreds of times larger than life.

■ ■ ■

This series of Yellow Pages ads show the changes in design over the years. From top, 1882, 1920, 1930s, and 1990s.

- *Colors.* Use bold, bright colors. The greatest impact is created by maximum contrast between two colors such as dark colors against white or yellow.[3]
- *Figure/ground.* Make the relationship between foreground and background as obvious as possible. A picture of a soft drink against a jungle background is hard to perceive when viewed from a moving vehicle at a distance. The background should never compete with the subject.
- *Typography.* Use simple, clean, uncluttered type that is easy to read at a distance by an audience in motion. The industry's legibility research recommends avoiding all-capital letters, fanciful ornamental letters, and script and cursive fonts.
- *Product Identification.* Focus attention on the product by reproducing the label or package at a huge size.
- *Extensions.* Extend the frame of the billboard to expand the scale and break away from the limits of the long rectangle.
- *Shape.* For visual impact, create the illusion of three-dimensional effects by playing with horizons, vanishing lines, and dimensional boxes. Inflatables create a better 3-D effect than most billboards can, even with superior graphics. Made of a heavyweight, stitched nylon, inflatables can be free-standing, or they can be added to outdoor boards as an extension.
- *Motion.* Add motors to boards to make pieces and parts move. Disklike wheels and glittery things that flicker in the wind create the appearance of motion, color change, and images that squeeze, wave, or pour. Use revolving panels, called kinetic boards, for messages that change.

Art Reproduction

There are two general types of printed images: **line art** and **halftone**. A drawing or illustration is called line art because the image is solid lines on a white page, as in the Oklahoma City ads. Photographs, which are referred to as *continuous tone* or *halftone,* are much more complicated to reproduce because they have a range of gray tones between the black and white, as shown in Figure 14.5. Printers create the illusion of shades of gray by converting continuous-tone art and photos to halftones by shooting the original photograph through a fine **screen**. The screened image is converted to a pattern of dots that gives the illusion of shades of gray—dark areas are large dots that fill the screen and light areas are tiny dots surrounded by white space. The quality of the image depends on how fine the screen is. A coarse screen, usually 65 lines per inch (called a 65-line screen), is used by newspapers while magazines use fine screens, which may be 120 and up to 200 lines per inch.

Screens are also used to create various **tint blocks**, which can be either shades of gray in black-and-white printing or shades of color. A block of color can be printed solid or it can be screened back to create a shade. These shades are expressed as a range of percentages, from 100 percent (solid) down to 10 percent (very faint). Figure 14.6 gives examples of screens in black-and-white and color.

Color Reproduction   It would be impossible to set up a printing press with a separate ink roller for every hue and value in a color photo. How, then, are these colors reproduced? Full-color images are reproduced using four distinctive shades of ink called **process colors**,

14.5 **Line Art and Halftone Art**
An example of a figure reproduced as line art (left) and as a halftone (right).

in a process called **four-color printing**. These colors are *magenta* (a shade of pinkish purple), *cyan* (a shade of bright blue), *yellow,* and *black.* Printing inks are transparent, so when one ink overlaps another, a third color is created and that's how the full range of colors is created. For example, red and blue create purple, yellow and blue create green, yellow and red create orange. The black is used for type and, in four-color printing, adds depth to the shadows and dark tones in an image. The process printers use to reduce the original color image to four halftone negatives is called **color separation**. In photographing the original (or scanning on a computer), a separate color filter screens out everything but the desired hue for each of the four process colors. Figure 14.7 illustrates the process of color separation.

Printing Processes

Here are the most common printing processes used in advertising and a brief description of how they work. Art directors have to understand how these various printing processes work because they all impact the design in some way.

10%   100%

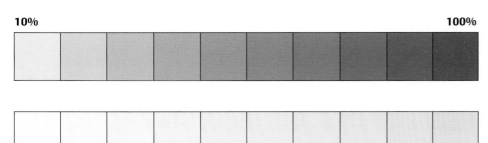

14.6

Screen Values and Tint Blocks
These are different screens for black-and-white image tints for a color tint.

(a)

(b)

(c)

(d)

(e)

(f)

FIGURE 14.7

The Color Separation Process

The six photos starting here illustrate the process of creating four-color separations: (a) Yellow plate, (b) Magenta plate, (c) Yellow and Magenta combined plate, (d) Cyan plate. (Note: After cyan is added, there would also be combined plates showing it added first to yellow, then to magenta, then to the combined yellow and magenta. These steps were left out to simplify the presentation.) (e) Black plate, (f) the finished ad with all four process colors combined.

- *Letterpress.* A process used for numbering items (such as tickets and so on) and specialty printing effects such as embossing. With **letterpress** printing, a raised surface gets inked; then when it strikes the surface of the paper, the image is transferred.
- *Offset Lithography.* The most popular type of printing for newspapers and most magazines. **Offset printing** uses a smooth-surface and chemically treated plate to transfer the image. Based on the principle that oil and water don't mix, the oil-based ink adheres to parts of the image but not to other parts. The offset plates are produced photographically.
- *Rotogravure.* A process used for long print runs with high-quality photographic reproduction. **Rotogravure** printing uses an incised surface. The images are engraved into

the plate and ink collects in these little wells. When the plate strikes the surface of the paper, ink is transferred from the wells to the paper.

- *Flexography.* A procedure that prints on unusual surfaces and shapes such as mugs and balls. **Flexography** uses a rubber-surface printing plate that can be bent to print on irregular surfaces. The plate transfers ink similarly to offset printing.
- *Silkscreen.* A type of printing used to print posters, T-shirts, and point-of-sale materials. **Silkscreen printing** uses a porous screen of silk, nylon, or stainless steel mounted on a frame. A stencil image is made either by hand or using a photographic process and the stencil is adhered to the screen. The nonprinting areas are blocked by the stencil and the areas to be printed are left open. Using a squeegee, ink is forced through the screen onto the printing surface.

If an ad is going to run in a number of publications, there has to be some way to distribute a reproducible form of the ad to all of them. The duplicate material for offset printing is a slick proof of the original mechanical. These proofs are called **photoprints** or **photostats**, which are cheap to produce. **Veloxes** or **C-prints** are better-quality proof prints but are more expensive.

Digitization   A recent trend in print production is the **digitization** of images, whether type or art, that uses computer technology to break them into tiny grids, each one coded electronically for tone or color. This is also how computers now handle the color reproduction process. These digitized images can then be transmitted electronically to printers or clients, across a city for local editions of newspapers, or by satellites for regional editions of magazines and newspapers such as *USA Today*. Agencies also use this method for transmitting ad proofs within the agency network, as well as to clients.

Desktop publishing, the process of producing print documents on personal computers with easy-to-use software is taking over the inexpensive end of typesetting and printing. Designers, writers, and editors can create page layouts and advertising layouts on a personal computer, sometimes with very little training or understanding of design principles. At the higher end, typesetting systems use sophisticated computer-based pagination equipment that combines computer typesetting with page layout capabilities. More sophisticated computers and software can produce the printing plates directly from the layout.

Binding and Finishing   Art directors can enhance their ads and other printed materials by using a number of special printing effects. For example, US Robotics, a maker of minicomputers, once used a small brochure the actual size of a Palm Pilot to demonstrate its minicomputer's size. The shot of the Palm Pilot was glued to a photo of a hand. As the ad unfolded, it became a complete product brochure that visually demonstrated the actual size of the minicomputer. Other mechanical techniques include:

- *Die-Cutting.* A sharp-edged stamp, or die, used to cut out unusual shapes. A common **die-cut** shape you're familiar with is the tab on a file folder.
- *Embossing or debossing.* The application of pressure to create a raised surface (**embossing**) or depressed image (**debossing**) in paper.
- *Foil-Stamping.* The application of a thin metallic coating (silver, gold) molded to the surface of the image with heat and pressure is called **foil stamping**.
- *Tip-ins.* **Tip-ins** are separate preprinted ads provided by the advertiser to be glued into a publication as the publication is being assembled, or bound. Perfume manufacturers, for example, tip in samples that are either scratch-and-sniff or scented strips that release a fragrance when pulled apart.

Consider This

1. What's the difference between newspapers and magazines in terms of their production requirements? What does a designer have to consider when using one or the other?
2. Explain how color separation works.

TELEVISION ART DIRECTION

Where does our art director start when putting together a commercial? Working within the framework of the creative strategy, art directors create the look of the TV commercial. The look of the award-winning "Cat Herders" commercial that the Minneapolis-based Fallon agency created for Electronic Data Systems (EDS) was that of the American West, much like a John Ford movie, with horses, craggy-faced cowboys who acted as cat wranglers, and stampeding animals (the cats).

The excitement and drama in a television commercial is created through the moving images. The visual storytelling is another responsibility of the art director. In the "Cat Herders" spot, the Fallon art director decided that the metaphor of herding cats meant that

A MATTER OF PRACTICE
Kitty Slickers and Cat Herders

EDS, a company that essentially invented the information technology (IT) industry back in the 1960s, found itself with an unhip Old Economy image as the New Economy exploded in the late 1990s. Although a leader in such New Economy areas as Web hosting, digital supply chain management, and networking, EDS got no respect from its would-be high-tech partners.

The assignment given to the Fallon agency (Minneapolis) was to change those perceptions and infuse energy and pride into the EDS workforce. Fallon's strategy was to leverage EDS's proven experience and its rock-solid infrastructure, which enabled it to tackle enormous IT problems. The strategy came together in the positioning statement: "EDS thrives on defeating complexity."

How do you depict an organization defeating complexity? A catch phrase popular in the Silicon Valley culture—"It's like herding cats"—was the perfect metaphor for how EDS wrangles technology and manages complexity. And that's what the Fallon creative team did: It filmed a team of rugged cowboys herding thousands of housecats.

The commercial, which was designed to run during the Super Bowl, not only won an EFFIE award, it won every online poll ranking Super Bowl commercials that year. And it did so by erasing the company's rigid and unapproachable image and supplanting it with a down-to-earth, tongue-in-cheek image that appealed to the cynical dot-com industry.

In addition to being the favorite Super Bowl commercial, the "Cat Herders" commercial started EDS's telephones ringing and its Web site overflowed with visitors. The company estimated it had 2 million hits on its Web sites the next day, 10 times the normal volume. In terms of Fallon's objectives, one of which was to create brand awareness and buzz in the industry, EDS estimated that its $8 million investment in the ad and its supporting campaign netted an additional $12 million in PR. The campaign was also designed to generate sales and new-business inquiries and EDS reported that its sales were up 20 percent and its new-business leads grew by 40 percent.

The campaign was also designed to energize the workforce. "Cat Herders" gave EDS employees an inspiring image of themselves as wranglers in an epic undertaking whose message is: "No job is too tough." The company's employee turnover rate dropped, and thousands of employees sent letters to the president thanking him for the inspiring symbol of the cat herder.

Consider This

1. What was the problem the "Cat Herders" advertisement was designed to overcome?
2. If you were asked to recommend an idea for the next year's advertising, what would it be? Would you build on this theme or move in some other direction? Why?

Sources: Adapted from the EDS EFFIE brief provided by EDS and Fallon. Also, from "Super Ad Has EDS Purring," *Washington Technology* (March 20, 2000): 46; Becky Ebenkamp, "Creative: On Location: Kitty Slickers," *Adweek* (January 17, 2000): 24–26.

the cats had to swim across a river, but is it possible? Here's how it was done: The trainers taught a few cats that weren't averse to water to swim by starting them out in a quarter inch of water and then gradually adding water to the pool until it was deep enough for the cats to swim. The "river" was actually a small pool warmed by a portable heater; art director Hanson described it as "a little kitty Jacuzzi." Multiple copies of the swimming kitties were made and manipulated using computer graphics until an entire herd had been created. And that's how this famous scene came about—from Hanson's unlikely vision of a herd of cats swimming a river.

Visual storytelling is important, even for abstract concepts, such as "empowered," "inspired," and "inventive," which are the focus of commercials in the PBS "Be More" campaign. In the "Be more empowered" commercial, a gold fish makes its escape from its little round bowl in an apartment and jumps from a puddle to a bottle to a river where it works its way upstream accompanying giant salmon who are leaping up waterfalls as they return upstream in their annual migration.

In another commercial titled "be more inspired," a composer agonizes over the right notes and eventually hits a point of total frustration. As he looks out the window, he sees a group of birds sitting on a set of five power and telephone wires that are conveniently aligned to look like a music staff. From the bird's positions he crafts a line of music that becomes the theme for his composition.

PBS uses these clever little visual stories to present itself as a creative force that inspires people to use their imaginations. For example, a commercial that brings to life the idea "Be more inventive" is set in a rural, Old World scene probably in Italy. A resident realizes the village's library is on fire and organizes a bucket brigade. Unfortunately there isn't enough water coming from the town pump to make a dent in the fire. An "inventive" solution to the problem is to reverse the direction of the effort and use the buckets to scoop up burning items and carry them outside.

■ ■ ■
Even though cats can be trained to do a number of things including sitting on a horse's saddle, the magic in the EDS "Herding Cats" commercial was found in the computer manipulation of the digitized images.

Video Graphics

Art directors are responsible for creating the graphic elements that appear on screen. The art director can arrange for filming, or choose to use **stock footage**—previously recorded images, either video, still slides, or moving film. Typical stock footage files are shots from a satellite, historical scenes such as World War II battles, or a car crash. Other graphic elements such as words, product logos, and still photos are digitized or computer generated right on the screen. A **crawl** is a set of computer-generated letters that appear to be moving across the bottom of the screen. All of these are designed or specified by the art director. The Thomasville Bogart commercial opens with letterboxed, black-and-white film shot as if viewers were watching a 1940s-style party in a movie with a Bogart look-alike actor. It then moves to full screen in color and ends with shots of the furniture that is complimentary to a contemporary home.

Sophisticated computer graphics systems, such as those used to create the *Star Wars* special effects, have pioneered the making of artistic film and video advertising on computers. Computer graphic artists brag that they can do anything with an image. They can look at any object from any angle or even from the inside out. One of the most creative video techniques is called **morphing**, in which one object gradually changes into another. Photographs of real objects can change into art or animation and then return to life. Computer graphics specialists use tools such as the Paint Box software to create, multiply (that's how 50 cats can be made to look like hundreds), and manipulate video images.

Principle
Visual storytelling in television commercials is constructed through the careful design of individual shots and the sequencing of moving images.

■ ■ ■

The classy image of movie
star Humphrey Bogart and his
Hollywood lifestyle was used
as a theme for this commercial
that announces Thomasville
Furniture's Bogart Collection.

TV and Film Requirements

The length of a TV commercial is important in its design. TV ads first got shorter (15 or 10 seconds) as television time got more expensive; then they got longer as advertisers discovered that infomercials could be used in inexpensive times. From a design standpoint, the short length means the ads must be simple enough for consumers to grasp quickly, yet visually intriguing to prevent viewers from switching channels. Infomercials, however, can be longer and provide time for in-depth explanations and demonstrations.

In addition to TV commercials, videos, CDs, and DVDs are also used for product literature, news releases, direct marketing, and training films and, like ads, these are also designed by art directors. The objective is to tell a longer product story, and sometimes the focus is as much on education as it is on selling the product. The car industry has been using videos for years as product "literature" to give potential customers a "test drive" on their television screens. Movie trailers are similar to television commercials but are generally longer and better produced because they must compete with the beautiful images found in most movies. Trailer messages are usually 45 seconds, 1 minute, or 2 minutes in length. The projection of larger-than-life images in a darkened theater is totally unlike the experience of watching television. The impact of the large screen makes for a compelling image that commands total attention.

Consider This

1. What does an art director do in the making of a television commercial?
2. Explain how the art director told the "kitty slickers" story through visuals.

BROADCAST PRODUCTION

Most local retail commercials are simple and inexpensive, shot and taped at the local station. The sales representative for the station may work with the advertiser to write the script, and the station's director handles the taping of the commercial. Creating a national TV commercial is more complex and requires a number of people with specialized skills. The ad agency crew usually includes the copywriter, art director, and producer. The producer oversees the production on behalf of the agency and client and is responsible for the budget, among other things. The director, who is the person responsible for the filming of the commercial, is usually someone from outside the agency. This person takes the art director's storyboard and makes it come to life on film.

The producer and director are the core of the production team. The commercial's effectiveness depends on their shared vision of the final commercial and the director's ability to bring it to life as the art director imagined it. In the case of the "Cat Herders" commercial, the director was chosen by the agency because of his skill at coaxing naturally humorous performances from nonprofessional actors. In this commercial he worked with real wranglers on their semiscripted testimonials about their work with kitties. Table 14.1 summarizes the responsibilities of broadcast production personnel.

Producing TV Commercials

There are a number of ways to produce a message for a television commercial. It can be filmed live or prerecorded using film or videotape. It can also be shot frame-by-frame using animation techniques. Let's look at these production choices. Typically the film is shot on 35-mm film or videotape and then digitized, after which the editor transfers the image to videotape for dissemination, a process called **film-to-tape transfer**. Film consists of a series of frames on celluloid; actually, each frame is a still shot. Film is shot at 24 frames per second. To edit on film, editors cut between two frames and either eliminate a segment or attach a new segment of film. The term **cut**, which comes from this editing procedure, indicates an abrupt transition from one view of a scene to another. Art directors work closely with editors, who assemble the shots and cut the film to create the right pacing and sequence of images as outlined in the storyboard.

TABLE 14.1   Who Does What in TV and Radio Production?

Copywriter	Writes the script, whether it contains dialogue, narrative, lyrics, announcements, descriptions, or no words at all.
Art Director	In TV, develops the storyboard and establishes the look of the commercial, whether realistic, stylized, or fanciful.
Producer (can be an agency staff member)	Takes charge of the production, handles the bidding and all production arrangements, finds the specialists, arranges for casting talent, and makes sure the expenses and bids come in under budget.
Director	Has responsibility for the actual filming or taping, including scene length, who does what, how lines are spoken and the characters played; in TV determines how the camera is set up and records the flow of action.
Composer	Writes original music and sometimes writes the lyrics along with the music.
Arranger	Orchestrates music for the various instruments and voices to make it fit a scene or copy line. The copywriter usually writes the lyrics or at least gives some idea of what the words should say.
Editor	Puts everything together toward the end of the filming or taping process; evaluates how to assemble scenes and which audio elements work best with the dialogue and footage.

Animation The technique of **animation** traditionally meant drawing images on film and then recording the images one frame at a time. Cartoon figures, for example, were sketched and then resketched for the next frame with a slight change to indicate a small progression in the movement of an arm or a leg or a facial expression. Animation is traditionally shot at 16 drawings per second. Low-budget animation uses fewer drawings, so the motion looks jerky. The introduction of computers has accelerated the process and eliminated a lot of the tedious hand work.

Animation effects can also be used to combine created characters such as the little green GEICO gecko with live-action figures, or even with other animated characters. The famous Aflac duck has been featured in a traditional "Looney Tunes" cartoon with the Road Runner, Wile E. Coyote, Bugs Bunny, and Daffy Duck. It was created as a collaboration between Warner Brothers and the Aflac agency, the Kaplan Thaler Group in New York.[4] More advanced techniques, similar to those used in movies like *Lord of the Rings* and *Matrix Reloaded,* create lifelike images and movement. A technique called "mental ray" was used in a Levi Strauss ad featuring 600 stampeding buffalo. Mental ray is so good it was able not only to create lifelike images, but even to add realistic hair on the animals.[5]

Stop Motion A particular type of animation is **stop motion**, a technique used to film inanimate objects like the Pillsbury Doughboy, which is a puppet. The little character is moved a bit at a time and filmed frame by frame. The same technique is used in **claymation**, which involves creating characters from clay and then photographing them one frame at a time. Both have been popular with art directors who create advertising where fantasy effects are desired, although new computer effects also are simplifying these techniques.

Music and Action Specifying the music is usually done as part of the copywriting, but matching the music to the action is an art director's or producer's responsibility. In some cases, as in high-production song-and-dance numbers, the music is the commercial. Other times, it is used to get attention, set a mood, and lock the commercial into memory. For example, a recent JanSport commercial for its Live Wire Euphonic Pack, a backpack with built-in earphones and volume controls, cries out for a musical demonstration. The unlikely song picked for the spot, which targets the MTV crowd, was "Do-re-mi" from the 1959 *Sound of Music* musical. You might wonder why the creative team at the DDB Seattle agency would choose such a piece. Actually the rendition is not from the early recording but rather an ethereal, techno-pop version. The stick-in-the-head lyrics match the action on screen in a contemporary version of the boy meets girl, boy loses girl, boy finds girl story.[6]

■ ■ ■
Finding the talent—real wranglers as well as trained cats—was important in the "Cat Herders" commercial for EDS.

The TV Production Process

For the bigger national commercials, there are a number of steps in the production process that fall into four categories: message design (which we've already discussed), preproduction, the shoot, and postproduction. Figure 14.8 shows the steps in the TV production process.

Preproduction The producer and staff first develop a set of **production notes**, describing in detail every aspect of the production. These notes are important for finding talent and locations, building sets, and getting bids and estimates from specialists. In the "Cat Herders" commercial, finding the talent was critical. Some 50 felines and their trainers were involved in the filming. Surprisingly, different cats have different skills; some were able to appear to be asleep or motionless on cue, others excel as runners or specialize in water scenes.

Once the bids for production have been approved, the creative team and the producer, director, and other key players hold a preproduction meeting to outline every step of the production process and anticipate every problem that may arise. Then the work begins: The talent agency begins casting the roles; the production team finds a location and arranges site use with owners, police, and other officials. If sets are needed, they have to be built. Finding the props is a test of ingenuity, and the prop person may wind up visiting hardware stores, secondhand stores, and maybe even the local dump. Costumes may also have to be made, located, or bought.

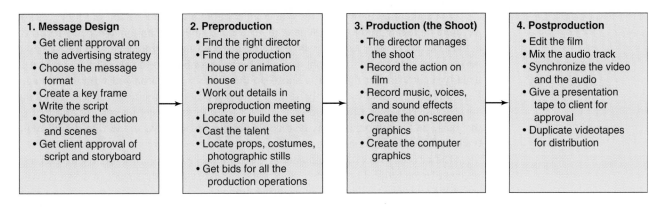

1. Message Design	2. Preproduction	3. Production (the Shoot)	4. Postproduction
• Get client approval on the advertising strategy • Choose the message format • Create a key frame • Write the script • Storyboard the action and scenes • Get client approval of script and storyboard	• Find the right director • Find the production house or animation house • Work out details in preproduction meeting • Locate or build the set • Cast the talent • Locate props, costumes, photographic stills • Get bids for all the production operations	• The director manages the shoot • Record the action on film • Record music, voices, and sound effects • Create the on-screen graphics • Create the computer graphics	• Edit the film • Mix the audio track • Synchronize the video and the audio • Give a presentation tape to client for approval • Duplicate videotapes for distribution

FIGURE 14.8   **TV Production Process**

In general, there are four steps in the production of a television commercial.

The Shoot   The film crew includes a number of technicians all of whom report to the director. For both film and video recording, the camera operators are the key technicians. Other technicians include the *gaffer*, who is the chief electrician, and the *grip*, who moves props and sets and lays tracks for the dolly on which the camera is mounted. The script clerk checks the dialogue and other script details and times the scenes. A set is a busy, crowded place. Table 14.2 offers definitions of terms common to television commercial production.

TABLE 14.2   Television Terminology

Shot Information	
Distance (camera to image)	Long shot (LS), full shot (FS), medium shot (MS), wide shot (WS), close-up (CU), extreme close-up (ECU or XCU).
Camera Movement	
Zoom in or out	The lens on the camera manipulates the change in distance. As you zoom in, the image seems to come closer and get larger; as you zoom out, it seems to move farther away and get smaller.
Dolly in and out	The camera itself is wheeled forward or backward.
Pan right or left	The camera is stationary but swings to follow the action.
Truck right or left	The camera itself moves right or left with the action.
Boom crane shoot	Camera mechanism moves over a scene; scene is shot from above.
Shot Transitions	
Cut	An abrupt, instantaneous change from one shot to another.
Dissolve	A soft transition in which one image fades to black while another image fades in.
Lap dissolve	A slow dissolve with a short period in which the two images overlap.
Superimposition	Two images held in the middle of a dissolve so they are both on-screen at the same time.
Wipe	One image crawls across the screen and replaces another.
Action	
Freeze frame	Stops the scene in mid-action.
Stop motion	Shots are taken one at a time over a long period. Used to record animation, clay-mation, or something that happens over a long period of time, such as a flower blooming.
Slow motion	Suspends the normal speed of things by increasing the number of frames used to record the movement.
Speeded-up motion	Increases the normal speed by reducing the number of frames used to record the movement.
Reverse motion	The film is run backward through the projector.

The audio director records the audio either at the time of the shoot, or, in the case of the more high-end productions, separately in a sound studio. If the sound is being recorded at the time of shooting, a *mixer,* who operates the recording equipment, and a mic or boom person, who sets up the microphones, handle the recording on the set. In the studio it is usually recorded after the film is shot—so the audio is synchronized with the footage. Directors often wait to see exactly how the action appears before they write and record the audio track. However, if the art director has decided to set the commercial to music, then the music on the audio track may be recorded before the shoot, as in the "Do-re-mi" audio track, and the filming done to the music.

The director shoots the commercial scene by scene, but not necessarily in the order set down in the script. Each scene is shot, called a **take**, and all the scenes in the storyboard are shot and then assembled through editing. If the director films the commercial on videotape, it is played back immediately to determine what needs correcting. Film has to be processed before the director can review it. These processed scenes are called **dailies**. **Rushes** are rough versions of the commercial assembled from cuts of the raw film footage. The director and the agency creative team view them immediately after the shoot to make sure everything's been filmed as planned. In some rare cases, an entire commercial is shot as one continuous action and there are no individual shots that are edited together in postproduction. Probably the most interesting use of this approach is an award-winning commercial for Honda, named "Cog." The principle in filming this kind of commercial is get it right, even if you have to do it over and over.

Postproduction For film and video, much of the work happens after the shoot in **postproduction**—when the commercial begins to emerge from the hands and mind of the editor. The objective of editing is to assemble the various pieces of film into a sequence that follows the storyboard. Editors manipulate the audio and video images creating realistic 3D images and combining real-life and computer-generated images. The postproduction process is hugely important in video because so many digital effects are being added to the raw film. In the "Cat Herders" commercial, Fallon could not film the cats and horses at the same time because of National Humane Society regulations. The director had to film the horses, background, and kitties separately. An editor fused the scenes together during postproduction, editing seamlessly to create the illusion of an elaborate cat drive.

Another goal of *video editing* is to manipulate time, which is a common technique used in commercial storytelling. Condensing time might show a man leaving work, then a cut of the man showering, then a cut of the man at a bar. The editor may extend time. Say a train is approaching a stalled car on the tracks. By cutting to various angles it may seem that the train is taking forever to reach the car—a suspense tactic. To jumble time, an editor might cut from the present to a flashback of a remembered past event or flash forward to an imagined scene in the future. All of these effects are specified by the art director in the storyboard.

The result of the editor's initial work is a **rough cut**, a preliminary edited version of the story that is created when the editor chooses the best shots and assembles them to create a scene. The editor then joins the scenes together. After the revision and reediting are completed, the editor makes an **interlock**, which means the audio and film are assembled together. The final version with the sound and film mixed together is called an **answer print**. The answer print is the final version printed onto a piece of film. For the commercial to air on hundreds of stations around the country, the agency has to make duplicate copies—a process called **dubbing**. The dubbed copies are called **release prints** and are usually in video form.

Consider This

1. List and explain the steps in the production of a television commercial.
2. What happens in postproduction? Why is it such an important step in the creating the look of a finished commercial?

A MATTER OF PRINCIPLE

Honda "Cog" Gets It Right, But Not the First Time

A two-minute commercial made in Britain for Honda by Wieden + Kennedy/London had viewers shaking their heads in disbelief and asking if it was for real. The spot shows all the many parts of a car, each set up in a domino fashion, that fall together piece by piece ultimately creating a new Honda that drives away at the end. It's tempting to think it was created through computer animation, but, no, it was filmed in real time without any special effects. It took 606 takes for the whole thing to work.

The lengthy process begins with a rolling transmission bearing, and moves through valves, brake pedals, tires, the hood, windshield wipers, and so forth. Every step of the process was carefully choreographed so that the part would do what it had to do exactly as planned. If there were any mistakes, and there were 605, then the filming started all over again from the beginning.

The commercial ends with the car driving away and Garrison Keillor, the star of the *Prairie Home Companion* radio show, asking "Isn't it nice when things just work?" The director and all the other people involved in the commercial were asking the same thing when it finally did work on the 606th take.

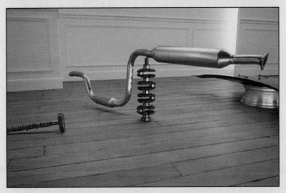

Because it was filmed using a British model that isn't sold in the United States and also because the cost of running a two-minute commercial would be prohibitive, the commercial was not shown in the United States, other than on news and feature shows and videos of award show winners. One of the most talked-about spots ever made, the publicity given to the commercial was probably even more valuable than an advertising buy.

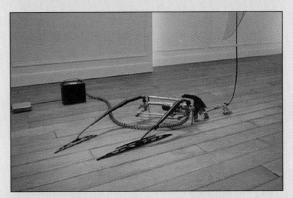

The "Cog" commercial won a Grand Clio (a creative award show), as well as a Gold Lion at the Cannes film festival, which also recognizes outstanding advertising. Even though it was never shown on air in the United States, it picked up no fewer than 20 awards from various British and international organizations.

The spot can be seen at http://home.attbi.com/~bernhard36/honda-ad.html.

Consider This

1. What makes the Honda "Cog" commercial so attention getting?
2. Do you think this commercial has a strong selling point? Explain your viewpoint.

Source: Stuart Elliott, "Is That Honda Commercial Real?" The New York Times Direct, June 10, 2003, NYTDirect@nytimes.com; "Honda's Cog Does It Again, Taking the Grand Clio," AdForum Alert, May 19, 2004, info@adforum.net.

EFFECTIVE WEB DESIGN

Web design includes creating ads that run on the Web as well as the Web site itself. Banner ads are designed more like outdoor boards than conventional print ads because their small space puts intense requirements on the designer to make the ad communicate quickly and succinctly, and yet attract attention and curiosity in order to elicit a click-through response. You can check out banner ads online at www.banneradmuseum.com.

Designers know that Web pages, particularly the first screen, should follow the same layout rules as posters: The graphics should be eye-catching without demanding too much downloading time; type should be simple, using one or two typefaces and avoiding all capitals and letter spacing that distorts the words. Because there is often a lot to read, organizing the information is critical. In terms of legibility, black type on a high-contrast background usually is best; all the design elements—type and graphics—should be big enough to see on the smallest screen.

Sometimes the illustrations, as well as the photos, are obtained from clip-art services, or rather **click art**, such as that provided by www.eyewire.com or www.1stoppictures.net. Actually, any image can be scanned and manipulated to create a Web image, which is causing a copyright problem for artists. Because of the magic of digitizing, Web pages can combine elements and design styles from many different media: print, still photography, film, animation, sound, and games. The combination of interactive navigation, live streaming video, online radio, and 360-degree camera angles creates Web pages that may be more complex than anything you see on TV, which is why ease-of-use is a factor in Web site design. The Inside Story describes research on the best and worst site design practices conducted by Forrester Research, a company that specializes in monitoring the effectiveness of Internet advertising.

Web designers use a completely different toolbox than other types of art directors. Animation effects, as well as sophisticated *navigation paths,* are designed using software programs such as Flash, Director, Blender, Squeak, and nonlinear editing tools such as Premier, FinalCut, and AfterEffects, among others. It's such a rapidly changing design world that it's difficult to keep track of the most recent innovations in Web design software. An example of a good Web site design is crewcuts.com, which was designated as the Best Web site by the Internet Professional Publisher's Association. It's hard to convey here why the site is effective because of the animation, so check out www.crewcuts.com. One source for tips on Web site design is www.eMarketers.com. Table 14.3 lists eMarketers' 10 rules

TABLE

14.3 **eRules for eDesign**

Rule One: Manage your image. Projecting and protecting your brand identity are no less important online than in any other medium.

Rule Two: Simple navigation. Retail stores don't stay in business unless their customers can find what they want, easily. The same applies to Web sites. Remember K.I.S.S. (Keep It Simple, Stupid)?

Rule Three: Don't waste time. Do you like to wait in line? Do you go back to stores where sales clerks don't respond? Make sure your consumers find the information they're looking for—fast.

Rule Four: Keep your product fresh. Spiders may constantly comb the Web, but if anyone finds cobWebs on your site, they won't come back.

Rule Five: Give it away. If your site doesn't offer real value, there's no real reason for anyone to visit.

Rule Six: Information-in-the-end. When someone takes the time to link through to your site, don't let them come up empty. Reward them with content, content, content.

Rule Seven: Get interactive! Mass media are passive; the new media are interactive. In which direction do you think the world is going?

Rule Eight: Follow the Rule of Ten. Ten is enough for God and David Letterman, so learn from them. Keep your lists short, too.

Rule Nine: Promote your site. "Build it and they will come" was a nice theme for the movie *Field of Dreams.* But if you want customers, not virtual ghosts, on your site, get smart about promotion—in the real world.

Rule Ten: The rules will change. No one who does "business as usual" today is going to be in business tomorrow. So move often and as intelligently as possible. Keep up with fast-changing online business trends.

THE INSIDE STORY
The Best and Worst of Site Design

Harley Manning, Vice President, Research, Forrester Research

Over the past five years, Forrester has graded the quality of user experience on hundreds of Web sites with a technique called "heuristic evaluation." Today, variations on this methodology are used by virtually every interactive design agency and testing lab to judge the effectiveness of sites. It's also used in-house by many companies, including Ford and Johnson & Johnson.

We introduced version 4.0 of our own methodology in late 2003. To identify some of the best and worst examples of Web design at the time, we used it to grade five sites in each of four industries: automotive, media, retail, and travel. When we published the results we kicked up quite a storm because we named names.

The retail category came out best overall, with the highest low score (JCPenney) as well as the highest high score (Lands' End). This finding was consistent with the results from the 375 sites we had graded previously, using versions 2 and 3 of our methodology. In our earlier studies, the retail category averaged several points higher than sites in the next-best category, financial services.

The automotive sites we graded laid firm claim to the cellar, with both the lowest low score (Toyota) and the lowest high score (MINI USA). This, too, was consistent with our earlier studies, in which the automotive manufacturer category ranked last among industry categories.

What explains the relatively poor showing of automotive sites versus retail sites? One reason is that online retailers' business success ties directly to the quality of customer experience on their sites: When customers can't find a product or complete the checkout process, it shows up immediately in lost sales. This feedback loop drives retail site designers to quickly find and fix problems like inadequate product information, confusing menus, and poor reliability.

In contrast, managers of automotive sites struggle to even measure business results, like dealer leads that actually result in a sale. And when Web traffic logs show car shoppers wandering around their sites, it's hard to tell whether the prospects are fascinated or just lost.

Source: As part of Forrester's Customer Experience research team, Harley Manning focuses on design and testing strategies for Web sites and software. Harley came to Forrester after spending 18 years designing and building interactive services for a variety of companies including Dow Jones, AT&T, MCI, Prodigy, and Sears. He received a Master of Science degree in Advertising from the University of Illinois, Urbana, in 1977.

Nominated by the late Professor and Dean Kim Rotzell, University of Illinois.

for Web site design. For more examples of excellence in Web site design and reviews of the top Web sites, check out:

www.netroadmap.com   www.clioawards.com
www.imarvel.com   www.oneclub.com
www.topsiteslinks.com   www.ippa.org

Action and Interaction

Web advertisers are continuing to find ways to bring dramatic action to the small screen in order to make the imagery more engaging. For example, Ford used a banner on the Yahoo! home page with the familiar Ford oval and a bunch of little black birds on a wire. Then three of the birds flew down to the middle of the page and started pecking at what looked like birdseed, uncovering an image of the new Explorer. The link read: "click to uncover the next territory." Those who did click probably expected a pop-up image, but instead the page shook, the birds scattered, and a big red Ford Explorer drove up to the front of the screen, replacing most of the content. It was a surprising, highly involving, and very effective announcement of the car.

Because users can create their own paths through the Web site, designers have to make sure that their sites have clear **navigation**. Users should be able to move through the site easily, find the information they seek, and respond. Ideally, users who visit a site regularly should be able to customize the site to fit their own interests. If a site is well designed, people may want to interact with the organization sponsoring the site. For example, Texture/Media, a Boulder, Colorado–based Web design firm, created a seven-episode series over five months that detailed the journey of two men attempting to climb the Meru Sharksfin summit in India, for client Marmot Mountain Works. Called ClimbMeru.com, it chronicled the team's training and trip, and hosted contest give-aways that helped gather information about Marmot's customers. Texture/Media's objective with its award-winning Web sites is to make the consumer a participant in its brand stories.[7]

Consider This

1. Explain how the need for navigation is a factor in Web site design.

2. Researchers have found that banners have a relatively low click-through rate. Why do you suppose that is so? What can be done with their design to increase their effectiveness?

IT'S A WRAP

IMAGINE A LEGENDARY LIFESTYLE

■ ■ ■

The $60 billion furniture category is unusual in that there are more than 5,000 furniture manufacturers with very little brand differentiation among them. Thomasville Furniture is a key player but it, like all its competitors, struggles to create a brand identity for its products and a brand relationship with consumers.

The "Collection of a Lifetime" campaign for the Hemingway Collection generated $100 million in sales, which was six times the original sales objective and the largest launch in the company's history. Not only that, the Hemingway campaign, as well as the newer Bogart Collection, also created a halo effect over the entire Thomasville line. Sales across all lines increased by 39 percent immediately following the launch of the "Collection of a Lifetime" campaigns.

In terms of effectiveness measures, the unaided brand awareness of Thomasville increased from 14 percent to 27 percent after the line's first year of advertising; however, the awareness of the Hemingway line jumped from zero to 41 percent during that same one-year period. That level exceeded the brand awareness levels of established competition, such as Henredon, which was at 28 percent awareness at the end of that same introductory year. *Furniture Today,* a leading trade journal, declared that the Hemingway launch was "one of the most successful new lines in industry history." And that was the reason "The Collection of a Lifetime" launch was selected as an EFFIE-award winner.

■ ■ ■ Summary

1. **Explain how visual impact is created in advertising.** Visual communication is important in advertising because it creates impact. It grabs attention, maintains interest, creates believability, and sticks in memory.

2. **List the principles of layout, and explain how design is affected by media requirements.** A layout is an arrangement of all the ad's elements. It gives the reader a visual order to the information in the ad; at the same time, it is aesthetically pleasing and makes a visual statement for the brand. Principles that designers use in print advertising include direction, dominance, unity, white space, contrast, balance, and proportion.

Newspaper ads accommodate the limitations of the printing process by not using fine details. Magazine ads, because they are printed on good paper, offer quality images and good color reproduction. For directory ads, designers keep in mind that people are searching for information, particularly about location and how to contact the company, and so these ads are focused on directional information. Visibility and the need for simple messages are the primary concerns of poster and outdoor board designers. Interior transit ads are designed for reading; exterior cards work like billboards.

3. **Describe how art and color are reproduced.** Illustrations are treated as line art and photographs are reproduced through the halftone process by using screens to break down the image into a dot pattern. Full-color photos are converted to four halftone images, each one printed with a different process color—magenta, cyan, yellow, and black—through the process of color separation.

4. **Explain how the art director creates TV commercials.** TV art directors are responsible for the "look" of a commercial. They also design the on-screen graphic elements as well as the presentation of the action through visual storytelling. Computer graphics are playing a more important role in the creation of special effects, particularly animation.

5. **Identify the critical steps in planning and producing broadcast commercials.** Commercials are planned using scripts (and storyboards for TV). Radio commercials are scripted, taped, and mixed. TV commercials are shot live, shot on film or videotape, or created "by hand" using animation, claymation, or stop action. There are four stages to the production of TV commercials: message design (scripts and storyboards), preproduction, the shoot, and postproduction.

6. **Summarize the techniques of Web design.** Web advertising can include ads and banners, but the entire Web site can also be seen as an advertisement. Art on Web pages can be illustrations or photographs, still images as well as moving ones, and may involve unexpected effects such as 360-degree images. When designers plan a Web page, they need to consider navigation—how people will move through the site. They also need to consider how to incorporate elements that allow for interaction between the consumer and the Web page company.

▪▪▪ Key Terms

all capitals, 392	film-to-tape transfer, 407	newsprint, 399	sans serif, 392
animation, 408	flexography, 403	offset printing, 402	screen, 400
answer print, 410	flush left, 392	photoprints or photostats, 403	semicomps, 396
claymation, 408	flush right, 392	picas, 392	serif, 392
click art, 412	foil stamping, 403	points, 392	silkscreen printing, 403
clip art, 388	font, 392	postproduction, 410	spot color, 390
color separation, 401	four-color printing, 401	probono campaign, 387	stock footage, 405
comprehensives, 396	halftone, 400	process colors, 400	stop motion, 408
C-print, 403	high-resolution film, 397	production notes, 408	surprinting, 394
crawl, 405	interlock, 410	ragged left, 392	take, 410
cut, 407	justified type, 392	ragged right, 392	thumbnail sketches, 396
dailies, 410	layout, 394	registration, 399	tint blocks, 400
debossing, 403	letterpress, 402	release prints, 410	tip-ins, 403
desktop publishing, 403	line art, 400	reverse type, 392	typography, 391
die cut, 403	mechanicals, 396	rotogravure, 402	unjustified type, 392
digitization, 403	morphing, 405	rough cut, 410	veloxes, 403
dubbing, 410	navigation, 413	rough layouts, 396	visualization, 388
embossing, 403	negative space, 395	rushes, 410	white space, 395

▪▪▪ Review Questions

1. What are the six reasons why visual impact is so powerful in advertising?
2. List the eight design principles and explain each one.
3. Explain the difference between line art and halftones.
4. What does the phrase four-color printing mean? What are the four process colors?
5. Explain the four steps in the video production process.
6. What are five rules to remember in designing a Web site?

■ ■ ■ Discussion Questions

1. What are the differences between using an illustration and using a photograph? Give an example of a product category where you would want to use an illustration and another example where you use a photograph. Explain why.

2. What principles govern the design of a magazine ad? Collect two samples, one that you think is a good example of effective design and one that you think is not effective. Critique the two ads and explain your evaluation based on what you know about how design principles work in advertising layouts.

3. Choose an ad from this textbook that you think demonstrates a good layout with a clear visual path. Take a piece of tracing paper, as we have done with the Porsche ad in Figure 13.5, and convert the key elements to geometric shapes to see what kind of pattern emerges. Illustrate on your tracing how the eye moves around the page. Put an X on the dominant element on your tracing.

4. One of the challenges for creative ad designers is to demonstrate a product whose main feature cannot be seen by the consumer. Suppose you are an art director on an account that sells shower and bath mats with a patented system that ensures that the mat will not slide (the mat's underside is covered with tiny suction cups that grip the tub's surface). Brainstorm some ways to demonstrate this feature in a television commercial. Find a way that will satisfy the demands of originality, relevance, and impact.

5. Think of a television commercial you have seen recently that you thought was creative and entertaining. Then find one that you think is much less creative and entertaining. Analyze how the two commercials work to catch and hold your attention. How do the visuals work? What might be done to make the second commercial more attention getting? You can also use online sources to find commercials at www.adcritic.com and at www.badads.org.

6. One approach to design says that a visual image in an ad should reflect the image of the brand. Find a print ad that you think speaks effectively for the personality of the brand. Now compare the print ad with the brand's Web site. Does the same design style continue on the site? Does the site present the brand personality in the same way as the print ad?

■ ■ ■ Class Projects

1. Select a product that is advertised exclusively through print. Examples of such products are business-to-business and industrial products, school supplies, many over-the-counter drugs, and some food items. Your objective is to develop a 30-second television spot for this product. Divide the class into groups of four to six. Use a creative brief (see Chapter 12) to summarize the ad's strategy. In your small groups, brainstorm about ways to develop a creative idea for the commercial. Then write a script and develop a storyboard to present your idea for this product. In the script include all the key decisions a producer and director would make. Present your work to the class.

2. You have been asked to design a Web page for a local business or organization (choose one from your local community). Go to www.1stoppictures.net and choose a visual to illustrate the Web site by trying to match the personality of the organization to a visual image. Then identify the primary categories of information that need to be included on the page. Develop a flowchart or map that shows how a typical user would navigate through the site. What other image could you find on 1stoppictures that might be used on inside pages to provide some visual interest to this business's online image? Now consider interactivity: How could this site be used to increase interactivity between this company and its customers? Create a plan for this site that includes the visual elements and a navigation flowchart.

HANDS-ON

The Future Definition of Advertising

You could call October 29, 1998, a historic day, for on that date John Glenn, the then 77-year-old former astronaut and senator, returned to space aboard the shuttle *Discovery,* making him the oldest person to ever go into orbit. In perhaps somewhat less dramatic fashion, history was made another way that day, because network coverage of Glenn's mission included the first five TV commercials ever broadcast in high definition (HDTV). Historic, yes, but the special quality of these five Proctor & Gamble commercials probably went unnoticed by most viewers, since in 1998 HDTV's were still very rare in the United States. In fact, even as late as 2005, despite intense efforts by broadcasters and television manufacturers, HDTV sets could be found in only about 10 million homes, and only about 2 million of these had the tuners required to watch HDTV programming.

HDTV is a special kind of digital format, one that provides movie theater–quality pictures and stereo-quality audio. However, its growth has been slowed by the expense of HDTV-ready televisions and the limited selection of HDTV channels on many cable systems. Many industry forecasters expect HDTV to begin a period of rapid growth in 2005 since there are now thousands of hours of programming broadcast in the format each week.

The advertising world is beginning to take notice too. During the 2004 Super Bowl only one advertiser chose to run an ad in high definition, whereas almost a third of advertisers planned to do so for the 2005 game. Why? Well, as *Advertising Age* put it:

> Imagine watching the Super Bowl this year in high definition on your new big-screen plasma TV. Watch the quarterback's eyes dart from side to side as he calls a play in Dolby surround sound. Watch nervous defensive ends drip sweat as they wait for the call. Cut to commercial, and suddenly the screen shrinks from a wide screen to a small squared-off box with a flat and dull-looking product inside it. Now imagine you're the brand manager of that product. Imagine picking up the phone and calling your advertising agency to query, "I paid $2.4 million for that?"

What challenges face an advertiser told by its agency to film a commercial in HD? As you might expect, cost is an issue, since ads filmed in the format can cost 10–15 percent more than analog commercials. Given the current low penetration of HDTV, it may strike some advertisers as an unnecessary expense. However WPP Group's Michael Bologna points out that the extra cost is relatively small, especially for a Super Bowl advertiser. "If you're willing to spend $2.4 million on a Super Bowl Spot, at least convert it to high definition; that's what we're recommending to our clients."

At least one industry survey, sponsored by the iNDemand Network, suggests benefits for advertisers who choose to use HD. According to the survey, 62 percent of respondents say they enjoy watching commercials in HD; 51 percent believe they pay more attention to HD commercials, and 69 percent think advertisers that show commercials in HD are "more cutting edge."

HD may offer some good news for revenue-hungry networks as well, because it may attract advertiseres that have traditionally avoided television. An example is fashion companies, which have usually favored print ads to show off their wares. One fashion consultant, Mathew Evins of Evins Communications, argues, "You can't see the subtleties of fabrics and designs on regular TV, but when HDTV becomes mainstream, my guess is we'll start to see more high-end designers use it to showcase fashions . . . it will be like Imax for TV commercials."

Consider This

1. Evaluate the arguments for and against creating high-definition ads. Under what conditions would you counsel an advertiser to spend the extra money on this new format?
2. Adoption of HDTV has been slower than expected. What will have to happen for consumers to embrace the technology?
3. Explain how production considerations, such as the use of HDTV, might influence the planning and design of a television commercial. How would you determine if using HDTV is effective?

Sources: Kate Fitzgerald, "Visuals Only Get Better," *Advertising Age* (February 24, 2003); Bradley Johnson, "TV-Set Brands Carefully Enter Digital Future," *Advertising Age* (November 9, 1998); Jennie L. Phipps, "Digital Debate: Video vs. Film, *Advertising Age* (June 18, 2001); Beth Snyder Bulik and Kirs Oser, "High Time for Ads to Move to High Def," *Advertising Age* (December 13, 2004); Phillip Swann, "HDTV: The Price Is Right: But the Consumer Electronics Industry Must Do a Better Job of Letting People Know," September 29, 2004, http://www.tvpredictions.com/hdtvprice092904.html.

PART-ENDING CASE

Part 4
Effective Advertising
Messsages

You do not have to be a big brand with millions of dollars to have great advertising. The Chick-fil-A "Eat Mor Chikin®" campaign is a great example. Chick-fil-A competes in one of the largest and most competitive industries: fast food. It is outnumbered 15 to 1 in store count and outspent 60 to 1 in media by the likes of McDonald's, Burger King, and Wendy's.

Faced with these disadvantages in the marketplace, Chick-fil-A and its advertising agency set out to develop a brand campaign that would increase top-of-mind awareness, increase sales, and earn Chick-fil-A a spot in consumers' consideration list of fast-food brands. To do this effectively, the campaign positioned Chick-fil-A chicken sandwiches as the premium alternative to hamburgers.

The company could not outspend the competition. It couldn't even afford a national campaign on television, which is where most of its competitors were advertising. So it decided to advertise where its competitors weren't—on outdoor billboards. The challenge was: How to build a brand using outdoor billboards as the primary medium? After all, common sense suggests that billboards are used to let people know where to exit or how many miles to travel, not to build brands.

Well, for Chick-fil-A and its agency, overcoming the challenge would be easier than expected. Chick-fil-A's "Eat Mor Chikin" three-dimensional billboard campaign helped break the fast-food hamburger pattern. The witty use of a Holstein cow encouraging the target audience to "Eat Mor Chikin" instead of beef provided a bold personality that broke through industry clutter. Why? The message and execution were simple, the cows were funny, the creative idea was unexpected, and the call to action was powerful.

This lighthearted, unconventional campaign has helped increase sales every year. In 1995, when the campaign first began, Chick-fil-A reported $501,639,680 in sales. Today, the company reports nearly $2 billion in sales and its unaided brand awareness has grown 81 percent since 1996.

Chick-fil-A and its agency have found a creative way to use outdoor successfully in building the Chick-fil-A brand without spending millions of media dollars.

Source: Information courtesy of Mike Buerno, The Richards Group.

Consider This

1. What are the risks of using a humorous creative approach?
2. What other creative approaches do you think they could use?

Integration and Effectiveness: The Big Picture

Hundreds of different communication activities can deliver brand messages both formally through planned marketing communication programs and informally through other activities and operations. This book is focused on those formal programs and hopes to provide a framework for you to understand how all these programs and tools can work together to send target audiences consistent, persuasive messages that promote a brand's objective.

In Part 5 we will introduce a collection of these key marketing communication tools—direct response, sales promotion, events and sponsorships, and public relations—whose activities need to be coordinated with advertising to prevent inconsistent messages that might conflict with each other and with the overall brand strategy. This section of the book deals with the complexities of marketing communication. What holds everything together in an integrated program is a strong "big idea," as well as a strong commitment to a coherent brand position and image. The end result is brand integrity. Note that integration and integrity come from the same Latin root.

The best campaigns are developed from the company's mission or philosophy of business, particularly when it is customer-focused. Southwest Airlines, for example, has become the most profitable airline in the country on the basis of understanding its customers' needs and serving them well. A brand is integrated when there is integrity in the various messages used in the campaign.

Messages that create brand integrity may also be the ones that are most effective. So the final chapter in this section develops the concept of effectiveness in terms of evaluation—how marketing communication messages are tested to determine if they deliver on their objectives. An effective message strategy, then, is one in which advertising and all the other marketing communication tools work together to create synergy. By working together to create brand integrity, the effectiveness of the integrated campaign is greater than the sum of its individual pieces.

NO. I'VE DECIDED TO OPT FOR A SMALL AND RATHER UNEVENTFUL LI

You could eat up a lifetime pondering what to do with your days on earth. Or you could take one look at a machine like the Wide Glide.® And let gut instinct take it from there. Get a load of the high handlebar and stretched-out profile. We didn't hold anything back in building this ride. So what's holding you back? 1-800-443-2153 or www.harley-davidson.com. The Legend Rolls On.®

Direct Response

What's Holding You Back from a Harley?

Award:
Direct Marketing Association Echo Leader Award
EFFIE® Silver

Organization:
Harley-Davidson

Agency:
Carmichael Lynch

Campaign:
"What's Holding You Back"

CHAPTER OBJECTIVES

After reading this chapter, you will be able to:

1. Define and distinguish between direct marketing and direct-response advertising.

2. Explain the types of direct marketing.

3. Name the players in direct marketing.

4. Evaluate the various media that direct-response programs can use.

5. Explain how databases are used in direct marketing.

6. Discuss the role of direct marketing in integrated marketing programs.

Throughout this book, we have introduced chapters with EFFIE award–winning campaigns. The direct-marketing industry has its own award equivalent to the EFFIEs, called the Echo Award. You can read about the Echo award at www.dma-echo.org, but in this chapter we will introduce you to a campaign that has won this award, which is given for excellence in response rates, marketing strategy, and creative components

Harley-Davidson is one of the world's best-known brands and its advertising has won many awards over the years. However, in the early 2000s, Harley found itself riding uphill as competitors cut into its market share. Working with the Carmichael Lynch agency, Harley was able to overcome a worrisome customer trend with a direct-response campaign designed to generate leads.

The Marketing Situation

Harley-Davidson had managed to hold on to its mystique over the years, but its customer base was aging. The average age of Harley owners had increased from 37 to 45 during the 1990s, yet investors continued to press the company to increase its sales and profitability as it had in the past. Quantitative and qualitative research showed that price is an overwhelming barrier, particularly for younger riders. The perception of younger customers was that the normal price tag of a Harley was in the neighborhood of $20,000. In fact, the $6,500 Sportster model was the entry-level, rider-friendly model that Harley wished to market to this younger segment.

The challenge given to the Carmichael Lynch agency was to reach out to these younger buyers and convince them that a Harley-Davidson motorcycle was attainable.

Campaign Strategy

The objectives for the Harley ad campaign were ambitious: (1) reach new prospects, (2) break down barriers to purchase (namely price misperception), and (3) generate leads to develop a new, younger customer base for the entry-level model.

A carefully tailored communication program was designed to reach 25 to 44-year-old prospects, including those who had never owned a motorcycle, as well as previous owners and owners of competitive brands. Their median household income was $45,000+. Their lifestyle was dominated by sports, entertainment, and music. They were also characterized as cost conscious, making price an important decision criterion.

Message Strategy

The message was designed to have a youthful appeal and be somewhat edgy, while still focusing on the fundamental values that have built Harley's brand—freedom of spirit, adventure, and individualism. By using Harley's traditional rebellious attitude and tone to communicate the reasonable price of a Sportster, the campaign was able to stay consistent with Harley's position. Even as it acknowledged consumers' perception of Harley's high price, it also stressed that "now is the time to get out and start living your life, fulfilling your dream." A tagline provided the fundamental question for this target market: "What's holding you back? A mere $6,500 will get you a Harley."

Media Strategy

The first step of the campaign strategy was to generate leads in order to capture key qualifying information and begin an ongoing dialogue with prospects. The next step delivered customized information based on the prospect's riding status. These messages focused on the products and programs that would help the prospects overcome their barriers to purchase and take steps toward making Harley ownership a reality.

Harley had a very limited budget for this campaign, so its strategy for using media was quite selective. To generate leads, magazine ads were used in a few categories that complemented the target audience's interests, such as sports or fitness. The focus was on publications read by active young men like the *Sport's*

Illustrated swimsuit issue and *Rolling Stone.* In the spring, commercials ran on national cable stations such as ESPN.

The magazine ads ran with a Business Reply Card (BRC) that communicated the price message for the Sportster and invited interested readers to sign up, via mail or toll-free phone number, for a "How-to-Get-a-Harley" package. Qualifying information on the card helped Harley dealers determine the level of qualification, riding experience, and demographics or the prospect.

The campaign was highly successful and was rewarded with an EFFIE award for its effectiveness. The It's a Wrap section at the end of this chapter will tell you more about the campaign's results.

Source: Adapted from information in the 2003 Echo entry and the EFFIEs Brief provided by Harley-Davidson and Carmichael Lynch and from personal interviews with the marketing team in 2004.

A big change is taking place in marketing and advertising as marketers are moving to more direct forms of communication with their customers. In the past, marketing communication was a monologue: Advertisers talked to anonymous consumers through the mass media. Now communication is becoming a dialogue. Using computers and the Web, mail, video, and the telephone, advertisers can talk directly with, rather than at customers. This advertising dialogue is achieved through *direct marketing.* In this chapter we'll discuss the practice and process of direct marketing and database marketing, as well as the key players and tools of direct marketing, and the principles of integrated direct marketing.

THE PRACTICE OF DIRECT MARKETING

Direct marketing is big business, with total expenditures in 2001 of $241.1 billion. Advertisers use direct marketing in every consumer and business-to-business category. IBM, Xerox, and other manufacturers selling office products use direct marketing, as do almost all banks and insurance companies. Airlines, hotels, and cruise lines use it. Packaged-goods marketers such as General Foods, Colgate, and Bristol Myers; household product marketers such as Black and Decker; and automotive companies use it. Direct marketing shows up in membership drives, fund-raising, and solicitation for donations by nonprofit organizations such as the Sierra Club and the Audubon Society, political associations, and the Denver Rescue Mission.

There is some confusion in marketing departments and the advertising industry over what people mean when they use the term "direct marketing." Although the direct-marketing industry continues to be in a state of flux, Figure 15.1 depicts the components that currently constitute direct marketing. **Direct marketing (DM)** occurs when a seller and customers deal with each other directly rather than through an intermediary, such as a wholesaler or retailer. As noted in Figure 15.1, it includes a strong focus on marketing research to guide strategy; and database development, to better target customers. The four strategic tools of direct marketing are: catalog, direct mail, telemarketing, and direct-response advertising. In turn, each of these tools provides an infrastructure whereby the transaction can actually take place.

When considering these four tools of direct marketing, there is recognition that catalog, direct mail, telemarketing, and direct-response advertising are also types of communication devices. All four are delivering persuasive messages and the focus is on actually producing a sale. As noted repeatedly, producing a sale is the goal of all businesses, and identifies the primary reason why direct marketing is growing in popularity. And sales, or other actions, are measurable, meaning that the marketer always knows how it is doing relative to its investment in direct marketing. Its effectiveness is easy to evaluate.

Principle
Direct marketing is a growth area because it produces measurable results, particularly sales, which makes it easy to evaluate its effectiveness.

The Direct-Marketing Industry
The direct-marketing industry focuses on research and database building. Its main tools are catalogs, direct mail, telemarketing, and direct-response advertising.

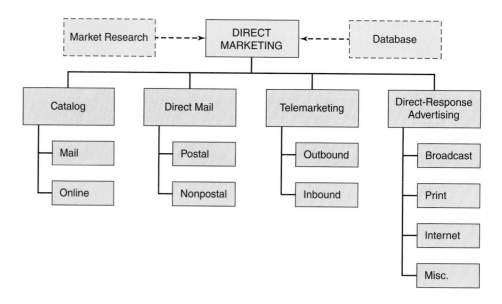

Advantages and Disadvantages of Direct Marketing

Advantages of direct marketing over indirect marketing, such as advertising, include the following:

- Direct-marketing technology allows for the collection of relevant information about the customer contributing to the development of a useful database and selective reach, which reduces waste.
- Products have added value through the convenient purchase process and reliable, quick delivery mechanisms of direct marketing. Purchase is not restricted to a location.
- The marketer (rather than the wholesaler or retailer) controls the product until delivery.
- Advertising carrying direct-marketing components is easier to evaluate.
- It affords flexibility in both form and timing, as the Battelle case (see page 426) illustrates.

As with all concepts, direct marketing has some weaknesses. Most notably, consumers are still reluctant to purchase a product sight unseen. This problem is changing with the increase in credible direct marketers, along with the ability of the Internet to simulate actual shopping and touching. The other weakness is the annoyances associated with direct marketing, such as too many catalogs, junk mail, and calls during dinner. Finally, direct-marketing strategies are unable to reach everyone in the marketplace. With improvement of databases, the problem is diminishing.

Direct Marketing and Direct-response Advertising

Since this text focuses on advertising, it is necessary to clearly distinguish between direct marketing and direct-response advertising. Direct marketing includes one or more components that allow for **lead generation**—which refers to the way marketers identify prospective customers—as well as actual purchase.

Direct-response advertising is a type of marketing communication that combines the characteristics of advertising (attention-getting visuals, interesting copy, and relevant timing) but also includes an element that allows the reader, viewer, or listener to make a direct response to the advertiser. The contact element can be a toll-free 800 or 900 phone number, an order coupon, a request-for-information device, or a Web site or e-mail address. In contrast to traditional advertising, which offers a long-term implicit promise and delayed action, direct-response advertising provides a short-term explicit result and the opportunity for immediate action. Therefore, the return on investment is significantly higher for direct-response advertising.

The Direct-marketing Process

As outlined in Figure 15.2, there are five basic steps in direct marketing: (1) setting objectives and making strategic decisions (research helps advertisers target and segment

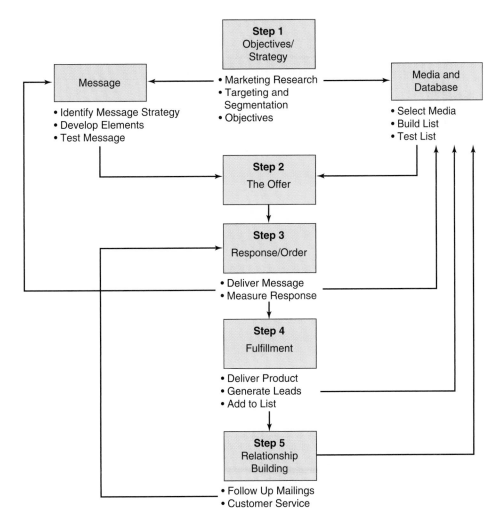

Step 1
Objectives/
Strategy

• Marketing Research
• Targeting and
  Segmentation
• Objectives

Message

• Identify Message Strategy
• Develop Elements
• Test Message

**Media and
Database**

• Select Media
• Build List
• Test List

Step 2
The Offer

Step 3
Response/Order

• Deliver Message
• Measure Response

Step 4
Fulfillment

• Deliver Product
• Generate Leads
• Add to List

Step 5
Relationship
Building

• Follow Up Mailings
• Customer Service

FIGURE 15.2

The Direct-marketing Process
The direct-marketing process
has five main steps. The direct
marketer's challenge is to manage
these steps and build a relationship
with the consumer.

prospects, as well as set objectives); (2) the communication of an offer (the message) by the seller through the appropriate medium; (3) response, or customer ordering; (4) fulfillment, or filling orders and handling exchanges and returns; and (5) maintenance of the company's database and customer service.

Objectives and Strategies   As in all planning processes, we begin by delineating the specific objective to achieve. Direct marketing has three primary objectives:

1. *Lead Generation.* Providing basic information on companies or individuals who are potential customers.
2. *Traffic Generation.* Motivating customers to visit an event, retail outlet, or other location.
3. *Action.* Order products and make payments or take some other action, such as visiting a dealer, returning a response card, or visiting a Web site.

The planner can then make these three basic objectives more concrete by specifying such factors as timing, amount of increase, and the consumer's specific behavior, such as where they see the product or what kind of action they might engage in. For example, a local Volvo dealership might expect its direct-marketing program to increase showroom traffic by 60 percent during the next 90 days.

The direct-marketing tools that achieve these objectives are: direct-response advertising, catalog, direct mail or e-mail, or telemarketing—separately or in some combination. Our Volvo dealer purchases a database of consumers who meet the criteria for a potential Volvo owner and sends out a direct-mail piece that offers $50 to anyone taking a test drive on a specific set of dates. This offer is repeated in the local newspaper. This whole process is known as prospecting. **Prospecting** is a technique of mining the information in databases

to uncover prospective buyers whose characteristics match those of users. Let's look more closely at "the offer."

The Offer   All direct marketing (DM) contains an *offer,* typically consisting of a description of the product, terms of sale, and payment and delivery information. In its offer, a successful DM campaign must communicate benefits to buyers by answering the enduring question: "What's in it for me?" Direct marketers might tell potential buyers of product benefits promotional tactics, such as buy-one-get-one-free.

An effective DM offer, as with all marketing offers, clearly calls on the buyer to take some action, as the TigerDirect.com cover illustrates. All the variables that are intended to satisfy the needs of the consumer are considered part of the offer. These variables include the price, the cost of shipping and handling, optional features, future obligations, availability of credit, extra incentives, time and quality limits, and guarantees or warranties. The offer is supported by a message strategy, a media strategy, and the database.

Message and Media Strategy   There are general guidelines that apply to message development in direct marketing. First, the message is often longer and contains more

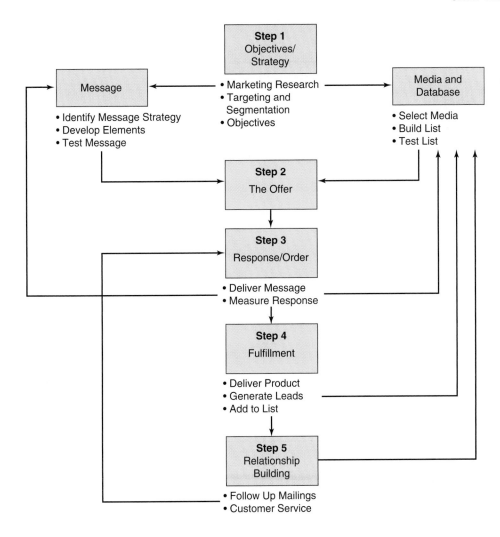

FIGURE
15.2

The Direct-marketing Process
The direct-marketing process has five main steps. The direct marketer's challenge is to manage these steps and build a relationship with the consumer.

prospects, as well as set objectives); (2) the communication of an offer (the message) by the seller through the appropriate medium; (3) response, or customer ordering; (4) fulfillment, or filling orders and handling exchanges and returns; and (5) maintenance of the company's database and customer service.

Objectives and Strategies   As in all planning processes, we begin by delineating the specific objective to achieve. Direct marketing has three primary objectives:

1. *Lead Generation.* Providing basic information on companies or individuals who are potential customers.
2. *Traffic Generation.* Motivating customers to visit an event, retail outlet, or other location.
3. *Action.* Order products and make payments or take some other action, such as visiting a dealer, returning a response card, or visiting a Web site.

The planner can then make these three basic objectives more concrete by specifying such factors as timing, amount of increase, and the consumer's specific behavior, such as where they see the product or what kind of action they might engage in. For example, a local Volvo dealership might expect its direct-marketing program to increase showroom traffic by 60 percent during the next 90 days.

The direct-marketing tools that achieve these objectives are: direct-response advertising, catalog, direct mail or e-mail, or telemarketing—separately or in some combination. Our Volvo dealer purchases a database of consumers who meet the criteria for a potential Volvo owner and sends out a direct-mail piece that offers $50 to anyone taking a test drive on a specific set of dates. This offer is repeated in the local newspaper. This whole process is known as prospecting. **Prospecting** is a technique of mining the information in databases

SHOWCASE

■ ■ ■

As part of an award-winning corporate identity program, the accounting firm Battelle & Battelle created a flexible kit composed of a pocket folder that could accommodate inserts of various kinds including simple sheets of information, a series of trifold brochures outlining the firm's services, and business cards. The new materials were launched with a series of postcards that invited prospective clients to learn more about the firm's capabilities. These materials were contributed by Amy Niswonger, designer at the Dayton-based Nova Creative Group, and a 2001 graphic design and marketing graduate from Miami University (Oxford, Ohio).

to uncover prospective buyers whose characteristics match those of users. Let's look more closely at "the offer."

The Offer   All direct marketing (DM) contains an *offer*, typically consisting of a description of the product, terms of sale, and payment and delivery information. In its offer, a successful DM campaign must communicate benefits to buyers by answering the enduring question: "What's in it for me?" Direct marketers might tell potential buyers of product benefits promotional tactics, such as buy-one-get-one-free.

An effective DM offer, as with all marketing offers, clearly calls on the buyer to take some action, as the TigerDirect.com cover illustrates. All the variables that are intended to satisfy the needs of the consumer are considered part of the offer. These variables include the price, the cost of shipping and handling, optional features, future obligations, availability of credit, extra incentives, time and quality limits, and guarantees or warranties. The offer is supported by a message strategy, a media strategy, and the database.

Message and Media Strategy   There are general guidelines that apply to message development in direct marketing. First, the message is often longer and contains more explanation and detail than regular advertising; especially in light of the fact that DM products are often unavailable in traditional retail outlets. Messages must contain clear comparisons or characteristics such as price, style, convenience, and so forth. Second, copy tends to be written in a personal, one-to-one conversational style. Third, the message should reflect whether the offer is a one-step offer or a two-step offer. A **one-step offer** asks for a direct sales response; it is crucial that there is a mechanism for responding to the offer. A **two-step offer** is designed to gather leads, answer consumer questions, drive to a computer store, or set up appointments. The design of the message must account for all these possibilities.

There are two types of media employed in direct marketing. In the case of direct-response advertising, traditional mass media are used to deliver the offer. Various print, broadcast, Internet, and other miscellaneous media are considered. The second kind is called **controlled media**, in that the direct marketer either owns the medium or contracts for a company to deliver the message using carefully controlled criteria. These media include catalogs, telemarketing, and direct mail. They also differ from traditional mass media in their ability to better target the consumer and deliver more complete information.

The Response/Order

Unlike advertising, in which the initial objective is to generate awareness, and the ultimate objective is to contribute to sales, all direct marketing aims to generate a behavioral response, especially sales. Generating a response is the third step in the direct-marketing process (see Figure 15.2). Consumer response may take the form of direct action (purchase, donation, subscription, and membership) or behaviors that precede purchase (attending a demonstration, participating in a taste test, test-driving a car, or asking for more information). Direct marketing prompts behavior by making a relevant offer and providing a mechanism for convenient purchase and fast delivery. KitchenAid's direct-response success story is the focus of an ad by direct-marketing company Respond2. To create urgency, the direct-marketing message may also include a promotional device such as a gift or limited-time-only price deal.

Fulfillment and Customer Maintenance

The next step in the direct-marketing process is called **fulfillment**—that is, getting the product to the customer who ordered it. Fulfillment includes all the back-end activities that the company's infrastructure is designed to make easy for the customer to respond to. The types of customer service offered, such as toll-free telephone numbers, free limited-time trials, and acceptance of several credit cards, are important techniques for overcoming customer resistance to buying through direct-response media. The most critical aspect of successful direct marketing, however, is maintaining a customer relationship. Direct marketers use a database to track customer interactions and transactions, the last step in Figure 15.2.

Evaluation

Direct marketing is not a "shot-in-the-dark" approach. DM professionals are able to continually evaluate and accurately measure the effectiveness of various offers in a single campaign. By employing such measurement tools as tracking printed codes on mail-in responses that identify different offers, and using different telephone numbers for

The cover of the TigerDirect.com mail-order magazine demonstrates how an effective direct marketer makes the offer, as well as the call to action, clear. The response numbers are also easy to find.

each commercial (by time slot, station, or length), the DM professional can clearly identify those offers that yield the best results, and modify the campaign to take advantage of them. Because of this constant evaluation, there is an emphasis in DM to learn what works and employ that information in succeeding efforts. Such accurate measurements and adjustments are largely responsible for DM's success.

Consider This

1. What is the greatest advantage of direct marketing? Why is it a growth industry?
2. What are the steps in the direct-marketing program?

DATABASE MARKETING

A database is at the heart of direct marketing. Direct marketers use **databases** to keep track of customers and identify prospective customers, and as a segmentation tool for communicating offers to customers and prospects. On one hand, building a database is the end of the direct-marketing process: Data are collected based on the customer's behavior and interaction with the company. However, if you look at relationship-driven communication programs as the ultimate goal of direct-response marketing, then the information gathered through customer interaction feeds back into the process and becomes an input for the next round of communication efforts. The database is important both at the beginning of the direct-marketing process, where it is a critical source of information, and at the end of the process, where it captures and updates information for the next interaction.

A direct-response company Respond2 (www.respond2.com) uses mini cases to demonstrate its success stories for new clients. This case explains how the legendary KitchenAid mixers found success over the Internet.

Database marketing is possible because of innovations in computer technology that have helped companies keep up with their customers. People move, have children, marry, divorce, remarry, retire, change purchase behavior, and so forth. The purpose of the database is to produce up-to-date information on customers and prospects, as well as their interactions with the company. **Database marketing** is a practice that uses databases to predict trends and monitor consumers to more effectively implement direct-marketing strategies. According to the Direct Marketing Association (DMA), a marketing database has four primary objectives:[1]

- To record names of customers, expires (names no longer valid), and prospects.
- To provide a vehicle for storing and then measuring results of advertising (usually direct-response advertising).
- To provide a vehicle for storing and then measuring purchasing performance.
- To provide a vehicle for continuing direct communication by mail or phone.

The database marketing process is illustrated in Figure 15.3. It begins with an initial information-collection point (and also ends with data collection). This could be the completion of a warranty card, entering a contest or sweepstake, opting in on a Web site, or filling out a card at a trade show, to name a few. The second stage is to enter the data into the computer to merge it with other information already in the file or added at the same time. Stage 3 allows the marketer to assess the data and determine the relevant level of detail. In stage 4, the direct marketer can

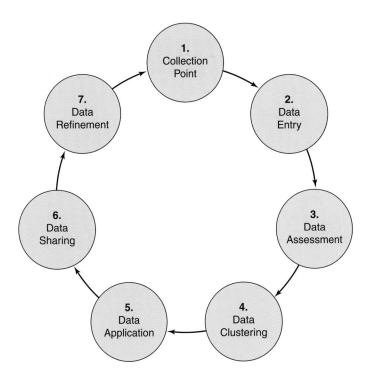

The Database Marketing Process
Using database marketing, advertisers can continually improve the effectiveness of their campaigns.

create clusters of characteristics and behaviors representing valuable consumer segments or target markets (audiences). Stage 5 applies the database to the specific marketing problems or strategies. An example might be sending coupons to a particular customer segment. In stage 6, the direct marketer makes decisions about data sharing and partnerships. A manufacturer may decide its retail outlets could use the data. Finally, the database goes through a refinement process that includes corrections, updates, additions, and deletions—information that is fed back into the planning process.

Principle
A reliable database of customer and prospect contact information lies at the heart of effective direct marketing.

If either expertise or resources are lacking, a company can obtain commercial databases from firms whose sole purpose is to collect, analyze, categorize, and market an enormous variety of detail about the American consumer. Companies such as National Decision Systems, Persoft, and Donnelly Marketing Information Systems are only a few of the firms that provide these relational databases (that is, their databases contain information useful in segmenting, as well as the contact information). Donnelly, for example, developed Hispanic Portraits, a database of households that segments the U.S. Hispanic population into 18 cluster groups.

Lists

As Spiller and Baier explain in their book, "Lists and data are at the very core of direct marketing."[2] Direct-mail **lists** that match market segments identified in the advertising plan can be purchased or rented from list brokers. Direct-mail **list brokers** have thousands of lists tied to demographic, psychographic, and geographic breakdowns. They have classified their data on such characteristics as hobbies, affiliations, and personal influence, such as the Roman Alliance database of decision makers. Geography is a common classification and Americans' households can be broken down to their postal carrier routes. For instance, one company has identified 160 zip codes it calls "Black Enterprise" clusters, inhabited by "upscale, white-collar, black families" in major urban fringe areas.

New lists can be created by merging and purging. If you want to target older women in New England who play tennis, most major firms would be able to put together a list for you by combining lists, called **merging**, and deleting the repeated names, called **purging**. For example, you may want to develop a list of people who are in the market for fine furniture in your city. You could buy a list of new homebuyers and combine that with a list of people who live in a desirable census tract. These two lists together—a compiled list—

This is a postcard mailed to businesses involved in direct marketing. It offers 47 "buying influence selectors" including such things as job function, industry, and decision making.

would let you find people who have bought new homes in upscale neighborhoods. There are three types of lists: house lists, response lists, and compiled lists.

- *House List.* A **house list** of the marketer's own customers or members, its most important target market, probably its most valuable list. Stores offer credit plans, service plans, special sale announcements, and contests that require customers to sign up to maintain this link. Some stores, such as Radio Shack, fill in customers' names and addresses at the cash register, and those customers join the list.
- *Response List.* Derived from people who respond to something such as a direct-mail offer or solicitation, a **response list** is similar to the advertiser's target audience. For example, if you sell dog food, you might like a list of people who have responded to a magazine ad for a pet identification collar; such lists are usually available for rent from the original direct-mail marketer. Those on the list indicate a willingness to buy pet items, and possibly, by direct mail.
- *Compiled List.* A **compiled list** is rented from a direct-mail list broker. It is usually a list of some specific category, such as sports car owners, new homebuyers, graduating seniors, new mothers, association members, or subscribers to a magazine, book club, or record club.

Data-driven Communication

Gathering information about customers and prospects is also the beginning of a new round of interaction. Using the insights captured from previous interactions to create **data-driven communication**, companies are better able to respond to and interact with their customers. Keeping track of interactions lets the company respond with some sense of the customer's interests, as well as the history of the customer's relationship with the company. Ultimately, the knowledge in the database is the tool used to build and maintain customer relationships, as the Matter of Principle box explains.

Principle

Data-driven communication lets the brand speak with a sense of the history of the customer relationship because it tracks the customer's interactions with the brand.

Today, computers and database software programs are getting smarter. Services such as Prodigy not only provide the user with online buying services, but also remember purchases and, over time, can build a purchase profile of each user. This kind of information is valuable to marketers, resellers, and their agencies. It's also of concern to consumer activists and consumers who worry about privacy.

Nintendo uses its 2-million-name database when it introduces more powerful versions of its video game system. The names and addresses are gathered from a list of

A MATTER OF PRINCIPLE
The Principles of Data-driven Relationships

Don Peppers and Martha Rogers, PhD

Enterprises that are building successful customer relationships understand that becoming customer focused doesn't begin with installing technology. It's not better-targeted and more efficient harassment (although you can't tell it when you look at a lot of the current efforts of "database marketing").

Becoming a customer-centric enterprise is about using insights into individual customers to gain a competitive advantage. It is an enterprise-wide approach to understanding and influencing customer behavior through meaningful communications, to improve customer acquisition, customer retention, and customer profitability. Defined more precisely, however, and what makes "one-to-one" into a truly different model for doing business and competing in the marketplace, is this: It is an enterprise business strategy for achieving customer-specific objectives by taking customer-specific actions. In essence, one-to-one is about treating different customers differently.

The overall business goal of this strategy will be to optimize the long-term profitability of the enterprise by increasing the value of the customer base. Building the value of customers increases the value of the "demand chain," the stream of business that flows from the customer up through the retailer all the way to the manufacturer. A customer-centric enterprise interacts directly with an individual customer.

Relationships are the crux of the customer-focused enterprise. The exchange between a customer and the enterprise becomes mutually beneficial, as customers give information in return for personalized service that meets their individual needs. This interaction forms the basis of the **learning relationship**, an intimate, collaborative dialogue between the enterprise and the customer that grows smarter and smarter with each successive interaction. The learning relationship works like this:

If you're my customer and I get you to talk to me, I remember what you tell me, and I get

smarter and smarter about you. I know something about you my competitors don't know. So I can do things for you my competitors can't do, because they don't know you as well as I do. Before long, you can get something from me you can't get anywhere else, for any price. At the very least you'd have to start all over somewhere else, but starting over is more costly than staying with us.

Even if a competitor were to establish exactly the same capabilities, a customer already involved in a learning relationship with the enterprise would have to spend time and energy—sometimes a lot of time and energy—teaching the competitor what the current enterprise already knows. This creates a significant *switching cost* for the customer, as the value of what the enterprise is providing continues to increase, partly as the result of the customer's own time and effort. The result is that the customer becomes more loyal to the enterprise, because it is simply in the customer's own interest to do so. As the relationship progresses, the enterprise becomes more valuable to the customer, allowing the enterprise to protect its profit margin with the customer, often while reducing the cost of serving that customer.

Learning relationships provide the basis for a completely new arena of competition, quite separate and distinct from traditional, product-based competition. An enterprise cannot prevent its competitor from offering a product or service that is perceived to be as good as its own offering.

Consider This

1. What do Peppers and Rogers mean by one-to-one marketing, and what are its advantages?
2. What is a learning relationship, and why is that important to a company or brand?

Don Peppers and Martha Rogers, PhD, are the founders of the Peppers and Rogers Group, a management-consulting firm that specializes in customer-based business strategy. Among their many accomplishments, Peppers and Rogers have authored numerous works, including the influential books *The One to One Future* and *Enterprise One to One*.

subscribers to its magazine, *Nintendo Power*. The company believes that many of its current customers will want to trade up systems and this direct communication will make it possible for Nintendo to speak directly to its most important target market about new systems as they become available. Nintendo began its database in 1988 and credits database marketing with helping it maintain its huge share of the $6 to $7 billion video game market.

Customer Relationship Management (CRM)

One of the most powerful tools to emerge from database marketing, **customer relationship management (CRM)**, is a result of the improved management of information contained in customer databases. CRM identifies and analyzes patterns in customer behavior to maximize the profitability of each relationship. It has been described as integrating and aligning "the people, processes, and technologies of all the business functions that touch the customer—marketing, sales, and customer service."[3] In Figure 15.2, customer relationship management is step 5, but notice that it begins at step 3, the response/order.

Behind CRM is highly developed database software that establishes links between transactions and the corresponding customers' characteristics. Armed with this knowledge, the company can pursue strategies to improve services that are important to its most profitable customers, attract new customers with similar characteristics, reward best customers, and identify and eliminate those customer relationships that drain company resources.

There are many examples of the successful use of CRM to improve customer relationships and services. Consider the true story of someone who flies nearly 2 million miles annually on American Airlines. While he was preparing to fly from San Diego to New York on a recent trip, the plane developed mechanical problems on the ground. Before this person even started to inquire, an American Airlines' Special Services person came aboard, escorted him off the plane, handed him a ticket for another flight to San Diego, and sent him on his way. These positive experiences are based on the ultimate principle of CRM: identifying a company's most profitable customers and giving them something that makes them feel prized and privileged.

Consider This

1. What is the role of databases in direct marketing?
2. Why is data-driven communication considered to be more customer focused than more traditional mass-media advertising?

THE KEY PLAYERS

There are four main players in direct-response marketing: advertisers who use direct response to sell products or services; agencies that specialize in direct-response advertising; the media that deliver messages by phone, mail, or the Web; and consumers, who are the recipients of the information and sometimes the initiator of the contact.

The Advertisers

More than 12,000 firms are engaged in direct-response marketing. Their primary business is selling products and services by mail or telephone. This number does not include the many retail stores that use direct marketing as a supplemental marketing communication program. Traditionally, the types of companies that have made the greatest use of direct marketing have been book and record clubs, publishers, insurance companies, sellers of collectibles, manufacturers of packaged foods, and gardening firms.

Dell has built a huge direct-marketing business selling computers directly to consumers rather than through dealers, as its competitors do.[4] Why don't Compaq, Hewlett-Packard, and IBM copy the Dell model and sell computers directly? For one thing, their retail dealers, who deliver big sales to these companies, would retaliate if these companies started experimenting with direct sales. Furthermore, it takes a lot of effort and infrastructure to set up a direct-marketing business. Rather than an army of sales reps, Dell employs an army of people in fulfillment who take the order, find the product, handle the money, and arrange for the shipping.

The Agencies

The four types of firms in direct-response advertising include advertising agencies, independent direct-marketing agencies, service firms, and fulfillment houses, as the list below outlines.

- *Advertising Agencies.* Agencies whose main business is mass-media advertising either have a department that specializes in direct response or own a separate direct-response company. Even if there isn't a special division or department, the staff of the agency may still be involved in producing direct-marketing pieces as the Inside Story explains.
- *Independent Agencies.* The independent, full-service, direct-marketing agencies specialize in direct response, and many of them are quite large. The largest direct-marketing agencies include some firms that specialize in only direct response and others that are affiliated with major agencies.
- *Service Firms.* Service firms specialize in supplying printing and mailing, and *list brokering.*
- *Fulfillment Houses.* The fulfillment house is a type of service firm that is vital to the success of many direct-marketing strategies. This is a business responsible for making sure consumers receive whatever they request in a timely manner, be it a catalog, additional information, or the product itself.

The Media Companies

Direct-marketing media include mail, phone, Web sites, and e-mail. In other words, all those can be used by the seller to make a contact with a prospect and by the customer to place an order or inquiry. One of the most active direct-mail marketers is the U.S. Postal Service. There are also thousands of telemarketing and Web marketing firms that handle contact with consumers.

The Customers

Although people might dislike the intrusiveness of direct-response advertising, many appreciate the convenience. It is a method of purchasing goods in a society that is finding itself with more disposable income but with less time to spend it. Stan Rapp, an expert on direct marketing, described this type of consumer as "a new generation of consumers armed with push-button phones and a pocket full of credit cards getting instant gratification by shopping and doing financial transactions from the den or living room."[5] The

These three little brochures were created by the U.S. Postal Service to explain the benefits of direct-mail advertising. Each one is focused on a different consumer response from interest, to awareness, to sales.

THE INSIDE STORY
Shaping the World of Miss Hall's School

Peter Stasiowski, Art Director, Gargan Communication, Dalton, Massachusetts

Gargan Communication was hired by Miss Hall's School, a small, upscale New England girls' prep school, to produce a series of direct-mail pieces for its annual fund-raising campaign. It was primarily a design assignment. The client came to us already having a carefully maintained mailing list, a theme, format, and vision of the desired size of the pieces.

The target market was former students and past donors and the client provided us with samples of direct-mail pieces they've used in previous years, and the theme: Shape the World. Based on this theme, we decided that a series of brochures, each focusing on a current student, "her story," and how the school has influenced her maturation would be a solid concept to develop further. The girls featured in the pieces were selected by the school, interviewed by one of our writers, and photographed.

The photography came out wonderfully, so I decided to make it the cornerstone of the design. I also wanted to make a connection between the photography and the theme of Shape the World.

Sometimes the most effective design concepts are the ones right in front of your face: Shape the World? How about Shape OF the World! Thinking that an overt "globe" theme might be a bit clichéd, I decided to use long arcs and subtle lines, reminiscent of the longitude and latitude lines seen on a globe, to create the feeling of Shape the

World without making the piece look like it was designed by a geography buff. It was a delicate balance.

Once the arcs and lines were in place, I created a small visual for the theme that not only reinforced the concept, but gave the design a much needed visual anchor; after all, the arcs and lines looked nice, but without context, "they're really just arcs and lines," I thought. At the meeting where we presented the original rough of the idea to the client, we decided that since there were seven girls to be featured, we should choose seven different background colors to pick up on the colors in the photography, and at the same time, communicate the cultural diversity of the school's student body.

The production of the pieces required some detailed and time-consuming Photoshop work, a few rounds of press proofs, and the extension of a deadline or two, but by that time everyone involved was completely sold on the concept and execution; these issues became secondary to creating a final piece to be proud of.

This process will begin again soon, as we have been asked to design the direct-mail pieces for next year's campaign.

Peter Stasiowski, a Massachusetts native, graduated in 1991 from the University of West Florida with a BA in Communication Arts with an emphasis in advertising and public relations. He is presently an art director at Gargan Communication, a marketing and advertising agency in Dalton, Massachusetts.

Nominated by Professor Tom Groth, University of West Florida

push-button shopper is joined by an even larger group of mouse-clicking shoppers. It takes some daring to order a product you can't see, touch, feel, or try out. These consumers are confident and willing to take a chance but don't like to be disappointed.

Consider This

1. Who are the key players in direct marketing?
2. What are the risks you face in buying something through direct marketing?

THE TOOLS OF DIRECT MARKETING

Direct marketing employs five primary tools to achieve its objectives. These strategic tools are direct mail, catalogs, telemarketing, and direct-response advertising as well as Web-based e-marketing.

Direct Mail

Direct mail is the granddaddy of direct response and still commands big marketing dollars. A direct-mail piece is a print advertising message for a product or service that is delivered by mail. It may be as simple as a single-page letter or as complex as a package consisting of a letter, a brochure, supplemental flyers, and an order card with a return envelope. A 2 to 5 percent response rate is considered typical. Most direct mail is sent using the third-class bulk mail permit, which requires a minimum of 200 identical pieces. Third class is cheaper than first class, but it takes longer for delivery. Estimates of nondelivery of third-class mail run as high as 8 percent. As summarized in Table 15.1 direct mail has a number of advantages and disadvantages.

TABLE 15.1   Advantages and Disadvantages of Direct Mail

Advantages	Description
Tells a story	The medium offers a variety of formats and provides enough space to tell a complete sales story.
Engages attention	Because direct mail has little competition when it is received, it can engage the reader's attention.
Personalizes the message	Because of the use of databases, it is now possible to personalize direct mail across a number of consumer characteristics, such as name, product usage, purchase history, and income.
Builds in feedback	Direct mail is particularly conducive to marketing research and can be modified until the message design matches the needs of the desired target audience.
Reaches the unreachable	Direct mail allows the marketer to reach audiences who are inaccessible by other media.

Disadvantages	Description
Negative perceptions	The main drawback of using direct mail is the widespread perception that it is junk mail. According to a Harris-Equifax Consumer Privacy Survey, about 46 percent of the public see direct-mail offers as a nuisance, and 90 percent consider them an invasion of privacy.
Cost	Direct mail has a higher cost per thousand than mass media. A great deal of this high cost is a result of postage. (However, it reaches a more qualified prospect with less waste.) Another cost factor is the maintenance of the database.
Mailing list	To deliver an acceptable response rate, the quality of the mailing list is critical. It must be maintained and updated constantly.
Response rate	Because of the changing nature of mailing lists, as well as the difficulty of keeping relevant data in the database, the response rate can be as low as 2 or 3 percent. Even with that low response, however, database marketers can still make money.
Vulnerability	Direct-mail delivery is vulnerable to natural disasters as well as catastrophes such as the 9/11 terrorist attacks.

Direct-mail Message Design   How it looks is as important as what it says. Progressive direct marketers, supported by research findings, have discovered that the appearance of a direct-response ad—the character and personality communicated by the graphics—can enhance or destroy the credibility of the product information. The functions of a direct-mail message are similar to the steps in the sales process. The message must move the reader through the entire process, from generating interest to creating conviction and inducing a sale. And it's all done with a complex package of printed pieces. The Practical Tips box is a helpful guide for putting together direct-mail pieces.

Practical Tips

Creating Effective Direct Mail

* Get the attention of the targeted prospect as the envelope comes from the mailbox.
* Create a need for the product, show what it looks like, and demonstrate how it is used.
* Answer questions, as a good salesperson does, and reassure the buyer.
* Provide critical information about product use.
* Inspire confidence, minimize risk, and establish that the company is reputable.
* Make the sale by explaining how to buy, how to order, where to call, and how to pay for the purchase.
* Use an incentive to encourage a fast response.

Most direct-mail pieces follow a fairly conventional format. The packaging usually consists of an outer envelope, a letter, a brochure, supplemental flyers or folders, and a reply card with a return envelope. These can be one-page flyers, multipanel folders, multi-page brochures, or spectacular **broadsheets** that fold out like maps big enough to cover the top of a table. The most critical decision made by the target is whether to read the mailing or throw it away, and that decision is based on the outer envelope. The envelope should state the offer on the outside and spark curiosity through a creative idea.

A mailing for the Denver Rescue Mission used a most unusual mailer—a brown paper lunch bag—to get people's attention. Because 80 percent of its funds are collected in the last four months of the year, the Mission needed to create a unique campaign to help fund its annual Thanksgiving dinner for the homeless as well as its other year-long services. In addition to the simple brown paper sandwich bag, the mailer included a message explaining how donors could buy a Thanksgiving dinner for a homeless person for $1.79 and a peel-off label they could use to send their check to the Denver Mission. The bag had "a second life," to make it more than a direct-mail piece: Donors could reuse it for their own lunch as a reminder of the meals they were giving others. The campaign proved very effective, with responses 51 percent higher than campaigns for the previous three years. It provided for more than 2,600 dinners and was awarded the Direct Marketing Association's Gold Echo award for the most innovative use of direct mail.

Historically, the letter has been the most difficult element in a direct-mail package. Over the years many techniques have proven effective in getting consumers to read a direct-mail letter. Dean Rieck, an internationally respected direct-response copywriter, designer, and consultant, offers these hints for writing an effective letter.[6]

1. *Attention.* To grab attention or generate curiosity, use pictures and headlines that tout the product's benefits.
2. *Personalize.* Use a personalized salutation. If the individual's name is not available, the salutation should at least be personalized to the topic, such as, "Dear Cat Lover."
3. *Lead-in.* The best way to begin a letter is with a brief yet compelling or surprising statement—"Dear Friend: I could really kick myself!"
4. *The Offer.* Make the offer as early in the body of the letter as possible.

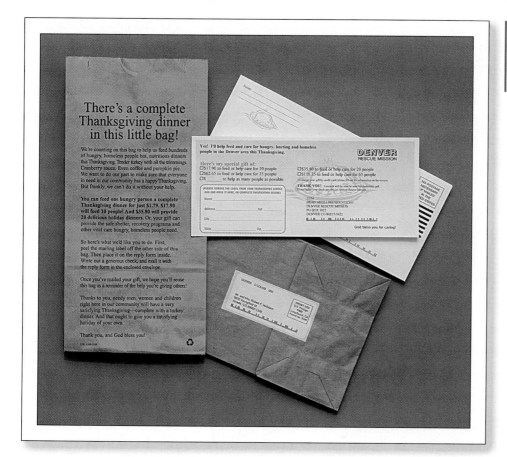

The Denver Rescue Mission used an unusual—and attention-getting—mailing that featured a brown lunch bag.

5. *The Letter.* The letter should use testimonials or other particulars that clearly describe benefits to the customer.
6. *The Closing.* The closing of the letter should include a repetition of the offer, additional incentives or guarantees, and a clear call to action.

Catalogs

A **catalog** is a multipage direct-mail publication that shows a variety of merchandise. The big books are those produced by such retail giants as JCPenney and L.L.Bean. As databases improve, catalog marketers are refining their databases and culling consumers who receive catalogs but don't order from them. Even though catalog marketers are cutting back on the waste in their mailings, there are still a lot of catalogs in mailboxes. L.L.Bean mails to more than 115 million customers and Lillian Vernon mails more than 175 million catalogs a year. Catalogs are the chief beneficiaries of the social changes that are making armchair shopping so popular. However, the catalog marketer must make sure the ordering process is easy and risk free. Catalogs have become so popular that direct-response consumers receive mailings offering them lists of catalogs available for a fee. People pay for these catalogs the way they pay for magazines and an increasing number of catalogs can be purchased at newsstands.

Some of these retailers have their own stores, such as Williams-Sonoma and Tiffany's. Banana Republic began as a catalog marketer and then moved into retailing. Others, such as Hanover House and FBS, offer their merchandise only through catalogs or other retailers. Some of the merchandise is inexpensive, such as the Hanover line, which usually offers items for $10 or less. In contrast, marketers such as Dell computer offer more expensive products costing hundreds of dollars.

The real growth in this field is in the area of specialty catalogs. There are catalogs for every hobby, as well as for more general interests. There are catalogs specifically for

Alsto's is an example of a home-catalog direct marketer that employs beautiful photography and high-quality paper and printing to convey its upscale image.

purses, rings, cheese and hams, stained-glass supplies, garden benches, and computer accessories, to name just a few. Balducci's fruit and vegetable store in Greenwich Village, New York, produces a catalog promising overnight delivery of precooked gourmet meals. There are advantages and disadvantages of catalogs. They are listed in Table 15.2.

A number of advertisers are using video catalogs because these provide more information about their products. Consumers can also go online and review several catalogs, make comparisons, and place orders. Buick developed an electronic catalog on CD. The message is interactive and features animated illustrations. It presents graphic descriptions and detailed text on the Buick line, including complete specifications, that lets you custom-design your dream car. The electronic catalog has also been marketed to readers of computer magazines.

Telemarketing

More direct-marketing dollars are spent on **telemarketing**—ads delivered through phone calls—than on any other medium. That's because telemarketing is almost as persuasive as personal sales, but a lot less expensive. A personal sales call may cost anywhere from $50 to $100 after factoring in time, materials, and transportation. A telephone solicitation may range from $2 to $5 per call, or a CPM of $2,000 to $5,000. That is still expensive if you compare the cost of a telephone campaign to the CPM of an advertisement placed in any one of the mass media ($10–$50); however, the returns are much higher than those generated by mass advertising.

A typical telemarketing campaign usually involves about 75 people making 250,000 calls over three months.[7] These callers work in **call centers**, which are rooms with large banks of phones and computers. Most calls are made from databases that contain prospects who were previously qualified on some factor, such as an interest in a related product or a particular profile of demographics and psychographics. Occasionally **cold-calling** is used, which means the call center staff are calling unqualified numbers, sometimes just randomly selected, and this practice has a much lower response rate.

Types of Telemarketing   There are two types of telemarketing: inbound and outbound. An **inbound** or incoming **telemarketing** call originates with the customer. The consumer can be responding to an ad or a telemarketing message received earlier. L.L.Bean's advertising often draws attention to its telephone representatives' friendly and helpful manner. Calls originating with the firm are outgoing; these **outbound telemarketing** calls are the ones that generate the most consumer resistance.

Criticisms of Telemarketing   Telemarketing does have its drawbacks. Perhaps the most universally despised telemarketing tool is **predictive dialing**. Predictive dialing technology makes it possible for telemarketing companies to call anyone—even those with unlisted numbers. Special computerized dialing programs use random dialing. This explains why, from time to time, when you answer your phone you simply hear a dial tone; the predictive dialer has called your number before a call agent is free. For many people, such an interruption is only a nuisance; but because some burglars have been known to call a house to see if anyone's home before they attempt a break-in, many people find such calls alarming.

TABLE
15.2   **Advantages and Disadvantages of Catalogs**

Advantages	Description
Targeted	Can be directed at specific market segments.
Engages attention	Employs high-quality design and photography (see Alsto's cover).
Complete information	Extensive product information and comparisons are provided.
Convenience	Offer a variety of purchase options.

Disadvantages	Description
Negative perceptions	Catalogs are viewed as junk mail by many recipients.
Costs	The cost per thousand of catalogs is higher than mass media.
Response rate	The response is relatively low at 3 to 4 percent.
Mailing list	Databases must be constantly maintained.

Another problem associated with telemarketing, and one that has tarnished its reputation, is fraudulent behavior, such as promising a product or service in exchange for an advance payment, convincing consumers they need some kind of financial or credit protection that they don't really need, or enticing consumers to buy something by promising them prizes that are later discovered to be worthless. In response to these abuses in telemarketing, the Federal Trade Commission enacted the Telemarketing Sales Rule (TSR) in 1995 to protect consumers. Among other things, the TSR prohibits telemarketers from calling before 8 A.M. or after 9 P.M.; it imposes strict informational disclosure requirements; it prohibits misrepresentative or misleading statements; and it provides for specific payment collection procedures. More recently, FTC regulations require telemarketing firms to identify themselves on caller ID.[8]

The most serious restriction on telemarketing is coming from various state and national "do-not-call" lists. Some 30 states have set up these lists and a national do-not-call list took effect in 2003. The national Do Not Call Registry had 31.6 million sign-ups even before it took effect.[9] (To register go to donotcall.gov and sign up.) The effect has been to drastically reduce the number and size of call centers. Telemarketing companies have responded by challenging the legality of these lists in court based on what they believe to be an illegal restriction on commercial free speech. Telemarketers were unhappy in late 2004 when the U.S. Supreme Court let stand a lower-court ruling that the industry's free-speech rights were not violated by the national do-not-call list.[10]

Phone companies also offer their customers a service called "Privacy Manager" that screens out sales calls.[11] For customers who have Caller ID, numbers that register as "unavailable" or "unknown" are intercepted by a recorded message that asks callers to identify themselves. If the caller does so, the call rings through.

Telemarketing Message Design   The key point to remember about telemarketing solicitations is that the message has to be simple enough to be delivered over the telephone. If the product requires a demonstration or a complicated explanation, then the message might be better delivered by direct mail. The

Call centers are large rooms with multiple stations for staff who make the calls (outbound) or answer calls from people placing orders (inbound).

message also must be compelling. People resent intrusive telephone calls, so there must be a strong initial benefit or reason-why statement to convince prospects to continue listening. The message also must be short; most people won't stay on the telephone longer than 2 to 3 minutes for a sales call.

Direct-response Advertising

The common thread that runs through all types of direct-response advertising is that of *action.* The move to action is what makes direct-response advertising effective. However, some advertisers see direct response as less effective than brand or image advertising because it doesn't reach as many people or, if it does, the cost of reaching each individual is very high. This is believed to be justified because the objective is action rather than recall or attitude change. Today the high-cost argument is being reconsidered. Although it costs a lot per impression, direct-response advertising, particularly direct mail, is well targeted. It reaches a prime audience; people who are likely, for reasons related to their demographics or lifestyles, to be interested in the product.

Print Media Ads in the mass media are less directly targeted than are direct mail and catalog but they can still provide the opportunity for a direct response. Ads in newspapers and magazines can carry a coupon, an order form, an address, or a toll-free or 900 telephone number. The response may be either to purchase something or to ask for more information. In many cases the desired response is an inquiry that becomes a sales lead for field representatives.

In their book *MaxiMarketing,* direct-marketing experts Stan Rapp and Tom Collins discuss the power of double-duty advertising that combines brand-reinforcement messages with a direct-response campaign by using a premium, a sample, or a coupon.[12] American Express used this double-duty concept when it launched *Your Company,* a quarterly mailed to more than 1 million American Express corporate card members who own small businesses. Four sponsors launched *Your Company:* IBM, United Parcel Service, Cigna Small Business Insurance, and American Express Small Business Services. Such efforts combine the editorial direction of a magazine with direct advertising's ability to target a narrow audience based on demographics and lifestyle. Magazines have been trying to do this with demographic editions and selective bindings as well.

In magazines, response cards may be either **bind-ins** or **blow-ins**. Both are free-standing cards that are physically separate from the ad they support. Bind-in cards are stapled or glued right into the binding of the magazine adjoining the ad. They have to be torn out to be used. Blow-in cards are attached to the magazine after it is printed by special machinery that puffs open the pages. These cards are loose and may fall out in distribution, so they are less reliable.

Broadcast Media Television is a good medium for direct marketers who are advertising a broadly targeted product. A direct-response commercial on radio or TV can provide the necessary information (usually a toll-free 800 phone number or Web address) for the consumer to request information or even make a purchase. Direct-response advertising on television used to be the province of the late-night TV with pitches for vegematics and screwdrivers guaranteed to last a lifetime. Radio's big advantage is its targeted audience. For example, teenagers are easy to reach through radio. Also, radio has had some success selling products such as cellular phones and paging systems specifically to a mobile audience. Radio is often used to supplement other forms of direct response. For example, publishers use radio to alert people that a sweepstakes mailing is beginning and to encourage participation.

Cable television lends itself to direct response because the medium is more tightly targeted to particular interests. QVC and the Home Shopping Network reach more than 70 million households and service their calls with huge phone banks. As more national marketers such as GEICO move into the medium, the direct-response commercial is becoming more general in appeal, selling clothes and entertainment, as well as insurance and financial services.

Direct-response TV also makes good use of the infomercial format. The Salton-Maxim Juiceman infomercial took the company from $18 million to $52 million in sales overnight and made a marketing superstar of George Forman. Infomercials blur the lines

A MATTER OF PRACTICE
GEICO Delivers a "Good News" Story

How do you sell car insurance by direct marketing? GEICO is the leading direct-response auto insurer in a low-involvement category dominated by major brands, such as Allstate and State Farm. Its biggest marketing challenge is to generate inquiries for rate quotes, to motivate people to call or go online to find out how they can save money, which is reflected in its long-standing brand promise, "15 minutes could save you 15 percent or more on car insurance."

GEICO's advertising, under the direction of the Martin Agency, is guided by aggressive objectives that include significant increases in total rate-quote volume and in new policies written as a result of these quotes, as well as a continual upward trend in key advertising indicators including brand awareness and ad recall.

The advertising has used humor to stand out from the pack, particularly in the use of its unique brand character, the little green GEICO gecko. To face the growing competition, the Richmond, Virginia–based agency recommended a new "Good News" TV campaign that largely spoofs TV and radio programming. For example, a "Baseball" TV spot airs during baseball season and a "Soap Opera" spot during daytime TV. Other parodies and their media programs include weather and traffic spots, hair-growth infomercials, home-improvement shows, as well as a congressional investigation reported as a newscast.

The idea was to associate the "Good News" scenario with the idea of saving money in unexpected ways. In addition to a national average for savings, the spots could be modified to use specific savings figures for a particular market. The memorable and entertaining campaign not only communicated the savings message, but it also associated GEICO with the "good news." The campaign was so successful that it was parodied by ESPN, the *Today Show*, Jim Carrey on the *Conan O'Brien Show*, comic strips, and local newscasters, and even in an announcement by an airline pilot.

It was most successful, however, in overcoming consumer inertia, driving customers to their phones and the Internet, and accomplishing its aggressive objectives—resulting in the highest level of inquiries in company history.

With success like this, you can understand why GEICO's "Good News" and Gecko campaigns have received so much industry attention.

Consider This

1. What is the biggest problem selling car insurance by direct marketing?
2. How did GEICO overcome this problem?

Source: EFFIEs brief and DMA ECHO brief provided by The Martin Agency and GEICO.

between retail and direct response. The Salton commercial made Juiceman the brand to buy, whether direct from television or from a local department store or mass merchant. Infomercials have been around since the emergence of the cable industry and have become a multibillion-dollar industry. An infomercial is typically 30 or 60 minutes long and tends to be played during non-prime-time periods.

Today, the infomercial is viewed as a viable medium because: (1) consumers now have confidence in infomercials and the products they sell; (2) with the involvement of upscale

■ ■ ■

Television shopping networks handle sales orders by using hundreds of customer service agents.

advertisers, the quality of infomercial production and supportive research has improved; (3) consumers can be better segmented and infomercials are coordinated with respect to these audiences; and (4) infomercials can easily be introduced into foreign markets. Finally, advertisers might use the infomercial format if their product needs to be demonstrated, is not readily available through retail outlets, and has a relatively high profit margin.

The Internet and Direct Response

Direct marketers saw the Internet's potential early. Actually, direct marketing—particularly catalog marketing—is the model for e-commerce. The Internet provides the same components found in direct mail and telemarketing. Amazon.com is the leader of the pack but other companies that sell merchandise direct include Columbia House Online (www.columbiahouse.com), L.L.Bean (www.llbean.com), Wal-Mart Online (www.walmart .com), Gridland (www.gridland.net), and CDNow (www.cdnow .com). The Web is moving marketers much closer to one-to-one marketing.

Another feature of Internet direct marketing is greater sampling opportunities. Online music stores now have hundreds of thousands of music clips for shoppers to listen to before making a purchase. Eddie Bauer lets site visitors "try on" clothes in a virtual dressing room. It also sends them e-mail messages offering special prices on items based on their past purchasing patterns.

The Internet is also providing companies with new ways to gather information on consumers. One of the more ambitious is allowing consumers to create their own network of contacts for marketers to promote across. The giant bookseller Amazon.com owns PlanetAll, a Web-based address book, calendar, and reminder service. A subscriber enters friends' information and then Amazon can not only remind these subscribers about upcoming birthdays, but also suggest books that those friends and relatives have indicated they'd like to receive as gifts.

The technology of the Internet has produced dramatic changes in the direct-mail industry. At a most basic level, the Internet has facilitated the ease in producing and distributing traditional direct mail. Take USA Direct, which introduced the USAMailNow Web site in early 2001. This company identified the most frustrating and time-consuming processes of direct-mailing campaigns and constructed a Web site that does these processes for companies. USAMailNow's streamlined process allows a company of any size to point and click its way through a series of choices to make predesigned mailer templates priced and sorted by industry, mailing lists, and various mail media (postcards, letters, flyers, or newsletters), which customers can customize with their logo and other proprietary images or copy.

The use of e-mail as a marketing tool has not been restricted to the usual e-commerce companies. Well-known corporate brands such as BMW now are getting into the act. In one campaign, it requested existing and prospective customers to view a collection of Web movies about new BMW models. Another campaign notified BMW owners of a new section at BMW.com that was reserved strictly for their use. Called the "Owner's Circle," the section allowed owners to obtain special services and set up profiles that tracked maintenance items specific to their cars. Shortly after the mailing, enrollment in the Owner's Circle doubled, and participation in BMW's financial services program tripled.[13]

On a more sophisticated level, the Internet has begun to reconcile an ongoing conflict within the direct-mail industry: the debate over sending small, personalized mailings or big, mass mailings. With their long letters, ornate brochures, free gift enclosures, and other attention-grabbing devices, personalized mailings were thought to grab consumers' attention. However, this attention came at a high per-unit price and so personalized mailings have a limited scope. In contrast, cheaper mass media (postcards, short form letters, flyers, and newsletters) were particularly well suited to boosting a company's reach and frequency. Unfortunately, they lacked much of the allure of their more personalized cousins. How has the Internet helped reconcile this debate? Today, the utilization of extensive database information and innovative e-mail technology, combined with creative marketing strategies, has brought the benefits of highly personalized, inexpensive messages to far-reaching mass campaigns.

Spam and Permission Marketing   Although e-mail marketing has enjoyed increased success, the practice has received intense criticism for generating too much unwanted e-mail, otherwise known as **spam**. The FTC has determined that 90 percent of all spam involving business and investment opportunities contains false or misleading information. The problem also exists with nearly half of the messages advertising health products and travel and leisure. This is why Congress passed the CAN-SPAM Act in 2003.[14] The problem is so big that some industry experts estimate that more than half of all e-mail messages are spam.[15] Amazon has filed lawsuits in U.S. and Canadian courts to stop e-mail spammers it says have been fraudulently using its identity to send out spam, a practice known as **spoofing**.[16] One of the largest telemarketing companies, OptInRealBig, has been sued by the State of New York, as well as by Microsoft, whose Explorer service is bombarded with e-mail spam, for allegedly sending misleading and fraudulent e-mail solicitations.[17]

This is a huge problem for legitimate direct marketers who have responded to the criticism in two ways. For one, companies now search their rich databases for customers' buying habits or recent purchases. They then send these customers e-mail that offer deals on related products and connect it to their customer's previous interactions with the company. More recently, direct marketers have used a second approach called **permission marketing** to reduce criticism about spam. Permission marketing gives customers an opportunity to *opt-in* to a notification service from a company. The e-mail will ask if the recipient wants further e-mails and wants to be on the mailing list. When opting-in, customers are often asked to complete a questionnaire about their purchasing habits or other information, which is used to personalize the service.

Permission marketing also gives customers an opportunity to *opt-out* of the service when they no longer need a company's product or services. They can sometimes even *opt-down* by reducing how frequently they receive messages. So customers gain control over the amount and type of e-mail messages they receive, and companies reduce wasted resources on marketing to uninterested individuals. They also gain valuable insight into their customers' habits and interests. The concept at the heart of permission marketing is that every customer who opts-in to a campaign is a qualified lead.[18]

Consider This

1. What are the primary direct-marketing tools?
2. Which of these tools do you feel is most useful to direct marketers trying to build a long-term customer relationship? Why?

INTEGRATED DIRECT MARKETING

Historically, direct marketing is the first area of marketing communication that adopted an integrated marketing approach. In fact, it would be appropriate to rename direct marketing *integrated direct marketing*. As technology has provided more and better ways to interact with customers, the challenge to direct marketers has been to integrate direct mail, catalogs, telemarketing, Web sites, e-mail, text messaging, and instant messaging with other marketing communication, such as advertising.

One reason integration plays so well in the direct-response market is because of its emphasis on the customer. The coordination problem is exacerbated by the deluge of data bombarding direct marketers from many different channels. The only way to manage the information is to focus it around customer needs and interests. By using databases, companies can become more sensitive to customer wants and needs and less likely to bother them with unwanted commercial messages. **Integrated direct marketing (IDM)**, also known as **integrated relationship marketing**, can be defined as a systematic way to get close to your best current, and potential customers. Sharon Henderson, CEO of a direct-marketing agency, explains that "in the last couple of years the big marketers are saying 'we want integrated relationship marketing' and that means integrating at every customer touch point." For her agency that means developing total business-solution programs.[19]

Linking the Channels

Instead of treating each medium separately, as advertising agencies tend to do, integrated direct-marketing companies seek to achieve precise, synchronized use of the right media at the right time, with a measurable return on dollars spent. Here's an example: Say you do a direct-mail campaign, which generates a 2 percent average response. If you include a toll-free 800 number in your mailing as an alternative to the standard mail-in reply—with well-trained, knowledgeable people handling those incoming calls with a carefully thought-out script—you can achieve a 3 to 4 percent response rate. If you follow up your mailing with a phone call within 24 to 72 hours after your prospect receives the mailing, you can generate a response two to eight times as high as the base rate of 2 percent. So, by adding your 800 number, you bring the response rate from 2 percent to 3 or 4 percent. By following up with phone calls, you bring your total response rate as high as 5 to 18 percent.

The principle behind integration is that not all people respond the same way to direct-response advertising. One person may carefully fill out the order form. Someone else may immediately call the 800 number. Most people, if an ad grabs them, tend to put it in the pending pile. That pile grows and grows, and then goes into the garbage at the end of the month. But if a phone call follows the direct-mail piece, the marketer may get the wavering consumer off the fence. Hewlett-Packard, AT&T, Citibank, and IBM have all used integrated direct marketing to improve their direct-marketing response rates.

Safeway Stores have become interested in integrated direct marketing. Essentially, Safeway has signed up manufacturers such as the Quaker Oats Co. and Stouffer Food Corp. (owned by Nestlé) for a database marketing program that provides trade dollars in exchange for quality customer data. The program exemplifies the convergence of two trends: Grocers are looking for manufacturers to supplement their own shrunken marketing budgets, and manufacturers eager to allocate new field marketing support dollars are working closer as partners. A number of manufacturers, whose products are carried in the store, contribute to Safeway's quarterly mailings in exchange for in-store support and sales data.

A common failure in direct-marketing integration is that direct-marketing messages and advertising messages often do not reinforce each other as well as they should because the two functions—advertising and direct marketing, which often are handled by different agencies—don't talk to one another. This will change, however, as clients demand more coordination of their marketing communication programs.

Creating Loyalty

Changing the attitude of the consumer toward direct marketing has not been easy because consumers resent companies that know too much about them. If the company can demonstrate that it is acting in the customer's best interest rather than just trolling for dollars, it might gain consumers' loyalty. Saks Fifth Avenue identified the customers who account for half of all sales and offered the group exclusive benefits through a program call Saks First. The benefits include fashion newsletters and first crack at all sales.

Perhaps the most ambitious attempt to create consumer loyalty is through a concept called **lifetime customer value (LCV)**. LCV is an estimate of how much purchase volume companies can expect to get over time from various target markets. To put it formally, LCV is the financial contribution through sales volume of an individual customer or customer segment over a length of time. The calculation is based on known consumption habits plus future consumption expectations. The estimate of the contribution is defined as *return on investment*—that is, revenue gains as a function of marketing costs. In simpler terms, by knowing your consumers' past behavior, you can decide how much you want to spend to get them to purchase and then repurchase your product; you can track your investment by measuring the response.

Consider This

1. What is integrated direct marketing, and why is it important?
2. Explain lifetime customer value. Are you a customer of value to any marketer? Can you estimate your annual value (expenditures) to that brand or company?

GLOBAL CONSIDERATIONS IN DIRECT MARKETING

The direct-marketing industry is growing fast in many Far Eastern and European countries—in some places, even faster than in the United States. The global trend is fueled by the same technological forces driving the growth of direct marketing in the United States: the increasing use of computer databases, credit cards, toll-free phone numbers, and the Internet, and the search for more convenient ways to shop. The growth may be even greater in business-to-business marketing than in consumer marketing.

Direct marketing is particularly important in countries that have tight restrictions on advertising and other forms of marketing communication. However, there are restrictions on direct marketing, as well. The privacy issues are even more intense in some European countries than in the United States. In some countries, lists are not available or they may be of poor quality. Databases can be more freely transferred between European countries than they can between the United States and European countries.[20]

Governmental regulation of the postal service may also place limitations on the use of direct mail. For example, the format of the address has to be exactly correct in some countries, such as Germany, where the Deutsche Post has strict rules about correct address formats. For example, in Hungary the street name is in the third line of the address, whereas it is on the second line along with the postal code in Germany. Presorted mail in a wrong format may result in charges to the end user that significantly raise the cost of the mailing.

IT'S A WRAP

LIVING THE HARLEY DREAM

Direct marketing and its various tactics have evolved from "junk mail" to a highly regarded, effective means of marketing communication. This chapter has introduced you to these new direct-marketing tactics along with the trends for the future.

The results of Harley's "Attainability" campaign were impressive, gathering a higher than expected number of leads from the under-45-year-old category. The number of total leads generated exceeded the previous year by 8 percent.

The campaign was deemed to be a resounding success based on a number of quantifiable measurements:

- 81 percent of the leads were new to the Harley brand, and of this amount 38 percent did not currently own a motorcycle and 43 percent were current or previously owners of a competitive model.
- 62 percent were planning to purchase a motorcycle within the year.
- 60 percent were 44 years or younger.

Not only were the leads higher than expected, the conversion from simply being interested to actually visiting a dealership and/or buying a Harley was higher than expected.

• 60 percent of the leads visited a Harley dealer as a result of the campaign.
• More than 12 percent purchased a Harley, which was more than double the objective.
• Of the leads that did not purchase, 65 percent indicated that they anticipated buying a motorcycle in the future.

Finally, the campaign was determined to be highly cost-effective with the return on investment estimated at $1 : $17. In other words, for every dollar invested in the campaign, $17 dollars were received in sales.

Most importantly, the campaign reversed the trend of diminishing numbers among younger buyers. These were the results that led the "Attainability" campaign to be selected as an EFFIE winner and as a DMA Echo Award winner.

■ ■ ■ Summary

1. **Define and distinguish between direct marketing and direct-response advertising.** Direct marketing always involves a one-on-one relationship with the prospect. It is personal and interactive and uses various media to effect a measurable response. Direct-response advertising can use any advertising medium, but it has to provide some type of response or reply device to facilitate action.

2. **Explain types of direct marketing.** The direct-marketing industry includes direct-response advertising, database marketing, direct mail, catalog, and telemarketing.

3. **Name the players in direct marketing.** The four players in direct marketing are the advertisers, the agencies, the media, and the consumers.

4. **Evaluate the various media that direct-response programs can use.** Direct-response media include direct mail,

catalogs, telemarketing, print media, broadcast media, and the Internet.

5. **Explain how databases are used in direct marketing.** Direct-marketing advertising has benefited from the development and maintenance of a database of customer names, addresses, telephone numbers, and demographic and psychographic characteristics. Advertisers use this information to target their campaigns to consumers who, based on demographics, are likely to buy their products

6. **Discuss the role of direct marketing in integrated marketing programs.** Because direct marketing is close to the customer and is interactive, it fits very well into an integrated program. Direct marketers are accustomed to linking the channels of communication and delivering the same message using multiple sources that reinforce one another.

■ ■ ■ Key Terms

bind-ins, 440
blow-ins, 440
broadsheets, 436
call centers, 438
catalog, 437
cold-calling, 438
compiled list, 430
controlled media, 427
customer relationship management (CRM), 432
databases, 428
database marketing, 428

data-driven communication, 430
direct mail, 435
direct marketing (DM), 423
direct-response advertising, 424
fulfillment, 427
house list, 430
inbound telemarketing, 438

integrated direct marketing (IDM), 444
integrated relationship marketing, 444
lead generation, 424
learning relationship, 431
lifetime customer value (LCV), 444
lists, 429
list brokers, 429
merging, 429

one-step offer, 427
outbound telemarketing, 438
permission marketing, 443
predictive dialing, 438
prospecting, 425
purging, 429
response list, 430
spam, 443
spoofing, 443
telemarketing, 438
two-step offer, 427

■■■ Review Questions

1. What principle, or objective, separates direct-response from other types of advertising?

2. What are the five steps in the direct-marketing process?

3. What is a database, and how do direct marketers use it?

4. Describe the four types of agencies involved in direct marketing.

5. What are the five tools used in direct-marketing programs?

6. How is integrated direct marketing used in an IMC program?

■■■ Discussion Questions

1. Most people hate telemarketing. Say you work for the local campus environmental organization. How could you conduct a campus and community telemarketing effort that would not generate resistance? How would you develop a telemarketing program to promote campus fund-raising? Would it be better to solicit money directly or indirectly by having people attend specially designed events? Your primary targets are students, faculty, and staff.

2. We know that copy and illustration are vital parts of a successful direct-mail campaign, but there must be some priorities. All of the components of creativity are important, but which are most important for direct-response creativity? What principles drive message design for direct marketing?

3. Hildy Johnson, a recent college graduate, is interviewing with a large garden-product firm that relies on television for its direct-response advertising. "Your portfolio looks very good. I'm sure you can write," the interviewer says, "but let me ask you what is it about our copy that makes it more important than copy written for Ford, or Pepsi, or Pampers?" What can she say that will help convince the interviewer she understands the special demands of direct-response writing?

4. One of the smaller, privately owned bookstores on campus is considering a direct-response service to cut down on its severe in-store traffic problems at the beginning of each semester. What ideas do you have for setting up some type of direct-response system to take the pressure off store traffic?

5. How does the recent fervor surrounding personal privacy affect direct marketing—specifically, telemarketing? In addition to legal issues, what consumer issues must media planners consider when designing a direct-marketing campaign?

6. The success of infomercials helps validate direct marketing as a revenue generator. What characteristics of a product must you consider when determining whether to use a direct-marketing campaign? An infomercial?

7. Amazon.com is one of the most-well-known direct marketers on the Internet. Browse the company's Web site and identify what direct-marketing strategies the company employs. Which do you think are the most successful? Why? Which are the least effective? Why? What does Amazon expect to gain from direct marketing?

■■■ Class Projects

1. Divide the class into groups. Each group should select a consumer product that normally is not sold through direct marketing, but could be. Create a direct-marketing campaign for this product. Be sure to specify your objectives and indicate the parts of the offer as well as the medium used. Develop a mockup of some of the campaign's pieces that illustrates your ideas about message design.

2. Visit a few direct-marketing organizations online such as: The Direct Response Forum, Inc., www.directresponse.org; Direct Marketing Association, www.the-dma.org; and Direct Marketing News, www.dmnews.com. Pick an issue that, judging from these sites, is a threat to direct marketing. Explain what you, as a direct-marketing team, would do to overcome this threat.

HANDS-ON
CASE

I Won't Be Calling, But Let's Talk: Telemarketers Respond to the Do-Not-Call Registry

It's a good bet that most consumers would rank telemarketing near the bottom of their list of favorite ad appeals. So when Congress proposed legislation for creating a Federal Do-Not-Call Registry, which would make it illegal for companies to call people who choose to "opt out" of telemarketing calls, there was broad public support. The legislation passed in October 2003 and a year later telemarketers lost a Supreme Court appeal to declare the list unconstitutional.

The years leading up to the creation of the Registry were ones of phenomenal growth for telemarketing. In 2002 alone, telemarketers spent $80 billion and placed 16 million calls. This effort yielded $274 billion in sales, up from just $10 billion in 1980. But telemarketing's phenomenal success may have helped to create its own downfall. Andy Orr, a newspaper circulation consultant, suggests that Congress stepped in after consumers had had enough. "After the 1980s everyone got on the [telemarketing] bandwagon and consumers began to feel assaulted. Then, computerized dialing machines came on the scene and became a nuisance. To protect themselves, people began paying for caller ID, they demanded that companies develop internal do-not-call lists and they lobbied for legislation to create statewide registries."

The Registry has proven immensely popular; as of early 2005 more than 63 million Americans have signed up to "opt out" of telemarketing calls. Each call made to someone registered on the list can be punishable with a fine of up to $11,000. Phone services giant AT&T received unwanted publicity when the FCC accused it of contacting people on the Registry just two days after it went into effect. The company eventually settled by agreeing to pay a fine of close to half a million dollars. Shortly thereafter AT&T decided to discontinue all telemarketing activities.

In the time since its passage it appears the Registry has affected telemarketers in different ways. For some organizations the new law has meant little; groups such as charities and political organizations are exempted. Other companies, which used telemarketing as a small component of their marketing mixes, have shifted their spending elsewhere without much effect. But a few companies have been unable to replace telemarketing as a tool for building business. AT&T, MCI, Scholastic, and Gannett all publicly blamed financial losses in 2004 on their inability to market via the phone.

Several companies have taken a fresh look at what might be considered an even more intrusive strategy for building customers: "door-to-door" sales efforts. Door-to-door selling has declined over the years in response to demographic changes like dual-working couples and gated communities. But businesses that formerly relied on the phone are finding that knocking on front doors can also be successful. Cable company Comcast found that by going door-to-door in 2004 it was able to win back 40,000 customers from its competitors. AT&T also sent people door-to-door after intensively training salespeople to avoid such no-no's as tramping dirt on hallway carpets or asking to use homeowner bathrooms. Newspapers have used door-to-door to build circulation, and have tried to turn a problem into an opportunity: The Do-Not-Call Registry, says National Association of Newspapers vice president John Murray, "is forcing people to do what they should have done long ago: balance multiple sales sources."

Other companies have found ways to legally telemarket by taking advantage of gaps in the law. Companies can still legally phone individuals with whom they have an "existing relationship," which in practice means the consumer has bought a service and/or product or has contacted the company within the previous 18 months. Individuals in the Registry can also give up their immunity if they subsequently agree to let marketers contact them. A company called CoolSavings, based in Chicago, takes advantage of this Registry "loophole" by gathering information from visitors to third-party Web sites who indicate they would be receptive to offers. CoolSavings makes money by then selling the contact information to companies that can now safely call the newly "unregistered" individuals.

And figuring that a carrot always beats a stick when it comes to relationship building, Coke, the Weather Channel, and Proctor & Gamble are all hoping they can convince cell phone users to call them. P&G supports its "Herbal Essences" brand by offering young cell phone users branded content, including downloadable music and pictures. Callers can also use the Herbal Essences mobile Web site to play games and send messages. The bill for all of this activity is paid by the cell phone user who is charged by his or her carrier. Sometimes it really is better when they call you.

Consider This

1. Analyze why telemarketing is simultaneously an effective way to market and yet is widely disliked by many consumers.
2. Could the telemarketing industry have prevented the Do-Not-Call Registry? Or was it inevitable that legislators would step in?
3. Can you think of products or services about which many people would not mind being contacted either by phone or in person by a salesperson?

Source: Yuki Noguchi, "New Ad Frontier: Cell Phones. Marketers Bet Consumers Will Ask for Text Messages," MSNBC News, November 7, 2003, http://msnbc.msn.com/id/3403665/; Jim Edwards, "A Year After Do Not Call, Some Hangups Remain," *Brandweek* (October 4, 2004): 9; Anne Lallonde, "Telemarketing's Aftermath: Circulation Executives Seek and Find New Ways to Make the Sale," Newspaper Association of America, January 23, 2004, http://www.naa.org/artpage.cfm?AID=5917&SID=541; "Justices Uphold "Do Not Call" Registry," *New York Times* (October 5, 2004): C2; Jane Spencer, "Ignore That Knocking: Door-to-Door Sales Make a Comeback," *Wall Street Journal* (April 30, 2003): D.1; Brian Steinberg, Suzanne Vranica, and Yochi Dreazen, " 'Do Not Call' Registry Is Pushing Telemarketers to Plan New Pitches," *Wall Street Journal* (July 2, 2003): A1.

Sales Promotion, Events, and Sponsorships

History's Lost and Found Auction Block

Marketer:
The History Channel

Agency:
Clarion Marketing

Award:
2004 REGGIE® Bronze New Media Promotion

Promotion:
"History's Lost and Found"

CHAPTER OBJECTIVES

After reading this chapter, you will be able to:

1. Explain the principles that drive the use of sales promotion and discuss why advertisers are spending increasing sums of money on sales promotion.

2. List and explain the use of various consumer promotions.

3. Summarize the types and purposes of trade promotions.

4. Describe the use of other types of promotions: sponsorships, specialties, interactive promotions, loyalty programs, and co-marketing programs.

5. Explain the strategic use of promotions in marketing, in terms of brand building, new-product launches, integration, and effectiveness.

W e've introduced you to the EFFIE awards program, as well as the Echo awards for direct marketing. This chapter's story focuses on the winner of a REGGIE award, given in the sales promotion industry. The History Channel, a member of the A&E Television Networks, is a core cable network that reaches more than 79 million subscribers throughout the United States. In only its seventh year of operation, the History Channel's proprietary "Where the Past Comes Alive" positioning and unique, award-winning programming have catapulted it into the top echelon of television networks.

History's Lost and Found is the network's wild scavenger hunt through history that tracks down long-lost objects and artifacts that have significantly changed the world. Focusing on everyday personal objects that truly bring history to life, the show weaves amazing stories of history's most compelling people, places, and events.

The objectives of "History's Lost and Found Auction Block" were to: (1) develop a model of convergence of television and new-line media by integrating programming content with the Internet; (2) provide a unique and entertaining experience within an auction format to create the opportunity to "own a piece of history"; (3) develop a strategic alliance with a major auction site to maximize exposure and awareness of the History Channel; (4) drive *History's Lost and Found* viewership and broaden the channel's audience; (5) drive traffic to the channel's Web site; and (6) maintain and enhance the integrity and significance of the History Channel brand into a global online collectors' marketplace.

The History Channel forged a strategic marketing alliance with eBay, the world's largest online person-to-person trading community. Important to the partnership was the fact that eBay owns Butterfields Auction House, which was able to research, procure, and authenticate all auction items that were part of this programming and promotion alliance.

A new segment of *History's Lost and Found,* "Auction Block" was featured at the beginning of each week, when show hosts introduced an item, detailed its historical significance, and opened the bidding. Viewers were directed to the eBay and History Channel Web sites to view and bid on the featured item as well as to preview future auction items. For the balance of the week, viewers were reintroduced to the item and kept abreast of the latest bid. The Friday show concluded the auction, revealed the winning bid, and previewed the following week's item. During the nine-month promotion, auctioned items included a letter signed by "Buffalo Bill" Cody, a kamikaze pilot's helmet, a book typeset by Benjamin Franklin, and John F. Kennedy's briefcase.

"History's Lost and Found Auction Block" was promoted on eBay via online merchandising, a History Channel button on its home page, banners, a gallery page with a tune-in message, AOL placement, and e-mail sent to its database. Off-line merchandising included direct mailings to Butterfields' customers, inclusion in Butterfields' catalog, a publicity campaign, and promotion to eBay power sellers.

The History Channel supported the promotion with on-air programming, which featured eBay significantly in the "History's Lost and Found Auction Block" segment. Additional on-air promotions included tune-in spots and a call to action encouraging visits to the eBay Web site. More than 2,000 spots aired during the life of the promotion. The promotion was so successful it won a Reggie award from the Promotion Marketing Association (PMA). The results of this effort will be described later in the It's a Wrap feature at the close of this chapter.

Source: "Reggie Awards Case Studies: History's Lost and Found Auction Block," Promotion Marketing Association Inc., http://www.pmalink.org/awards/reggie/2002reggie winners3.asp; "Vintage Clothes Can Be Worth Thousands," CNN Saturday Morning News, May 12, 2001, http://transcripts.cnn.com/TRANSCRIPTS/o0105/19/smn.12.html.

The History Channel's scavenger hunt through history is an example of an award-winning promotion that captivated viewers and involved them personally in building the History Channel into a powerful new media brand. This chapter is about the fun, creative, and exciting ideas that the sales promotion industry uses to spur action and build strong brand relationships. In this chapter we will explain the difference between consumer and trade promotions, as well as other programs—such as loyalty programs, tie-ins, and sponsorships—that cross the line between advertising and promotion. First let's discuss the concept and basic principles of sales promotion.

THE PRACTICE OF SALES PROMOTION

Whenever a marketer increases the value of its product by offering an extra incentive to purchase a brand or product it is creating a sales promotion, which is the subject of this chapter. In most cases the objective of sales promotion is to encourage action, although promotion (we will use the word *promotion* to refer to sales promotion) can also help build brand identity and awareness, as the History Channel case illustrated. Similar to advertising, sales promotion is a type of marketing communication. Although advertising is designed to build long-term brand awareness, sales promotion is primarily focused on creating action.

As **sales promotion** has evolved, so too has the way experts define it. In 1988 the American Marketing Association (AMA) offered this definition of sales promotion: "media and nonmedia marketing pressure applied for a predetermined, limited period of time in order to stimulate trial and impulse purchases, increase consumer demand, or improve product quality."[1] More recently, the Council of Sales Promotion Agencies offered a somewhat broader definition: "Sales promotion is a marketing discipline that utilizes a variety of incentive techniques to structure sales-related programs targeted to consumers, trade, and/or sales levels that generate a specific, measurable action or response for a product or service."[2]

Let's examine the latter definition. First, it acknowledges that consumers are an important target for promotions, but so are other people, such as the company's sales representatives and members of the trade (distributors, retailers). Second, the definition recognizes that sales promotion is a set of techniques that prompts members of three target audiences—consumers, sales representatives, and the trade (distributors, retailers, dealers)—to take action, preferably immediate action. Simply put, sales promotion offers an extra incentive to act—usually in the form of a price reduction—but it also may be additional amounts of the product, cash, prizes and gifts, premiums, special events, and so on. It may also be just a fun brand experience, as the History Channel's "Lost and Found" promotion illustrates. Although an action response is the goal of most sales promotions, some programs, such as the History Channel campaign, are designed to build awareness first, but always with action as the ultimate goal.

Principle
Sales promotion is primarily designed to motivate people to act by offering incentives.

Changes in the Promotion Industry

Until the 1980s, advertising was the dominant player in the marketing communication arena. But during the 1980s more marketers found themselves driving immediate bottom-line response through the use of sales promotion. As a result, in the 1980s and particularly in the 1990s the budget share switched from 60 percent advertising and 40 percent sales promotion to the reverse: 40 percent advertising and 60 percent sales promotion. That trend reversed again in the late 1990s as the dot-com companies spent huge sums on advertising to establish their brands. Even though the promotion industry continued to grow, with spending increasing 8.1 percent, that growth rate was slower than that of advertising, which saw spending increase by 9.8 percent in the early 2000s.[3] The industry has continued to grow and in 2003 the growth rate was 9.7 percent for a total sales promotion expenditure of $288.3 billion.[4]

A *Promo* magazine report found that "the migration of marketing dollars away from media advertising gained steam in 2003." Of the total spent on advertising and sales promotion in 2003, 28.5 percent was spent on consumer promotion and 17.5 percent on consumer media advertising. The remaining 54 percent was spent on trade promotions.[5] So over the years, advertising and sales promotion have been battling for their share of the marketing communication budget but sales promotion, particularly trade promotion, is now winning that budget battle.

The accompanying table lists consumer sales promotion categories and their percentage of the marketing communication mix as collected by *Promo* magazine for 2003.[6] Retail merchandising led the way at 35.3 percent, followed by couponing and co-marketing activities. We'll be explaining all these categories and tools in the discussion that follows.

Brands Spent Most On . . .

Retail merchandising	35.3
Couponing	31.3
Co-marketing	31.3
Promotional ads	30.2
Trade shows	29.4
Event marketing	27.8
Entertainment tie-ins	27.1
Games, contests, sweepstakes	25.3
Interactive (online and phone)	23.9
P-o-P (in-store displays)	23.7
Premiums, incentives, ad specialities	20.1
Loyalty marketing programs	18.8

Note: Three responses allowed, so does not total 100%

Source: Adapted from "Upward Bound," *Promo,* April 1, 2004, http://promomagazine.com/mag/marketing upward bound/index.html.

Reasons for the Growth of Sales Promotion

Why are companies spending more money on sales promotion? The chief reasons are the pressure for short-term profits and the need for accountability for marketing communication efforts. Sales promotions are relatively easy to evaluate in terms of their impact on sales, as the Matter of Practice box illustrates. There are also consumer factors.

In terms of accountability, most U.S. companies focus on immediate profits, a drive that sales promotion satisfies. Product managers are under pressure to generate quarterly sales increases. Because advertising's benefits are often more apparent in the long term, companies invest more money in sales promotion when they want quick results. Advertisers also cite economic reasons for the shift. Traditional media costs have escalated to the point where alternative types of media must be considered. As the networks raised their advertising prices, the networks' share of prime-time television viewers has dropped dramatically. Advertisers, therefore, are exploring marketing communication forms that cost less and produce immediate, tangible results. Sales promotion is able to deliver these results.

Another reason for sales promotion's accountability is that it is relatively easy and quick to determine whether a sales promotion strategy has accomplished its objectives because there is usually an immediate response of some kind.

From the consumers' perspective, sales promotion reduces the risk associated with a purchase by giving them something of *added value* such as a coupon, rebate, or discounted price. Promotions typically offer the consumer added value, or "more for less," as a Diet Coke ATM card promotion illustrates. Developed in conjunction with MasterCard International, it used ATM cash cards to reward consumers for buying Coke.

Other reasons for the move to sales promotion match changes in the marketplace, such as these:

- *Consumer Behavior.* Shoppers today are better educated, more selective, and less loyal to brand names than in the past, which means they are more likely to switch brands.

Principle
Sales promotion reduces the risk of trying a new product by giving something of added value to motivate action.

- *Pricing.* Consumers have come to expect constant short-term price reductions such as coupons, sales, and price promotions.
- *Market Share.* In most industries, the battle is for market share rather than general product growth. Sales promotion encourages people to switch products, increasing market share.
- *Parity Products.* Sales promotion is often the most effective strategy for increasing sales of a parity product when the products in the category are largely undifferentiated. When products are similar, promotions become the tie-breaker in the consumer's decision making.
- *The Power of the Retailer.* Dominant retailers, such as Safeway, Wal-Mart, Toys "R" Us, and Home Depot, demand a variety of promotional incentives before allowing products into their stores.

This ad includes not only a price discount, but also several other deals to encourage store visits.

Categories of Sales Promotion

The most common sales promotion strategies target the three audiences of promotions: consumer, trade, and sales force. The first two—customer sales and trade support—have direct implications for advertising and are the focus of this chapter. In the third category, sales-force promotions include two general sets of promotional activities directed at the firm's salespeople to motivate them to increase their sales levels. The first set of activities includes programs that better prepare salespeople to do their jobs, such as sales manuals, training programs, sales presentations, and supportive materials (training films, slides, videos, and visual aids). The second set of activities deals with promotional efforts or incentives that motivate salespeople to work harder. Contests dominate this category. We will include contests as part of our trade promotion discussion, but first we examine consumer promotions.

Consider This

1. Why is sales promotion a growth area?
2. What are the three general types or categories of sales promotion?

CONSUMER PROMOTIONS

Although trade promotion claims the greatest percentage of the promotion budget, we'll start with consumer promotions because it is the most familiar to most people. Consumer sales promotions are directed at the ultimate user of the good or service. They are intended to provide an incentive so that when consumers go into a store they will look for a particular brand. The primary strengths of consumer sales promotions are their variety and flexibility.

Types of Consumer Promotions

There are many promotion techniques that a product manager can use and combine to meet almost any objective. Sales promotion works for all kinds of businesses. Here's a summary of the most common types of consumer promotions.

- *Price Deals.* A popular sales promotion technique is a **price deal**, a temporary price reduction or a sale price, as in the Pearle Vision and Amazon.com ads. There are four common price deals: (1) A *cents-off deal* is a reduction in the normal price charged for a good or service (for example, "was $1,000, now $500," or "50 percent off")

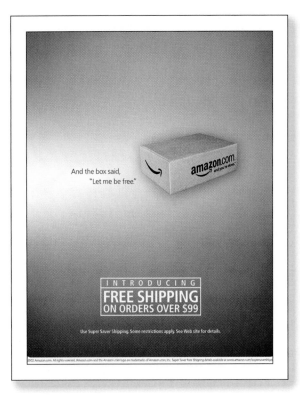

■ ■ ■

The Amazon.com ad seeks to persuade consumers to buy more by giving free shipping on large orders.

announced at the point of sale or through mass or direct advertising; (2) *Price-pack deals* provide the consumer with something extra through the package itself—a prize in a cereal box, for instance; (3) *Bonus packs* contain additional amounts of the product free when consumers purchase the standard size at the regular price. For example, Purina Dog Food may offer 25 percent more dog food in the bag; and (4) *Banded packs* are more units of a product sold at a lower price than if they were bought at the regular single-unit price. Sometimes the products are physically packaged together, such as bar soap and six-packs of soft drinks.

• *Coupons.* There are two general types of **coupons**, which provide a discount on the price of a product: retailer and manufacturer. Retailer-sponsored coupons can be redeemed only at the specified retail outlet. Manufacturer-sponsored coupons can be redeemed at any outlet distributing the product. They are distributed directly (direct mail, door-to-door), through media (newspaper and magazine ads, free-standing inserts), in or on the package itself, or through the retailer (co-op advertising). Manufacturers pay retailers a fee for handling their coupons.

• *Refunds and Rebates.* A **refund** or **rebate** is a marketer's offer to return a certain amount of money to the consumer who purchases the product. Sometimes the refund is a check for a certain amount of money but other times it may be a coupon to encourage repeat use.

• *Sampling.* Allowing the consumer to try the product or service is called **sampling**. Advertisers can distribute samples to consumers in numerous ways. Sampling tables, particularly for food products, can be set up in stores, such as Johnsonville Sausage did with its Brown Sugar and Honey breakfast links. Small samples of products can show up with newspapers and on house doorknobs, in doctors' and dentists' offices, and, most commonly, through the mail. Advertisers can design ads with coupons for free samples, place samples in special packages, or distribute samples at special in-store displays.

• *Contests and Sweepstakes.* Contest and sweepstakes promotions create excitement by promising "something for nothing" and offering impressive prizes. **Contests** require participants to compete for a prize or prizes based on some sort of skill or ability. **Sweepstakes** require only that participants submit their names to be included in a drawing or other chance selection. A *game* is a type of sweepstake. It differs from a one-shot drawing type of sweepstake because the time frame is longer, so it establishes continuity requiring customers to return several times to acquire additional pieces (such as bingo-type games) or to improve their chances of winning. There are legal as well as ethical issues with contests, sweepstakes, and games. McDonald's, for example, got burned in 2000 when its "Who Wants to Be a Millionaire" and "Monopoly" games turned into scams. One of the employees of the company hired to run the games distributed winning game pieces to a network of accomplices. McDonald's didn't return to game promotions until 2003, after it had developed strict security procedures.[7]

• *Premiums.* A **premium** is a tangible reward for a particular act, usually purchasing a product or visiting the point-of-purchase. Premiums are a type of incentive that work by adding value to the product. Examples of premiums are the toy in Cracker Jacks, glassware in a box of detergent, and a radio given for taking a real estate tour. Premiums are either free or low in price. The two general types of premiums are direct and mail. Direct premiums award the incentive immediately, at the time of purchase. There are four variations of direct premiums: (1) store premiums, given to customers at the retail site; (2) in-pack premiums, inserted in the package at the factory; (3) on-pack premiums, placed on the outside of the package at the factory; and (4)

A MATTER OF PRACTICE

Brown Sugar and Honey: I Love Those Links!

Here's the problem. You work for Kerker, a Minneapolis-based sales promotion company, whose client is Johnsonville, maker of Brown Sugar and Honey breakfast sausage links. The line has been around for a couple of years without much promotional support and no one knows about it. The flavor wins raves, but how do you get consumers to try it? The relaunch of the new flavor was complicated by several factors:

1. Johnsonville is better known for its bratwurst line even though it has had a breakfast line for years.
2. The window of opportunity for ownership of this new flavor is small as the larger competitors are bound to launch their own versions and the opportunity to be first to market will be lost if the Johnsonville product doesn't immediately establish itself.
3. Johnsonville is definitely a little guy in the breakfast sausage category with distribution in only 60 percent of the country, compared to 90 percent for competitors.
4. Johnsonville's hallmark product, bratwurst—a distinctive grilled dinner sausage with a German heritage that's boiled in beer and eaten at tailgate parties in football stadiums—doesn't carry over to the breakfast sausage target.
5. The much larger competing brands are filling the market with new packaging, two-for-one pricing strategies, and eight times the media support in advertising.

How can promotions be used most effectively in support of this launch? How can a promotion gain trial, overcome the noise in the category, and deliver a distinctive message that doesn't just say "new from Johnsonville"?

The specific objectives were:

1. Increase trial: Increase Johnsonville Brown Sugar and Honey breakfast sausage dollar sales by 10 percent and share by 2 points during a 12-week promotion period.
2. Lift the line: Increase total Johnsonville breakfast sausage sales by 20 percent and share by 5 points during the 12-week promotion period.
3. Build on success: Sustain sales and share increases beyond the promotion period.

The primary target audience was identified as women age 35–54 who are current Johnsonville breakfast sausage users. The goal was to get current users to increase purchase volume and frequency, not just to trade their current Johnsonville links for the new flavor.

To grow Johnsonville's share of the market, the campaign would also need to convert users from other brands. The secondary target was therefore younger women age 25–35 who are consumers of competing breakfast sausages. The idea was that this audience is more likely to switch brands and have younger children, who are often big consumers of breakfast links.

The grocery story sample line was the perfect venue for introducing this product to moms. Store sampling implies newness and drives home the flavor and brand ID. Plus, the campaign message "You all come back again and again" encourages repeat sales and helps lift the sales of the entire Johnsonville line.

To support the sampling effort, spot television was used regionally to reach moms through intelligent, informative entertainment programming. The campaign schedule emphasize key holiday weeks, as well as key shopping days.

The campaign won an EFFIE award because it delivered on its objectives. The first objective—to drive trial of the Brown Sugar and Honey links with a 10 percent sales increase—resulted in a 74 percent sales increase from the previous year. The performance was more than seven times the sales objective. The share objective, which predicted growth of 2 points, was reached when the share actually grew more than 3 points.

Objective #2 was to lift sales of the entire Johnsonville breakfast sausage line by 20 percent. The actual sales increase was 31 percent and share increased 8 points (the objective was 5 points).

The third objective focused on sustained success beyond the promotional period and, in fact, satisfied customers kept coming back for more. Three months afterward, Johnsonville became the number-one national brand in dollar sales, proving that the promotion not only encouraged current users to buy more, but also attracted new users to the brand.

Source: 2003 EFFIE Brief, provided by Johnsonville and Kerker.

container premiums, in which the package is the premium. Mail premiums require the customer to take some action before receiving the premium. A **self-liquidating premium** usually requires that a payment be mailed in along with some proof of purchase before the customer receives the premium. The payment is sufficient to cover the cost of the premium. Another type of mail premium requires the customer to save coupons or special labels attached to the product that can be redeemed for merchandise.

- *Specialties.* **Specialty advertising** presents the brand's name on something that is given away as a reminder—calendars, pens and pencils, T-shirts, mouse pads, tote bags, water bottles, and so forth. The ideal specialty is an item kept out in the open where other people can see it, such as a coffee mug.

How to Use Consumer Promotions

To demonstrate the strategy behind the use of these tools in a new-product launch, let's suppose we are introducing a new corn chip named Corn Crunchies. Promotion is particularly useful to launch the corn chip because it has a number of tools designed to encourage trial, but it can also be used later in the brand's life to maintain or increase its share of market, as well as remind and reward its loyal customers.

Awareness　Our first challenge is to create awareness of this brand, which is the real strength of advertising and, you may remember from Chapter 5, the first step in consumer decision making. However, sometimes awareness can be increased when advertising is combined with an appropriate promotion to call attention to the brand name in order to get people to try the product, as the Johnsonville Sausage case illustrated. Awareness-building promotion ideas for this new corn chip might include colorful point-of-purchase displays, sponsorship of a Corn Crunchies team, or a special event that will attract people in the target market.

Trial　Creating awareness will only take the product so far, however. Consumers must also perceive Corn Crunchies as offering some clear benefit compared to the competition. Sales promotion does this by arranging for experiences, such as special events where people can try the product or see it demonstrated. Trial is one of sales promotion's most important objectives; however, the important thing is to get the right people—the targeted audience—involved with the product. The Inside Story explains how a promotion was used to target a select group for a test drive for a new car.

Sales promotion has other tools that lead to trial, such as sampling. An effective way to get people to try Corn Crunchies is to give away free samples at events, in stores, or through direct mail to the home. Sampling is an effective strategy for introducing a new or modified product or for dislodging an entrenched market leader by enticing potential users to try the product. As a general rule of thumb, retailers and manufacturers maintain that sampling can boost sales volume as much as 10 times when used with a product demonstration and 10 percent to 15 percent thereafter. Sampling is generally most effective when reinforced on the spot with product coupons. Most consumers like sampling because they do not lose any money if they do not like the product. To be successful, the product sampled must virtually sell itself with minimal trial experience.

Another way sales promotion can motivate people to try a new product like Corn Crunchies is to offer a price deal: *You try this product and we will give it to you cheaper than the usual price.* These price deals are usually done through coupons, refunds, rebates, or premiums. Refunds and rebates are effective because they encourage consumers to purchase a product before a deadline. In addition, refunds stimulate sales without the high cost and waste associated with coupons.

Coupons mainly encourage trial, induce brand switching, and reward repeat business. The main advantage of the manufacturer's coupon, such as those that run in consumer magazines, is that it allows the advertiser to lower prices without relying on cooperation from the retailer to distribute them. Announcements for cents-off deals include the package itself and signs near the product or elsewhere in the store. Advertising for these deals includes sales, flyers, newspaper ads, and broadcast ads.

THE INSIDE STORY

The Phaeton Test Drive Program at W Hotels™

Jennifer Montague, Former Phaeton Manager, San Francisco Market
Currently National Accounts Director with Swivel Media, San Francisco

In 2003, Volkswagen, "the people's car," made a bold move and introduced the Phaeton, a luxury car to rival Mercedes, BMW, and Lexus. Recognizing that the Phaeton was not a car for the masses (prices start at $65,000), Volkswagen turned to Arnold Brand Promotions to develop an exclusive promotion to introduce the car to targeted prospects before it was available for purchase in the United States. Program objectives were to expose targeted drivers to the Phaeton; to increase awareness, consideration (willingness to consider the brand), and traffic in the showroom; and to reach aggressive sales goals.

The Phaeton Experience incorporated a number of different marketing communication elements to interest consumers and entice them to test-drive. At the cornerstone of the program was a partnership with the W Hotels™. Volkswagen customers who were invited to take part in this exclusive program came to the W Hotel in San Francisco, Los Angeles, Chicago, or New York to receive the Phaeton for an up to 4-hour test drive. The partnership was a natural fit because the design philosophy behind the Phaeton and VW's approach to luxury were consistent with the W Hotels™ brand. This relationship would help build the foundation for the public's perception of VW as a luxury brand. As part of the partnership, VW customers were offered a special "Phaeton Rate" at the Hotel and W Hotel™. VIPs and preferred guests were invited upon check-in to schedule a Phaeton shuttle ride or the opportunity to test-drive for up to four hours.

The initial direct-mail effort garnered an 11 percent response rate. The program goal over 16 weeks was 1,400 test drives, and was exceeded by 38 percent on average, for a total of 1,933 test drives in four markets. Not only were numbers exceeded, but feedback from Volkswagen prospects and W Hotel™ guests was overwhelmingly positive. Both the program and car were extremely well received, which generated buzz among consumers. More than 2,600 prospects and guests contacted a Phaeton dealer as a result of the program. Arnold Brand Promotions was recently honored for excellence and innovation in promotional marketing at the annual meeting of the Promotional Marketing Association in Chicago. The Phaeton Test Drives at W Hotels™ Program took home the gold Reggie Award in the "Local, Regional, or Target Market Promotion (Budget over $1,000,000)."

Whether or not a luxury car from Volkswagen will be accepted by the market remains to be seen. However, if this program's success is any indicator, then the chances are indeed good!

Jennifer Montague, who received an IMC master's degree from the University of Colorado, was the former Phaeton manager for the San Francisco market, before moving to Swivel Media in San Francisco where she is National Accounts Director.

Nominated by Professor Sandra Moriarty, University of Colorado.

Maintain or Increase Market Share In addition to encouraging trial of a new product, another purpose of price deals is to convince prospective users to switch from an established competing brand, such as Doritos in the Corn Crunchies case. Later, after the Corn Crunchies brand is established, a price deal can be used to reward loyal users in order to encourage their repeat business. Price deals are particularly effective in those situations where price is an important factor in brand choice or if consumers are not brand loyal.

To maintain a brand's presence or increase its market share after it is launched, markets use promotional tools such as coupons, premiums, special events, and contests and sweepstakes. The Blue Bunny brochure was used as a Sunday newspaper supplement. It features the entire Indulge line of low-carb and low-fat products, as well as coupons to encourage trial.

In addition to serving as a reward for buying a product, premiums can enhance an advertising campaign or a brand's image. Characters like the Campbell Soup Kids, Tony the Tiger, Cap'n Crunch, and Ronald McDonald are used on premiums, such as soup or cereal bowls, to reinforce the consumer's association of the brand with the character. Cereal manufacturers are among the biggest users of in-pack premiums as reminder devices. Kellogg distributed millions of special anniversary promotions across its Corn

■ ■ ■
The Blue Bunny brochure uses strong appetite appeal in its visuals to emphasize the good taste of its low-carb and low-fat products.

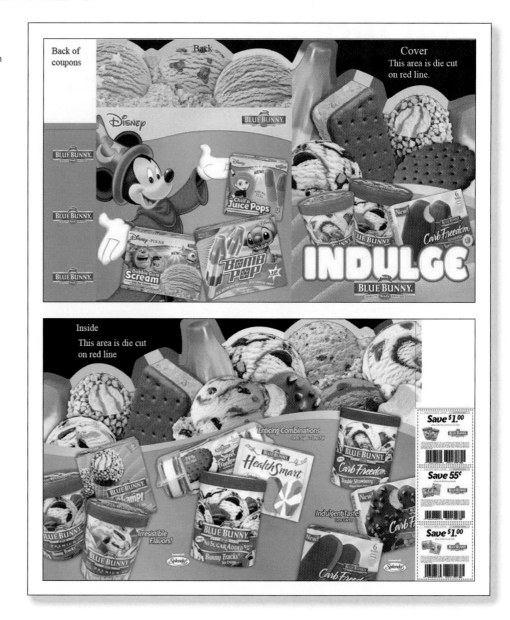

Flakes, Rice Krispies, and Froot Loops brands to celebrate the company's ninetieth anniversary. The cereal boxes offered consumers commemorative Matchbox trucks, utensils, and other collectible items. In addition, Kellogg's Special K cereal teamed with Reebok and Polygram to offer an on-pack, special-edition Reebok Versa Training exercise video; and a recipe and coupon offer good for free Sun Maid Dried Fruit appeared on packages of Kellogg's Low Fat Granola cereal. All of these special promotions were designed to increase excitement for the anniversary event.

Brand Reminder   In addition to new-product launches, promotions are also used in the *reminder stage.* This means that you change advertising copy to remind customers about the positive experience they had with the product, and use sales promotion to reinforce their loyalty with coupons, rebates, and other rewards. After the initial purchase we want the customer to remember the brand and repeat the purchase, so specialty items, such as a Corn Crunchies snack bowl, can serve as a brand reminder. Specialty advertising serves as a reminder to the consumer—a reminder to reconsider the product. Specialties also build relationships, such as items given away as new-year or thank-you gifts (the calendar hanging in the kitchen). Advertisers use specialty items to thank customers for patronage, to reinforce established products or services, and to generate sales leads.

TRADE PROMOTIONS

Consumer awareness and desire mean nothing unless Corn Crunchies is available where the consumer thinks it should be. Somehow the trade must be convinced that the product will move off the shelves. Marketers know that they must engage the trade in the program if their consumer promotions are to be effective. In such programs, *trade* refers to all the people involved in the channel of distribution—buyers, brokers, distributors, wholesalers, dealers, franchisees, retailers, and so on.

Typically companies spend more than 50 percent of their total promotion budget on promotions directed at the trade (distributors, dealers, retailers). The *Promo* magazine 2003 report mentioned earlier found that companies directed 54 percent to the trade or channel market and 29 percent to the consumer market, which is to say that although consumer promotion is highly visible, trade promotion is more important as a marketing communication strategy. So let's look at the types of trade promotion.

Principle
Consumer promotion is of little use if the product isn't available where the consumer can find it.

Types of Trade Promotion

Trade advertising directed at wholesalers and retailers provides trade members with information about the new product and its selling points. In addition, trade promotion techniques, especially price discounts, point-of-purchase displays, and advertising allowances, motivate retailers to provide shelf space for products and consumer promotions. Resellers (the intermediaries in the distribution channel) are the 1.3 million retailers and 338,000 wholesalers who distribute the products manufacturers make. The Corn Crunchies manufacturer will be more encouraged that the product is acceptable if resellers are willing to carry and push it. Many promotional devices designed to motivate resellers to engage in certain sales activities are available to the manufacturer. Here are the most common types of trade promotion tools.

- *Point-of-Purchase Displays.* A manufacturer-designed display distributed to retailers who use it to call their customers' attention to product promotions is known as a **point-of-purchase (POP) display**. Another popular POP form is the merchandising display, which retailers use to showcase their products and create a personality for their stores. Although POP forms vary by industry, they can include special racks, display cartons, banners, signs, price cards, and mechanical product dispensers, among other tools (see Table 16.1).
- *Retailer (Dealer) Kits.* Materials that support retailers' selling efforts or that help representatives make sales calls on prospective retailing customers are often designed as sales kits. The kits contain supporting information, such as detailed product specifications, how-to display information, and **ad slicks**—print ads that are ready to be sent to the local print media as soon as the retailer or dealer adds identification, location, promotion price, or other information.

TABLE 16.1   Types of POP Displays

Carton displays	Banners
Floorstands	Inflatables
Sidekicks	Product dispensers
Counter units	Chalkboards
Dump bins	Mirrors and clocks
Kiosks	Lightboxes
Literature holders	Posters
Neon signs	Decals
Menus and menuboards	CD listening stations
Table tents	Video units
Shelf talkers	Motion units
Signs (metal, cardboard, wood, paper, plastic, etc.)	

- *Trade Incentives and Deals.* Similar to consumer price deals, a manufacturer may reward a reseller financially for purchase of a certain level of a product or support of a promotion. These retailer promotional efforts can take the form of special displays, extra purchases, superior store locations, or greater local promotion. In return, retailers can receive special allowances, such as discounts, free goods, gifts, or cash from the manufacturer. The most common types of **trade deals** are buying allowances for increasing purchases and advertising allowances, which include deals on cooperative advertising and display allowances—that is, deals for agreeing to use promotional displays.
- *Contests.* As in the case of consumer sales promotion, advertisers can develop contests and sweepstakes to motivate resellers. Contests are far more common than sweepstakes, mainly because resellers find it easy to tie contest prizes to the sale of the sponsor's product. A sales quota is set, for example, and the retailer or person who exceeds the quota by the largest percentage wins the contest.
- *Trade Shows and Exhibits.* The **trade show** is where companies within the same industry gather to present and sell their merchandise, as well as to demonstrate their products. Exhibits are the spaces that are designed to showcase the product.

How to Use Trade Promotion

The ultimate gauge of a successful trade promotion is whether sales increase. Trade promotions are primarily designed to get the cooperation of people in the distribution channel and to encourage their promotion of the product to the consumer. Sales promotion brings resellers to that point of conviction. There are two primary roles for a trade promotion:

- *Trade Support.* To stimulate in-store merchandising or other trade support (for example, feature pricing, superior store location, or shelf space).
- *Excitement.* To create a high level of excitement about the product among those responsible for its sale.

In addition, trade promotion is also used to accomplish other marketing objectives, such as manipulating levels of inventory held by wholesalers and retailers and expanding product distribution to new areas of the country or new classes of trade.

Demand: Push-and-Pull Strategies As we said earlier, manufacturers hope to see their trade partners push a product. To understand the role of trade promotion, consider how sales promotion is used in push-and-pull strategies (see Figure 2.3). Consumer and trade promotions interact through complementing push-and-pull strategies. If people really want to try Corn Crunchies, based on what they have heard in advertising and publicity stories, they will ask their local retailers for it, which is called a **pull strategy**; that is, by asking for it they will pull the product through the distribution channel. Sometimes the advertising and publicity are focused on a sales promotion, which can be used to intensify demand for the product. By conducting a contest in conjunction with sampling, for example, we can increase the pull of a promotion at the same time we get people to try the new product.

However, you might use a **push strategy** to push the product through the channel by convincing (motivating or rewarding) members of the distribution network to carry Corn Crunchies. For example, we want grocery stores to not only carry them, but also allocate good shelf space in the crowded chip aisle. Here are the most common types of incentives and trade deals used with retailers as part of a push strategy.

- *Bonuses.* A monetary bonus (also called push money or *spiffs*) is paid to a store's salesperson based on the units that salesperson sells over a period of time. For example, an air-conditioner manufacturer might give salespeople a $50 bonus for the sale of one model and $75 for a fancier model, within a certain time frame. When time is up, each salesperson sends in evidence of total sales to the manufacturer and receives a check for the bonus amount.
- *Dealer Loaders.* **Loaders** are premiums (comparable to a consumer premium) that a manufacturer gives to a retailer for buying a certain amount of a product. A buying loader rewards retailers for buying the product. Budweiser offered store managers a

free trip to the Super Bowl if they sold a certain amount of beer in a specified period of time. Display loaders reward retailers by giving them the display after the promotion is over. For example, Dr Pepper built a store display for the July fourth holiday that included a gas grill, picnic table, basket, and other items. The store manager was awarded these items after the promotion ended.

- *Buying Allowances.* A manufacturer pays a reseller a set amount of money, or a discount, for purchasing a certain amount of the product during a specified time period.
- *Advertising Allowances.* The manufacturer pays the wholesaler or retailer a certain amount of money to advertise the manufacturer's product. This allowance can be a flat dollar amount or it can be a percentage of gross purchases during a specified time period.
- *Cooperative Advertising.* In a contractual arrangement between the manufacturer and the resellers, the manufacturer agrees to pay a part or all of the advertising expenses incurred by the retailers.
- *Display allowance.* A direct payment of cash or goods is given to the retailer if the retailer agrees to set up the point-of-sale display. Before issuing the payment, the manufacturer requires the retailer's signature on a certificate of agreement.

Attention   Some trade promotions are designed not only to get the attention of the trade members, but also to grab the attention of customers. POP displays, for example, are designed to get the attention of shoppers when they are in the store and to stimulate impulse purchases. They are used by retailers, but provided by manufacturers. As we moved to a self-service retail environment in which fewer and fewer customers expect help from sales clerks, the role of POP continues to increase. The Point-of-Purchase Advertising International Association (POPAI) released a study that examined the effect of various POP forms on sales. Topping the POP list were displays communicating a tie-in with entertainment, sports, or charities.[8]

In addition to getting attention in crowded aisles and promoting impulse purchases, marketers are designing POP efforts to complement other promotional campaigns. As part of getting attention, retailers appreciate POP ideas that build store ambience.[9] Club Med designed a floor display for travel agents that featured a beach chair with a surfboard on one side and a pair of skis on the other to show that Club Med has both snow and sun destinations. Advertisers must consider not only whether POP is appealing to the end user, but also whether the trade will use it; retailers will use a POP only if they are convinced that it will generate greater sales.

Motivation   Most trade promotions are designed to motivate in some way trade members to cooperate with the manufacturer's promotion. Incentives such as contests and trade deals are used. If conducted properly with a highly motivating incentive or prize, contests can spur short-term sales and improve the relationship between the manufacturer and the reseller. They encourage a higher quantity of purchases and create enthusiasm among trade members who are involved with the promotion. Trade incentive programs are used to stimulate frequency and quantity of purchase and encourage cooperation with a promotion.

Information   Trade shows display products and provide an opportunity to sample and demonstrate products particularly for trade buyers (people who buy for stores). The food industry has thousands of trade shows for various product categories and the manufacturer of Corn Crunchies would want to make sure that there was an exhibit featuring the new corn chip at the appropriate food shows. Trade shows permit companies to gather information about their competition. In an environment where all the companies are attempting to give a clear picture of their products to potential customers, competitors can easily compare quality, features, prices, and technology.

Advertisers use POP displays to call attention to a product and increase sales.

Consider This

1. What is the difference between consumer and trade sales promotion?
2. What are the strengths of both consumer and trade promotions?

PROMOTIONS THAT CROSS THE LINES

So far we have looked at consumer sales promotions and trade promotions. But marketers have other promotion techniques at their disposal. In this section, we focus on sponsorships, event marketing, interactive and Internet promotions, loyalty programs, and co-marketing or partnership promotions. Many of these promotion techniques, such as sponsorships and event marketing, blur the lines between promotions, advertising, and public relations.

Sponsorships and Event Marketing

Sponsorships occur when companies support an event—say a sporting event, concert, or charity—either financially or by donating supplies and services. **Event marketing** means building a product's marketing program around a sponsored event, such as the Olympics or a golf tournament. Sponsorships and event marketing include: sports sponsorships (events, athletes, teams); entertainment tours and attractions; festivals, fairs, and other annual events; cause marketing (associating with an event that supports a social cause); and supporting the arts (orchestras, museums, etc). They typically cost a lot of money. Sponsors for major golf tournaments, for example, are expected to invest between $6 million and $8 million.[10]

Companies undertake sponsorships to build brand associations and to increase the perceived value of the brand in the consumer's mind. The important thing is that the event must project the right image for the brand. That's particularly important in troubled economic times when companies with budget problems find it hard to justify spending money on glitzy events. Companies that use sponsorships focus their efforts on supporting causes and events that matter most to employees and customers.[11]

Hundreds of companies sponsor NASCAR cars in order to not only reach those fans but also link their brand to a winning car and driver. Johnsonville Sausage, for example, is a co-sponsor of a car that features the brand name and logo on the car. But the sponsorship also ties into the brand's "Big Taste Grills" campaign and the car is displayed with a grill strapped to its grille. IBM, General Motors, and Sony spend millions of dollars to be official sponsors of the Olympics. Lipton sponsors golf tournaments. Texaco sponsors car races, and Siemens sponsors international men's tennis. These events also give sales representatives the opportunity to interact with prospective and current customers in a social environment as opposed to a less relaxed business setting, so it's building the image and reputation of the company, as well as supporting lead generation and customer-reward programs.

In an EFFIE award–winning promotion, the Marines elected to sponsor the ESPN X-Games, as well as local related events. The idea was to use the "Xtreme" sports angle to show the connection between the Marines and youths' "can do" attitudes: The challenge of becoming a Marine and the challenge of Xtreme sports push people to limits they did not know they could reach. At the national level, the Marines sponsored ESPN's X-Games and X-Games Tour. In addition, a "Marines Xtreme" digital banner was placed on ESPN's "Sports Zone" home page and hot linked to the Marine Corps' home page. "Sports Zone" is a site their target age group visits often. On the local level, the Marine Corps sought to use its larger-than-life image to engage prospects in an extreme challenge. It sponsored a "Hoop Camp" as a 50-city, three-on-three basketball tournament. The Corps also sponsored a "Chin-up Challenge" at fairs, concerts, and sporting events and produced an on-site video so that attendees could learn more about becoming a Marine. All of these events got prospective Marines involved with the Corps as part of its recruitment program.

Ambush marketing is the term given to promotional stunts used at events, such as the Olympics and the soccer and rugby world cups, by companies that are not official sponsors. Ambush marketing typically occurs when "one big brand is trying to dilute the presence of a rival that is sponsoring an event, thus diminishing the return on the official sponsor's investment."[12] In 2002 Nike, for example, ran its own soccer competition against the World Cup whose official sponsor was Adidas. Because of the publicity, many consumers assumed Nike was the official World Cup sponsor.

The term *event marketing* describes the marketing practice of linking a brand to an event, such as the Jose Cuervo beach volleyball tournament. Marketers use related promotional events, such as a tour or the appearance of the product or its spokesperson at a mall or sporting event, to gain the attention and participation of people in the target audience who attend the event. The event showcases the brand, often with sampling, coupons, and other incentives. Business-to-business promotions also use events to reach trade audiences, which can include the sales staff, distributors, retailers, and franchisees. These stakeholders are invited to participate in the event as a reward for their support.

To be successful the event must match the brand to the target market's lifestyle. Johnsonville, for example, used the "World's Largest Touring Grill," the Johnsonville Big Taste Grill, to reach NFL fans, who are big part of its bratwurst market. The Grill weighed more than 53,000 pounds and extended to a length of 65 feet. It required its own semi-truck to haul it to each location where 12 grill masters cooked more than 750 brats at a time, approximately 2,500 per hour.[13] Reebok, immersed in lifestyle marketing, even has a director of events marketing.

Other Promotional Support

Advertisers will use blimps, balloons, and inflatables—even skywriting planes—to capture attention and create an aura of excitement at events. Everybody has probably heard of the Goodyear blimp, but other companies such as MetLife, which uses characters from the popular "Peanuts" comic strip in its advertising, has two blimps, Snoopy I and Snoopy II, to connect with the corporate campaign and provide brand-reminder messages. Inflatables, giant models of products, and packages are used at all kinds of events, including grand openings, sporting events, parades, trade shows, beaches, malls, and other places where they can make an impression for a new-product rollout. Giant inflatables, such as the Whipper Snapple bottle, demand attention and provide an entertaining and highly memorable product presentation. Its effectiveness comes from its huge size and three-dimensional shape.

Interactive and Internet Promotions

There are a number of ways that advertisers can use the Internet for sales promotion programs, including sampling, sweepstakes and contests, price deals, and coupons. Internet promotion is one of the hot areas of sales promotions with the highest level of client spending increases (15.5 percent) in 2003 in the sales promotion industry.[14] Many advertising campaigns include a campaign-dedicated Web site, such as the "microsite" designed as a tie-in for Heineken and the *Matrix* movies. The site included an online merchandise sweepstakes.[15]

Sampling has been a mainstay of interactive promotions on the Internet. Some companies offer samples from their own home pages; however, most farm out the efforts to online companies that specialize in handling sample offers and fulfillment. Some of these online sampling companies are: freesampleclub.com, startsampling.com, freesamples .com, and sampleville.com. There are also freebie portals such as amazingfreebies.com, nojunkfree.com, and the freesite.com that have endless offers for gratis goodies. Sampling over the Internet is not cheap for companies. Although traditional store sampling costs 17 cents per sample and event sampling runs about 25 cents per sample, online sampling costs 75 to 90 cents.[16] The reason for the high cost is the money it takes to set up and run the Web site.

Sweepstakes and contests are effective promotional tools for driving people to marketers' Internet sites. America Online has conducted numerous promotions to drive users to its advertisers' sites. One recent promotion gave visitors a chance to win a $1 million drawing, one of the dozens of daily prizes including merchandise emblazoned with the online service's logo. The results from Internet sweepstakes can be huge. According to Seth Godin, president and founder of Yoyodyne, an online marketing and sweepstakes company, "We basically say, if you give us permission to e-mail you information about a product or a site, we'll give you a chance to win a house." He explains, "We get a 36 percent response rate every time we send an e-mail, which is about 30 times what you get with direct mail marketing." Steven Krein, president and chief executive of Webstakes, an online sweepstakes company, says, "Sweepstakes, combined with the Internet's direct marketing tools, equals sweepstakes on steroids. You're not just filling in information on a card. There's so much more interaction, that's why the results can be astronomical."[17]

Giant inflatables, such as the Whipper Snapple Bottle by Boulder Blimp, demand attention.

Some sites offer price promotions only to online purchasers. The promotions might be discounted prices, rebates, or free offers such as frequent flier miles. *Promo* magazine has found that consumers are more receptive to rebates online than offline.[18] Incentive programs offered by online marketers CyberGold (www.cybergold.com), FreeRide Media (www.freeride.com), Intellipost (www.bonusmail.com), MotivationNet (www.mypoints .com), and Netcentives (www.clickrewards.com) offer discounts to customers who enroll with them before buying from other merchants.

Coupons can be delivered via the Internet. Several sites have been designed for this. Catalina's ValuPage Web site (www.valupage.com) allows users to print coupons that they can use at 7,000 supermarkets. The coupon is printed with a bar code and is used with the shopper's store card. If Corn Crunchies were to offer coupons this way, the site could link the shopper's Internet information with store card information, which the Corn Crunchies brand manager could use in determining whether the coupon strategy was effective.

Loyalty Programs

Another type of program that crosses the line between advertising and promotion is frequency, or loyalty, programs. A **loyalty program**, also called a **continuity** or **frequency program** (such as airline frequent flier programs), is a promotion to increase customer retention. Marketers typically define loyalty programs as ones created to keep and reward customers for their continued patronage, which is why they are called continuity programs. Typically, the higher the purchase level, the greater the benefits. The Practical Tips box lists the four mandates of loyalty programs.

Practical Tips

Four Mandates of Loyalty Programs

1. Identify your best customers.
2. Connect with those best customers.
3. Retain the best customers, usually by rewarding them for their patronage.
4. Cultivate new "best customers."

Source: Vicki Gerson, "Marketer's Best Friend," *Integrated Marketing and Promotion* (March/April 1998): 35.

Today loyalty programs are synonymous with the word *frequent.* Frequent flier clubs, created by United and American Airlines in 1981, are the model for a modern continuity program. They offer a variety of rewards, including seat upgrades, free tickets, and premiums based on the number of frequent flier miles accumulated. Continuity programs work in competitive markets in which the consumer has difficulty perceiving real differences between brands. TGI Friday's, for example, has used a "Frequent Friday's" program with several million members. Members receive 10 points for every dollar they spend in the restaurant. Bonuses include 500 enrollment points and double, triple, and double-triple points for special promotions. Members who accumulate 1,250 points receive a free appetizer and 5,750 points are good for a $15 dining certificate.

Marketers like membership programs because they also generate information for customer databases. The enrollment application at TGI Friday's, for example, captures name, address, telephone number, birth date, and average visit frequency. The database can also record the restaurant locations, date, time, purchase amount, and items you ordered for each visit. Marketers can then use this information to more specifically target customers with promotions and advertising materials.

Partnership Programs

Another promotion tool that crosses the lines is the *partnership program.* **Co-marketing** is where manufacturers develop marketing communication programs *with* their main retail accounts, instead of *for* them. If done right, they strengthen relationships between manufacturers and retailers. Co-marketing programs are usually based on the lifestyles and purchasing habits of consumers who live in the area of a particular retailer. The partnership means that the advertising and sales promotions build equity for both the manufacturer and the retailer. For example, Procter & Gamble and Wal-Mart might develop a spring-cleaning promotion directed at Wal-Mart shoppers that features P&G cleaning products sold at reduced prices or with premium incentives.

Co-branding   When two companies come together to offer a product the effort is called **co-branding**. An example of co-branding is when American Airlines puts its logo on a Citibank Visa card and awards AAdvantage points to Citibank Visa card users. Both companies are equally present in the product's design and promotion and both get to build on the other company's brand equity.

Licensing   Legally protected brand-identity items, such as logos, symbols, and brand characters, must be licensed: A legal contract gives another company the right to use the brand-identity element. In brand licensing, a company with an established brand "rents" that brand to other companies, allowing them to use its logo on their products and in their advertising and promotional events. Fashion marketers such as Gucci, Yves St. Laurent, and Pierre Cardin have licensed their brand names and logos for use on everything from fashion accessories to sunglasses, ties, linens, and luggage, and they do this because it makes them money and extends their brand visibility. The PGA Tour is a golf brand that has become recognizable through an elaborate, integrated marketing campaign. Charles Schwab, the financial investment house, has used the Tour logo as a part of its advertising. This lets the company associate its brand with a golf event that has a lot of interest and positive associations for their target audiences.

■ ■ ■
The PGA licenses the use of its logo to other advertisers who want to associate themselves with the PGA Tour event and pros.

Tie-Ins   Another type of cooperative marketing program is a **tie-in**, which is an effective strategy for marketers using associations between complementary brands to make one-plus-one equal three. For example, Doritos may develop a tie-in promotion with Pace salsa in which bottles of salsa are displayed next to the Doritos section in the chip aisle (and vice versa). The intention is to spur impulse sales. Ads are also designed to tie the two products together and the sponsoring companies share the cost of the advertising. The biggest tie-in deals are arranged around movies and other entertainment events. The movie series *Lord of the Rings* was accompanied by a Burger King global marketing program at more than 10,000 of its restaurants where "Rings" characters toys were offered for sale or as prizes to young customers. In an unusual tie-in, Victoria's Secret launched its "bad girl" look called the Rock Angel Collection by having models arrive at the retailer's flagship Manhattan store on Harley-Davidson motorcycles.[19]

The reason for the tie-in success stories is that brands can leverage similar strengths to achieve a bigger impact in the marketplace. Typically, marketers align themselves with partners that provide numerous complementary elements, including common target audiences, purchase cycle patterns, distribution channels, retailer penetration, and demographics to drive their products and promotions through retail channels and into the minds of consumers.

Consider This

1. Identify all the different promotional tools used in the History Channel's "Lost and Found" promotion.
2. Why do we say that sponsorships and loyalty programs cross the line between advertising and promotion?

PROMOTION STRATEGY

As we explained in Chapter 3, promotions are just one element of the marketing communication mix available to marketers. Here we discuss the strategy behind the use of promotions, as well as how advertising and promotions complement each other, particularly in building brands.

Promotion Objectives

Our earlier discussion of the use of promotion identified a number of reasons for using promotions and these can easily be translated into objectives; many of the reasons focused on the use of promotions in a new-product launch, and how that can deliver trial. Promotions can offer consumers an immediate inducement to try or buy a product, often simply by making the product more valuable. Sales promotion can make consumers who know nothing about the brand develop awareness and trial, as well as persuade them to buy again once they've tried it. It can push the product through the distribution channel by generating positive brand experiences among resellers and buyers in many places along the channel and purchase continuum.

In addition to helping introduce a new product and create brand awareness, promotions can build a brand over time by reinforcing advertising images and messages. Promotions can create an affinity between brands and buyers and provide new channels for reaching audience segments. They can create brand involvement and positive experiences that people associate with the brands.

There are other things that promotions cannot do very effectively. Promotions alone cannot create an image for a brand, for example. They cannot do much to change negative attitudes toward a product, overcome product problems, or reposition a brand. Brand building, however, is an interesting challenge to promotion, so let's look at it in more depth.

The Issue of Brand Building

For years there has been a heated debate concerning sales promotion and brand building. Advertisers claim that the strength of advertising is creating and maintaining brand image and that sales promotion's price deals negate all their hard work by diverting the emphasis from the brand to the price. The result, sales promotion critics complain, is a brand-insensitive consumer. Consider McDonald's, which has long based its image on everyday value, one of the four pillars of McDonald's marketing mantra: Quality, Service, Cleanliness, and Value (QSC&V). Price promotions like a 99-cent Big Mac damage more than its bottom line because the price promotion undercuts the value pillar. In other words, if value is central to McDonald's pricing, then it wouldn't need to have special sale prices.[20]

Procter & Gamble's division manager of advertising and sales promotion explains it this way: "Too many marketers no longer adhere to the fundamental premise of brand building, which is that [brand] franchises aren't built by cutting price but rather by offering superior quality at a reasonable price and clearly communicating that value to consumers. The price-cutting patterns begun in the early 1970s continue today, fostering a short-term orientation that has caused long-term brand building to suffer."[21] Critics point to a general decline in consumer brand loyalty as just one negative result of price-based promotions.

The problem is that brand building is a long and time-consuming process of establishing the brand's core values. Promotion, whether a sale price, a premium, a coupon, or some other incentive, is inherently short term, so the promotion can undermine the brand's established values if not handled carefully. But sales promotion experts argue that sales promotion can help to build brand image. They refer to many cereal brands, rental car companies, airlines, and hotels that have used a variety of well-planned sales promotion strategies (like loyalty programs, for example) to enhance their brand images. Second, they acknowledge that continuous promotion—particularly continuous price promotion—does not work well with brand building, except for discount marketers, whose image is built on the notion of sale prices.

According to one industry expert, the solution to the debate is to make advertising more accountable and promotion more brand focused. He explained, "In isolation, neither traditional advertising nor promotion can deliver the level of long-term image and profitable volume-building that's now required."[22] In other words, the advertising and promotion need to work more closely together and, in particular, short-term campaigns shouldn't be at odds with one another, which is why there is a need for more integration in the planning of marketing communication programs.

Promotion Integration

Advertising and promotion both contribute to the effectiveness of a marketing communication plan, primarily because they do different things and have different objectives. In an effective plan, the two work together, along with other marketing communication tools, to accomplish the overall marketing communication objectives.

The major differences between advertising and sales promotion concern their methods of appeal and the value they add to the sale of the product or service. Advertising is primarily used to create a brand image and high levels of brand awareness over time; promotions are primarily used to create immediate action. To accomplish this immediate goal, sales promotion may rely heavily on rational appeals, such as price deals. In contrast, advertising often relies on emotional appeals to promote the product's image. In other words, advertising tends to add intangible value—brand personality and image—to the good or service. Promotions add tangible value to the good or service and contribute greatly to the profitability of the brand. Table 16.2 summarizes the differences between these two marketing tools in terms of their primary orientations.

Some of the objectives that advertising and promotion share include increasing the number of customers and increasing the use of the product by current customers. Both objectives attempt to change audience perceptions about the product or service, and both attempt to make people do something. Of course, advertisers accomplish these tasks in different ways. In most cases, advertising is needed to support promotions. Price deals, for example, are advertised as a way to build traffic in a store. Contests, sweepstakes, and special events won't work if no one knows about them.

Another area needing cooperation and integration is the use of direct marketing to announce a promotion. For example, we mentioned earlier that marketers often choose direct mail when they want to deliver samples. An EFFIE-winning campaign by Sears titled "Umpteen Appliances" combined direct mail with an advertising specialty mailed to the home as part of its Home Central™ appliance repair service launch. The specialty was a branded refrigerator magnet that provided a visible daily reminder of the new Sears brand of

■ ■ ■
This is a coupon that encourages increasing the quantity purchased.

TABLE

16.2 **The Differences between Advertising and Sales Promotion**

Advertising	*Sales Promotion*
Creates a brand image over time	Creates immediate action
Relies on emotional appeals	Added value strategies rely on rational appeals; impulse appeals use emotion
Adds intangible value to the product or service through image	Adds tangible value to the product or service
Contributes moderately to short-term profitability	Contributes greatly to short-term profitability

appliance repair. This promotion was also supported with magazine advertising announcing this value-added program and the idea of one simple phone number, 1–800–4-REPAIR.

In terms of the integration of promotion with other marketing communication activities, *Promo* magazine conducted a survey[23] in which it asked marketers how well sales promotion was integrated into their overall marketing communication plan. More than 82 percent said it was a part of the integrated effort and 31 percent of those marketers said it was the core component. In other words, most of them were planning promotion as part of an integrated marketing communication program:

A component of our integrated marketing plan	51%
The core component of our integrated marketing plan	31.4%
A separate program not integrated into the overall plan	13.7%

Promotion Effectiveness

Since promotions are so focused on action, it makes sense that sales is the primary measure of their effectiveness. After all, they are called "sales promotions." Response rate—consumers calling the company, sending back a card—is also important to sales promotion. So are redemption rates, which are the rates at which people redeem coupons, refunds, and rebates, which are used to evaluate the effectiveness of these promotional programs. All of these will be discussed in more detail in Chapter 19.

An important dimension of sales promotion effectiveness that should be mentioned here is **payout planning**. An example of poor payout planning comes from Maytag and an ill-fated U.K. promotion. It was a simple offer: Customers in Great Britain and Ireland were offered two free airline tickets to the United States or Continental Europe when they purchased at least $150 worth of Hoover products. Hoover planned to use the commissions it made from land arrangements, such as hotel reservations and car rentals, to help pay for the airline tickets. How did the promotion turn into a catastrophe? Unfortunately, the commissions were less than anticipated and the ticket demand was far greater. Maytag's travel agents began attaching unreasonable demands to the free tickets, expensive extras, inconvenient airports, and undesirable departure dates to discourage acceptance of the offer. All these strategies turned happy winners into complaining customers. In the aftermath, Hoover fired three top executives and set up a $30 million fund to pay for the airline tickets.

The trade press is full of stories about poorly designed or performing promotions. Such failures hurt companies' reputations, waste money, and sometimes even hurt consumers. For example, in 2001, Burger King had to recall 400,000 toy boats given away with kids' meals after reports that children had been stuck with metal pins that came off the boats too easily. That recall came a week after McDonald's recalled a Happy Meal "Scooter Bug" toy. In 1999 the fast-food industry reeled from the deaths of two infants who suffocated from containers used in a Pokémon promotion. About 25 million of those toys were recalled. So promotions that work can deliver sales to a company, but if they are not well planned they can also negatively affect the brand's reputation.

Consider This

1. Explain the debate over sales promotion and its impact on branding.
2. How do you determine whether a sales promotion is effective?

IT'S A WRAP

HISTORY CHANNEL FINDS A WINNING PROMOTION IDEA

■ ■ ■   Consumer sales promotions are directed at the ultimate user of the good or service. They are intended to add value to a product, providing an incentive so that when consumers go to a store they will look for a particular brand. Trade promotion is used to encourage channel members to support a promotion and push a product. Both are designed to create an immediate response.

The History Channel's "Lost and Found" promotion resulted in a significant increase in viewership with a total of 16.9 million unique viewers watching *History's Lost and Found* in the third quarter, which represented a 26 percent increase in total audience. "History's Lost and Found Auction Block" generated more than 572 million online impressions worth an estimated $29 million. Featured on the *Today Show* and in *Newsweek* along with other media coverage, the promotion achieved significant publicity, while generating more than 110 million impressions. Traffic to historychannel.com was boosted significantly, and the Lost and Found section averaged 50,000 views per month during the promotion.

■ ■ ■ Summary

1. **Explain the principles that drive the use of sales promotion and discuss why advertisers are spending increasing sums of money on sales promotion.** Sales promotion offers an "extra incentive" to take action. It gives the product or service additional value and motivates people to respond. Sales promotion is growing rapidly for many reasons. It offers the manager short-term bottom-line results; it's accountable; it's less expensive than advertising; it speaks to the current needs of the consumer to receive more value from products; and it responds to marketplace changes.

2. **List and explain the use of various consumer promotions.** Sales promotions directed at consumers include price deals, coupons, contests and sweepstakes, refunds, premiums, specialty advertising, continuity programs, and sampling. Their purpose is to pull the product through the distribution channel.

3. **Summarize the types and purposes of trade promotions.** Sales promotions directed at the trade include point-of-purchase displays, retailer merchandising kits, trade shows, contests, and price deals such as discounts, bonuses, and advertising allowances. These are used to push the product through the channel.

4. **Describe the use of other types of promotions: sponsorships, specialties, interactive promotions, licensing, loyalty programs, and co-marketing programs.** Sponsorship is used to increase the perceived value of a brand by associating it with a cause or celebrity. The purpose of specialty advertising is to serve as a reminder. Internet promotions can be used to drive people to a sponsor's Web page. Licensing "rents" an established brand to other companies to use on their products. Loyalty programs are designed to increase customer retention. Co-marketing programs are designed to build stronger relationships between manufacturers and retailers.

5. **Explain the strategic use of promotions in marketing in terms of brand building, new-product launches, integration, and effectiveness.** Promotion offers an incentive to action and it stimulates trial, which is important in launching a new product. In brand building it can reinforce advertising images and messages and encourage or remind consumers to buy the brand again. It can be used to push or pull a product through the distribution channel by creating positive brand experiences. Interactive promotions are more involving. Sales promotion is used with advertising to provide immediate behavioral action. It is effective when the return on the investment more than covers the cost of the promotion.

Key Terms

ad slicks, 461
ambush marketing, 464
co-branding, 467
co-marketing, 466
contests, 456
continuity program, 466
coupons, 456
event marketing, 464

frequency program, 466
licensing, 467
loaders, 462
loyalty (continuity, frequency)
  program, 466
payout planning, 470
point-of-purchase display
  (POP), 461

premium, 456
price deal, 455
pull strategy, 462
push strategy, 462
rebate, 456
refund, 456
sales promotion, 453
sampling, 456

self-liquidator premium,
  458
specialty advertising, 458
sponsorship, 464
sweepstakes, 456
tie-ins, 467
trade deal, 462
trade show, 462

Review Questions

1. Define sales promotion and explain its primary contribution to a marketing program.
2. List the primary tools of consumer promotions.
3. Why is trade promotion so important?
4. What are the primary trade promotion tools?
5. What is the difference between sponsorships and event marketing?
6. What's the role of sales promotion in an integrated marketing communication program?

Discussion Questions

1. You have just been named product manager for Bright White, a new laundry detergent that will be introduced to the market within the next six months. Would you use a push or a pull strategy? Why?
2. Tom Jackson's marketing professor is covering some promotion methods, explaining that in selecting the consumer sales promotion, planners must know the brand situation and objectives before techniques are chosen. Some techniques tend to increase product use and others are used to get new consumers to try the product. "Which methods belong with which objective and why?" the professor asks. How should Tom answer this question?
3. Janice Wilcox is a brand manager for a new line of eye cosmetics. She is about to present her planning strategy to division management. Janice knows her company has been successful in using sales promotion plans lately, but she has strong misgivings about following the company trend. "This new line must create a consumer brand franchise, and promotion isn't the best way to do that," she thinks to herself. How is sales promotion weak in building and maintaining a brand? Should Janice propose no promotion, or is there a reasonable compromise for her to consider?
4. Jambo Products' promotion manager, Sean Devlin, is calculating the cost of a proposed consumer coupon drop for March. The media cost of a free-standing insert for the coupon and production charges is $125,000. The distribution will be 4 million coupons, with an expected redemption of 5 percent. The coupon value is 50 cents, and Devlin has estimated the handling and compensation to the store to be 8 cents per redeemed coupon. Based on these estimates, what will be the cost to Devlin's budget?

Class Projects

1. Look through your local newspaper and identify a retailer who is engaging in co-op advertising. Interview the store manager and determine the specific arrangements that exist between the advertiser and the retailer. What is the attitude of the retailer toward this arrangement? Write a two-page report.
2. Select a print ad for a national marketer. Redesign the ad, including the use of a consumer sales promotion. Show both the before version and the after version to five people. Assess whether the second version has increased their intention to buy.

3. Check the Web site for Camp Jeep® (www.jeep.com then type the "campjeep" keyword). Explain how the event works to build and reinforce customer relationships. Find another company that uses a special event to create a relationship-building program. Explain that program and compare it to Camp Jeep. Which do you believe is the most effective special event and why?

HANDS-ON

Upromise Uses Values Marketing to Pay for College

Most consumers are familiar with loyalty programs from airlines, hotel chains, and car-rental companies. Airlines call them frequent flier miles, and people who choose a particular airline each time they fly can accumulate them to get a free flight or an upgrade. The program rewards heavy fliers and encourages fliers to remain loyal to an airline for a reason besides low fares.

Many people probably believe it would be great if loyalty programs like these existed for the places where most consumers spend the bulk of their money—for example, grocery stores and gas stations. In fact, such a program does exist. Upromise, a college-savings loyalty network, was started in 2001 by Michael Bronner and George Bell. The idea is simple. When consumers shop at participating stores, a portion of the receipts is set aside for a college-savings plan in the consumer's name. There is no cost for the shopper, other than the time necessary to sign up for the program.

One obvious benefit of participation is the opportunity for people to make painless, regular contributions to their children's college savings. The National Center for Education Statistics estimates that in order to have tuition and board for a child attending a private college in 2010, parents would have needed to save $800 a month starting in 1998. At those prices, parents probably want any help that they can get. Of course many people do not spend enough on groceries and gas to generate even $100 a month, but Upromise allows families to pool contributions. That means grandparents and other relatives can use their grocery purchases to help as well. What if you've just graduated from college? Upromise allows recent grads to enroll in the program to pay off their student loans.

Helping people to pay a big expense is an important benefit of the Upromise program, but some see much more. "As a marketer, I am giving money and I'm expecting the customers to say 'I'm going to do more business with them because I like their values,'" says Rick Barlow, chairman-CEO of Frequency Marketing. "It's a brilliant and a powerful idea because it combines an aspirational and an altruistic goal." Bronner puts it this way, "I see the evolution from value marketing to values marketing."

There are benefits for participating Upromise sponsors, too. Companies can track participant purchases because people in the program have to use either a major credit card (such as Citibank cards) or a grocery chain card. A small brand can build customer loyalty and encourage consumers to switch by offering a larger credit than its competitors.

In just three years Upromise has proven very successful. The company has signed partnerships with major brands including ExxonMobil, AOL, Citibank, and Publix supermarkets. Marketing costs are low since program sponsors do the bulk of the advertising. And consumers are signing up in droves. The program currently has 5 million participants, and membership is growing by about 50 percent a year.

Consider This

1. What are the risks for brands that become Upromise sponsors? What are the risks for those that don't?
2. Although the program seems like a "win-win" for consumers and marketers, some critics have pointed out that most people will not be able to save for a college education exclusively by participation in Upromise. In addition, some suggest that people are spending in an unhealthy way in order to maximize their credits. How should Upromise respond to these criticisms?
3. How does the use of a sales promotion, such as the Upromise program, benefit a brand? How would you recommend evaluating the effectiveness of the promotion?

Sources: Cara Beardi, "Been There, Done That," *Advertising Age* (July 23, 2001); Dale Buss, "Giving Credit Where It's Due," *Brandweek* (July 26, 2004); Anne Marie Chaker, "How Shopping Can Pay for College; Rewards Programs Offering Tuition Benefits Emerge as a Popular Savings Tool," *Wall Street Journal* (September 23, 2004): D2; Kaja Whitehouse, "Shopping Rebates Promise to Ease College Tuition Costs," *Wall Street Journal* (June 12, 2002): D2.

Mark Lawson stuffs a 26th hot dog into his mouth, just enough to win an annual contest held in Beachwood, NJ.

ELSEWHERE IN AMERICA, 12 MILLION CHILDREN ARE FIGHTING HUNGER.

THE SOONER YOU BELI
or visit feedingchild

Kim Werther hands out one of the 2,300 antacid tablets she served to overstuffed participants at Monroe County's annual Chili Cookoff.

ELSEWHERE IN AMERICA, 12 MILLION CHILDREN ARE FIGHTING HUNGER

THE SOONER YOU BELIEVE IT, THE SOONER WE CAN END IT. Call 1-800-FEED-KIDS.
or visit feedingchildrenbetter.org to learn about child hunger in America.

I tell my children little white lies.

I tell them we're skipping lunch today so we have more time to spend at the park. I tell them the refrigerator is broken so we can't keep any food in it. I don't tell them that because I bought medicine there's no money left for food. When I was little, I was told that telling little white lies isn't really a sin. I hope that wasn't a little white lie.

Food or medicine? **1 in 5 kids in A**
like this. To help in your co
feedingchildrenbetter.org. Hunge

Insert Your Local Food
or Food Rescue Progra

Ad Council

Julie is cold. She has chicken skin she says.
She woke up in the middle of the night shivering be
I turned the heat down. I'm afraid if my bill gets t
I won't have any money left for food. I pull Julie cl
hug her tight. She says she will be fine - she kno
not really a chicken.

Heat or food? **1 in 5 kids in America face hu**
like this. To help in your community, cal
feedingchildrenbetter.org. Hunger. A choice n

Insert Your Local Food Bank
or Food Rescue Program Here

Ad Council

Public Relations

**Kids Are Hungry.
Believe It!**

Award:
Silver EFFIE®

Organization:
Ad Council

Agency:
*Powell Communications/
BBH*

Campaign:
*"Feeding Children Better:
Child Hunger"*

CHAPTER OBJECTIVES

After reading this chapter, you will be able to:

1. Explain what public relations is and how it differs from advertising.

2. Describe the most common types of public relations programs.

3. Analyze the key decisions in public relations planning.

4. Explain the most common types of public relations tools.

5. Discuss the importance of measuring the results of public relations efforts.

Over 14 million children in the United States live with hunger today. But, the American public is not even aware that child hunger is a U.S. issue, especially in such great proportions. This is so because the face of child hunger is hidden in America. We do not see emaciated children with distended bellies as in photos from "third world" countries. Yet, one-fifth of all American children live with hunger every day. (By hunger, we mean that millions of children skip meals unwillingly each day based on their families' unfortunate economic situation.) And not only are people not aware of the U.S. child hunger issue, but there is also great resistance to recognizing the problem. People just do not believe child hunger could possibly be a *real* U.S. issue. After all, we live in a country with such wealth and an abundance of resources.

Also, if any American children are suffering from hunger, people blame the parents for being abusive, unemployed, lazy, or drug-

475

addicted. Yet, the reality is that over one-third of adults seeking food assistance for their families are employed but still struggling to make ends meet. Sometimes, they have to choose between paying the rent or feeding their children. That's the problem the nonprofit Ad Council faced with its Child Hunger campaign. (The Ad Council is a network of agencies and media that donate their time and services to good causes.) The New York–based Powell Communications/BBH took on the assignment to bring this message to the American people.

The PSA Strategy

The campaign was designed to educate people and create awareness of the seriousness of child hunger in the United States by putting a realistic face on the problem while not stigmatizing the suffering families. It also needed to challenge stereotypes and allow no emotional "escape route" such as scapegoating the parents. The objectives were to:

* Maximize media exposure.
* Change perception: Make people believe that child hunger in the United States is real and get them to empathize with the victims—not judge them.
* Inspire action: Get people to call the 1-800 number and visit the Web site.
* Generate collective concern and discussion.

The strategy was to use a *public service campaign,* which relies on donated services and media time and space. In terms of targeting, the campaign had to first move the public service advertising (PSA) directors at TV or radio stations, those people responsible for deciding which PSAs are used. The ads needed to strike a strong emotional chord with this group. Given that the Ad Council would have no control over the media schedule since the time is donated by the station, the audience would include all adults in the market. However, to be more realistic the planners decided that those who would pay attention to these messages were people who showed more interest in and involvement with both children and charities. To reach these people, the agency's consumer research showed that the campaign needed to make people feel they were walking in the shoes of someone dealing with child hunger.

Message Strategy: Disarming through Sympathy

Powell's research found that Americans really think this issue is someone else's, not ours. And if U.S. child hunger was such a huge concern, the public questions why we aren't hearing or reading more about it in the news. These insights led to the message *U.S. child hunger is real*—and to the strategy of developing a supporting publicity program that provided information to the media. The agency enlisted Joe Pytka to direct as he is known for depicting reality in an understated way and working with nonactor talent. Pytka donated his services to shoot the campaign.

In order to get people to recognize the truth, the agency team wanted to disarm people by openly acknowledging their disbelief in the campaign's tagline "The sooner you believe it, the sooner we can end it." In the TV commercials, the agency team chose to put a realistic face on child hunger through narrative stories uncovered by talking to workers and client families at food shelters in various states. The print and outdoor advertising showed visuals of

American excess (a hot dog–eating contest, a Las Vegas buffet, etc.) and juxtaposed these with the shocking child hunger statistics.

The results of this highly effective campaign are detailed in the It's a Wrap feature at the end of the chapter.

Source: EFFIE brief provided by Powell/BBH and the Ad Council.

Handling a campaign assignment calls for extraordinary public relations skills and a well-thought-out plan. This chapter considers the role of public relations in an organization and how goodwill can be used effectively in a marketing communication program. It discusses many aspects of public relations, including the types of PR programs, PR planning, and PR tools. As we introduce these topics, we will learn more about the development of the EFFIE-winning Child Hunger campaign.

THE PRACTICE OF PUBLIC RELATIONS

Public relations is used to generate goodwill for an organization. That mission is as broad in scope as the definition from the Public Relations Society of America (PRSA) suggests: **Public relations** (PR) helps an organization and its publics relate to each other to the benefit of both.[1] So public relations is focused on all the relationships that an organization has with its various publics. By **publics**, we mean all the groups of people with which a company or organization interacts: employees, media, community groups, shareholders, and so forth. Another term for this is **stakeholders**, which refers more specifically to people who have a stake (financial or not) in a company or organization. Although public relations has a distinguished tradition, people often mistake it for **publicity**, which refers to getting news media coverage. Publicity is focused on the news media and their audiences, which is just one aspect of public relations. The focus on bringing various interests into harmony is apparent in PRSA's Code of Ethical Practice, shown here.

PRSA Code of Ethical Practice

As a member of the Public Relations Society of America:
I base my professional principles on the value and dignity of the individual, holding that the free exercise of human rights, especially freedom of speech, freedom of assembly, and freedom of the press, is essential to the practice of public relations.

In serving the interests of clients and employers, I dedicate myself to the goals of better communication, understanding, and cooperation among the diverse individuals, groups, and institutions of society, and of equal opportunity of employment in the public relations profession.

www. prsa.org

Public relations is practiced by a wide range of organizations: companies, governments, trade and professional associations, nonprofit organizations, the travel and tourism industry, educational systems, labor unions, politicians, organized sports, and the media. Most organizations have in-house public relations departments that handle the firms' public relations work, although many also hire outside public relations agencies.

On one level, public relations is a tactical function in that PR staff produce a variety of communication tools to achieve corporate image objectives. On a higher level, it is a management function that monitors public opinion and advises senior corporate managers on how to achieve positive relationships with various audiences (publics) in order to effectively manage the organization's image and reputation. Its publics may be external (customers, the news media, the investment community, the general public, government bodies) and internal (shareholders, employees). Martin Sorrell, CEO of WPP Group, one of the largest advertising and marketing services groups in the world, believes that "public relations and public affairs are probably higher up the CEO's agenda than advertising, market research, or other forms of specialist communication." As Sorrell notes, public relations practitioners have "access to the CEO's office," which gives them more influence on corporate policies.[2]

Public Opinion

Public relations programs are built on an understanding of public opinion on issues critical to the organization, such as how a company's practices impact on the environment and its local community; or workers' rights and how a company deals with its employees. **Public opinion**, the label describing what a group of people think, is "a belief, based not necessarily on fact but on the conception or evaluation of an event, person, institution, or product."[3] The public relations strategist researches the answers to two primary questions about public opinion to design effective public relations programs. First, which publics are most important to the organization, now and in the future? Second, what do these publics think? Particular emphasis falls on understanding the role of **opinion leaders**, important people who influence the opinions of others. The Matter of Practice box illustrates a campaign designed to change public opinion.

Reputation: Goodwill, Trust, and Integrity

Public **goodwill** is the greatest asset any organization can have. A well-informed public with a positive attitude toward an organization is critical to the organization's survival— and that is why creating goodwill is the primary goal of most public relations programs. A public relations program that is tuned to creating goodwill operates as the conscience of the organization. Howard Rubenstein, an elder statesman in public relations, advises clients and colleagues that deliberately deceiving is "a career limiting move." He has a paperweight in his office in his 50-year-old agency that says, "If you tell the truth, you don't have to remember anything."[4]

Principle

Public relations is the conscience of the company with the objective of creating trust and maintaining the integrity of the organization.

The trust on which goodwill is based comes from corporate integrity. In these post-Enron days many companies have dedicated more resources and efforts to creating an integrity platform for the company. Some companies have even created a chief integrity officer (CIO) position or made that assignment an important part of the PR office's mission.[5]

Integrity involves more than image. **Image** is a perception based on messages delivered by the advertising and other marketing communication tools. **Reputation**, however, is based on an organization's actual behavior. Image mirrors what a company says about itself but reputation reflects what other people say about the company.[6] Here are a set of public relations principles that guide an organization's integrity and create trust:[7]

- Our goal is integrity.
- We have constructive aspirations.
- We live a philosophy of integrity.
- We have a commitment to compliance and good conduct.
- We recognize those who achieve the best work in the best way.
- Our vigilance is driven by our principles, priorities, and conscience.
- Everyone is committed to integrity.

Comparing Public Relations and Advertising

Designing ads, preparing written messages, and buying time or space are the key concerns of advertisers. Their objective is to create the consumer awareness and motivation that deliver sales. The goal of public relations specialists is communicating with various stakeholders, managing the organization's image and reputation, and creating positive public attitudes and goodwill toward the organization. Ultimately, the difference between advertising and public relations is that public relations takes a longer, broader view of the

A MATTER OF PRACTICE
"I Love Smoke-Free NYC"

The scene is set for a knock-down, drag-out fight over a smoking ban in New York City bars and restaurants. On one side are bar and restaurant owners, smokers, and tourism groups who fear the ban will hurt business and violate smokers' rights. On the other side are the New York City Department of Health, the U.S. Environmental Protection Agency (EPA), people who don't smoke, and waiters and waitresses who object to secondhand smoke.

The city had passed one of the toughest smoking bans in the nation in 2003 and a new state smoking ban was also being considered by the state legislature. Opponents of the ban were trying to overturn the law by implying that the majority of New Yorkers opposed the law and that the ban would hurt the city's nightlife and hinder recovery from the effects of 9/11 and the recession. They also argued that the secondhand smoke claims were bogus. Bar owners rallied at City Hall and at the state capital and they held town meetings across the five NYC boroughs to pressure lawmakers to modify or overturn the bans.

Thirty days before the ban was to take effect media coverage was dominated by stories about unhappy smokers, as well as restaurant and bar owners. The state vote was pending in the legislature and vulnerable to the drumbeat of opposition. A coalition of the ban's supporters contacted the Fleishman-Hillard agency, with a tiny budget of $100,000 to mount a campaign to counter opposition to the ban by presenting the facts about secondhand smoke and the ban's widespread support. The phrase, "I Love Smoke-Free NYC," which is a variation on the city's famous slogan, gave the campaign an easily recognized theme.

The effort was focused on the five-day countdown to the law's effective date. The countdown started with a launch event held at the popular Bryant Park Grill located near the city's historic library. With its airy dining room and floor-to-ceiling windows, it was a perfect symbol of a smoke-free atmosphere. The city's health commissioner was the keynote speaker, but the centerpiece of the event was the announcement by the Bryant Park Grill's manager that the restaurant was going smoke free five days early in honor of the countdown. Bartenders and wait staff also gave testimonials about the hardships they faced with secondhand smoke. Speakers from the American Lung Association and the American Cancer Society underscored the benefits of a smoke-free environment with statistics.

The launch was followed with a postcard campaign to officials. The www.nycsmokefree.org Web site presented information about the campaign but also made it possible for New Yorkers to send e-cards to officials. A series of events similar to the launch were held around the city including celebrations when the ban went into effect. "I Love Smoke-Free NYC" buttons were worn by supporters of the ban, particularly wait persons. Articles were pitched to City Hall beat reporters and health and lifestyle writers to get them to present the facts about the secondhand smoke issue, as well as cover the events.

As a result of the publicity effort, every major media outlet in the city covered the launch and provided coverage for the four follow-up event celebrations. The launch event received lengthy segments on two of the major stations with repeated segments throughout the day. All stories showed happy New Yorkers supporting or enjoying the ban. Here's a tally of the results:

- The publicity during the five-day countdown period resulted in 15.2 million print impressions and nearly 10 million broadcast impressions.
- The campaign gathered tens of thousands of signatures and e-mails to officials in support of the city and state bans.
- Citywide public opinion surveys showed 62 and then 70 percent support for the ban. A statewide survey found 63 percent support for the state ban.

Most importantly, the NYC ban was preserved and the state law was supported despite the concerted campaign by the opposition. Furthermore, the campaign was transformed into a statewide "I Love Smoke-Free NY" campaign for the state law and adopted by county tobacco control coalitions across the state. Its effectiveness is what led the Public Relations Society of America (PRSA) New York Chapter to recognize the campaign with a Big Apple Award.

Consider This
1. What problems did this campaign have to overcome?
2. What public relations tools were used to get the message out in support of the campaign?

Source: Big Apple Award brief provided by Fleishman-Hillard.

importance of image and reputation as a corporate competitive asset and addresses a greater number of target audiences. Public relations and advertising also differ in how they use the media, the level of control they have over message delivery, and their perceived credibility. Credibility was a major factor in the Child Hunger campaign.

Media Use   In contrast to buying advertising time and space, public relations people seek to persuade media gatekeepers to carry stories about their company. **Gatekeepers** include writers, producers, editors, talk show coordinators, and newscasters. This aspect of public relations is called *publicity* and carries no direct media costs. Even when public relations uses paid-for media such as advertising, the message focuses on the organization, with little or no attempt to sell a brand or product line.

Control   In the case of news stories, the public relations strategist is at the mercy of the media gatekeeper. There is no guarantee that all or even part of a story will appear. PR writers write the story, send it to the media, and cross their fingers that this story will appear. In fact, there is the real risk that a story may be rewritten or reorganized by an editor so that it no longer means what the strategist intended. In contrast, advertising runs exactly as the client who paid for it has approved. And it runs as scheduled.

Credibility   The public tends to trust the media more than they do advertisers. This consumer tendency is called the **implied third-party endorsement** factor. For example, when Tom Brokaw delivered a two-minute story on the NBC *Nightly News* about an Eli Lilly pharmaceutical breakthrough, he was more credible than a print ad sponsored by Eli Lilly.[8] Thomas Harris, in his book *Value-Added Public Relations,* observes that today's sophisticated and skeptical consumers know when they are being informed and when they are being "sold to." He explains, "PR closes the marketing credibility gap because it is the one marketing communication tool devoted to providing information, not salesmanship."[9]

Types of Public Relations Programs

The word *relations* in public relations refers to relationships with various stakeholders. In fact, the main subspecialties in the field—public affairs, media relations, employee relations, and financial relations—call attention to important relationships with such groups as the general public, the media, employees, and the financial community. Figure 17.1 outlines the various publics, or stakeholders, for a multinational company. The term **relationship marketing** introduces a point of view in marketing planning that resembles that of public relations.[10]

The key publics addressed by relationship management programs in public relations are media, employees, the financial community (including a company's shareholders), government, and the general public.

Media Relations The area that focuses on developing media contacts—knowing who in the media might be interested in the organization's story—is called **media relations**. When you say "public relations," most people immediately think about publicity, which indicates the importance of this media function. The organization initiates publicity and provides pertinent information to the media. A successful relationship between a public relations person and the editor is built on a PR person's reputation for honesty, accuracy, and professionalism. Once this reputation is tarnished or lost, the public relations person cannot function effectively as a liaison between a company and the media.

Employee Relations Programs that communicate information to employees are called **employee relations**. This function may belong to public relations, although it may also be the responsibility of human resources. A related program is called **internal marketing**, which is communication efforts aimed at informing employees about marketing programs and encouraging their support.

Financial Relations All the communication efforts aimed at the financial community, such as press releases sent to business publications, meetings with investors and analysts, and the annual report, which the federal government requires of publicly held companies, are referred to as **financial relations**.

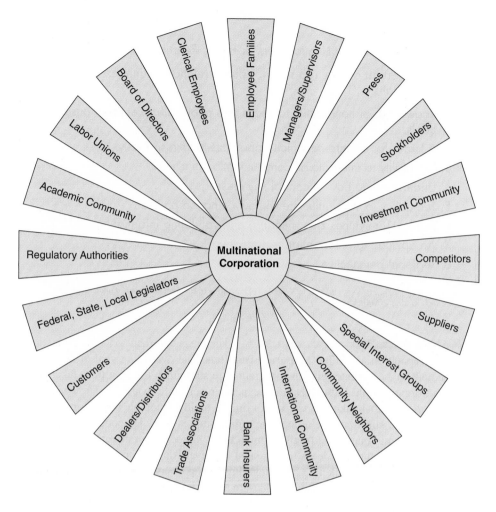

Twenty Key Publics
Of the 20 key publics of a typical multinational corporation, relationship management programs focus on the media, employees, the financial community, government, and the general public.

Source: Fraser P. Seitel, *The Practice of Public Relations* (Upper Saddle River, NJ: Prentice Hall, 1998), 10.

Public Affairs Corporate communication programs with government and with the public on issues related to government and regulation are called **public affairs**. For example, a company building a new plant may need to gain the approval of government health and public safety regulators. Public affairs also includes **lobbying**, when the company provides information to legislators in order to get their support and vote on a particular bill. It also includes communication efforts with consumer or activist groups who seek to influence government policies. **Issue management** is another term for this function. In addition to government relations, public affairs programs also monitor public opinion about issues central to the organization's interest and develop programs to communicate to and with the public about these issues.

Fund-raising **Fund-raising** is the practice of raising money by collecting donations. It is used by nonprofit organizations, such as museums, hospitals, and emergency groups (such as the Red Cross) and directed to potential donors. Professional fund-raisers know how to make the initial contacts that inspire other people to participate, how to use other marketing communication tools such as advertising, and how to make the best use of special events and public recognition. At universities fund-raising is called *development.*

Cause Marketing When companies associate themselves with a good cause, providing assistance as well as financial support, the practice is called **cause marketing**. This topic—as well as related areas, such as nonprofit marketing, public communication campaigns, social marketing, and mission marketing—will be discussed in more detail in Chapter 18.

   Other areas of public relations, such as corporate reputation management, crisis management, marketing public relations, and public communication campaigns are distinctive because of their focus rather than their target audience.

Practical Tips

Test Yourself: Would I Like to Work in Public Relations or Public Affairs?

Here's a short list of required skills for public relations managers or public affairs specialists:

1. Knowledge of how public relations and public affairs support business goals.
2. A knack for discerning which opponents to take seriously.
3. The ability to integrate all communication functions.
4. Understanding how to control key messages.
5. The ability to have influence without being too partisan.
6. A talent for synthesizing, filtering, and validating information.
7. An aptitude for information technology.
8. A global perspective.

Source: Doug Pinkham, "What It Takes to Work in Public Affairs and Public Relations," *Public Relations Quarterly* (Spring 2004): 15.

Corporate Reputation Management   The areas that focus on an organization's image and reputation are called **corporate relations**. The overriding goal of **reputation management** in a corporate relations program is to strengthen the trust that stakeholders have in an organization. Public relations expert Fraser Seitel warns in *The Practice of Public Relations* that "it takes a great deal of time to build a favorable image for a corporation but only one slip to create a negative public impression." He continues, "In other words, the corporate image is a fragile commodity."[11] Since corporate reputation is a perception, it is earned through deeds, not created by advertising. In an article on corporate reputation management, marketing consultant Prema Nakra says, "A company's reputation affects its ability to sell products and services, to attract investors, to hire talented staff, and to exert influence in government circles." She concludes that "once lost—or even tarnished—[it is] incredibly difficult to regain."[12]

Principle
Reputation is earned based on what you do, not what you say about yourself.

Crisis Management   There is no greater test for an organization than how it deals with a crisis. The key to **crisis management** is to anticipate the possibility of a disaster and plan how to deal with the bad news and all the affected publics. For example, Jack-in-the-Box restaurants has had a difficult time recovering from the public relations disaster it faced when a 2-year-old child ate a Kid's Meal from the Jack-in-the-Box restaurant in Tacoma, Washington, and 10 days later died of kidney and heart failure. Soon reports came in that more than 300 people had been stricken with the same E. coli bacteria responsible for the Tacoma death. Most victims had eaten recently at Jack-in-the-Box outlets in Idaho, Nevada, and Washington. Others apparently got sick after contact with restaurant customers.

The company's 12-person crisis team did some things right: It quickly scrapped nearly 20,000 pounds of hamburger patties prepared at meat plants where the bacteria were suspected of originating. It also changed meat suppliers, installed a toll-free number to field consumer complaints, and instructed employees to turn up the cooking heat to kill the deadly germ. But it took nearly a week for the company to admit publicly its responsibility for the poisonings. Even then, the admission seemed half-hearted. At a Seattle news conference, the company's president attempted to deflect blame, first criticizing state health authorities for not telling his company about new cooking regulations, then pointing a finger at the meat supplier. The damage to the company's reputation has been long lasting.

An effective crisis plan can help to both avoid crises and ease the damage if one occurs. A plan outlines who contacts the various stakeholders who might be affected (employees, customers, suppliers, civic and community leaders, government agencies), who speaks to the news media, and who sets up and runs an on-site disaster-management center. Companies also should conduct unannounced crisis training during which staff must drop everything and deal with a simulated crisis as it unfolds.

Marketing Public Relations   One area where advertising and public relations overlap is **marketing public relations (MPR)**. Tom Harris, author of *The Marketer's Guide to Public Relations,* says MPR is the fastest-growing area of public relations. He defines MPR as the process of planning and delivering programs that encourage sales and contribute to customer satisfaction by providing communication that addresses the needs and wants of consumers. MPR is different from a more general public relations approach in its consumer and sales focus. However, the need to establish a credibility platform is similar in both; that's what PR brings to marketing and is PR's greatest strength in an integrated marketing communication program. In other words, MPR supports marketing's product and sales focus by increasing brand credibility and the company's credibility with consumers.

Public Communication Campaigns   Used as a way to change public opinion, **public communication campaigns** also discourage socially harmful behaviors, such as discouraging driving in areas with air-pollution problems. Sometimes they are engaged in *counter-marketing* as they try to counter other advertising messages. For example, the Florida "Truth" campaign by the Porter-Novelli agency was designed to argue against the big tobacco companies' advertising and appeal to teenagers. The strategy was to get young people to rebel against the tobacco industry. An extension of that campaign by Crispin, Porter & Bogusky, a Miami-based advertising agency, featured teens in one award-winning commercial piling body bags outside Phillip Morris's New York headquarters. The campaign produced the largest single-year decline in teen smoking in nearly 20 years.

This postcard from the "Truth" campaign was mailed to Hollywood stars with a personal message on the back asking them to protest smoking in movies. Several stars, including supermodel Christy Turlington, talk show host Leeza Gibbons, and Melrose Place star Antonio Sabato Jr., publicly pledged to fight the entertainment industry's depiction of tobacco.

Consider This

1. In how many different ways does the concept of "relationships" represent a public relations program focus?
2. In what situations would you use public relations rather than advertising?

PUBLIC RELATIONS PLANNING

Planning for a public relations campaign is similar to planning an advertising campaign. The plan should complement the marketing and advertising strategies so the organization communicates with one clear voice to its various publics. The plan also identifies the various key publics and the public relations activities that PR people use to address the interests of its various publics. In addition to identifying key targets, public relations plans also specify the objectives that give direction to the PR program or campaign.

Research and SWOT Analysis

Research is used by an organization, as well as outside PR agencies, throughout the planning and implementation of a PR plan. It's also used afterward to determine if the effort was successful and if the organization is spending its money wisely on the public relations efforts. For example, to better understand the Child Hunger problem, the Powell/BBH creative team went where child hunger lived, such as shelters and soup kitchens. It was there that the team heard the real stories that would be the foundation for the advertising. They learned, sadly, that people can be terribly creative when they're hungry. Mothers gather ketchup packets to make "ketchup soup" for their families, water down powdered milk to make it stretch, and even send a sick child to school in order to give them a meal. These insights formed the advertising idea of using real stories to dramatize the problem and build sympathy.

The PR effort may also begin with a more formal type of background research, called a **communication audit**, to assess the internal and external PR environment that affects the organization's audiences, objectives, competitors, and past results. An annual audit or a campaign-specific audit can be used to ensure that a program is on track and performing as intended. Often **benchmarking** is used to identify baselines from previous audits or audits of other related companies and industries so there is a point of comparison.[13] A **gap analysis**, which measures the differences in perceptions and attitudes between groups or between the organization and its publics, may be part of the analysis.[14]

Since public opinion is so central to public relations programs, companies often use ongoing research to monitor opinions and attitudes. Trend-tracking services such as the Intelligence Factory (www.intelligencefactory.com) monitor trends important to companies and organizations. The Porter Novelli agency annually tracks American institutions' credibility, as well as consumers' concerns about such topics as health, nutrition, and their lifestyles. The company analyzes the findings in terms of seven different personality types, from "Hard-Living Hedonists" (people who smoke, drink, and eat cheeseburgers without even a twinge of guilt) to "Decent Dolittles" (people who pay attention to health issues but can't bring themselves to do much about it). The agency believes such information is useful in identifying people's orientation to health messages. It's also helpful in targeting various types of publics based on their general attitudes toward key issues, such as antismoking. The survey has consistently found that the credibility of institutions such as government, the media, and corporations is declining. The agency interpreted these findings to mean that America "is deeply mired in the Age of Cynicism."

As in marketing or advertising planning, a PR plan begins with background research leading to a **situation analysis**, or **SWOT** analysis, that evaluates a company's **s**trengths, **w**eaknesses, **o**pportunities, and **t**hreats. This analysis creates a general understanding of the difficulty of changing people's attitudes about issues like child hunger. Understanding the nature of the problem makes it easier to determine the appropriate communication objectives and the target stakeholder audiences, or publics, who will be addressed by the PR efforts. In public relations planning, the situation analysis can include such topics as changes in public opinion, industry and consumer trends, economic trends, governmental regulations and oversight programs, and corporate strategies that affect a company's relationships with stakeholders.

Targeting

As in advertising and other marketing communication areas, it is important to understand the target audience before designing the campaign. Research is conducted to identify the appropriate "publics" to which to address the public relations message.

The CIGNA insurance company, for example, realized that consumers have little empathy for insurance companies and view the industry as one that takes your money, gives back reluctantly, and raises premiums when its costs go up. In order to launch its "Power of Caring" campaign, which was a philanthropic sponsorship program that featured well-known personalities and their charitable causes, CIGNA conducted primary research to identify the "conscientious consumer." Having this information kept CIGNA from inadvertently putting out a campaign that its target audience might have found irritating or self-serving. The research determined that a conscientious consumer is someone who:

- shows higher propensity for action and involvement in areas such as family and health.
- is usually the decision maker in the purchase of CIGNA's health, financial, and insurance products.
- is more inclined to purchase from companies that support charitable causes.
- has a higher propensity for community volunteer work.
- represents approximately 30 percent of the U.S. population.

Objectives and Strategies

A variety of objectives guide a PR plan, and the company can use a number of strategies to carry out the plan. Public relations objectives are designed by PR planners to make changes in the public's knowledge, attitudes, and behaviors related to a company, brand, or organization. Usually, these objectives focus on creating credibility, delivering information, and building positive images, trust, and corporate goodwill, as well as changing behavior as the "Truth" campaign attempted to do.

Principle

Before changing behavior, a communication program may need to change beliefs, attitudes, and feelings.

As Bettinghaus and Cody explain,[15] the ultimate goal of persuasive communication like the "Truth" campaign often is to change behavior, and that is a difficult task. Before changing behavior, a communication effort may need to first change people's beliefs, attitudes, and feelings. In many PR efforts, these communication effects are easier to accomplish and measure than behavior change. Typical public relations objectives include:

- Creating a corporate brand
- Shaping or redefining a corporate reputation
- Positioning or repositioning a company or brand
- Moving a brand to a new market or a global market
- Launching a new product or brand
- Disseminating news about a brand, company, or organization
- Providing product or brand information

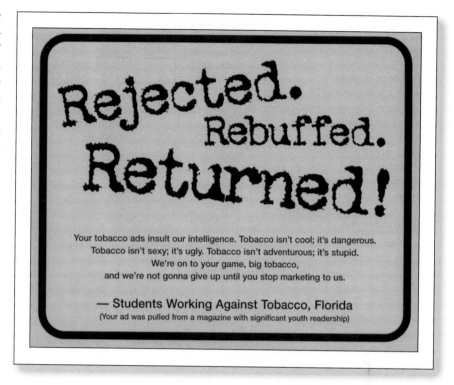

- Changing stakeholder attitudes, opinions, or behaviors about a brand or company
- Creating stronger brand relationships with key stakeholders, such as employees, shareholders and the financial community, government, members (for associations), and the media
- Creating high levels of customer (member) satisfaction
- Creating excitement in the marketplace
- Creating buzz (word of mouth)
- Involving people with the brand, company, or organization through events and other participatory activities
- Associating brands and companies with good causes

The Florida "Truth" campaign was designed to deliver action. Its SWAT team members sent cigarette ads back to the ad companies' CEOs adorned with a neon-orange "Rejected. Rebuffed. Returned!" sticker.

Change-agent Strategies   Changing the attitudes that drive behavior is central to public relations programs. **Change-agent programs** can be internal strategies focused on employees (sometimes called *internal marketing*) or external and focused on other publics, such as customers and other stakeholders. Regardless of the reason for change, "communication with principal stakeholders ranks high in the hierarchy of factors that predict success. Communication is second only to the main stakeholders' participation in the process."[16]

The objectives for the "Truth" antismoking campaign incorporate a change strategy that, according to the Centers for Disease Control and Prevention (CDC), has three steps:

1. Generate awareness.
2. Change attitudes.
3. Change behaviors.

As noted before, the last step, changing behaviors, is the most difficult, but the antismoking behavior-change "Truth" campaign was an award winner because it achieved its objective and actually produced a decrease in the number of teens taking up smoking. Figure 17.2 diagrams the change strategy behind the "Truth" campaign, but this diagram also describes the basic logic behind many change strategies.

Involvement Strategies   Public relations uses participation to intensify stakeholder involvement with a company or brand. Involvement can create interest and a feeling of excitement, but more importantly it can drive loyalty.[17] Getting people to participate in an action plan is one way to drive behavior change. For example, the "Truth" campaign included a Teen Summit in Seattle attended by 1,000 teenagers.

FIGURE 17.2

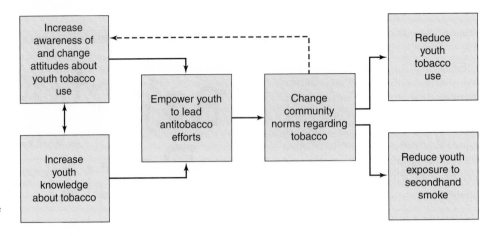

FTPP Change Strategy

The change strategy behind the "Truth" campaign involved first increasing youth awareness and knowledge about tobacco use, then empowering youth to lead antitobacco efforts that would lead to changing community norms. The hoped-for result was a reduction in both youth tobacco use and exposure to secondhand smoke.

Source: Youth Tobacco Prevention in Florida, a report prepared for the Florida Department of Health by the University of Miami, December 15, 1999, 3.

The Big Idea

Creative ideas are just as important in public relations as in advertising. And for the same reason: to get attention. For another example, the Clark County Desert Conservation Program in Nevada wanted to promote desert environments and inform about threats to their ecology. Mojave Max, a 50- to 60-year-old desert tortoise, became the group's mascot and announces the arrival of spring, just like Punxsutawney Phil does in the East. Who would have thought you could make a media star of a tortoise? Nevertheless, the 15-pound tortoise has become the poster reptile for desert ecology and attracts the attention of children as well as adults.

Stunts designed to get publicity are also part of the promotional arsenal. Janet Jackson's big exposé during the 2004 Super Bowl is an example of a stunt that got lots of visibility for the performer. Critics say the overexposure was in poor taste, but other PR experts say it was an example of a stunt that will be talked about for years. Jackson also gathered twice the number of U.S. press mentions as the commercials on the Super Bowl did.[18]

■ ■ ■

Mojave max is a desert tortoise used as a mascot for a desert conservation program in Navada.

PR's Role in IMC

In integrated programs, advertising and public relations aim at different targets with different but complementary messages. As one researcher observed, "In IMC, company assets and product assets are managed at the same time."[19] In many companies, advertising and public relations are separate, uncoordinated functions. People working in public relations are often trained as journalists, with little background in marketing, and they focus on corporate image rather than product sales. These different orientations can sometimes create inconsistencies in a company's communication efforts.

The truth is that public relations use a variety of marketing communication tools just as advertising does. Advertising is particularly useful in corporate image and reputation programs. Direct marketing is sometimes useful in sending out corporate books, videos, and CD-ROMs. The Internet is important because the corporate Web site is one of the primary ways to disseminate information about an organization. And PR activities, such as publicity and special mailings of CD-ROMs, can help drive traffic to the corporate Web site. Sales promotion is used in support of PR activities, such as special events. In some cases, it's hard to know whether an event is a sales promotion or public relations effort. But it's not just the use of these tools that makes PR a viable IMC function; it's the fact that PR can contribute some valuable effects, such as credibility.

Consider This

1. Describe the PR planning process.
2. What kind of objectives is public relations particularly good at accomplishing?

PUBLIC RELATIONS TOOLS

The public relations practitioner has many tools, which we can divide into two categories: controlled media and uncontrolled media. **Controlled media** include house ads, public service announcements, corporate (institutional) advertising, in-house publications, and visual presentations. The sponsoring organizations pay for these media. In turn, the sponsor maintains total control over how and when the message is delivered. **Uncontrolled media** include press releases, press conferences, and media tours. The most recent new media are electronic and they can be categorized as **semicontrolled**. Corporate Web sites, for example, are controlled by the company, but other Web sites (particularly those that are set up by critics and disgruntled ex-employees) and chat rooms about the company are not controlled.

Likewise, special events and sponsorships are set in place by the company, but participation by the press and other important publics is not under the control of the sponsoring company. Word of mouth, or buzz, is important to PR programs because of the persuasive power of personal conversation. PR programs, particularly the employee communication programs, may be designed to influence what people say about the company, but ultimately the comments are outside the control of the company.

The Child Hunger campaign is an example of a public relations effort for a nonprofit, with a supporting PR outreach program. The television ads were launched in the summer when children, without access to school lunch programs, are at the greatest risk of going hungry. The spots, as well as the print efforts, were submitted to the media with press releases in the hopes of moving the various media outlets to do stories on the issue and on children going hungry during the summer. To open up communication channels, provide additional information, and make action easy, the campaign invited people to visit www. feedingchildrenbetter.org, or call 1-800-FEED-KIDS. Table 17.1 summarizes these tools used with such PR programs.

Advertising

Public relations programs sometimes employ advertising as a way to create corporate visibility or increase its goodwill with its various stakeholder audiences. The primary uses of advertising are house ads, public service announcements, and corporate advertising.

House Ads   A company (or a medium, such as a newspaper, magazine, or broadcast station) may prepare a **house ad**, which is an ad for use in its own publication or programming. Consequently, no money changes hands. For instance, a local television station may run a house ad announcing its new fall programming or a local promotional event within its evening news program; likewise, a company may run an ad advocating a point of view or promoting a special employee benefit program within its corporate magazine. These house ads are often managed by the public relations department.

Public Service Announcements   The ads for charitable and civic organizations that run free of charge on television or radio or in print media are **public service announcements (PSAs).** The United Way, American Heart Association, and local

■ ■ ■
The Advertising Council has sponsored a number of public service advertising campaigns in support of good causes. The participating agencies donate their time and talent and media donate the time and space to run the PSAs. This ad by the FCB advertising agency recognizes one of the Ad Council's best-known campaigns.

Happy Birthday, Smokey.

TABLE 17.1 Public Relations Tools

Controlled Media	Uncontrolled Media
(company controls the use and placement)	*(media control the use and placement)*
• House ads	• The news release (print, audio, video, e-mail, faxes)
• Public service ads	• Features (pitch letters)
• Corporate, institutional, advocacy advertising	• Fillers, historical pieces, profiles
• Publications: brochures, flyers, magazines, newsletters	• The press conference and media advisory (media kits, fact sheets, background info)
• Annual reports	• Media tours
• Speakers	• Bylined articles, op/ed pieces, letters to the editor
• Photographs	• Talk and interview shows
• Films, videos, CD-ROMs	• Public service announcements
• Displays, exhibits	
• Staged events	
• Books	

Semicontrolled Media

(some aspects are controlled or initiated by the company, but other aspects aren't)

• Electronic communication (Web sites, chat rooms)
• Special events and sponsorships
• Word of mouth (buzz)
• Weblogs (blogs)

arts councils all rely on PSAs. These ads are prepared just like other print ads or commercials, and in most instances ad agencies donate their expertise and media donate time and space to run the ads.

The Advertising Council represents a PR effort for the entire advertising industry and has produced most of the PSAs you see on television and in print, such as the "Just Say No" antidrug campaign, the United Negro Colleges ("A mind is a terrible thing to waste."), Keep America Beautiful antilitter campaign, and the more recent "Dads" parenting campaign. The classic "Smokey the Bear" campaign ("Only you can prevent forest fires") is one of its longest-running and best-recognized efforts.

The "Child Hunger" campaign showed that getting donated time and space is not easy. The PSA directors at various media receive a barrage of public service campaigns every week on different issues and they have to choose which ones to run. There is no guarantee which markets will see the campaign elements and there is no guarantee that the same people will see the print and the TV. Some PSA campaigns do not get any airtime or print placements at all. The Powell/BBH agency learned that PSA directors were more likely to run ads that directly related to their local communities. So, regional food organizations were invited to "localize" the end of each ad with their own tag. This localizing strategy also made the ads more effective because it brought the problem to the local community.

Studies of PSA effectiveness help guide nonprofit organizations. For instance, a look at PSAs to combat drunk driving, particularly among the college population, found that the usual anti-drunk-driving messages are not as relevant to this audience as they might be. They do not address the students' greatest fear: being pulled over and charged with a DUI. The study also found that a localized PSA, one that mentions or uses a local community angle, is more meaningful to the college-age group.[20]

Corporate Advertising With **corporate advertising**, a company focuses on its **corporate image** or viewpoint. There is less emphasis on selling a particular product unless it is tied in to a good cause. For that reason, the ad or other campaign materials may originate in the public relations department rather than the advertising department.

An example of corporate advertising that is tied to a socially redeeming program is the Target Guest Card. In order to increase the use of the card, the Martin/Williams agency of Minneapolis had to find a compelling reason for people to shop at Target and use the card. Target's typical customer is female, aged 25 to 54, and her most important concern is her family. The agency team proposed a "Take Charge of Education" campaign, a simple fund-raising program for local schools tied to use of the Target Guest Card. One percent of the value of the purchases made with the card would go to a qualifying K–12 school of their choice. The fund-raising program for schools showcased Target's commitment to education, an area of great importance to Target customers. The Target "Take Charge of Education" campaign included a number of other public initiatives such as Arts in Education Grants, Good Neighbor Volunteers, and an environmental club for kids called EarthSavers, all of which reflect a strong public affairs orientation.

Corporate identity advertising is another type of advertising that firms use to enhance or maintain their reputation among specific audiences or to establish a level of awareness of the company's name and the nature of its business. Johnson & Johnson targeted its "Healthy Start" institutional campaign at pregnant women to position itself as a concerned company. Companies that have changed their names, such as Nissan (formerly Datsun), have also used corporate identity advertising. To polish its corporate image, the CIGNA insurance company has attempted to brand an intangible: a caring business philosophy. Edward A. Faruolo, CIGNA marketing communications vice president, stated: "If we could build our brand around the concept of caring, we could not only obtain a highly coveted position in the marketplace, but also earn the trust and loyalty of our customers and our employees."[21]

Sometimes companies deliver point-of-view messages called **advocacy advertising**. Oil companies, for example, will advertise that they support the environment and their extraction procedures do not do any lasting damage to the environment. To combat the antismoking campaigns, tobacco companies will run ads that explain their point of view—that they have a right to advertise a legal product.

Publicity

Moving away from controlled messages, consider the various tools and techniques used by media relations specialists to get publicity in the news media on behalf of a company or brand. Apple, for example, has received tremendous media coverage of its iPod, iTunes, and the Mini iPod. *Newsweek,* for instance, gave Apple's Steve Jobs and the iPod a cover and an eight-page story in full color. PR expert Tom Harris calls that "an endorsement that money can't buy."[22]

Media relations is often seen as the most important core competency for PR professionals.[23] Media relations specialists know media that would be interested in stories about their companies. They also develop personal contact with reporters and editors who write regularly on topics related to their organization's industry.[24] As Carole Howard, author of a media relations book, explains, "Good media contacts proliferate once they are established."[25] In addition to personal contact, the primary tool used in media relations is the news release, but they also use press conferences and media tours.

News Releases The **news release** is the primary medium used to deliver public relations messages to the various external media. Although the company distributing the news release controls its original form and content, the media decide what to present and how to present it. What the public finally sees, then, is not necessarily what the originating company had in mind, and so this form of publicity is uncontrolled by the originating company.

The decision to use any part of a news release at all is based on an editor's judgment of its news value. News values are based on such things as timeliness (something just happened or is about to happen), proximity (a local angle), impact (importance or significance), or human interest. Figure 17.3 illustrates how product categories rank in terms of news value to editors.

News releases must be written differently for each medium, accommodating space and time limitations. Traditional journalism form is followed, which means the 5W format

Media Assessment of News Values

This figure shows how product categories rank in terms of news value to editors.

Source: Adapted from Thomas L. Harris, *The Marketer's Guide to Public Relations* (New York: Wiley, 1993), 58.

	High News Value	Low News Value
A	Computers Cars Entertainment	Beer Soft Drinks Athletic Shoes **C**
B	Soup Cereal Aspirin	Cigarettes Car Mufflers Cookies **D**

A High news value

B Less interesting than A, but still considered to have a high news value

C Low news value

D Lower interest value than C

is standard—in other words, the release should lead with answers to questions of who, what, why, when, where, and how. The more carefully the news release is planned and written, the better the chance it has of being accepted and published as written. Note the tight and simple writing style in the news release from the Florida "Truth" campaign.

The news release can be delivered in a number of ways: in person, by local delivery service, by mail, by fax, or by e-mail. Sometimes a company that specializes in distribution, such as the U.S. Newswire, is hired. Originally sent by mail or delivery services, news releases are now more likely to be distributed electronically through satellite and Web-based networks. PR Newswire, U.S. Newswire, and BusinessWire are services that provide targeted distribution to special-interest media outlets or handle mass distribution of news releases, photos, graphics, video, audio, and other materials. If your organization decides to use e-mail, here is a set of guidelines for their delivery:[26]

- Use only one reporter's name and address per "to" line.
- Keep subject line header simple.
- Boldface "FOR IMMEDIATE RELEASE" on the first line above the date.
- Catch attention with a good headline.
- Limit length (shorter than print's 500-word limit).
- Use the 5W format.
- No attachments!
- Link to a URL where other background info and photos are posted.
- Remember readability and use short paragraphs, bullets, numbers, lists to keep it scannable.
- Put contact info below the text.
- Close with conventional end signs such as "30" or ######.

Video news releases (VNRs) contain video footage for a television newscast. They are effective because they show target audiences the message in two different video environments: first as part of a news report and then reused later in an advertisement. Of course, there is no guarantee that a VNR will be used. One study found that VNRs aired in the Miami market had high visual quality and simple stories.[27]

Pitch Letters Ideas for **feature stories**, which are human-interest stories rather than hard-news announcements, have to be "sold" to editors. This is done using a **pitch letter** that outlines the subject in an engaging way and sells a story idea. Companies use this to feature some interesting research breakthrough, employee, or corporate cause. Not only is the distribution of press releases moving online, so are the letters pitching editors with story ideas. Ragan Communications, publisher of *Interactive Public Relations,* lists some tips for getting reporters and editors to read e-mail pitch letters. (See the Practical Tips box.)

Practical Tips

How to Write E-mail Pitch Letters

1. Never list all recipients in the "To:" line. No one wants to see all the reporters who received the pitch, since these story ideas are supposed to be made available to the medium on an exclusive basis—in other words, no other medium will be offered that story.

For Immediate Release
February 12, 1999

Contact: Carlea Bauman
850-488-5959
Damien Filer
850-488-6809

Florida Teens Preparing Tobacco Industry Attack
at Second Annual Teen Tobacco Summit

(Tarpon Springs, FL) - More than 1,000 teenagers representing Florida's 67 counties will gather here at the second annual Teen Tobacco Summit, February 25 – 28, 1999. Their mission: Defending their generation from a lame addiction that kills.

Last year, 600 teenagers gathered in central Florida for the inaugural Summit. There, youth brainstormed on how to reach their peers with an effective anti-tobacco message. From that meeting, the "Truth" campaign and its activist organization, Students Working Against Tobacco (SWAT), were born. The goals for this year's Summit are just as ambitious.

"We've got a lot of strong momentum going against Big Tobacco," said SWAT Chairwoman Chrissie Scelsi, 17. "But we aren't through. The tobacco industry knows it is about to lose a lot of customers. They're going to turn up the heat on us. We have to be ready."

SWAT's teen leaders will lead the Summit. Participants will hold rallies, review SWAT's plans for the coming year and attend sessions on how to become more powerful advocates. The teens will be developing new advertising to publicize SWAT's role in the anti-tobacco movement. The heart of the counter-marketing effort, the "Truth" campaign, has already enjoyed remarkable success to date. In a survey taken six months after the launch of "Truth," more than 90 percent of Florida teens could identify at least one aspect of the campaign. What's more, teen attitudes about tobacco are already changing.

Additional sessions will give teens a chance to talk with professional athletes and coaches about how tobacco can make an athlete lose his or her edge. Other sessions will provide participants with the latest information on tobacco possession laws, cessation programs and the dangers of second-hand smoke. (See attached session descriptions and timelines for more detailed information.)

"The goal of the Summit is to inform and empower," said Susan Medina, a SWAT leader who has appeared in some of the "truth" commercials. "There is nothing more threatening to Big Tobacco than a teen who is armed with the truth and is feeling pretty mad about being lied to for so long."

While the Summit schedule includes serious activities, the weekend won't be all work for the teens.

- The opening session on Thursday, February 25th will focus on SWAT's project. "Reel Truth," which began during last summer's Truth Train. "Reel Truth" took the entertainment industry to task for irresponsibly depicting tobacco use in films and on television. Antonio Sabato, Jr., star of *Melrose Place* and *General Hospital*, will be on hand for a panel discussion on the issue and other celebrities, such as Leeza Gibbons, will send video-taped messages of support for the teens. Folk rock singer Leslie Nuchow, who received national attention for rejecting a Virginia Slims sponsorship offer, will also perform during the opening session.
- The teens will learn leadership and teamwork by tackling a ropes/obstacle course. As the teens face these challenges, they will gain the confidence, strength and leadership skills necessary to win the fight against Big Tobacco.
- On Saturday night, February 27th, teen participants will be treated to a live concert by the number one R & B band, Divine, who will perform their hit single, "Lately."

Several of the state's VIPs will also attend the Summit. Lt. Governor Frank Brogan will address the teens at breakfast and Secretary of Health, Robert G. Brooks, M.D., at lunch on Friday, February 26th. Following lunch, Secretary Brooks will tour the teen training sessions. Education Commissioner Tom Gallagher and Secretary of State Katherine Harris will be on hand for the closing ceremonies Sunday, February 28th. Also on Sunday, Ed Chiles, youngest son of the late Governor and Mrs. Chiles, will be on hand to announce the winners of the Lawton Chiles Youth Advocate of the Year Awards. The recipients, chosen for their anti-tobacco efforts, will receive scholarships to any public Florida university of their choosing. The scholarship is funded by the Lawton Chiles Foundation.

Foreign and national anti-tobacco experts will also be in attendance. Says Peter Mitchell, Acting Director of the Florida Tobacco Pilot Program: "As the 'Truth' campaign and SWAT become a bigger force in the tobacco war, more people want to study us; to see what works and why." Among the experts attending will be Bill Novelli, President of the Campaign for Tobacco Free Kids.

The Teen Tobacco Summit 2 is funded by the Florida Tobacco Pilot Program, which was created by the state's historic settlement with the tobacco industry in 1997.

For up to the minute information on Teen Tobacco Summit 2, check out our web site at www.state.fl.us/tobacco.

This is a typical news release. It has the release information in the upper left corner and contact information in the upper right. A headline summarizes the point of the news release. It closes with the Web site address for additional information.

2. Avoid attachments. They take time to open and to read, and busy reporters often dismiss them. They can also carry viruses.

3. Keep your pitches less than a page in length. The first paragraph should capture the who, what, and why of the story.

4. Help reporters do their jobs. Some reporters won't rewrite a news release because they want to write the story their own way. For those reporters, provide them with a great story idea, including visuals and other resources, and with contacts, so they can round out the story.

5. Make it personal. Use their first names and mention the publication name.

6. Keep subject-line headers to fewer than four or five words. The header should be clear and to the point; don't waste the space running the term "press release" itself.

7. Never follow up an e-mail pitch by asking, "Did you get it?" Instead, call to ask reporters if they need more information and call within an hour (things move quickly in the online world).

Source: "Seven Tips for Getting Your E-mail Pitches Read," direct mailing from Ragan Communications, September 2000.

Press Conferences A **press conference**—an event at which a company spokesperson makes a statement to media representatives—is one of the riskiest public relations activities because the media may not see the company's announcement as being real news. Some companies have successfully introduced new products, such as Gillette's Sensor, Sensor for Women, and, more recently, the Mach III, through press conferences and other publicity events, and then followed up the launch news events with an advertising campaign. But companies often worry about whether the press will show up for a press conference. Will they ask the right questions, or will they ask questions the company cannot or does not want to answer?

To anticipate some of these problems, companies may issue a **media kit**, usually a folder that provides all the important background information to members of the press, either before or when they arrive at the press conference. The risk in offering media kits (also called press kits) is that they give reporters all the necessary information so that the press conference itself becomes unnecessary. The SWAT "Truth Tour" featured a "Watch Out" media kit, which the media found useful because it provided a more detailed explanation of the antismoking campaign and its events.

Media Tours A **media tour** is a press conference on wheels. The traveling spokesperson makes announcements and speeches, holds press conferences to explain a promotional effort, and offers interviews. The Florida "Truth" campaign featured a 10-day, 13-city whistle-stop train tour and concert series across the state of Florida. Governor Lawton Chiles rode the train, joining the teen spokespeople, who conducted their own press conferences at every stop. SWAT members trained their peers in advocacy and media relations along the way, empowering teens throughout the state to join in the movement's rebellion against the tobacco industry.

Publications

Organizations may provide employees and other publics with pamphlets, booklets, annual reports, books, bulletins, newsletters, inserts and enclosures, and position papers. An example of a publication is found in the education part of the Florida "Truth" campaign, which included a book for children in grades 1, 2, and 3 titled *The Berenstain Bear Scouts and the Sinister Smoke Ring.* A companion Student Activity Workbook took the prevention message into an interactive format. For fourth- and fifth-grade students a jazzy, high-tech "Science, Tobacco and You" program was incorporated into two *Crush It!* magazines, which integrated the antismoking message into science, math, language arts, and social studies classes.

The Securities and Exchange Commission (SEC) requires that each publicly held company publish an **annual report.** You can review annual reports at www.sec.gov. A company's annual report is targeted to investors and may be the single most important document the company distributes. Millions of dollars are spent on the editing and design of annual reports.

Some companies publish material—often called **collateral material**—to support their marketing public relations efforts. Corning Fiberglass Insulation offers a free booklet on home insulation do's and don'ts as an integral part of its promotion effort. The booklet is highlighted in its advertising campaign.

Corporate publication, marketing, and sales promotion departments and their agencies also produce training materials and sales kits to support particular campaigns. Target's Coordinators Kit, for instance, was produced by Target for school representatives to help run the "Take Charge of Education" campaign. Target also used a number of different brochures, such as a series included in a "School Fundraising Made Simple" kit designed to train and support school representatives involved in the "Take Charge of Education" campaign.

Videos/DVDs, CDs, and Books

Videotapes, DVDs, CD-ROMs, and corporate books have become a major public relations tool for a great many companies. Corporate books have also become popular with the advent of simplified electronic publication.[28] Costing $1,000 to $2,000 per minute to make, videos are not cheap. However, they are an ideal tool for distributing in-depth information about a company or program. Because they are easier to duplicate, CD-ROMs are reducing this cost. Research has found that 90 percent of people that receive video cassettes in the mail do watch them and the conversion rates for video cassettes in direct marketing are as high as 23 percent.[29] For a company such as Target, mailing videotapes to schools as part of the "Take Charge of Education" announcement package was a worthwhile investment.

Speakers and Photos

Many companies have a **speakers' bureau** of articulate people who will talk about topics at the public's request. Apple Computer, Harvard University, and the Children's Hospital in Houston, Texas, all have speakers' bureaus that will provide speakers for local groups and classes. Some publics—particularly the news media—may want pictures of people, products, places, and events. That's why PR departments maintain files of photographs that are accurate and well composed. The permissions for ads in this book were provided because they present the advertisers in a positive light. Companies seldom give permission to use ads that authors intend to criticize.

Displays and Exhibits

Displays and exhibits (as well as special events and tours) may be important parts of both sales promotion and public relations programs. Displays include booths, racks and holders for promotional literature, and signage. A model of a new condominium complex, complete with a literature rack that has brochures about the development, is an example of a display. Exhibits tend to be larger than displays; they may have moving parts, sound, or video, and usually are staffed by a company representative. Booth exhibits are important at trade shows, where some companies may take orders for much of their annual sales.

Special Events and Tours

Some companies stage events to celebrate milestones, such as Scrabble's fiftieth anniversary and the thirtieth anniversary of the Big Mac. These are high-visibility activities designed to get maximum publicity. Special events can be the public relations manager's responsibility, as well as a sales promotion activity.

Staged events include open houses and even birthday celebrations. For example, when Barnum's Animal Crackers turned 100, Nabisco invited people to decide what new critters should join the circus of 17 animals in the traditional box. The use of fancier staged events has seen the most growth. Corporate sponsorship of various sporting events has evolved into a favorite public relations tactic. For example, *Sports Illustrated* magazine

■ ■ ■

Scrabble celebrated its fiftieth anniversary and Big Mac celebrated its thirtieth with oversized versions of their products.

developed an elaborate events strategy to attract new advertisers. The centerpiece of that strategy is the Sports Festival, a 70,000-square-foot exhibition that tours Time Warner's Six Flags theme parks during the summers, spending 10 days at each park. The exhibition includes interactive games that allow participants to slam-dunk a basketball or race against Carl Lewis.

Events can also be important in internal communication. Learning objectives are often accomplished through meetings, seminars, and workshops sponsored by a company, as well as training materials and other publications. To facilitate internal marketing, **town hall forums** are sometimes used.[30] This is an opportunity for management to make a presentation on some major project, initiative, or issue and invite employees to discuss it. Table 17.2 summarizes some of the marketing PR activities.

In addition to media tours, tours of all kinds are used in public relations programs, such as plant tours and trips by delegates and representatives. The Inside Story box explains how 37 Spokane business leaders, travel suppliers, and trade professionals embarked on a four-day mission to Calgary, Alberta. The tour was focused on showcasing Spokane's regional travel opportunities to Calgary's travel trade and travel consumers.

TABLE

17.2 **Marketing Public Relations Tours and Events**

Client	Event or Tour
Victoria's Secret	Victoria's Secret's supermodels, the "Angels," toured major cities via the "Angels" jet. At each stop they modeled the retailer's holiday gift collection and interacted with shoppers and fans. Supported by a one-hour special on VH1.
Best Buy	Uniformed Best Buy teams hit streets with branded CD samplers and store coupons; 30,000 people received tickets for a Sting concert in Central Park sponsored by Best Buy.
Intimo (men's underwear)	A "Thong-a-Thon" run featured some 10 guys in Intimo black thong underwear and a black Intimo running bib on a route through New York streets.
Häagen-Dazs Gelato	Three Italian chefs compete in an ice-cream scoop-off; winner gets a $25,000 charity donation in his or her name; onlookers get to sample gelato.
Levi Strauss & Co.	Old UPS trucks painted in Levi's colors, with mock college dorm rooms inside, toured raves, clubs, and other youth hangouts; and sold jeans from the truck.

THE INSIDE STORY

The Spokane Stampede: A Sales Mission to Calgary

John Brewer, President and General Manager,
Spokane Regional Convention and Visitors Bureau

In September of 2003, the Spokane Regional Convention and Visitors Bureau* and the International Trade Alliance in Spokane, Washington, were partners in an ambitious sales and marketing program to reintroduce the Canadian audience to the Spokane region for trade and tourism. With a much stronger Canadian dollar and greatly improved buying power, we had a terrific opportunity to reach this reemerging Canadian market.

In the past decade Canadian travel to the United States grew 9 percent, but Spokane did not feel that impact because of lack of visibility in the Canadian marketplace. With a more favorable exchange rate for Canadian visitors, and negative world events and border-crossing issues becoming somewhat less concerning, the CVB felt it was an opportune time to become more visible to our friends in Alberta and British Columbia.

The Spokane delegation networked with Alberta and Calgary dignitaries, and local travel professionals—along with taking time to tour the area and explore best-practice models for Canadian tourism.

As a first-time event of this nature, establishing goals was a priority to evaluate the mission's success, but it was also very difficult to set achievable goals without any historical perspective. We established specific and trackable goals based upon a best-case scenario: (1) showcase the Spokane region to 170,000 potential leisure travelers at the Spruce Meadows consumer show; (2) generate new contacts and sales to 450 qualified travel agents, meeting planners, and tour operators through industry trade shows in Calgary and Edmonton; (3) gain media hits in the Calgary market by meeting with 10 area journalists; (4) develop a reciprocal trade mission from Calgary tourism planners and industry professionals; and (5) provide a high level of satisfaction for the 37 participants from the Spokane region making the trip.

We chartered a new 50-passenger motor coach and placed marketing messages on the vehicle to act as a traveling billboard. The 10-hour road trip provided attendees the opportunity to learn more about each other's businesses and develop strategies to cross-promote. During stops along the way, we took the opportunity to plan media conferences relating to our mission and the rollout of our new Canadian promotion offering rates at par for the Canadian dollar.

"Team Spokane," as we came to be known, was outfitted in team vests and shirts developed specifically for the mission. Once we arrived in Calgary, the agenda was aggressive. We broke into teams to attend four industry trade shows and one consumer travel show. The cornerstone of our mission related to the Masters Horse Jumping Tournament at Spruce Meadows, one of Canada's premier sporting events. This venue allowed us the opportunity to host a special suite for dignitaries and offered a defined setting for a select audience to whom we could promote the assets and amenities of our region. We also developed a luncheon and trade show featuring giveaways, and a dynamic luncheon speaker who talked about "Selling your clients on travel below the border: At par prices. Above par experiences."

This theme was carried out through all of our multimedia pieces. We developed plastic "credit cards" that featured the campaign theme: "Spokane: Above par experiences. At par prices." and distributed nearly 10,000 of them. The prime objective of this card was to drive people to the CVB Web site, have visitors click on the Canadian button on the home page, then take advantage of the discounts offered by local hospitality partners.

We developed a *splash page* on our Web site listing all the participating businesses that offered specials to Canadian travelers in the Spokane region. Prior to departing for Calgary, we contracted with two companies in Canada to promote our campaign and sales mission through fax blasts and direct mail.

The mission was a phenomenal success. Our goals were very aggressive, and we were pleased to reach such a high number of leisure travelers, and also pleased with such a high ranking of participant satisfaction. Although we did not achieve 100 percent of our goals, we now have benchmark figures for subsequent campaigns. We deemed the Stampede successful because Spokane left an indelible impression on our core audience, and we benefited in ways we had not anticipated.

---

*The Spokane Regional Convention & Visitors Bureau is a nonprofit organization whose mission is to create economic growth for Spokane County by effectively marketing the Spokane region as a preferred convention and visitor destination. Our vision is to make the Inland Northwest one of the nation's top-of-mind visitor destinations.

John Brewer is a 1992 graduate from the University of West Florida. He specializes in tourism promotion and has worked as an account executive, public relations specialist at agencies in Montana before being named President of the Spokane Regional Convention & Visitors Bureau.

Nominated by Professor Tom Groth, University of West Florida

■ ■ ■
Named the Spokane Stampede, the mission allowed Spokane County hospitality suppliers to network and conduct business with Calgary media, travel agents, meeting and tour group planners, and potential leisure travelers. This visit was a step toward developing stronger ties between Canada and the Spokane region for economic development and community relations.

Online Communication

PR practitioner and author Fraser Seitel says, "No Website question about it, the Internet phenomenon, pure and simple, has been a revolution."[31] The new electronic media are making the biggest change in the communication landscape. E-mail, **intranets** (which connect people within an organization), **extranets** (which connect people in one business with its business partners), Internet advertising, and Web sites have opened up avenues for public relations activities.

External Communication   "The World Wide Web can be considered the first public relations mass medium in that it allows managed communication directly between organizations and audiences without the gatekeeping function of other mass media."[32] The Florida "Truth" campaign developed a Web site (www.whole truth.com) based on ideas from the Teen Tobacco Summit. The site contains facts and statistics on cigarettes and chewing tobacco, as well as information on how to join SWAT teams. It also provides updates on the program's activities.

Corporate Web sites have become an important part of corporate communication. These sites can present information about the company and open up avenues for stakeholders to contact the company. Web site newsrooms distribute a company's press releases to the media and other interested stakeholders. One study noted that the interactive dimension is particularly important: "If you built a highly interactive and informative Web site, then you can capitalize on building brand and corporate image through longer and more intense exposures than any other type of campaign." The study also found that interactivity—being able to contact the company—is more important than the actual information.[33]

In addition to Web sites, the Internet has become the favorite tool of media relations professionals, as well as journalists. E-mail is now used more frequently to contact reporters than the telephone, in person, or the fax and reporters indicate that corporate Web sites are their most important source of financial information.[34] Furthermore, most press releases are now distributed online by sending them either directly to reporters or to such services as PR Newswire, which then does mass distributions online to appropriate publications.

Internal Communication   E-mail is a great way for people in separate locations to communicate. You can get a fast reply if people on the other end are checking their mail regularly. It is also an inexpensive form of internal communication. Internal company e-mail may have its public relations downside, however. It can be used in court. Some of the most damaging evidence the federal government presented against Microsoft in its antitrust suit came from e-mail messages exchanged within the company.

Internal company networks do have great benefits. Intranets and corporate portals (an extensive collection of databases and links that are important to people working in a company) encourage communication among employees in general and permit them to share company databases, such as customer records and client information. Some companies urge employees to set up personal home pages as part of the company portal, which allows them to customize the material they receive and set up their own links to crucial corporate information such as competitor news, product information, case histories, and so forth.

Web Challenges   The Internet presents at least as many challenges to public relations professionals as it does opportunities. Search engine optimization is a major issue for online experts, who continually try to improve the process of keyword searching that leads interested Web users to their sites.[35]

The Internet makes it possible to present the company's image and story without going through the editing of a gatekeeper. On the other hand, it is much harder to control what is said about the company on the Internet. According to Parry Aftab, a lawyer specializing in computer-related issues, "It used to be that you could control the information because you'd have one spokesman who represented the company. Now where you have thousands of employees who have access to an e-mail site, you have thousands of spokesmen."[36] All employees have "an inside view" of their company, whether sanctioned by the PR department or not. Every employee becomes a spokesperson.

Gossip and rumors can spread around the world within hours. Angry customers and disgruntled former employees know this and have used the Internet to voice their complaints. A number of these people have set up Web sites such as the Official Internet AntiNike Web site; alt.destroy.microsft; I Hate McDonald's; ToysRUs Sucks; GTE Sucks; Why America Online Sucks; Packard Bell Is Evil; and BallySucks. As a defense against this negative press, some companies are registering domain names that might cause them trouble. For example, JP Morgan Chase bank owns IHateChase.com, ChaseStinks.com, and ChaseSucks.com, but not chasebanksucks.com, which is an active Web site critical of the company.

Some companies monitor the Internet to see what is being said about them so they can respond to protect their reputations. Thousands of companies have hired eWatch, a firm that provides Web-monitoring services, to collect such information.

Consider This

1. List the most common tools used by public relations practitioners.
2. How does public relations use advertising?

■ ■ ■
Companies such as Burelle's Information Services specialize in tracking press coverage.

EFFECTIVENESS AND PR EXCELLENCE

The Institute for PR has developed a set of measurement standards to help evaluate the effectiveness of public relations. As in advertising, public relations evaluation is based on setting measurable objectives in the beginning of the planning. Objectives that specify the impact the program seeks to have on the various publics can be evaluated by the PR manager if they contain benchmarks and target levels.

Figure 17.4 illustrates how research company Delahaye Medialink evaluates the effectiveness of public relations programs' controlled, semi-controlled, and uncontrolled messages (www. delahayemedialink.com). The model identifies exposure, awareness, and understanding (which leads to behavior change) as categories of effects that need to be measured in an evaluation program.

Public relations practitioners track the impact of a campaign in terms of output (how many news releases lead to stories or mentions in news stories) and outcome (attitude or behavior change). Such tracking is done to prove the effectiveness of the PR program, and so that they learn from their efforts and fine-tune future campaigns. To get a comprehensive picture of PR's impact, practitioners evaluate process (what goes out) and outcome (media use; effect on the target audience).

The Burrelle's ad describes the difficulty of tracking such publicity and offers its services as an

NOW WHAT?

PRESS CLIPPINGS

OK hotshot. So you ran a sensational PR campaign and the clips are pouring in. Now what do you do? Your bosses want to know what it all means. What do you show them...a big box of clips?

Not bad for a start, but what do they **really** mean? What is the true impact of your public relations effort...in terms of exposure, circulation, audience? What is the quality of the pickup you're getting? Which products or services are getting covered? Is the tone favorable, or neutral?

What is the advertising equivalence in real dollars? There's more...but we think you get the idea.

It's time you received NewsClip Analysis from Burrelle's. Burrelle's can create detailed, accurate, and visually stimulating reports that give you a true evaluation of your public relations effort. Burrelle's NewsClip Analysis reports are timely, and they won't break your budget.

So call today for more information. Then, next time you're rolling in the clips, instead of saying "Now What?" you'll be saying "Look At This!"

NewsClip Analysis

Burrelle's Information Services
75 East Northfield Road, Livingston, NJ 07039
Telephone: 1-800-631-1160, In NJ: 201-992-6600

BURRELLE'S
Intelligence through media monitoring.

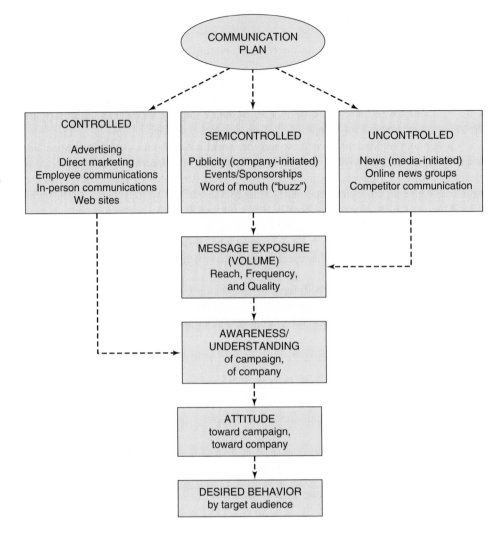

FIGURE 17.4

The Delahaye Medialink Model of Public Relations Evaluation

Research company Delahaye Medialink uses this model to evaluate the effectiveness of PR programs.

Source: Adapted from Delahaye Medialink New Business Kit, Portsmouth, New Hampshire (www.delahayemedialink.com).

outside company (www.burrelles.com) that specializes in tracking and monitoring press coverage. The "Truth" campaign was deemed successful because it resulted in more than 590,476,000 *impressions*—the number of times a person in the target audience is reached by one or more of the messages. In this case, the target audience was teens, parents, and influencers (teachers, role models).

Excellence in Public Relations

Another aspect of PR evaluation was showcased in Professor James Grunig's mammoth study of excellence in PR, sponsored by the International Association of Business Communicators (IABC).[37] The study concluded that there are 14 factors of excellent PR, grouped into four categories: program level, departmental level, organizational level, and effects of excellent public relations. As an example of how Grunig's factors can be used, one study used the 14 factors to investigate the forest industry. It found that based on these factors, the major companies investigated were making great efforts to identify and communicate effectively with their publics.[38]

Consider This

1. What's the difference between output and outcome evaluation?
2. What determines excellence in public relations?

IT'S A WRAP

∎∎∎

CHILD HUNGER IS REAL

The Ad Council and Powell/BBH realized that child hunger is a very curable epidemic in the United States but their biggest challenge was to communicate the extent of the problem. The "Child Hunger" campaign generated huge amounts of publicity for the child hunger issue. The campaign and the issue were also covered on the *Today Show* and the campaign was written up in the trade publication *Shoot Magazine* as being one of this year's "best campaigns."

Objective 1: Maximize media exposure. For the first 10 months, the campaign received $45.3 million in donated TV time. Most Ad Council campaigns receive an average of $28.6 million in donated media over the same time span so it was much more effective at eliciting donated time and space.

Objective 2: Change people's perceptions. The Ad Council realizes that it is hard to "move the needle" on social change issues, however the number of people who say child hunger is a problem in the United States and in their communities rose. There was a 36 percent increase in the number of people who agreed that "child hunger is a problem in my community."

Objective 3: Inspire action. More than 500,000 unique visitors were counted at the Web site during the first year of the campaign. In the first month alone, the Web banner advertising had 20.3 million impressions and 28,410 clicks, making a click-through rate of .14, which is above the Ad council's average of .10.

Objective 4: Generate collective concern. As a direct result of the groundswell of media coverage of the campaign, the USDA (U.S. Department of Agriculture) donated 9 million lunches in the summer to schools for children in need.

From the advertising and publicity stories, more than 57.5 million people either read, watched, or heard about the issue of child hunger as a result of this PSA campaign. The campaign had great results after its launch, which is why it is an EFFIE winner.

∎∎∎ Summary

1. **Explain what public relations is and how it differs from advertising.** Public relations is a management function that communicates to and with various publics to manage an organization's image and reputation. Advertising focuses on enhancing brand value and creating the awareness and motivation that deliver sales.

2. **Identify the most common types of public relations programs.** In addition to the key areas of government, media, employee, and investor relations, PR programs also include marketing public relations (MPR), corporate relations and reputation management, crisis management, and nonprofit public relations.

3. **Describe the key decisions in public relations planning.** Planning for a public relations campaign begins with a SWOT, or situation analysis, that is used as background for the identification of the target audience and the develop-

ment of objectives and strategies. Research is needed when planning a PR program and evaluating its effectiveness.

4. **Explain the most common types of public relations tools.** Uncontrolled media tools include the news story that results from a news release or news conference. Controlled media are tools that the company uses to originate and control content. Semicontrolled tools are controlled in that the company is able to initiate the use of the tool, but also uncontrolled in that the content is contributed by others.

5. **Discuss the importance of measuring the results of public relations efforts.** Public relations evaluation usually focuses on outputs and outcomes and may include relationship management and excellence. The evaluation effort is made to determine how well a PR program meets its objectives.

▪▪▪ Key Terms

advocacy advertising, 489
annual report, 492
benchmarking, 484
cause marketing, 481
change-agent program, 485
collateral material, 493
communication audit, 483
controlled media, 487
corporate advertising, 488
corporate identity
 advertising, 489
corporate image, 488
corporate relations, 482
crisis management, 482
employee relations, 480

extranets, 496
feature stories, 490
financial relations, 480
fund-raising, 481
gap analysis, 484
gatekeepers, 480
goodwill, 478
house ad, 487
image, 478
implied third-party
 endorsement, 480
internal marketing, 480
intranets, 496
issue management, 481
lobbying, 481

marketing public relations
 (MPR), 483
media kit, 492
media relations, 480
media tour, 492
news release, 489
opinion leaders, 478
pitch letter, 490
press conference, 492
public affairs, 481
public communication
 campaigns, 483
public opinion, 478
public relations, 477

public service announcement
 (PSA), 487
publicity, 477
publics, 477
relationship marketing, 480
reputation, 478
reputation management, 482
semicontrolled media, 487
situation analysis
 (SWOT), 484
speakers' bureau, 493
stakeholders, 477
town hall forums, 494
uncontrolled media, 487
video news releases
 (VNRs), 490

▪▪▪ Review Questions

1. Explain why public opinion is important to the success of public relations.

2. How does the practice of advertising differ from the practice of public relations?

3. What are the key strategic decisions in a PR plan?

4. In analyzing PR tools, compare the use of controlled and uncontrolled media. Explain the difference between the two categories.

5. In evaluating the effectiveness of public relations, explain the difference between output and outcome evaluations.

▪▪▪ Discussion Questions

1. Why is public opinion so important to the success of public relations? In how many different ways does it affect the success of a program like the "Truth" campaign?

2. What is reputation management, and how does it intersect with advertising programs? How did the CIGNA "Cares" campaign impact on the reputation of the company? Find another corporate reputation campaign and analyze its effectiveness.

3. Wendy Johnson and Phil Draper are having a friendly disagreement before class. Wendy claims that she is not interested in advertising as a career because she dislikes the "crass commercialism" of promoting products and services that many people don't need. Phil counters by saying that

public relations is doing the same thing by "selling ideas and images," and its motives are usually just as money centered as those of advertising. If you overheard this discussion, would you take Wendy's or Phil's side? Could you offer advice on ethical considerations for both careers?

4. Suppose you belong to a campus group planning a special weekend event on campus to raise public support and funds for a local charity. This will cost your organization time and money. Although contributions at the event will be some measure of the effectiveness of your public relations program, what other steps could you take to evaluate your success?

▪▪▪ Class Projects

1. Divide the class into groups of three to four people. Each group should adopt a local cause that operates on a low budget and needs public relations help. As a team, develop a public relations plan for that nonprofit organization.

2. Consult the two teen-targeted antismoking Web sites given below and compare them in terms of their appeal to a teen audience. Which one do you think is the most interesting to this age group? Which one is the least interesting? Compile the best ideas from both of them and write a report to your instructor on why the ideas are good and what else a Web site can do to reach a teen market.

 www.thetruth.com
 www.generationfree.com

HANDS-ON

CASE

Oprah Helps People Live Their Wildest Dreams, with Some Help from Pontiac

The first show of Oprah Winfrey's nineteenth season was a big one; 11 lucky audience members would win a new car. The show's theme was "wildest dreams," and the 11 shrieking winners probably did feel like a dream was coming true as Oprah handed them keys to a new Pontiac G6, Pontiac's sleek, sporty successor to the Grand Am. After things finally calmed down, Oprah had even better news. Studio guests would receive gift boxes, and one out of every three also contained keys to a new G6. After Oprah counted to three, paper and ribbons were torn apart and general pandemonium broke loose: Every guest was a winner.

Viewers at home, who might have been tempted to feel just a bit of envy at the good fortune of the show's guests, learned that this was no ordinary audience. Everyone in Oprah's studio that day had been personally selected by the host herself on the basis of testimonials from friends and loved ones explaining how a new car would change the recipient's life. In all, 276 people received a new Pontiac. The cars themselves were fully loaded, bringing the value of each prize to just under $30,000. Total cost of the giveaway: over $7 million.

Oprah Winfrey is one of the most successful and highly paid talents on television, with an annual salary of well over $100 million. But Oprah didn't actually buy the cars that her studio guests took home that day. The cost of the giveaway was borne by Pontiac. Was it worth it? Definitely, according to Aaron Walton, a president with Omnicom Group. He called the program "emotionally uplifting. It is an A-plus in marketing and brand entertainment. . . . There's an emotional connection. It is something you couldn't have paid for." In addition to the giveaways, the program featured footage of Oprah visiting Pontiac's Orion, Michigan, plant and even helping out on the production line. Winfrey was seen marveling over several G6 features including the optional Onstar navigation system (Onstar helped cover some of the promotional costs as well). To build on the show's impact, the G6 was the exclusive sponsor of Oprah's Web site for three months. Visitors to the site found a "Dream it. Win it." sweepstakes offering the chance to win one of four Pontiacs. Entering the contest brought users to Pontiac's Web site. According to Mark-Hans Richer, marketing director for the G6, a record 500,000 people visited the site in the days following the show.

The press response was immediate and positive. *USA Today* described the giveaway as "one of the great promotional stunts in the history of television." The Associated Press claimed Pontiac had created "an event that marketing executives say could set a new bar for product placement." And the *Wall Street Journal* suggested "GM couldn't

afford to buy all the free publicity." According to New York–based publicity tracker Video Monitoring Service, 674 TV news reports covered the giveaway during the days that followed the program, the most ever for an automotive event. And Pontiac and Oprah are not finished. Future program segments will show how the new cars changed the lives of some of the winners.

Not everyone seemed to think the promotion was such a slam dunk, though. Robert Cosmai, CEO at Hyundai America, sniffed, "I don't think we would need to spend $7 million to accomplish the same thing in publicity." Sour grapes from an outflanked competitor? Perhaps. But there were doubters within Pontiac itself. Only a couple of days before Winfrey's visit to the Michigan plant, mid-level managers wrote a memo objecting to the deal, arguing it would have a negligible impact on sales. When Pontiac marketing reps pitched the Oprah promotion to higher-ups at GM, the reps were given a green light, but were also told they would have to find the money for the promotion from their own budget. To come up with the money they canceled several ad buys on network television. Others within the organization wondered whether the same publicity could have been obtained by giving away only 100 cars rather than almost 300. And some within Pontiac were confused about how the promotion would ultimately help the G6 succeed with its intended demographic, young male drivers.

Consider This

1. Do you recall hearing about the giveaway? Did you discuss it with anyone? Was the brand a part of what you remember about it?

2. The costs of the promotion were substantial. Were they justifiable? What criteria, ultimately, are important in assessing whether Pontiac made the right call in spending its marketing budget as it did?

3. Why was the Pontiac G6 promotion considered a public relations success story? How would you recommend evaluating the effectiveness of such a program?

Sources: Jean Halliday and Claire Atkinson, "Madison+Vine: Pontiac Gets Major Mileage Out of $8 Million 'Oprah' Deal," *Advertising Age,* (September 20, 2004): 12; Jean Halliday, "Pontiac," *Advertising Age* (November 1, 2004); BBC News, "Cars Galore in Oprah Giveaway," September 14, 2004, http://news.bbc.co.uk/2/hi/americas/3654062.stm; Jason Stein, "Media Gush over G6 Group Giveaway," *Automotive News* (September 20, 2004): 45; Jason Stein, "GM Was Split on Oprah Deal; Some Tried to Stop Costly Car Giveaway," *Automotive News* (September 20, 2004): 1.

SEARCH ENGINE:

IT consultant who actually finds ways to make you money.

That new system was going to save you money. Only it wound up costing you. Big time. That's when you call in Novell. Our Ngag[...] provide you with IT consultants who have real-world experience. They don't go around ripping and replacing. They just find ways to [...] you have work. And make you money doing it. If you'd like them to apply their expertise for your company, give us a call at 1-800-[...] visit http://www.novell.com/ngage. ⊛ **WE SPEAK YOUR LANGUAGE.**

N[o...]

Special Advertising Situations

Novell Speaks Your Language

Award:
BtoB Best Awards;
American Association of
Advertising Agencies (4As)
Account Planning Award;
Grand AME Award
(Advertising and Marketing
Effectiveness)

Company:
Novell

Agency:
J. Walter Thompson

Campaign:
"We Speak Your
Language"

CHAPTER OBJECTIVES

After reading this chapter, you will be able to:

1. Discuss retail advertising and what makes it distinctive.

2. Explain the basics of B2B advertising.

3. Identify the basic goals and operations of nonprofit and social marketing.

4. Describe the strategic decisions behind international advertising and IMC.

hat does *RAM* mean to a businessperson? Or *cursor, megahertz, search engine,* or *ERP*?

Humorous definitions of these common technology terms were used as the creative link between IT (information technology) staff and their C-level bosses. C-level refers to senior executives, the target audience for this campaign for the Novell software company, who have *chief* in their title, such as chief executive officer (CEO), chief financial officer (CFO), or chief information officer (CIO).

So what do those terms mean? Here are the answers, which also served as headlines in an award-winning campaign for Novell by the J. Walter Thompson agency:

RAM: Attempt by certain large vendors to shove their proprietary technology solutions down your enterprise.

Cursor: CIO who discovers that his expensive new integration system needs yet another integration system.

Megahertz: How you'll feel if all your competitors attend Novell BrainShare and you don't.

Search Engine: IT consultant who actually finds ways to make you money.

ERP: Sound made by CIO when people see data they shouldn't.

The point of this award-winning campaign, which was titled, "We Speak Your Language," is that Novell is unlike other technology companies that speak in "techno-babble." Rather Novell's products and expertise can connect technology to business needs by selling the products' benefits as tools to make money or cut costs.

The brilliant insight behind this campaign is that the C-level executives don't understand techno-speak, so to get their attention, IT folks have to talk about what they do understand—the bottom line.

The Novell "We Speak Your Language" campaign was designed to promote Novell's best-known product, Netware, but it also needed to introduce the broad range of solutions the company offered—everything from consulting to Web services. Beyond Netware, four other products needed to be explained. The biggest goal, however, was to speak about these products in a way that demonstrated how Novell's products could make or save money for its customers.

The media plan, whose goal was to surround the executive throughout the course of the day, made it possible for the creative to stand out in the cluttered B2B market and attract attention. Executives saw the ads in their morning newspapers, on CNBC when they flipped it on in the office, on TV when they went home at night, and in business publications like the *Economist, Forbes,* and *Fortune* when they unwound at home.

This was the core campaign message and media strategy, but since Novell is an international company, JWT had to find a way to use the "language" strategy and message to executives around the world. The It's a Wrap feature at the end of the chapter will explain just how effective this campaign was at delivering a positive bottom-line message for Novell.

Sources: AME brief provided by Novell and J. Walter Thompson; Kate Maddox, "Integrated Marketing Success Stories," *BtoB,* June 7, 2003, www.btobonline.com; "2003 BtoB Best Awards," *BtoB* (December 8, 2003): 22.

The Novell case is about an integrated international business-to-business campaign. It combines two of the subjects we cover in this chapter, business-to-business and international advertising. Other topics in this chapter are retail and nonprofit. All these specialized areas use many of the basic advertising principles; however, there are some distinct differences that we will call to your attention in this chapter. We'll start with retail.

RETAIL ADVERTISING

Retail marketing is about selling (the company's viewpoint), but also it is about shopping (the consumer's viewpoint). Sometimes shopping is a chore, but many times it is

■ ■ ■
Best Buy uses surreal
advertising to convey the idea
that it has a huge selection
and offers a lot of choice to
shoppers.

fun, entertaining, or an adventure. Sporting goods store Galyans (renamed Dick's) tries
to make its store a hero (rather than the product) to its sports fanatic, heavy shopper target that Galyans identifies as "seekers." Galyans not only provides the newest, most
innovative products on the market, it even markets products that aren't yet on the market .[1] In addition to fun, shoppers also base their decisions on choice and selection as the
Best Buy ad illustrates.

   The face of retailing is changing as malls convert to open-air markets, eBay operates
an international flea market, and the Internet becomes the primary information source for
buyers. Clicks and bricks are changing places as store-based retailers set up Web sites and
e-marketers set up stores. NikeTown stores sells sports (and sporting clothes) as entertainment and ESPN takes X Games to malls. The more the retail world changes, the more there
is need for information and promotion. Retail advertising accounts for nearly half of all the
money spent on advertising.

Retail Advertising Strategies

Retail advertising occurs on local, national, and international levels. Retailers such as
Sears, Office Max, Macy's, Home Depot, and Best Buy advertise nationally. Some retailers, such as Toys "R" Us, advertise internationally, but most retail advertising is local. By
local advertising, we mean advertising targeted at consumers who live close to a retail
store. As the table shows, many types of organizations use retail advertising to reach consumer audiences. The types of organizations are diverse, ranging from independently
owned stores to restaurant chains.

Type	Examples
Locally owned stores	The local independent record or book store, auto parts shop, or bakery.
Service businesses	A local beauty salon, health clinic, or the local branch of a bank.
Local branches of retail store chains	Staples, Macy's, Wal-Mart.
Franchised retail businesses	Texaco, Holiday Inn, or Hertz.
Dealerships	Toyota or Ford auto dealerships, AT&T phone stores.
Restaurant and entertainment	Applebee's, TGI Friday's, the local bagel shop, movie theaters, sports arenas and teams, theater troupes.

Principle
The first strategic consideration in retail advertising is geography.

In targeting consumers, a retailer's first concern is geography: Where do my customers live? How far will they drive to come to my store? The next concern is consumer taste. National retailers also are trying to develop offers that appeal to consumers in different parts of the country as well as in different neighborhoods in the same suburb. H.E.B. Supermarkets operates its stores in both central and south Texas. In San Antonio, the stores located in Mexican American neighborhoods carry a merchandise assortment, as well as advertising program, very different from that in stores in other locations.

Retail advertising has a number of objectives. The primary one is to build store traffic, and advertising does that by emphasizing a reduced price on a popular item or by promoting the store image through focusing on unusual or varied merchandise, friendly and knowledgeable clerks, or prestige brands. Other objectives are:

- Build store brand awareness.
- Sell a variety of products and brands by creating consumer understanding of items or services offered.
- Deliver sales promotion messages.
- Create and communicate a store image or personality.
- Establish a store brand that resonates with the local audience.
- Create consumer desire to shop at this particular store.

In addition, most retailers use advertising to help attract new customers, build store loyalty, increase the amount of the average sale, maintain inventory balance by moving out overstocks and outdated merchandise, and help counter seasonal lows.

Differences between Retail and Brand Advertising   Retail advertising differs from brand advertising in various ways. First, local retail advertising is targeted to people living in the store's community and is customized to match their particular needs, wants, and culture. National and international brand advertisers (Sony, Calvin Klein, Chevrolet) typically deliver a more standardized, general message. Second, national brand advertising supports only the advertiser's brand, while retail advertising may promote several different brands or even competing brands. Third, retail advertising has an inherent urgency. Everything about the ad pushes the consumer toward a behavior—typically visiting the store. National retail brand advertising is more concerned with image. The fourth difference is that local retail advertising advertises a specific local store or stores and includes contact information such as the store's address, telephone number, and business hours.

For several reasons local retail advertising is generally more utilitarian than national advertising. It is more short term. Most retail ads deal with price and run for only a few days, while a national ad may run for months or years. Also, local retail advertisers can't justify high production costs for advertising. National advertisers can easily spend $5,000 to produce a newspaper ad when they are paying $200,000 to run it in 100 large markets. That's why local retailers often rely on their media sales representatives to design and produce their ads rather than outside agencies.

Cooperative Advertising   One way local retailers can compensate for their smaller budgets and limited expertise is to take advantage of **cooperative (co-op) advertising** (as discussed in Chapters 2 and 8), in which the national brand reimburses the retailer for part

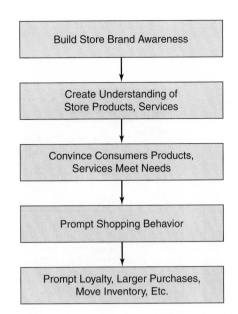

Retail Advertising Objectives
To build and maintain store traffic, a retail ad strives to meet these objectives.

or all of the advertising expenses. Co-op funds, sometimes called **ad allowances**, have become so common that most retailers won't even consider taking on a new brand, especially one in a heavily advertised category, without receiving some support. Retailers may also seek reimbursement for local advertising from suppliers as part of a retailer's vendor support program. Large drug and discount chains, for instance, periodically schedule a special advertising supplement. Their suppliers are offered an opportunity to buy space in this supplement. Suppliers generally are promised that no competing brands will be included.

Institutional and Product Retail Advertising   Two general types of retail advertising are institutional and product promotion. **Institutional retail advertising** is image advertising that sells the retail store as a brand. Retailers who want to build a brand identity must clearly and consistently communicate that identity to consumers. Product retail advertising presents specific merchandise for sale at a certain price and urges customers to come to the store to buy it. When a sales price dominates the ad, it is called **promotional** or **sales advertising**. Retailers use any reason they can find to have a sale (President's Day, tax time, overstocks). Stores search for themes, such an exotic place (Madras, India, was the theme of a special JCPenney sale) or period (see the '70s sale by Virgin Megastore). In contrast, **nonpromotional advertising** talks about merchandise that is new, exclusive, and of superior quality and designs.

Creating the Retail Ad

Prior to actually writing copy or drawing a layout, creative advertising experts Jeweler and Drewniany suggest that advertisers answer this question: Why would you shop in your store? Possible answers to this question can provide direction for the creative process. They suggest these typical reasons:[2]

• Store's personnel
• Store's location
• Store's pricing policy
• Store's products
• Store's history
• Store's stand on social responsibility issues

   The store's image is another reason. For retail operations that sell products and services that have little differentiation—such as gasoline, banking, and car rentals—a positive, distinctive image is a valuable asset. Image is also important for upscale retailers like Louis Vuitton. The retailer can convey this image through advertising, other forms of marketing communication, pricing, and location.

SHOWCASE

For Virgin Megastore's "Forever '70s" sale, Chris Hutchinson came up with the idea of a character who was stuck in the '70s—his music, his style, his lingo, his attitude. Where to find this cool cat? The perfect person turned out to be the art director himself, who worked out a great outfit: a huge Afro, tight bell-bottoms, and an "orange" leather jacket that his father wore in the real 1970s. The photographer shot on the run to get a semidocumentary look. The client loved the print so the art director directed himself in a set of TV spots, as well. The sale was a huge success nationwide. At the time he worked for San Diego–based Bulldog Drummond but he has since moved to Portland, Oregon, where he works as at Weiden + Kennedy.

Price also can be a factor in establishing a store's image and a reason for shopping. Most discount stores signal their type of merchandise with large, bold prices. Other retailers emphasize price by offering coupons in their print advertising. Featuring prices doesn't necessarily apply only to ads that give the store a bargain or a discount image, however. Price can help the consumer comparison shop without visiting the store.

Because the main object of retail ads is to attract customers, store location (or telephone number, if advertising is a service) is essential. For merchandise that is infrequently purchased, such as cars, furniture, wallpaper, and hearing aids, the ad should include a map or mention a geographic reference point (for example, three blocks north of the state capitol building) in addition to the regular street address.

Production   Small and medium-sized retailers often save money by using stock artwork. All daily newspapers subscribe to clip-art services that provide a wide range of photographs and line art drawings. Larger retailers or upscale specialty retailers, such as

Tiffany's, generally have their art designed by a staff or agency designer, which gives all of their ads a similar look and a distinct image. Some manufacturers also provide a **dealer tag**, which is time left at the end of a radio or television spot or space left at the bottom of print materials, where the local store is mentioned. Retailer chains make their television production more efficient by using a **donut format** in which the opening and closing sections are the same, while the middle changes to focus on different merchandise or different stores.

Who Creates the Retail Ad? Most retail advertising is created and produced by one or a combination of the following: local media, in-house staff, ad agencies, and freelancers. The larger the retail operation, the more likely it is to have an in-house advertising staff. All local media create and produce ads for retailers. With the exception of television, most provide this service free. The medium- and larger-sized newspapers and stations often have people whose only job is to write and produce ads. Some retail ads are created by agencies, particularly in-house agencies. Generally outside agency work is the most costly way to produce retail ads on a regular basis so agencies are used instead to create image ads for the retailer. Also, because agencies work for many different clients, they cannot always respond as quickly as an in-house agency can. Few agencies are prepared to handle the large number of day-to-day copy changes and the fast deadlines that are characteristic of major retail advertising.

Television spots, particularly if they are more image oriented instead of focused on product or price, may also be created by outside agencies. For example, office superstore Staples used the Cliff Freeman agency to create award-winning back-to-school campaigns that use humor to distinguish Staples' brand image. In one broadcast ad that used the song, "It's the Most Wonderful Time of the Year," a deliriously happy father is skipping down the aisles, gleefully dropping school supplies into a shopping cart. His kids look on with unhappy faces.

This brand image ad for a new Louis Vuitton store provides basic retail information—location and merchandise—as it also builds store traffic.

The Media of Retail Advertising

At the national level, retailers use a variety of traditional and nontraditional media—magazines, television, outdoor, the Internet—for their image or institutional advertising. They are also using new and nontraditional media. The upscale department store Bloomingdales, for example, publishes its own glossy high-fashion magazine called *B* that highlights clothes, travel, entertaining, and celebrity stories. Limited Too, the retailer for preteen girls, sells "Fast Friends," a series of fiction books about four friends.[3]

Aside from traditional newspaper ads, local retailers can use a host of store-based media to communicate their promotions. Manufacturers also provide window banners, bill inserts, and special direct-mail pieces, such as four-color supplements for the local paper that carry the store's name and address. Other media used by retailers include banners, posters, shelf talkers (signs attached to a shelf that let the consumer take away some piece of information or a coupon), end-of-aisle displays, and shopping cart ads. New interactive electronic kiosks with touch-screen computers, CD-ROM databases, full graphics, and product photos are moving into the aisles in many stores, where they provide more information about more products than the store can ever stock on its shelves.

Local Retail Media Strategy Unlike national advertisers, local retailers generally prefer *reach* over frequency. Because retailers can choose from many local media, they are careful to use media that minimize wasted reach. That's why direct mail is now the second-largest advertising medium used by retailers, next to newspapers. Media competition at the local level has increased significantly. Nearly all major markets now have at least one local independent station and a public television station and that has created many more local television opportunities. Radio is used by local retailers because it has a low cost, a high degree of geographic and audience selectivity, and it provides flexibility in scheduling. Many of the top-50 markets in the United States have at least one local magazine offering retailers high-quality, four-color ads to reach upscale consumers and many national magazines have regional or metropolitan editions that enable local retailers to buy exposure to the audience within their trading area only.

Newspapers have always made up the bulk of the retailer's advertising because the local newspaper fits the retailer's desire for geographic coverage and immediacy. Retailers can gain some measure of audience selectivity by advertising in specific sections of the paper, such as sports and financial pages. In addition to special rates for local advertisers, newspapers in major markets provide retail advertisers with their zip code circulation reports, which identify the circulation level for that newspaper in the various zip codes. This information, combined with zone editions of the paper (certain versions of the paper go to certain counties and suburbs), increases targeting efficiency.

Free-distribution newspapers called **shoppers**, dropped off at millions of suburban homes once or twice a week, are popular advertising outlets for retailers. **Preprints** are advertising circulars furnished by a retailer for distribution as a free-standing insert in newspapers. For instance, preprints account for more than 80 percent of Wal-Mart's advertising budget. Retail advertising is a huge part of the advertising industry, but so is business-to-business advertising, so let's look at that specialty area in more depth.

Consider This

1. What makes retail advertising different from other types of brand or product advertising?
2. What are the key characteristics of a retail advertisement?

BUSINESS-TO-BUSINESS ADVERTISING

Advertising directed at people in business who buy or specify products for business use is called **business-to-business advertising**. Business marketing is the marketing of goods and services to business markets, as the Matter of Practice box demonstrates. Although personal selling is the most common method of communicating with business buyers, business advertising is used to create product awareness, enhance the company's reputation, and support salespeople and other channel members by generating new business leads.

Types of Business-to-Business Advertising

Businesses are grouped according to **The North American Industry Classification System (NAICS),** which was formerly known as *The Standard Industrial Classification (SIC) system.* which was established by the U.S. government to group organizations on the basis of the major activity or product or service provided (see www.census.gov/epcd/www/naics.html). The NAICS system, which classifies more than 4 million manufacturers, allows a business advertiser to find its customers' NAICS codes and then obtain lists that include the publications each NAICS group uses. This information means the advertiser can select media that will reach the businesses in a certain NAICS. As we see in Figure 18.2, the industries are classified as industrial, government, trade, professional, and agricultural.

- *Industrial Advertising.* Original equipment manufacturers (OEMs), such as IBM and General Motors, purchase industrial goods or services that either become a part of the final product or aid business operations. **Industrial advertising** is directed at OEMs. For example, when General Motors purchases tires from Goodyear, information needs focus on whether the purchase will contribute to a high-quality finished product. When Goodyear purchases packaging materials to ship the tires it manufactures, information needs focus on prompt, predictable delivery.

A MATTER OF PRACTICE

Fred Makes the IT Manager a Hero

A business-to-business advertising campaign has to make a strong sales argument but that doesn't mean they have to be dull.

CDW, for example, sells computer systems and peripherals to its business clients direct via the Internet and over the telephone. Its primary competitor is Dell, which outspends CDW on advertising 10 to 1.

In the early 2000s the market for high-technology products hit bottom responding to the pressure of the dot-com bust. In the middle of this economic downturn, CDW asked the JWT Technology agency to help it continue sales growth.

The target audience for the campaign was the information technology (IT) manager. This group is primarily male between the ages of 35–44. Research determined that they generally feel misunderstood and underappreciated by their peers, who tend to badger them with unreasonable requests stemming from a lack of knowledge of technology.

In light of the massive spending directed to this target by the competition, the agency team felt it needed to not only present a strong selling message but touch the right emotional buttons of the IT manager who is often thought of as the ultimate geek.

The message strategy was to create a character, "Fred," a highly dedicated IT manager with whom this target could identify. Using empathetic humor, Fred demonstrated the exasperations of the IT manager whose life is filled with the trials and tribulations of dealing with non-tech co-workers. In this campaign Fred gets continuously harassed by dimwitted employees and turns to CDW for solace. The intent was to communicate that CDW truly knows what it's like to be in IT—and that CDW is equipped with the right products and services to make the IT manager's job a little easier. The campaign also used a tagline that communicated the selling point in a powerful way: "The Right Technology. Right Away."

The campaign used trade publications, online advertising, and television in very selected programs that had a high index for this target audience, such as science fiction and comedy channels. The largest part of the budget went to television because it provided the most dramatic platform for delivering the empathetic humor in the message strategy.

One indication of the success of the campaign was the response of the audience. Fred definitely connected with the IT target, which was clear from the flood of letters and e-mails to CDW's corporate offices. It was obvious that IT managers identified with Fred and wanted to share their own trying buying experiences with a company they knew would understand—CDW. The agency realized this response was a gold mine and acted quickly to capture these stories. They were compiled into a book and sent as a direct-mail piece to CDW's best customers. The book was

also sold on CDW's Web site in an area called "Fred's Corner," where customers could view the ad campaign and send in their own stories for inclusion in follow-up books.

The "Fred" campaign created for CDW by JWT Technology not only elicited a great response from IT managers who wanted to share their own stories about clueless co-workers, it also more than accomplished its objectives. Sales in the quarter that followed the launch of the campaign were 16 percent higher than the previous year—making it the highest quarterly sales in the history of the company. The effectiveness of this campaign in meeting its objectives set CDW's "Fred" campaign apart as an EFFIE award winner.

Consider This

1. What problem did the message strategy seek to overcome?
2. How was the effectiveness of this campaign determined?

Source: EFFIES Brief provided by JWT Technology and CDW Corp.

Types of Business Markets
The overall B2B market has five distinct markets, each of which purchases products and services differently.

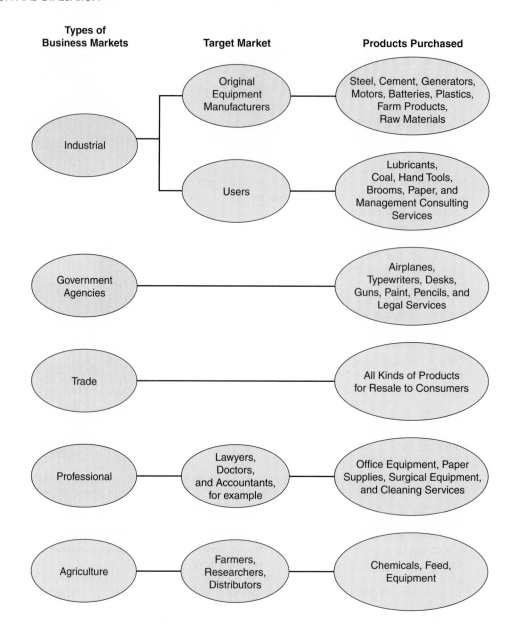

Figure 18.2

| Types of Business Markets | Target Market | Products Purchased |

Industrial → Original Equipment Manufacturers → Steel, Cement, Generators, Motors, Batteries, Plastics, Farm Products, Raw Materials

Industrial → Users → Lubricants, Coal, Hand Tools, Brooms, Paper, and Management Consulting Services

Government Agencies → Airplanes, Typewriters, Desks, Guns, Paint, Pencils, and Legal Services

Trade → All Kinds of Products for Resale to Consumers

Professional → Lawyers, Doctors, and Accountants, for example → Office Equipment, Paper Supplies, Surgical Equipment, and Cleaning Services

Agriculture → Farmers, Researchers, Distributors → Chemicals, Feed, Equipment

- *Government Advertising.* The largest purchasers of industrial goods in the United States are federal, state, and local governments. These government units purchase virtually every kind of good, from $15 hammers to multimillion-dollar missiles. Such goods may be advertised in *Federal Computer Week, Commerce Business Daily,* or *Defense News.* However, you seldom see advertisements targeted directly to government agencies because these purchases are usually made by bids and contracts and the decision is made on price.

- *Trade/Channel Advertising.* **Trade advertising** is used to persuade distribution channel members, such as resellers, wholesalers, and retailers, to stock the products of the manufacturer. *Chain Store Age, Florist's Review,* and *Pizza and Pasta* are examples of trade publications and there are thousands of these covering every possible product category. Resellers want information on the profit margins they can expect to receive, the product's major selling points, and what the producer is doing in terms of consumer advertising and other promotional support activities.

- *Professional Advertising.* Advertising directed at a group of mostly white-collar workers such as lawyers, accountants, technology consultants, doctors, teachers, funeral directors, and advertising and marketing specialists is known as **professional adver-**

tising. Advertisers interested in attracting professionals advertise in publications such as the *Music Educators' Journal* and *Advertising Age.*

- *Agricultural Advertising.* Agricultural advertising promotes a variety of products and services, such as animal health products, seeds, farm machinery and equipment, crop dusting, and fertilizer. Large and small farmers alike want to know how industrial products can assist them in the growing, raising, or production of agricultural commodities. They turn to such publications as *California Farmer* and *Trees and Turf* for such assistance.

B2B Buying Behavior

Business marketing differs from consumer marketing in three ways: who buys a product, what the buying motive is, and how the decision is made. In business markets, organizations buy products or services to support (1) their production requirements or (2) their business needs. Buying decisions are often made by committees and influenced by others in the organization from different functional areas: people from marketing, manufacturing, purchasing, or other different functional areas who have varying information needs. In general, those involved in making decisions for businesses are professionals who have technical knowledge and expertise and who use rational criteria when comparing choices.

Purchasing Objectives As you can see in the AIG advertisement, purchasing objectives in B2B center on rational, pragmatic considerations such as price, service, quality of the product or service, and assurance of supply. For that reason, B2B advertising tends to use rational strategies and focus on reasons and benefits.

- *Price.* Because of the size of most business purchases, buyers in the business arena are more concerned with price. In evaluating price, businesses consider a variety of factors that generate or minimize costs, such as: What amount of scrap or waste will result from the use of the material? What will the cost of processing the material be? How much power will the machine consume?
- *Service.* Business buyers require multiple services, such as technical assistance, repair capability, training, and technical support. Thus, the technical contributions of suppliers are important considerations wherever equipment, materials, or parts are being purchased.
- *Quality.* Business customers search for quality levels that are consistent with company standards, so they are reluctant to pay for extra quality or to compromise quality for a reduced price. The crucial factor is uniformity or consistency in product quality.
- *Assurance of Supply.* Interruptions in the flow of parts and materials can shut down the production process, resulting in costly delays and lost sales. To guard against interruptions in supply, business firms rely on a supplier's established reputation for delivery, especially on-time delivery.

Creating B2B Advertising

Although business advertising is an economical means of reaching large numbers of buyers, it is used primarily to assist and support the personal selling function. As a result, B2B advertising objectives center on creating company awareness, increasing overall

Business-to-Business Objectives
B2B advertising has six main
objectives.

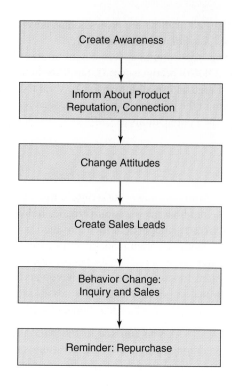

selling efficiency, and supporting distributors and resellers. When buyers are aware of a company's reputation, products, and record in the industry, salespeople are more effective. Advertising in trade magazines and general business publications often can reach the influencers more easily than a salesperson can (see Figure 18.3).

As in consumer advertising, the best business-to-business ads are relevant and understandable and strike an emotional chord in the prospective client. CDWs' "Fred" campaign demonstrates that a B2B ad can resonate with the target audience at the same time it delivers a compelling sales message. Business-to-business advertisers follow these guidelines to create effective ads:

- Make sure the ad selects the strongest benefit and presents it prominently and persuasively.
- Dramatize the most important benefit, either by showing the product in action or by visualizing the problem and offering your product or service as a solution.
- Make sure the visual is relevant to the key message. It should help readers understand how your product or service works or instantly show that you understand the problem.
- The offer must be clear. What exactly do you want the reader to do as a result of seeing your ad?
- Provide contact information. It should be easy for the potential customer to follow through with a response.

B2B Advertising Media

Although some business advertisers use traditional consumer media, most rely on general business or trade publications, industrial directories, direct marketing, or some combination of media. Novell's "We Speak Your Language" campaign was an IMC effort that used a variety of traditional and nontraditional media to reach its B2B audience—newspapers, magazines, cable television, airport billboards, outdoor, direct mail, a Web site, buttons, postcards—as well as a variety of marketing communication tools, including a conference and a direct-marketing effort that captured over 7,000 leads.

General Business and Trade Publications   As we saw in Chapter 8, general business and trade publications are classified as either horizontal or vertical. **Horizontal publications** are directed to people who hold similar jobs in different companies across different industries. For example, *Purchasing* is a specialized business publication targeted to people across industries who are responsible for a specific task or function. The magazines read by accountants or software engineers are other examples of horizontal publications. In contrast, **vertical publications**, such as *Iron Age and Steel* or *Advertising Age,* are targeted toward people who hold different positions in a particular industry.

Directory Advertising   Every state has an industrial directory, and there are also a number of private ones. One of the most popular industrial directories is the New York–based *Thomas Register.* The 19-volume *Register* contains 50,000 product headings and listings from 123,000 industrial companies selling everything from heavy machine tools to copper tubing to orchestra pits.

Consumer Media   Sometimes businesses advertise in consumer magazines (such as *Golf, Time,* or *Newsweek*) in the hope of building widespread brand recognition, such as the "Intel Inside" campaign. Consumer advertising can also be used to influence consumers to pull the brand through the channel by requesting a brand at their retail store. In general, consumer publications receive less than 5 percent of the total dollar amount spent on B2B advertising, and broadcast advertising receives less than 1 percent. There has been growth in business television programming. For example, Financial Network News (FNN) produces its own business shows and carries the syndicated business shows *This Morning's Business* and *First Business.* Introduced in 1989, CNBC's programming focuses more on personal finance.

The Web and B2B Advertisers   The Internet is a key medium for B2B advertisers. Company Web sites allow business clients to view product lists, place orders, check prices and availability, and replace inventories automatically. One of the most popular B2B sites on the Internet is FedEx's site, which allows its business clients all over the world to track their packages, obtain price information, and learn about FedEx software and services. It receives 1.7 million tracking requests a month, 40 percent of which probably would have been called in to the 800 number if the Web site had not been available. Because handling each call costs approximately $1, the Web site saves the company as much as $8 million in customer costs.

B2B Direct Marketing   Direct mail has the capacity to sell the product, provide sales leads, and lay the groundwork for subsequent sales calls. Business advertisers use various direct-marketing vehicles, such as direct mail, catalogs, and data sheets, to reach their markets. Catalogs and data sheets support the selling function by providing technical data about the product and supplementary information concerning price and availability. Technology developments allow direct-mail marketers to personalize the message to specific customers. Long copy, quality illustrations, diagrams, and specification sheets can be distributed easily through direct mail.

Consider This

1. What makes B2B advertising different from other types of brand or product advertising?
2. What are the key characteristics of a B2B advertisement?

NONPROFIT OR SOCIAL MARKETING

If a company wants to increase its integrity and positive reputation among customers, it must prove by its actions that it is a good corporate citizen. **Social marketing**, which refers to the use of marketing programs and marketing communication tools for the good of society, can be approached as either a corporate strategy or a strategy used by nonprofit organizations.

Let's first consider the corporate viewpoint. Concern for social issues is important to for-profit companies who use their marketing communication tools in support of a social responsibility position. A **societal marketing philosophy** describes the operations of companies whose corporate mission reflects their desire to do good—the business philosophies of Ben & Jerry's, Tom's of Maine, and the Body Shop, for example. Their commitment is

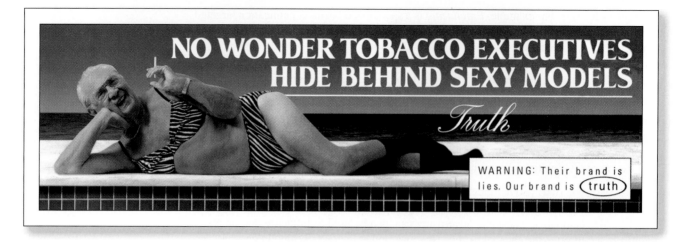

The antismoking and antidrug campaigns are a type of social marketing effort. This ad is from the "Truth" campaign featured in Chapter 17.

expressed in the way they design and produce their products, as well as market them. In addition to a societal marketing business philosophy, corporate public relations activities are sometimes designed to create a positive company image by emphasizing a company's concern for social issues and the steps that it takes to make a positive contribution to society. This happens through the use of cause or mission marketing.

Cause and Mission Marketing

Cause marketing means adopting a good cause and sponsoring its fund-raising and other community-oriented efforts. Sometimes called "sales promotion with a PR spin," *cause marketing* is described as "doing good things and getting credit for it."[4] For example, American Express has made it possible for its card users to donate money to aid the homeless with each purchase. Carol Cone, president of the Cone agency, develops dramatic programs for her clients based on what Cone calls *passion branding,* because it links brands to causes that people feel passionately about.[5] The Great American Bake Sale in the Matter of Principle box is an example of a how companies can use a great cause to build a positive association for themselves.

Principle

Cause marketing and mission marketing are driven by the passion employees and other stakeholders, as well as customers, feel for a good cause.

In addition to societal marketing, other companies also display a corporate commitment to the community (Target), the environment (Patagonia), a relevant target market cause (Avon and breast cancer research), and positive employee relations (Starbucks). If this commitment reflects the company's core business strategy, as in Tom's of Maine and Ben & Jerry's environmental commitment, it is called **mission marketing**. Mission marketing links a company's mission and core values to a cause that connects with the company's interests. It is more of a commitment than cause marketing and reflects the long-term brand-building perspective of IMC because the mission becomes the focal point for integrating all the company's marketing communication.[6] It also unites the entire organization and its stakeholders, particularly its employees, through their commitment to the effort.

Nonprofit Marketing

Socially responsible marketing is also be used by nonprofit organizations—such as hospitals, government agencies, zoos, museums, orchestras, religious organizations, charities, and universities and schools to "sell" their services, programs, and ideas. As these nonprofit organizations have become more competitive in their drive for public support, their marketing and marketing communication efforts have become more sophisticated. Social marketing is marketing communication used by nonprofits to affect attitudes or behaviors toward some idea or cause, as the Florida "Truth" campaign in Chapter 17.

Nonprofit organizations have a number of goals, such as *membership* (AARP, labor unions), *donations* (Red Cross, United Way, American Cancer Society), *participation*

A MATTER OF PRINCIPLE
The Great American Bake Sale Cooks Up Donations

Hunger and poverty affect more than 13 million children in the United States. One organization, Share Our Strength, the national antihunger, antipoverty organization, has organized the Great American Bake Sale and mobilized a group of dedicated corporate sponsors to deal with the issue. From the media come *Parade Magazine* and ABC Entertainment, who have helped to get the word out about the activities of other co-sponsors such as Tyson Foods and Betty Crocker.

In 2004 more than 600,000 Americans baked, bought, and sold brownies, muffins, and cookies as part of the second annual Great American Bake Sale to end child hunger in America. The groundbreaking program, which ran in July, raised more than a million dollars at bake sales around the country. Thousands of companies, youth groups, faith-based organizations, and civic and community groups registered to host an official Great American Bake Sale.

The funds raised through the Bake Sales were sent to Share Our Strength to distribute to the highest-need areas in America and awarded as grants to innovative child-hunger programs working at the local, state, and national level.

Betty Crocker sponsorship included ads with bake sale tips and recipes. The company's ad pointed out that every cookie, brownie, or muffin sold at 75 cents could feed at least four at-risk kids.

Tyson Foods advertised that for every product purchased from May to July the company would donate a pound of chicken, beef, or pork to the Share Our Strength organization. The company estimates that its donations helped serve 90 million protein-enriched meals to poor families across the country.

Other community partners who have worked with Share Our Strength include Youth Service America, the Points of Light foundation and Volunteer Center National Network, the National Council of Churches, and the National Association of RSVP Directors.

Share Our Strength is the nonprofit group spearheading this huge event. *Parade* and ABC are supporters who are engaged in cause marketing and give it tremendous publicity. Betty Crocker and Tyson are corporations whose missions involve feeding people so their involvement is at a different level, one that we refer to as mission marketing.

Consider This

1. What do the media and corporate sponsors get from their association with this event?
2. Explain how Share Our Strength, a small nonprofit, was able to enlist the participation and contributions of thousands through this special event.

Sources: David Oliver Relin, "They Won't Go Hungry Tonight," *Parade* (June 6, 2004): 14; Bill Shore, "The Hunger in America's Midst," *Christian Science Monitor*, June 3, 2004, http://www.csmonitor.com/2004/0603/p09s02-coop.html; www.strength.org; www.greatamericanbakesale.org; www.bettycrocker.com; www.tyson.com.

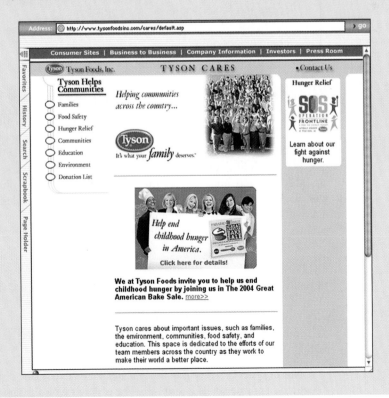

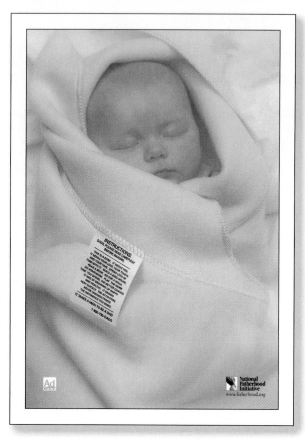

The Advertising Council has sponsored a number of public communication campaigns in support of good causes. The participating agencies donate their time and talent and media donate the time and space to run the PSAs. This one is for new dads and encourages them to learn more about parenting.

(Habitat for Humanity), *sales* (museum gift shops), *recruitment* (the military, universities), *attitude change* (political parties), *advocacy* (Weyerhauser for forest management), and *visits* or *attendance* (state tourism programs, art museums).

Fund-raising   Another activity that almost all nonprofits do is fund-raising, often under the guidance of a *development officer,* who is a professional specializing in fund-raising. Groups such as Save the Children use sophisticated segmentation and message strategies to target audiences.

Capital campaigns, which are designed to raise a specified amount of money in a given time period, are common for universities and other operations trying to finance buildings and other programs, such as museums and hospitals. They operate with a carefully designed strategy that involves sophisticated motivation strategies based on segmentation, targeting, goal setting, and leadership identification. Events and direct marketing are important tactical tools.

Public Communication Campaigns   Social marketing is also called public communication. **Public communication campaigns** are undertaken by nonprofit organizations as a conscious effort to influence the thoughts or actions of the public. For example, the Partnership for a Drug-Free American has used advertising and public relations to fight teen drug use. The biggest and longest-running program is the Advertising Council, which is a network of advertising agencies, media, and suppliers that donate their services to create ads and campaigns on behalf of socially important causes.

Consider This

1. What is the difference between social marketing done by a company and social marketing done by a nonprofit?
2. What are the most common types of objectives used by nonprofit marketing communication?

INTERNATIONAL ADVERTISING AND MARKETING COMMUNICATION

The globalization of marketing communication is driven by the development of international media and global brands. Increasing use of the Internet and English as an international language is helping to spread Western ideas of marketing. The tendency toward globalization is also a product of a healthy economy and those countries and regions that are modernizing (China, Eastern Europe) are more open to globalization than are countries with stagnant or depressed economies.[7] In this section we examine the issues and stages of international marketing communication, the planning of international advertising campaigns, and the organization of international marketing communication programs.

Stages of Market Development

Virtually every product category can be divided into local (or national), regional (trading bloc), and international markets and brands. Typically this is a process with a local company moving to a few foreign markets, perhaps to a group of markets in a region (Europe, Asia, for example), and eventually to a more global perspective with brands sold in many regions of the world. It is described as:

• *Exporting.* The first step requires placing the product in the distribution system of another country, a practice called *exporting.* The exporter typically appoints a distributor or importer, who assumes responsibility for marketing and advertising in the new country.

Some companies prefer to appoint a local distributor who knows the language and the distribution system and can handle customers and government better than a foreigner could.

- *Internationalization.* As sales of the imported line grow, management and manufacturing may transfer from the home country to the foreign one, with key marketing decisions focusing on acquiring or introducing products specifically for the local market, such as BMW setting up a U.S. manufacturing plant to build American versions of its German cars. Once the exporter becomes nationalized in several countries in a regional bloc, the company often establishes a regional management center and transfers day-to-day management responsibilities from the home country to that office.

- *Globalization.* An **international** or **global brand** is one marketed in two or more of the four major regional market blocs: North America, Latin America, Europe, and Asia-Pacific. The ultimate goal of any organization in attaining a global perspective is to leverage its operations in such a way that it benefits from currency exchange, tax or labor rates; the education and skill base of the labor force; natural resources; and industrial or government infrastructures. Another characteristic of globalized companies is that the "country of origin" label doesn't apply anymore. Nokia and Motorola, even though they are not U.S. companies, are both familiar brands to U.S. consumers.

There is an old axiom, "All business is local." But this should be modified to read: "Almost all transactions are local." Although advertising campaigns can be created for worldwide exposure, the advertising is intended to persuade a reader or listener to do something, which is usually a transaction that is completed at or near home or in the office.

The Global Versus Local Debate

A classic *Harvard Business Review* article by Harvard Business School professor Theodore Levitt ignited a debate over how to conduct global marketing. Levitt argued that companies should operate as if there were only one global market. He believed that differences among nations and cultures were not only diminishing but should be ignored because people throughout the world are motivated by the same desires and wants. Levitt argued further that businesses would be more efficient if planned for a global market.[8] The point is that some cultural habits and values cut across national and regional boundaries. Other scholars, such as Philip Kotler, marketing professor at Northwestern University, disagreed with Levitt. Kotler felt that Levitt misinterpreted the overseas success of Coca-Cola, PepsiCo, and McDonald's and pointed out that they did not offer the same product everywhere.[9]

People who study cultural differences, such as Dutch scholar Geert Hofstede, believe that the impact of national culture on business, the workplace, and consumption patterns is huge and should be accommodated in marketing and advertising strategies. Hofstede's conclusions were based on a study of 116,000 IBM employees around the world, which found their cultural differences to be stronger than the legendary IBM corporate culture that Hofstede had thought would be a standardizing influence.[10] Hofstede found that the American values of taking initiative, personal competency, and rugged individualism are not universal values and that some cultures prize collective thinking and group norms rather than independence.

Other researchers, however, have found some universal values, and global advertisers who are using strategies based on the following may have a useful platform for a more standardized campaign:[11]

- Protecting the family
- Honesty
- Heath and fitness
- Self-esteem
- Self-reliance
- Justice
- Freedom
- Friendship
- Knowledge
- Learning

FIGURE
18.4

Totally	Standardized	Standardized	Totally
Standardized	Strategy,	Strategy,	Localized
Strategy and	Translated	Modified	Strategy and
Execution	Execution	Execution	Execution

The Adaptability Continuum
Most global companies fall in the middle and right side of the continuum in their global strategies.

The outgrowth of this debate has been three main schools of thought on advertising in another country:

- *Standardization.* The **standardization** school of thought contends that differences between countries are a matter of degree, so advertisers must instead focus on the similarities of consumers around the world. Product category is important: There are enough similarities in certain categories, such as high-tech products and high-fashion cosmetics, that their advertising can be largely standardized across borders.
- *Localization (adaptation).* The **localization** or **adaptation** school of thought argues that advertisers must consider differences among countries, including local culture, stage of economic and industrial development, stage of life cycle, media availability, research availability, and legal restrictions.
- *Combination.* This school of thought reasons that a combination of standardization and localization may produce the most effective advertising. Some elements of brand identity and strategy, for example, may be standardized, but advertising executions may need to be adapted to the local culture.

Principle
Globalization is a fact, so marketers strive for a consistent brand strategy that still allows them to honor cultural differences when those differences are relevant to the brand's marketing strategy.

The reality of global advertising suggests that a combination approach is best. Still, the trend toward global markets is inescapable. The challenge for advertisers is to balance variations nationally or regionally with a basic global brand plan that maintains brand consistency. The Adaptability Continuum shown in Figure 18.4 elaborates on these three perspectives.

Procter & Gamble, one of the biggest worldwide marketers with more than 250 products in more than 140 different countries, has a flexible brand-management philosophy and uses all three approaches for its various brands. For example, at one end of the continuum, P&G's global laundry business markets a number of different brands—and brand strategies—in one category such Ariel, Cheer, Bold, Yes, Dreft, Gain, and Tide because consumer laundry habits are highly varied from country to country. On the other end of the continuum, the company markets its Pampers brand in most of the countries in which P&G competes because Pampers' global position is consistent around the globe. But when it comes to translating this position into precise communication strategies and advertising executions, Pampers does allow for regional and local variations in the messages.[12]

Note that most companies use the combination approach or lean toward localization. Starbucks uses localization. Tea is offered in stores in the Far East, stronger coffees in Europe, and gourmet coffees in the United States. Accordingly, Starbucks has standardized its product name, logo, and packaging to maintain brand consistency even though there is variation in its product line. See the Practical Tips box for the benefits of standardization and local strategies.

Practical Tips

Global Advertising: Standardize or Adapt?

When to Use a Standardization Advertising Strategy
- Standardization will lead to savings through economies of scale (advertising production, planning, control).
- Standardization ensures that advertising messages of a product are complementary and reinforcing.
- The company maintains control over the image projected by advertising for the brand.
- Global media create opportunities for global marketing.

- Converging buyer wants and needs means that buyers everywhere will increasingly want the same products and product benefits.
- There is little or no competition in many foreign markets.
- Graphic and visual advertising approaches can be used to overcome cultural differences.

When to Use a Localized Advertising Strategy

- A better fit with local markets means the advertiser is less likely to overlook local variations that affect buyer behavior.
- As a general rule, the fewer the people who have to approve decisions, the faster they can be made.
- Getting local managers and employees involved and motivated is much easier if those people have a say in the advertising decisions.
- Any cost reductions resulting from globalization often are offset by mistargeted ads.
- The chance of cultural blunders decreases.
- Strategically sound advertising is more likely to be successful.

Planning Global Marketing Communication Programs

Global marketing is inherently more complex than local marketing. Companies often offer local brands, as well as international and global brands. Sometimes the same product will be marketed under different brand names in different countries. Likewise, marketing communication may use a single-country approach, as well as campaigns that are regional or global in scope.[13] The marketing communication strategy can be complex if a multitude of IMC functions are being used. In order to keep all the various functions working together on strategy, it is also necessary to articulate a consistency platform for the use of certain key elements, such as the brand identity cues, a campaign theme, and, perhaps, the brand position.

Market or Culture Orientation   There are two basic ways to approach this planning: The market-orientation model is focused on the local market, or the cultural orientation is focused on the local culture. The **market-orientation model** compares data from several countries. The two major variables are (1) the share of market of brands within a category, and (2) the size of the category. For example, the brand's percentage share of the category market might vary substantially in four countries. We might look at the size of the market and see that as the critical factor. However, if that market is already dominated by global brands, no matter how big it is, then perhaps another country might be a better target because there is more opportunity for growth.

■ ■ ■
Starbucks has become a major global brand but it still follows a localization strategy and tailors its offerings to the tastes of different countries.

The second approach, the **culture-orientation approach**, emphasizes the cultural differences among peoples and nations. This school of thought recognizes that people worldwide share certain needs, but it also stresses the fact that these needs are met differently from culture to culture. San Diego State University professor Barbara Mueller believes that strategic decisions about international advertising should first of all accommodate cultural norms and values, but also consider political systems, economic policies, and social contexts in which the product is used and advertised.[14] For example, China recently banned certain products—feminine hygiene products, hemorrhoid medication, athlete's-foot ointment—from television commercials because Chinese viewers believe them to be offensive to discuss in mixed company.[15] How do cultural differences relate to advertising? Although the same emotions are basic to all humanity, the degree to which these emotions are expressed publicly varies. The camaraderie typical in an Australian business office would be unthinkable in Asia. The informal, first-name relationships common in North America are frowned on in Germany.

According to the high-context/low-context theory,[16] although the function of advertising is the same throughout the world, the expression of its

High-Context

Japanese

Chinese

Arabic

Greek

Spanish

Italian

English

French

North American

Scandinavian

German

Low-Context

FIGURE
18.5

High- to Low-context Cultures
The language of advertising messages is not as easy to craft in high-context cultures as in low-context cultures, where the meaning of a sentence is not so dependent on surrounding sentences.

message varies in different cultural settings. The major distinction is between **high-context cultures**, in which the meaning of a message can be understood only when contained within context cues, and **low-context cultures**, in which the message can be understood as it stands. In other words, in Japanese a word can have multiple meanings. Listeners or readers will not understand the exact meaning of a word unless they clearly understand the context in which the word is used. In contrast, English is a low-context language: Its words have clearly defined meanings that are not highly dependent on the words surrounding them. Figure 18.5 lists cultures from the highest to lowest context, with Japanese being the highest-context culture. This model helps explain the difficulties of advertising in other languages.

Advertising messages constructed by writers from high-context cultures might be difficult to understand in low-context cultures because they may offer too much detail to make the point clearly. In contrast, messages authored by writers from low-context cultures may be difficult to understand in high-context cultures because they omit essential contextual detail.

Central Control versus Local Adaptation   As noted earlier, some advertisers develop tightly controlled global campaigns with minimum adaptation for local markets. Others develop local campaigns in every major market. Most companies are somewhere in the middle. Even though Novell's "We Speak Your Language" campaign was designed with a consistent theme, there was still a need for adjustment in different markets. Novell realized that the business needs of an executive in Brazil are much different from those of a Japanese executive and those differences were reflected in the **pool-outs** or localized variations from the core campaign.

How are global campaigns created? International advertising campaigns have two basic starting points: (1) success in one country, and (2) a centrally conceived strategy. Planning approaches also include variations on the central campaign and bottom-up creativity.

- *Local Initiative* In the first starting point, a successful advertising campaign, conceived for national application, is modified for use in other countries. "Impulse," the body spray, started in South Africa with a campaign showing a woman being pleasantly surprised when a stranger hands her flowers. That strategic idea has been used all over the globe, but in most markets the people and the setting are localized. Wrigley, Marlboro, IBM, Waterman, Seiko, Philips, Ford, and many other companies have taken successful campaigns from one country and transplanted them around the world.
- *Centrally Conceived Campaigns* The second starting point, a centrally conceived campaign, was pioneered by Coca-Cola and is now used increasingly in global strategies. Microsoft uses a centralized strategy for its Xbox because, since it was a new brand, a consistent marketing strategy was deemed to be essential.[17] Although the centralization concept is simple, the application is difficult. A work team, task force, or action group (the names vary) assembles from around the world to present, debate, modify if necessary, and agree on a basic strategy as the foundation for the campaign. Cost is a huge factor. If the same photography and artwork can be used universally, this can save the $10,000 or more that *each* local variation might cost.
- *Variations on Central Campaigns* Variations on the centrally conceived campaign also exist. For example, Xerox may handle its European creative development by asking the European offices of Young & Rubicam to develop a campaign for a specific product. The office that develops the approved campaign would be designated the **lead agency** and would develop all the necessary elements of the campaign and prepare a standards manual for use in other countries. This manual would include examples of layouts and broadcast spots (especially the treatment of the logo or the product) and design standards for all elements. Because photography, artwork, television production, and color printing are very costly, developing these items in one location and then overlaying new copy or re-recording the voice track in the local language saves money. However, since some countries, such as Malaysia, require that all ads be locally produced, this approach gives direction to the message but still allows for local requirements to be met.
- *Bottom-Up Creativity* Sometimes a central campaign idea may be established but the executions can be developed locally and submitted to headquarters for use globally. For example, to extend McDonald's youth-targeted "I'm Lovin' It" campaign, McDonald's global chief marketing officer, Larry Light, held a competition among McDonald's ad

agencies all over the world. One winner, which became part of the international pool of ads, came from China, which is developing a lively creative advertising industry that produces edgy, breakthrough ads for young people. Light explained that McDonald's strategy was not just to do the creative work in the United States but rather to "Let the best ideas win."[18]

The Mr. CONTAC case from Japan is an example of a locally developed campaign idea that has been borrowed for use in other countries. The campaign with its Japanese-created brand character, Mr. CONTAC, helped rejuvenate the stagnant brand in Japan.

Planning a Global Advertising Strategy

Assuming that the ad campaign has been approved centrally, with a local application approach its execution must be adapted to suit the local market and that may involve modifying basic strategy decisions, such as objectives, targeting, and perhaps even positioning.

■ ■ ■
In the mid-1990s Glaxo Smithkline's CONTAC brand needed to be revitalized. When a reformulated "CONTAC 600 SR" was launched by Glaxo Smithkline, the assignment to create a new advertising campaign was given to Dentsu Inc., which is the largest agency not only in Japan, but also in the world.

Global Advertising Objectives   Just as every domestic advertising plan begins with a statement of objectives, global advertising plans originate with a similar statement. The problem of managing brand consistency is largely responsible for limiting most global marketing objectives to *awareness* and *recall*—two effective yet easily attainable marketing communication measures, although more specific objectives may be needed in individual markets. For example a brand may be well-known in one market and its primary objective, then, is reminder. At the same time it may be newly launched in another country and the objective there is focused on trial.

Targeting Issues   The globalization/localization debate is really about targeting. The question is whether people in the target are similar across borders or whether their national and cultural differences are great enough so that, to be effective, the message strategy has to be modified country by country. For example, in support of Levitt's argument about standardization, Procter & Gamble's Pampers marketing chief observed that "babies' bottoms are the same everywhere." In other words, mothers of infants who are buying diapers have very similar concerns and their decision is less affected by cultural differences.

Marketers of high-technology products, such as computers, and products sold to business travelers have found their target audiences to be moved by similar appeals. The MTV, music, pop culture is another group that tends to cut across national borders, one that has been described as a "surprisingly homogeneous global youth customer segment."[19] You can look out of a hotel window in Beijing or Brazil and see similar fashions on teenagers—Nikes, Chicago Bulls T-shirts, Oakley sunglasses—and hear similar music coming from their MP3 players. Unfortunately, this is also a trend-driven market with a short attention span.[20] Music is important in targeting this group, and a strong musical theme, especially typical of Coke and Pepsi, makes the transfer from one country to another even smoother because popular music has become an international language.

On the other hand, target audiences for food products have quite different tastes depending upon their national cultures. The British are less interested in hot, spicy products than are the Italians or Mexicans. The French use more sauces and delicate, nuanced flavors than do the British or Americans.

Positioning the Global Brand   Research must be conducted to identify the problems and opportunities facing the product in each of the international markets to be entered, as the Charmin commercial illustrates. The situation analysis portion of the advertising plan develops the information needed for positioning the product in the foreign markets. Particularly important is a good understanding of consumer buying motives in each market. This is almost impossible to develop without locally based consumer research. If analysis

THE INSIDE STORY
The "Mr. CONTAC" Campaign in Japan: A Case Study

Masura Ariga, Dentsu Inc.

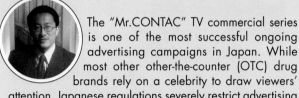

The "Mr.CONTAC" TV commercial series is one of the most successful ongoing advertising campaigns in Japan. While most other other-the-counter (OTC) drug brands rely on a celebrity to draw viewers' attention, Japanese regulations severely restrict advertising claims, so CONTAC effectively used a fictional character to boost sales as well as rebuild its lagging brand equity.

The brand situation when a reformulated "CONTAC 600 SR" was launched by Glaxo Smithkline was summarized as follows: (1) CONTAC was perceived as a strong, effective, and reliable cold remedy; however, for some consumers, it was perceived as potentially too strong. (2) The brand was strongly associated with the capsule product form.

The communication strategy was designed to focus on the brand's competitive advantage: long-lasting symptom relief through unique tiny time-pill action. There was a risk, though, that focusing on the consumer benefit of this feature alone meant that other product variants without it, which accounted for a quarter of total brand sale, could not be actively promoted.

Three very different creative ideas were developed by the agency's creative team:

1. Mr. CONTAC, a capsule character with a distinct regional dialect and personality
2. Godzilla with a cold, in which CONTAC is the hero that relieves the monster's symptoms
3. Humorous slice-of-life

These ideas were pretested using **animatics** (still photos presented as key frames in a television commercial). In the end, the Mr. CONTAC idea was selected based on the following reasons:

- **Campaignability.** The idea allowed for countless executions. It could also be expanded, allowing multiple characters to be created for each distinct product variant. The idea could cover future product development.
- **Ownability.** The advertising property could be owned, controlled, and managed by the client and the agency. Use of the Godzilla character for other product endorsements could not be controlled.

- **Uniqueness.** A talking capsule character would be unique within the Japanese OTC cold remedy category.
- **Fit with brand/product.** The CONTAC product story is very visual. One half of the capsule is transparent, revealing the tiny time pills, which release medicine gradually, relieving symptoms longer than the competition. The Mr. CONTAC creative idea brought that product story to life; the character *is* the product story.

The brand character was launched in 1996 and has been running in the Japanese market as a brand-building tool since then. Consumer response to the Mr. CONTAC character has been overwhelming. Sales, market share, awareness, and brand image numbers all increased significantly. Sales of variants not promoted were also expanded, benefiting from the campaign's "halo effect." This naturally led to extensions of the Mr. CONTAC creative idea into other activities. For example, a Mr. CONTAC Internet home page was developed (http://glaxosmithkline.co.jp/contac/funzone/index.html), and character goods were produced for on-pack promotions. In fact, some of these promotion goods have been snatched up by the public and privately sold for hundreds of dollars apiece. The company has been approached by toy companies and makers of home video games for sublicenses of the Mr. CONTAC character. However, the company has rejected these offers, and has maintained focus on only those activities directly supporting business objectives.

It has required discipline to maintain that focus. The campaign has been running for almost a decade now, with new executions of the same strategy being done each year. Over time, and with discipline, MR.CONTAC has become an equivalent of the Pillsbury Doughboy. The biggest compliment for any big idea is to be copied. The Mr. CONTAC creative idea is now being tested or implemented in other sister markets.

Masura Ariga graduated with a BA in Political Science from Waseda University in Tokyo in 1985. In 1992 he was in the first graduating class from the new IMC Master's program at Northwestern University. His graduate education was sponsored by Dentsu and he has been working for that agency ever since.

reveals that consumer buying behavior and the competitive environment are the same across international markets, it may be possible to use a standardized positioning throughout. In exploring the international marketing opportunity for Gatorade, Quaker discovered that the active, outdoor lifestyle that created demand for sports beverages was an international, not a domestic phenomenon.

Setting the Budget All the budgeting techniques discussed in Chapter 7 have possible application in foreign markets. When preparing a single advertising plan for multiple markets, many companies use an objective-task budgeting approach that uses a separate budget for each foreign market. (Remember that this approach looks at the objectives for each activity and determines the cost of accomplishing each objective.) This technique adds some flexibility to localize campaigns as needed. However, local practices also may affect the budget decision. Most notably, the exchange rate from country to country may affect not only the amount of money spent in a particular market, but also the timing of the expenditures. The cost of television time in Tokyo is approximately twice what it is on U.S. networks, and, rather than being sold during an up-front market every spring, Japanese TV time is wholesaled several times during the year.

Executing the International Campaign The execution of a global campaign is usually more complex than a national plan. The creative may need to be reshot with local models and settings, as well as language. The Novell campaign had serious language challenges in moving to an international message that could be launched in 10 languages. Language is always a problem for a campaign that is dependent on words rather than visuals as the primary carrier of meaning. Some of the Novell technology terms were commonly understood but others weren't. So a team of language experts was needed to adjust the terms and carry over the meanings in the different languages.

Government approval of television commercials can be difficult to secure in some countries. As advertisers move into international and global advertising, they also face many of the same ethical issues that advertisers in the United States deal with, such as the representation of women and advertising to children, but they may also have to deal with questions about the Americanization or Westernization of local cultures.[21] In terms of the media buy, the global corporation typically has operating companies locally registered in most major countries and advertising might have to be bought through these local entities for maximum tax benefits or to meet local laws of origination. The media planner might only be able to establish the media strategy for the target audience and set the criteria for selecting media.

Adjustments may need to be made for seasonality. For example, a campaign in the Southern Hemisphere, especially for consumer goods, requires major changes from a Northern Hemisphere campaign. In the Southern Hemisphere, summer, Christmas, and back-to-school campaigns are all compressed from November through January. Holidays also differ based on local history and religion. Christmas, for example, is celebrated in Christian lands and Ramadan in Muslim countries.

Everything takes longer internationally—count on it. The New York business day overlaps for only three hours with the business day in London, for two hours with most of Europe, and for one hour with Greece and not at all with Japan, Hong Kong, the Middle East, or Australia. For these reasons e-mail that permits electronic transfer and telecopy transmission is a popular mode for international communication. E-mail and fax numbers have become as universal as telephone numbers on stationery and business cards in international companies. Time is an enemy in other ways. France and Spain virtually close down in August for vacation.

Organizing for the International Campaign Agencies have to develop an organizational structure to manage global brand messages. The organizational structure depends heavily on whether the client company is following a standardization or localization strategy. Some agencies exercise tight control, while others allow more local autonomy. All these approaches fall into three groups: tight central international control, centralized resources with moderate control, and matching the client's organization (if the client is highly centralized, then the agency account structure will be highly centralized).

The IMC Factor in Global Advertising

Integrated marketing communication means that all the messages a consumer receives about a brand work together to create a coherent brand impression. To do that on a global level there must be both horizontal and vertical coordination. The vertical effort represents

■ ■ ■
Positioning is one of the key strategic elements that brands usually try to keep consistent from country to country. Charmin, for example, continues to emphasize softness through the device of a cuddly bear, even in Mexico where this commercial ran. Note that it is largely a nonverbal execution, which is easier to use for global campaigns than those with a lot of words.

	Country A	Country B	Country C	Country D
Advertising Target: Position: Objectives: Strategies/Tactics Brand Consistency				
Direct Response Target: Position: Objectives: Strategies/Tactics Brand Consistency				
Sales Promotion Target: Position: Objectives: Strategies/Tactics Brand Consistency				
Public Relations Target: Position: Objectives: Strategies/Tactics Brand Consistency				
Events/Sponsorships Target: Position: Objectives: Strategies/Tactics Brand Consistency				

FIGURE 18.6 **Global IMC Planning Worksheet**

A planning sheet for a global IMC program outlines the various tools used and their strategies across all the company's international markets.

the coordination of the key planning decisions, such as targeting, positioning, objectives, strategies, and tactics across all the various tools used in the communication program. The horizontal level requires coordination across all the countries and regions involved in the plan.[22] Figure 18.6 represents a planning sheet used in plotting the strategic coordination across country and IMC tool, including the designation of elements that maintain brand consistency. Such a worksheet in a much expanded format is useful in spotting potential consistency problems.

Figure 18.6 illustrates a planning sheet that incorporates two factors: strategy and country, but there are other factors that might be included in a different variations of this worksheet. For example, some companies sell not just one brand but a portfolio of brands or brand extensions and the challenge is to maintain brand consistency across different product lines. In working through this analysis, marketers might use the brand line as the vertical dimension and compare its presentation across countries. For example, MTV wants to maintain a coordinated approach to advertising sales, marketing, and new program formats across a global portfolio of products that includes 34 Nickelodeon channels, 42 MTV services, and 11 VH1 channels.[23]

Consider This

1. What is the nature of the global/local debate?
2. What factors do global marketers have to consider in creating effective advertising for international markets?

IT'S A WRAP

GIVING VOICE TO THE BOTTOM LINE

How do you define *system upgrade*? In the "We Speak Your Language" campaign, Novell defined it as "What happens when the technology you invest in actually makes you money." And that's what happened to Novell's bottom line after this award-winning campaign ran.

In the first three months of the campaign, Novell's advertising awareness jumped from 21 percent to 36 percent, an increase of 71 percent. Novell's familiarity among C-level executives went from 7 percent to 20 percent, an increase of nearly 300 percent. In terms of sales of the new products, the Management and Service products' brand identity link increased by 36 percent from the previous year.

The campaign redefined the language of technology on Novell's terms and gave the words specific meanings that increased the company's competitive voice in the clamorous IT market. It got Novell into the C-level conversation. One of Novell's business partners expresses the kind of response this award-winning campaign generated: "WOW!! I love the creative. Thanks for reviving Novell Marketing. And . . . did I mention I love the creative! It is a clear, hard-nosed, focused, CEO-specific value proposition." And did I mention that I love the creative!"

Summary

1. **Discuss retail advertising and what makes it distinctive.** Retailers are merchants who sell directly to consumers. Most retail businesses are locally owned and advertise at the local level. However, retail advertising at the national and international levels is becoming more common. Co-op advertising with manufacturers and service providers is common. Retail advertising directed at a local audience typically focuses on attracting customers through price and promotion information. It may also focus on store image, product quality, and style. The main medium used for retail advertising is newspapers. However, retailers also use shoppers, preprinted inserts, magazines, television, radio, and the Web. Apart from traditional store retailing, some businesses engage in nonstore retailing, including use of the Web.

2. **Explain the basics of B2B advertising.** Business-to-business advertising is used to influence demand and is directed at people in the business arena who buy or specify products for business use. Its objectives include creating company awareness, increasing selling efficiency, and supporting channel members. Compared to the consumer market, the market for business goods is limited; decision making tends to be shared by a group of people and purchasing decisions center around price, services, product quality, and assurance of supply. Business-to-business media consist of general business and trade publications, directories, direct mail, catalogs, data sheets, the Web, and consumer media.

3. **Identify the basic goals and operations of nonprofit and social marketing.** Social marketing uses marketing programs and marketing communication tools for the good of society. It can be a corporate strategy or a strategy used by a nonprofit organization.

4. **Describe the strategic decisions behind international advertising and IMC.** Marketing begins with a local brand, expands to a regional brand, and, finally, goes global. Advertising follows the same path. Basically global advertising is either market oriented or culture oriented. Ultimately, such campaigns should be centrally controlled and centrally conceived. There should also be local applications and approval. The biggest strategic decision involves how much of the marketing communication strategy is globalized or localized.

▪▪▪ Key Terms

ad allowances, 507
adaptation, 520
animatics, 524
business-to-business
    advertising, 510
capital campaigns, 518
cause marketing, 516
cooperative (co-op)
    advertising, 506
culture-orientation model, 521
dealer tag, 509
donut format, 509

global brand, 519
high-context culture, 522
horizontal publications, 514
industrial advertising, 510
institutional retail advertising,
    507
international brand, 519
lead agency, 522
local advertising, 505
localization, 520
low-context culture, 522
market-orientation model, 521

mission marketing, 516
nonpromotional advertising, 507
North American Industry
    Classification System
    (NAICS), 510
pool-outs, 522
preprints, 510
professional advertising, 512
promotional advertising, 507
public communication
    campaigns, 518
retail advertising, 505

retail marketing, 504
sales advertising, 507
shoppers, 510
social marketing, 515
societal marketing philosophy,
    515
standardization, 520
trade advertising, 512
vertical publications, 515

▪▪▪ Review Questions

1. How does retail advertising differ from national consumer brand advertising? Which is the more difficult to create?

2. How do retail advertising objectives differ from business-to-business objectives?

3. Explain how social marketing can be used by both for-profit companies and nonprofit organizations.

4. What are the differences between local, regional, and international brands?

5. Explain how a global IMC program is more complex than an IMC program operated nationally.

▪▪▪ Discussion Questions

1. Choose a restaurant in your community. What types of people does it target? Would you recommend that its advertising focus on price or image? What is (or should be) its image? Which media should it use?

2. Tom and Wendi Promise have just purchased a sandwich shop. They found a good lease in a neighborhood shopping center, but the costs of franchising, leasing, and other charges have left them very little for advertising. With limited funds, Tom and Wendi can afford only one of the following options: a Yellow Pages display ad, a series of advertisements in the area's weekly "shopper" newspaper, or advertising in the area's college newspaper (the campus is six blocks from the store). Which of these media will best help Tom and Wendi get the awareness they need?

3. Select a print retail advertisement. Think about how this ad could be converted into a television commercial. Give examples of when and on what channel this broadcast ad would be aired. Support your recommendations with an explanation.

4. You work for a large chain of local sporting goods stores that would like to focus all of its local philanthropic activities in one area. You believe the company could benefit from a mission-marketing program. Develop a proposal for the marketing VP that explains mission marketing and present an example of a mission-marketing project that might work for the company.

5. Biogen Corporation's mission is to become a leading company in genetic research and development for health industries. Privately held at the time of incorporation, it decided to go public and have its stock traded. How would corporate advertising assist Biogen in its mission? What audience targets should be priorities for its communication programs? Should it develop more than one campaign?

6. Although personal selling is a vital marketing tool for business-to-business companies, advertising also has a significant role. What if a limited budget means expanding one at the sacrifice of the other? Suppose you were making a decision for a company that is beginning a marketing effort for a new set of products; you'll need approximately six new salespeople. If an advertising campaign to introduce the firm would mean hiring four salespeople instead of six, is the advertising worth it? Explain the strengths and weaknesses of this idea.

7. Dean Bennett has gotten a new assignment for an upscale pen made in Switzerland under the brand name of Pinnacle. Its primary advantage is that it has an extremely long-lasting cartridge, one that is guaranteed to last for at least five years. The pen is available in a variety of forms—roller ball, felt tip—and a variety of widths from fine to wide stroke. Use the adaptability continuum to analyze the globalization or localization options for launching this pen first in Europe and then globally including North America and Asia. What would your recommendation be on standardizing the advertising?

8. Define the difference between a high-context and a low-context culture, and illustrate the difference by finding two ads that you think effectively demonstrate these two message strategies. Explain how they work.

▪▪▪ Class Projects

1. To demonstrate the problems of language in advertising, divide the class into teams of five or six. Each team should choose a print advertisement it believes would have universal appeal. Take the headline and one paragraph of body copy to a language professor or someone who is proficient in a language other than English. Next, take that translation to another professor or native-language speaker of the same language and ask for a back translation into English. Compare and report on how well the concept translated.

2. Compare the speed, convenience, and content of the following three business-to-business sites: americanexpress.com, dell.com, officedepot.com. Write a one- to two-page report on your analysis of these sites. What would your team recommend to improve their usefulness to consumers?

HANDS-ON CASE

A New Alliance Turns Google Yellow

For young 30-somethings Steve Bryn and Larry Page, the moment in August 2004 when shares of their young company were first offered to the public must have felt awfully good. That moment represented years of hard work and substantial risk following their first meeting in the mid-1990s as computer science grad students at Stanford. Bryn and Page disagreed about almost everything, but they shared a passion for solving an important computer problem: how to efficiently find bits of information scattered across enormous amounts of data. Running up substantial debt buying computers and hard drives, the two succeeded in creating a technology that sorted search results based on the number of pages linked to a Web site.

Their initial plan to license the technology foundered when companies failed to see that search engines might be a "killer app." So instead the two started their own company, and when Google shares went public in 2004 Bryn and Page were both instant billionaires. Today, for many, "googling" is a word synonymous with Web search and almost half of all Internet searches are done with Google's technology.

The company's success has always rested on two important pillars: a fast-growing number of loyal users and the ability to generate accelerating revenue and profits. The company is profitable because companies that want to advertise on the Web love Google's business model. Advertisers bid on "AdWords," with higher bidders receiving more prominent listings in the advertiser section of search results. In addition, the money spent advertising with Google is results driven, because companies only pay for click-throughs—that is, for people who actually view their sites, not for showings. Innovations such as Froogle, an easy-to-use shopping portal, and Gmail, a free e-mail service that offers virtually limitless storage capacity, are just some of the ways Google has tried to stay ahead of well-funded competitors like Yahoo! and Microsoft. Based on most performance indicators, Google has thus far been successful.

But for all the company's successes, Google has fallen short with one important market: the estimated 20 million small to medium-sized businesses that are local advertisers

and spend the bulk of their ad budgets on Yellow Pages ads. Small-business owners, many of whom are not technologically sophisticated, may have a difficult time understanding why they should shift dollars to a global medium like the Internet when they sell goods or services to local markets. Compounding Google's problem: Almost half of local advertisers do not even have a Web site.

In an effort to make inroads in this important market, in late 2004 Google announced a partnership with former rival (and classic "old media" company) BellSouth, publisher of a popular Yellow Pages directory in the southeastern United States. Under terms of the partnership, Google will share its brand name and search technologies with BellSouth. In return, BellSouth's 2,000-person workforce will market AdWords to local advertisers, who will also get personal assistance in choosing keywords for Internet searches, setting reasonable Internet ad budgets, and even setting up and designing company Web pages. And, in a break from its bidding model for AdWords, Google will let BellSouth market the product to local advertisers for a fixed fee. According to Laurie Scholl, marketing director for BellSouth, "Our advertisers are different. They prefer to pay a flat rate, as they're used to with our print yellow pages. They're busy running their business day-to-day, so they're looking for a full-service approach."

Consider This

1. BellSouth and Google had viewed one another as competitors prior to signing this agreement. What are the partnership's advantages and disadvantages for each company?

2. How useful will the Web be for local advertisers in the next few years? Does this medium offer significant benefits for small companies?

Source: Kevin Newcomb, "Google. BellSouth Team for Local Search Sales," October 28, 2004, www.clickz.com/news/article.php/3428411; Kris Oser, "2008 Market for Local Search Engine Ads: $2.5 Billion: Why the Google-BellSouth Yellow Pages Deal Happened," *Advertising Age* (November 2004); Danny Sullivan, "Up Close with Google AdWords," March 4, 2002, http://searchenginewatch.com/sereport/article.php/2164591.

"I've been using three different companies for **international, overnight and ground.** Now I just call Brown." It's all part of a simpler lifestyle I'm trying out."

Your world is complicated enough. Simplify it. Let Brown handle all your shipping. In return, we'll give you the peace of mind that comes from using just one, perfectly integrated shipping network. One company that can deliver international, overnight and ground shipments to your customers, on time. Guaranteed. It's as simple as that.

INTERNATIONAL. OVERNIGHT. GROUND. SYNCHRONIZED.

UPS.com® 1-800-PICK-UPS®

UPS

WHAT CAN BROWN DO FOR YOU?®

"I run my company out of my garage. But Brown r I'm listed on Wall Stre I'm cool

At UPS.com,® shipping is fast and easy no matter what size your company is. Print labels, track packages, schedule a pickup; it's all simple. Pay with a credit card? We're cool with that.

SMALL BUSINESS SHIPPING. SYNCHRONIZED.

UPS

WHAT CAN BROWN DO FOR YOU?®

UPS.com® 1-800-PICK-UP

Evaluation of Effectiveness

Changing Perceptions from the Mailroom to the Board Room

Award:
Gold EFFIE®

Client:
UPS

Agency:
The Martin Agency

Title:
"Brown"

CHAPTER KEY POINTS:

After reading this chapter, you will be able to:

1. Demonstrate that you understand why and how advertising evaluation is conducted.

2. List and explain the stages of copy testing.

3. Identify the key areas of media evaluation.

4. Discuss how campaigns and IMC programs are evaluated.

When you ask business people what they think of when they hear UPS, they tend to reply "brown and ground." In other words, UPS specializes in ground package delivery. But if managers want to send an overnight or international package, then they use Federal Express. Consumer research identified that the perception was strong: UPS for ground and FedEx for overnight and international. UPS, however, had upgraded and built impressive capabilities in logistics, systems integration, and supply chain management. So how could the image of UPS catch up with the sophistication of its services? That was the assignment given to the Richmond, Virginia–based Martin Agency.

Target Audiences
The Martin team's research determined that there were at least four different audiences and they each had different needs:

- **Shipping Managers.** "Make my job easier." Shipping managers already have a good UPS relationship but just for ground shipping. If they used UPS for all their shipping needs, including overnight and international, it could make their job easier.

- **Small-Business Owners.** "Help me grow my business." UPS's new logistics could make shipping easier and more convenient for small-business owners and free them for more strategic thinking.

- **Front-Office Managers and Receptionists.** "Let me focus on my work." With long to-do lists, managers and receptionists want the reliability and efficiency of UPS's new systems that lets them check off shipping, at the same time giving them more control.

- **Senior Management.** "Help me compete." Senior management could care less about shipping but UPS's supply chain services could provide them with an important competitive advantage and more profit for the company.

Objectives

The same perception problem—"ground and brown"—affected all these audiences. In order to create the perception shift, the Martin team identified three critical objectives:

1. **Break through:** Achieve high levels of campaign awareness *and* high levels of brand linkage (UPS had historically reached 20–40 percent correct attribution of the ad to the brand among those aware of the advertising).

2. **Break the inertia:** Re-energize the brand for shipping decision makers.
   a. Maintain ground shipping volume and revenue.
   b. Make inroads into and grow overnight and international delivery service volume and revenue.

3. **Expand relevance:** Make UPS relevant to senior management.
   a. Increase nonpackage, supply chain services revenue.
   b. Evolve perceptions of the brand beyond shipping, to become a trusted partner and player in supply chain and logistics management.

Message and Media Strategy

The Martin planners found from consumer research that the problem wasn't with "brown"; it was with its narrow association with "ground." In fact, everyone recognized brown as a symbol of UPS: hardworking efficiency, humanity, and a get-it-done attitude.

So instead of running away from "brown," Martin embraced it. In fact, the team decided to use it as a synonym for UPS. "Brown" provides immediate brand familiarity and lets the brand speak with unexpected energy and attitude. The idea of calling UPS "Brown" was the perfect platform for the reappraisal and relevance the team was looking for. The tagline "What can Brown do for you?" challenged the customer to think about UPS differently.

Because a one-size-fits-all approach wouldn't work with these audiences, Martin's media planners designed four tailor-made individual media plans. The key was to find media that generated conviction and loyalty. The Martin planners didn't just want GRPs (gross rating points) and insertions; they wanted programs the audience can't wait to see. The resulting plan included "appointment viewing" television programs (programs people schedule themselves to watch), as well as their top-preference radio stations, and magazines that they read cover-to-cover.

To further break the inertia, UPS coupled the "push" power of the "Brown" campaign with the "pull" of an integrated direct-mail campaign, which was focused on closing the sale: profitably generating incremental shipping volume and revenue in all products—international, overnight, and ground. And UPS rewarded customers who attained minimum shipping volumes with remote-controlled minireplicas of the UPS truck and Dale Jarrett's #88 stock car, connecting the "Brown" brand campaign with the hugely successful UPS NASCAR "Race the Truck" advertising.

The campaign was a great success and won a Gold EFFIE award. Check the It's a Wrap feature at the end of the chapter for more on this campaign's results.

Source: EFFIE brief provided by UPS and The Martin Agency.

There are four categories of work that get evaluated in advertising and marketing communication programs: the message execution, the media, the campaign, and the other marketing communication areas and their synergistic effect as part of an IMC program. This chapter will discuss the basic concept of the evaluation of effectiveness and then look at those four areas.

EVALUATING EFFECTIVENESS

The final section in a campaign plan is evaluating the effectiveness of the marketing communication program or campaign. Similarly, the final step in implementation is to assess the outcome or results of the plan.

Why do evaluation? The first reason is that the stakes in making an advertising misstep are high. By the time an average 30-second commercial is ready for national television, it has cost about $200,000 in production costs. If it is run nationally, its sponsor can invest several million dollars in airtime. The second reason is advertising optimization; that means reducing risk by testing, analyzing, tracking performance, and making changes where possible to increase the performance of the advertising. The third reason is to learn what works and what doesn't—in other words, to identify best practices so a brand's advertising continues to improve.

Types and Stages of Evaluation

Evaluation is done through testing, monitoring, and measurement. Testing is used to predict results; monitoring tracks performance; and measurement evaluates results. In other words, advertisements typically are tested before they run as a way to predict their effectiveness, a practice, as we've seen, called *copy testing*. Ideally, the results of evaluative research should be available before large sums of money are invested in finished work or in media buys. As a campaign unfolds, the performance is tracked to see whether any elements need to be changed. Sales may fall, or they may not increase as rapidly as expected. Is the advertising at fault? The results, the actual effects, are measured after the ad or campaign runs. Diagnostic research also is used in all stages of a campaign to deconstruct an advertisement in order to spot message problems. These are the four types of research used in evaluation:

1. ***Developmental research*** through pretesting estimates the likelihood that an ad idea will work or that one idea is better than another.

2. *Concurrent research* using tracking studies and test marketing monitors the way the campaign is unfolding and how the messages and media are working.

3. *Posttesting research* evaluates the impact after the campaign is over or after the ad ran. In order for postcampaign research to be useful, benchmark or baseline studies are needed, in order to gauge movement. These can be research company norms or they can be based on previous campaigns by this brand.

4. *Diagnostic research* deconstructs an ad to see what elements are working or not working. Researchers who evaluate commercials use frame-by-frame or moment-by-moment analysis to identify strengths and weaknesses in a commercial.

Factors to Be Evaluated

Most advertisers would be happy if evaluation could simply tell them how much the advertising contributed to their sales effort. That's difficult for a number of reasons: There are factors other than the advertising that affect sales, and that makes it hard to isolate advertising in order to determine its impact. Furthermore, advertising effects tend to be delayed, so it's difficult to link the advertising seen at one time to a purchase made days or weeks later. In some cases, such as direct-response advertising, sales can be measured as a direct response to an advertising message.

Usually, however, advertising is measured in terms of its communication effects, which become surrogate measures for sales impact. Such factors as purchase intention, preference, and liking all suggest that the advertising message can make a positive contribution to an eventual purchase decision. According to research professionals at Ipsos-ASI, the largest U.S. provider of advertising pretesting, "Ads work best when they engage viewers' interest, when consumers enjoy watching them, when they are relevant, and when they tell their story in a unique and interesting way."[1] Those are some of the dimensions of effectiveness, but there are others that also are important, as we know from Chapter 4.

Good evaluation plans, and the objectives found in them, are based on a model of human response to an advertisement—an idea about how advertising works. So the best starting point in setting objectives is a model that identifies key effects and guides their evaluation, which is what we developed with our Facets Model in Chapter 4. Table 19.1 groups the key factors of effectiveness and then matches them to the types of research questions that advertisers can use to determine effectiveness.

Principle
Good evaluation plans, as well as effective professional work, are guided by a model of how people respond to advertising.

Copy-testing Services

Copy-testing companies have different specialties focusing on different effectiveness dimensions. The most successful of these companies have conducted enough tests that they have developed **norms** for common product categories. In other words, after they pretest the ad, they are able to compare its score with others that reflect how comparable ads perform on the factors they test. Norms allow the advertiser to tell whether a particular advertisement is above or below the average for the brand or its product category. Without norms the advertiser would not know whether a score of 23, for example, is good or bad.

Most of these companies have also developed diagnostic methods that identify strong and weak points of the ad. Here is a list of some of the more common companies and the types of tests they provide:[2]

- *Ameritest:* brand linkage, attention, motivation, communication, flow of attention and emotion through the commercial
- *ARS:* persuasion, brand or ad recall, communication
- *Diagnostic Research:* brand recall, main idea, attribute statements (importance, uniqueness, believability)
- *IPSOS-ASI:* recall, attention, brand linkage, persuasion, (brand switch, purchase probability), communication
- *Mapes & Ross:* brand preference change, ad or brand recall, idea communication, key message delivery, like or dislike, believability, comprehension, desire to take action, attribute communication

TABLE
19.1 **Effectiveness Research Questions**

Effect	Research Questions
Perception	
Awareness/Noticed	What ads do you remember seeing? What ads were noted?
Attention/Interest	What ads did you find interesting? Did you read/watch most of them?
Brand Linkage	What brand is being advertised in this ad?
Recognition (Aided)	Have you seen this ad/this campaign?
	Sort elements into piles of remember/don't remember.
Relevance	How important is the product message to you? Does it speak to your aspirations?
Cognition	What thoughts came to your mind?
Clarity	What happened in the commercial?
Comprehension	Are the claims/product attributes/benefits understood?
Confusion	What is the main message? What is the point of the ad? Is there anything in the ad you don't understand?
Recall (Unaided) and Brand Recall	What do you remember seeing in the ad? What brands were advertised? (In open-ended responses, was the brand named?)
Differentiation	What's the difference between Brand X and Y?
Emotion	How did it make you feel? What feelings did the ad stimulate?
Liking	Do you like this brand? This ad message?
	What did you like or dislike In the ad?
Persuasion	
Attitude change	In ?? category (or product set), which brand would you choose? (usually a pre- and posttest)
Preference	What brand do you prefer?
Intention	Do you intend to try it or buy it?
Argument	What are the customer's reasons to buy it?
Believability	Do you believe the reasons, claims, proof statements?
Association	What is the personality of the brand?
	When you think of this brand, what (products, qualities, attributes, people, lifestyles, etc.) do you think of?
Action	How many responded (called, sent back card, used coupon, clicked, visited Web site, visited dealer, visited booth, etc.)?

- *Millward Brown:* branding, enjoyment, involvement, understanding, ad flow, brand integration, feelings to ad, main stand-out idea, likes or dislikes, impressions, persuasion, new news, believability, relevance
- *RoperASW:* overall reaction, strengths and weaknesses, understanding, clutter busting, attention, main message, relevance, appeal, persuasiveness, motivate trial, purchase intent

Consider This

1. What are the most common types of evaluation used in advertising?
2. Based on Table 19.1, how can the Facets Model be used in advertising evaluation?

STAGES OF COPY TESTING

Copy testing is a general term that describes various kinds of research used at different stages in the advertising process—before, during, and after an ad or campaign has run.

THE INSIDE STORY
Volvo Road Tests the "Starting a Family" Campaign

John W. Butler, Jr., Senior Marketing and Communications Strategist,
Witeck-Combs Communications, Inc.

After years of seeing general market ads, gay, lesbian, bisexual and transgender (GLBT) consumers now expect to see ads with tailored messages and images to earn their loyalty.

Ford Motor Company and its Volvo brand took this into account when developing a campaign to reach GLBT customers. Ford conducted extensive quantitative research to determine automotive buying differences between GLBT and non-GLBT consumers. This led to further qualitative research to understand how GLBT consumers felt about Volvo and its advertising.

The research, which was conducted in partnership with Harris Interactive, indicated Volvo's messaging needed to communicate safety, family, quality, and diversity. Volvo had to reiterate these attributes in its products, and make the brand relevant to GLBT consumers. They needed to speak directly to GLBT consumers about Volvo's diverse family of vehicles, drawing a connection between GLBT families and Volvo's family of vehicles, both diverse, coming in all shapes and sizes.

A creative plan and various concepts were developed by Prime Access, Inc. in collaboration with Witeck-Combs Communications, Inc. The concepts represented a range of GLBT-specific imagery and copy. Ford and Volvo selected their top three choices and used online message testing to assess the copytesting constructs of Branding, Communication, and Persuasion, including the concept of Consumer Connection (the ability of the ad to move consumers closer to the brand on Cognitive, Behavior, Emotional and Aspirational dimensions).

Across the three executions, "Starting a Family" was most likely to deliver to Volvo's strategy. The other two were less successful in engaging respondents, more con-

WHETHER YOU'RE STARTING A FAMILY

OR CREATING ONE AS YOU GO.

VOLVO
for life

fusing, and gave less positive impressions of Volvo. "Starting a Family" was more successful because consumers said, "It was more believable, likely to 'speak to me' and leave me with a positive impression of Volvo."

After the "Starting a Family" ad was chosen, it was further refined to reflect current Volvo advertising standards. The ad then appeared in a variety of gay and lesbian publications, including the Advocate and Out magazines. The campaign was so successful that Volvo extended and resized it for regional gay and lesbian newspapers at the request of local retailers.

John W. Butler, Jr., a graduate of George Mason University with a degree in Integrated Studies, is a senior marketing and communications strategist for Washington, D.C.-based Witeck-Combs Communications, Inc. Butler plays a critical role in the strategic development and implementation of GLBT communications campaigns for some of the country's most powerful companies and non-profit organizations including American Airlines, Ford Motor Company, Volvo Cars of North America, Jaguar North America, Land Rover North America, Gay and Lesbian Alliance Against Defamation (GLAAD), National Lesbian and Gay Journalists Association (NLGJA), and the Human Rights Campaign (HRC)

Message Development Research

Deciding what facts to convey in advertisements is never easy. Research is needed to develop and test alternative message strategies.

Message Strategy   Planners conduct research with members of the target audience to develop the message strategy and test the relative effectiveness of various selling premises—hard-sell or soft-sell, informational or emotional, and so forth. Insights into consumer motivations and purchasing decisions help solve the often-difficult puzzle of selecting the most relevant information and motivating promise, as well as the emotional appeal that best engages the audience.

Concept Testing   Advertising and other marketing communication messages usually incorporate a "Big Idea," a creative concept that is attention getting and memorable. Research in **concept testing** compares the effectiveness of various creative ideas. This testing often relies on a *key concept card,* which is an artist's drawing of the visual idea with a sentence underneath that captures the essence of the idea. A researcher may use a pack of three, five, or more idea cards to elicit consumer responses in a mall or through discussions in a focus group.

Pretesting Another type of evaluative research called **pretesting** helps marketers to make final go/no-go decisions about finished or nearly finished ads. Pretesting differs from concept testing or message strategy research, which reveals the strengths and weaknesses of different versions of a concept or approach as marketers develop them. Pretesting assesses the strength of the finished message and predicts how well it will perform.

In terms of print advertisements, the ideas to be tested are often full mockups of the ad. In television, advertisers can test the commercials as storyboard ideas or **photoboards** (still photos arranged as a storyboard), but more often commercials are in the form of *animatics* (drawings or still photos shot on videotape synchronized with a rough version of the audio track). Advertisers can show these versions of the commercial to individuals, to focus groups, or to groups in a theater testing situation. They follow the viewing of the advertisement with a survey, a more open-ended interview, or a set of questions for a group discussion.

Diagnostics Many advertisers and agencies are moving away from copy-testing methods that rely on single scores to evaluate an ad and are turning to methods that are more focused on diagnosing strengths and weaknesses. The reason is that they believe an advertisement is too complex to be reduced to one factor and one simple score. Instead they are using research methods that are designed to diagnose strengths and weaknesses of their advertising ideas in order to improve the work while it is still in development or to learn more from the ad in order to improve subsequent advertisements.

In theater tests for TV commercials, for example, respondents may have a black-box device and can press a button to record different types of responses—indicating what they liked or didn't like or how long they paid attention by letting up on the button when their attention shifts.

Principle
Advertising effects are too complicated to be reduced to a single score.

Moment-by-moment tests of commercials, as described in the Matter of Practice box, provide an analysis of the impact of the internal logic of the commercial. The procedure includes showing a **clutter reel** (a group of commercials that includes the test commercial and competitors' commercials as well as others), and conducting interviews afterward. The Ameritest company, whose work is described in the box, also uses a **picture sort** to diagnose the viewer's attention to and emotional engagement with different elements in the commercial. The viewers receive a deck of key frames from the commercial and sort them into images they remember seeing and ones they don't remember. Then they sort them into five categories from strong positive to strong negative. Researchers tabulate the sets to depict a flow of impact for both attention and emotion. In particular, they want to analyze key moments in the commercial such as the solution to a problem, or the introduction of the brand, and analyze them in terms of viewers' attention and emotion.[3]

During Execution: Concurrent Testing

Concurrent testing takes place while the advertising is actually being run. There are three primary techniques: coincidental surveys, attitude tests, and tracking studies. The first two assess communication responses; tracking studies evaluate actual behavior.

The **coincidental survey** technique is most often used with broadcast media. Random calls are made to individuals in the target market. By discovering what stations or shows people are seeing or hearing, the advertiser can determine whether the target audience is getting the message and, if so, what information or meaning the audience members receive. This technique can be useful in identifying basic problems. For example, several years ago Pepsi discovered that the use of Madonna as a spokesperson was a terrible mistake.

Tracking Studies Studies that follow the purchase activity of a specific consumer or group of consumers over a specified period of time are **tracking studies**. These in-market studies combine conventional marketing research data with information on marketing communication spending and provide a more complete view of the market. Researchers use market tracking for both concurrent testing and posttesting. It may serve two basic

A MATTER OF PRACTICE

Research Finds Moments of Truth for IBM

Infrastructure? What's that? And why should business marketers care?

As e-business has developed, managers have learned that their success or failure often depends upon the "back end" of the business—the information technology (IT) software and hardware needed to manage an online business and handle customers' orders. Managing this infrastructure is a complicated operation that, in addition to taking care of the customer's business, challenges existing systems to work together and share information.

Building infrastructure is what IBM does. So the emergence of the Internet also created a whole new world of business opportunity for the company. IBM's e-business infrastructure campaign was designed by the Ogilvy and Mather agency to highlight e-business problems and solutions. It was called "Moment of Truth" because it was designed to deliver maximum impact at the point where a customer's infrastructure problem was solved.

One of IBM's requirements of its advertising is that everything must be pretested and proven to be effective before it goes on air or appears in print. That's where Ameritest, an Albuquerque-based advertising research company, comes in. Ameritest tests television and print advertising to diagnose its problems and estimate its potential to deliver on the strategy.

For the infrastructure campaign, O&M developed a prototype commercial called "Crash Site." Ameritest used its two proprietary methods—Flow of Attention and Flow of Emotion—to do a moment-by-moment analysis of the ad. Here is how the research methods were used to deconstruct the way the commercial built understanding of "The Moment of Truth" into the message.

Using the diagnostics from the prototype ad, another 16 commercials were developed, with 9 testing above IBM's historical average based on its Ameritest benchmarks. The research diagnostics were used to improve the lower-scoring commercials before they ran.

The campaign was highly effective with IBM, resulting in a 6-point increase in its motivation (persuasion) scores in the ads tested by Ameritest. In brand-tracking studies, unaided association with the term "e-business infrastructure" rose to an indexed score of 113 (13 percent higher than an average score). In more general terms the campaign exceeded its new-business revenue goal in just over nine months and the revenue exceeded IBM's target by 354 percent.

The role of research in driving this highly effective "Moments of Truth" campaign is the reason the Advertising Research Foundation named it the Grand Winner (ARF) David Ogilvy Awards.

Sources: "Ameritest Shares the 2003 Grand Ogilvy Research Award with IBM, Along with First-in-Category Win!," www.ameritest.net, April 2003; "Spotlight Shines Brightly on IBM Research," ARF Press Release, April 11, 2003, www.arf.site.org; Amy Shea, "IBM E-business Infrastructure IBM Ogilvy Submission, May 2003, PowerPoint presentation.

objectives: (1) to show how the marketer's product sales or market share compares with the competition after implementing some marketing communication; and (2) to conduct reassessment—that is, to help the marketer understand how the market responds to changes made in the marketing communication strategy.

Tracking studies evaluate copy and media against changes in sales. The higher the sales, of course, the better the strategy. Tracking studies lead to decisions such as pulling advertising to changing copy to altering a campaign strategy.

Brand tracking is an approach that tracks the performance of the brand, rather than the ad, as Figure 19.1 shows. The assumption is that with fragmented media and an abundance of high-quality but similar products, it is more important to track the brand because it reflects the quality of the customer's brand relationship. Instead of focusing on attributes and claims about a product, this research identifies how customers are involved with the brand and whether they are more favorably disposed toward it than toward other brands.

Because spending information enters the analysis, much of the focus of tracking studies is on the target market, the selection of media vehicles, the schedule, the marketing communication mix, and the media mix. Account planners use several methods to collect tracking data: attitude tests, wave analysis, consumer diaries, pantry checks, and single-source tracking.

- *Attitude Tests.* In Chapter 4 we discussed the relationship between an attitude—a favorable or unfavorable disposition toward a person, thing, idea, or situation—and consumer behavior. Researchers survey individuals who were exposed to the ad, ask-

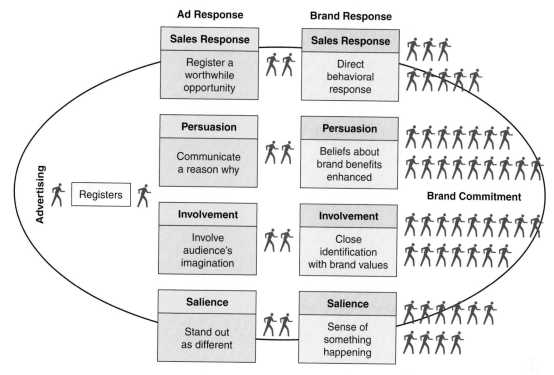

A Brand-tracking Framework

Hall & Partners is a research firm that has pioneered a type of brand tracking that focuses more on the brand response than the consumer response to the advertising.

ing questions about the spokesperson, the tone of the ad, its wording, and so forth. Results that show strong negative attitude scores may prompt the advertiser to pull an ad immediately. A favorable attitude indicates that people are more likely to purchase a brand than they would with an unfavorable attitude.

- *Wave Analysis.* **Wave analysis** looks at a series of interviews during a campaign. The tracking begins with a set of questions asked of a random sample of consumers on a predetermined date. After the person is qualified as hearing or seeing the ad, the researcher asks a series of follow-up questions. The answers serve as a benchmark and allow adjustments in the message content, media choice, and timing. Perhaps two months later, the researcher makes another series of random calls and asks the same questions. The second wave is compared with the first until management is satisfied with the ad's market penetration and impact.

- *Consumer Diaries.* Sometimes advertisers ask a group of representative consumers to keep a diary during a campaign. The advertiser asks the consumers to record activities such as brands purchased, brands used for various activities, brand switches, media usage, exposure to competitive promotions, and use of coupons. The advertiser can then review these *consumer diaries* and determine factors such as whether the message is reaching the right target audience and whether the audience is responding to the message as intended. One common unfavorable finding from consumer diaries is that no attitude or behavioral change occurred because of exposure to the campaign.

- *Pantry Checks.* The **pantry check** provides much of the same information as the diary method but requires little from the consumer. A researcher goes to homes in the target market and asks what brands or products they have purchased or used recently. In one variation of this procedure, the researcher counts the products or brands currently stocked by the consumer. The consumer may also be asked to keep empty packages, which the researcher then collects and tallies.

- *Test Marketing.* A **test market** might serve to test product variations, as well as elements of a finished ad, a campaign, or a media mix in two or more potential markets.

In a typical test market, one or more of the test cities serve as controls while the others are the test. In the control markets the researcher can either (a) run no advertising or (b) continue to run the old ad. The new ad is used in the test cities. Before, during, and after running the advertising, marketers compare sales results in the test cities by checking inventories in selected stores representative of the target market. Some cities, such as Buffalo, Indianapolis, and San Antonio, are considered excellent test markets because their demographic and socioeconomic profiles are representative of either the United States or a particular target market. Furthermore, they are relatively isolated as media markets so the advertising impact is less likely to be affected by what is happening in other markets.

The possibilities for isolating variables in test markets are almost limitless. Researchers can increase the frequency of advertising or try a different media schedule. They can see whether an ad emphasizing product convenience will stimulate sales to two-career families. They can try an ad that plays up the product's fiber or vitamin content or compare the effectiveness of a two-for-one promotion and a cents-off coupon.

Posttesting: After Execution Research

Evaluative research occurs after the ad has been run to determine if it met its objectives. Here are the most common evaluative research techniques that account planners use: memory tests, persuasion tests, direct-response counts, frame-by-frame tests, in-market tests, and brand tracking.

Memory Tests   Memory tests are based on the assumption that an advertisement leaves a mental residue with the person who has been exposed to it. One way to measure an advertisement's effectiveness, then, is to contact consumers who saw the ad and find out what they remember. Memory tests fall into two major groups: recall tests and recognition tests.

One way to measure memory is to show the advertisement to people and ask them whether they remember having seen it before. This kind of test is called a **recognition test**. In a **recall test**, respondents who have read the magazine are asked to report what advertisements or brands they remember seeing. The interviewer may go through a deck of cards containing brand names. If the respondent says, "Yes, I remember seeing an advertisement for that brand," the interviewer asks the interviewees to describe everything they can remember about the ad.

Similarly, a TV commercial is run on network television within a regular prime-time program. The next evening, interviewers make thousands of random phone calls until they have contacted about 200 people who were watching the program at the exact time the commercial appeared. The interviewer then asks a series of questions, such as the following:

- Do you remember seeing a commercial for any charcoal briquettes?
- (If no) Do you remember seeing a commercial for Kingsford Charcoal briquettes? (Memory prompt)
- (If yes to either of the above) What did the commercial say about the product? What did the commercial show? What did the commercial look like? What ideas were brought out?

The first type of question is called **unaided recall** because the particular brand is not mentioned. The second question is an example of **aided recall**, in which the specific brand name is mentioned. The answers to the third set of questions are written down verbatim. The test requires that the respondent link a specific brand name, or at least a specific product category, to a specific commercial. If the commercial fails to establish a tight connection between the brand name and the selling message, the commercial will not get a high recall score.

Persuasion Tests   Another evaluative research technique is a **persuasion test**, or attitude change test. The basic format is to ask consumers how likely they are to buy a specific brand. Next they are exposed to an advertisement for that brand, usually as part of a collection of brands. After exposure, researchers again ask them what they intend to purchase.

The researcher analyzes the results to determine whether *intention to buy* has increased as a result of exposure to the advertisement. This test is sometimes referred to as an intend-to-buy or **motivation test**. The validity of a persuasion test depends in part on whether participants in the experiment represent a good sample of the prospects the advertiser is trying to reach. A dog food advertiser, for example, would not be interested in responses from people who do not own dogs.

Likability Tests   A study by the Advertising Research Foundation (ARF) compared a variety of different copy-testing methods to see if any of them were better able to predict sales impact. Surprisingly, it wasn't awareness, recall, communication, or persuasion measures that won out but rather **likability tests**. Likability, however, is not easy to measure because it's difficult to know if the consumer likes the ad, the brand, or some other factor (the person giving the test). A number of the copy-testing companies do offer a likability score but they suggest it needs to be interpreted relative to other consumer responses. Questions that try to evaluate likability investigate such things as *personally relevant, important to me, stimulates interest or curiosity, creates warm feelings, enjoyable, entertaining,* and *fun.*

Inquiry Tests   A form of action response, **inquiry tests** measure the number of responses to an advertisement. The response can be a call to a toll-free number, an e-mail or Web site visit, a coupon return, a visit to a dealer, an entry in a contest, a call to a salesperson, or an actual transaction. Inquiry tests are the primary measurement tool for direct-response communication, but they also are used to evaluate advertisements and sales promotions when the inquiry is built into the message design. Inquiry tests also are used to evaluate the effectiveness of alternative advertisements using a *split-run technique* in magazines, where there are two versions of the magazine printed, one with ad A and the other with ad B. The ad (or direct-mail piece) that pulls the most responses is deemed to be the most effective.

Scanner Research   Many retail outlets, but especially supermarkets, use electronic scanners at the checkout to collect consumer information. When you shop at your local Safeway, each product you buy has an electronic bar code that contains the name of the product and its price. The regional Safeway system may decide to establish a consumer panel so it can track sales among various consumer groups. In **scanner research**, you would be asked to join the panel, which might contain hundreds of other customers. You would complete a fairly extensive questionnaire and be assigned an ID number. You might receive a premium or a discount on purchases for your participation. Each time you make a purchase, you also submit your ID number. Therefore, if Safeway runs a two-page newspaper ad, it can track actual sales to determine to what extent the ad worked. Various manufacturers who sell products to Safeway can do the same kind of testing. Your panel questionnaire will also contain a list of media that you use, so media can also be evaluated.

■ ■ ■

Scanner research reads the information from a shopper's identification card and records that along with product information. Many retail outlets use electronic scanners to track sales among various consumer groups.

Single-Source Research   Thanks to scanners, combined with computer technology and data and the use of electronic media, researchers are closer to showing a causal relationship between advertising and sales because of **single-source research**. Single-source research companies arrange to control the television signal of a community's households. The company divides the households into equivalent matched groups. It then sends advertisements to one group but not to the other and collects exact records of what every household purchases. This information is collected through the scanners found at the supermarket cash register. Because advertising is the only manipulated variable, the method permits an unambiguous reading of cause and effect. The data collected in this way are known as single-source data because advertising and product-purchasing data come from the same source.

Syracuse professor John Philip Jones, who spent many years at J. Walter Thompson, has used single-source data from JWT combined with Nielsen TV-viewing data to prove that advertising can cause an immediate impact on sales. His research has found that the strongest campaigns can triple sales, while the weakest campaigns can actually cause sales to fall by more than 50 percent.[4]

Although fairly expensive, single-source data can produce exceptionally dependable results. Real advertisements are received under natural conditions in the home and the resulting purchases are actual purchases made by consumers. However, the method usually requires more than six months to produce usable results. Critics also say that single-source research is better for short-term immediate sales effects and doesn't capture very well other brand-building effects.

Consider This

1. What are the three stages of copy testing?
2. How is diagnostic research used in advertising evaluation?

MEDIA EVALUATION

Advertising has little chance to be effective if no one sees it. Analyzing the effectiveness of the media plan, then, is another important part of evaluation. Did the plan actually achieve reach and frequency objectives? Did the newspaper and magazine placements run in the positions expected and produce the intended GRP and CPM levels?

Evaluating Audience Exposure

The estimates in the media plan are checked against the performance of each vehicle. The critical evaluation is whether the reach and frequency objectives were obtained.

Verifying the audience measurement estimates is a challenge. Media planners are working sometimes with millions of dollars and they can't afford to get it wrong. In Chapter 11 we discussed how various media channels measure their audiences. For print, services such as the Audit Bureau of Circulations (ABC), Simmons-Scarborough (SMRB), and MediaMark (MRI) provide data. Likewise for broadcast, Arbitron, RADAR, and A.C. Nielsen provide audience monitoring. These estimates are used initially by media planners to develop a media plan but they are also used by media buyers to verify the accumulated impact of the media buy after the campaign has run.

Media-planning oversight is usually handled in-house by the media buyer, but it can also be contracted by the advertiser to independent companies who specialize in conducting media audits of the agency's media-planning and -buying operations.[5] Nissan, for example, as well as the giant package-goods company Procter & Gamble have hired outside media-auditing firms to test the work of their media-buying activities.[6]

As the job gets more complex, media planners are being asked to prove the wisdom of their recommendations in an area where the data they use are sometimes suspect or unreliable, particularly if there are problems with the media measurement companies' formulas and reporting systems. Nielsen, for example, has been subject to much criticism for its television ratings.

In order to better understand the problems in media evaluation, let's look at two specific areas where media performance is hard to estimate: outdoor and the Internet. As you would expect, accurately measuring the mobile audience for outdoor advertising is challenging. Traffic counts can be gathered but the problem is that traffic does not equal exposure. Just because a car drives by a board, doesn't mean that the driver or the passengers see it, particularly since some outdoor boards are more attention getting than others, as the "road rage" board illustrates.

Similarly, the measures of effectiveness used to evaluate off-line campaigns don't seem to transfer well to the online world. Is the Web site visitor or banner ad viewer similar to print or broadcast audiences? The industry hasn't been able to establish equivalencies

for GRPs and CPMs. Similarly, the industry is still trying to define what makes an effective Internet ad, as well as develop a system that accurately measures online advertising effectiveness. At the heart of the problem is the question of what exactly is to be measured and how that equates to other media—readers, viewers, visitors, hits, click-throughs, minutes spent with a site.

Advertising ROI and Media Efficiency

Advertisers continue to search for *advertising ROI* (return on investment, which means the costs of creating and running the advertisement versus the revenue it generates). ROI measures the relationship between output (sales; surrogate measures) and input (budget; dollars spent on message creation and delivery). Another way to look at is the cost-to-sales ratio.

Since the dollar impact for advertising, and also public relations, is hard to measure, ROI is difficult to calculate. The campaigns must be carefully designed not only to move the sales needle, but also to ensure that advertisers can isolate the impact of the message and verify that it caused the increase in sales. ROI is easier to calculate for direct marketing (because there are fewer variables between the message and the sales) and for sales promotion (because there is an immediate response, which is easier to link to the message).

One question related to ROI is: How much is too much? How do you determine whether you are overadvertising (or underadvertising)? That's one of the key reasons to use test marketing. If a campaign is launched in several different, but matched cities, at different levels of media activity, a comparison of the campaigns results (sales or other kinds of trackable responses) can determine the appropriate level and type of media spending.

Wearout   The point where the advertising gets tired and there is no response or less response than at the launch is called **wearout**. This is also the point where recall stabilizes or declines and irritation levels increase because people are tired of hearing or seeing the same ad replayed.

Wearout is a combination of creative impact and media buying. The more intrusive the creative technique, the higher the level of irritation. It's like a joke: You may pay attention the first couple of times you hear it but then it gets wearisome. Other types of advertising are less prone to wearout. Jingles, for example, can be repeated almost endlessly, and the more people like to hum along with the tune, the less likely there will be a wearout problem because of irritation.

Media Optimization   Ultimately the biggest challenge in media planning is accountability. Advertisers want to know their dollars are being spent in the most efficient way and for the greatest impact. You may remember from Chapter 11 that media planners operate with computer media-optimization models of media performance that they use in making decisions about media selection, scheduling, and weights (amount of budget). Models are always theoretical, so one result of postevaluation is that the actual performance of a plan can be compared with the results projected by the media planner's model. The goal in testing media planning is always to optimize the budget—to get the most impact possible with the least expenditure of money. That is the critical finding derived from the comparison of performance with projections. In addition to meeting the reach and frequency objectives, was the media plan efficient?

Consider This

1. Explain media optimization.
2. How does wearout relate to media efficiency?

CAMPAIGN AND IMC EVALUATION

The last stage in the development of a campaign plan is preparing a proposal stating how the campaign will be evaluated. Evaluation is the final and, in some respects, the most important step in an advertising campaign because it determines whether the campaign effort was effective. A campaign evaluation will assess the campaign's performance in terms of its message and media objectives. It employs either internal performance data or results from an outside research organization that monitors brand performance, such as Gallup-Robinson, Decision Analyst Inc., and Millward Brown.

As we said earlier, when all the pieces work together, the whole is greater than the sum of its parts. That's called *synergy,* and it's the reason why advertisers run campaigns rather than one-shot ads. Synergy is difficult to evaluate, so usually it is done in terms of the overall brand position and brand perception. In other words, has the image become stronger on critical dimensions of the image, such as personality and positioning cues, because of the campaign?

Marketing Communication Evaluation

Even though this book focuses on advertising, we recognize that advertising is just one part of the market communication mix, along with sales promotion, public relations, direct marketing, events and sponsorships, personal sales, packaging, point of purchase (PoP), and specialties. As Table 19.2 illustrates, marketers can also use the Facets Model to identify the objectives commonly associated with the various marketing communication areas, as well as the types of measures used to evaluate performance. The idea is that certain marketing communication areas, such as public relations and sales promotion, do some things better than other areas; therefore, in an integrated plan, we would use the best tool to accomplish the desired effect. In Table 19.2 the main effects are located in column 1, with a collection of surrogate measures identified in column 2 (this list is not inclusive, it's just a sample). The last column lists the communication tool or tools that may be most appropriate for achieving the objective.

An examination of Table 19.2 shows that advertising is particularly effective in accomplishing several objectives—for instance, creating exposure, awareness, and brand image. It is also good at providing brand reminders to the customer and encouraging repurchase. However, other marketing communication tools, such as sales promotion, are better at getting people to respond with an immediate purchase and public relations is particularly strong at building credibility. Let's look briefly at these other marketing communication areas in terms of their evaluation.

Evaluation doesn't just happen at the end of a campaign or after the ad is run. It has to be planned into the campaign from the very beginning, as this planning meeting illustrates.

TABLE
19.2 **Message Effectiveness Factors**

Key Message Effects	Surrogate Sales Measures	Communication Tools
Perception	Exposure	Adv Media; PR, PoP
	Attention	Adv; Sales Promo, Packaging; PoP
	Interest	Adv; SP; PR, Direct; PoP
	Relevance	Adv; PR; Direct; PoP
	Recognition	Adv; PR, Pkging; PoP, Specialties
Cognitive	Understanding	Adv; PR; Sales; Direct
	Recall	Adv; SP; PR, PoP, Specialties
		Adv; PR; Pkging
Affective	Emotions & Liking	Adv; Sales Promo, Pkging; PoP
	Appeals	Adv; PR; Sales; Events/Spnsrshps
	Resonate	Adv; PR; Events/Spnsrshps
Persuasion	Attitudes	Adv; PR; Direct
	Preference/Intention	Adv; PR; Sales Promo
	Credibility	PR
	Conviction	PR; Sales; Direct
	Motivation	Adv; PR; Sales; Sales Promo
Brand Assoc.	Brand Image	Adv; PR, Events/Spnsrshps
Action	Trial	SP; Sales; Direct, PoP
	Purchase	SP; Sales; Direct
	Repeat Purchase	Adv; SP; Sales; Direct, Specialties

Direct Response   The objective of direct-response communication is to drive a transaction or generate some other type of immediate behavioral response, such as a donation or a visit to a dealer. What makes this marketing communication tool so attractive to marketers is that response is so easily measurable, as is its efficiency or cost-effectiveness.

We evaluate ads containing elements that can be returned by using **direct-response counts**. Some advertisements request direct response via a toll-free number, a mail-in coupon, a Web site or e-mail address, or an offer embedded in the body copy. Instead of depending on consumers' memory or ads' persuasion or some other indirect indication of effectiveness, the advertiser simply counts the number of viewers or readers who request more information or buy the product. (See the Arm & Hammer ad.)

In some ways, direct-response mechanisms are the easiest marketing communication tool to evaluate both in terms of the message effectiveness and in terms of ROI efficiency—the sales-to-cost ratio. The efficiency of the direct-response offer is measured in terms of cost per thousand (CPM) and response per thousand (RPM). CPM is used to compare the cost estimates from various suppliers (printing, postage, mailing labels, fulfillment). The formula is:

$$\frac{\text{Total cost}}{\text{Total quantity}} \times 1,000$$

For example, one direct-marketing firm might give a quote of $5,000 for 10,000 brochures and a competitor estimates $6,000 for 15,000 brochures. On the face of it the first company is cheaper, but when you calculate the CPM, then you can see that the fist company is charging $500 per thousand and the second is charging $400 per thousand, which makes it a more cost-efficient buy.

To calculate the RPM, use the following formula:

$$\frac{\text{Total responses}}{\text{Total mailed}} \times 1,000$$

Principle
Advertising is particularly effective in accomplishing such objectives as creating exposure, awareness, and brand image, and delivering brand reminders.

■ ■ ■
This print ad includes a coupon that allows advertiser Arm & Hammer to count the responses to the ad as part of its evaluation program.

That calculation lets you compare the response rate of alternative mailings. For example, if one mailing of 15,000 pulled 750 responses, then the RPM was 50 per 1,000. If a different mailing of 12,000 pulled 800 responses, then the RPM was 66 per 1,000, making it a more effective offer.

Sales Promotion   Sales promotion programs are complicated in that it may be necessary to evaluate both trade and consumer promotions. Marketers are finding that promotions are most effective when they catch consumers' interest. They are also finding that the best way to listen to consumers may be through qualitative tests.[7] By using focus groups and in-depth interviews, for example, researchers can identify the level of interest the target market has for certain sports and events and analyze how that interest might work in a future brand promotion. In a *Promo* magazine survey,[8] marketers reported that they used the following evaluation measures:

Measure	% used
Sales	45.8
Response Rates	19.4
Awareness	10.2
Other Mix	8.8
Redemption Rates	4.2

In terms of channel (trade promotions), store audits can record the pre–post shelf space allocated to the brand and the use of dealer or retailer promotional materials. Nielsen does formal retail audits to monitor the effectiveness of trade promotions. Store audits can also record consumer response to in-store promotions. Promotions that contain a response device have a built-in evaluation measure. Redemption of coupons is another common form of sales promotion monitoring.

The efficiency of a sales promotion can be evaluated in terms of its financial returns more easily than advertising. We compare the costs of the promotion, called a **payout plan**, to the forecasted sales generated by the promotion. A type of payout plan called **breakeven analysis** seeks to determine the point at which the total cost of the promotion

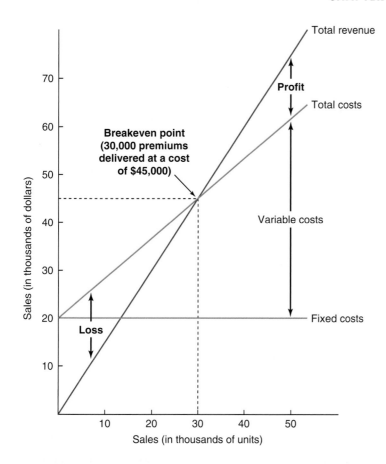

**A Sales Promotion
Breakeven Analysis**
At the breakeven point, where
30,000 premiums are delivered at a
cost of $45,000, the sales revenues
exactly cover, but do not exceed,
total costs. Below and to the left of
the breakeven point (in the portion
of the diagram marked off by dashed
lines) the promotion operates at a
loss. Above and to the right of the
breakeven point, as more premiums
are sold and sales revenues climb,
the promotion makes a profit.

exceeds the total revenues, identifying the point where the effort cannot break even. Figure 19.2 depicts this analysis.

Public Relations   The evaluation of public relations examines the success of the program in getting the message out to the target audience in terms of *output* (materials produced and distributed) and *outcomes* (acceptance and impact of the materials), as well as public opinion and relationship tracking. The output/outcome evaluation is conducted by asking such questions as: How many placements (news releases that ran in the media) did we get? How many articles were published? How many times did our spokesperson appear on talk shows? How much airplay did our public service announcements receive? The results are presented in terms of counts of minutes, mentions, or inches.

Content analysis also helps us determine the favorability of the coverage, share of voice, and issue and competitor coverage.[9] Ongoing public opinion tracking studies consider such questions as: Has there been a change in audience knowledge, attitudes, or behavior (as measured in the pretesting and posttesting)? Can we associate behavior change (for example, product trial, repeat purchase, voting, or joining) with the public relations effort?

The table summarizes the most common measures of output and outcomes in public relations.

Output Objectives Achieved:

- *Production.* Number of PR products, such as news releases or brochures, generated.
- *Distribution.* Number of media outlets (TV stations, newspapers) receiving PR products.
- *Coverage.* Number and size of clips, column inches, seconds, or minutes of time or space.
- *Impressions.* Media placements multiplied by circulation or broadcast reach.
- *Advertising value.* Equivalent ad costs for time or space.
- *Systematic Content Analysis.* Positive or valence (whether the story or mention seems to be more positive or negative), key messages (the idea in the story), sources, and prominence.

Outcome Objectives Achieved:

• *Awareness.* Aided and unaided recall in the target audience.
• *Attitudes.* Perceptions, preferences, and preference or intent to buy.
• *Behavior.* Did they do what you wanted them to do?

The search for methods to tie public relations activities to bottom-line business measures, such as ROI (return on investment) is like the quest for the "Holy Grail." PR practitioners would like to demonstrate ROI because it would provide even more support for the importance of PR effects. Unfortunately research methods and analytical techniques that provide this support are elusive.[10] A surrogate ROI measure can be based on shareholder value, which Fombrun identifies as a company's or brand's reputation capital. For example, research conducted on companies with the most effective employee-communication programs has determined that they provide a much higher total return to shareholders.[11]

IMC Consistency

IMC is a new discipline and the research is only now being developed that proves the effectiveness of advertising in combination with other marketing communication areas. John Philip Jones, in his landmark research using single-source data, has determined that sales promotion by itself, for example, is much less effective than when it is combined, planned and executed as part of an integrated program.[12]

Integration is an outcome and it can be evaluated using an IMC audit.[13] The first step is a *content analysis,* which collects all the materials produced by an organization and codes its use of agreed-upon consistency elements, such as brand identity cues, slogans, design format, tone of voice, colors, the expression of core values, and positioning cues. The content analysis also looks for materials that are coded as off strategy and diagnoses the ways in which deviant messages are being sent. In addition to a content analysis, IMC researchers use observational tools such as *mystery shopping* and *phantom phone calls,* which refers to researchers who visit a retail store or service outlet or who contact a company by phone or e-mail and then observe and record the interactions and communication pattern.

The complexity of an IMC program complicates evaluation because there are multiple efforts with multiple objectives and many of them demand different types of research techniques. Ongoing research or tracking studies against some general measures such as brand reputation give a general indication of how the various message strategies are coming together to create a coherent brand impression.

Special Advertising Situations

The special situations identified in Chapter 18 are evaluated using many of the same tools as advertising; let's look now at these areas in terms of their particular objectives and how they are evaluated.

Retail Advertising   The primary objective of retail advertising is to generate store traffic and that is usually created through a combination of marketing communication programming. Sales promotion contributes the most to traffic building with sale prices and loss leaders, contests, and special events. All of these, however, have to be announced to customers, and public relations and advertising are the most cost-effective way to get the word out. The results of traffic-building promotions and advertising are simple counts of people coming through the door or down an aisle.

Visibility is another objective of retail advertising and that also is attained through special promotions and events, announced through publicity and advertising. Special events are often used to build visibility, for example, radio broadcasts from the store, particularly for grand-opening celebrations. Similarly, some stores create programs that contribute positively to the store image through partnership promotions, such as sponsorships of charitable programs, like Habitat for Humanity. Educational programs such as the "how-to" classes that Home Depot offers are good relationship-building programs. All of these can be measured by participation counts as well as sign-up and fill-out forms that may also ask for feedback related to the store's image and consumer perception of the events and supporting promotional activities. Another important retail objective is loyalty and that is fostered through frequency clubs and measured in terms of participation.

B2B Advertising   The primary objective of B2B advertising is to generate a response, particularly sales leads. So a common form of evaluation is a lead count based on calls, e-mails, and cards returned to the advertiser. Another common objective is called **conversion** and that refers to the number of leads that turn into customers who make a purchase. Conversion rates, which are percentages of the leads, are also calculated for most marketing communication tools used in B2B programs.

Although few business marketers today rely exclusively on their sales forces to reach potential buyers, many business people still wonder about the effectiveness of business advertising. The Advertising Research Foundation (ARF) and the Association of Business Publishers (ABP) have studied the link between business advertising, industrial-product sales, and profits.[14] The researchers monitored product sales and the level and frequency of their advertising schedules for one year. To ensure that the study's findings could apply to a wide range in industries and products, three very different products were monitored: a portable safety device that sold for less than $10, a commercial transportation package that sold for around $10,000, and highly specialized laboratory equipment priced between $5,000 and $10,000.

Despite the diversity in price, product life, purchase complexity, and distribution channels, the study found that for all three products:

- Business-to-business advertising created more sales than would have occurred without advertising.
- It paid to advertise to both dealers and end users when the product was sold through dealers.
- Increased advertising frequency increased sales leads and generated higher profits.
- It took four to six months to see the results of the advertising program.
- The use of color in the advertising made a dramatic difference.
- The advertising campaign was effective long after the campaign had ended.
- Advertising favorably affected purchasers' awareness of and attitudes toward industrial products.

International Advertising   A strong effectiveness evaluation program is particularly important for international advertising. Intuition serves the advertiser poorly as an evaluation method because most managers lack familiarity with foreign markets. International advertising most often takes place out of the advertising manager's sight and is difficult to control. Advertising managers face special problems that make evaluation of international programs difficult.[15] First, many markets with distinctive characteristics must be analyzed, not just the markets in one country. Furthermore, the costs of running evaluation programs in smaller markets may not be cost effective. There may also be incompatibilities among various measurement systems and data analysis techniques that make it difficult to compare the data from one market with similar data from another market.

The effectiveness of an international evaluation program for advertising should focus, at least initially, on pretesting. Unfamiliarity with the culture, language, and consumer behavior can result in major miscalculations. Pretesting helps the advertiser correct major problems before miscommunication.

The best approach is to test two ads that are both based on the global advertising strategy: a locally produced version of the advertising and an original ad produced locally. As a general rule of thumb, the global strategy usually works around 60 percent of the time. If the locally produced advertising wins, the improvement must be decisive or the cost of creating a local version of the campaign may not be affordable. Cost efficiency, in other words, always favors a standardized approach, but that must be tempered by questions of whether the standardized approach is equally effective at the local level. Global companies must remain flexible enough to adapt the strategy that emerges as the winner to local markets.

Consider This

1. Compare the evaluation of direct response, sales promotion, and public relations with the evaluation of advertising.
2. How is consistency evaluated in an IMC campaign?

IT'S A WRAP

WHAT CAN BROWN DO FOR YOU?

Evaluation through testing is a risk-reduction practice, one that's needed because it's difficult to predict how effective an ad idea will be. There are a lot of variables and a lot of factors that can't be controlled, such as how consumers think and respond to a message. Some evaluation is informal and based on the personal judgment of an experienced manager; some can be built into the plan as structured feedback such as response cards and calls; but usually the evaluation effort involves a more formal research project.

UPS knew from its customer research that to break out of the "brown and ground" perception, the company had to overcome the inertia of shipping managers and other front-office customers who use UPS for ground packages and FedEx for overnight and international. The company also had to engineer a perception shift in the minds of senior executives moving from a company that handles packages to a strategic partner in systems planning. The "Brown" campaign by The Martin Agency successfully achieved those goals and delivered the following results:

Objective 1: Breaking Through
- Awareness of the Brown campaign outpaced *all* past UPS advertising measured in the 10+ year history of its tracking study.
- Among those aware of the campaign, correct brand linkage to UPS was 95–98 percent across all audiences (compared to a historical average of 20–40 percent for past UPS advertising).
- "What can BROWN do for you?" has taken hold in popular culture. For instance, recently both *Saturday Night Live* and *Trading Spaces* mentioned the tagline and campaign in their shows which boosts the campaign's impressions.

Objective 2: Breaking the Inertia Trance
- International shipping profitability increased 150 percent and overnight volume spiked by 9.1 percent after the campaign ran. The targets' total package volume increased by 4.39 percent.
- From the start of the campaign in March to the year-end, annual ground shipping revenue grew by $300 million.
- With shipping decision makers, the brand is showing steady and significant gains in key measures like, "Helps my operation run more smoothly," "Dynamic and energetic," and "Offers a broad range of services."
- The campaign was a hit in terms of response with a 10.5 percent response rate and an ROI of 1:3.5. (That means every dollar spent of the campaign generated $3.5 dollars in revenue.)

Objective 3: Breaking the Relevance Trance
- At the start of the campaign, annual non package (supply chain) revenue was approximately $1.4 billion. By the end of the year, nonpackage revenue had almost doubled to $2.7 billion.
- For the first time in the 10+ year history of the brand tracking study, UPS leads FedEx in all image measures among C-level and senior-level decision makers. All significant brand image measures continued upward.
- Among C-level and senior decision makers, the *biggest* gains were in key measures like, "For people like me," "Acts as a strategic partner to my company," "Helps in distribution and supply chain operations," and "Provides global competitive advantage."

Research determined that the "Brown" campaign was successful in changing the perception of UPS by addressing the right audience with the right messages. It convinced shipping managers that UPS could make their jobs easier; it convinced small-business owners that UPS could help grow their business; it convinced front-office workers that UPS could take a load off their desks and make them more efficient; and it convinced senior management that UPS could contribute as a strategic partner. Most of all, it convinced the EFFIE judges that this was a highly effective campaign that deserved a Gold EFFIE.

Summary

1. **Demonstrate that you understand why and how advertising evaluation is conducted.** Advertising evaluation is used to test, monitor, measure, and diagnose advertising messages. The factors tested are the key effects outlined in a model of advertising effectiveness.
2. **List and explain the stages of copy testing.** Copy testing is conducted before (pretesting), during (tracking), and after (posttesting) an ad or campaign has run. Diagnostic evaluation can be conducted at all three stages.
3. **Identify the key areas of media evaluation.** Media evaluation begins by verifying the media exposure in terms of the

achievement of the reach and frequency objectives, as well as the audience measurement reports of the media used. Media ROI evaluation considers such questions as how much is enough, particularly in terms of advertising wearout.

4. **Discuss how campaigns and IMC programs are evaluated.** A campaign's performance is assessed in terms of how well it meets its message and media objectives. IMC plans also assess the performance of the various marketing communication tools, as well as the synergistic effect of the elements working together.

Key Terms

aided recall test, 540
breakeven analysis, 546
clutter reel, 537
coincidental survey, 537
concept testing, 536
conversion, 549
direct-response counts, 545

inquiry tests, 541
likability tests, 541
moment-by-moment tests, 537
motivation test, 541
norms, 534
pantry check, 539
payout plan, 546

persuasion test, 540
photoboards, 537
picture sort, 537
pretesting, 537
recall test, 540
recognition test, 540
scanner research, 541

single-source research, 541
test market, 539
tracking studies, 537
unaided recall test, 540
wave analysis, 539
wearout, 543

Review Questions

1. What are the four categories of work that are evaluated in assessing the performance of advertising and marketing communication?
2. What are the three stages where advertising evaluation is conducted, and what is being evaluated at each stage?
3. What is media efficiency, and how does that relate to ROI?
4. How is an IMC campaign evaluated?

Discussion Questions

1. Research professionals recommend using focus groups to help develop a campaign strategy or theme, but many are opposed to using focus groups to choose finished ads for the campaign. Is this advice contradictory? Why or why not?
2. Many creative people feel that formal copy-testing research doesn't do justice to their ideas. In particular, they feel that research results are designed to reward cognitive approaches and don't do a good job of evaluation for brand image ads and emotional ads. From what you have read in this chapter about copy testing, why do they feel that way? Do you believe that is a legitimate criticism of copy testing?
3. Most clients want a quick and easy answer to the question of whether the ad works. Advertising professionals, how-

ever, tend to believe that a one-score approach to copy testing is not appropriate. Why would they feel that way? If you were helping an agency prepare for a presentation on its copy-testing results, what would you suggest the agency say to explain away the idea that you can evaluate an ad with a single test?

4. In the dot-com craze of the late 1990s, new Internet companies emerged almost daily. What types of strategic or evaluative research do you think many of these companies conducted, if any? Do you believe research would have helped any of these companies make decisions that might have helped them survive the dot-com crash? Why or why not? What particular decision might have been considered?

■■■Class Projects

1. Put together a portfolio of ads for a product category targeted to a college audience. Set up a focus group with participants recruited from among your friends and ask them to evaluate the ads. Identify the top ad in unaided awareness and the bottom ad. Ask the focus group participants to analyze the headline, the visual, and the brand identification of each ad. How do the two ads compare in terms of their ability to get attention and lock the brand in memory?

2. As a team, explore the Web sites for two copy-testing companies such as Ameritest (www.Ameritet.net), Ipsos-ASI (www.ipsos.com), Dianostic Research (www.diagnostic.com) or the ARS Group (www.ars-group.com) and compare the services they offer to their clients. If your team were looking for a company to pretest a campaign for a cosmetic product, which one would you prefer? Why?

HANDS-ON
CASE

Lovin' It at McDonalds Again

In 2003 McDonald's, one of the biggest advertisers in the world, decided to consolidate its media-buying operations, which are responsible for placing nearly a billion dollars of advertising each year. Cost savings were not the reason for the change. "We don't believe we were getting our money's worth out of our media," claimed company official Larry Light. "We're not trying to see how much we can cut in our advertising. We're looking to be the most powerful voice in advertising, to be more effective." McDonald's also launched a global campaign featuring the tagline "I'm lovin' it." *Ad Age* critic Bob Garfield was unimpressed, writing "If 50 Cent were kidnapped by the New Christy Minstrels, and forced to record a video soundtrack commissioned by Mentos, you'd have the introduction to the new McDonald's campaign. Alert the media: The clown is dead, and the Pepsi Generation is on Ecstasy." But McDonald's had the last laugh, as its stores have seen double-digit sales growth, far outpacing the competition.

McDonald's, like other large advertisers, is interested in creating effective ads. But what is the metric of effectiveness? Every client, of course, wants to see sales increase, but is that a fair standard for an agency's work? Agencies have long pointed out that great advertising cannot make a substandard brand succeed. And in point of fact, McDonald's instituted a number of other changes at the same time it refocused its advertising, including adding new healthier product lines, like salads and fruit and yogurt. The company also changed its promotional relationship with Disney and focused hard on improving the consumer experience at its restaurants. So how does one separate the effects of the ads from the other changes?

Most people probably believe effective ads are the ones they like and talk about, and there is logic to that. After all, if consumers like an ad they should be willing to watch it over and over, reducing wearout, and perhaps they will also think about the brand more positively; marketing research suggests that a consumer's attitude toward an ad influences his or her attitude toward the brand. In real life it doesn't always seem to work out that way, though. One of the most popular campaigns of the late 1990s was one for Taco Bell that featured a talking Chihuahua. But when sales at franchises grew stagnant, Taco Bell fired the agency that developed the campaign, and replaced it with an agency that got rid of the dog and focused more on the product.

BBDO's efforts for KFC had the same result. BBDO's ads, featuring *Seinfeld* alum Jason Alexander, were well received by consumers and were among the most highly recalled of 2002. But KFC's same-store sales over the time period were actually negative, and the agency was fired. Poor advertising? Perhaps, but other explanations are possible too. Branding consultant Michael Markowitz points out that "The fundamental product offering—fried chicken—has been countertrend for years. Fried chicken is not a first-tier choice for people any longer." He adds, "No matter how clever the ads are, it can't mask or disguise the fundamental weaknesses in business." Besides, if a company fails to achieve its sales targets, "shoot the agency seems to be the rule," observes Ron Paul, a food-service consultant. "It doesn't mean that it's their fault, but it's an easy place to point the finger."

Paul's point probably suggests that the key to McDonald's success is both improved advertising and an improved product. That seems like a sound way for any advertiser to be effective.

Consider This

1. Most clients seem interested in sales increases as a benchmark for judging the quality of their agency's work. From a client perspective, why does this make sense?

2. From an agency perspective, defend the idea that increased product sales is not always an appropriate benchmark. If short-term sales gains are not the metric of success, what metrics would you propose agencies use for their work?

3. What would you propose for a more comprehensive evaluation program for the McDonald's campaign? Using the Facets Model as an outline, how would you determine the effectiveness of the campaign?

Sources: Richard Gibson, "McDonald's Hopes to Increase Effectiveness of Its Advertising," *Wall Street Journal* (Eastern edition) (December 3, 2003): 1; Emma Hall, "Spotlight," *Advertising Age* (April 12, 2004); Kathryn Kranhold, "Omnicom Group to Measure How Ads Do," *Wall Street Journal* (Eastern edition) (October 21, 1999): B16; Kate MacArthur, "Rivals Not Lovin' McD's Comeback," *Advertising Age* (July 26, 2004); Brian Steinberg and Suzanne Vranica, "KFC Seeks a Crisp Take on Its Ads; Fried-Chicken Chain Aims to Revive Sluggish Sales with a Fresh Campaign," *Wall Street Journal* (Eastern edition) (August 1, 2003): B6.

Part 5
Integration and
Evaluation

Chick-fil-A and its advertising agency, The Richards Group, have developed one of the most successful integrated brand campaigns in the fast-food industry, one that has been executed across all media.

For Chick-fil-A, the extendable brand idea was the "Eat Mor Chikin" campaign, which featured cows persuading consumers to eat more Chick-fil-A chicken. The campaign rolled out initially as a three-dimensional billboard. This medium provided Chick-fil-A with a unique platform for being heard and getting noticed. The billboards were and are still very successful; however, the campaign didn't stop there. The "Eat Mor Chikin" campaign continues to evolve and make its way into every point of contact with the customer.

If cows could climb up on a billboard, why couldn't they stand in front of a Chick-fil-A encouraging people to "Eat Mor Chikin"? A 7-foot-tall, standup cow soon became part of a complete in-store point-of-purchase kit that also included banners, table tents, cups, bags, and register toppers. This marked the beginning of campaign integration.

From there, the campaign has moved into other print materials such as direct mail and ads. In no time, the print campaign found itself in promotions, events, TV, radio, the Web, clothing, and merchandise. In 1998 Chick-fil-A began producing calendars featuring the cows. Due to high calendar demand, production numbers have jumped every year from 470,000 calendars in 1998 to more than 2.3 million in 2005. The cows and their quirky antics have become a key symbol of Chick-fil-A's marketing communication.

Public relations also has played a major role in the success of the campaign. Since 1996, the Chick-fil-A cows have received over $10 million in free media on both local and national levels. Chick-fil-A may never have the advertising budgets of its competitors, but the influence and success of an integrated campaign is making up the difference.

Source: Information courtesy of Mike Buerno, The Richards Group.

Consider This

1. Has Chick-fil-A developed a truly integrated campaign? Why or why not?
2. Suggest how this campaign could be better integrated.

Glossary

A

Account management *(p. 49)* People and processes at an ad agency that facilitate the relationship between the agency and the client.

Account planner *(p. 50)* The person responsible for the strategy and its implementation in the creative work.

Account planning process *(p. 195)* A process of using research to gain information about the brand in its marketplace, the consumer's perspective, or both, and to use that research to contribute directly to advertising development.

Acquired needs *(p. 138)* A driving force learned from culture, society, and the environment.

Ad allowances *(p. 507)* In cooperative advertising, funds are provided by manufacturers to retailers who feature the manufacturers' products in the retailers' local advertising.

Added value *(p. 36)* A marketing activity, such as advertising, makes a product more appealing or useful.

Adese *(p. 360)* Formula writing that uses clichés, generalities, stock phrases, and superlatives.

Advertainment *(p. 282)* A form of persuasive advertising in which the commercials look like TV shows or short films, and provide entertainment as opposed to high levels of information.

Advertiser *(p. 11)* A person or organization that initiates the advertising process.

Advertising *(p. 5)* Paid nonpersonal communication from an identified sponsor using mass media to persuade or influence an audience.

Advertising department *(p. 13)* A department within the company that acts as a facilitator between outside vendors and internal advertising management.

Advertising plan *(p. 13, 184)* A plan that proposes strategies for targeting the audience, presenting the advertising message, and implementing media.

Advocacy advertising *(p. 489)* A type of corporate advertising that involves creating advertisements and purchasing space to deliver a specific, targeted message.

Affective response *(p. 109)* A response caused by or expressing feelings and emotions.

Affiliate *(p. 251)* A station that contracts with a national network to carry network-originated programming during part of its schedule.

Agency-of-record *(p. 14, 45)* An advertising agency that manages the business between a company and the agencies it has contracts with.

AIDA *(p. 102)* A hierarchy of effects identified as Attention, Interest, Desire, and Action.

Aided recall *(p. 106)* When one can remember an idea after seeing a cue.

All capitals *(p. 392)* Type set in all capital letters.

Ambush marketing *(p. 464)* In event marketing, a competitor advertises in such a way that it steals visibility from the designated sponsor.

Analysis *(p. 174)* Making sense of all the data collected and figuring out what the information means for the future success of the brand or product.

Animation *(p. 408)* A film or video technique in which objects or drawings are filmed one frame at a time.

Annual report *(p. 492)* A financial document legally required of all publicly held companies.

Answer print *(p. 410)* The finished version of the commercial, with the audio and video recorded together.

Aperture *(p. 293)* The ideal moment for exposing consumers to an advertising message.

Appeal *(p. 340)* An advertising approach that connects with some need, want, or emotion that makes the product message attractive, attention getting, or interesting.

Argument *(p. 114)* A cognitive strategy that uses logic, reasons, and proof to build convictions.

Art director *(p. 357)* The person who is primarily responsible for the visual image of the advertisement.

Association *(p. 110)* The process used to link a product with a positive experience, personality, or lifestyle.

Attention *(p. 105)* Concentrating the mind on a thought or idea.

Attitude *(p. 114)* A learned predisposition that we hold toward an object, person, or idea.

Attribute trade-offs An application of embedded research in which a list of most preferred products for an individual is generated from customer-provided quantitative ratings of their preferences for specific attributes, such as brand, price, and features.

Audiometer *(p. 257)* A measuring instrument attached to a TV set that records which channel a TV is tuned to.

Average frequency *(p. 299)* The average number of times an audience has an opportunity to be exposed to a media vehicle or vehicles in a specified time span.

Awareness *(p. 105)* The degree to which a message has made an impression on the viewer or reader.

B

Back translation *(p. 381)* The practice of translating ad copy into a second language and then translating that version back into the original language to check the accuracy of the translation.

Banner ad *(p. 277)* Small, often rectangular-shaped graphic that appears at the top of a Web page.

Banners See "banner ad."

Benchmarking *(p. 189, 484)* Comparing a result against some other known result from a comparable effort.

Benefits *(p. 341)* Statements about what the product can do for the user.

Big Idea *(p. 327)* A creative idea that expresses an original advertising thought.

Bind-ins *(p. 440)* Cards bound into the binding.

Bleed *(p. 224)* A full-page ad with no outside margins—the color extends to the edge of the page.

Blind headline *(p. 363)* An indirect headline that gives little information.

Blog *(p. 276)* A personal diary-like Web page.

Blow-ins *(p. 440)* Cards blown in loose between the pages of a publication.

Body copy *(p. 360)* The text of the message.

Brag-and-boast copy *(p. 360)* Self important copy that focuses on the company rather than the consumer.

Brainstorming *(p. 333)* A creative thinking technique using free association in a group environment to stimulate inspiration.

Brand *(p. 8, 33)* A name, term, design, or symbol that identifies the goods, services, institution, or idea sold by a marketer.

Brand equity *(p. 35)* The value associated with a brand; the reputation that the brand name or symbol connotes.

Brand image *(p. 33, 113)* A special meaning or mental representation created for a product by giving it a distinctive name and identity.

Brand management *(p. 37)* An organizational structure that places a manager or management team in charge of a brand's total marketing efforts.

Brand mark *(p. 35)* The part of the brand that cannot be spoken, also known as the logo.

Brand name *(p. 35)* The part of the brand that can be spoken, such as words, letters, or numbers.

Branding *(p. 33)* The process of creating a unique identity for a product.

Break-even analysis (payout planning) *(p. 546)* A type of payout plan that seeks to determine the point at which the total cost of the promotion exceeds the total revenues, identifying the point where the effort cannot break even.

Brief *(p. 198)* A strategy document that explains the consumer insight and summarizes the message and media strategy.

Broadband *(p. 254)* A bandwidth that has more capacity to send data and images into a home or business through a cable television wire than the much smaller capacity of a traditional telephone wire or television antenna system.

Broadcast media *(p. 243)* Media, such as radium television, and interactive media, which transmit sounds or images electronically.

Broadsheet *(p. 215)* A newspaper with a page size eight columns wide and 22 inches deep.

Broadsheets *(p. 436)* A full-size news page sheet.

Business marketing *(p. 510)* The marketing of goods and services to organizations.

Business strategic plan *(p. 182)* A business plan that deals with the broadest decisions of the organization.

Business-to-business advertising *(p. 17, 510)* Targets other businesses.

Buzz *(p. 22, 342)* Gossip created by people over a popular interest in something.

C

Cable television *(p. 251)* A form of subscription television in which the signals are carried to households by a cable.

Call centers *(p. 438)* Facilities with banks of phones and representatives who call prospects (outbound) or answer customer calls (inbound).

Call-out *(p. 361)* A block of text separate from the main display copy and headline where the idea is presented.

Call to action *(p. 253, 344, 365)* A concluding line that tells people how to buy the product.

Campaign *(p. 185)* A comprehensive advertising plan for a series of different but related ads that appear in different media across a specified time period.

Captions *(p. 363)* Text which explains what is happening in a corresponding photo or illustration.

Car cards Small advertisements that are mounted in racks inside a vehicle.

Carryover effect *(p. 307)* A measure of residual effect (awareness or recall) of the advertising message some time after the advertising period has ended.

Casting *(p. 376)* Finding the right person for the role.

Cause marketing *(p. 516)* Sponsoring a good cause in the hope that the association will result in positive public opinion about the company.

Catalog *(p. 437)* A multipage direct-mail publication that shows a variety of merchandise.

Cease-and-desist order *(p. 68)* An FTC remedy for false or deceptive advertising that requires an advertiser to stop its unlawful practices.

Central processing When the brain is searching for information and evaluating it critically.

Change agent program *(p. 485)* A program designed to intervene in corporate culture and change stakeholder behaviors.

Channel of communication *(p. 99)* The media through which an advertisement is presented.

Channel of distribution *(p. 39)* People and organizations involved in moving products from producers to consumers.

Chat room *(p. 275)* A web site that allows users to share information.

Circulation *(p. 212)* The number of copies sold.

Claim *(p. 338)* A statement about the product's performance.

Classified advertising *(p. 217)* Commercial messages arranged in the newspaper according to the interests of readers.

Claymation *(p. 408)* A stop-motion animation technique in which figures sculpted from clay are filmed one frame at a time.

Click through *(p. 279)* The act of clicking on a button on a Web site that takes the viewer to a different Web site.

Clip art *(p. 388)* Generic, copyright-free art that can be used by anyone who buys the book or service.

Close *(p. 364)* The last paragraph of the body copy that often refers back to the creative concept and wraps up the Big Idea.

Closing *(p. 315)* Represents the last date to send an ad to production.

Closure A gestalt principle which states that missing parts of a shape will automatically be added on perception.

Clutter *(p. 101)* The excessive number of messages delivered to a target audience.

Clutter reel *(p. 537)* A reel of commercials used in ad testing on which one ad is the one being tested and the others are included to simulate the clutter of a typical advertising break in a program.

Co-branding *(p. 467)* A product offered by two companies with both companies' brands present.

Cognition *(p. 106)* How consumers respond to information, learn, and understand.

Cognitive dissonance *(p. 139)* A tendency to justify the discrepancy between what you receive and what you expected to receive.

Cognitive learning *(p. 108)* When advertisers want people to know something new after watching or hearing a message.

Coincidental survey *(p. 537)* Random phone calls made to viewers to determine what shows they are watching at that time.

Cold calling *(p. 438)* Sales calls made to individuals and businesses who haven't been informed in advance of the call.

Collaborative filtering An application of embedded research in which customers can see product recommendations based on predictive models that classify them with others who have similar profiles of attitude or behavior.

Collateral materials *(p. 367, 493)* Brochures and other forms of product literature used in support of an advertising, public relations, or sales promotion effort.

Color separation *(p. 401)* The process of splitting a color image into four images recorded on negatives; each negative represents one of the four process colors.

Co-marketing *(p. 466)* Programs through which manufacturers partner with retailers in joint promotions.

Commercial speech *(p. 64)* Our legal right to say what we want to promote commercial activity, as defined by the First Amendment.

Commission *(p. 51)* The amount an ad agency charges to the client, often a percentage of media cost.

Communication audit *(p. 483)* A type of background research that assesses the internal and external PR environment that affects the organization's audience, objectives, competitors, and past results.

Communication brief *(p. 198)* A strategy document that explains the consumer insight and summarizes the message and media strategy.

Comparative advertising *(p. 81)* A message strategy that explicitly or implicitly compares the features of two or more brands.

Competitive advantage *(p. 190)* Features or benefits of a product that let it out perform its competitors.

Compiled list *(p. 430)* In database marketing, a list that is created by merging several lists and purging duplicate entries.

Comprehensives *(p. 396)* A layout that looks as much like the final printed ad as possible.

Concept testing *(p. 165, 536)* When a simple statement of an idea is tried out on people who are representative of the target audience in order to get their reactions to the Big Idea.

Conditional learning *(p. 108)* Learning through association by connecting a stimulus to a reward through repeated exposure to a stimulus that eventually leads to the reward.

Consent decree *(p. 68)* A formal FTC agreement with an advertiser that obligates the advertiser to stop its deceptive practices.

Consumer behavior *(p. 126)* The process of an individual or group selecting, purchasing, using, or disposing of products, services, ideas, or experiences to satisfy needs and desires.

Consumer magazine *(p. 221)* A publication oriented to a general (non-business) audience.

Consumer market *(p. 41)* Selling products to a general (non-business) audience.

Consumer research *(p. 157)* A type of market research that identifies people who are in the market for a product.

Contact points *(p. 200)* The media, as well as other places and ways, where a consumer engages in a brand experience.

Content analysis *(p. 165, 548)* Research that analyzes articles, news stories and other printed materials for themes and positive or negative mentions of a brand or company.

Contest *(p. 456)* A form of promotion that requires participants to compete for a prize or prizes based on some sort of skill or ability.

Continuity *(p. 307)* Even, continuous advertising over the time span of the advertising campaign.

Continuous strategy *(p. 307)* A media strategy that spreads the advertising evenly over a period.

Controlled media *(p. 427, 487)* Media that the direct marketer either owns or has delivered through carefully controlled criteria by a contracted company.

Conversion *(p. 549)* In sales, changing a prospect into a customer.

Conviction *(p. 114)* A particularly strong belief that has been anchored firmly in one's attitudes.

Cookies *(p. 273)* Web "bugs" that can be placed on your computer by a Web server to track your online movements.

Co-op advertising *(p. 44, 217, 506)* Also called cooperative advertising; an arrangement between a retailer and manufacturer in which the manufacturer reimburses the retailer for all or part of the retailer's advertising costs.

Cooperative advertising See Co-op advertising.

Copycat advertising *(p. 327)* Using some other brand's creative idea.

Copy-testing *(p. 165, 330)* Evaluating the effectiveness of an ad, either in a draft form or after it has been used.

Core values *(p. 128)* Underlying values that govern a person's (or a brand's) attitudes and behavior.

Copywriter *(p. 357)* The person who writes the text for an ad.

Corporate advertising *(p. 488)* A type of advertising used by firms to build awareness of a company, its products, and the nature of its business.

Corporate culture *(p. 129)* The values and attitudes that shape the behavior of an organization and its employees.

Corporate image *(p. 488)* A perception of a company that its stakeholders create in their minds from messages and experiences with the company.

Corporate relations *(p. 482)* Relations between a corporation and the public involving an organization's image and reputation.

Corrective advertising *(p. 69)* An FTC directive that requires an advertiser to run truthful ads to counter deceptive ads.

Cost Per Rating (CPR) A method of comparing media vehicles by relating the cost of the message unit to the audience rating.

Cost Per Thousand (CPM) *(p. 305)* The cost of exposing each 1,000 members of the target audience to the advertising message.

Coupons *(p. 456)* Legal certificates offered by manufacturers and retailers that grant specified savings on selected products when presented for redemption at the point-of-purchase.

Coverage *(p. 247)* The degree to which a particular advertising medium delivers audiences within a specific geographical area.

C-prints *(p. 403)* High quality proofs used in printing.

Crawl *(p. 405)* Computer-generated letters that move across the bottom of the screen.

Creative brief *(p. 198, 345)* The document that outlines the key strategy decisions and details the key execution elements.

Creative concept *(p. 327)* A Big Idea that is original, supports the ad strategy, and dramatizes the selling point.

Creative director *(p. 331)* The person responsible for managing the work of the creative team.

Creative platform *(p. 345)* A document that outlines the message strategy decisions for an individual ad.

Creative strategy *(p. 334)* The determination of the right message for a particular target audience, a message approach that delivers the advertising objectives.

Crisis management *(p. 482)* Management of people and events during times of great danger or trouble.

Cross-functional management A practice that uses teams to coordinate activities that involve different areas in and outside a company.

Cultural and social influences *(p. 128)* The forces other people exert on your behavior.

Cultural imperialism *(p. 62)* Imposing a foreign culture on a local culture; usually referred to as the impact of Western culture, products, and lifestyles on a more traditional culture.

Culture *(p. 128)* The complex whole of tangible items, intangible concepts, and social behaviors that define a group of people or a way of life.

Culture-orientation model *(p. 521)* A strategy that emphasizes the cultural differences between people.

Customary pricing *(p. 45)* Using a single, well-known price for a long period of time.

Customer-focused marketing All communication within an advertisement that is evaluated in terms of the consumer's response.

Customer *(p. 127)* Current or prospective purchaser of a product.

Customer relationship management (CRM) *(p. 53, 432)* A database process that identifies and analyzes patterns in customer behavior to maximize the profitability of each relationship.

Cut *(p. 407)* An abrupt transition from one shot to another.

Cutouts *(p. 228)* Irregularly shaped extensions added to the top, bottom, or sides of standard outdoor boards.

D

Dailies *(p. 410)* Processed scenes on film that a director reviews to determine what needs correcting.

Databases *(p. 428)* Lists of consumers with information that helps target and segment those who are highly likely to be in the market for a certain product.

Database marketing *(p. 428)* A tool and industry that utilizes databases to predict trends and monitor consumers in order to more effectively implement direct-marketing strategies.

Data-driven communication *(p. 430)* Communication strategy used in direct marketing that is based on customer information and previous interactions with the brand.

Data sheets *(p. 515)* Advertising that provides detailed technical information.

Daypart *(p. 247)* The way the broadcast schedule is divided into time segments during a day.

Dealer tag *(p. 509)* Time left at the end of a manufacturer's TV or radio commercial to insert local retail store information.

Debossing *(p. 403)* A depressed image created on paper by applying heat and pressure.

Deceptive advertising *(p. 66)* Advertising that misleads consumers by making claims that are false or by failure to fully disclose important information.

Delayed effects *(p. 109)* An advertisement's impact occurs at a later time (than its time of delivery).

Demand creation *(p. 61)* An external message creates a want or need.

Demography *(p. 131)* The study of social and economic factors that influence how individual consumers behave.

Demographics *(p. 131)* Human traits such as age, income, race, and gender.

Diaries *(p. 170)* In advertising research, consumers record their consumption activities, including media use.

Die cut *(p. 403)* A sharp-edged stamp used to cut irregular shapes.

Differentiate *(p. 42)* The way products are unique or different from competitors.

Digitization *(p. 403)* Converting art into computer-readable images.

Directional advertising *(p. 233)* Tells people where to go to find goods and services.

Direct-action headline *(p. 362)* A headline that is straightforward and informative and leads to some kind of action.

Direct mail *(p. 435)* A type of direct marketing that sends the offer to a prospective customer by mail.

Direct marketing (DM) *(p. 44, 423)* A type of marketing that uses media to contact a prospect directly and elicit a response without the intervention of a retailer or personal sales.

Direct-response advertising *(p. 17, 424)* A type of marketing communication that achieves an action-oriented objective as a result of the advertising message.

Direct-response counts *(p. 545)* Evaluative tests that count the number of viewers or readers who request more information or who purchase the product.

Discretionary income *(p. 135)* The money available for spending after taxes and necessities are covered.

Display advertising *(p. 217)* Sponsored messages that can be of any size and location within the newspaper, except the editorial page.

Display copy *(p. 360)* Type set in larger sizes that is used to attract the reader's attention.

Distribution chain or channel *(p. 39)* The companies involved in moving a product from the manufacturer to the customer.

Donut format *(p. 509)* A format for a radio commercial where the manufacturer records the beginning and end and the local retailer drops in the middle.

Double-page spread *(p. 224)* An advertisement that crosses two facing pages in a magazine.

Dubbing *(p. 410)* The process of making duplicate copies of a videotape.

E

E-business *(p. 271)* The practice of conducting business online.

E-commerce Selling goods and services through electronic means, usually over the Internet.

Effective frequency *(p. 300)* A planning concept that determines a range (minimum and maximum) of repeat exposures for a message.

Effects *(p. 19)* The impact created by an advertisement and the target audiences response to the message.

Embedded research *(p. 173)* Research that is measured through real purchase and use situations which benefits the consumer, manufacturer, and retailer.

Embossing *(p. 403)* The application of pressure to create a raised surface image on paper.

Emotional appeals *(p. 110)* Message strategies that seek to arouse our feelings.

Employee relations *(p. 480)* Relations between the company and its workers.

Endorsement or testimonial *(p. 83)* Any advertising message that consumers reasonably believe reflects the opinions, beliefs, or experiences of an individual, group, or institution.

Ethics *(p. 75)* A set of moral principles that guide our actions.

Ethnographic research *(p. 169)* A form of anthropological research that studies the way people live their lives.

Evaluative research *(p. 157)* Research that determines how well the ad or campaign achieved its goals.

Event marketing *(p. 464)* Creating a promotion program around a sponsored event.

Exchange *(p. 32)* The process whereby two or more parties transfer something of value to one another.

Exclusive distribution When only one distributor is allowed to sell the brand in a particular market.

Execution *(p. 520)* The different variations used to represent the message of a campaign.

Exposure *(p. 105, 212)* The opportunity for a reader, viewer, or listener to see or hear an advertisement.

Extensions *(p. 228)* Embellishments to painted billboards that expand the scale and break away from the standard rectangle limitations.

Exterior transit advertising *(p. 231)* Advertising posters that are mounted on the sides, rear, and tops of vehicles.

Extranets *(p. 274, 496)* Networked systems of electronic communication that allow employees to be in contact with each other in one business with its business partners.

F

Family *(p. 130)* Two or more people who are related by blood, marriage, or adoption and live in the same household.

Feature *(p. 338)* A product attribute or characteristic.

Feature story *(p. 490)* In the media, these are human-interest stories, in contrast to hard news.

Feature analysis *(p. 190)* A comparison of your product's features against those of competing products.

Federal Communications Commission (FCC) *(p. 70)* A U.S. government agency that regulates broadcast media and can eliminate ads that are deceptive or offensive.

Federal Trade Commission (FTC) *(p. 66)* A U.S. government agency responsible for regulating several advertising issues including banning deceptive or misleading advertising.

Fee *(p. 51)* An hourly amount charged to the client by the agency.

Feedback *(p. 100)* Response to a message by a receiver that is conveyed back to the source.

Film-to-tape transfer *(p. 407)* A procedure by which film is shot, processed, and then transferred to videotape.

Financial relations *(p. 480)* Communications with the financial community.

First-run syndication *(p. 254)* Network shows that move into syndication even though new episodes are continuing to be produced.

Flexography *(p. 403)* A printing process that uses a flexible rubber printing plate in order to print on unusual shaped objects.

Flighting *(p. 307)* An advertising scheduling pattern characterized by a period of intensified activity called a flight, followed by a period of no advertising called a hiatus.

Focus groups *(p. 168)* A group interview led by a moderator.

Font *(p. 392)* The basic set of letters in a particular typeface.

Food and Drug Administration (FDA) *(p. 70)* A regulatory division of the Department of Health and Human Services that oversees package labeling and ingredient listings for food and drugs.

Four-color printing *(p. 401)* A printing process that replicates the full color of a photograph although it only uses four colors of ink.

Frame-by-frame tests Tests that evaluate consumers' reactions to the individual scenes that unfold in the course of a television commercial.

Free-standing insert advertisement *(p. 218)* Preprinted advertisement placed loosely in the newspaper.

Frequency *(p. 212)* The number of times an audience has an opportunity to be exposed to a media vehicle or vehicles in a specified time span.

Frequency *(p. 243)* The number of radio waves produced by a transmitter in one second.

Frequency distribution *(p. 299)* A media planning term describing exactly how many times each person is exposed to a message by percentage of the population (reach).

Frequency program *(p. 466)* A loyalty program that rewards customers for repeat purchases.

Friendship focus groups *(p. 169)* Group interviews with people who know one another and have been recruited by the person who hosts the session, which is usually held in that person's home.

Fulfillment *(p. 427)* The back-end operations of direct marketing, which include receiving the order, assembling the merchandise, shipping, and handling returns and exchanges.

Full-service agency *(p. 47)* An agency that provides clients with the primary planning and advertising services.

G

Gaffer *(p. 409)* Chief electrician on a film shoot.

Gap analysis *(p. 484)* A research technique that measures the differences in perceptions and attitudes between groups or between them and the organization.

Gatefold *(p. 224)* Four or more connected pages that fold in on themselves.

Gatekeepers *(p. 480)* Individuals who have direct relations with the public such as writers, producers, editors, talk-show coordinators, and newscasters.

Geodemographic clusters Distinct types of neighborhoods.

Geomarketing Marketing that is geared to increasing diversity in consumer tastes and preferences.

Global brand *(p. 519)* One that is marketed with the same name, design, and creative strategy in most or all of the major regional market blocs.

Global perspective A corporate philosophy that directs products and advertising toward a worldwide market.

Globalization *(p. 23)* The deepening relationships and broadening interdependence among people from different countries.

Grip *(p. 409)* Individual who moves the props and sets on a film shoot.

Gross impressions *(p. 212)* The sum of the audiences of all the media vehicles used within a designated time span.

Gross Rating Points (GRPs) *(p. 258)* The sum of the total exposure potential of a series of media vehicles expressed as a percentage of the audience population.

Guerrilla marketing *(p. 285)* A form of unconventional marketing, such as chalk messages on a sidewalk, that is often associated with staged events.

Gutter *(p. 224)* The white space, or inside margins, where two facing magazine pages join.

H

Habit Something learned so well, it has become second nature.

Halftone *(p. 400)* (Continuous tone): Image with a continuous range of shades from light to dark.

Hard sell *(p. 6, 335)* A rational, informational message that emphasizes a strong argument and calls for action.

Headline *(p. 360)* The title of an ad; it is display copy set in large type to get the reader's attention.

Hierarchy-of-effects *(p. 102)* A set of consumer responses that moves from the least serious, involved, or complex up through the most serious, involved, or complex.

High context culture *(p. 522)* The meaning of a message is dependent on context cues.

High involvement *(p. 116)* Perceiving a product or information as important and personally relevant.

High-involvement decision process *(p. 116)* A decision process that relates to higher-risk products purchased infrequently.

Hit *(p. 279)* The number of times a Web site is visited.

Horizontal publications *(p. 221, 514)* Publications directed at people who hold similar jobs.

House ad *(p. 487)* An ad by an organization that is used in its own publication or programming.

Household *(p. 130)* All those people who occupy one living unit, whether they are related or not.

HUT *(p. 212)* A measure of Households Using TV.

I

Image *(p. 478)* The use of intangible attributes to create a specific perception.

Image advertising *(p. 342)* A type of advertising that creates a unique brand meaning.

Image transfer *(p. 304, 369)* When the presentation in one medium stimulates the listener or viewer to think about the presentation of the product in another medium.

IMC research *(p. 157)* Research used to plan and evaluate the performance and synergy of all marketing communication tools.

Impact The effect of the message on the audience.

Implied third-party endorsement *(p. 480)* When the media endorse a product and the public finds it credible.

Impression *(p. 212)* In media planning, one person's opportunity to be exposed to an advertising message.

Inbound telemarketing *(p. 438)* Incoming calls initiated by the customer.

In-depth interview *(p. 168)* One-on-one interview using open-ended questions.

Industrial advertising *(p. 510)* Advertising that targets original equipment manufacturers (OEM).

Indirect advertising *(p. 71)* Advertising that features one product instead of the primary (controversial) product.

Indirect marketing *(p. 44)* Distributing a product through a channel structure that includes one or more resellers.

Indirect-action headlines *(p. 362)* Headlines that aim to capture attention although they might not provide much information.

Industrial advertising *(p. 510)* Advertising directed at suppliers or original equipment manufacturers (OEMs).

In-house agency *(p. 15)* An agency within an advertiser's organization that performs all the tasks an outside agency would provide for the advertiser.

In-market tests Tests that measure the effectiveness of advertisements by measuring actual sales results in the marketplace.

Innate needs *(p. 135)* Primary needs connected with survival.

Inquiry tests *(p. 541)* Evaluation that measures the number of responses to a message.

Instant messaging *(p. 285)* Exchanging text-based messages in real time via an Internet communications service.

Institutional retail advertising *(p. 507)* Advertising that focuses on the image of the store rather than selling merchandise.

Integrated direct marketing *(p. 444)* A method of achieving precise, synchronized use of the right mediums at the right time, with a measurable return on dollars spent. Also known as integrated relationship marketing.

Integrated marketing *(p. 52)* The process of meeting customers' needs through the coordination of the marketing mix and the other business functions.

Integrated Marketing Communication (IMC) *(p. 23)* The practice of unifying all marketing communication efforts so they send a consistent, persuasive message to target audiences.

Integrated media strategy A media strategy in which advertisers understand which media fit particular advertising needs, which media are complementary, and which detract from each other.

Intensive distribution Stocking the product in as many outlets as possible.

Interactive communication *(p. 100)* Personal conversations between two people.

Interactive technology Technology such as the Internet.

Interactive TV *(p. 254)* A television with computer capabilities.

Interconnects *(p. 252)* A special cable technology that allows local advertisers to run their commercials in small geographic areas through the interconnection of a number of cable systems.

Interest *(p. 105)* Activities that engage the consumer.

Interior transit advertising *(p. 231)* Advertising posters that are mounted inside vehicles such as buses, subway cars, and taxis.

Interlock *(p. 410)* A version of the commercial with the audio and video timed together, although the two are recorded separately.

Internal marketing *(p. 200, 480)* Providing information about marketing activity and promoting it internally to employees.

Internal service departments Departments such as the traffic department, print production, financial services, and human resources or personnel, which serve the operations within the agency.

International advertising *(p. 52)* Advertising designed to promote the same product in a number of countries.

International brand *(p. 52, 519)* A brand or product that is available in most parts of the world.

Internet *(p. 271)* A linked system of international computer networks.

Intranets *(p. 274, 496)* Networked systems of electronic communication that allow employees to be in touch with one another from various locations.

Involvement *(p. 116)* The intensity of the consumer's interest in a product.

Issue management *(p. 481)* The practice of advising companies and senior management on how public opinion is coalescing around certain issues.

J

Jingles *(p. 244, 368)* Commercials set to music.

Justified type *(p. 392)* A form of typeset copy in which the ends of the lines in a column of type are forced to align by adding space between words in the line.

K

Kiosks *(p. 231)* Multisided bulletin board structures designed for public posting of messages.

L

Layout *(p. 394)* A drawing that shows where all the elements in the ad are to be positioned.

Lead *(p. 364)* The first paragraph of the body copy.

Lead agency *(p. 522)* In international marketing, the agency that develops the campaign.

Lead generation *(p. 424)* The identification of prospective customers.

Lead time *(p. 307)* Production time; also time preceeding a sesonal event.

Legibility *(p. 392)* How easy or difficult a type is to read.

Letterpress *(p. 402)* A printing process that prints from a raised surface.

Licensing *(p. 467)* The practice whereby a company with an established brand "rents" it to another company.

Lifestyle *(p. 135)* The pattern of living that reflects how people allocate their time, energy, and money.

Lifestyle analysis *(p. 141)* Examining the ways people allocate their time, energy, and money.

Lifetime customer value *(p. 444)* An estimate of the revenue coming from a particular customer (or type of customer) over the lifetime of the relationship.

Likability tests *(p. 541)* Evaluation of positive responses to an ad.

Line art *(p. 400)* Art in which all elements are solid, with no intermediate shades or tones.

Lists *(p. 429)* Databases of prospects' and customers' contact information.

Loaders *(p. 462)* Trade promotions that encourage retailers to stock up on a product.

Lobbying *(p. 481)* A form of public affairs involving corporations, activist groups, and consumer groups who provide information to legislators in order to get their support and to get them to vote a certain way on a particular bill.

Local advertising *(p. 17, 505)* Advertising targeted to consumers who live within the local shopping area of a store.

Local brand *(p. 52)* A brand that is marketed in one specific country.

Local cable *(p. 252)* Cable scheduling that allows advertisers to show their commercials to highly restricted geographic audiences through interconnects.

Localization (Adaption) *(p. 520)* A strategy in international advertising that adapts the message to local cultures.

Locking power Creative approach that captures the attention of the consumer.

Low-context cultures *(p. 522)* The meaning of a message is obvious without needing a sense of the cultural context.

Low-involvement *(p. 116)* Perceiving a product or information as unimportant.

Low-involvement decision process *(p. 116)* A decision process that relates to products purchased frequently with low risk.

Low-power FM *(p. 244)* Nonprofit, noncommercial stations that serve a small are market, such as a college campus.

Loyalty program *(p. 466)* A program designed to increase customer retention by rewarding customers for their patronage.

M

Make-goods *(p. 315)* Compensation that media give to advertisers in the form of additional message units. These are commonly used in situations involving production errors by the medium and preemption of the advertiser's programming.

Market *(p. 39)* An area of the country or a group of buyers.

Market aggregation strategy *(p. 147)* An undifferentiated segmentation strategy that treats consumers as homogenous.

Market orientation model *(p. 521)* A strategy in international marketing that emphasizes the differences in cultures.

Market research *(p. 157)* A type of marketing research that investigates the product and category, as well as consumers who are or might be customers for the product.

Market segmentation *(p. 148)* The process of dividing a market into distinct groups of buyers who might require separate products or marketing mixes.

Market selectivity *(p. 214)* When the medium targets specific consumer groups.

Market tracking studies Studies that follow the purchase activity of a specific consumer or group of consumers over a specified period of time.

Marketer *(p. 37)* The company or organization behind the product.

Marketing *(p. 8)* Business activities that direct the exchange of goods and services between producers and consumers.

Marketing communications *(p. 8)* The element in the marketing mix that communicates the key marketing messages to target audiences.

Marketing communication mix *(p. 42)* A combination of marketing communication activities, such as personal selling, advertising, sales promotion, marketing public relations, and packaging, to produce a coordinated message strategy.

Marketing concept *(p. 31)* An idea that suggests that marketing should focus first on the needs and wants of the customer, rather than finding ways to sell products that may or may not meet customers' needs.

Marketing imperialism *(p. 62)* Marketing practices that result in imposing foreign cultural values on a local cutlure with different vlaues and traditions.

Marketing mix *(p. 8)* A blend of four main activities: designing, pricing, distributing, and communicating about the product.

Marketing mix modeling A modeling technique that allows marketers to determine the precise impact of the media plan on product sales.

Marketing plan *(p. 45, 183)* A written document that proposes strategies for using the elements of the marketing mix to achieve objectives.

Marketing Public Relations (MPR) *(p. 483)* A type of public relations that supports marketing's product and sales focus by increasing the brand's and company's credibility with consumers.

Marketing research *(p. 162)* Research that investigates all elements of the marketing mix.

Mass customization A product development process that relies on flexible manufacturing to customize products for select markets or individuals.

Mechanicals *(p. 396)* A finished pasteup with every element perfectly positioned that is photographed to make printing plates for offset printing.

Media *(p. 15, 211)* The channels of communication that carry the ad message to target audiences.

Media-buying services *(p. 49)* Service providers that specialize in the purchase of media for their clients.

Media kit *(p. 492)* Also called a press kit, a packet or folder that contains all the important information for members of the press.

Media mix *(p. 212)* Selecting the best combination of media vehicles, nontraditional media, and marketing communication tools to reach the targeted stakeholder audiences.

Media objective *(p. 212)* A goal or task a media plan should accomplish.

Media planning *(p. 212)* A decision process leading to the use of advertising time and space to assist in the achievement of marketing objectives.

Media relations *(p. 480)* Relationships with media contacts.

Media reps *(p. 213)* Media salespeople who sell media time and space for a variety of media outlets.

Media salespersons *(p. 213)* People who work for a specific medium and call on media planners and buyers in agencies to sell space or time in that medium.

Media strategy *(p. 300)* The decisions media planners make to deliver the msot effective media mix that will reach the target audience and satisfy the media objectives.

Media tour *(p. 492)* A traveling press conference in which the company's spokesperson travels to different cities and meets with the local media.

Media vehicle *(p. 212)* A single program, magazine, or radio station.

Medium *(p. 101)* A single form of communication (television, billboards, online media).

Merging *(p. 429)* The process of combining two or more lists of data.

Message *(p. 99)* The words, pictures, and ideas that create meaning in an advertisement.

Message strategy *(p. 334)* The determination of the right message for a particular target audience that delivers the advertising objectives.

Mission marketing *(p. 516)* Linking the mission of the company to a good cause and committing support to it for the long term.

Mission statement *(p. 183)* A business platform that articulates the organization's philosophy, as well as its goals and values.

Mixer *(p. 410)* The individual who operates the recording equipment during a film shoot.

Moment-by-moment tests *(p. 537)* A research method that evaluates viewers' response to a commercial frame by frame.

Morning drive time *(p. 247)* On radio the day part that reaches people when they are commuting to work.

Morphing *(p. 405)* A video technique in which one object gradually changes into another.

Motivation (motive) *(p. 114)* An unobservable inner force that stimulates and compels a behavioral response.

Motivation test *(p. 541)* Research that evaluates consumers' intention to act.

N

Navigation *(p. 413)* The action of a user moving through a Web site.

Needs *(p. 108)* Basic forces that motivate you to do or to want something.

Negative space *(p. 395)* In a layout, the white (unprinted) space surrounding the ad's elements.

Network *(p. 250)* When two or more stations are able to broadcast the same program that originates from a single source.

Network cable *(p. 252)* Cable scheduling that runs commercials across an entire subscriber group simultaneously.

Network of associations *(p. 113)* The linked set of brand perceptions that represent a person's unique way of creating meaning.

Network radio *(p. 246)* A group of local affiliates providing simultaneous programming via connection to one or more of the national networks through AT&T telephone wires.

Newsprint *(p. 399)* An inexpensive paper with a rough surface, used for printing newspapers.

News release *(p. 489)* Primary medium used to deliver public relations messages to the media.

Niche markets *(p. 149)* Subsegments of the general market which have distinctive traits that may provide a special combination of benefits.

Noise *(p. 100)* Anything that interferes with or distorts the advertising message's delivery to the target audience.

Nonprofit *(p. 18)* Noncommercial organizations.

Nonpromotional product advertising *(p. 507)* A form of advertising that talks about merchandise that is new, exclusive, and of superior quality and design.

Nontraditional delivery *(p. 223)* Delivery of magazines to readers through such methods as door hangers or newspapers.

Norms *(p. 128, 534)* Simple rules that each culture establishes to guide behavior.

North American Industry Classification System (NAICS) *(p. 510)* The federal system of grouping businesses based on the major product or service provided.

O

Objective *(p. 19)* The goal or task an individual or business wants to accomplish.

Objective-task method *(p. 193)* Budgeting approach based on costs of reaching an objective.

Observation research *(p. 169)* Qualitative research method that takes researchers into natural settings where they record people's behavior.

Off camera *(p. 374)* In television, a voice is coming from an unseen speaker.

Off-network syndication *(p. 254)* Reruns off network shows.

Off-line advertising *(p. 278)* Advertising in traditional media that is designed to drive consumers to an advertiser's Web site.

Offset printing *(p. 402)* A printing process that prints an image from a smooth surface chemically treated printing plate.

One-order, one-bill *(p. 218)* When media companies buy newspaper advertising space for national advertisers and handle the rate negotiation and billing.

One-step offer *(p. 427)* A message that asks for a direct sales response and has a mechanism for responding to the offer.

On location *(p. 374)* Commercials shot outside the studio.

Open-ended questions *(p. 168)* A qualitative research method that asks respondents to generate their own answers.

Open pricing A pricing a method in which prices are negotiated on a contract-by-contract basis for each unit of media space or time.

Opinion leaders *(p. 478)* Important people who influence others.

Opt in (Opt out) *(p. 281)* In e-mail advertising (and direct mail) consumers agree to be included or not included in the list.

Outbound telemarketing *(p. 438)* Telemarketing sales calls initiated by the company.

Outdoor advertising *(p. 227)* Advertising on billboards along streets and highways.

Out-of-home advertising *(p. 227)* All advertising that is displayed outside the home, from billboards, to blimps, to in-store aisle displays.

Overlines *(p. 361)* Text used to set the stage and lead into the headline of copy.

P

Pace *(p. 376)* How fast or slowly the action progresses in a commercial.

Package goods *(p. 41)* Products sold for personal or household use.

Painted bulletin *(p. 228)* A type of advertisement that is normally created on-site and is not restricted to billboards as the attachment.

Pantry checks *(p. 539)* A research checks home-owners' pantries to determine their purchases.

Participation marketing A method of direct marketing in which the company knows its customers, generates feedback at every opportunity, involves the customers and prospects as much as possible, markets according to the customer's schedule, and makes the customer feel vested in the company's success.

Participations *(p. 256)* An arrangement in which a television advertiser buys commercial time from a network.

Payout plan *(p. 470, 546)* A way to evaluate the effectiveness of a sales promotion in terms of its financial returns by comparing the costs of the promotion to the forecasted sales of the promotion.

People meters *(p. 259)* Boxes on a TV set that record viewing behaviors.

Perceived risk *(p. 144)* The relationship between what you gain by making a certain decision and what you have to lose.

Percentage-of-sales method *(p. 194)* A budgeting technique based in the relationship between the cost of advertising and total sales.

Perception *(p. 104)* The process by which we receive information through our five senses and acknowledge and assign meaning to this information.

Peripheral processing Quick decision making based on simple factors for low-involvement purchases such as smell or a catchy slogan.

Permission marketing *(p. 53, 443)* A method of direct marketing in which the consumer controls the process, agrees to receive communication from the company, and consciously signs up.

Permission to believe *(p. 342)* Credibility building techniques that increase consumers' conviction in making decisions.

Personal selling *(p. 45)* Face-to-face contact between the marketer and a prospective customer that intends to create and repeat sales.

Personality *(p. 140)* The consistent attitudes and behaviors that make us an individual.

Persuasion *(p. 113)* Trying to establish, reinforce, or change an attitude, touch an emotion, or anchor a conviction firmly in the potential customer's belief structure.

Persuasion test *(p. 540)* A test that evaluates the effectiveness of an advertisement by measuring whether the ad affects consumers' intentions to buy a brand.

Photostats *(p. 403)* Photoprint proofs that are cheap to produce.

Photoboards *(p. 537)* A mockup of a television commercial that uses still photos for the frames.

Pica *(p. 392)* A unit used to measure width and depth of columns; there are 12 points in a pica and 6 picas in an inch.

Picture sort *(p. 537)* Viewers receive a deck of photos and sort them into categories as requested by the researcher.

Pitch letter *(p. 490)* A letter to a media outlet that outlines a possible story idea that the PR person would like to provide.

Point *(p. 392)* A unit used to measure the height of type; there are 72 points in an inch.

Point of differentiation *(p. 338)* The way a product is unique from its competitors.

Point-of-Purchase (POP) display *(p. 461)* A display designed by the manufacturer and distributed to retailers to promote a particular brand or line of products.

Pool-outs *(p. 522)* Variations on a core campaign theme.

Population *(p. 168)* An entire group of people from which a sample is drawn.

Positioning *(p. 42, 190)* The way in which consumers perceive a product in the marketplace.

Poster (panels) *(p. 228)* A type of advertisement that is created by designers, printed, and shipped to an outdoor advertising company who prepastes and applies it in sections to the poster panel's face on location.

Postproduction *(p. 410)* In TV production, assembling and editing the film after the film has been shot.

Predictive dialing *(p. 438)* Technology that allows telemarketing companies to call anyone by using a trial and error dialing program.

Preference *(p. 114)* Favorable positive impression of a product that leads to an intention to try or buy it.

Preferred frequency The percentage of audience reached at each level of repetition (exposed once, twice, and so on).

Preferred positions *(p. 217)* Sections or pages of print media that are in high demand by advertisers because they have a special appeal to the target audience.

Premium *(p. 456)* A tangible reward received for performing a particular act, such as purchasing a product or visiting the point-of-purchase.

Preprints *(p. 510)* Advertising circulars furnished by a retailer for distribution as a free-standing insert in newspapers.

Press conference *(p. 492)* A public gathering of media people for the purpose of establishing a company's position or making a statement.

Pretesting *(p. 537)* Evaluative research of finished or nearly finished ads that leads to a go/no go decision.

Price *(p. 44)* An amount a seller sets for a product that is based not only on the cost of making and marketing the product, but also on the seller's expected profit level.

Price copy *(p. 45)* A term used to designate advertising copy devoted to information about the price and the associated conditions of a particular product.

Price deal *(p. 455)* A temporary reduction in the price of a product.

Price lining A strategy where a company offers variations of a particular product and prices them accordingly.

Primary research *(p. 42, 159)* Information that is collected from original sources.

Primary research suppliers *(p. 159)* Research firms that specialize in interviewing, observing, recording, and analyzing the behavior of those who purchase or influence the purchase of a particular good or service.

Prime time *(p. 250)* Programming on TV that runs between the hours of 8 and 11 p.m.

Print production *(p. 51)* A department that takes a layout, type, and artwork and turns it into a reproducible format.

Printed poster *(p. 228)* A type of billboard that uses printed formats in standardized sizes that are pasted to the board's surface.

Privacy policy *(p. 273)* A statement on a company's Web site that explains what user data it collects and how it uses the data.

Problem solution format *(p. 345)* A message strategy that sets up a problem that the use of the product can solve.

Process colors *(p. 400)* Four basic inks—magenta, cyan, yellow, and black—that are mixed to produce a full range of colors found in four-color printing.

Product-as-hero *(p. 345)* A form of the problem-solution message strategy.

Product category *(p. 8, 43)* Classification to which a product belongs.

Product differentiation *(p. 190)* A competitive marketing strategy that tries to create a competitive difference through real or perceived product attributes.

Product management *(p. 37)* An organizational structure that places a brand manager or management team in charge of a brand's total marketing effort.

Product placement *(p. 263)* The use of a brand name product in a television show, movie, or event.

Product retail advertising Advertising that focuses on selling merchandise.

Production notes *(p. 408)* A document that describes in detail of every aspect of a commercial's production.

Professional advertising *(p. 512)* Advertising that is targeted at professionals.

Profile *(p. 150)* A composite description of a target audience using personality and lifestyle characteristics.

Program preemptions Interruptions in local or network programming caused by special events.

Program sponsorships *(p. 253)* Commercial announcements used in public broadcasting to underwrite programming costs.

Promise *(p. 341)* Found in a benefit statement, it is something that will happen if you use the product.

Promotional advertising *(p. 507)* Retail advertising that is focused on price or a special sale.

Prospecting *(p. 425)* In database marketing, this is the process of identifying prospects based on how well they match certain user characteristics.

Psychographics *(p. 140)* All psychological variables that combine to share our inner selves and help explain consumer behavior.

Psychological pricing *(p. 45)* A strategy that tries to manipulate the customer's purchasing judgment.

Public affairs *(p. 481)* Relations between a corporation, the public, and government involving public issues relating to government and regulation.

Public communication campaigns *(p. 483, 518)* Social issue campaigns undertaken by nonprofit organizations as a conscious effort to influence the thoughts or actions of the public.

Public opinion *(p. 478)* People's beliefs, based on their conceptions or evaluations of something, rather than on fact.

Public relations *(p. 477)* A management function enabling organizations to achieve effective relationships with various publics in order to manage the image and reputation of the organization.

Public Service Announcements (PSAs) *(p. 487)* A type of public relations advertising that deals with public welfare issues and typically is run free of charge.

Publicity *(p. 477)* Information that catches public interest and is relayed through the news media.

Publics *(p. 477)* All groups of people with which a company or organization interacts.

Puffery *(p. 81)* Advertising or other sales representation that praises a product or service using subjective opinions, superlatives, and similar techniques that are not based on objective fact.

Pull strategy *(p. 44, 462)* A strategy that directs marketing efforts at the consumer and attempts to pull the product through the channel.

Pulsing strategy *(p. 307)* An advertising scheduling pattern in which time and space are scheduled on a continuous but uneven basis; lower levels are followed by bursts or peak periods of intensified activity.

Purging *(p. 429)* The process of deleting duplicative information after lists of data are combined.

Push strategy *(p. 44, 462)* A strategy that directs marketing efforts at resellers, where success depends on the ability of these intermediaries to market the product, which they often do with advertising.

Q

Qualitative research *(p. 160)* Research that seeks to understand how people think and behave and why.

Quantitative research *(p. 160)* Research that uses statistics to describe consumers.

R

Ragged right *(p. 392)* In typesetting, the line endings of the right side of the column fall where they will. Also called "unjustified".

Ratings, Rating Points *(p. 213, 247, 258)* Percentage of population or households tuned to a program.

Reach *(p. 212)* The percentage of different homes or people exposed to a media vehicle or vehicles at least once during a specific period of time. It is the percentage of unduplicated audience.

Reason why *(p. 341)* A statement that explains why the feature will benefit the user.

Rebate *(p. 456)* A sales promotion that allows the customer to recover part of the product's cost from the manufacturer in the form of cash.

Recall test *(p. 540)* A test that evaluates the memorability of an advertisement by contacting members of the advertisement's audience and asking them what they remember about it.

Receiver *(p. 100)* The audience for an advertisement.

Recognition *(p. 106)* An ability to remember having seen something before.

Recognition test *(p. 540)* A test that evaluates the memorability of an advertisement by contacting members of the audience, showing them the ad, and asking whether they remember having seen it before.

Reference group *(p. 129)* A group of people that a person uses as a guide for behavior in specific situations.

Refund *(p. 456)* An offer by the marketer to return a certain amount of money to the consumer who purchases the product.

Regional brand *(p. 52)* A brand that is available throughout a regional trading block.

Registration *(p. 399)* When the four-colors used in full-color printing are perfectly aligned with the image.

Relationship marketing *(p. 53, 480)* The ongoing process of identifying and maintaining contact with high-value customers.

Release prints *(p. 410)* Duplicate copies of a commercial that are ready for distribution.

Relevance *(p. 105)* The message connects with the audience on a personal level.

Reliability *(p. 172)* In research, reliability means you can run the same test over again and get the same results.

Reminder advertising *(p. 344)* An advertising strategy that keeps the brand name in front of consumers.

Reputation *(p. 478)* A general estimation in which a company is held by the public, based on its practices, policies, and performance.

Resonance *(p. 110)* A message that rings true because the consumer connects with it on a personal level.

Response list *(p. 430)* In direct marketing, a list that is compiled of people who respond to a direct-mail offer.

Retail advertising *(p. 17, 505)* A type of advertising used by local merchants who sell directly to consumers.

Retainer *(p. 51)* Agency monthly compensation based on an estimate of the projected work and its costs.

Rich media *(p. 278)* Messages are effective in grabbing people's attention because of their novelty and entertainment value.

Rotogravure *(p. 402)* A printing process used for long press runs that provides high-quality phographic reproduction.

Rough cut *(p. 410)* A preliminary edited version of the commercial.

Rough layout *(p. 396)* A layout drawn to size but without attention to artistic and copy details.

Run-of-paper rate *(p. 217)* In newspaper advertising, a rate based on a locaton that is at the discretion of the publisher.

Rushes *(p. 410)* Rough versions of the commercial assembled from unedited footage.

S

Sales advertising *(p. 507)* Advertising in which the sales price dominates the ad.

Sales promotion *(p. 453)* Marketing activities that add value to the product for a limited period of time to stimulate consumer purchasing and dealer effectiveness.

Sampling *(p. 456)* Allowing the consumer to experience the product at no cost.

Sans serif *(p. 392)* A typeface that does not have the serif detail at the end of the strokes.

Scanner research *(p. 541)* Research that tracks consumer purchases and compares the marketing communication received by the consumer's household.

Script *(p. 369)* A written version of a radio or television commercial.

Search engine *(p. 274)* Internet services that locate information based on key words.

Search marketing *(p. 274)* Marketing communication strategies designed to aid consumers in their search for information.

Secondary research *(p. 42)* Information that already has been compiled and published.

Secondary research suppliers *(p. 158)* Research firms that gather and organize information around specific topic areas for other interested parties.

Segmenting *(p. 147)* Dividing the market into groups of people who have similar characteristics in certain key product-related areas.

Selective distortion *(p. 138)* The process of interpreting information in a way that is consistent with the person's existing opinion.

Selective distribution The use of more than one, but fewer than all, of the intermediaries who are willing to carry the company's product.

Selective exposure *(p. 138)* The ability to process only certain information and avoid other stimuli.

Selective perception *(p. 104)* The process of screening out information that doesn't interest us and retaining information that does.

Selective retention *(p. 138)* The process of remembering only a small portion of what you are exposed to.

Self-liquidator *(p. 458)* A type of mail premium that requires a payment sufficient to cover the cost of the item.

Selling premise *(p. 341)* The sales logic behind an advertising message.

Semicomps *(p. 396)* A layout drawn to size that depicts the art and display type; body copy is simply ruled in.

Semicontrolled media *(p. 487)* Media, such as the Internet, whose messages can be controlled by an organization in some ways, but that also contains totally uncontrolled messages.

Semiotic analysis *(p. 165)* A qualitative research method designed to uncover layers and types of meaning.

Serif *(p. 392)* Typeface in which the end of each stroke is finished off with a little flourish.

Set *(p. 408)* A constructed setting in which the action of a commercial takes place.

Share of audience *(p. 258)* The percent of viewers based on number of sets turned on.

Share of market *(p. 39)* The percentage of the total market in a product category that buys a particular brand.

Share of mind *(p. 336)* The extent to which a brand is well known in its category.

Share of voice *(p. 295)* One brand's percentage of advertising messages in a medium compared to all messages for that product or service.

Showings *(p. 229)* The percentage of the market population exposed to an outdoor board during a specific time.

SIC Code (See NAICS)

Signal *(p. 243)* A series of electrical impulses used to transmit radio and television broadcasting.

Silkscreen printing *(p. 403)* A printing process that uses a porous screen to transfer a stencil-like image.

Single-shot ads Ads that are designed to work alone rather than as part of an ongoing campaign.

Single-source research *(p. 541)* A test that is run after an ad campaign is introduced that shows a causal relationship between marketing communication and sales.

Situation analysis *(p. 42, 186, 484)* The first section in a campaign plan that summarizes all the relevant background information and research and analyzes its significance.

Skyscrapers *(p. 277)* Extra-long narrow ads that run down the right or left side of a Web site.

Slice-of-life format *(p. 345)* A type of problem-solution ad in which "typical people" talk about a common problem.

Slogans *(p. 363)* Frequently repeated phrases that provide continuity to an advertising campaign.

SMCR model *(p. 99)* A communication model that identifies the Source, Message, Channel, and Receiver.

Social class *(p. 129)* A way to categorize people on the basis of their values, attitudes, lifestyles, and behavior.

Social marketing *(p. 515)* Marketing with the good of society in mind.

Social responsibility *(p. 87)* A corporate philosophy based on ethical values.

Societal marketing concept *(p. 515)* A business philosophy that describes companies whose operations are based on the idea of socially responsible business.

Soft sell *(p. 6, 335)* An emotional message that uses mood, ambiguity, and suspense to create a response based on feelings and attitudes.

Sound effects *(p. 368)* Lifelike imitations of sounds.

Source *(p. 99)* The sender of a message, the advertiser.

Source credibility *(p. 114)* Belief in a message one hears from a source one finds most reliable.

Spam *(p. 281, 443)* Blasting millions of unsolicited e-mail ads.

Speaker's bureau *(p. 493)* A public relations tool that identifies a group of articulate people who can talk about an organization.

Specialty advertising *(p. 458)* Free gifts or rewards requiring no purchase and carrying a reminder advertising message.

Sponsorship (cause or event) *(p. 464)* An arrangement in which a company contributes to the expenses of a cause or event to increase the perceived value of the sponsor's brand in the mind of the consumer.

Sponsorship (television) *(p. 255)* An arrangement in which the advertiser produces both a television program and the accompanying commercials.

Spot announcements *(p. 257)* Ads shown during the breaks between programs.

Spot color *(p. 390)* The use of an accent color to call attention to an element in an ad layout.

Spot radio advertising *(p. 246)* A form of advertising in which an ad is placed with an individual station rather than through a network.

Stakeholders *(p. 23, 477)* Groups of people with a common interest who have a stake in a company and who can have an impact on its success.

Standard advertising unit (SAU) *(p. 215)* A standardized system of advertising sizes in newspapers.

Standardization *(p. 520)* In international advertising, the use of campaigns that vary little across different cultures.

Stereotyping *(p. 76)* The process of positioning a group of people in an unvarying pattern that lacks individuality and often reflects popular misconceptions.

Stock footage *(p. 405)* Previously recorded film, video, or still slides that are incorporated into a commercial.

Stop motion *(p. 408)* An animation technique in which inanimate objects are filmed one frame at a time, creating the illusion of movement.

Storyboard *(p. 377)* A series of frames sketched to illustrate how the story line will develop.

Strategic business unit (SBO) *(p. 182)* A division of a company focused on a line of products or all the offerings under a single brand name.

Strategic planning *(p. 181)* The process of determining objectives, deciding on strategies, and implementing the tactics.

Strategic research *(p. 157)* All research that leads to the creation of an ad.

Strategy *(p. 181)* The means by which an individual or business accomplishes objectives.

Streaming video *(p. 278)* Moving images transmitted online.

Structural analysis *(p. 349)* Developed by the Leo Burnett agency, this method evaluates the power of the narrative or story line, evaluates the strength of the product or claim, and considers how well the two aspects are integrated.

Subculture *(p. 129)* Groups of people that are similar in some way, usually characterized by age, values, language, or ethnic background.

Subheads *(p. 363)* Sectional headlines that are used to break up a mass of "gray" type in a large block of copy.

Subliminal message *(p. 81)* A message transmitted below the threshold of normal perception so that the receiver is not consciously aware of having viewed it.

Subscription TV *(p. 251)* Television service provided to people who sign up for it and pay a monthly fee.

Supplements *(p. 218)* Syndicated or local full-color advertising inserts that appear in newspapers throughout the week.

Suppliers *(p. 21)* Organizations, professionals, and specialized businesses that provide goods and services.

Support *(p. 341)* The proof, or substantiation needed to make a claim believable.

Survey research *(p. 168)* Research using structured interview forms that ask large numbers of people exactly the same questions.

Sweepstakes *(p. 456)* Contests that require only that the participant supply his or her name to participate in a random drawing.

SWOT analysis *(p. 42, 186, 484)* An analysis of a company or brand's strengths, weaknesses, opportunities, and threats.

Symbolic meaning *(p. 110)* Communication conveyed through association.

Syndication *(p. 246)* This is where local stations purchase television or radio shows that are reruns or original programs to fill open hours.

Synergy *(p. 544)* The principle that when all the pieces work together, the whole is greater than the sum of its parts.

T

Tabloid *(p. 215)* A newspaper with a page size five to six columns wide and 14 inches deep.

Tactic *(p. 181)* The specific techniques selected to reflect the strategy.

Taglines *(p. 363)* Clever phrases used at the end of an advertisement to summarize the ad's message.

Talent *(p. 376)* People who appear in television commercials.

Targeting, Target audience *(p. 147)* People who can be reached with a certain advertising medium and a particular message.

Target market *(p. 8, 148)* The market segment(s) to which the marketer wants to sell a product.

Teaser *(p. 336)* A message strategy that creates curiosity as the message unfolds in small pieces over time.

Telemarketing *(p. 438)* A type of marketing that uses the telephone to make a personal sales contact.

Test market *(p. 539)* A group used to test some elements of an ad or a media mix in two or more potential markets.

Testimonial *(p. 83)* See endorsement.

Theater of the mind *(p. 367)* In radio advertising, the story is visualized in the listener's imagintion.

Think-Feel-Do model *(p. 103)* A model of advertising effects that focuses on the cognitive, emotional, and behavioral responses to a message.

Thumbnail sketches *(p. 396)* Small preliminary sketches of various layout ideas.

Tie-ins *(p. 467)* A promotional tool that promotes two products together to increase both brands' visibility.

Tint blocks *(p. 400)* A screen process that creates shades of gray or colors in blocks.

Tip-ins *(p. 403)* Preprinted ads that are provided by the advertiser to be glued into the binding of a magazine.

Touch points *(p. 200)* The contact points where customers interact with the brand and receive brand messages.

Town hall forums *(p. 494)* Meetings within an organization as part of an internal marketing program to inform employees and encourage their support.

Tracking studies *(p. 537)* Studies that follow the purchase of a brand or the purchases of a specific consumer group over time.

Trade advertising *(p. 512)* A type of business-to-business advertising that targets members of the distribution channel.

Trade deal *(p. 462)* An arrangement in which the retailer agrees to give the manufacturer's product a special promotional effort in return for product discounts, goods, or cash.

Trade show *(p. 462)* A gathering of companies within a specific industry to display their products.

Trademark *(p. 35, 63)* When a brand name or brand mark is legally protected through registration with the Patent and Trademark Office of the Department of Commerce.

Traditional delivery *(p. 223)* Delivery of magazines to readers through newsstands or home delivery.

Traffic department *(p. 51)* People within an agency who are responsible for keeping track of project elements and keeping the work on deadline.

Trailers *(p. 262)* Advertisements shown in movie theaters before the feature.

Transformation *(p. 111)* Creating meaning for a brand that makes it a special product, one that is differentiated within its category by its image.

Two-step offer *(p. 427)* A message that is designed to gather leads, answer consumer questions, or set up appointments.

Typography *(p. 391)* The use of type both to convey words and to contribute aesthetically to the message.

U

Unaided recall or recognition *(p. 106)* When one can remember an idea all by oneself.

Unbundling media services *(p. 316)* Media departments that separate themselves from agencies becoming separate companies.

Uncontrolled media *(p. 487)* Media that include the press release, the press conference, and media tours.

Underlines *(p. 362)* Text used to elaborate on the idea in the headline and serve as a transition into the body copy.

Understanding A conscious mental effort to make sense of information.

Undifferentiated or market aggregation strategy *(p. 147)* A view of the market that assumes all consumers are basically the same.

Unduplicated audiences *(p. 298)* Different members of an audience exposed to a message in a particular time frame.

Unique selling proposition (USP) *(p. 341)* A benefit statement about a feature that is both unique to the product and important to the user.

Unjustified type *(p. 392)* A form of typesetting where the line endings on the right side of the column are allowed to fall where they will.

Usage *(p. 144)* Categorizing consumers in terms of how much of the product they buy.

V

Validity *(p. 171)* The research results actually measure what they say they measure.

Value added, value added media *(p. 315)* A marketing or advertising activity that makes a product—or a media buy—more valuable.

Values *(p. 128)* The source of norms; values are not tied to specific objects or behavior, are internal, and guide behavior.

Values and Lifestyle System (VALS) *(p. 141)* A research method that caegorizes people into lifestyle groups.

Vampire creative *(p. 349)* Big ideas that are so powerful that they are remembered but not the brand.

Veloxes (C-prints) *(p. 403)* High quality proofs from printing.

Vendors *(p. 16)* A group of service organizations that assist advertisers, ad agencies, and the media; also known as freelancers.

Vertical publications *(p. 221, 515)* Publications targeted at people working in the same industry.

Video News Releases (VNRs) *(p. 490)* Contain video footage that can be used during a television newscast.

Viral marketing *(p. 101, 344)* A strategy used primarily in Web marketing that trelies on consumers to pass on messages about a product.

Virtual research *(p. 173)* Measures the effectiveness of ads through interactive media.

Visualization *(p. 388)* Imagining what the finished copy will look like.

Voice-over *(p. 374)* A technique used in commercials in which an off-camera announcer talks about the on-camera scene.

W

Wants *(p. 108)* Motivations based on desires and feelings.

Wasted reach *(p. 261)* Advertising directed at a disinterested audience that is not in the targeted audience.

Wave analysis *(p. 539)* In research, a series of interviews conducted at different points in a campaign.

Web page Computer-generated information, usually sponsored by one company or institution, that provides information about the entity and is accessible via the Web.

Web site *(p. 274)* Sometimes called a "home page", this is the online presence of a person or organization.

Webcasting *(p. 244)* Radio transmitted through audio streaming over the Internet.

Webisodes *(p. 284)* Web advertisements that are similar to TV programs with a developing storyline.

Weighting *(p. 304)* In media planning decision criteria are used to determine the relative amount of budget allocated to each medium.

White space *(p. 395)* Areas in a layout that aren't used for type or art.

World Wide Web *(p. 271)* The structure of the information interface that operates behind the Internet.

Y

Your-name-here copy *(p. 359)* Pompous writing used in corporate communication that contains generic claims that do not differentiate the company.

Z

Zero-based planning The practice of analyzing the strengths and weaknesses of the various marketing communication tools and then matching them to the problem identified in the situation analysis.

Credits

Notes

CHAPTER 1

1 Anusree Mitra and John G. Lynch Jr., "Toward a Reconciliation of Market Power and Information Theories of Advertising Effects on Price Elasticity," *Journal of Consumer Research* 21 (March 1995): 44–59.

2 "Ad Age Special Report: Comestic Advertising Spending by Category," *Advertising Age* (June 23, 2003): S–14.

3 John Burnett and Sandra Moriarty, *Marketing Communications: An Integrated Approach,* (Upper Saddle River NJ: Prentice-Hall, 1998): 14.

4 Tom Duncan and Sandra Moriarty, *Driving Brand Value: Using Integrated Marketing to Manage Profitable Stakeholder Relationships,* (New York: McGraw-Hill, 1997).

CHAPTER 2

1 Peter D. Bennett, *Dictionary of Marketing Terms* (Chicago: American marketing Association, 1988): 115.

2 John Gapper, "Why nobody sells the car we really want," *Financial Times* (June 29, 2004): 15.

3 Joshua Kurlantzick, "Most Valuable Players," *Entrepreneur* (June 2003): 68–71.

4 Brian Steinberg and Suzanne Vranica, "Chief Seeks to Help Leo Burnett Get Its Groove Back," *The Wall Street Journal* (October 12, 2003): l2B.

5 Noreen O'Leary, "The Incredible Shrinking Account Exec," *Adweek* (May 26, 2003) 22.

6 Erin White, "Linking Agency Fees to Ad Success," *The Wall Street Journal* (March 29, 2004): B4.

7 Tom Duncan and Sandra Moriarty, *Driving Brand Value: Using Integrated Marketing to Manage Profiitable Stakeholder Relationships* (New York: McGraw-Hill, 1998).

8 Duncan & Moriarty, 1998.

CHAPTER 3

1 "Sound can be a trademark," *The London Times Law Report* (December 4, 2003):73.

2 Robert J. Posch Jr., "Trademark Protection for Internet Domain Names," *Direct Marketing* (July 1998): 63–65.

3 Barbara Martinez, "Gap Faces suit over Eyewear Used in Ad," *Wall Street Journal* (January 6, 1998): B10.

4 Rebecca Flass, "Done That," *Adweek* (April 22, 2002): 21.

5 Anne Cunningham, "Commonsense or Nonsense: Limiting First Amendment Protection of Commercial Speech,"

Proceedings of the American Academy of Advertising Conference, M.S. Shaw (ed.), (E. Lansing, MI: Michigan State University): 61–83.

6 Chris Adams, "Looser Lip for Food and Drug Companies?" *Wall Street Journal* (September 17, 2002): A4.

7 Doug McKenna, "Marketers Opt Out of Civil Society," *Boulder Daily Camera (*April 13, 2003): 38.

8 "Nike Vs Kasky: Case dismissed," *SriMedia report* (June 26, 2003). (www.srimedia.com/artman/publish/article-642.shtml; Wendy Melillo, "Ad Groups Back Nike In Supreme Court Brief," *Adweek* (March 3, 2003): 3; Adam M. Kanzer and Cynthia A. Williams, "The Future of Social Reporting Is on the Line," *Business Ethics,* 17:4 (Winter 2003); Roger Parloff, "Can we talk?," *Fortune* (September 2, 2002): 102–10.

9 "Letter to congress Explaining FTC'ls new Deception Policy," Advertising Compliance Service (Westport, CT: Meckler Publishing, November 21, 1983) and Ivan Preston, "A Review of the Literature on Advertising Regulation," in *Current Issues and Research in Advertising* (1983), James H. Leigh and Claude L. Martin, eds. (Ann Arbor: University of Michigan Press): 2–37.

10 Robert E. Wilkes and Jams B. Wilcox, "Recent FTC Actions: Implications for the Advertising Strategists," *Journal of Marketing* 38 (January 1974): 55–56.

11 Jack Neff, "Duracell Agrees to Modify Robo-War Duck Ad," *Advertising Age* (February 6, 2002) (http://www.adage.com/news.cms?newsid=339 81; Daniel Golden and Suzanne Vranica, "Duracell's duck Ad WilL Carry Disclaimer," *Wall Street Journal* (February 7, 2002): B7.

12 Tom McGhee, "Broomfield firm's penalty for ad: Drugs destroyed," *Denver Post* (April 18, 2002): 2C.

13 John J. Burnett, "Gays: Feelings about Advertising and Media Used," *Journal of Advertising Research* (January-February 2000): 75–86.

14 Stephen P. Durchslag, "Agency Liability Extends to False Advertising Claims," *Promo* (October 1992): 17.

15 Deborah Vence, "FDA seeks to clarify rules for pharma ads," *Marketing New* (March 3, 2003): 6.

16 Michael McCarthy, "Local ads stir up Utah controversy," *USA Today* (January 2, 2202): 7B.

17 Eli Pariser, MoveOn.org email (January 22, 2004).

18 Editorial, "Super Censored," *The Boulder Daily Camera* (January 30, 2004): 4B.

19 Robert Weller, "Breckenridge pulls ad campaign," *Boulder Sunday Camera* (September 8, 2002): 3B.

20 Roy F. Fox, "Hucksters Hook Captive Youngsters," *Mizzou* (Summer 2002): 22–27.

21 Lee Anne Peck, "Foolproof or Foolhardy? Ethical Theory in Beginning Reporting Texts," *Journalism & Mass Communication Educator* 58 (Winter 2004): 343–63.

22 Robert Weller, "Breckenridge pulls ad campaign," *Boulder Sunday Camera* (September 8, 2002): 3B

23 D. J. Ganahl, T. J. Prinsen, and S. B. Netzley, "A Content Analysis of Prime Time Commercials: A contextual Framework of Gender Representation," Broadcast Education Association, Las Vegas, NV (2001); M. R. Barner, "Sex-role stereotyping in FCC-mandated children's educational television," *Journal of Broadcasting & Electronic Media,* 43 (1999): 551–64; S. Coltrane and M. Adams, "Work-family imagery and gender stereotypes: Television and the Reproduction of difference," *Journal of Vocational Behavior* 50 (1997): 323–47.

24 Richard Linnert, "Take it like a man," *Advertising Age* (December 8, 2003): 40.

25 D. J. Ganahl, T. J. Prinsen, and S. B. Netzley, "A content Analysis of Prime time Commercials: A contextual Framework of Gender Representation," Broadcast Education Association, Las Vegas NV, (2001).

26 "Stereotypes of Women Persist in Ads," *Wall Street Journal* (October, 17, 2003): B4.

27 D. J. Ganahl, S. B. Netzley, William Hoon, and Kwangok Kim, "The Culture Clash in Television Commercials: Mainstreaming Black Stereotypes into Primetime Prototypes," unpublished manuscript, (2003).

28 Michelle Wirth Fellman, "Preventing Viagra's Fall," *Marketing News* (August 31. 1998): 1, 8.

29 Joan Voight, "Realistic or Offensive?" *Adweek* (September 2, 1003): 16–17.

30 Interview with Jean Kilbourne by Renee Montagne, NPR Morning Edition transcript (June 22, 2004).

31 Robert Gustafson, Mark Popovich, and Steven Thomsen, "The 'thin ideal'," *Marketing News* (March 15, 1999): 22.

32 Herbert Rotfeld, "Desires Versus the Reality of Self-Regulation," *Journal of Consumer*

Affairs 37 (Winter 2003): 424–27; Nanci Hellmich, "Weight-loss deception found ads for many of those pills, patches, creams, and wraps are grossly exaggerated," " *USA Today* (2002)

[33] Joe Morgan, "Barclays forced to withdraw 0% campaign by OFT," *The London Times* (November 19, 2003): 4M.

[34] Herbert J. Rotfeld and Kim B. Rotzoll, "Is Advertising Puffery Believed?" *Journal of Advertising* 9:3 (1980): 16–20, 45.

[35] Barry Newman, "Ad Ad Professor Huffs Against Puffs, but It's A Quixotic Enterprise," *Wall Street Journal* (January 24, 2003): A1; Ivan Preston, "A Problem Ignored: Dilution and Negation of consumer Information by Antifactual Content," *Journal of Consumer Affairs* 36 (Winter 2002): 263–83; Ivan Preston, "Dilution and Negation of Consumer Information by Antifactual Content: Proposals for Solutions," *Journal of Consumer Affairs* 37 (Summer 2003): 1–21.

[36] Stephanie Thompson, "Food fight: Kraft beats back critics," *Advertising Age* (January 20, 2003): 1, 37.

[37] Betsy Spethmann, "Tobacco's Two Tiers," *Promo Magazine* (January 2004): 24–28.

[38] Deborah Vence, "Match Game," *Marketing News* (November 11, 2002): 1, 11–12.

[39] Wendy Melillo, "FTC Reviews Ad Plans from Alcohol Clients," *Adweek* (May 26, 2003): 8.

[40] Christopher Lawton, "Lawsuits Allege Alcohol Makers Target Youths," *Wall Street Journal* (February 5, 2004): B1; Ira Teinowitz, "Marketers blast charges in alcohol suit," *Advertising Age* (December 1, 2003): 10.

[41] Chuck Ross and Ira Teinowitz, "Beer Ad Has Wide Underage Reach on MTV," *Advertising Age* (January 6, 1997): 4: Ira Teinowitz, "LFTC Governing of Beer Ads Expands to Miller, A-B," *Advertising Age* (April 7, 1997): 1, 50.

[42] Bill McInturff, "While Critics May Fret, Public Likes DTC Ads," *Advertising Age* (March 26, 2001): 24; David Goetzi, "Take a Heaping Spoon-ful," *Advertising Age* (November 6, 2000): 32; Angetta McQueen, "Watchdog Blames Ad Spending for High Drug Costs," *The Denver Post* (July 11, 2001): 4C.

[43] Gene R. Laczniak and Patrick E. Murphy, "Fostering Ethical Marketing Decisions," *Journal of Business Ethics* 10 (1991): 259–71.

[44] Carter McNamara, "Complete guide to Ethics Management: An Ethics Toolkit for Managers," Authenticity Consulting (http://www.managementhelp.org/ethics/ethxgde.htm), April 2004.

[45] "Public Rates Nursing as Most Honest and Ethical Profession," December 1, 2003 (www.gallup.com), April 2004.

[46] Peck, 2004.

CHAPTER 4

[1] Ennis Higgins, "Conversations with David Ogilvy," in *The Art of Writing Advertising* (Chicago: Advertising Publications, 1965).

[2] Simon London, "Choked by a data surfeit," *Financial Times* (January 29, 2004): 9.

[3] Thomas Barry and Daniel Howard, "A Review and Critique of the Hierarchy of Effects in Advertising," *International Journal of Advertising* (9:2, 1990): 429–35; Michael Ray, "Communication and the Hierarchy of Effects," in *New Models for Mass Communication Research,* P. Clarke, ed. (Beverly Hills, CA: Sage Publications, 1973): 147–75.

[4] Ivan Preston, "The Association Model of the Advertising Communication Process," *Journal of Advertising* 11:2 (1982): 3–14.

[5] "Stuart Elliott/In Advertising: Would You Trust Mini-me with Your Money." *New York Times Direct,* May 20, 2003, NYTimes.com.

[6] Walter Weir, "Another Look at Subliminal Facts," *Advertising Age* (October 15, 1984): 46.

[7] Dave Carpenter, "Hidden Messages are Back in Focus," *Rocky Mountain News* (September 17, 2000): 11G.

[8] Walter Shapiro, "Fear of subliminal advertising is irrational," *USA Today,* September 12, 2000 (www.usatoday.com/news/opinion/Shapiron/462.htm).

[9] "Subliminal Advertising," Advertising Law Resource Center: Advertising Compliance Service, JLCom Publishing, July 2004, (www.lawpublish.com/subliminal.html).

[10] David Stewart and David Furse, *Television Advertising: A Study of 1000 Commercials,* (Lexington, MA: Lexington Books, 1986).

[11] Jon D. Morris, Chongmoo Woo, James Geason, Jooyoung Kim, "The Power of Affect: Predicting Intention," *Journal of Advertising Research* (May/June 2002): 7–17.

[12] Russell I. Haley and Allan L. Baldinger, "The ARF Copy Research Validity Project," *Journal of Advertising Research*, (April/May 1991): 11–32.

[13] Ivan Preston, "The Association Model of the Advertising Communication Process," *Journal of Advertising* 3 (1982): 3–14; Ivan Preston and Esther Thorson, "Challenges to the Use of Hierarchy Models in Predicting Advertising Effectiveness," in *Proceedings of the 1983 American Academy of Advertising Conference,* Donald Jugenheimer, ed. (Lawrence KS: University of Kansas), 27–33.

[14] Bill Wells, "How advertising Works," speech to St. Louis AMA, September 17, 1986.

[15] Daniel J. O'Keefe, *Persuasion: Theory and Research,* (Newbury Park, CA: Sage, 1990), 17.

[16] Stuart Elliott, "HP Promotes High-Tech Recycling." *New York Times Direct,* July 29, 2003, NYTimes.com.

[17] Scott McCarthy, "You Free Flight To Maui is Hobbling the Airline Industry," *Wall Street Journal* (February 4, 2004): D1.

[18] Herbert Krugman, "The Impact of Television Advertising: Learning Without Involvement," *Public Opinion Quarterly*, (29:3, 1965): 349–56.

[19] John Rossiter, Larry Percy and Robert Donovan, "A Better Advertising Planning Grid," *Journal of Advertising Research* (October/November, 1991): 11–21. Also reprinted in Maureen FitzGerald & David Arnott, *Marketing Communications Classics,* (London: Thomson Learning, 2000): 84–97.

[20] Lee Bowman, "Drug ads can influence patients," *Daily Camera* (February 26, 2003): 11.

[21] John Philip Jones, *When Ads Work: New Proof that Advertising Triggers Sales* (New York: Lexington Books, 1995).

CHAPTER 5

[1] John Fetto, "One Size Doesn't Fit All: Today's Working Mothers Defy the Label 'Soccer Mom,'" *American Demographics* (May 2000): 44–45.

[2] Mary Sutler and Laurel Wentz, "U.S. Conexciones," *Advertising Age* (July 16, 2001): 14.

[3] Mindy Charski, "Old Navy to Tailor Message to Hispanics," *Adweek* (August 4, 2003): 9

[4] Jack Neff, Hillary Chura, "Buyer Cross Borders," *Advertising Age* (March 3, 2003): 54.

[5] Gary Silverman, "Hispanics in Tune with TV Advertising," *Financial Times* (March 4, 2004): 18.

[6] Joan Davis, "Blacks in Black and White," *PROMO* (August 2000): 37.

[7] Jennifer Lach, "The Color of Money," *American Demographics* (February 2000): 59–60.

[8] Arundhati Parmar, "Knowledge of Mature Market Pays Reward," *Marketing News* (April 28, 2003): 5–6.

[9] Thomas T. Semon, "Income Is Not Always Predictor of Spending," *Marketing News* (March 31, 2003): 6.

[10] Winston Fletcher, *A Glittering Haze* (Henley-on-Thames, UK: NTC, 1992).

[11] James W Peltier, John Schibrowsky, Don Schultz, and John Davis, "Interactive Psychographics: Cross-selling in the Banking Industry," *Journal of Advertising Research* March/April 2002): 7–22.

[12] Joseph T. Plummer, "The Concept and Application of Life-Style Segmentation," *Journal of Marketing* (January 1974): 34.

[13] David Lipke, "Head Trips," *American Demographics* (October 2000): 38–40.

[14] Yuri Kageyama, "The 'Cool Hunter' in Japan," *Boulder Daily Camera* (February 7, 2004): E1.

[15] Everett Rogers, *Diffusion of Innovations*, 3rd ed. (New York: The Free Press, 1983).

CHAPTER 6

[1] Karl Weiss, IMC Marketing Research course handout, University of Colorado, January 2001.

[2] "Analysis of a Commercial: OnStar and Batman," http://student.claytonstate.net/~csu11197/3901/project1/.

[3] Roger Wimmer and Joseph Dominick, *Mass Media Research*, 7th ed. (Belmont CA: Wadsworth/Thomson Learning, 2003).

[4] Weiss.

[5] Dennis W. Rook, "Out-Of-Focus." *Marketing Research* (Summer 2003): 10–15; Alison Stein Wellner, "The New Science of Focus Groups." *American Demographics* (March 2003): 29.

[6] Susan Mendelsohn, personal communication, December 20, 2003.

[7] Leigh Ann Steere, "Culture Club," *Print,* (March/April, 1999): 4–5.

[8] Shay Sayre, *Qualitative Methods for Marketplace Research* (Thousand Oaks: CA: Sage Publications, 2001), 31.

[9] Russell W. Belk, ed., *Highways and Buyways: Naturalistic Research from the Consumer Behavior Odyssey* (Provo, UT: Association for consumer Research, 1991).

[10] Sayre, 20.

[11] Thomas Davenport, Jeanne Harris, Ajay Kohli, "How Do They Know Their customers So Well?" *MIT Sloan Management Review* (Winter 2001): 63–72.

[12] Gerry Khermouch, "Consumers in the Mist," *Business Week* (February 26, 2001): 92–93; Alison Stein Wellner, "Research on a Shoestring," *American Demographics* (April 2001): 38–39.

[13] Wellner, "Research on a Shoestring."

[14] Roy S. Johnson, "Banking on Urban America," *Fortune* (March 2, 1998): 129–32.

[15] Emily Eakin, "Penetrating the Mind by Metaphor," February 23, 2002, NYTimes.com.

[16] Sandra Yin, "New or Me Too," *American Demographics* (September 2002): 28.

[17] Mendelsohn.

[18] Robin Couler, Gerald Zaltman, and Keith Coulter, "Interpreting Consumer Perceptions of Advertising: An Application of the Zaltman Metahor Elicitation Technique," *Journal of Advertising* 30: 4 (Winter 2001): 1–14; Emily Eakin, "Penetrating the Mind by Metaphor," February 23, 2002, NYTimes.com; Daniel Pink, "Metaphor Marketing," *Fast Company*, http://www.fastcompany.com/magazine/14/zaltman.html; HBS Division of Research, The Mind of the Market Laboratory, "ZMET," http://www.hbs.edu/mml/zmet.html.

[19] Catherine Arnold, "Hershey Research Sees Net Gain." *Marketing News* (November 25, 2002): 17.

[20] Paula Kephart, "Virtual Testing," *Marketing Tools* (June 1998).

CHAPTER 7

[1] "Comfort Zone," *Adweek* Special Planning Section (July 3, 1998): 31.

[2] Tom Duncan and Sandra Moriarty, *Driving Brand Value: Using Integrated Marketing to Manage Profitable Stakeholder Relationships*, (New York: McGraw-Hill, 1997).

[3] Research for R.O.I.; Communications Workshop, Chicago: DDB Needham (April 10, 1987).

[4] "What is Account Planning? (and what do account planners do exactly?)," Account Planning Group (APG) Web site, http://www.apg.org.uk

[5] Susan Mendelsohn, personal communication, January 8, 2004.

[6] Margaret Morrison, Tim Christy, Eric Haley, "The Integration of Account Planning In U.S. Advertising Agencies," Advertising Division, Association for Education in Journalism and Mass Communication, 2002 National Conference, Kansas City, MO.

[7] Laurie Freeman, "Planner 'Puts Clients in Touch With Soul of Brands,'" AdAge.com, February 8, 1999; http://www.adage.com/news.cms?newsID=34705.

[8] Jon Steel, *Truth, Lies and Advertising: The Art of Account Planning*, (New York: Wiley, 1998); "Tests ahead for account planning," *Advertising Age* (September 20, 1999): 36.

[9] Duncan and Moriarty.

CHAPTER 8

[1] Jon Fine, "Newspaper-industry Slide Worsens," *Advertising Age* (May 10, 2004): 59.

[2] James Poniewozik, "The People's Paper," *Time* (July 21, 2003): 49–50.

[3] Laurel Wentz and Mercedes Cardona, "Newspapers Turn to Hispanics," *Advertising Age* (January 5, 2004): 16.

[4] "Media," *2003 Marketing Fact Book* (July 7, 2003): 17.

[5] Kim Long, *The American Forecaster Almanac*, 1993 Business Edition.

[6] Magazine Reader Experience Study, Chicago: Northwestern University Media Management Center, www.mediamanagementcenter.org.

[7] Anne Marie Kerwin, "Magazines Blast Study Showing Reader Falloff," *Advertising Age* (March 8, 1999): 13, 55.

[8] Elizabeth H. Weise, "On-Line Magazines: Will Readers Still Want Them after the Novelty Wears Off," *The Marketing News* (January 29, 1996): 1, 14.

[9] Jonathan Asher, "Make the Most of Packaging Design Updates," *Marketing News* (September 18, 2000): 13.

[10] Cathy Frisinger, "Label Cuisine Remains an American Favorite," *The Tampa Tribune* (January 21, 2004): 3.

[11] Stuart Elliott, "Selling 'Nothing,'" March 16, 2004, NYTimes.com.

[12] "Media," *2003 Marketing Fact Book* (July 7, 2003): 17.

[13] *The Signage Sourcebook* (South Bend, IN: The Signage Foundation, 2003).

[14] Rebecca Gardyn, "Moving Targets," *American Demographics* (October 2000): 32–34.

[15] Almar Latour, "Amid High-Tech Turf Battles, Baby Bells Feel Heat on Cash Cow," *Wall Street Journal* (April 13, 2004): A1.

[16] Latour.

[17] Eugenia C. Daniels, "Critical Shift in Direction," *Advertising Age* (February 14, 2000): S12.

CHAPTER 9

[1] Leigh Gallagher, "Prairie Home Commercial," *Forbes* (August 6, 2001): 54–55.

[2] Beth Snyder, "Rolling Stone Radio Seeks New Revenue, Expands Mega Brand," *Advertising Age* (November 2, 1998): 40.

[3] Steve Jarius, "Marketing Issues Raised by LPFM Stations," *Marketing News* (August 28, 2000): 7.

[4] "Marketing Fact Book," special insert in *Marketing News* (July 15, 2004): 4.

[5] Joan Raymond, "Radio-Active," *American Demographics* (October 2000): 28–29.

[6] Alex Veiga, "Marketers Use Free CDs to Promote New Artists," *Daily Camera* (July 1, 2003): E1.

[7] Jonathan Karp, "Hey, You! How About Lunch?" *Wall Street Journal* (April 1, 2004): B1.

[8] Bob Garfield, "Why TV Can Only Get Better," *AARP Bulletin* (April 2004,): 10; John Consoli, "The Case of the Missing Young Male TV Viewers," *Adweek* (October 20, 2003): 7.

[9] Christopher Reynolds, "The Lost Demo," *Promo Magazine* (February, 2004): 16-17.

[10] Michael McCarthy, "Forecast: Public to Turn to Paid Media," *USA Today* (August 15, 2003): 12B.

[11] May Wong, "TiVo Views Clones as a Threat," *The Denver Post* (April 26, 2004): 2C; Eroc Taib, "'Cannot Imagine TV Without TiVo'," *The Denver Post* (March 22, 2004): 5C.

[12] Rudy Martzke, "Super bowl Ratings Edge Up," *USA Today*, (February 2, 2004): 1.

[13] Brooks Barnes, "Nielsen Postpones New York Launch of Rating System," *Wall Street Journal* (April 7, 2004): B3.

[14] [no author] "Is the End of the Ad Slump in Sight?" *Fortune* (January 12, 2004) p. 48.

[15] Alastair Ray, "Own-brand Broadcaster Tunes In," *Financial Times* (March 16, 2004) p. 10.

[16] Terry Lefton, "You Can't Zap these Ads," *The Industry Standard* (March 26, 2001): 54–55; James Poniewozik, "This Plug's For You," *Time* (June 18, 2001): 76–77.

[17] Ralph Atkins, BMW Says It Will Defy Downturn," *Financial Times* (March, 12, 2004): 12.

CHAPTER 10

[1] www.census.gov.

[2] Jefferson Graham, "For Google, Many Retailers Eagerly Jump Through Hoops," *USA Today* (February 5, 2004): 1.

[3] Dan Gillmore, "Blogs Getting Serious About Themselves," *Denver Post,* (April 26, 2004): 5C.

[4] Marcus Lillkvist, "Blogs are Growing Up; Ads on the sites are Taking off," *Business Plus* (March 22, 2004): 13.

[5] Suzanne Vranica, "U.S. Ad Spending Rose 6.1% in 2003," *Wall Street Journal* (March 9, 2004): B6.

[6] Lillkvist.

[7] Mylene Mangalindan, "Web Ads on the Rebound After a Multiyear Slump: Online Marketing Gets a Lift by Broadband, New Formats," (August 25, 2003): B1.

[8] Tobi Elkin, "Marketing Beyond the Pop-Up," *Advertising Age* (March 10, 2003): 4.

9 Jack Hitt, "Confessions of a Spam King," *New York Times Magazine*, September 28, 2003, NYTimes.com.

10 "New Beer Uses Pre-Launch Viral Email Vote to turn Consumers into Evangelists," June 24, 2003, www.MarketingSherpa.com.

11 Peter Fancese, "Media Blitzed," *American Demographics* (February, 2004): 40–41.

12 Pamela Paul, "Nouveau Niche," *American Demographics* (July/August 2003): 20–21.

13 Theresa Howard, "Brands Becoming Stars of the Show," *USA Today*, April 9, 2003, p. B1; Kate Macarthur, "Branded Entertainment, Marketing Tradition Tussle," *Advertising Age* (May 10, 2004): 6; Ruth Mortimer, "In the Picture: How Brands are Muscling in on Content," *Brand Strategy* (May 2003): 10–11.

14 Tobi Elkin, "Marketing Beyond the Pop-Up," *Advertising Age* (March 10, 2003): 4.

15 Brian Steinberg and Suzanne Vranica, "Burger King Seeks Some Web Heat," *Wall Street Journal* (April 15, 2004): B3.

16 Laura Rich, "That's Advertainmnet," *The Industry Standard* (June 25, 2001): 60–62.

17 Randall Rothenberg, "Ad of the Month," *Fast Company* (March 2003): 40.

18 "AmEx Plans Jerry Seinfeld-Meets-Superman Internet Show," *Advertising Age*, February 4, 2004, AdAge.com.

19 Kevin Delaney and Robert Guth, "Beep. Foosh. Buy Me. Pow." *Wall Street Journal*, (April 8, 2004): B1; Christopher Parkes, "Nielsen to Interact with Gaming Group," *Financial Times* (April 8, 2004): 24.

20 Richard Linnett. " Starcom's Play Targets Gamers," *Advertising Age* (June 9, 2003): 3. 62.

21 Delaney and Guth.

22 Pamela Paul.

23 Marcia Dunn, "The Space for Sale," *Sunday Camera* (October 14, 2001): 1DD.

24 Mark Harper, "Mobile Campaign Roots Around for Truth in Politics," *Daytona Beach News-Journal* (May 26, 2004): 3C.

CHAPTER 11

1 "Best Practice: Television Planning," *Admap* (June 2002): 11–12.

2 Hugh Cannon, John leckenby, Avery Abernethy, "Beyond Effective Frequency: Evaluating Media Schedules Using Frequency Value Planning," *Journal of Advertising Research* (November/December 2002): 33–47.

3 *Admap.*

4 Ian Brace and Louise Edwards, "Can Advertising Reach Everybody?" *Adweek* (July/August, 2002): 26–28.

5 "The Medium Shapes the Message," *Business 2.0* (July, 2003): 32.

6 Maura Clancey and Gale Metzger, "Building Survey-based, Media-mix Planning Tool," *Admap* (June 2002): 47–49.

7 Bradley Johnson, "Low CPM Can Spell Bargain for Buyers," *Advertising Age* (May 19, 2003): 10.

8 Hank Bernstein and Kate Lynch, "Media Scheduling and Carry-over Effects," *Admap* (October 2002): 40–42.

9 Kate Fitzgerald, "Trolling for Media Plan's Role," *Advertising Age Special Report* (March 3, 2003): S10-S12.

10 Claire Atkinson, "Coke Catapults Starcom MediaVest," *Advertising Age* (February 9, 2004): S6, S10.

11 Bradley Johnson, "Cracks in the foundation," *Advertising Age* (December 8, 2003): 1, 10.

12 Don E. Schultz, "Outdated Approach to Planning Needs Revamping," *Marketing News* (November 11, 2002).

13 Clancey and Metzger.

CHAPTER 12

1 A. Jerome Jewler and Bonnie L. Drewniany, *Creative Strategy in Advertising* (Belmont, CA: Wadsworth/ Thomson Learning, 2001), 3.

2 Jerri Moore and William D. Wells, *R.O.I. Guidebook: Planning for Relevance, Originality and Impact in Advertising and Other Marketing Communications* (New York: DDB Needham, 1991).

3 Alisa White, Bruce Smith, and Fuyuan Shen, "Rating creativity: Do advertising professionals and educators apply the same standards?" *Journal of Advertising Education,* 6:2 (Fall 2002): 37–46.

4 James Webb Young, *A Technique for Producing Ideas,* 3d ed. (Chicago: Crain Books, 1975).

5 John Eighmy, *The Creative Work Book* (Iowa City: University of Iowa, 1998), 1.

6 Thomas Russell and Glenn Verrill, *Kleppner's Advertising Procedure,* 14th ed. (Upper Saddle River, NJ: Prentice Hall, 2002), 457.

7 Linda Conway Correll, "Creative Aerobics: A Technique to Jump-Start Creativity," *Proceedings of the American Academy of Advertising Annual Conference,* Carole M. Macklin, ed. (Richmond, VA: AAA, 1997), 263–64.

8 Sheri J. Broyles, "The Creative Personality: Exploring Relations of Creativity and Openness to Experience." Unpublished doctoral dissertation, Southern Methodist University, Dallas, 1995

9 Broyles, "The Creative Personality."

10 A. Kendrick, D. Slayden, and S. J. Broyles, "Real Worlds and Ivory Towers: A Survey of Top Creative Directors," *Journalism and Mass Communication Educator* 51(2) (1996a): 63–74; A. Kendrick, D. Slayden, and S. J. Broyles, "The Role of Universities in Preparing Creatives: A Survey of Top U.S. Agency Creative Directors," in *Proceedings of the 1996 Conference of the American Academy of Advertising,* ed. G. B. Wilcox (Austin: University of Texas, 1996b): 100–106.

11 Graham Wallas, *The Art of Thought* (New York: Harcourt, Brace, 1926); Alex F. Osborn, *Applied Imagination,* 3d ed. (New York: Scribner's, 1963).

12 Sandra Moriarty and Brett Robbs, "Advertising," in *The Encyclopedia of Creativity,* Vol. 1 (San Diego, CA: Academic Press, 1999), 23–29.

13 William Wells, "How Advertising Works," speech to the St. Louis AMA, September 17, 1986.

14 Karen Lundegaard, "Buick Beats BMW: New Car Rankings," *Wall Street Journal* (March 9, 2004): D1.

15 Blythe Yee, "Ads Remind Women They Have Two Hands," *Wall Street Journal* (August 14, 2003): B5.

16 Jane Levere, "Celebrities Help Publicize National Parks, The New York Times Direct, August 5, 2003, NYTDirect@nytimes.com.

17 Stuart Elliott, "The Risky Business of 'Shockvertising,'" The New York Times Direct, February 10, 2004, NYTDirect@nytimes.com.

18 Rick Boyko, "Re-defining the ad," *one.a magazine* (Winter 2003):4–5.

19 Betsy Sharkey, "Super Angst," *Adweek* (January 24, 1993): 24–33.

CHAPTER 13

1 Yumiko Ono, "Some Times Ad Agencies Mangle English Deliberately," *Wall Street Journal* (November 4, 1997): B1

2 David Ogilvy, *Ogilvy on Advertising* (New York: Vintage, 1985).

3 Cynthia Crossen, "Clever Lines/Make Us Crave/Return to Days/Selling Burma-Shave," *Wall Street Journal* (August 20, 2003): 1A.

4 Sandra Dallas, "Road to Pave? Remember Burma-Shave!" *BusinessWeek* (December 30, 1996): 8; Frank Rowsome Jr., *The Verse by the Side of the Road* (New York: Dutton, 1965).

5 Paul D. Bolls and Robert F. Potter, "I Saw It on the Radio: The Effects of Imagery Evoking Radio Commercials on Listeners' Allocation of Attention and Attitude toward the Ad," *Proceedings of the Conference of the American Academy of Advertising,* Darrel D. Muehling, ed. (Lexington, KY, 1998), 123–30.

6 This was used with permission from the Radio Advertising Bureau in *Creative Advertising,* 2nd ed., Englewood Cliffs, NJ: Prentice-Hall (1991): 283.

7 Stuart Elliott, "'Everybody Eats' at an Italian-Food Chain," New York Times Direct, November 4, 2003, NYTDirect@nytimes.com.

8 Peter Hochstein, "Ten Rules for Making Better Radio Commercials," Ogilvy & Mather's *Viewpoint* (1981).

9 Adapted from A. Jerome Jewler and Bonnie Drewniany, *Creative Strategy in Advertising,* 7th ed. (Belmont CA: Wadsworth/Thomson): 177; A. Jerome Jewler, *Creative Strategy in Advertising* 4th ed. (Belmont, CA: Wadsworth, 1992), 164–65.

10 Adapted from John Burnett and Sandra Moriarty, *Marketing Communications: An Integrated Approach* (Upper Saddle River, NJ: Prentice-Hall, 1998), 296–97.

11 Blessie Miranda and Kuen-Hee Ju-Pak, "A Content Analysis of Banner Advertisements: Potential Motivating Features," Annual Conference Baltimore, AEJMC, August 1998.

CHAPTER 14

1 Sandra Dolbow, "Brand Builders," *Brandweek* (July 24, 2000): 19

2 Sandra Ernst Moriarty, *The ABCs of Typography*, 2nd ed. (Glenbrook, CT: Art Direction Book Company, 1996).

3 Noreen O'Leary, "Legibility Lost," *Adweek* (October 5, 1987): D7.

4 Stuart Elliott, "A Reader Asks," *The New York Times Direct,* March 9, 2004, NYTDirect @nytimes.com.

5 Charles Goldsmith, "Adding Special to Effects," *Wall Street Journal,* (February 26, 2003): B1.

6 Stuart Elliott, "JanSport Sings 'Do-Re-Mi' to Teens," The New York Times Direct, April 29, 2003, NYTDirect @nytimes.com.

7 Steve Jarius, "Marketing Issues Raised by LPFM Stations," *Marketing News* (August 28, 2000): 7.

CHAPTER 15

1 Lisa Spiller and Martin Baier, *Contemporary Direct Marketing,* (Upper Saddle River, NJ: Prentice Hall, 2004).

2 Pradeep K. Korgaonkar, Eric J. Karson, and Ishael Akaah, "Direct Marketing Advertising: The Assents, the Dissents, and the Ambivalents," *Journal of Advertising Research* (September/October 1997): 41–45.

3 Spiller and Baier, 44.

4 Matt Hasan, "Ensure success of CRM with a change in mindset," *Marketing News* (April 14, 2003): 16.

5 Daniel Lyons, "Games Dealers Play," *Forbes* (October 18, 1998): 132–34.

6 Stan Rapp and Tom Collins, *MaxiMarketing* (New York: McGraw-Hill, 1987).

7 Dean Rieck, "10 Basics for Writing Better Letters," *Direct Marketing* 3 (12) (April 2001): 52–53, 62.

8 Khozem Merchant, "Telesales called to account," *Financial Times,* (March 29, 2004): 20.

9 Jonathan D. Salant, "Rules require telemarketer identification," *Boulder Daily Camera* (January 29, 2004): 4E.

10 David Streitfeld, "Markters dialing before Oct. 1," *Boulder Sunday Camera* (August 24, 2003): F1.

11 Christine Tatum, "No-call lists force sellers to adjust," *The Denver Post* (January 25, 2004): 1K.

12 "Telemarketing Sales Rule Reaches Fifth Anniversary," *Direct Marketing* 64 (2) (June 2001): 8.

13 Stan Rapp and Tom Collins, *MaxiMarketing* (New York: McGraw-Hill, 1987).

14 Lance Arthur, "Clear cut lessons for effective E-mail," *Direct Marketing* 64 (1) (May 2001): 62–63.

15 "Targeting spammers," *Boulder Daily Camera* (December 26, 2003): 18A.

16 Dennis Berman, "Could Spam One day End Up Crushed Under Its own Weight?" (August 25, 2003): B1.

17 Fiona Harvey and Scott Morrison, "Amazon steps up fight against junk e-mail with legal action on 'spoofers" *Financial Times* (August 27, 2003): 1.

18 Clint Talbott, "'Spam king' didn't opt for this call," *Boulder Daily Camera* (January 30, 2004): 5B.

19 Janis Mara, "E-Mail Direct," *Adweek* (April 10, 2001): 116–17.

20 David McNickel, "Deeper, Closer, Faster, Smarter," *AdMedia* (April 2003): 36.

21 John Brown, "Taking the Stress out of International Direct Marketing," August 2003, http://www.the-dma.org/international/articles/.

CHAPTER 16

1 Russ Brown, "Sales Promotion," *Marketing & Media Decisions* (February 1990): 74.

2 Council of Sales Promotion Agencies, *Shaping the Future of Sales Promotion* (1990): 3.

3 2001 Annual Report, *Promo* (May 1, 2001), as reported in www.industryclick.com/magazinearticle.asp? magazinearticleid=99739&.

4 "Upward Bound," *Promo*, April 1, 2004, http://promomagazine.com/mag/marketing_upward_bound/index.html.

5 "Upward Bound."

6 "Upward Bound."

7 Dave Carpenter, "McDonald's unveils new game, but stock hits 10-year low," The Associated Press State & Local Wire (March 6, 2003), http://web.lexis-nexis.com/universe/document?_m=e0607584954c0d52b07aa058.

8 "Entertainment Marketing Awards: Who's Who," *Promo Special Reports,* May 1, 2001, www.industryclick.com/Microsites/Newsarticle.asp?newsarticleid=218986&srid=.

9 Matthew Kinsman, "The Last Stand," *Promo* (January 2001): 29–34.

10 Sam Walker, "The Bankers Behind the Woman," *Wall Street Journal* (May 23, 2003): W5.

11 Christine Tatum, "Firms more thoughtful in sponsoring of events," *Denver Post* (August 8, 2003): 4.

12 Emiko Terazono, "Ambush marketing tactics to be kicked into touch," *Financial Times* (September 2, 2003): 9.

13 "The Boomer Esiason foundation and Johnsonville Sausage Team Up for Monday Night Football, *PR Newswire,* September 4, 2003, http://prnewswire.com.

14 "Upward Bound".

15 Elizabeth Boston, "Heineken Aims to Nab 'Matrix' Ad Limelight," *Advertising Age* (May 26, 2003): 30.

16 Dan Hanover, "We Deliver," *Promo* (March 2001): 43–45.

17 Bob Tedeschi, "A Growing Ad Strategy: 'Click to Win!' " *New York Times,* August 21, 1998, www.nytimes.com/library/tech/98/08/cyber/articles/

18 "Walking the Tight Rope," *Promo* (March 2001): 48–49.

19 Samantha Critchell, "Bad girl biker look popular for fall," *Boulder Daily Camera* (August 28, 2003): 4D.

20 Jacques Chevron, "Branding and Promotion: Uneasy Co-habitation," *Brandweek* (September 14, 1998): 24.

21 Scott Hume, "Rallying to Brands' Rescue," *Advertising Age* (August 13, 1990): 3.

22 Jon Kramer, "It's Time to Tie the Knot with Promotion," *Integrated Marketing and Promotion* (September/October 1998): 77.

23 2001 Annual Report, *Promo*.

CHAPTER 17

1 www.prsa.org/pressroom/aboutpr.html.

2 Martin Sorrell, "Assessing the State of Public Relations," *The Strategist* 3(4) (Winter 1998): 48.

3 Doug Newsom, Alan Scott, and Judy Van Slyke Turk, *This Is PR: The Realities of Public Relations,* 4th ed. (Belmont, CA: Wadsworth, 1989), 99.

4 Claire Atkinson, "Rubenstein: PR maestro," *Advertising Age* (October 11, 2004): 46.

5 Jaqmes Lukaszewski, "Chief Integrity Officer is tailor-made for PR," *Odwyer's PR Services Report* (March 2004): 8.

6 Tom Duncan and Sandra Moriarty, *Driving Brand Value* (New York: McGraw-Hill, 1997).

7 Lukaszewski.

8 Kirk Hallahan, "No, Virginia, It's Not True What They Say about Publicity's 'Implied Third-Party Endorsement' Effect," Association for Education in Journalism and Mass Communication Annual Conference, August 1998, Baltimore, MD, 13.

9 Thomas L. Harris, *Value-Added Public Relations: The Secret Weapon of Integrated Marketing* (Lincolnwood, IL: NTC Business Books, 1998).

10 Sandra Moriarty, "IMC Needs PR's Stakeholder Focus," *AMA Marketing News* (May 26, 1997): 7

11 Fraser P. Seitel, *The Practice of Public Relations,* 9th ed. (Upper Saddle River, NJ: Prentice Hall, 2003), 115.

12 Prema Nakra, "Corporate Reputation Management: 'CRM' with a Strategic Twist?" *Public Relations Quarterly* 45(2) (Summer 2000): 35.

13 Barbara Palframan-Smith, "Employee Connection," *Communication World* (March–April 2004): 7.

14 Bernard Charkand, ""How Can Communicators Bridge the Gap Between Executives and Employees: Australia," *Communication World* (March–April 2004): 12.

15 Erwin Bettinghaus and Michael Cody, *Persuasive Communication,* 5th ed. (Fort Worth: Harcourt Brace, 1994), 7.

16 Tamara Gillis, "In Times of Change, Employee Communication Is Vital to Successful Organizations," *Communication World* (March-April 2004): 8.

17 E.W. Brody,"Have Made the Transition? Are You Practicing Public Relations In the 21st Century Rather Than the 20th?" *Public Relations Quarterly* (Spring 2004): 7–9.

18 Claire Atkinson, "PR Firms Praise Janet Jackson Breast Stunt," AdAge.com, February 9,

2004, http://www.adage.com/ news.coms?newsid=39756.

[19] Harris.

[20] Alyse R. Gotthoffer, "Exploring the Relevance of Localization in Anti-Drinking and Driving PSAs," in *The Proceedings of the American Academy of Advertising Conference,* Darrel D. Muehling, ed. (Lexington, KY: AAA, 1998), 214.

[21] Edward A. Faruolo, "A Business of Caring," *The Advertiser* (October 1998): 36–40.

[22] Thomas Harris, "iPod, Therefore iAm," *ViewsLetter* (September 2004): 3.

[23] Kathy Cripps, "PR is more than just media," letter to editor, *Advertising Age* (Ocotber 11, 2004): 24.

[24] Andrea Tanner, "Communicating Health Information and Making the News," *Public Relations Quarterly* (Spring 2004): 24–27.

[25] Carole Howard, "Working With Reporters: Mastering the Fundamentals To Build Long-Term Relationships," *Public Relations Quarterly* (Spring 2004): 36.

[26] Fraser P. Seitel, "E-mail news releases," *O'Dwyer's PR Wservices Report* (March 2004): 37.

[27] Anne R. Owen, "Avant-Garde or Passé: Using Video News Releases Internationally," in *The Proceedings of the American Academy of Advertising Conference,* Carole M. Macklin, ed. (St. Louis: AAA, 1997), 290.

[28] Brody, 7–9.

[29] Ben Tyson Sativa Ross, Steve Broderick, Susan Westa, "Getting Viewers to Your Website: A Study of direct Mail CD-Rom Effectiveness," *Public Relations Quarterly* (Sring 2004): 18–23.

[30] Marcia Xenitelis, "How Can Communicators Bridge the Gap Between Executives and Employees: Australia," *Communication World* (March–April 2004): 7.

[31] Seitel, *The Practice of Public Relations,* 441.

[32] Candace White and Niranjan Raman, "The World Wide Web as a Public Relations Medium," Association for Education in Journalism and Mass Communication Annual Conference, Baltimore, MD, August 1998.

[33] Michelle O'Malley and Tracy Irani, "Public Relations and the Web: Measuring the Effect of Interactivity, Information, and Access to Information in Websites," AEJMC Conference, Baltimore, MD, August 1998.

[34] Seitel, *The Practice of Public Relations,* 447.

[35] Jill Whalen, "Online Public Relations," *High Rankings Advisor,* Issue 109, August 18, 2004 (http://www.highrankings.com/issue109.htm)

[36] Michael Markowitz, "Fighting Cyber Sabotage," *Bergen Record* (October 4, 1998); retrieved online at www.bergen.com/biz/ online04199810041.htm.

[37] James E. Grunig, *Excellence in Public Relations and Communication Management* (Hillsdale, NJ: Erlbaum, 1992).

[38] Kimberly Gill, "Searching for Excellence in Public Relations," Association for Education in Journalism and Mass Communication Annual Conference, Public Relations Division, Baltimore, MD, August 1998.

CHAPTER 18

[1] Stuart Elliott, "Luring Customers With Bait From the Future," *New York Times,* September 9, 2003, NYTDirect@nytimes.com.

[2] Jerome Jeweler and Bonnie L. Drewniany, *Creative Strategy in Advertising,* 7th ed. (Belmont, CA: Wadsworth, 2001), 240–44.

[3] Lorri Grant, "Retailers take a novel approach to advertising," *Salt Lake Tribune* (June 22, 2003): E2.

[4] John A. Koten, "The Strategic Uses of Corporate Philanthropy," in the *Handbook of Strategic Public Relations and Integrated Communications,* Clarke L. Caywood, ed. (New York: McGraw-Hill, 1997), 149.

[5] "1999 Midsize Agency of the Year: Cone," *Inside PR* (Winter 1999): 11.

[6] Tom Duncan and Sandra Moriarty, *Driving Brand Value: Using Integrated Marketing to Manage Profitable Stakeholder Relationships* (New York: McGraw-Hill, 1997), 1997.

[7] Nick Chiarelli, "Has the global consumer changed?" *Admap* (May 2003): 29–31.

[8] Theodore Levitt, "The Globalization of Markets," *Harvard Business Review* (May–June 1983): S8–S9.

[9] Philip Kotler, *Marketing Management,* 6th ed. (Englewood Cliffs, NJ: Prentice-Hall, 1988).

[10] Morgen Witzel, The quantifier of culture," *Financial Times* (August 26, 2003): 7.

[11] Chiarelli, 29–31.

[12] P&G External Relations Department and Jack Neff, "P&G Flexes Muscle for Global Branding," *Advertising Age* (June 3, 2002): 53.

[13] Warren Keegan and Mark Green, *Global Marketing,* 3rd ed. (Upper Saddle River NJ: Prentice Hall), 524–25.

[14] Barbara Mueller, *Dynamics of International Advertising* (New York: Peter Lang, 2004).

[15] Geoffrey Fowler, "China Cracks Down on Commercials," *Wall Street Journal* (February 19, 2004): B7.

[16] Edward Hall, *Beyond Culture* (Garden City, NY: Anchor Press/Doubleday, 1976).

[17] Colin Grimshaw, "Why Global Firms Need Local Media," *Marketing* (May 15, 2003): 27.

[18] Geoffrey Fowler, "China's Edgey Advertising," *Wall Street Journal* (October 27, 2003): B1.

[19] Michael Solomon, *Conquering Consumerspace: Marketing Strategies for a Branded World* (New York: American Management Association, 2003); Arundhati Parmar, Global youth united," *Marketing News* (October 26, 2002): 1, 49.

[20] Ibid.

[21] Katherine Frith and Barbara Mueller, *Advertising and Societies: Global Issues* (New York: Peter Lang, 2002).

[22] Andreas Grein and Stephen Gould, "Globally Integrated Marketing Communications," *Journal of Marketing Communications* (2: 1996): 141–58.

[23] Tim Burt, "Veteran leads MTV's attack," *Financial Times* (August 12, 2003): 6.

CHAPTER 19

[1] David Brandt and Dave Walker, "Copy Testing Under the Gun?" *Ipsos Ideas* (August/September, 2003): 3.

[2] Tim Huberty, "Who's Who in Ad Copytesting," *Quirk's Marketing Research Review* (March 2002), www.quirks.com.

[3] Charles E. Young, "Capturing the Flow of Emotion in Television Commercials: A new Approach," *Journal of Advertising Research* (June 2004): 202–09; Chuck Young and John Kastenholz, "Emotion in TV ads," *Admap* (January 2004): 40–42.

[4] John Philip Jones, *When Ads Work: New Proof That Advertising Triggers Sales* (New York: Lexington Books, 1995).

[5] Erwin Ephron, "Media Audit's time is Come," *Advertising Age* (September 2, 2002): 16.

[6] Richard Linnett, "Nissan Seeks Media Audit for $1B Acc't," *Advertising Age* (January 5, 2004): 1. 24; Jack Feuer, "P&G Looks Outside For Media Auditing," *Adweek* (May 26, 2003): 6.

[7] Julie Zdziarski, "Evaluating Sponsorships," *Promo* (March 2001): 92–93.

[8] Ibid.

[9] Jeff Miller, "Media measurement: it's more than looking at ROI," *O'Dwyer's PR Services Report* (March 2004): 13.

[10] Ibid.

[11] Peter Vogt, "Awareness to Action," *Communication World* (March–April 2004): 22–26.

[12] Jones, 1995.

[13] Tom Duncan and Sandra Moriarty, *Driving Brand Value: Using Integrated Marketing to Manage Profitable Stakeholder Relationships* (New York: McGraw-Hill, 1997).

[14] Lynn G. Coleman, "The Crunch Has Come," *Marketing News* (March 4, 1991): 16.

[15] Warren Keegan and Mark Green, *Global Marketing,* 3rd ed. (Upper Saddle River, NJ: Prentice Hall, 2003), 241.

Index

A

AAAA. *See* American Association of Advertising Agencies
ABC. *See* Auditing Bureau of Circulations (ABC)
Accountability, 7
"Accountability Era," in advertising history, 21
Account executives, 50
Account management department, 49
Account managers, 195
Account planners, 199
Account planning, 50, 194–199
Account Planning Group (APG), 197
Ackerman McQueen, 156
Acquired needs, 138
Action, in direct marketing, 425
Actors, in television commercials, 376
Ad agencies. *See* Advertising agencies
Ad allowances, 507
Ad copy. *See* Copy; Copywriting
Ad Council, 475–477, 499
Added value, 35–36
Adese, 360
Adoption, 144
Adaptation advertising strategy, 520
Ad spending
    by medium, 211
    newspaper, 217
Advertainment, 282
Advertisers
    in direct marketing, 432
    as players, 11–13
    self-regulation of, 72–75
Advertising. *See also specific types*
    as communication, 99–102
    comparative, 74, 81–83
    corporate, 488–489
    corrective, 69
    current issues in, 21–24
    deceptive, 66–69, 80–81
    defining, 5
    effectiveness. *see* Effectiveness
    evolution of, 21
    false, 80–81
    functions of, 10, 18
    indirect, 71
    key concepts of, 5–6
    manipulative, 81
    media review of, 72

    offensive, 59–60, 75–76, 90
    players in, 10–17
    process, 13
    promotions and, 469–470
    as PR tool, 487–489
    vs. public relations, 478, 480
    roles of, 6–10, 18, 61–62
    societal role of, 61–62
    strengths of, 8
    subliminal, 106, 107
    timeline, 22–24
    types of, 17–18
Advertising agencies
    as advertising players, 13–15
    in direct marketing, 433
    in-house, 14–15
    legal responsibility of, 69
    organization of, 49–51
    professional ethics of, 87–88
    revenues of, 51
    top, 47
    types of, 47–49
    working with, 45, 47
Advertising and Marketing Effectiveness (AME) awards, 20
Advertising audits, 165
Advertising campaigns. *See also specific types*
    continuity of, 307–308
    duration of, 306–307
    evaluation of. *see* Evaluation
Advertising communication model, 99–102
Advertising departments, 13–14
Advertising executions, 6
Advertising expenditures, newspaper, 217
Advertising planning, 184
    research methods used in, 165–172
    strategic, 179–202
    uses of research in, 162–165
    see also Strategic planning
Advertising plans, 184, 185
Advertising regulations, 62–71
Advertising research. *See* Research
Advertising Review Council (ARC), 72, 73
Advertising review process, 72–75
Advertising ROI, 182, 543
Advertising strategies. *See* Strategies
Adweek, list of losers, 59–60, 90
AdWords, 529

AFA. *See* American Family Association (AFA)
Affective responses, 109–110
Affiliates, 251
AFLAC, 122–123
African Americans, 133
Age, 131–132
Agency-of-record (AoR), 14, 45
"Age of Print," in advertising history, 21
Agricultural advertising, 513
AIG, 513
AIDA model (attention, interest, desire, action), 102–103
Aided recognition, 106, 540
AIG, 513
Alcohol advertising, 85
Ali, Ryan, 89
All caps, layout, 392
All-you-can-afford budgeting, 194
Alternative media, 282–286
AMA. *See* American Marketing Association (AMA)
Amazon.com, 271–273, 456
Ambush marketing, 464–465
AME awards, 20
American Airlines, 467
American Association of Advertising Agencies, code of standards, 87
American Express, 284
American Family Association (AFA), 93
American Marketing Association (AMA), 31
Ameritest, 534
AM/FM stations, 243
Analogies, 330
Anderson, Cheri L., 143
Animation, 408
Announcers, 376
Annual reports, 492–493
Answer prints, 410
Antidrug ads, 118–119
Aperture concept, 293
APG. *See* Account Planning Group (APG)
Appeals, 340–341
Apple Computer, 4, 11, 12, 209–210, 235
Arbitron, 247, 248, 295
ARC. *See* Advertising Review Council (ARC)
Archipelago Exchange, 291–292, 301, 317–318
Arguments, 114
Arm & Hammer, 546

Army, U.S., 164
Arnold Worldwide, 3–4, 9, 13, 100
Arrangers, 407
ARS, 534
Art direction
    print, 389–398
    television, 404–406
Art directors, 331, 387–388, 407
Artifact creation, 171
Art reproduction, 400–401
Association, 108, 110–113
Association message strategy, 342, 344
Association networks, 113
Attention, 105
Attitudes, 114, 139
Attitude tests, 538–539
Attorneys General, 70
Attributes, 338
Audience
    Internet, 278–279
    magazine, 221
    measuring cost of, 305–306
    newspaper, 218–219
    television, 257–259
    unduplicated, 298
    see also Target audiences
Audience exposure, 542–543
Audio advertising, 249
    see also radio
Audio aspect, of television commercials,
    374
Audio directors, 410
Audiometers, 257
Auditing Bureau of Circulations (ABC),
    218
Average frequency, 299
Award shows, 20–21
Awareness, 105–106

B

B2B. See Business-to-business (B2B)
    advertising
B2B ad networks, 275
Baby Busters, 149
Backgrounding, 186
Background research, 165–166
Back translation, of ad copy, 381
Balance, in layout design, 395
Banner ads, 277, 278, 378, 380, 412
Barriers to purchase, 187
Batelle & Batelle, 426
BATF. See Bureau of Alcohol, Tobacco,
    and Firearms (BATF)
BBB. See Better Business Bureau
    (BBB)
BDI. See Brand development index (BD)
Beauty ads, 383
Beck, Heather, 309
Beer industry, 85
Behavior. See Consumer behavior

Behavioral influences, on consumer deci-
    sions, 144–145
Behavioral response, 116–118
Behavioral segmentation, 148
BellSouth, 377
"Be More" campaign, 405
Benchmarking, 189, 484
Benefits, 341
Benefit segmentation, 148
Benetton, 60
Best Buy, 494, 505
Best Western International, 170
Better Business Bureau (BBB), 74–75
Big Idea, 327–329, 334, 376, 486
    see also Creative strategies
Billboards, 228–229, 365–367, 399–400,
    418
Bindings, 403
Bind-ins, 440
Bleed pages, 224
Blimps, 465
Blind headlines, 363
Blogs, 276
Blow-ins, 440
BMW, 21–22, 284, 288
Body copy, 360, 361, 364–365
Body images, 79
Bonuses, 462
Books, 493
Bottom-up creativity, 522–523
Boycotts, 92–93
Brag-and-boast copy, 360
Brainstorming, 333
Brand advertising, 17
Brand affiliation, 205
Brand awareness, 381, 458
Brand building, 468
Brand communication, 111, 113
Brand development index (BDI), 303
Branded entertainment, 282
Brand equity, 35
Brand experiences, Web-based, 283
Brand identity, 111
Brand image, 33, 113
Brand information, 162
Branding, 33–35, 36, 39, 191, 204–205,
    342–344
Brand integrity, 419
Brand loyalty, 113, 114–115
Brand management, 37
Brand marks, 35
Brand names, 35
Brand personality, 113, 205
Brand promise, 113
Brand reminders, 460
Brands, 33
    defined, 8
    evoked set of, 146
    global, 52, 519, 523–524
    identifying problems with, 187
    local, 52

positioning, 113, 191–193, 204
power of, 176–177
regional, 52
researching, 165
transformation of, 111
Brand-tracking framework, 539
Breakeven analysis, 546–547
Breakthrough advertising, 323
Breckenridge Ski Resort, 76
Brewer, John, 495
Broadband, 254
Broadcast media, 241–265
    direct-response advertising and,
        440–442
    films, 262–263
    production of, 407–410
    product placements, 263
    radio, 243–249
    television, 249–262
    using effectively, 263–264
Broadsheet newspapers, 215
Broadsheets, 436
Brochures, 367
Brown Sugar and Honey sausages, 457
Bryn, Steve, 529
Budget cuts, 309
Budgeting, 193–194, 304, 308, 525
Bulletins, 228
Bureau of Alcohol, Tobacco, and Firearms
    (BATF), 70
Burelle's Information Services, 497–498
Burger King, 283, 467, 470
Business plans, 182–183
Business publications, 514–515
Business reply cards (BRCs), 423
Business-to-business (B2B) advertising,
    17–18, 510–515
    creating, 513–514
    decision making in, 146–147
    evaluation of, 549
    media for, 514–515
    objectives, 514
    types of, 510–513
Business-to-business (B2B) buyers, 513
Business-to-business markets, 39–41
Butler, John W., Jr., 536
Buying allowances, 463
Buzz, 22, 344

C

Cable television, 251–252
CAC. See Cinema Advertising Council
    (CAC)
California Avocados, 112
Call centers, 174, 438, 439
Call-outs, 361
Call to action, 253, 344, 361, 365, 369
Calvin Klein, 59–60
Campaign plans, 185, 544–549
Campaigns. See Advertising campaigns

Capital campaigns, 518
Capital letters, 392
Captions, 361, 363
Car industry, 406
CARU. *See* Children's Advertising Review Unit (CARU)
Casting, 376
Catalogs, 437–438, 439
Category development index (CDI), 303
"Cat Herders" commercial, 404–405, 408, 410
Cause marketing, 481, 516
CDI. *See* Category development index (CDI)
CDs, 493
CDW, 511
Cease-and-desist orders, 68–69
Celebrity endorsements, 342, 345, 376
Celestial Seasonings, 43
Cell phones, 284–285
Centrally conceived campaigns, 522
Change-agent programs, 485
Channel advertising, 512
Channel markets, 39–41
Channels, media, 15–16
Channels of distribution, 39, 42
Character types, 376
Charles Schwab, 467
Chat rooms, 275–276
Cheesecake strategy, 77
Chick-fil-A, 94, 204–205, 321–322, 418, 554–555
"Child Hunger" campaign, 475–477, 499
Children, ads targeting, 79–80
Children's Advertising Review Unit (CARU), 80
Children's Television Advertising Practice Act, 80
Choice Hotels, 135–137
Cigarette advertising, 84–85
Cinema Advertising Council (CAC), 262
Circulation, 212, 215–216
    controlled, 223
    magazine, 224–225
Citibank Visa, 467
Citizens Bank, 179–181, 184, 187, 188, 189–190, 201
Claims, 80–81, 338, 340
Claim substantiation, 67–68
Clarion Marketing, 451–453
Classified ads, 217
Claymation, 408
Click art, 412
Click-throughs, 279
Client information, 294
Clip art, 388
Closings, 364–365
Clutter, 101
Clutter reels, 537
Co-branding, 467
Coca-Cola, 147–148

Code of standards, 87–88
Coffee Rush, 366
"Cog" commercial, 411
Cognition, 106–109
Cognitive dissonance, 139
Cognitive learning, 108
Coincidental surveys, 537
Cold-calling, 438
Collateral materials, 367, 493
Color, use of in print ads, 390–391, 400
Color reproduction, 400–401
Color separation process, 401, 402
Co-marketing, 466–467
Comcast, 15
Commercial Closet, 76–77
Commercials. *See* Television commercials
Commercial speech, 64–65
Commissions, 51
Commonalities, 162
Communication
    advertising as, 99–102
    cross-cultural, 172
    data-driven, 430–431
    two-way, 173
    visual, 386–389
    wireless, 284–285
    see also Marketing communications
Communication audits, 483–484
Communication briefs, 198–199
Communication exchange, 33
Communication model, 99, 99–102
Communications planning, 319–320
Comparative advertising, 74, 81–83
Comparisons, 345
Competitive advantage, 190
Competitive advertising, 295
Competitive analysis, 165
Competitive budgets, 194
Compiled lists, 430
Composers, 407
Comprehensives, 396
Computer graphics, 405
Computer optimization modeling, 305
Concept testing, 165, 536–537
Concurrent research, 534
Concurrent testing, 537–540
Conditioned learning, 108, 110–111
Connection planning, 207
Consent decrees, 68
Consumer activist groups, 75
Consumer attitudes, 304
Consumer behavior
    decision process and, 145–147
    influences on, 127–145
    sales promotions and, 454
    understanding, 126–127
Consumer boycotts, 92–93
Consumer diaries, 539
Consumer information, 297
Consumer insight, 194, 195–198
Consumer insight research, 162–163

Consumer magazines, 221
Consumer markets, 39–41
Consumer promotions, 455–460
    types of, 455–458
    using, 458–460
Consumer redress, 69
Consumer research, 157, 166–171, 195
Consumer responses
    to advertising, 102–120, 188
    affective/emotional, 109–110
    association, 110–113
    behavioral, 116–118
    cognition, 106–109
    perception, 104–106
    persuasion, 113–116
Consumers
    categorizing, 127
    defined, 127
    understanding, 101
    ways to contact, 166
    see also Customers
Consumer to business (C to B), 288
Consumption patterns, 303
CONTAC 600 SR, 523, 524
Contact points, 200
Content analysis, 165
Contests, 456, 462, 465
Continuity, of advertising, 307–308
Continuity programs, 466
Continuous strategy, 307
Controlled circulation, 223
Controlled media, 427, 487, 488
Convergence, 285
Conviction, 114, 341–342
Cookies, 273
Cool hunters, 143
Cooperative (co-op) advertising, 44, 217, 463, 506–507
Copy
    body copy, 360, 361, 364–365
    effective, 358–360
    see also Copywriting
Copycat advertising, 64, 327–328
Copyright protection, 63–64
Copy testing, 165, 350, 535–542
Copy-testing services, 534–535
Copywriters, 331, 357–358, 407
Copywriting, 355–382
    in global environment, 380–381
    overview of, 357–360
    for print, 360–367
    for radio, 367–369
    retail ads, 507–509
    techniques, 363–365
    for television, 371–378
    tools of, 361, 368, 374, 376
    for the Web, 378–380
    writing styles, 358–360
Core values, 128
Corporate advertising, 488–489
Corporate culture, 129

Corporate identity advertising, 489
Corporate images, 488–489
Corporate relations, 482
Corporate reputation management, 482
Corrective advertising, 69
Cost per point (CPP), 305–306
Cost per thousand (CPM), 305–306
Coupons, 456, 458, 466
Coverage, radio, 247
C-prints, 403
Crain, Rance, 1
"Crave" campaign, 151
Crawl, 405
Creative advertising, 327–350
    Big Idea and, 327–329
    effectiveness and, 327–330
    strategies, 334–350
Creative aerobics, 330–331
Creative Black Book, 234
Creative boutiques, 49
Creative briefs, 198–199, 345–348
Creative concepts, 6, 327–329
Creative development department, 49
Creative leap, 329–330
Creative people, 331–332
Creative process, 332–333
Creative strategies, 334–345
    approaches to, 344–345
    attention-getting, 336–337
    branding, 342–344
    calls to action, 344
    for cognition, 338–340
    emotional, 340
    evaluating, 349–350
    facets of, 336–345
    global, 348–349
    persuasion, 340–342
    planning and managing, 345–350
    in public relations, 486
    see also Message strategies
Creative thinking, 330–331
Creativity, 7
    bottom-up, 522–523
    media planning and, 207
Credibility, 480
Crest Whitestrips, 197
Crisis management, 482
CRM. See Customer relationship management (CRM)
Cultural imperialism, 62
Cultural influences
    on consumer decisions, 128–135
    international advertising, 521–522
Culture-orientation approach, 521
Customary pricing, 45
Customer-centric enterprises, 431
Customer information, 272–274
Customer maintenance, 427
Customer relationship management (CRM), 53, 432

Customers
    defined, 127
    focusing on needs of, 31–32
    as players in direct marketing, 433, 435
    see also Consumers
Cut, 407
Cutouts, 228

D

Dailies, 410
Database marketing, 428–432
Databases, 428
Data-driven communication, 430–431
David Letterman Show, 297, 298–299
Dayparts, 247
DDB Needham, 187
Dealer kits, 461
Dealer loaders, 462–463
Dealer tags, 508
Debossing, 403
Deceptive advertising, 66–69, 80–81
DeGrasse, Tammie, 50
Delahaye Medialink Model, 498
Delayed effects, 109
Dell Computer, 32
Demand creation, 61
Demographics, 131–135
Demographic segmentation, 148
Demonstrations, 83, 344
Denver Rescue Mission, 436, 437
Designated marketing area (DMA), 297
Design personas, 167
Design principles, for print ads, 395–396
Desktop publishing, 403
Developmental research, 533
Diagnostic research, 534
Diaries, 170
Die-cutting, 403
Differentiation, 42, 108, 338
Digital video recorders (DVRs), 254–255
Digitization, of images, 403
Direct-action headlines, 362
Direction, in layout design, 395
Direct mail, 435–437
Direct-mail lists, 429–430
Direct-marketing agencies, 433
Direct marketing (DM), 44, 423–445
    advantages and disadvantages of, 424
    B2B, 515
    database marketing and, 428–432
    direct-response advertising and, 424
    global concerns in, 445
    integrated, 443–445
    Internet and, 442–443
    players in, 432–435
    practice of, 423–428
    process, 424–428
    tools of, 423, 435–443
Direct-marketing industry, 424

Directors, of television commercials, 407, 410
Directory advertising, 233–234, 365, 515
Direct-response advertising, 17, 421–424, 440–442, 545–546
Direct-response counts, 545–546
Discretionary income, 135
Disney, 15
Display advertising, 217–218
Display allowances, 463
Display copy, 360
Displays, 493
Distribution, 43–44
Distribution chain, 39
Distribution channels, 39, 42
Distributors, 39
Divergent thinking, 330
Diversity issues, 76–77
DM. See Direct marketing (DM)
DMA. See Designated marketing area (DMA)
Dominance, in layout design, 395
Do-Not-Call Registry, 448
DoubleClick, 276–277
Doublemint gum, 343
Double-page spreads, 224
Doughnut format, 508
Dove Firming, 383
DRADAR. See Radio's All-Dimension Audience Research (DRADAR)
Dramas, 336
"Drivers Wanted" campaign, 9, 17, 20, 334
Drug advertising, 116–117
Drugstore.com, 241–242, 264–265
Dubbing, 410
DVDs, 493
DVRs. See Digital video recorders (DVRs)

E

EBay, 269–271, 286
E-business, 271–272
Echo Award, 421
Economic impact, of advertising, 8, 10
Editors, 407
EDS. See Electronic Data Systems (EDS)
Education levels, 133–134
Effective frequency, 300
Effectiveness
    advertising, 1, 7, 19–21
    affective responses and, 109–110
    association and, 110–113
    behavioral response and, 116–118
    cognition and, 106–109
    creative aspect of, 327–330
    determining, 194
    evaluating, 533–551
    factors in, 545
    IMC, 548

message effects and, 102–120
perception and, 104–106
persuasion and, 113–116
of promotions, 470
of public relations, 497–498
qualities of advertising, 350
research questions, 535
of television commercials, 371
of visuals, 387
of Web design, 412–414
see also Evaluation
Effective reach, 300
EFFIE award, 20
Electronic Data Systems (EDS), 404–405
E-mail advertising, 281–282, 442–443
Embedded research, 173–174
Embossing, 403
Emotional appeals, 109–110
Emotional responses, 109–110
Emotional strategies, 340
Employee relations, 480
Endorsements, 83, 345, 480
Ethical Consumer, 92–93
Ethical issues, 75–90
ads targeting children, 79–80
body images, 79
comparative advertising, 81–83
controversial products, 84–85
demonstrations, 83
endorsements, 83
international standards, 88
manipulative advertising, 81
misleading advertising, 80–81
offensive advertising, 75–76
personal ethics, 88–89
professional ethics, 87–88
puffery, 81
social ethics, 86–87
stereotypes, 76–79
Ethnicity, 132–133
Ethnic stereotypes, 78
Ethnographic research, 169–170
Evaluation
of B2B advertising, 549
campaign, 544–549
in direct marketing, 427–428
of effectiveness, 533–551
factors to consider in, 534
of international advertising, 549
of marketing communications, 544–548
media, 542–544
of PR, 547–548
of retail advertising, 548
of sales promotions, 546–547
types and stages of, 533–534
see also Effectiveness
Evaluation research, 163, 165
Event marketing, 464–465
Exchange, 32–33
Exhibits, 493

Exporting, 518–519
Exposure, 105, 297–298
Extranets, 274, 496

F

Facets Model of Advertising Effects, 103–104, 188, 334
Fallon agency, 404
False advertising, 80–81
Family, 130–131
FCB. *See* Foote, Cone & Belding (FCB)
FCC. *See* Federal Communications Commission (FCC)
FDA. *See* Food and Drug Administration (FDA)
Feature analysis, 190, 191
Features, 338–339
Feature stories, 490
Federal Communications Commission (FCC), 70
Federal Trade Commission Act, 67
Federal Trade Commission (FTC), 66–69
Feedback, 100, 102
Fee system, 51
Female stereotypes, 77–78, 79
Fill-in-the-blanks, 170
Film editing, 407, 410
Films, 262–263, 406
Film-to-tape transfers, 407
Financial relations, 480
Finishings, of print ads, 403
First Amendment, 64–65, 72
First-run syndication, 254
FJ. *See* FootJoy (FJ)
Flexography, 403
Flighting strategy, 307–308
FM radio, 243
Focus groups, 168–169
Foil-stamping, 403
Fonts, 392
Food and Drug Administration (FDA), 70
Foote, Cone & Belding (FCB), 334
FootJoy (FJ), 97–98, 100, 111, 119–120
Foreign markets. *See* International advertising
Forrester Research, 413
Four-color printing, 401
Fox Sports Net, 60
Free association, 330
Free-standing inserts (FSIs), 218
Frequency, levels of, 212
Frequency distribution, 299–300
Frequency objective, 299–300
Frequency programs, 466
Friendship focus groups, 169
Frontier Airlines, 355–356, 371–373, 381
FSIs. *See* Free-standing inserts (FSIs)
FTC. *See* Federal Trade Commission (FTC)

FTC Improvement Act, 67
Fulfillment, in direct marketing, 427
Fulfillment houses, 433
Full-service agencies, 47
Fund-raising, 481, 518

G

Gaffers, 409
Galyans, 505
Gander Mountain, 38, 185–186, 339
Gap, 63–64
Gap analysis, 484
Gargan Communication, 434
Gatefolds, 224
Gatekeepers, 480
Gay community, 76–77
GEICO, 441
Gender, 132
Gender roles, 77–78
Generation Y, 149
Gen X, 149
Geographic segmentation, 148
Geography, 135, 303, 505–506
Glaxo Smithkline, 523
Global advertising. *See* International advertising
Global brands, 519, 523–524
Global environment
copywriting for, 380–381
direct marketing and, 445
marketing in, 518–527
see also International advertising
Globalization, 23–24, 172, 519, 520
G-mail, 273
Golden Rule, 86
Goodwill, 478
Google, 273, 529
"Got Milk" campaign, 327
Government advertising, 512
Governmental oversight, 62–71
Government organizations, statistics from, 157
Government reports, 159
Grammar, in copywriting, 360
Gray Market, 149
Great American Bake Sale, 517
Grips, 409
Gross impressions, 212–213, 297–298, 299
Gross rating points (GRPs), 258–259, 297–298, 299
GRPs. *See* gross rating points (GRPs)
Guerilla marketing, 285–286
Gutter, 224

H

Häagen-Dazs Gelato, 494
Halftone art, 400, 401
Hard-sell approaches, 6, 335

Harley-Davidson, 33, 36, 421–423, 445–446, 467
HDTV. *See* High-definition TV (HDTV)
Head and heart strategies, 334
Headlines, 360–363
Heavy-up schedules, 303
HE'R&NU', 260
Hierarchy-of-effects model, 102–103
High-context cultures, 522
High-definition TV (HDTV), 254, 417
High-involvement products, 116
"Hire" campaign, 21–22
Hispanic market, 132–133
History Channel, 451–453, 471
Honda, 411
Horizontal publications, 221, 514–515
House ads, 487
Household income, 135
Households, 130–131
Households using television (HUT), 212
House lists, 430
Hume, Amy, 232
Humor, 345
Hutchinson, Chris, 379
HUT (households using television), 212
Hybrid technologies, 285

I

IBM, 271, 386, 538
IDM. *See* Integrated direct marketing (IDM)
Illustrations, 389–390, 400
"I Love Smoke-Free NY" campaign, 479
Image, in public relations, 478
Image advertising, 342–344
Images, digitization of, 403
Image transfer, 304
IMC. *See* Integrated marketing communication (IMC)
Implied third-party endorsements, 480
Impressions, 212–213, 297–298
Impulse buyers, 145
Inbound telemarketing, 438
Income, 134–135
In-depth interviews, 168
Indirect-action headlines, 362–363
Indirect advertising, 71
Indirect marketing, 44
Industrial advertising, 510
Industrialization, 6
Industrial magazines, 221
Industrial markets, 39–41
"Industrial Revolution and Emergence of Consumer Society," 21
Inflatables, 465
Infomercials, 340, 440–442
Information, 108
    analysis of, 174
    client, 294
    consumer, 297

customer, 272–274
market, 162
media, 295, 297
search, 145
sources, 293–297
Informational strategies, 338–340
Information overload, 101, 174, 323
Ingredient branding, 39
In-house agencies, 14–15
Innate needs, 135, 138
Innovation, 144, 145
Inquiry tests, 541
Insight mining, 196–198
Instant messaging (IM), 285
Institute of Practitioners Award (IPA), 20
Institutional advertising, 18
Institutional markets, 39–41
Institutional retail advertising, 507
Integrated direct marketing (IDM), 443–445
Integrated marketing, 52–53
Integrated marketing communication (IMC), 22–23, 102
    evaluation, 548
    global advertising and, 525–527
    objectives, 200–201
    planning, 184, 185, 199–200
    PR's role in, 486
    research, 157
Integrated relationship marketing, 444
Interactive communication model, 99, 100, 102
Interactive media, 173, 271–282
    e-mail advertising, 281–282
    Internet, 271–281
Interactive promotions, 465–466
Interactive technology, 17
Interactive television, 254
Interconnects, 252
Interest, 105
Interlocks, 410
Internal marketing, 200
International advertising, 52, 518–527
    challenges of, 172
    copywriting for, 380–381
    creative strategies for, 348–349
    ethical standards in, 88
    evaluation of, 549
    execution of, 525
    IMC factor in, 525–527
    market development and, 518–519
    media planning for, 308–309
    objectives, 523
    planning, 521–525
    social considerations in, 62
    Web and, 280
International brands, 52
Internationalization, 519
International laws and regulations, 70–71
International marketing, 52
International Truck, 222

Internet, 271
    advertising, 276–281
    for B2B advertising, 515
    brand experiences on, 283
    customer information collected on, 272–274
    direct marketing and, 442–443
    e-business and, 271–272
    interactivity of, 271–273
    international advertising and, 280
    marketing communications and, 274–276
    media buying on, 317
    privacy issues and, 273–274
    as PR tool, 496–497
    research on, 158, 173074
    trends, 280–281
Internet promotions, 465–466
Interviews, 168
Intimo, 494
Intranets, 274, 496
Involvement, 116
Involvement strategies, 485
IPA. *See* Institute of Practitioners Award (IPA)
IPod, 209–210, 212, 235
IPSOS-ASI, 534
Issue management, 481
ITunes, 209–210, 235
Ivory Soap, 34, 35

J

Jack-in-the-Box, 482
Jaguar, 375
Jeep, 22
Jingles, 244, 368
Johnsonville Sausage, 457, 464, 465
Just for Feet, 60
Justification, of type, 392
"Just Say No" campaign, 118–119
J. Walter Thompson agency, 503–504

K

Kellogg's Special K, 232, 342
Kenneth Cole, 60
Key concept cards, 537
Key frames, 376
Key visuals, 337
KFC, 196, 552
King Thomas, Joyce, 353
Kiosks, 231
Krispy Kreme, 46

L

Lanham Act, 67, 82
Layouts, 394–397
Layout stages, 396–397
LCV. *See* Lifetime customer value (LCV)

Lead agencies, 522
Lead generation, 424, 425
Leads, 364
Lead time, 307
LeapFrog, 155–157, 162–163, 174
Learning relationships, 431
Lectures, 335–336
Legal environment, 62–64
Legibility, of type, 392, 394
Legislation, 67
Leo Burnett, 164
Letterpress, 402
Levi Strauss, 494
Licensing, 467
Lifestyle analysis, 141
Lifestyles, 130, 141
Lifetime customer value (LCV),
    444–445
Likeability tests, 541
Line art, 400, 401
Linkler, Josh, 203
List brokers, 429
Lists, direct-mail, 429–430
Loaders, 462–463
Lobbying, 481
Local advertising, 17, 505–506
Local brands, 52
Localization advertising strategy,
    520–521
Local television, 252–253
Logason, Ingvi, 192, 260
Logos, 337, 388, 389
"London Calling" campaign, 375
Low-context cultures, 522
Low-involvement products, 116
Low-power FM (LPFM), 244
Loyalty, 114–115, 444–445
Loyalty programs, 466

M

Macintosh (computer), 12
Magazines, 220–226, 238, 365, 399
Magnuson-Moss Warranty/FTC
    Improvement Act, 67
Make-goods, 315
Manipulative advertising, 81
Mann, Lara, 36
Manning, Harley, 167, 413
Mapes & Ross, 534
Marines, U.S., 464
Market aggregation strategy, 147–148
Market coverage strategy, 44
Market development, global, 518–519
Marketers, 37
Market information, 162
Marketing
    ambush, 464–465
    channel, 41
    database, 428–432
    defined, 8, 31–37

direct, 423–445
dynamics of, 52–53
event, 464–465
guerilla, 285–286
integrated, 52–53
internal, 200
international, 52
objectives, 19–20
permission, 53, 443
players in, 37–39
process, 41–45
relationship, 53, 480
strategies, 42–45
tools of, 8
viral, 101, 282, 344
Marketing communication mix, 42
Marketing communications, 8, 43
    evaluating effectiveness of, 533–551
    global, 518–527
    Internet and, 274–276
    personal sales and, 45
    tools of, 419
    see also Integrated marketing commu-
        nication (IMC)
Marketing concept, 31–32
Marketing imperialism, 62
Marketing mix, 8, 42–45, 184
Marketing plans, 45, 183–184
Marketing public relations (MPR), 483
Marketing spending, by media type,
    304
Market-orientation model, 521
Market research. See Research
Markets, types of, 39–41
Market segmentation, 147–150, 189–190
Market selectivity, 214
Market share, 39, 184, 455, 459–460
Market situation analysis, 183–184
Market strategies, undifferentiated,
    147–148
Martin Agency, 531–533
Maslow's hierarchy of needs, 135, 138
Mass communication, 8
    see also communication
Mass media, 15–16
    see also Media
MasterCard, 353
Maytag, 470
McCann-Erickson, 353
McDonald's, 468, 522–523, 552
Measurable objectives, 189
Mechanicals, 396
Media
    as advertising players, 15–16
    alternative, 282–286
    B2B, 514–515
    broadcast, 241–265
    controlled, 427, 487, 488
    creative use of, 6
    evaluation, 542–544
    interactive, 271–282

monitoring systems for, 317
optimization, 543–544
players in, 213
print, 213–235
of retail advertising, 509–510
semicontrolled, 487, 488
uncontrolled, 487, 488
Media aperture, 293
Media budget, 308
Media buyers, 213, 313–316
Media buying, 212, 313–317
Media-buying services, 49, 213, 293,
    316
Media companies, 433
Media departments, 49–50
Media efficiency, 543
Media flowcharts, 308
Media fragmentation, 173
Media industry, overview of, 211–213
Media information, 295, 297
Mediamark Research, Inc. (MRI), 160,
    161, 225, 295–296
Media mix, 212, 303–305
Media objectives, 297–300
Media planners, 213
Media planning, 207, 212, 293
    budgets and, 308
    challenges of, 316–317
    cost efficiency and, 305–306
    global, 308–309
    goal of, 212
    media mix and, 303–305
    media research and, 293–297
    media strategies, 300–309
    objectives of, 297–300
    scheduling strategies, 306–308
Media plans, 293–297, 310–313
Media relations, 480
Media reps, 213
Media research, 163, 293–297
Media researchers, 213
Media salespeople, 213
Media strategies, 195, 300–309
    in direct marketing, 426–427
    target audience strategies, 301–303
Media technology, new, 172–173
Media tours, 492
Media use
    by age, 131
    changes in, 302–303
    in public relations, 480
Media vehicles, 212
MediaVest, 256
Media weighting, 304
Medium, 101
Memory, 106, 108, 337
Mendelsohn, Susan, 195, 197
Mental states, 135
Mercedes-Benz, 233
Meredith, 315
Merging, of lists, 429

Message development, 163, 165
    in direct marketing, 426–427
    research, 165–172, 536–537
    in telemarketing, 439–440
Message effects, 102–104
Message execution, 347
Message objectives, 334
Messages, 101
    attention-getting, 336–337
    memorability of, 337
Message strategies, 195, 536
    aperture concept and, 293
    communication briefs for, 198–199
    dramas, 336
    hard-sell, 335
    head and heart strategies, 334
    lectures, 335–336
    soft-sell, 335
    see also Creative strategies
Metaphors, 171, 176–177, 330
Michelin, 330
Microsoft Network (MSN), 325–326,
    350–351
Millennium Generation, 149
Miller Light, 77
Millward Brown, 535
Minisites, 278
Miss Hall's School, 434
Mission marketing, 516
Mission statements, 183
Mobile phones, 284–285
"Modern Advertising Era," in advertising
    history, 21
Moment-by-moment tests, 537
Montague, Jennifer, 459
Montes, Sonia, 14, 343
Morning drive time, 247
Morphing, 405
Motivations, 114, 139
Motivation tests, 541
MoveOn, 72, 73
Movie trailers, 406
Mr. CONTAC, 523, 524
MRI, 225. See Mediamark Research, Inc.
    (MRI)
MSN. See Microsoft Network (MSN)
Multimedia research, 172–173
Music
    in radio, 368
    in television commercials, 374, 408

N

NAICS. See North American Industry
    Classification System (NAICS)
NASCAR, 203
National Advertising Division (NAD),
    73–74
National Advertising Review Board
    (NARB), 73–74
National Advertising Review Council, 73

Navigation, of Web sites, 413–414
Need recognition, 145
Needs, 108, 135, 138
Negative space, 395
Network of associations, 113
Network radio, 246
Network television, 250–251
"New advertising," 21–23
New media, 282–286
News Corp., 15
Newspapers, 214–220, 365
Newsprint, 399
News releases, 489–490, 491
Niche markets, 149–150
Nielsen Media Research, 295, 542
Nike, 36, 60, 65, 92, 97–98, 283, 464
1984 commercial, 12
Nintendo, 430–431
Niswonger, Amy, 426
Noise, 100–101
Nokia, 190
Nonprofit advertising, 18
Nonprofit marketing, 515–518
Nonpromotional advertising, 507
Norms, 128, 534–535
North American Industry Classification
    System (NAICS), 510
"Not Typical" campaign, 179–181, 201
Novell, 503–504, 527
Nuveen Investments, 90
NYNEX, 357

O

Objectives, 19–20
    analyzing, 189
    B2B, 513, 514
    defined, 181
    delivering on, 300–301, 345
    in direct marketing, 425
    frequency objective, 299–300
    global advertising, 523
    IMC, 200–201
    at marketing level, 184
    measurable, 189
    message, 334
    promotion, 468
    in public relations, 484–485
    reach, 298–299
    retail advertising, 507
    setting, 42, 188
Objective-task method, of budgeting,
    193–194
Observation research, 169
Occupations, 134
OEMs. See Original equipment manufac-
    turers (OEMs)
Offensive advertising, 75–76, 90
Off-line advertising, 278
Off-network syndication, 254

Offset printing, 402
Ogilvy, David, 99
Ogilvy & Mather, 383
One-step offers, 427
Online advertising, 276–281
    copywriting for, 378–380
    see also Internet
Online communications, 496–497
On location, commercials on, 374
On-premise signs, 230
OnStar, 166
Open-ended questions, 168
Open Show, The, 292, 317–318
Opportunities, identifying, 187
Opt-in, 281
Opt-out, 281–282
Orders, in direct marketing, 427
Original equipment manufacturers
    (OEMs), 510
Original ideas, tips for creating, 328–339
Orly "Chantilly Peach," 397
Outbound telemarketing, 438
Outdoor advertising, 227–230, 365–367,
    399–400, 418
Out-of-home advertising, 227–231
Overlines, 361

P

Pacific Life, 199
Package goods, 41
Packaging, 43, 226–227
Page, Larry, 529
Painted bulletins, 228
Pamphlets, 367
Pantry checks, 539
Parity products, 191, 455
Participations, 256
Partnership programs, 466–467
Payout planning, 470
Payout plans, 546
Pay-per-view television, 253
PBS, 253, 405
People meters, 259
Peppers, Don, 431
Pepsi, 93
Perceived risks, 144
Percentage-of-sales method, of budgeting,
    194
Perception, 104–106, 135, 138–139
Perception problems, 187
Perceptual maps, 191
Permission marketing, 53, 443
Personal ethics, 88–89
Personalities, 139–140
Personal sales, 45
Personal shoppers, 174
Personas, 167
Persuasion, 113–116
Persuasion tests, 540–541
Persuasive advertising, 340–342

PGA Golf Tour, 467
Phaeton, 459
Photoboards, 537
Photo elicitation, 171
Photographs, 389–391, 400
Photoprints, 403
Photo sorts, 171
Photostats, 403
Picas, 392
Picture sorts, 537
Pitch letters, 490, 492
Pizza Hut, 310–313
"Pods Unite" campaign, 4, 17, 20, 24–25
Point of differentiation, 338
Point-of-purchase (POP) displays, 461
Points, 392
Polaroid, 302
Political advertising, 260
Pontiac, 501
Pool-outs, 522
Pop-behind ads, 277
Populations, 168
Pop-up ads, 277
Positioning, 42, 190–193, 523–524, 525
Posters, 228, 230–231, 365, 399
Postproduction, of commercials, 410
Postpurchase evaluations, 146
Posttesting research, 534, 540–542
Powell Communications, 475–477, 499
Predictive dialing, 438
Preference, 114
Preferred-position rates, 217
Preferred positions, 315
Premiums, 456, 458
Preprints, 510
Preproduction, of commercials, 408
Prescription drugs, 85
Press conferences, 492
Pretesting, 537
Price, 43
Price deals, 455–456, 458, 459–460
Pricing, 44–45, 455
Primary needs, 135
Primary research, 42, 159–162, 165
Primary research suppliers, 159
Prime-time, 250
Print ad production, 399–403
Printed posters, 228
Printing processes, 401–403
Print media, 213–235
    art direction for, 389–398
    copywriting for, 360–367
    directory advertising, 233–234
    direct-response advertising and, 440
    magazines, 220–226
    newspapers, 214–220
    out-of-home advertising, 227–231
    packaging, 226–227
    production requirements, 399–400

relationship between advertisers and, 238
    using, 235
Print production department, 51
Privacy policies, 273–274
Problem solutions, 345
Pro bono campaign, 387
Process colors, 400–401
Proctor & Gamble (P&G), 34, 35, 37, 93, 319–320
Producers, of television commercials, 407
Product-as-hero, 345
Product categories, 8, 43
Product demonstrations, 83
Product differentiation, 42, 190–191, 338
Product features, 190
Production department, 49
Production notes, 408
Product literature, 367
Product management, 37
Product placements, 238, 263
Product reviews, 174
Products
    controversial, 84–85
    dangerous, 84–85
    defined, 32–33, 43
    elements of, 42
    parity, 191, 455
    positioning, 42, 190–193, 523–525
Product usage, 144
Professional advertising, 512–513
Professional ethics, 87–88
Professional magazines, 221
Profiles, 150
Proflowers, 338
Program sponsorships, 253
Program syndication, 253–254
Promises, 341
Promotional advertising, 507
Promotion industry, changes in, 453–454
Promotions. See sales promotions
Proportion, in layout design, 395–396
Prospecting, 425–426
PSAs. See Public service announcements (PSAs)
Psychographics, 140–141
Psychographic segmentation, 148
Psychological influences, on consumer decisions, 135–143
Psychological pricing, 45
Public affairs, 481
Publication frequency, of newspapers, 214–215
Publications, as PR tool, 492–493
Public broadcasting system (PBS) stations, 253, 405
Public communication campaigns, 483, 518
Publicity, 477, 489–492

Public opinion, 478
Public radio, 243–244
Public relations (PR), 293, 475–499
    vs. advertising, 478, 480
    effectiveness of, 497–498
    evaluation of, 547–548
    excellence in, 498
    planning, 483–487
    practice of, 477–483
    tools of, 487–497
    types of programs, 480–483
Public Relations Society of America (PRSA), 477
Publics, 477, 481
Public service announcements (PSAs), 18, 487–488
Public television, 253, 405
Puffery, 81
Pulling power, 336–337
Pull strategy, 44, 462–463
Pulsing strategy, 307
Puma, 29–31, 53
Purchase decisions, 146
Purchase intent, 160
Pure Food and Drug Act, 67
Purging, of lists, 429
Purpose-driven games, 170–171
Push strategy, 44, 462–463

Q

Qualitative research, 160, 162, 170–171
Quantitative research, 160, 171–172

R

Race, 132–133
Racial stereotypes, 78
Radio, 243–249, 266–267
Radio Advertising Bureau, 367
Radio copy, 367–369
Radio's All-Dimension Audience Research (DRADAR), 248
Radio scripts, 369
Radio signals, 243
Rate cards, 217
Rating points, 258–259
Ratings, 213, 247, 258
Reach, 212, 301–302
Reach objective, 298–299
Rebates, 456, 466
Recall, 106, 108
Recall tests, 540
Recognition, 106
Recognition tests, 540
Reference groups, 129–130
Refunds, 456
REGGIE award, 451
Regional brands, 52
Register-Guard, 370
Registration, 399

Regulatory issues, 62–71
    federal agencies, 66–70
    Federal Communications Commission
        (FCC), 70
    Federal Trade Commission (FTC),
        66–69
    Food and Drug Administration (FDA),
        70
    international, 70–71
    laws concerning, 62–65
    media review, 72
    self-regulation, 72–75
Relationship marketing, 53, 344, 480
Release prints, 410
Relevance, 105
Reliability, 172
Reputation, 478
Reputation management, 482
Rerailers, 39
Research, 42, 50, 155–177, 162, 295
    advertising, 157
    analysis of, 174
    background, 165–166
    challenges, 172–174
    consumer, 157, 166–171, 195
    consumer insight, 162–163
    defined, 157
    embedded, 173–174
    ethnographic, 169–170
    evaluation, 163, 165
    IMC, 157
    Internet, 158
    market, 157, 295
    marketing, 162
    media, 163, 293–297
    message development, 536–537
    methods, 165–172
    multimedia, 172–173
    on new media, 317
    observation, 169
    primary, 159–162, 165
    in public relations, 483–484
    qualitative, 160, 162, 170–171
    quantitative, 160, 171–172
    scanner, 541
    secondary, 157–159, 165
    single-source, 541–542
    strategic, 157
    survey, 168
    types of, 157–162
    used in evaluation, 533–534
    uses of, 162–165
    virtual, 173
Resonance, 110
Respond2, 428
Response, in direct marketing, 427
Response lists, 430
Retail ads, 507–509
Retail advertising, 17, 504–510
    vs. brand advertising, 506
    evaluation of, 548

    media of, 509–510
    objectives, 507
    strategies, 505–507
Retailer kits, 461
Retailers, power of, 455
Retail marketing, 504–505
Retainers, 51
Return-on-investment (ROI), 182, 327,
    543
Reverse type, 392
Review process, 72–75
Rich media, 278
Rieck, Dan, 436
Right-brain thinking, 330
Rockport, 184
Rogers, Martha, 431
ROI, 327. See Return-on-investment
    (ROI)
RoperASW, 535
Rotogavure, 402–403
Rough cuts, 410
Rough layouts, 396
Rubin coffee, 192–193
Run-of-paper (ROP) rates, 217
Rushes, 410

S

Sales advertising, 507
Sales geography, 294
Sales levels, 184
Sales promotions, 8, 42, 43
    vs. advertising, 469–470
    ambush marketing, 464–465
    categories of, 455
    consumer promotions, 455–460
    effectiveness of, 470
    evaluation of, 546–547
    event marketing, 464–465
    growth of, 453–455
    integration of, 469
    interactive, 465–466
    Internet, 465–466
    loyalty programs, 466
    objectives of, 468
    partnership programs, 466–467
    practice of, 453–455
    sponsorships, 464–465
    strategies for, 467–470
    trade promotions, 461–463
Salton-Maxim Juiceman, 440–441
Samples, 168
Sampling, 456, 458, 465
Sans serif typeface, 392
Satellite radio, 266–267
Satellite transmissions, 308
Satellite TV, 252
Satisfaction, 139
SAU. See Standard Advertising Unit
    (SAU)
Scanner research, 541

Scenes, in television commercials, 376
Scheduling strategies, 306–308
Schroeder, Karl, 245, 328, 335, 370
Scientific method, 171–172
Scott, Lee, 27
Scrabble, 493–494
Screened images, 400
Scripts, 377
Scuba-diving industry, 379
Sealey, Peter, 1
Search engines, 274
Search marketing, 274
Secondary research, 42, 157–159, 165
Secondary research suppliers, 158
Sega, 64
Segmentation, 42, 147–150, 189–190
Selection, 105
Selective perception, 104, 138–139
Self-images, 79
Self-liquidating premiums, 458
Self-regulation, 72–75
Selling premises, 341
Semicomps, 396
Semicontrolled media, 487, 488
Semiotic analysis, 165–166
Senior citizens, 78–79
September 11, 2001, 21
76 Ads, 329
Sex, 76, 77
Sexual orientation, 132
Share of audience, 258
Share of market, 39, 184
Share of mind, 336
Share of voice, 295
Shell, 86
Shockvertising, 345
Shoot, television commercial, 409–410
Shoppers, 510
Showings, 229
Signatures, 337
SignBoy, 98, 119–120
Silkscreen printing, 403
Simmons Market Research Bureau
    (SMRB), 160, 225
Simmons-Scarborough Syndicated
    Research Associates, 219
Simplicity, in layout design, 396
Single-source research, 541–542
Sirius, 266–267
Situational ads, 282
Situation analysis, 42, 186, 483–484
Skyscrapers, 277
Slice-of-life format, 345
Slogans, 337, 361, 363, 371
SMCR model of communication, 99–102
Social class, 129
Social ethics, 86–87
Social influences, on consumer decisions,
    128–135
Social marketing, 515–518
Social responsibility, 87

Societal marketing philosophy, 515–516
Societal roles, of advertising, 10, 61–62
Sociodemographic segments, 148–149
Soft-sell approaches, 6, 335
Sony Pictures, 80
Sorrell, Martin, 56
Sound effects, 368
Source credibility, 114
Southwest Airlines, 419
Spam, 281–282, 443
Speakers' bureau, 493
Special events, 493–494
Specialized agencies, 47, 49
Specialty television, 253
Spherical Branding, 204–205
Split-run tests, 362
Spokane Regional Convention and
    Visitors Bureau, 495
Spokespersons, 83, 345, 376
Sponsorships, 255–256, 464–465
Spoofing, 443
Spot announcements, 257
Spot buys, 253
Spot color, 390
Spot radio advertising, 246
Staged events, 493–494
Stakeholders, 23, 200, 477
Standard Advertising Unit (SAU), 215,
    216
Standard Directory of Advertisers and
    Advertising agencies (Red Book),
    234
Standardization advertising strategy,
    520–521
Starbucks, 256, 521
Stasiowski, Peter, 398, 434
Stereotypes, 76–79
Stern, Howard, 266–267
Stock footage, 405
Stop motion, 408
Stopping power, 336
Storyboards, 377
Story elicitation, 171
Strategic business units (SBUs), 182
Strategic decisions, 42
Strategic planning, 179–202
    account planning, 194–199
    budgeting, 193–194
    decisions, 185–194
    defined, 181
    IMC planning, 199–200
    positioning strategies, 190–193
    process, 182–184
Strategic research, 155–177, 157
Strategies, 5–6, 181
    advertising, 5–6
    in direct marketing, 425
    effect-based, 188
    positioning, 190–193
    for promotions, 467–470
    in public relations, 484–485

for retail advertising, 505–507
see also Creative strategies; Media
    strategies; Message strategies
Streaming video, 278
Structural analysis, 349–350
Stunts, 486
Subcultures, 129
Subheads, 361
Subliminal advertising, 81, 106, 107
Subscription television, 251–252
Substantiation, 67–68
Super Bowl, 249–250
Superstations, 252
Superstitials, 278
Supplements, newspaper, 218
Suppliers, 16, 38–39
Supply chains, 38
Surprinting, 394
Survey research, 168
Sweepstakes, 456, 465
SWOT analysis, 42, 186–187, 483–484
Symbolism, 110
Syndicated radio, 246

T

Tabloids, 215
Tactics, 181
Taglines, 337, 361, 363
Takes, 410
Talent, 376
Target audiences, 8, 16–17
    children as, 79–80
    measuring cost of, 305–306
    media strategies for, 301–303
    profiling, 150
    radio, 246–248
    reaching, through magazines, 225
    research on, 162–163
    tone of voice for, 359–360
Targeted reach, 301–302
Targeting, 42, 189–190
    in global environment, 523
    in public relations, 484
    segmentation and, 147–150
Teaser campaigns, 336–337
Teasers, 345
Technological advances, 172–173, 224
Technology, hybrid technologies, 285
Telchin, Eric, 272
Telemarketing, 438–440, 448
Telemarketing and Consumer Fraud Act,
    67
Television
    ad rates, 261
    advertising, 249–250, 255–257,
        259–261
    art direction, 404–406
    audience, 257–259
    children's advertising on, 80
    copywriting for, 369, 371–378

direct-response advertising and,
    440–442
exposure, 212
industry structure, 250–253
programming options, 253–255
ratings, 213
relationship between advertisers and,
    238
terminology, 409
trends in, 261–262
Television commercials
    art direction for, 404–406
    copy for, 369, 371–378
    planning, 376–378
    production of, 407–410
    production requirements for, 406
Testimonials, 83
Test markets, 539–540
Thaler, Linda Japlan, 122–123
"Thanks for Traveling" campaign,
    135–137
Theater of the mind, 367
Think-feel-do model, 103
Thomasville Furniture, 385–386, 387,
    390, 405, 406, 414
Thumbnail sketches, 396
Tie-ins, 467
Tiffany's, 33
Time-shifting, 254
Time Warner, 15
Timing strategies, 306–308
Tint blocks, 400, 401
Tip-ins, 403
TiVo, 254–255
Tobacco advertising, 84–85
Tom's of Maine, 183
Tone of voice, 347, 359–360
Touch points, 200
Tours, 493–494
Town hall forums, 494
Toyota, 60, 153
Tracking studies, 537–540
Trade advertising, 512
Trade associations, information from,
    157–158
Trade deals, 462
Trade incentives, 462
Trademarks, 35, 63
Trade papers, 221
Trade promotions, 461–463
    types of, 461–462
    using, 462–463
Trade publications, 514–515
Trade shows, 462, 463
Traffic department, 51
Traffic generation, 425
Trailers, 262
Transformation, 111
Transit advertising, 231
Trends, 143
Trend spotters, 143

Trials, 458
"Truth" campaign, 484–486
Tuners, 153
TV commercials. *See* Television commercials
TV scripts, 377
Two-step offers, 427
Type measurement, 392
Typography, 391–394, 400

U

Unaided recall, 540
Unaided recognition, 106
Unbundling media services, 316
Uncontrolled media, 487, 488
Underlines, 361, 362
Undifferentiated products, 191
Undifferentiated strategy, 147–148
Unduplicated audiences, 298
Uniform Commercial Code (UCC), 81
Unilever, 383
Unique selling propositions (USPs), 341
United Airlines, 32
Unity, in layout design, 395
Upromise, 473
UPS, 531–533, 550
USA Direct, 442
Usage behavior, 144
U.S. Army, 164
U.S. Postal Service, 70

V

Validity, 171–172
VALS. *See* Values and Lifestyle System (VALS)
Value-added media services, 315
Values, 61–62, 128, 139
Values and Lifestyle System (VALS), 141–143

Vampire creativity, 349
Veloxes, 403
Vendors, 16, 38–39
Vertical publications, 221, 515
Viacom, 15
Victoria's Secret, 467, 494
Video editing, 410
Video games, 284
Video graphics, 405
Video news releases (VNRs), 490
Videos, 262–263, 493
Viewing diaries, 257–258
Viral marketing, 30, 101, 282, 344
Virgin Megastores, 7, 508
Virtual research, 173
Visual aspect, of television commercials, 374
Visual communication, 386–389
Visual impact, 387
Visualization, 388
Visual storytelling, 405
Voice, in radio, 368
Voice-overs, 374
Volkswagon (VW), 3–4, 9, 11, 17, 20, 24–25, 334, 459
Volvo, 536
VW. *See* Volkswagon (VW)

W

Wal-Mart, 27
Walters, Trent, 38
Wants, 108, 135, 138
Warner-Lambert, 69
Wasted reach, 261
Waterford Crystal, 280
Wave analysis, 539
Wearout, 543
Web ads, 380
Webcasting, 244
Web design, 412–414

Webisodes, 284
Web sites, 274, 275
    corporate, 496–497
    interactive, 283–284
    see also Internet
Weighting, 304
Weight-loss advertising, 80
"We Speak Your Language" campaign, 503–504
Wheeler-Lea Amendment, 67
Whiskas, 349
Whitaker, Mark, 238
White Castle, 125–126, 151
White space, 395
Wholesalers, 39
W Hotels, 459
Winfrey, Oprah, 501
Wireless communication, 284–285
World Wide Web, 271
    copywriting for, 378–380
    see also Internet; Web sites
WPP group, 56
Writing styles, 358–360

Y

Y&R, 375
Yellow Pages, 233–234, 365, 399
YMCA, 115
Your-name-here copy, 359

Z

Zaltman, Gerlad, 176–177
ZMET (Zaltman Metaphor Elicitation Technique), 171, 176–177